THE JAPANESE TATTOO

THE JAPANESE TATTOO

火事と喧嘩は江戸の華

Fights and Fires Are the Flowers of Edo

Manami Okazaki

PRESTEL
MUNICH · LONDON · NEW YORK

CONTENTS

INTRODUCTION

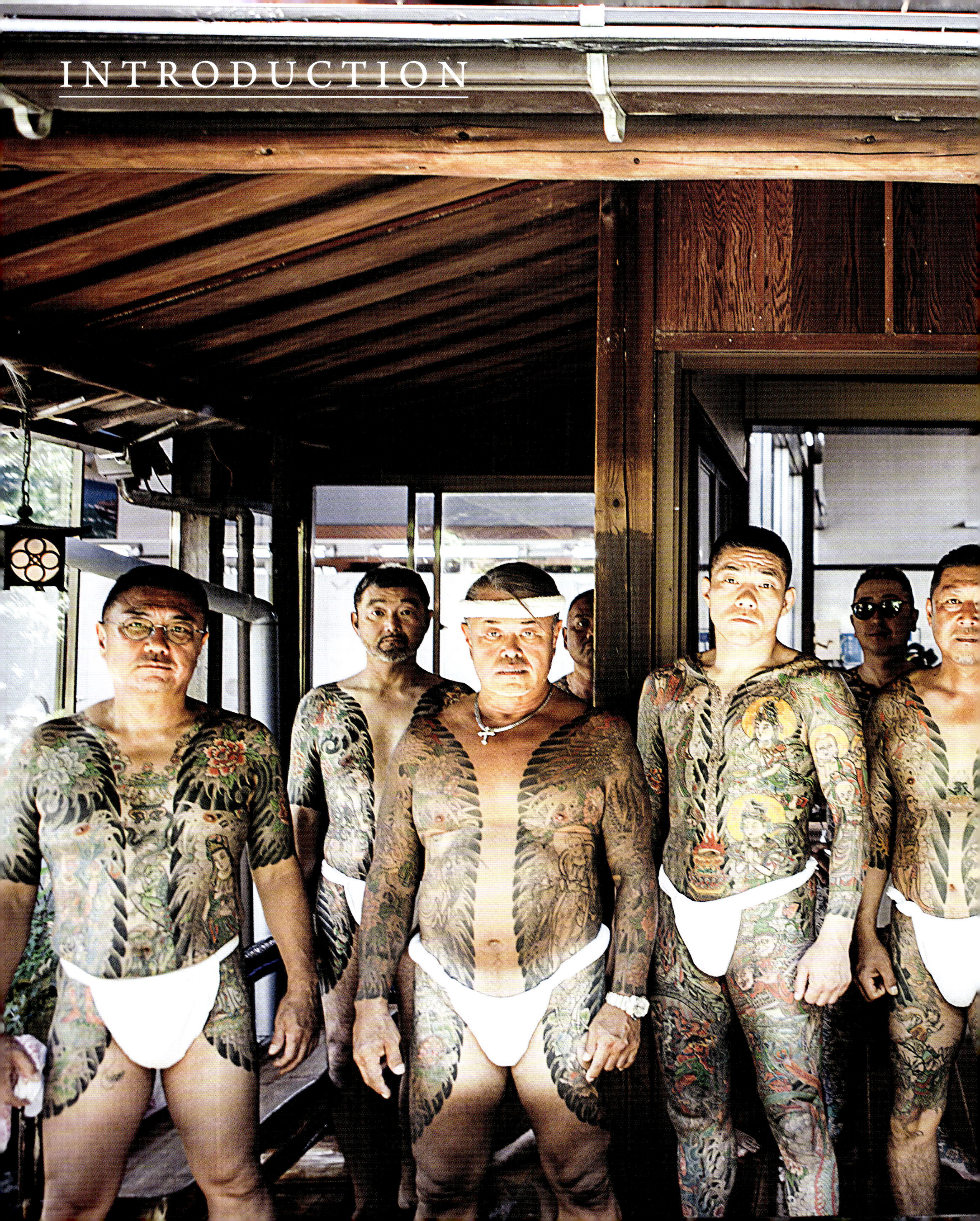

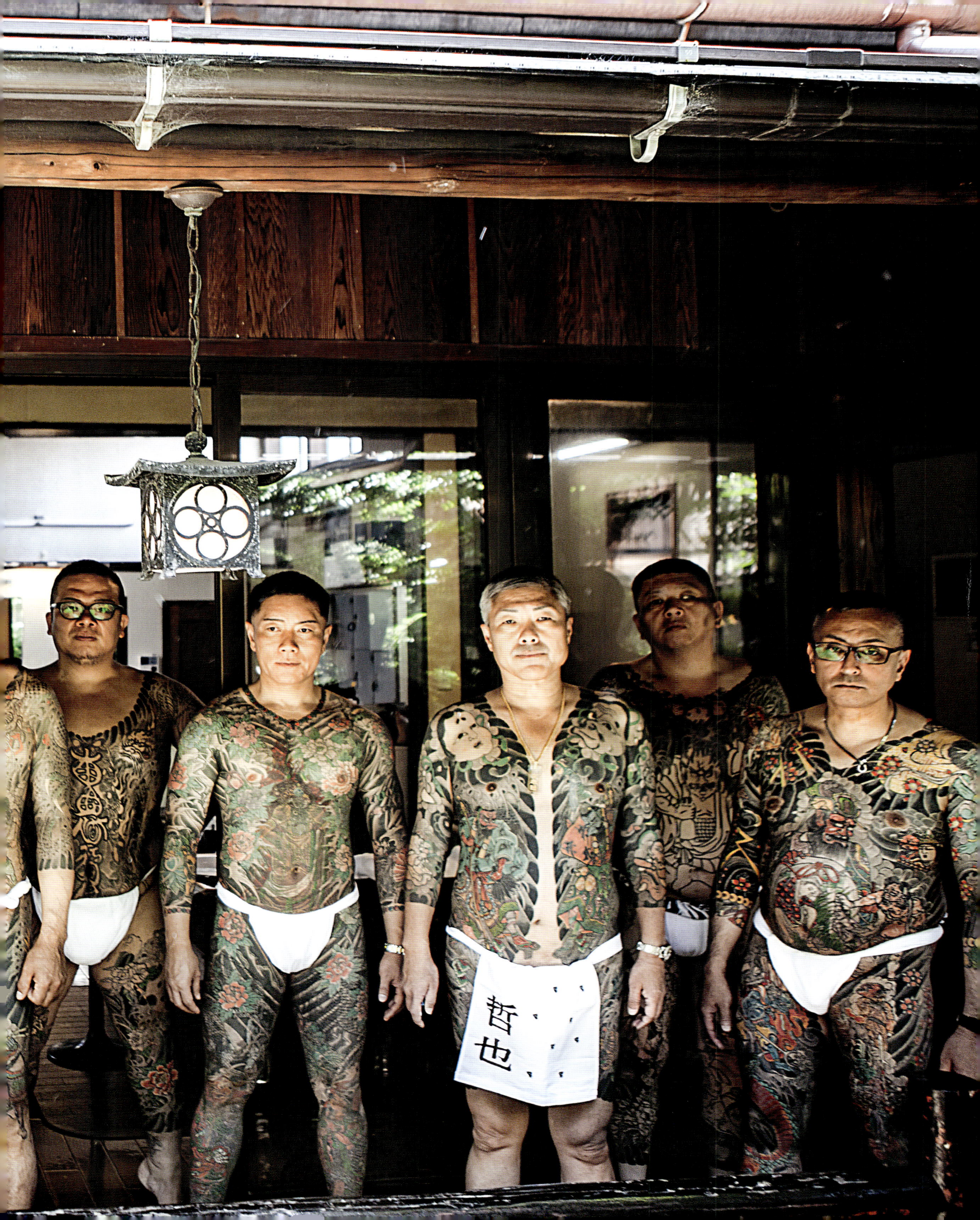
哲也

Japanese traditional tattoos (also known as *irezumi*, *horimono* and *wabori*, terms that will be used interchangeably throughout this book) are typified by narrative topics taken from Japanese folklore, religion and the natural world, which are then embellished with complementary iconographic elements from the relevant season of the year. The motifs range from famous warriors and divinities to animals both mythical and real, and the work in its entirety tells a vivid story. The tattoos are executed with incredible dexterity by master artists called *horishi*, who take decades to hone their skills. While there are many tattoo cultures all around the globe, Japanese tattoos are certainly some of the most powerful, aesthetically pleasing and compositionally balanced. They are nothing short of breathtaking when seen in the flesh.

The Japanese Tattoo will look at the nation's tattooing tradition, still alive and well today, that is a continuation of the Edo-period (1603–1868) tattoo culture which proliferated among Tokyo's working class in urban *shitamachi* (downtown) areas. Tattooed people of the time included craftsmen, carpenters, firefighters, couriers and artisans, as well as street gangsters. Many of these jobs were done half naked, and in shape and function the tattoos resembled workers' uniforms.

Wabori originally flourished alongside the phenomenally popular woodblock print artwork of the era, called *ukiyo-e*. While the majority of these prints depicted the daily lives of regular folks in a stratified society, it was the introduction of *Suikoden*, a classic literary tale adapted from the Ming Dynasty Chinese *Water Margin*, coupled with the imagination and dexterity of woodblock artists, that really elevated Japanese tattooing into a sophisticated art form. The exoticism, heroism and mystique of the imagery, and the association that commoners made between tattoos and valour, instigated a tattoo craze. Downtown heroes such as firefighters – who were like celebrities at the time – were embellished with increasingly elaborate protective water dwellers, both folkloric and real, giving specific talismanic meanings to their tattoos.

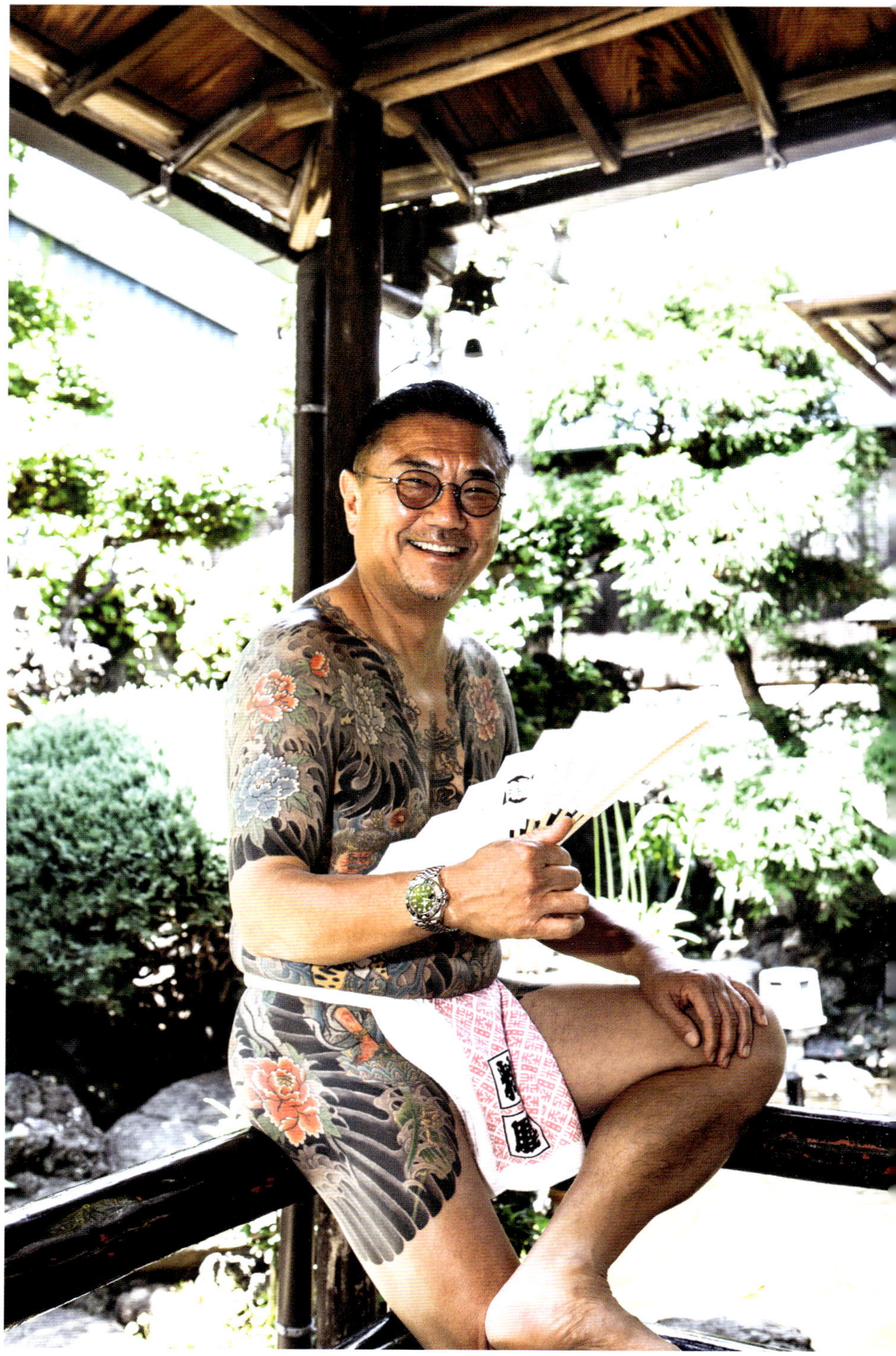

PREVIOUS SPREAD
Clients of the late Shodai Horikazu (Horizaku I) and his son Asakusa Horikazu, both master tattooers (*horishi*), at a *sento* (bathhouse) in Tokyo.

ABOVE
A client of the late Shodai Horikazu relaxes at a Tokyo bathhouse. Traditional Japanese tattoos are considered to be a 'hidden beauty', and some of the only places to see them are the *sento* and festivals (*matsuri*).

OPPOSITE
Some of the most heavily tattooed people in Japan are part of the MMA and jiu-jitsu worlds.

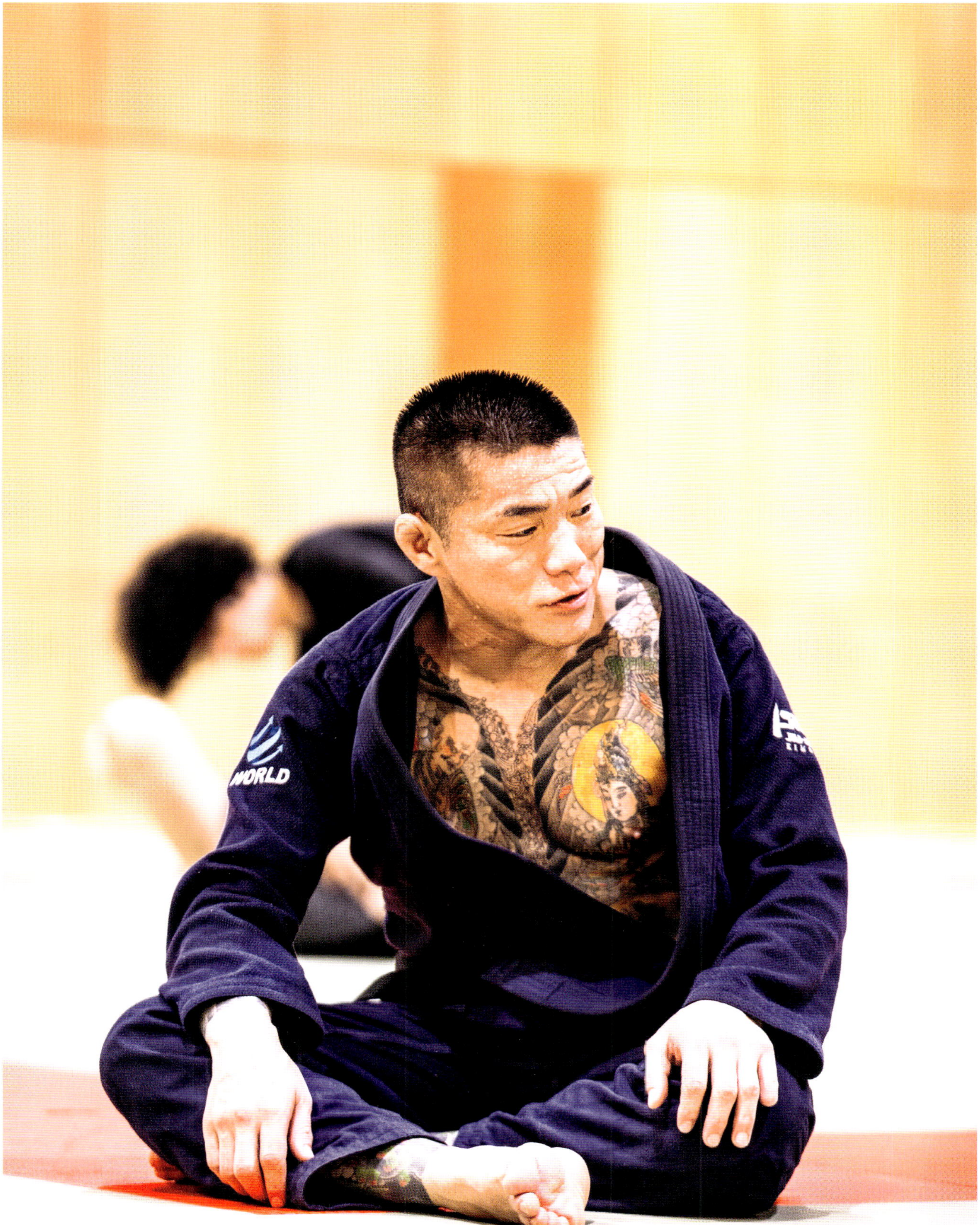

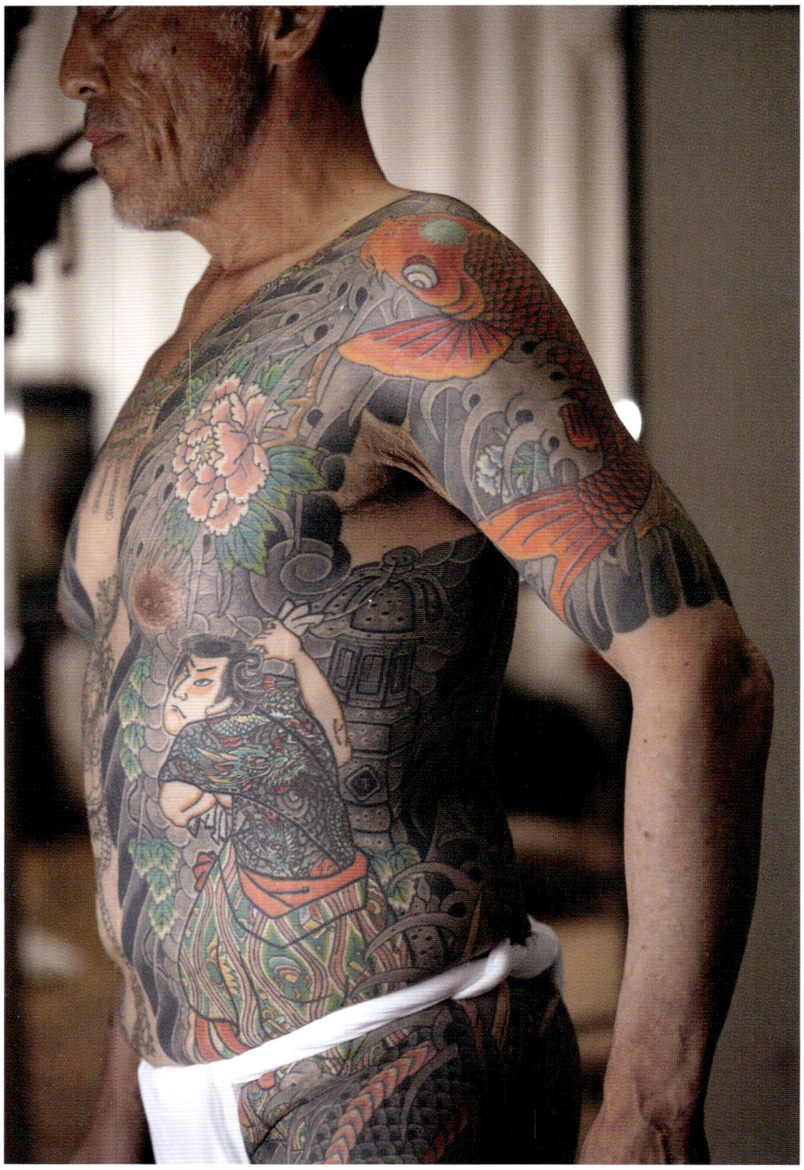

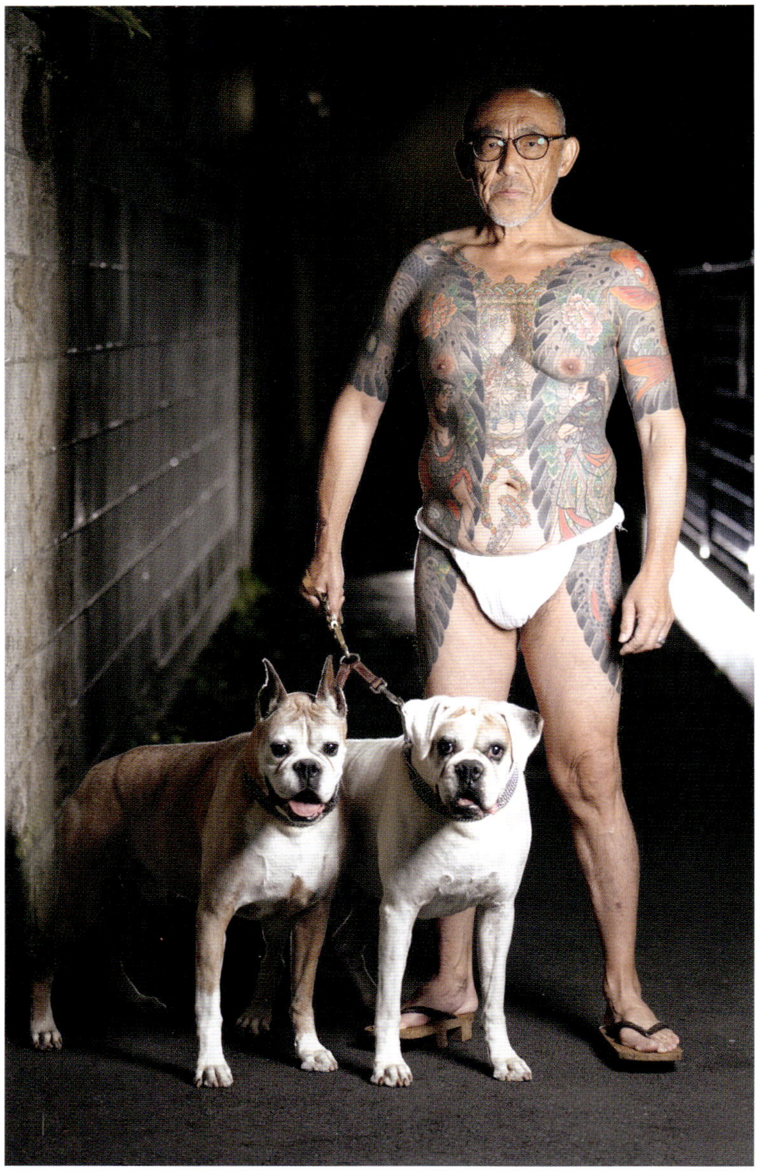

LEFT
Some of the most common motifs used in traditional Japanese tattoos come from *Suikoden* (adapted from the 14th-century Chinese novel *Water Margin*), a literary tale about tattooed outlaws who help the poor.

RIGHT
A heavily embellished client of the Horikazu dynasty.

The beauty of Japanese tattoos is multifaceted, from the splendour of the dark black gradations to the dramatic subjects. They were, and still are, made with *sumi* (black) ink created from soot. It is this shadowy *sumi* that gives the tattoos their rich yet illicit-feeling appearance. Everything has a prescribed significance and almost all the pieces are auspicious and offer good luck, including the ones that seem frightening (these are thought to be so terrifying that they ward off evil).

What is generally considered to be *wabori* (Japanese tattooing) as opposed to *yobori* (Western-style tattooing) is basically a continuation of an Edo-era tradition: masters usually insert the ink by hand and the work is large in scale, as opposed to what are referred to in Japanese as 'one points', or small Western-style tattoos.

Particularly since the Second World War, Japanese tattoos have had a strong association with the underworld and organized crime. Many *yakuza* (Japanese organized crime syndicate members) are covered in *wabori* to the degree that, until around 2010, a number of master *horishi* claimed that gangsters provided their main income streams. Recently, however, this has taken a complete turn. With a few exceptions, it's rare for *horishi* to tattoo *yakuza* at all – both because they have plenty of clients who want tattoos for purely aesthetic reasons, and because *yakuza* numbers are dropping owing to Japan's anti-organized-crime laws. However, socially sanctioned discrimination against tattooed people still exists in Japan. Because of this, much too often, the craftsmanship of *wabori* is overlooked by mainstream Japanese culture, and is not considered worthy of contemplation. As such, the industry has remained in the shadows, despite Western tattoos becoming fashionable and spreading across Japan.

In keeping with the old-school style, most Japanese *horishi* operate out of nondescript apartments and are extremely difficult to find. The studios they work from often don't have signage, and there is no indication on buildings that there are studios inside. Many of the top tattooers require an introduction to each client, and whether they will agree to tattoo someone or not is determined on a case-by-case basis.

Japanese *irezumi* are what enthusiasts often refer to as a 'hidden beauty'. Many fans of *wabori* don't attend modern-style tattoo conventions, so opportunities to actually witness ink in Japan are few and far between. The two main places to see *wabori* in their full glory are at local *sento* (public bathhouses) and *matsuri* (traditional festivals).

This book will explore the traditional tattoo scene as it exists today, with a focus on individuals who encapsulate the power, beauty and spirituality of Edo-era tattooing within a contemporary context. From the resplendent craftsmanship of Horitoku's dragons to the bold impact of Horimyo's work, the world of Japanese tattooing highlights the intersection between the nation's artisanal spirit, downtown lifestyle, festivals, woodblock prints and popular culture.

Much of *The Japanese Tattoo* will focus on the Horikazu dynasty. When the current Horikazu started he was known as Horikazuwaka; he adopted the name Horikazu after his father, the first Horikazu, died. The father and son encapsulate traditional tattooing in its entirety: the quality of the *tebori* (hand-carving), the hereditary nature of artisanship and the relationships that are forged in Tokyo's Asakusa community – which is the historic heartland of Edo commoner culture, and is where *wabori* as we know it today was born. Horikazu is the only *horishi* who also manages a *matsuri* festival community, and the people depicted in the Sanja *matsuri* section of the book (which is Tokyo's largest and most important festival), as well as Torigoe and Kawagoe *matsuri*, are clients of the Horikazu dynasty. The section on Buddhist and Shinto motifs features their clients too.

Horikazu's relationships in the tattoo world are formed through real-life interactions. His daily *sento* visits are where he networks with his current clients and sees his father's pieces on older clients, many of whom are from the underworld elite. Nowadays, he tattoos many other tattoo artists and

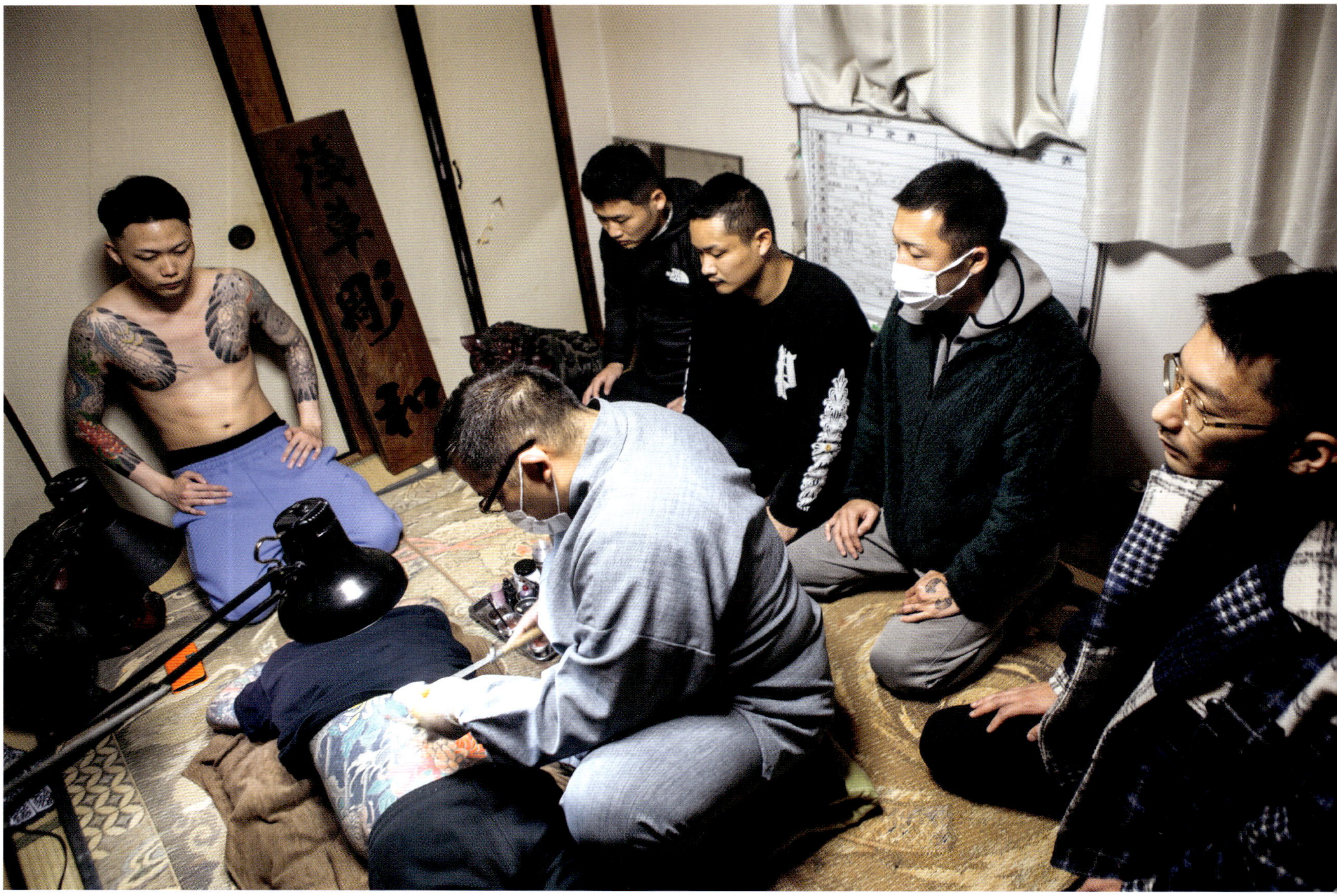

people in the Asakusa community, from chefs to artisans. In reality, Horikazu is a very rare case and the last of a few remaining *horishi* who operate like this, as many old-school tattooers have now retired or passed away. The majority of young *horishi* rely completely on Instagram or YouTube to attract clientele, and it has become a world where the most attention-seeking behaviour – such as giving away trade secrets on social media – wins the popularity contest.

Wabori has travelled across the globe as a fashion statement. Back in Japan, it has its roots as a ritual and lifestyle, and exists within a cultural context which I hope to share in this book.

Thank you to the *horishi*'s clients for allowing us to photograph their tattoos.

Note: For premodern times, the traditional naming system (family name first, given name last) is used.

ABOVE
Tattooing is an underground rite and a ritual, as demonstrated in a tense scene in Horikazu's studio.

OPPOSITE
The work of Horikazu on a female client. It is rare for women to have Japanese traditional tattoos. This one features a modest chest panel, or *hikae*, which is shaped to suit the female body.

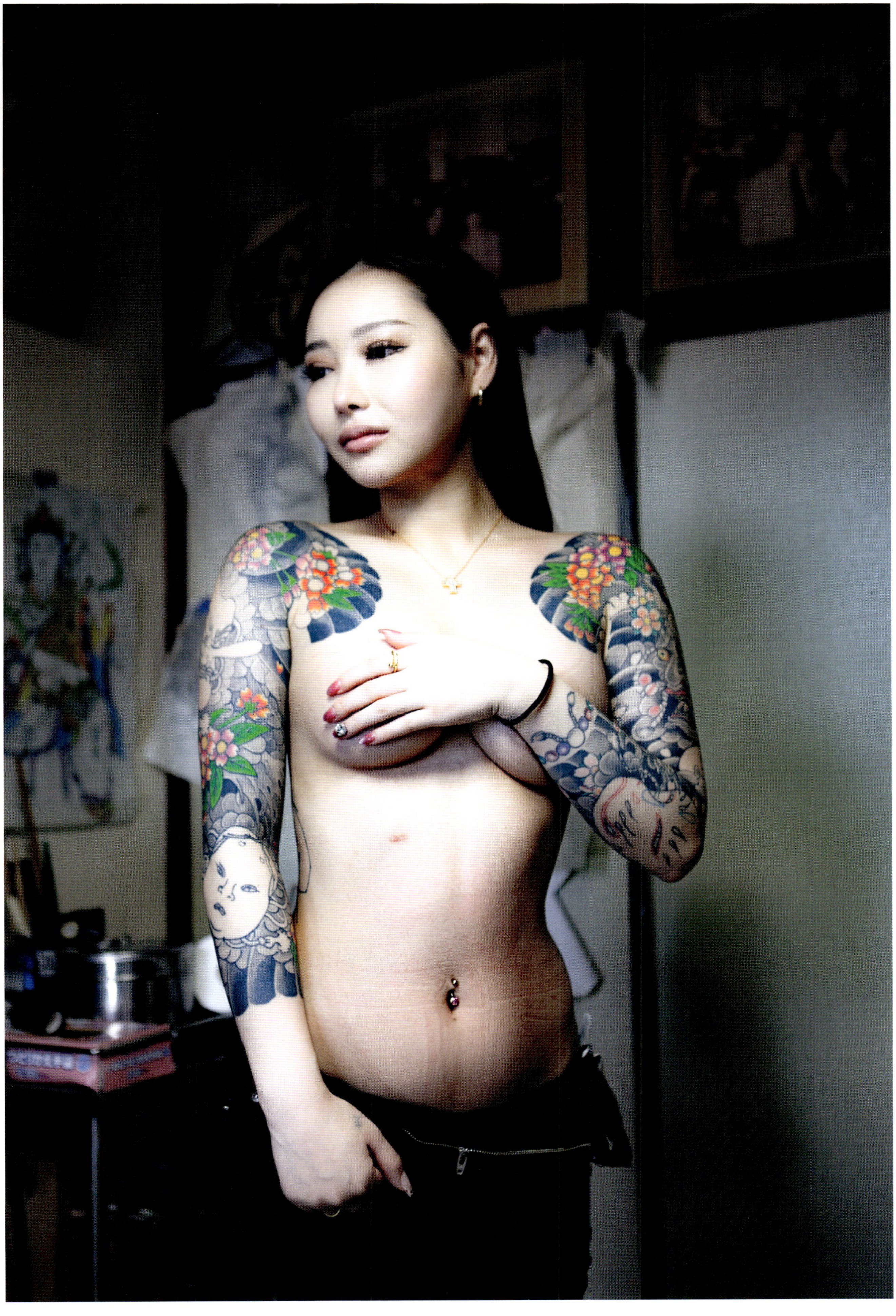

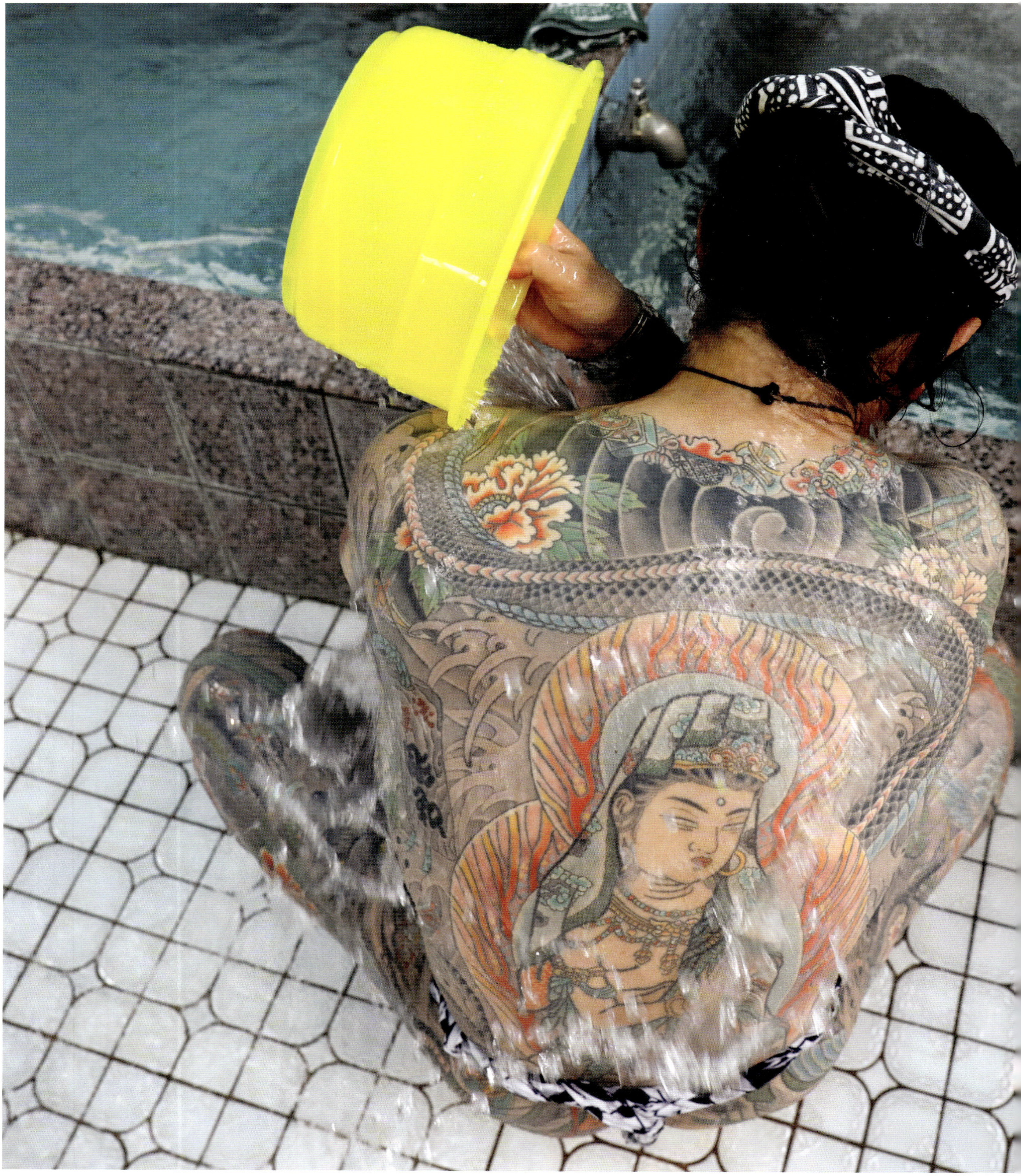

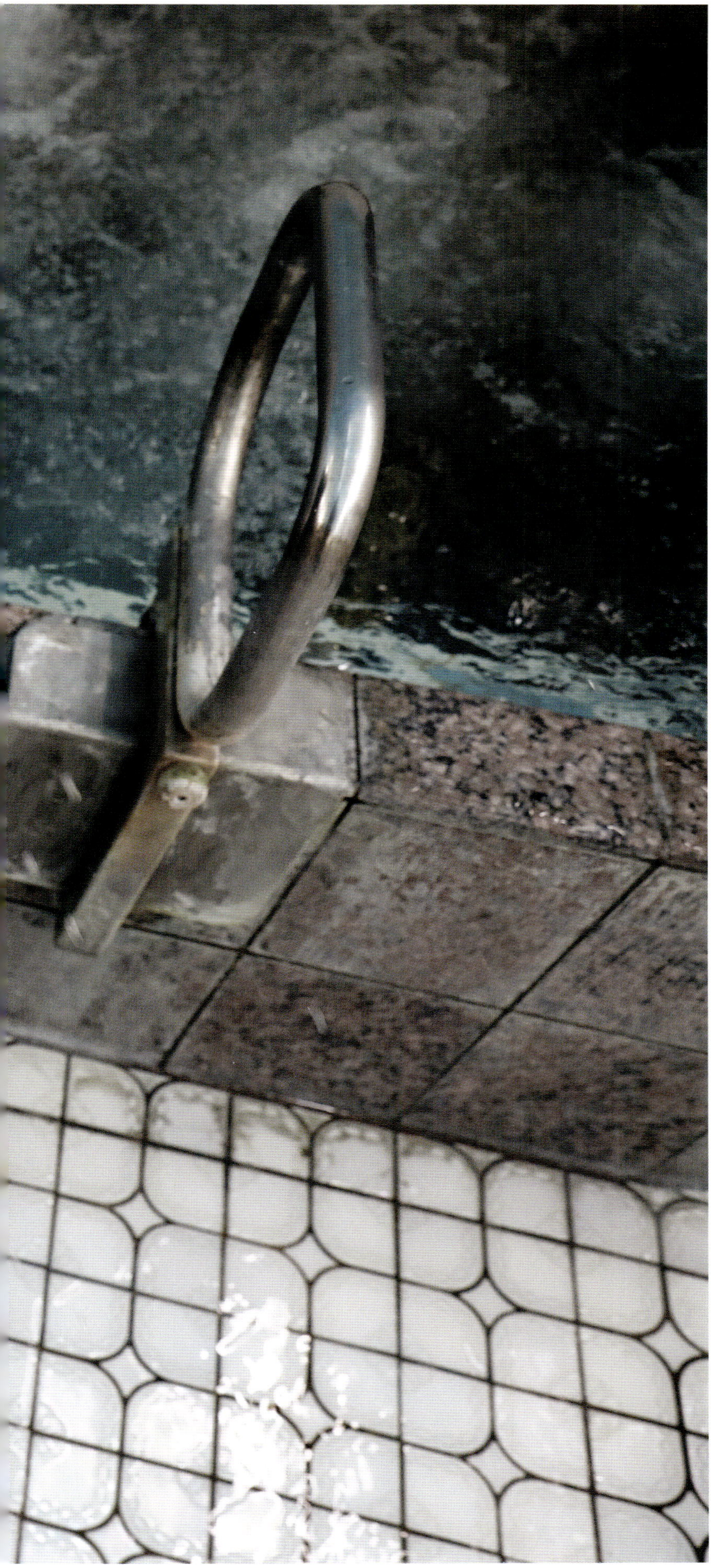

LEFT
Work by Horikazu on a *tobi* construction worker. The tradition of construction workers getting ink in Japan is a continuation of Edo-era culture.

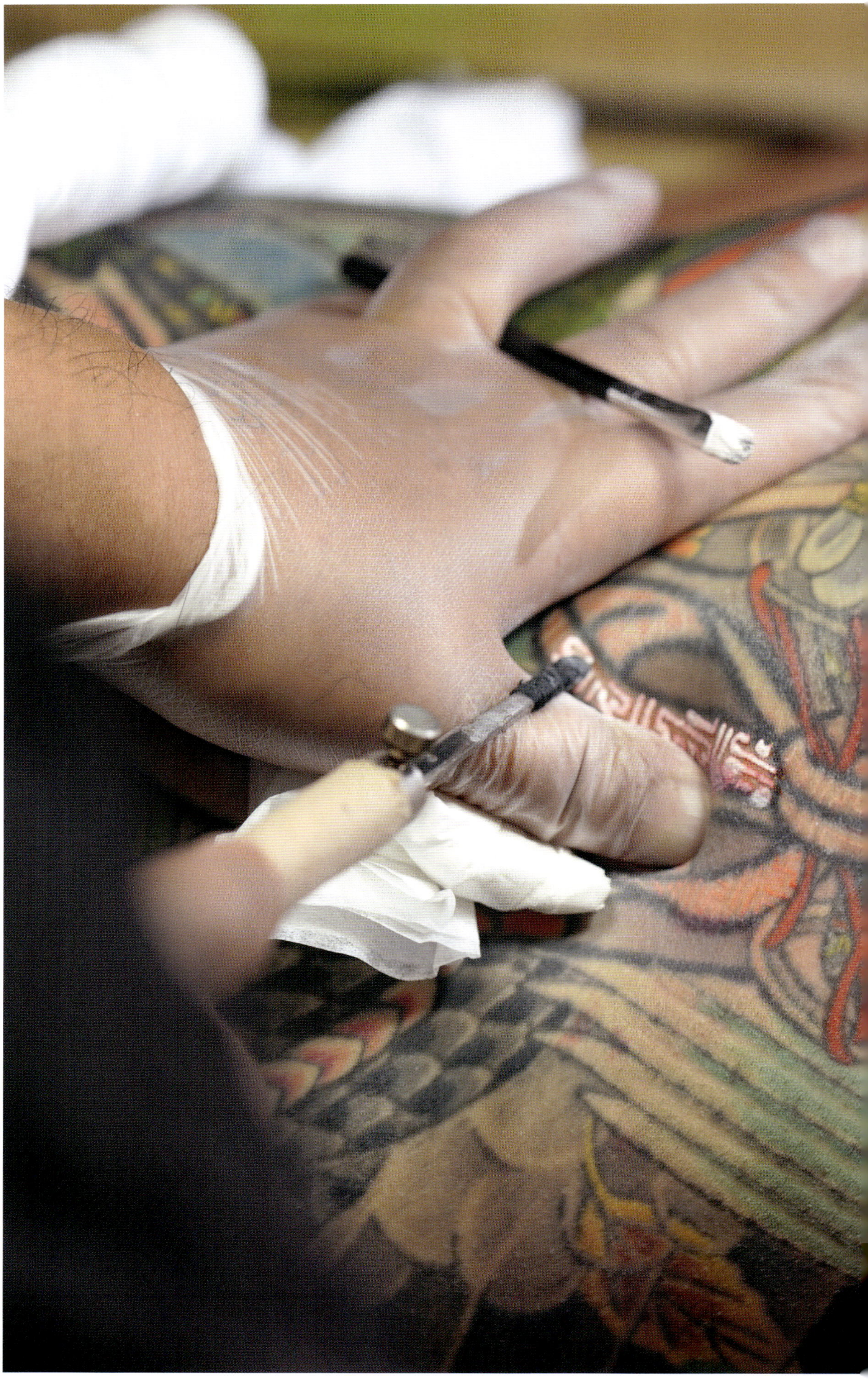

RIGHT
A *tennyo*, or Buddhist angel, being tattooed by Horikazu at his studio in Tokyo's Asakusa area, the heartland of the art form in Japan.

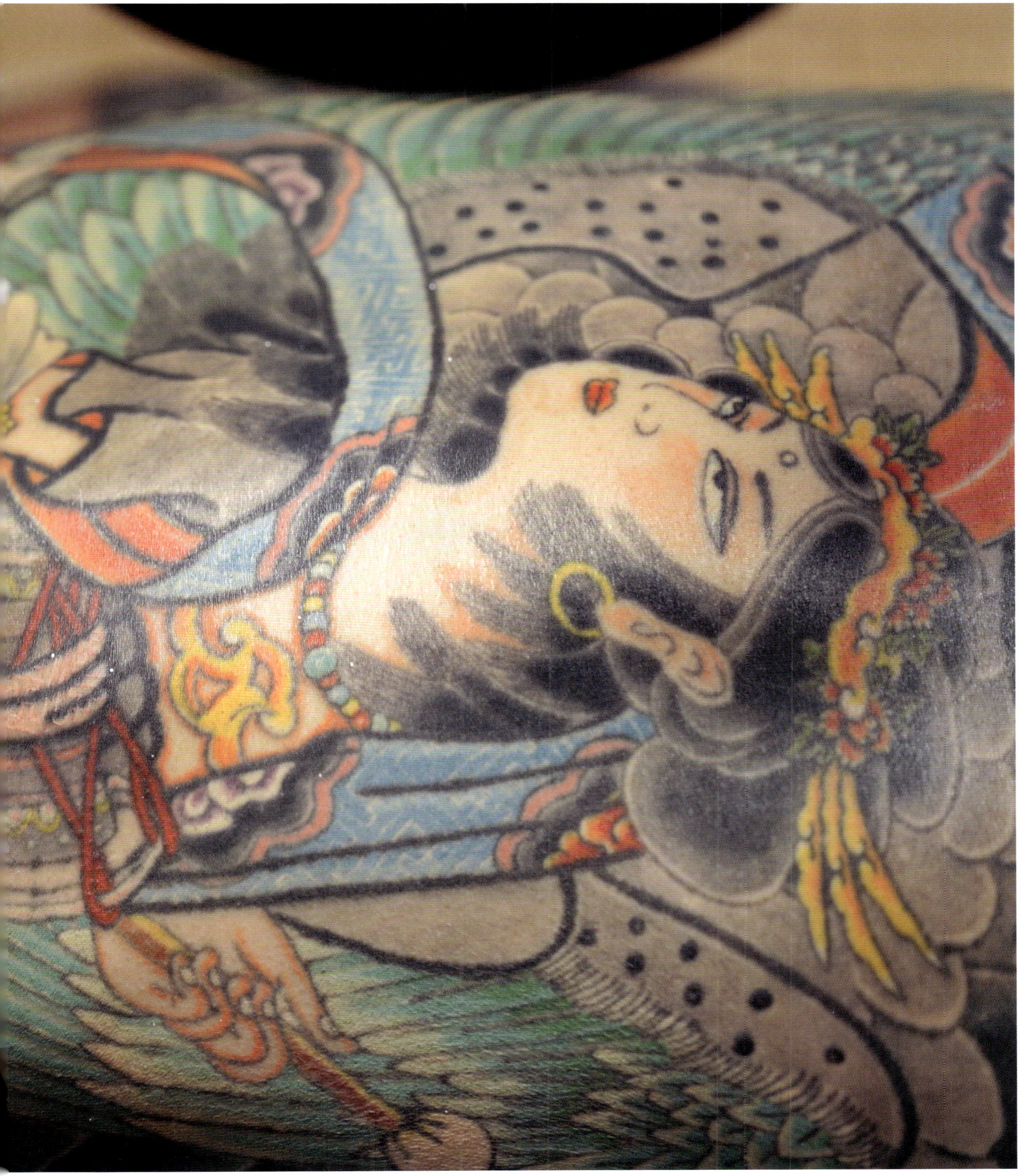

HISTORY

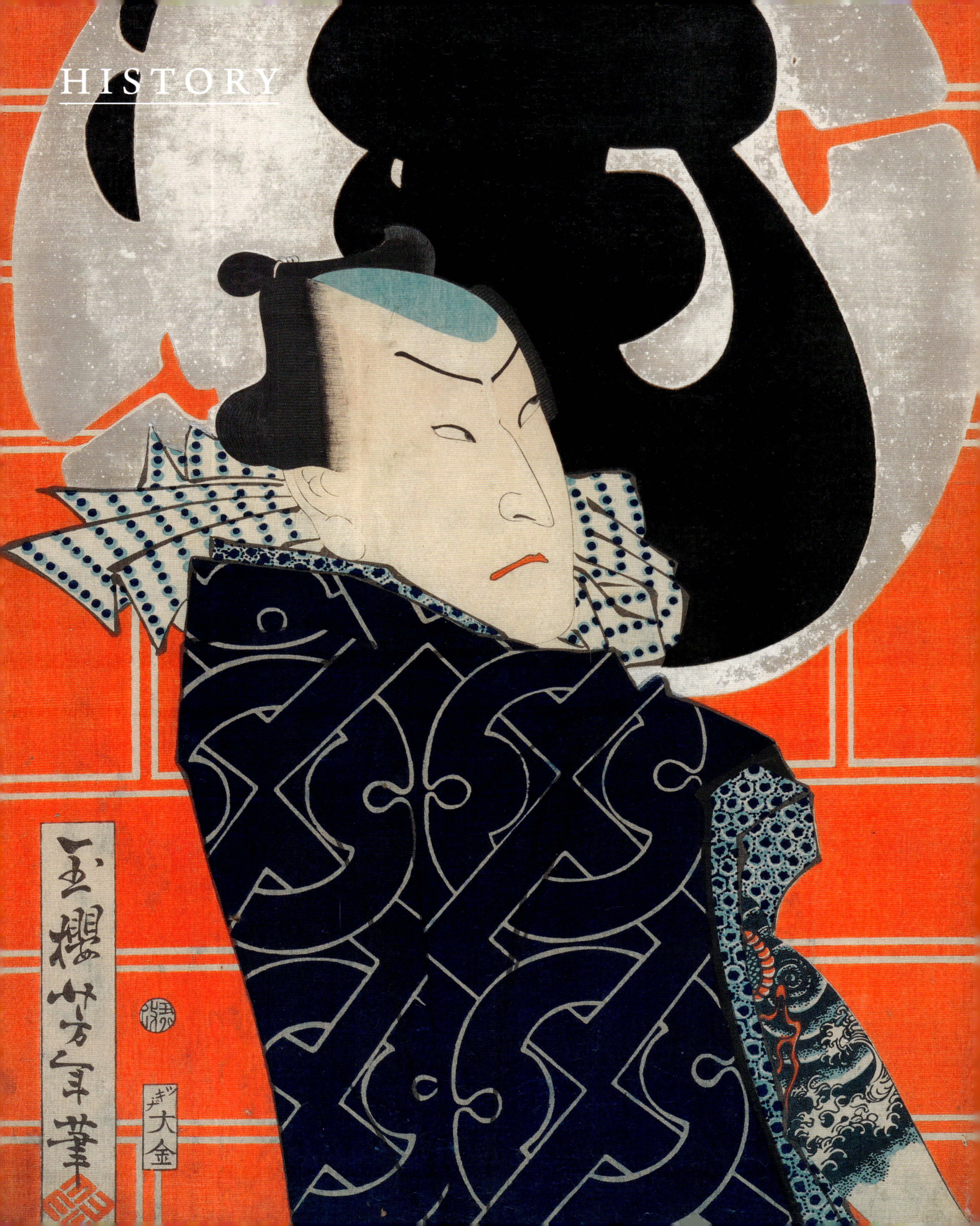

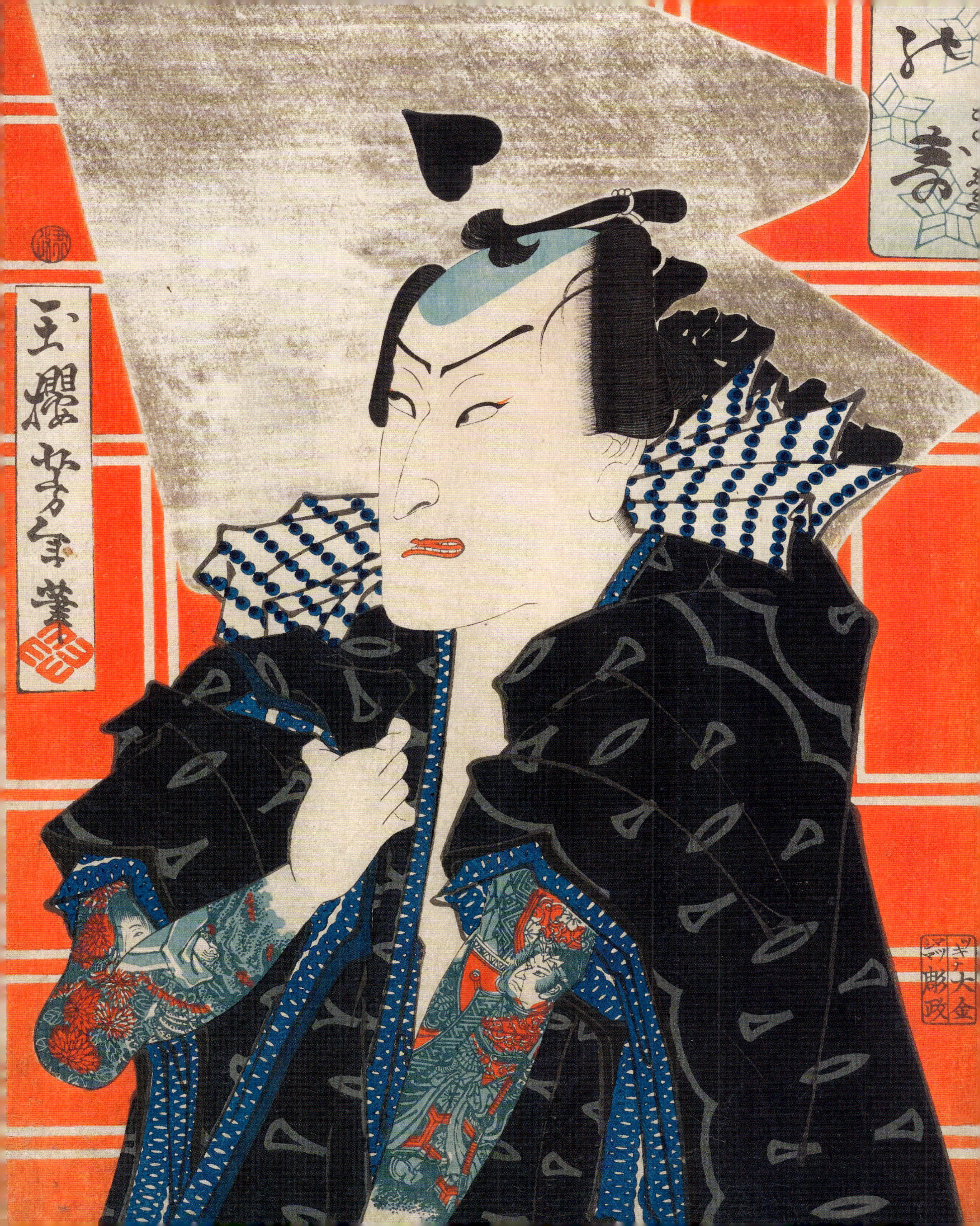
玉櫻芳幾筆

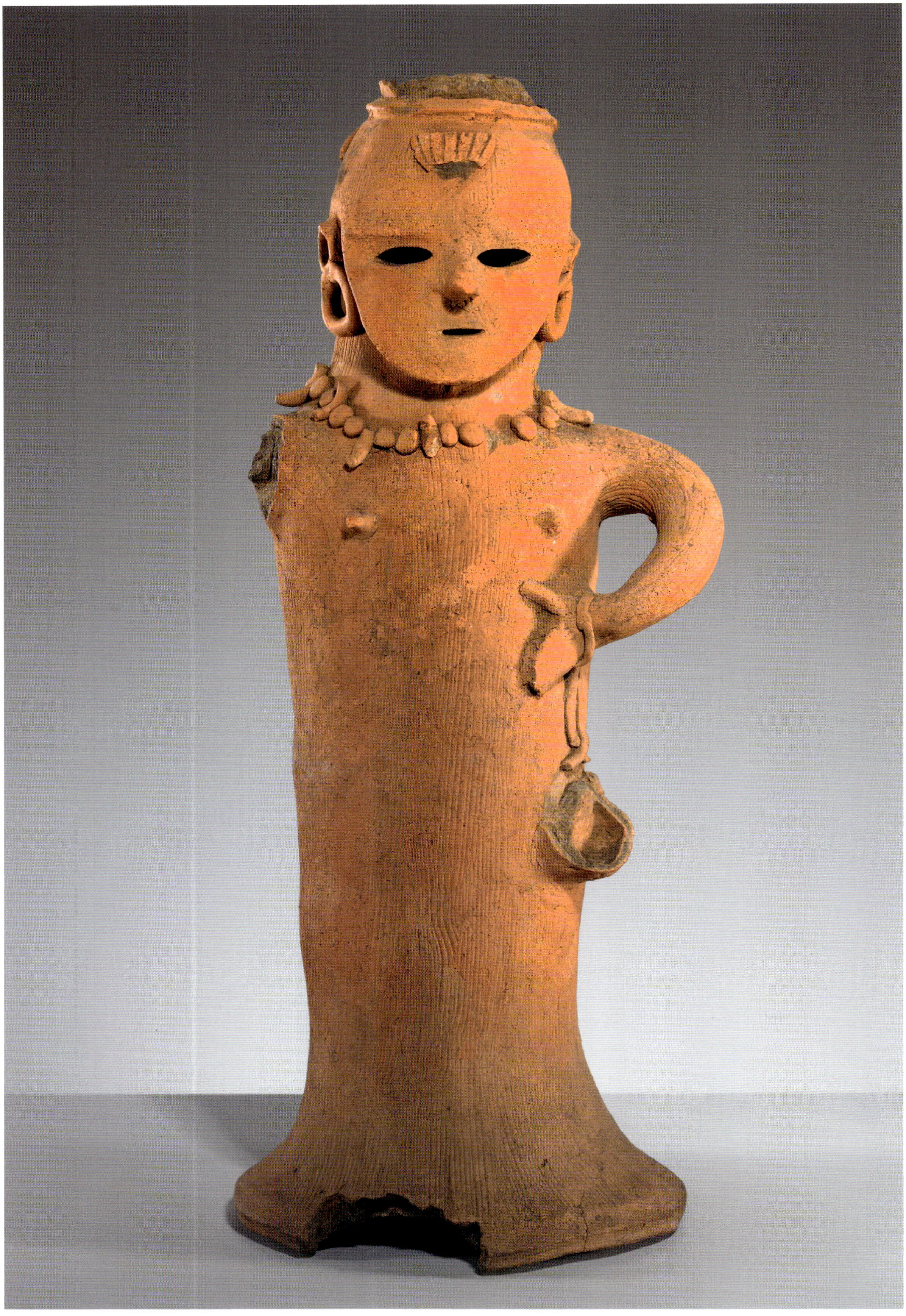

PREHISTORIC TATTOOING

Japanese tattoos have a dignified beauty dense with esoteric and auspicious symbolism, which exists in parallel to their dark atmosphere. By and large, their clandestine allure simultaneously draws curiosity while warning people to stay away. The reasons for these connotations are historic. While there is an innate human desire to transform and adorn the body, Japanese tattoos can seem inaccessible – a feeling made manifest through centuries of underworld associations. Having said that, the history of tattooing in Japan goes much further back than its subcultural roots.

It is thought that tattoos have existed in Japan since the Jomon period (about 10,000 BC to 300 BC), based on archaeological markings found on clay figures. Archaeology scholars have debated the question of whether the Jomon people had written language, and inferences have been made that the markings on these artefacts represent facial tattooing that was practised during the time, since decorative customs existed all over the world within primitive societies.

In the Yayoi period (300 BC to AD 300), Chinese travellers who came to Japan chronicled observations of tattooed people there in a historic manuscript called the *Wei zhi*, which describes Japan during the Wei dynastic period. It includes accounts of seafood divers who ascribed talismanic meaning to their tattoos, which were said to protect them from large fish and birds.

There are multiple records of tattoos from the Nara period (710–794) – such as in the *Kojiki*, Japan's oldest literary chronicle, which was compiled in 712 – but tattooing was not yet common. In the *Nihon Shoki*, compiled in 720, there is also mention of the use of *irezumi*. Early texts describe the insertion of ink as a form of punishment for people who had committed crimes, such as treason, in peripheral regions.

After the Nara period, records of tattoos were mostly absent for the next several hundred years, until the Edo era, suggesting that tattooing was not a prominent practice during that time. There are various theories about why this was, one being that the influence of China on Japanese culture led to the cessation of these kinds of bodily adornments. In the Kofun period (AD 250–538), Japanese rulers had taken on much of Chinese ideology, and Confucian Chinese beliefs had permeated Japanese cultural values. Accordingly, tattoos were looked upon negatively and seen as barbaric. From the mid-7th century onwards, a lot of emphasis was placed on clothing, and the culture of tattooing only really flourished much later, in the Edo era.

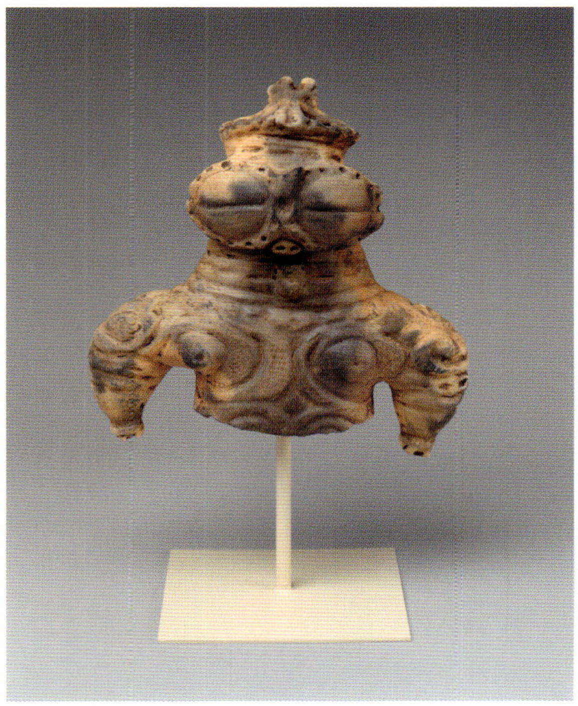

PREVIOUS SPREAD
Tsukioka Yoshitoshi (carver: Matsushima Masakichi), *A Celebration of Bravery*, 1865, woodblock print. In Japan during the Edo period, firefighters, who were heavily tattooed, were exalted as protectors of the city, and were often depicted in Edo- and Meiji-era *ukiyo-e* woodblock prints and *kabuki* theatre.

OPPOSITE
Haniwa (clay figure) of a woman, 6th century. Her necklace suggests she is a *miko*, or shrine attendant. Traces of red pigment on her face indicate tattoos or ceremonial face paint.

RIGHT
Clay figure of a woman, 1000–300 BC, from Tohoku, thought to have functioned as a fertility symbol. The cord-shaped markings suggest tattoos.

INDIGENOUS TATTOOING TRADITIONS

Separate to the Edo-era tattooing culture that is featured in this book, there have been other distinct tattooing traditions in Japan. The insertion of ink was widespread among women in the Ryukyu Islands (the region between Kyushu and Taiwan, including Okinawa), who marked their hands and wrists, as well as women in Ainu indigenous communities in northern Japan, who tattooed their mouths, cheeks and arms.

The Ainu people were colonized by the Japanese and in the 19th century were subject to forced assimilation. Okinawa was formerly an autonomous kingdom known as the Ryukyu Kingdom. It was annexed into Japan in 1879 and transformed into Okinawa prefecture. Both the Ainu and the Uchinanchu (Ryukyu people) have had a long struggle to preserve their heritage. More recently, in Okinawa, there are Ryukyu artists like Moeko Heshiki, who are active locally. Members of the global Okinawan diaspora have been trying to preserve *hajichi* (Ryukyu-style tattooing) culture, too. Hawaii-based tattooer Erin Nagamine's family is originally from Okinawa; her grandfather immigrated to Hawaii in 1919 to work on a sugar plantation. Nagamine sees *hajichi* as a way to connect to her heritage, as well as an opportunity to inspire the world to respect these traditional practices: 'When I first began my journey, *hajichi* was a gateway to connect to my roots and family,' she explains. 'Now, what *hajichi* means to me has blossomed into connecting with other people within our community and learning from them. Traditionally, the symbolism of *hajichi* was to honour milestones of womanhood. Women are said to have a connection to the spiritual realm, so the symbols are a reflection of that belief. Giving and receiving *hajichi* is about more than just pride in my heritage. It is a symbol of responsibility to continue learning about how to honour my ancestors and loved ones, the responsibility to help inspire other Uchinanchus through *hajichi*, and most of all, the responsibility to also honour and ground myself.'

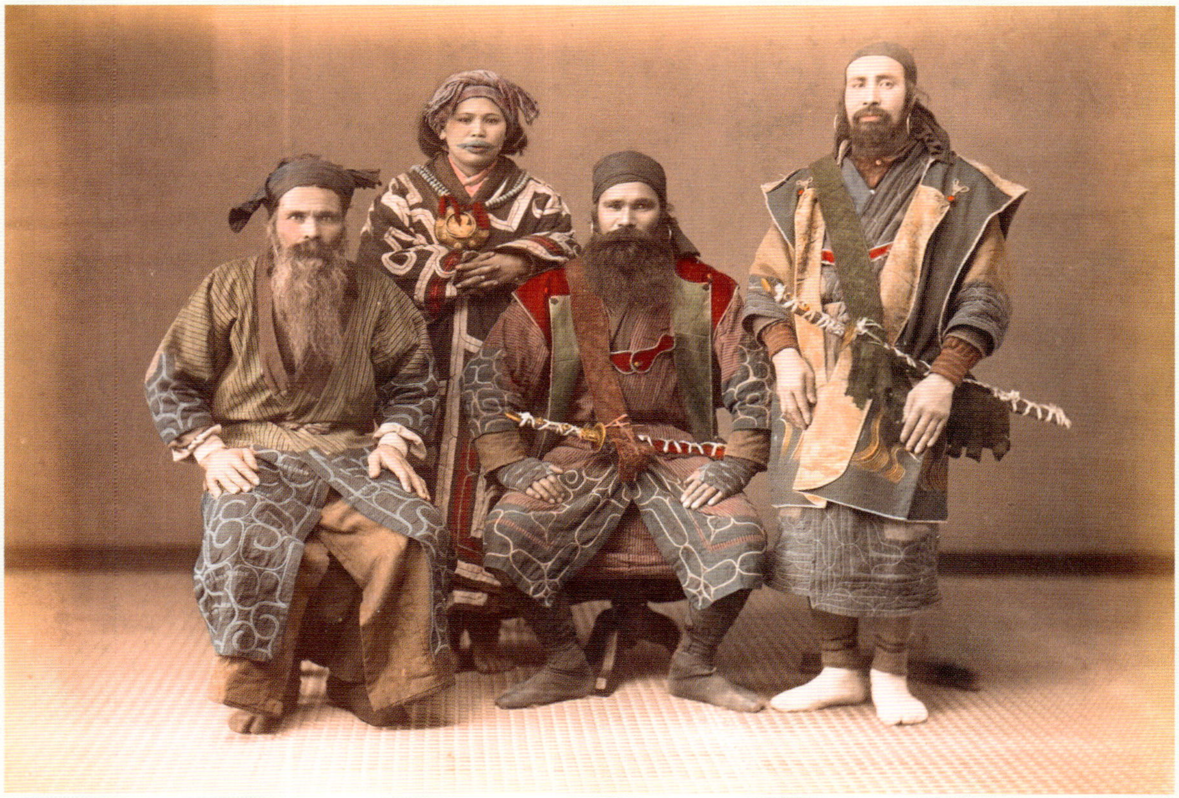

LEFT
Indigenous Ainu people from northern Japan, around 1900. Ainu women were known for tattooing their mouths, cheeks and arms.

OPPOSITE TOP
Jan Takahashi and her daughter Willow getting *hajichi* (Ryukyu Islands-style tattooing) from Hawaii-based tattooer Erin Nagamine.

OPPOSITE BOTTOM
An example of Nagamine's work. She feels strongly about the preservation of the *hajichi* art form as the result of learning about her cultural identity and the history of the colonization of the Ryukyu people.

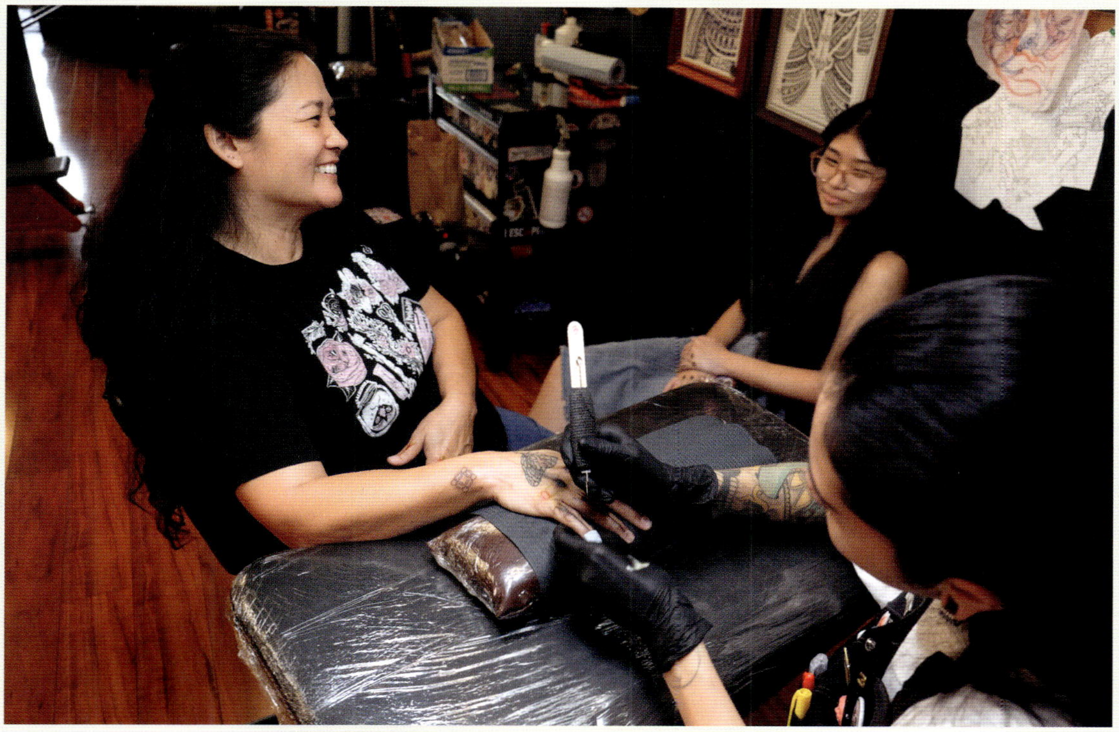

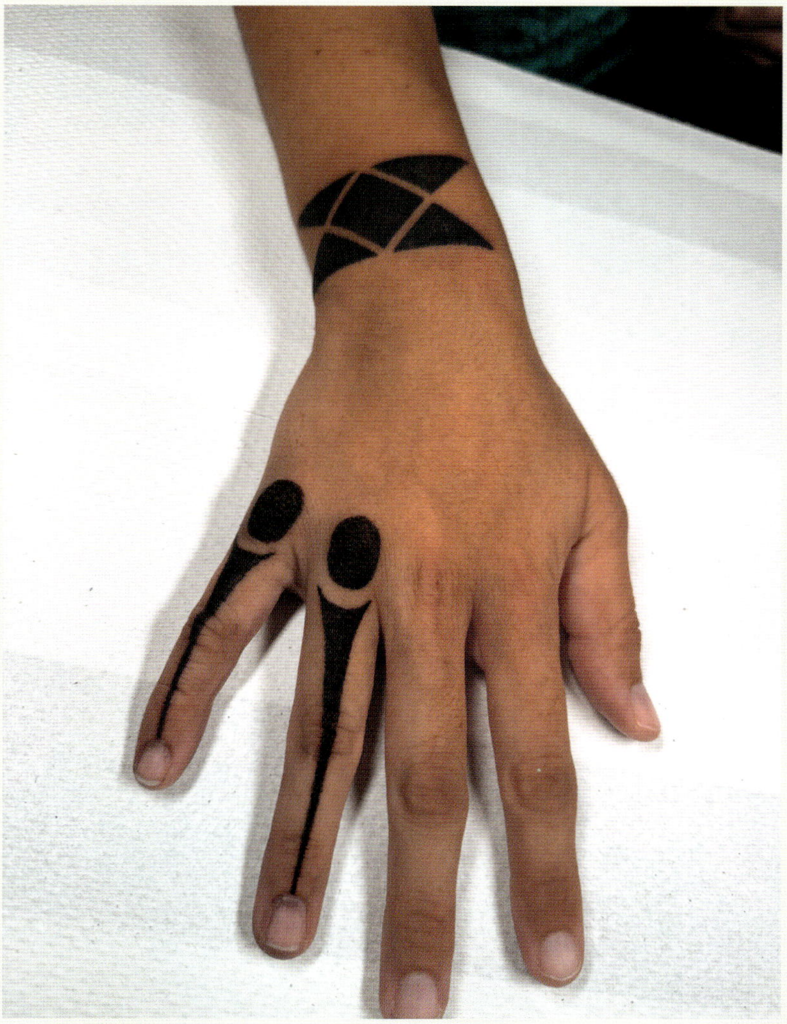

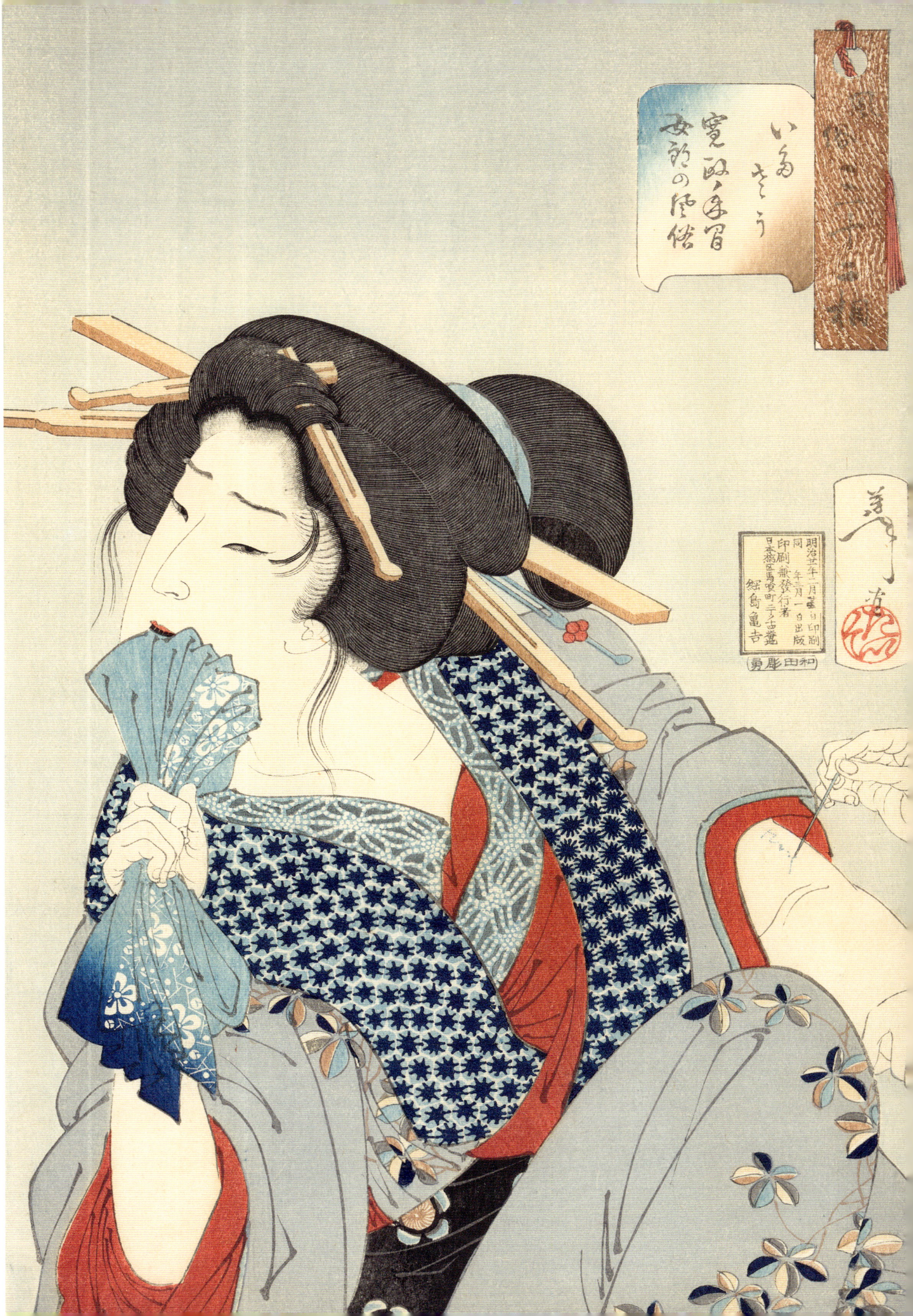
いたさう
寛政年間
女郎の風俗

THE EDO ERA

During Japan's Edo period, there was a formal type of punishment that saw criminals tattooed with either bands on their arms or letters on their foreheads, among other types of markings. The nature of these tattoos varied from clan to clan and depended on the severity of the crimes in question. Some criminals eventually got cover-ups on their arms to hide the markings.

Soon, Japanese tattooing began to flourish, centred around downtown Edo (now Tokyo), and spawning from the merchant and artisan culture of the time. Edo was the newly urbanized nation's capital and the arts thrived there in many guises. Under the prevailing Tokugawa shogunate class system, which was in place from 1603 to 1868, there was a hierarchy that saw samurai at the top, followed by farmers, artisans and finally merchants at the bottom (although artisans often took on the role of merchants as well, as they sold their own wares). Working-class people were restricted to the marshy *shitamachi* (downtown) part of Edo, where they were segregated from the ruling class (who lived in the uptown region, where west Tokyo is now). Hence, the art and entertainment of the area – *kabuki* theatre, *ukiyo-e* woodblock prints, festivals and the region's huge red-light district, the Yoshiwara – were purely created for commoners, by commoners, forming an independent culture in clear contrast to the high society of the elite. Tattoos were a celebration of the working class, but also a manifestation of a counterculture that was in opposition to the corrupt shogunate. Overall, though, the Edo era was a time of peace, unlike previous periods in Japanese history that were fraught with civil conflict. There was a sense of freedom and wealth, even among the lower classes.

Japanese tattooing as it is practised today has its roots in the 'floating world', or *ukiyo*, a term that expressed Edo-era social conditions for the everyday people of Tokyo, Osaka and Kyoto. *Ukiyo* is the Buddhist notion that everything is temporary, and encapsulates a sorrowful sense of the ephemeral. However, this awareness that all is fleeting evolved into a hedonistic, live-for-the-moment attitude. In fact, some of the first known examples of Edo-era tattoos were done in the pleasure quarters, where prostitutes made declarations of loyalty to their clients by getting pledge tattoos featuring discreet dots or names.

Inked bodysuits were common among people engaged in occupations that necessitated a certain level of bravado, such as *tobi* construction workers, and in particular firefighters – who were celebrated like stars, as fires were so rife in downtown Edo. These firefighters – who often had tattoos of dragons, which were thought to bring rain – embodied the fleeting nature of life in Edo. There was a

OPPOSITE
Tsukioka Yoshitoshi (carver: Wada Yūjirō), *Appearing in Pain, Behaviour of a Prostitute of the Kansei Era*, 1888, woodblock print. Japanese tattoos are inextricably intertwined with the nation's *kabuki* theatre and *ukiyo-e* woodblock print traditions. Tokyo's downtown, including the red-light district Yoshiwara, essentially gave birth to this now-global art form.

notion that their existence could go up in flames at any moment. The famous poetic phrase 'Fights and fires are the flowers of Edo' describes this everyday drama of downtown life; there is an appreciation of the beauty of transience. Other tattooed folks at the time included labourers and delivery people.

Kyokaku and *otokodate* (street gangsters) were also among the tattooed people of the period, and were exalted in the popular imagination as defenders of commoners against the corrupt samurai. Many lower-class townsfolk sought their protection, and saw inspiration in the Robin Hood-esque narrative of *Suikoden* – a folkloric tale adapted from the Chinese *Water Margin* in the 18th century – which is about a group of chivalrous, tattooed bandits who fight the injustices of the overlords. *Otokodate* were often tattooed with the likenesses of these courageous antiheroes.

The three art forms of *ukiyo-e*, *kabuki* and *irezumi* grew in parallel, in terms of both complexity and popularity. *Kabuki* was a form of commoner theatre, with its flamboyance and sensational dramatizations of everyday affairs. *Kabuki* actors were the celebrities of the time, and people sought out woodblock prints that featured them standing in their trademark exaggerated poses. Many of the protagonists represented the working class, such as the *otokodate*, for example, in the popular play *The Summer Festival*. Theatregoers felt an affinity with these handsome, tattooed brutes, who would mete out street justice to corrupt authoritarian forces. As such, the *kabuki* was also a place where *irezumi* symbolism flourished, and these plays in turn inspired more tattoo-themed woodblock prints.

While sumptuary laws of the time tried to restrict commoners from flaunting ostentatious wealth and engaging in hedonistic pursuits, tattoos flourished and served as symbols of rebellion and anti-authoritarianism. At the same time, they were an indication of community belonging and identification with the *iki* (cool) sensibilities of the Edo townsfolk and the floating world.

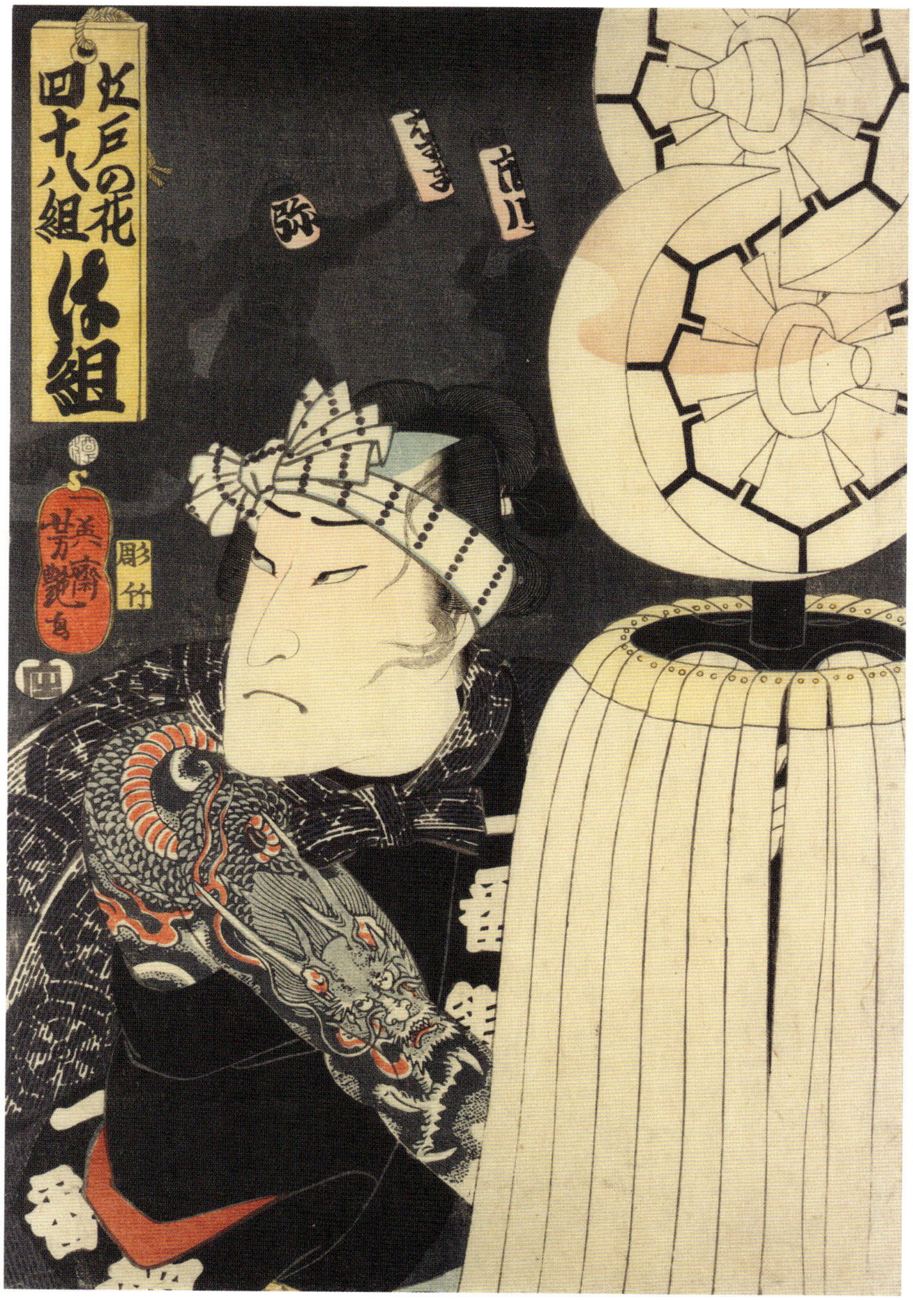

ABOVE
Utagawa Yoshitsuya, *Ha Brigade*, from the series *Flowers of Edo: 48 Brigades*, 1861, woodblock print.

OPPOSITE TOP
The Firefighters Memorial Service at Yutenji, Tokyo, held to commemorate the lives of firefighters who died while working from the Edo to the Showa era.

OPPOSITE BOTTOM
Celebrating Edo-era firefighting culture during an annual New Year's performance of firefighters in Tokyo. During the Edo era, fires were rife. Firemen of the time were seen as heroes and were often tattooed with motifs they thought were talismanic.

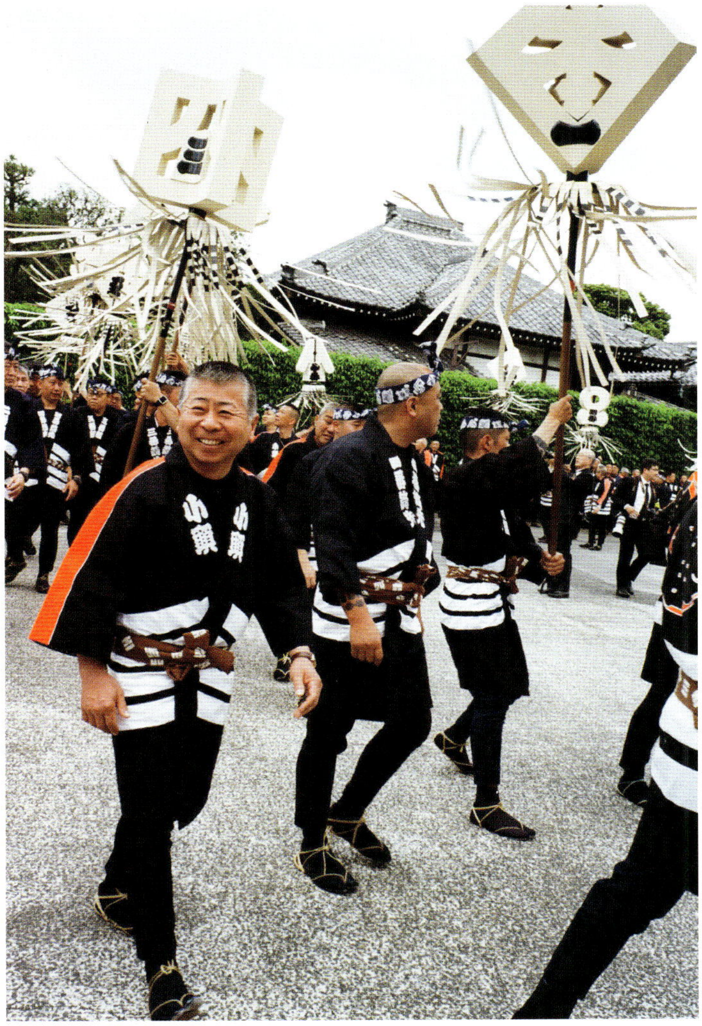

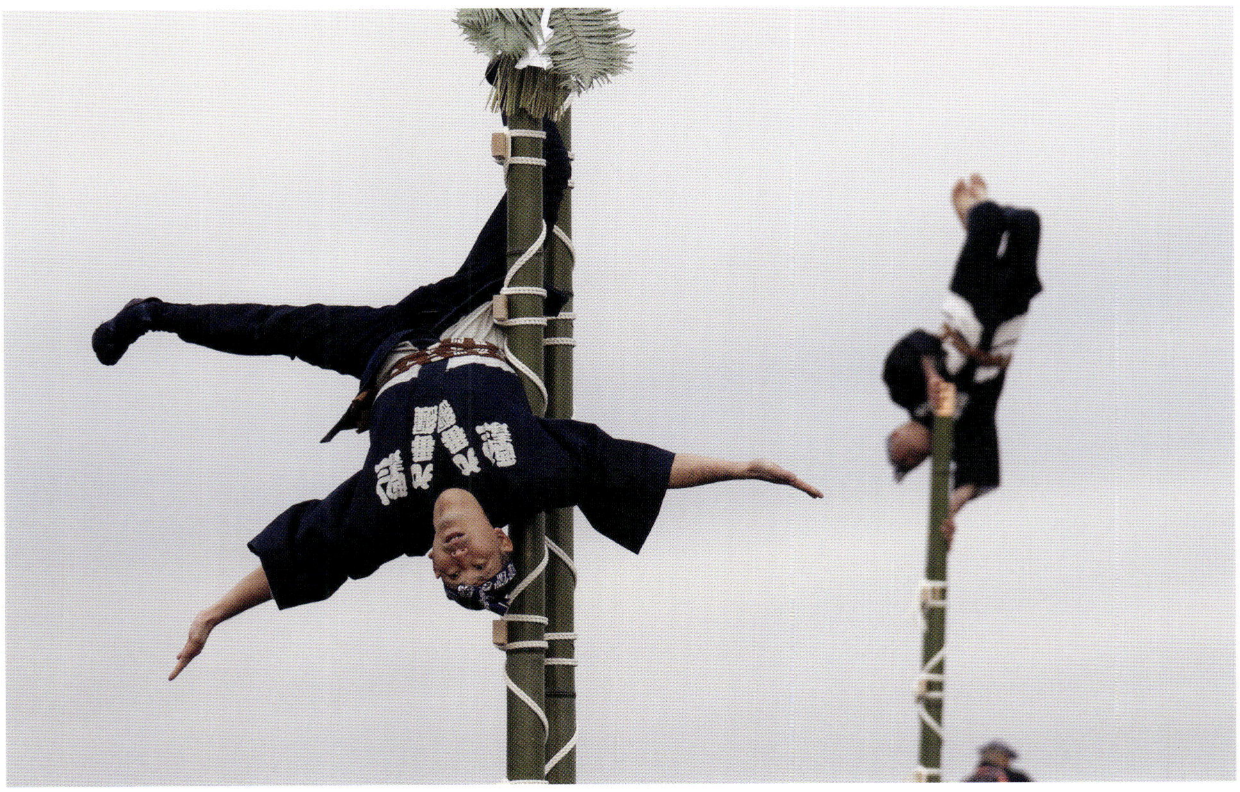

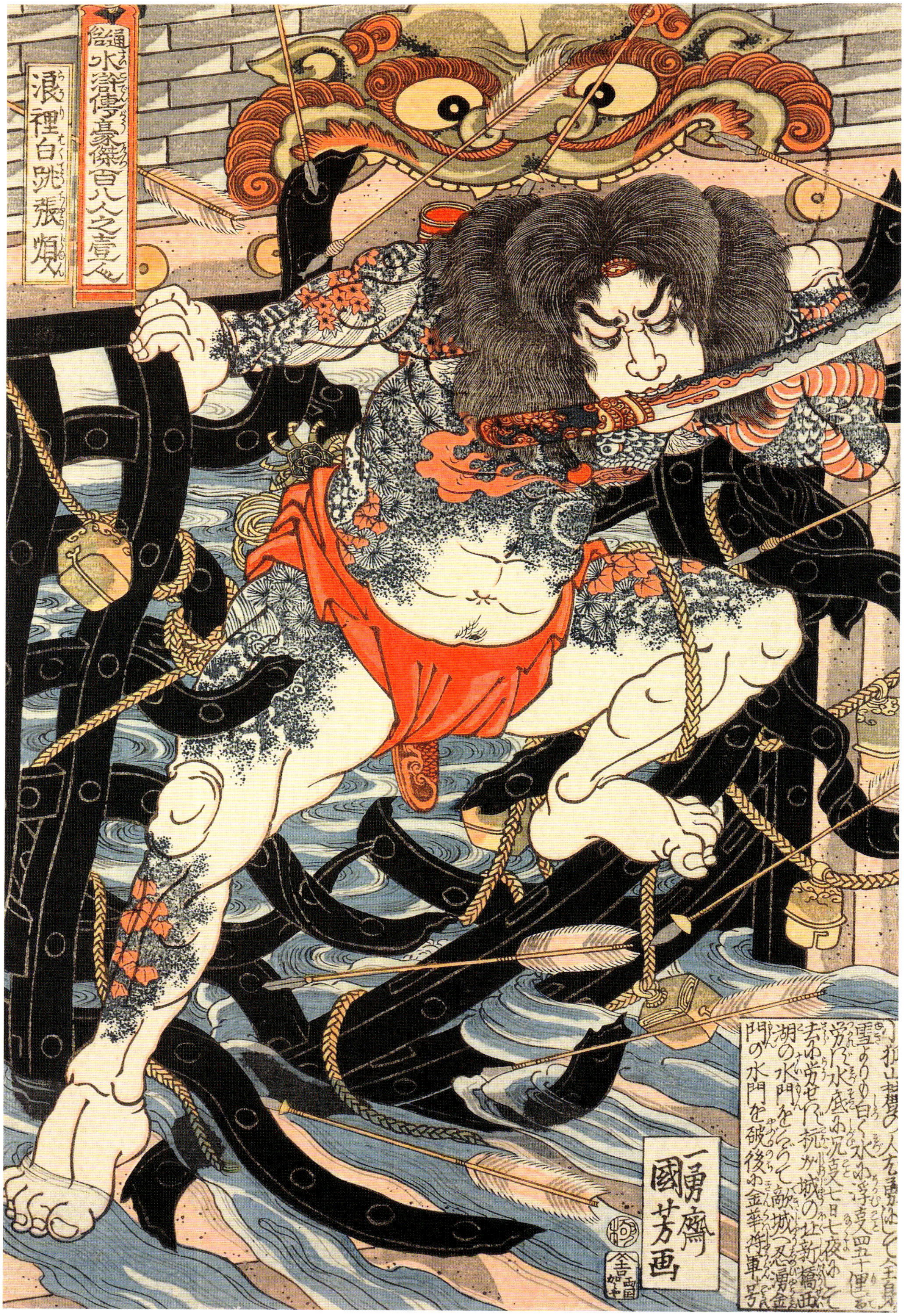
通俗水滸傳豪傑百八人之壹人
浪裡白跳張順
一勇齋國芳画

UKIYO-E WOODBLOCK PRINTS

When considering the visual qualities of Japanese tattoos, the composition, motifs and aesthetic sensibilities are the result of the relationship *wabori* has with *ukiyo-e* woodblock prints. *Ukiyo-e* prints were a form of print media and art that flourished during the Edo period, when the Tokugawa government unified the country. The scenes depicted in *ukiyo-e* were a reflection of the times: there is a positivity, an exultation of spirit and *joie de vivre* in the works.

The first *ukiyo-e* master is said to have been Hishikawa Moronobu (1618–1694), who was born in present-day Chiba prefecture. His family was in the textile industry and he used this knowledge in his prints, the subjects of which were often beautiful women. Early *ukiyo-e* were rendered in black *sumi* ink until full-colour prints started to be mass-produced in the mid-Edo era, when Suzuki Harunobu (1725–1770) created them in gorgeous hues. Called *nishiki-e*, these intricate, polychrome, layered prints were developed using multiple woodblocks, and *ukiyo-e* became an increasingly sophisticated art form as a result.

Woodblock printing required the work of four artisans: an artist, a carver, a printer and a publisher (who often commissioned the works). The artist first conceived of an image, which was then transferred to paper. This paper was pasted to a cherrywood block, and the carver engraved the wood so that lines were raised. Ink was then applied to this block for printing. Colours were carved on separate blocks (up to twenty of them for each artwork), which were printed on *washi*, fibrous Japanese paper made from mulberry tree bark. Thousands of works could be printed from a single set of blocks using this technology.

Ukiyo-e artists were members of the commoner class, while their clients were predominantly wealthy merchants. Many of the historic prints show everyday scenes and floating-world life as people then knew it, with the most frequent themes being individuals in the entertainment industry, such as *kabuki* actors, and courtesans, such as those of the Yoshiwara red-light district. Numerous *ukiyo-e* artists, like Utagawa Kuniyoshi, used tattoos as a narrative device in their designs. Some of Kuniyoshi's most well-known works were of the 108 *Suikoden* heroes, all of which he created over the course of three years, starting in 1827. The popularity of *Suikoden* inspired an entire genre of warrior artworks, a theme that remains widespread in the tattoo world, even today. Other notable artists, such as Utagawa Kunisada, Tsukioka Yoshitoshi and Toyohara Kunichika, also depicted inked bodies in their woodblock prints from the Edo era to the Meiji period (1868–1912).

Enamoured with the bravado of *kabuki* stars, fans copied these tattoo-design prints during the 17th century. In turn, *ukiyo-e* masters made the tattoos in their artworks ever more complex and beautiful, which is the genesis of Japanese decorative tattooing as it is known today. From the carving of cherrywood to the carving of skin, *horimono* is a reflection of the spirit and energy of downtown Edo.

OPPOSITE
Utagawa Kuniyoshi, *Rorihakucho Cho Jun*, from the series *One Hundred and Eight Heroes of the Popular 'Water Margin'*, *c.* 1827–30, woodblock print. Kuniyoshi, a favourite *ukiyo-e* artist of the Edo era, is known for the sense of freedom in his work, his fresh ideas and his rebellious spirit. Even though various sumptuary laws were foisted on Japanese commoners during the time he was working – including bans on prints featuring courtesans and *kabuki* actors – he continued to challenge the authorities and make large quantities of them.

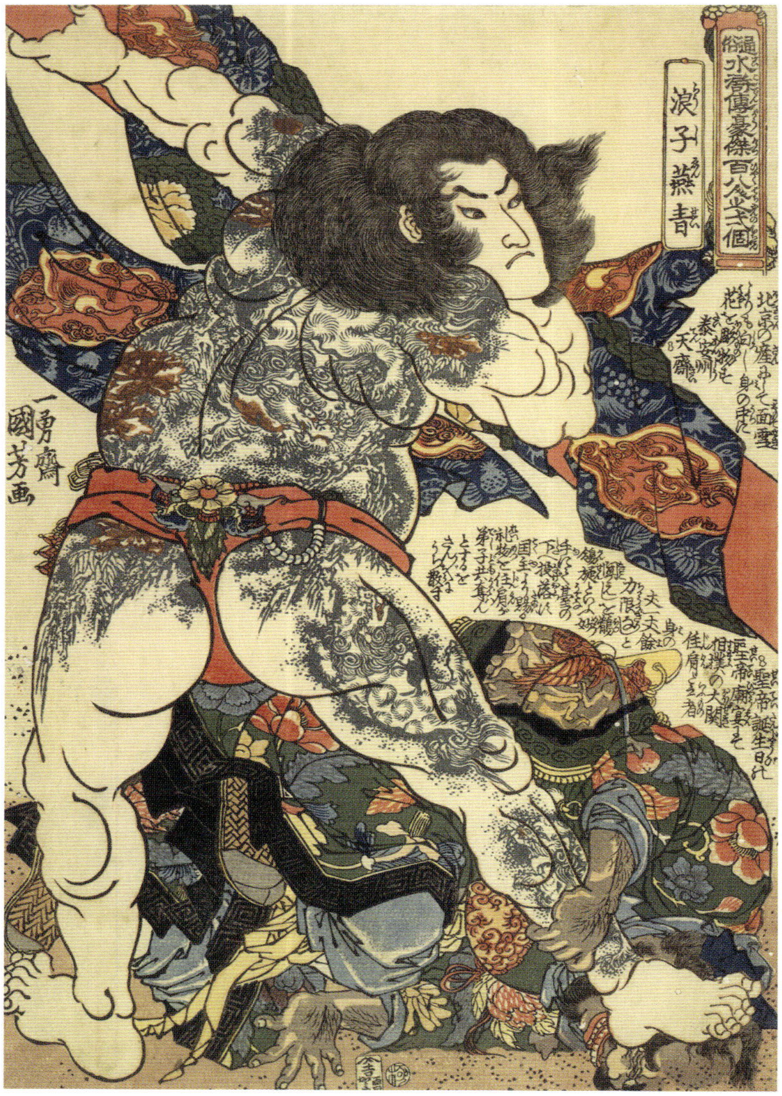

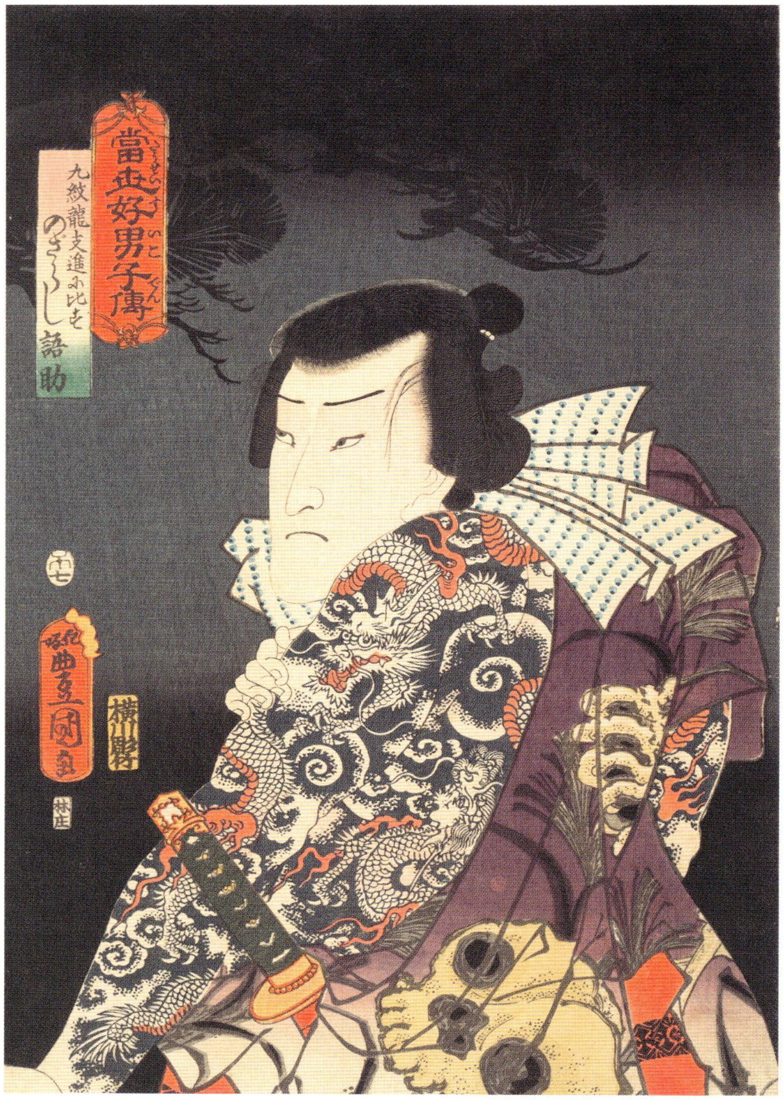

LEFT
Utagawa Kuniyoshi, *Roshi Ensei*, from the series *One Hundred and Eight Heroes of the Popular 'Water Margin'*, *c.* 1827–30, woodblock print.

RIGHT
Utagawa Kunisada, *The Actor Ichikawa Ichizo III as Nozarashi Gosuke, Likened to the Kyumonryu Shishin*, from the 'Pine' triptych of the series *A Modern Water Margin*, 1854, woodblock print.

OPPOSITE
Utagawa Kuniyoshi, *Tammeijiro Genshogo*, from the series *One Hundred and Eight Heroes of the Popular 'Water Margin'*, *c.* 1823, woodblock print. The bandit Tanmeijiro Genshogo from *Suikoden* is depicted fighting underwater, as one of his skills is being able to stay submerged for a long time. He is covered in tattoos.

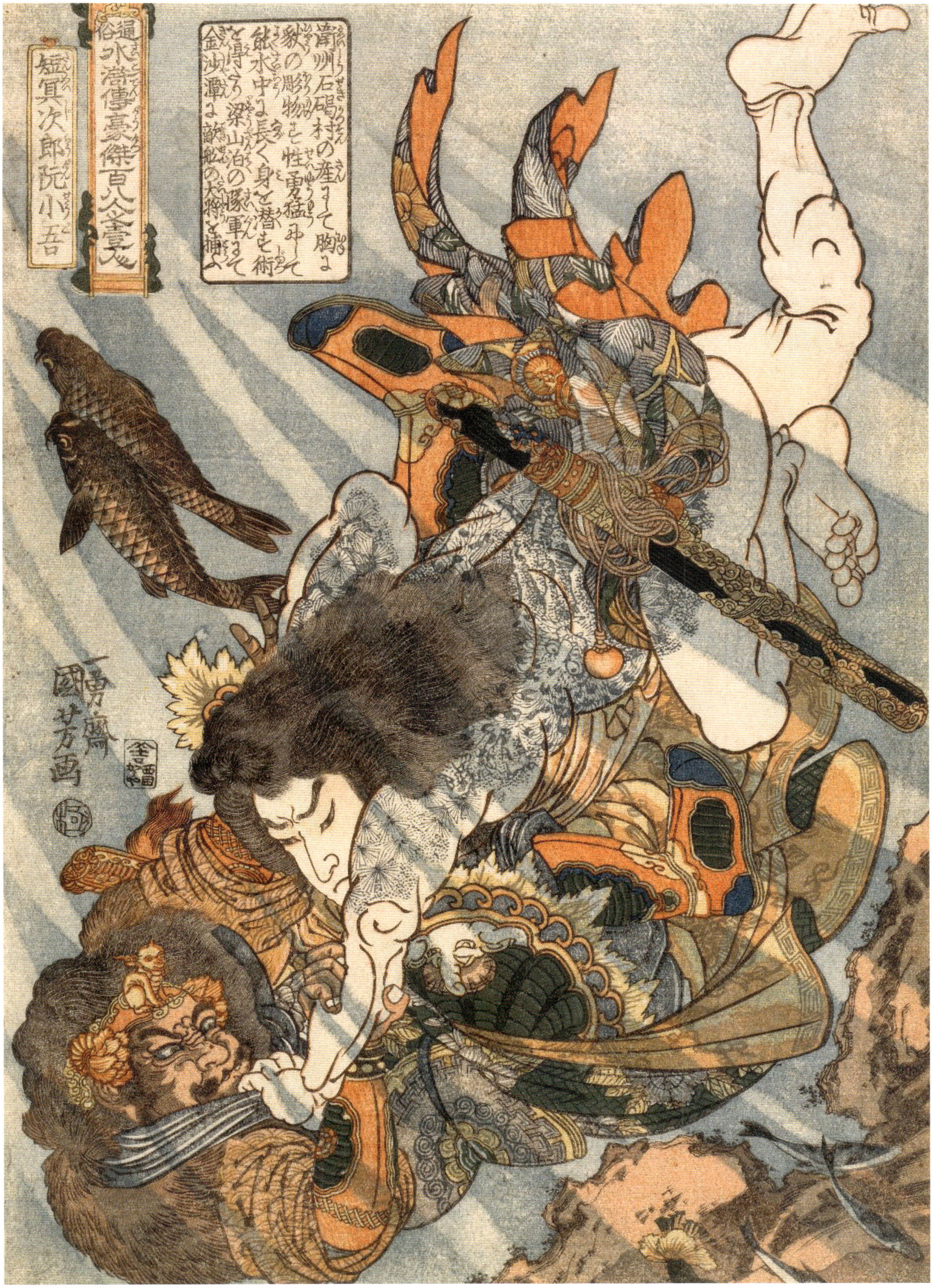
通俗水滸傳豪傑百八人之壹人
短冥次郎阮小吾
一勇齋國芳画

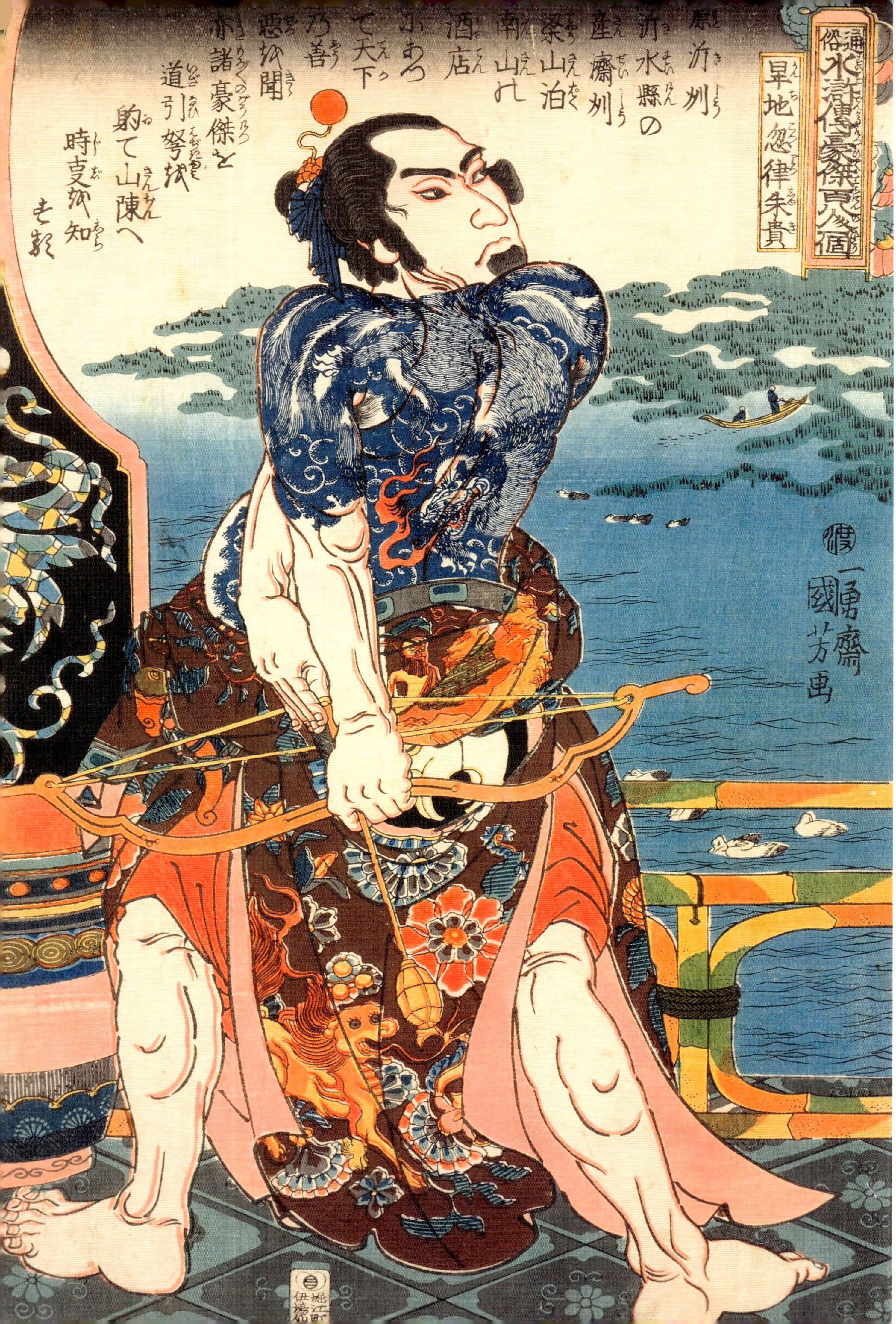
通俗水滸傳豪傑百八人之一個
旱地忽律朱貴
一勇斎國芳画

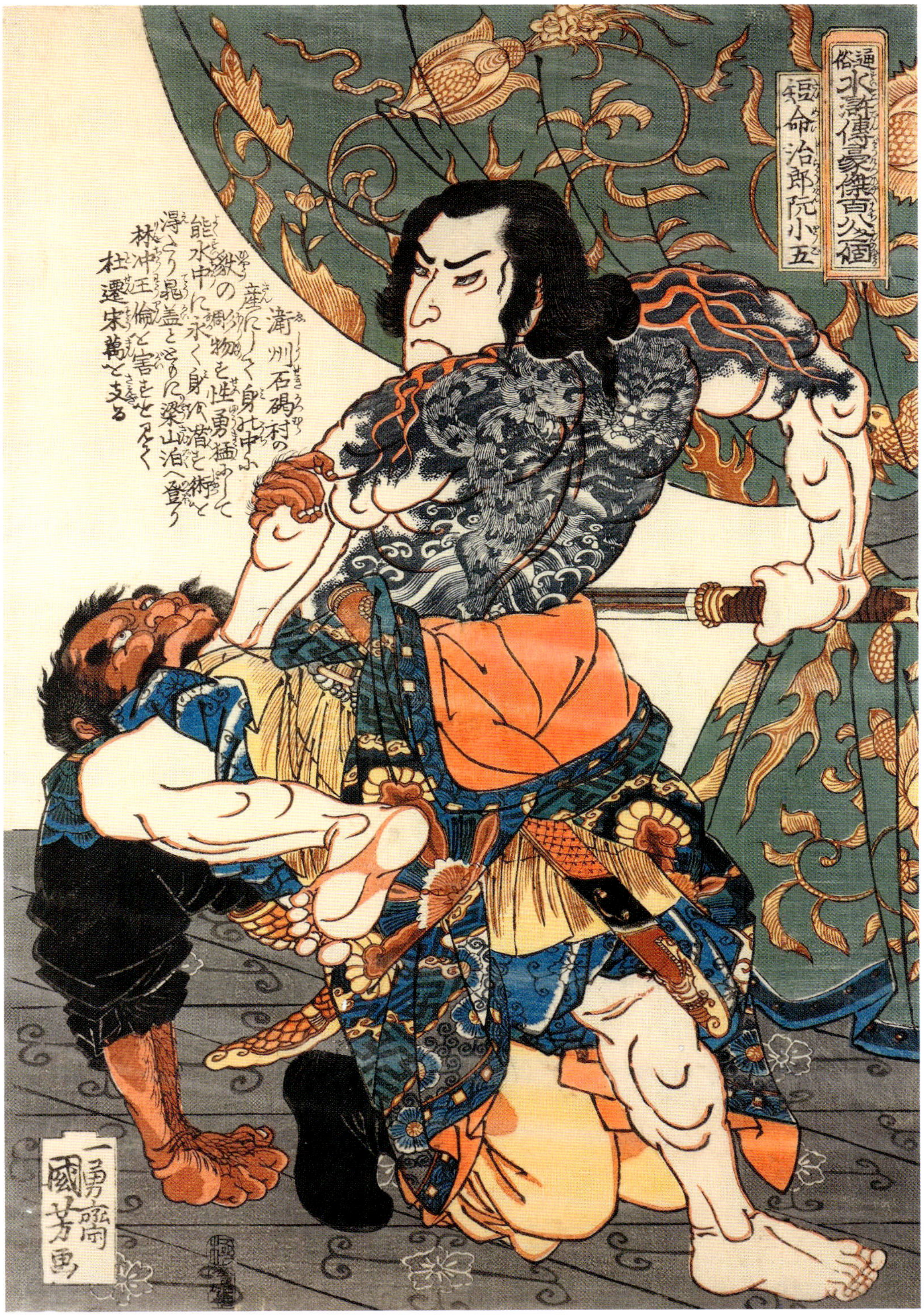

OPPOSITE
Utagawa Kuniyoshi, *Zhu Gui, the Dry-Land Crocodile*, from the series *One Hundred and Eight Heroes of the Popular 'Water Margin'*, *c.* 1827–30, woodblock print. The hero Zhu Gui has a tattoo of a nine-tailed fox on his back.

ABOVE
Utagawa Kuniyoshi, *Tanmeijiro Genshogo*, from the series *One Hundred and Eight Heroes of the Popular 'Water Margin'*, *c.* 1827–30, woodblock print. Tanmeijiro Genshogo has a tiger tattoo on his back.

OVERLEAF LEFT
Utagawa Kunisada, *The Actor Nakamura Fukusuke I as Asahina Tōbei, Likened to Lu Zhishen the Tattooed Priest*, from the 'Pine' triptych of the series *A Modern Water Margin*, 1854, woodblock print.

OVERLEAF RIGHT
Toyohara Kunichika, *Ichimura Uzaemon XIII in a Role as a Tattooed Man with a Tiger Pelt, possibly Takemon no Toramatsu*, 1863, woodblock print. Kunichika was known for his spectacular depictions of *kabuki* culture, which often featured the best-known stars of his era in the roles of tattooed bandits and outlaws, rendered in vivid colours imported from overseas.

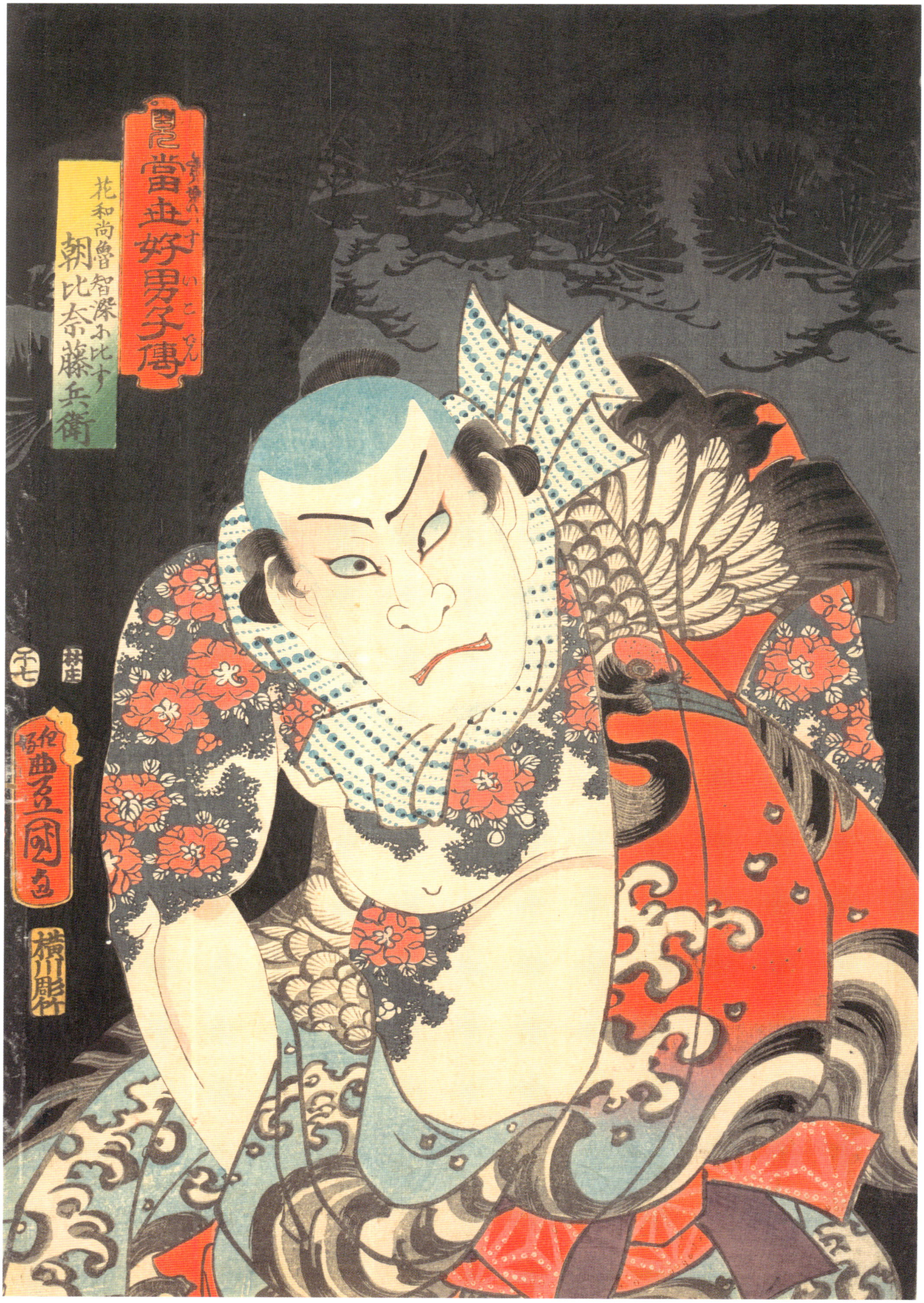
當世好男子傳
花和尚魯智深ニ比す
朝比奈藤兵衛
横川彫竹

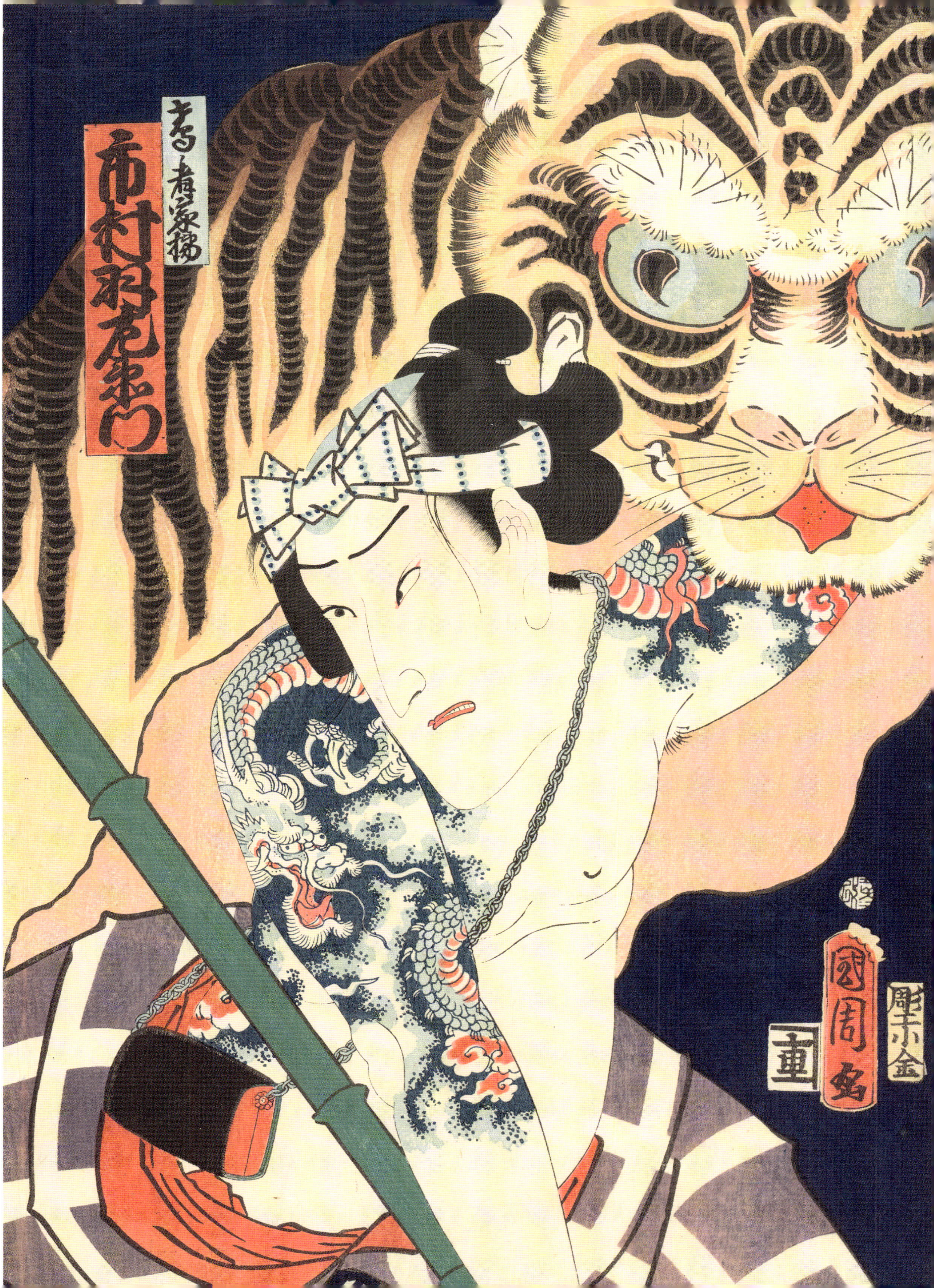
市村羽左衛門
國周画

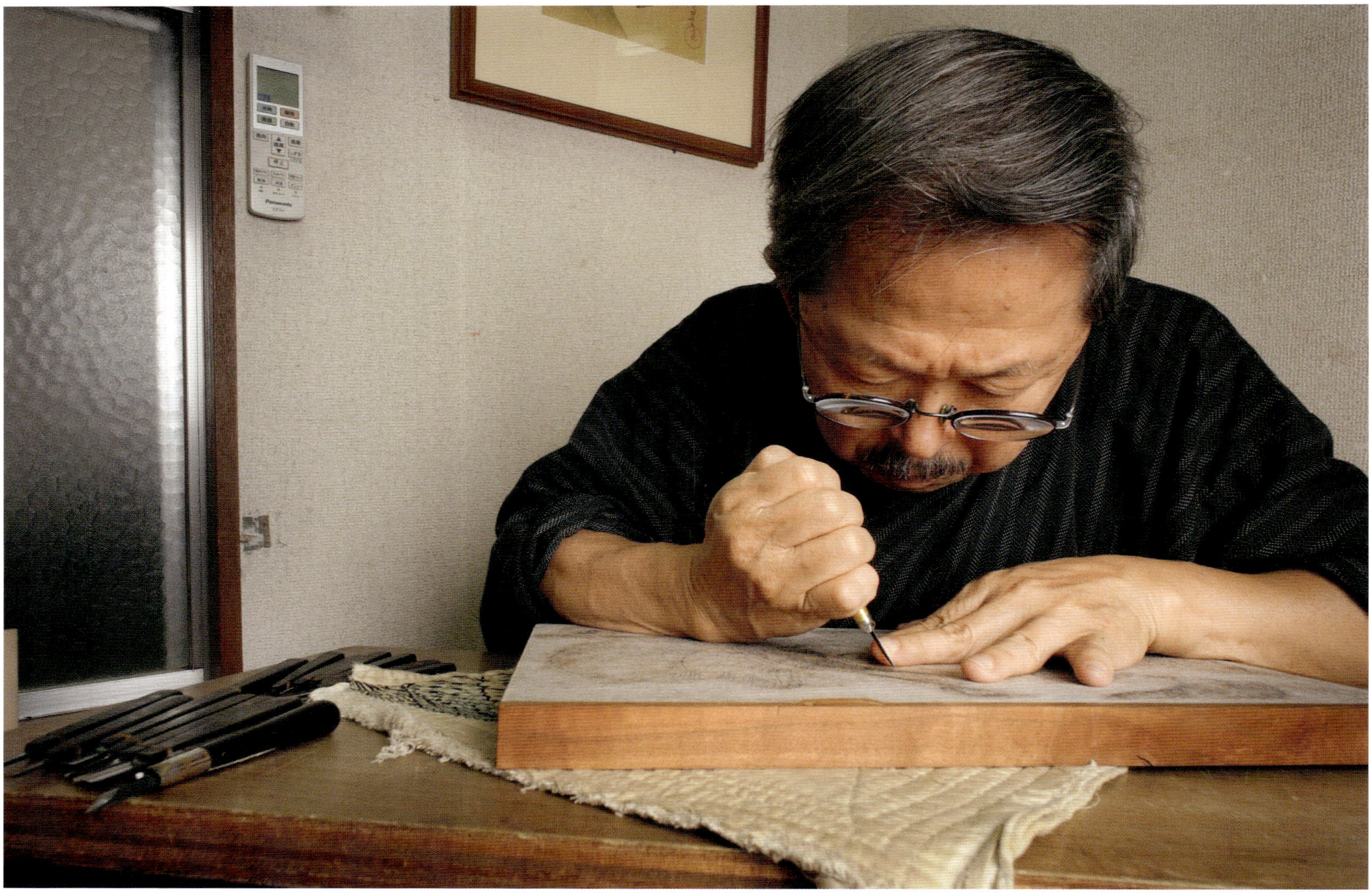

ABOVE
Motoharu Asaka is a woodblock print artisan who collaborates with *horishi*. Of the appeal of *ukiyo-e*, he says, 'When you turn them over, the colour seeps through the back of the paper, and it is only *ukiyo-e* that has this kind of technology to permeate the *washi* paper elements like this. Handmade things have a warmth; your soul shows in the work.'

OPPOSITE LEFT
A collaboration between Asaka and tattoo artist Horiyoshi III. '*Wabori* has heritage and a narrative,' Asaka explains. 'Likewise, *ukiyo-e* depicts Edo culture. I think the Edo era was a brilliant time when there was still this sense of freedom and *iki* (coolness).'

OPPOSITE RIGHT
Collaboration between Asaka and movie director 'Beat' Takeshi Kitano.

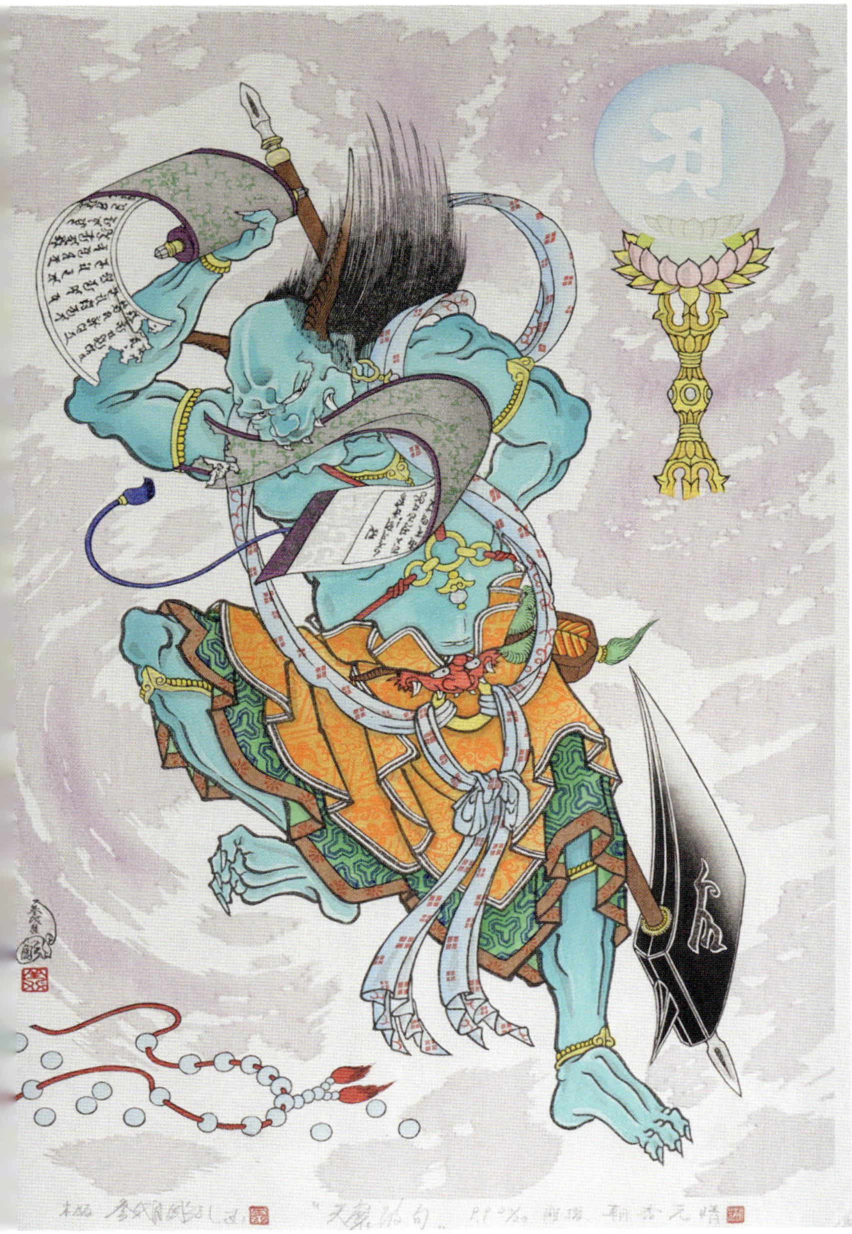

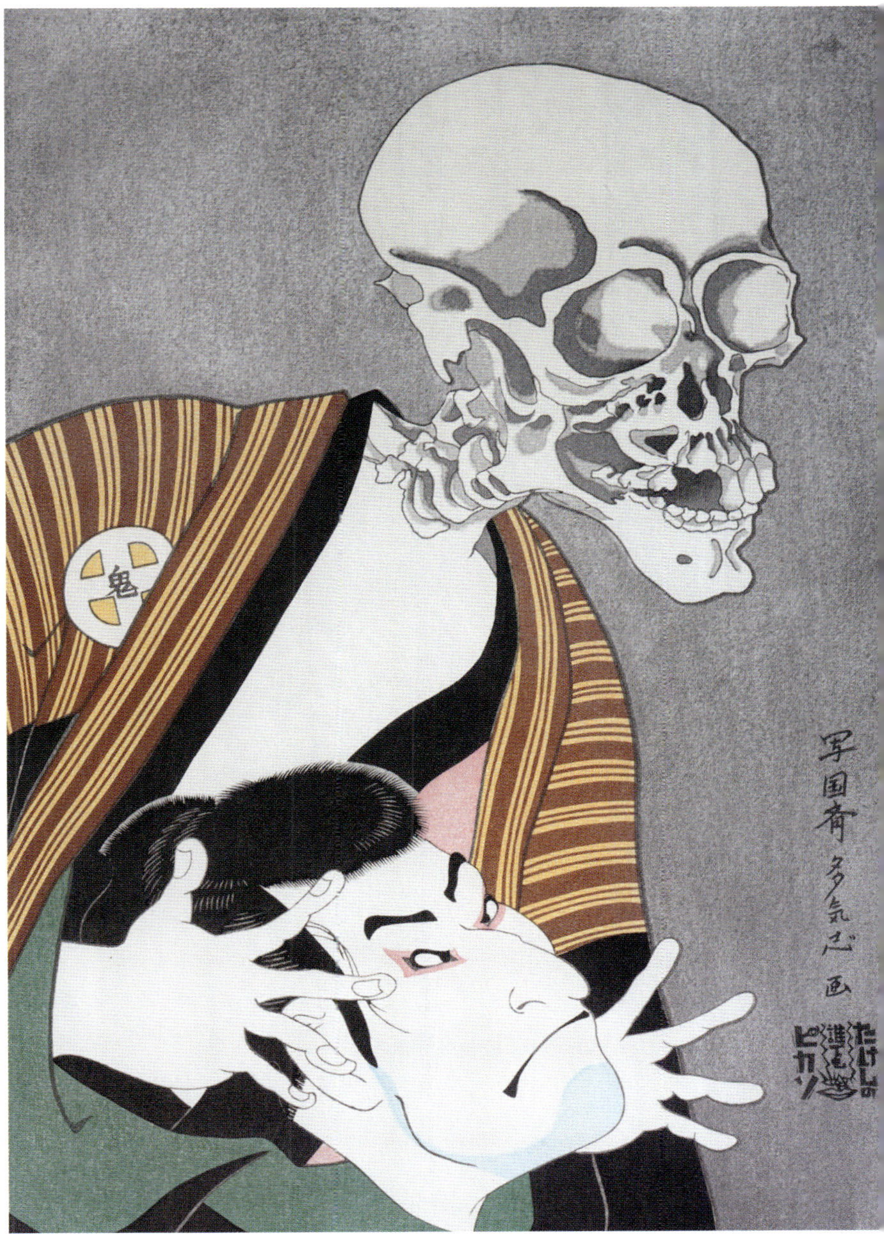

CONTEMPORARY TATTOO CULTURE

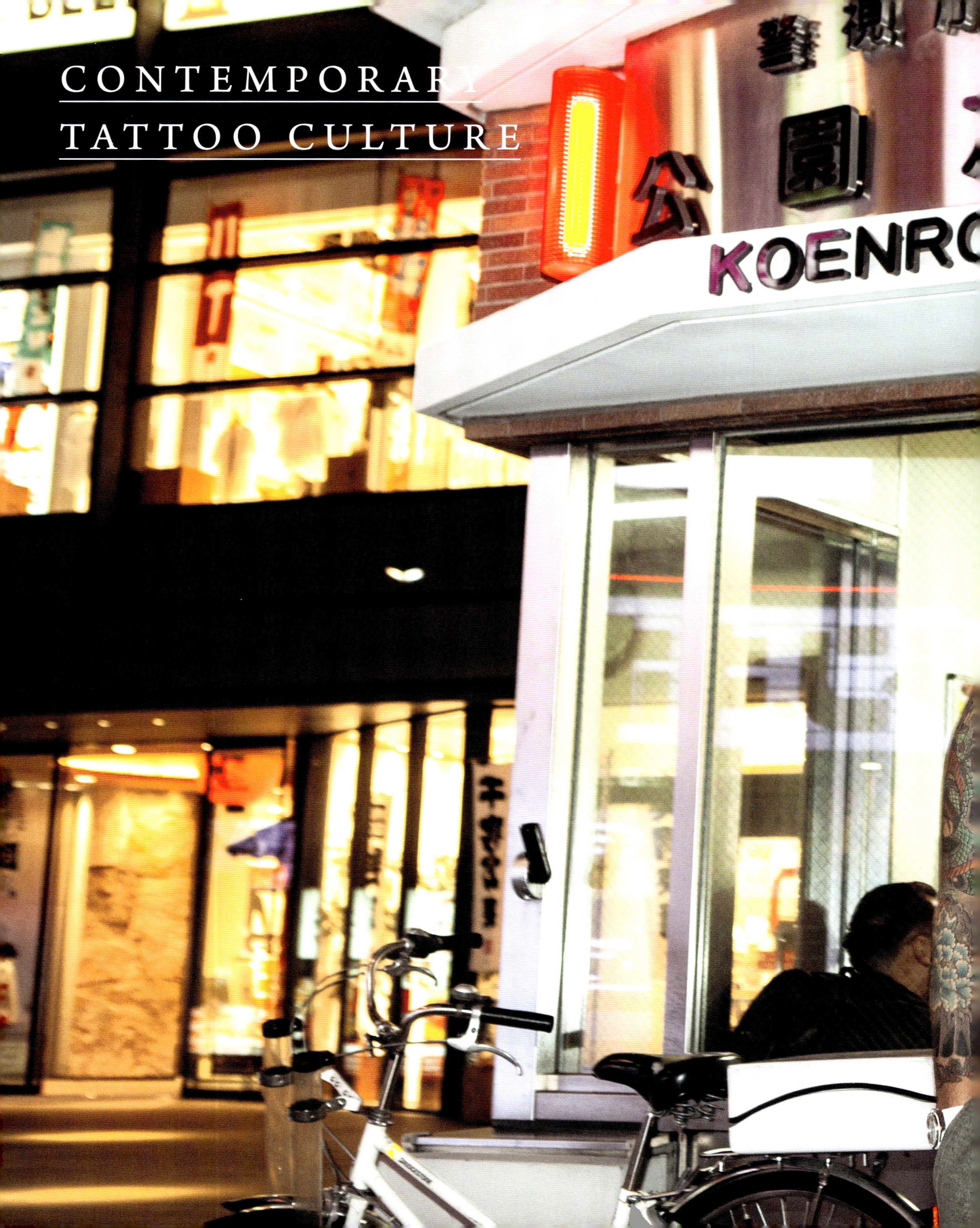

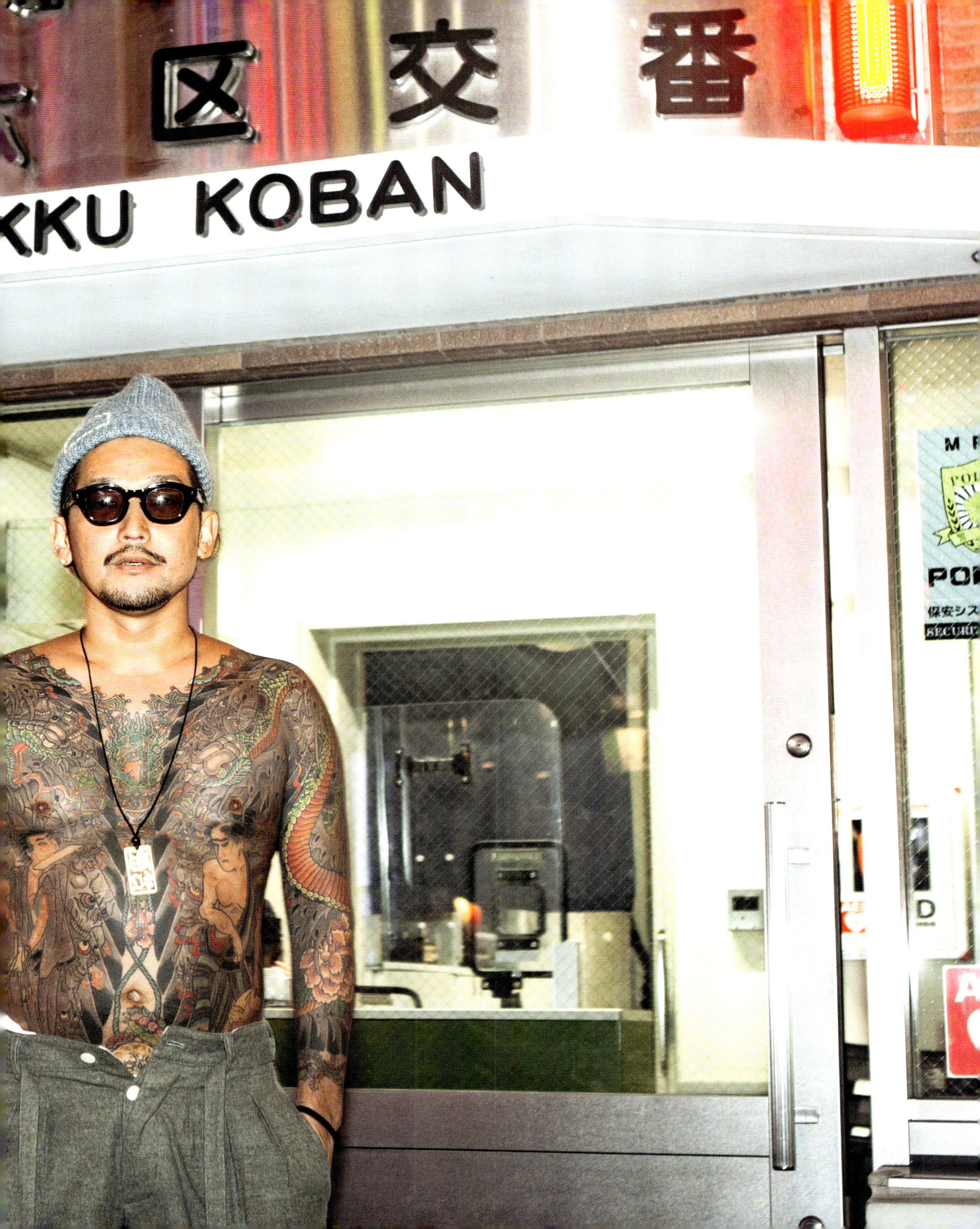
区交番
KKU KOBAN

When the American Commodore Matthew Perry and his four ships sailed into the Tokyo Bay harbour in 1853, Japan opened up to world trade after an isolationist period that had lasted for over 250 years. The Meiji era saw an end to feudalism and brought about rapid modernization, with an initial phase of intense Westernization. The Japanese government banned tattoos in 1872, as they were concerned about the critical scrutiny of foreigners, whom they thought might be repelled by this seemingly backward practice. During this time of prohibition, tattoo artists were forced to move studios regularly to avoid the authorities. However, *irezumi* never ceased. Ironically, rather than being disgusted, many foreigners, including royals such as George V of England and Nicholas II of Russia, received tattoos while in Japan. However, the ban wasn't officially lifted until the post-Second World War American occupation, when *horishi* were tattooing American servicemen.

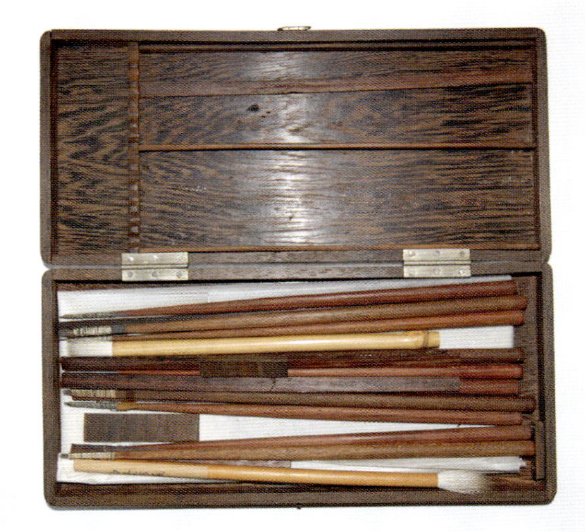

By and large, the tattoo world in Japan during the post-war era was a subterranean affair, mostly supported by the *yakuza*, whose members were adorned with full bodysuits as a sign of gang affiliation. In 1988, Western-style tattoo artists Kishi and Uchiyama approached traditional tattoo master Horitoku and became his students shortly afterwards. This instigated a major shift, causing Western-style tattoos to seep into Japan via the media, fashion and subcultures in the 1990s. During that period, Horitoku appeared on a TV show with Akira Uno, an illustrator with whom he had collaborated on a rather avant-garde backpiece on a woman, leading to further national exposure. Kishi and Uchiyama were among the first artists to create tattoo shops like those seen overseas. Eventually, a full-blown boom in the 2000s flourished in Japan, leading to the founding of over 500 tattoo shops across the nation, as well as numerous tattoo magazines and almost weekly conventions of various sorts.

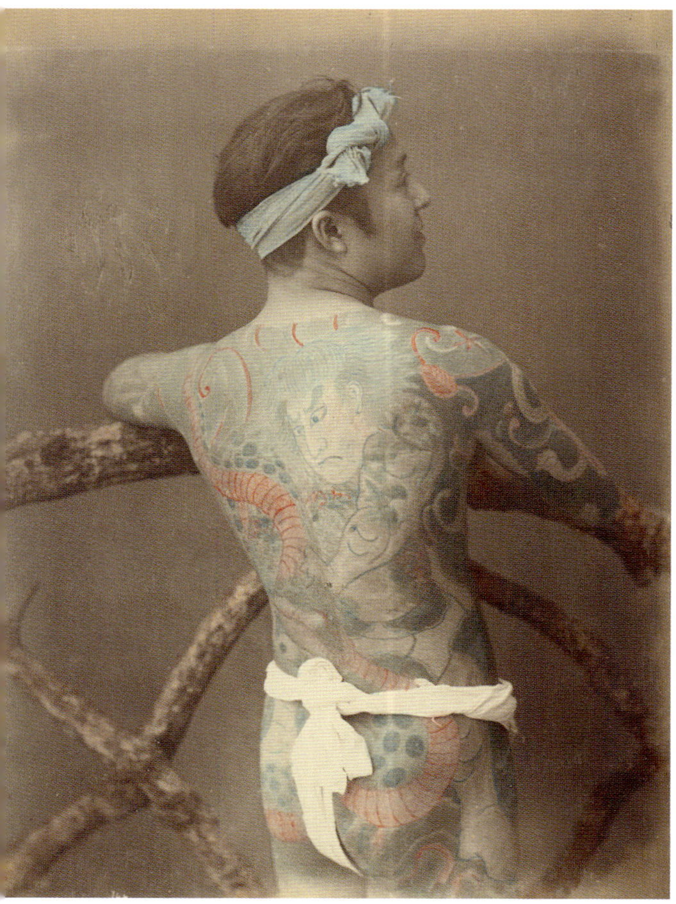

Miho Kawasaki, editor from 1999 to 2011 of *Tattoo Burst*, Japan's leading tattoo magazine, points to a significant shift in the 1980s and '90s. 'Tattoos became a cool culture from overseas: the pinnacle of fashion, trending with the youth. In the '80s, if something was in fashion, everyone would get the same thing, but the '90s was about street culture, individualism and self-expression. Remix culture was at the fore. Tattoos were connected to identity. Kishi and Uchiyama received a lot of media attention.'

PREVIOUS SPREAD
One of Horizaku's clients in front of a police station. While the number of gang-related clients is decreasing in the tattoo world, there is still a strong association between outlaws and tattoos in Japan. For some people who are not gang-affiliated, this counterculture vibe is one of the appealing aspects of tattoos.

LEFT
Tattooed Tokyo denizen in the late 1800s.

ABOVE
Portable box of tattooing equipment from the Meiji era.

OPPOSITE
Wabori on a man's back, *c.* 1875.

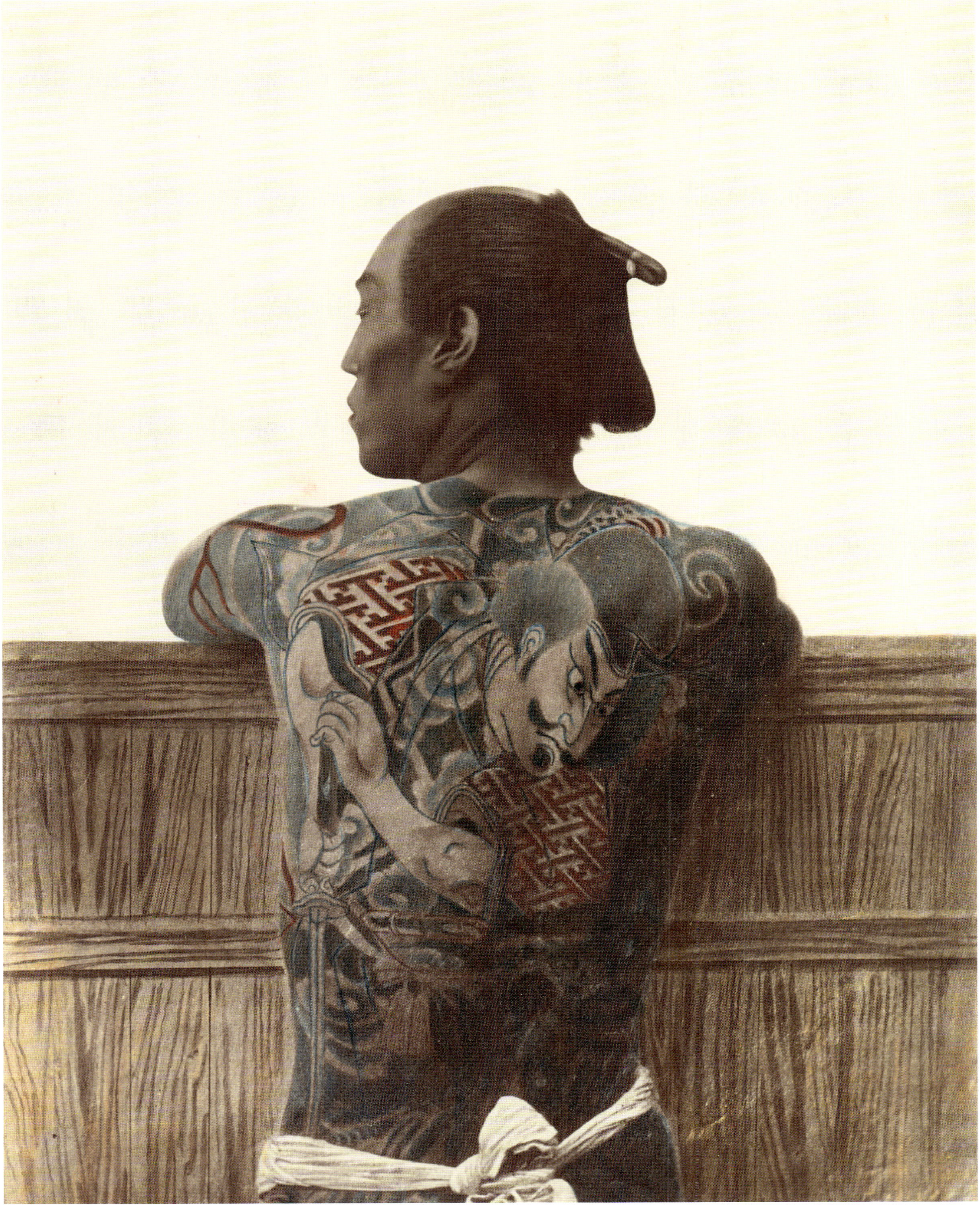

Despite the ensuing tattoo boom, in 2001, the Ministry of Health, Labour and Welfare declared tattooing to be a medical practice, meaning that only licensed medical professionals would legally be able to tattoo. Given that tattooers are generally not doctors, almost all of them were suddenly working in an unregulated legal grey zone, which made them liable to criminal prosecution.

Eventually, the tattooing bubble of the 1990s and 2000s burst. The 2011 tsunami in Tohoku, which took over 20,000 lives, led to a morbid national atmosphere in which people felt guilty about having fun. Various incidents from the time made it clear that tattoos were seen unfavourably in mainstream society. For example, in 2012, the mayor of Osaka, Toru Hashimoto, ordered public servants working for the city to undertake an ethically dubious survey as to whether they had tattoos or not, including giving details of their size and location on the body. Kawasaki explains that at this time a culture sprang up where people would harass others anonymously online and via official complaints to media channels. 'People got scared and the atmosphere was suffocating. Eventually people felt the pressure to stop living freely.'

In 2015, a lengthy legal battle took place after tattooer Taiki Masuda appealed an order to pay a fine of 150,000 yen (about £750, or $1,000) for tattooing three people, violating the Medical Practitioners' Act. Usually, artists would just pay the fine and continue working, but he fought back, leading the Japanese Supreme Court to recognize that tattooing requires artistic skill and is not part of the medical field. This landmark case led to tattooing finally being recognized, more or less, as a legitimate job.

The largest recent changes in Japanese tattoo culture have come about due to social media, with many artists who travel overseas having incredible online followings. New technology, such as tattoo pens, means that anyone can try inking, leading to tattoos that Kawasaki describes as 'dreadful'. Another trend that veteran *horishi* Horitoku observes is that absolutely everyone is getting tattooed. 'In [hip Tokyo neighbourhood] Okubo, they even have their faces tattooed,' he explains. 'As a workplace habit, I can't help staring at strangers' tattoos. I'm like, "That isn't very good quality." The old-school sensibility that is inherited from the Edo era, which involves *tebori* insertion by hand, not wanting to put out flashy shop signs, and hiding their sleeves even when putting out the rubbish, is being eroded. Western-style tattooers here get good, then they want to learn *wabori*. But overseas tattooers are doing a mix of Japanese and Western tattoos, and the Japanese are copying that. The aesthetic of tattoos has changed and there are very few people doing real traditional work.'

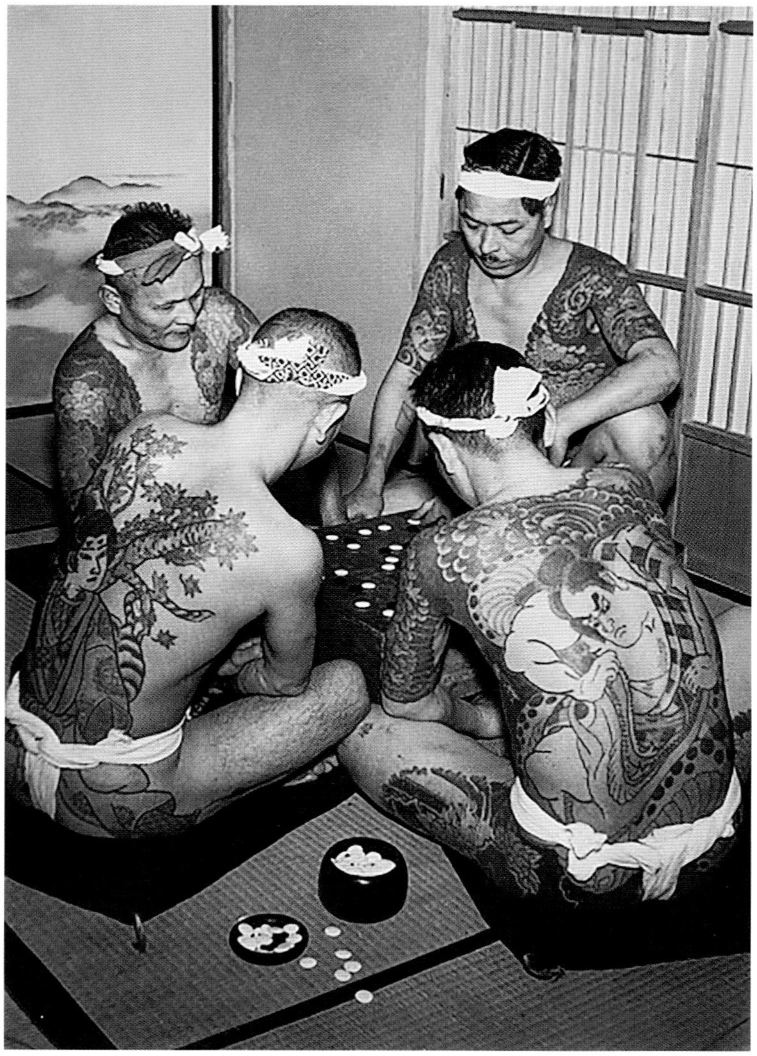

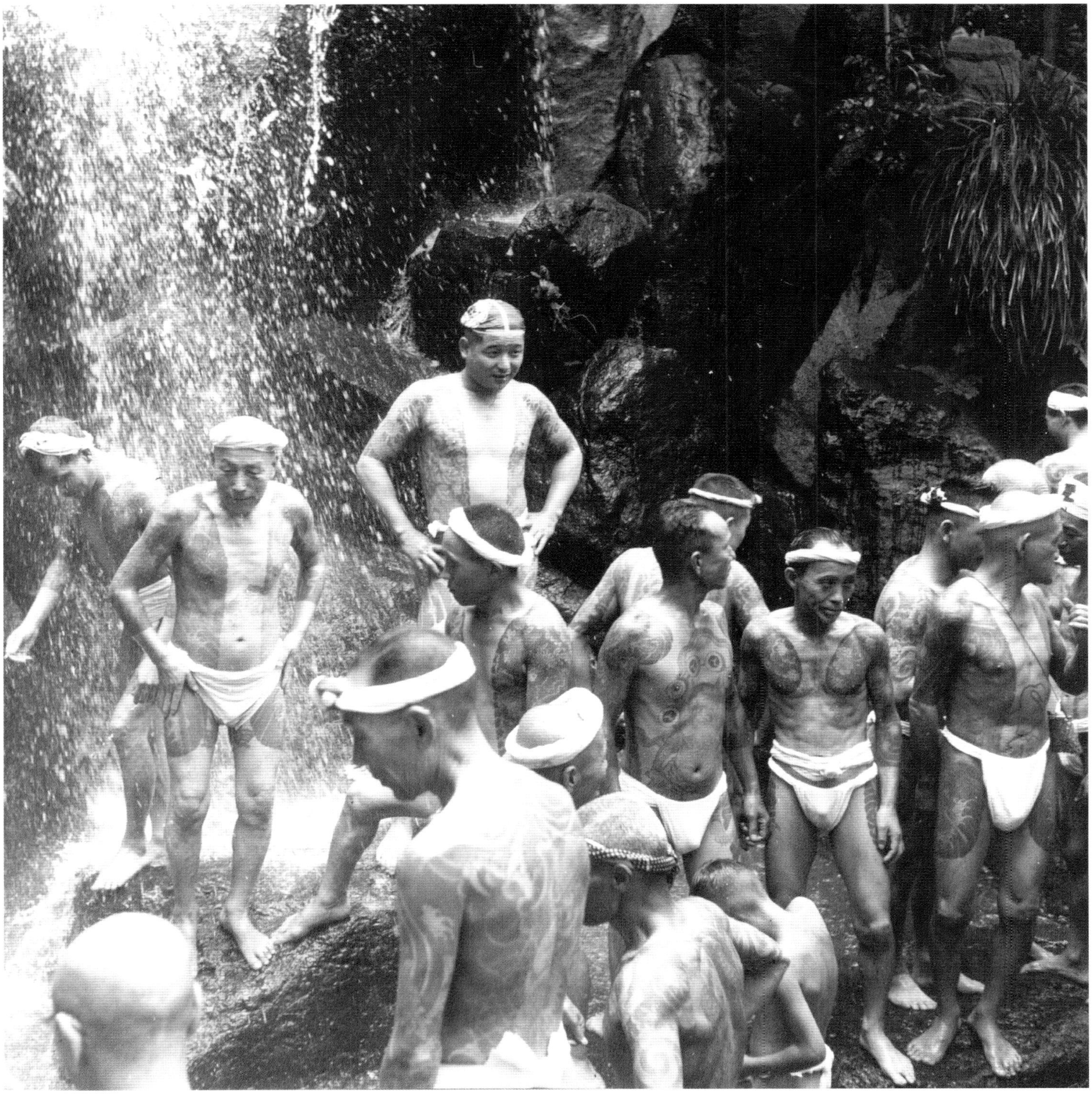

OPPOSITE
Heavily tattooed men playing the strategy board game Go, *c.* 1955.

ABOVE
Men from the Edo Choyukai tattooers' association, 1955.

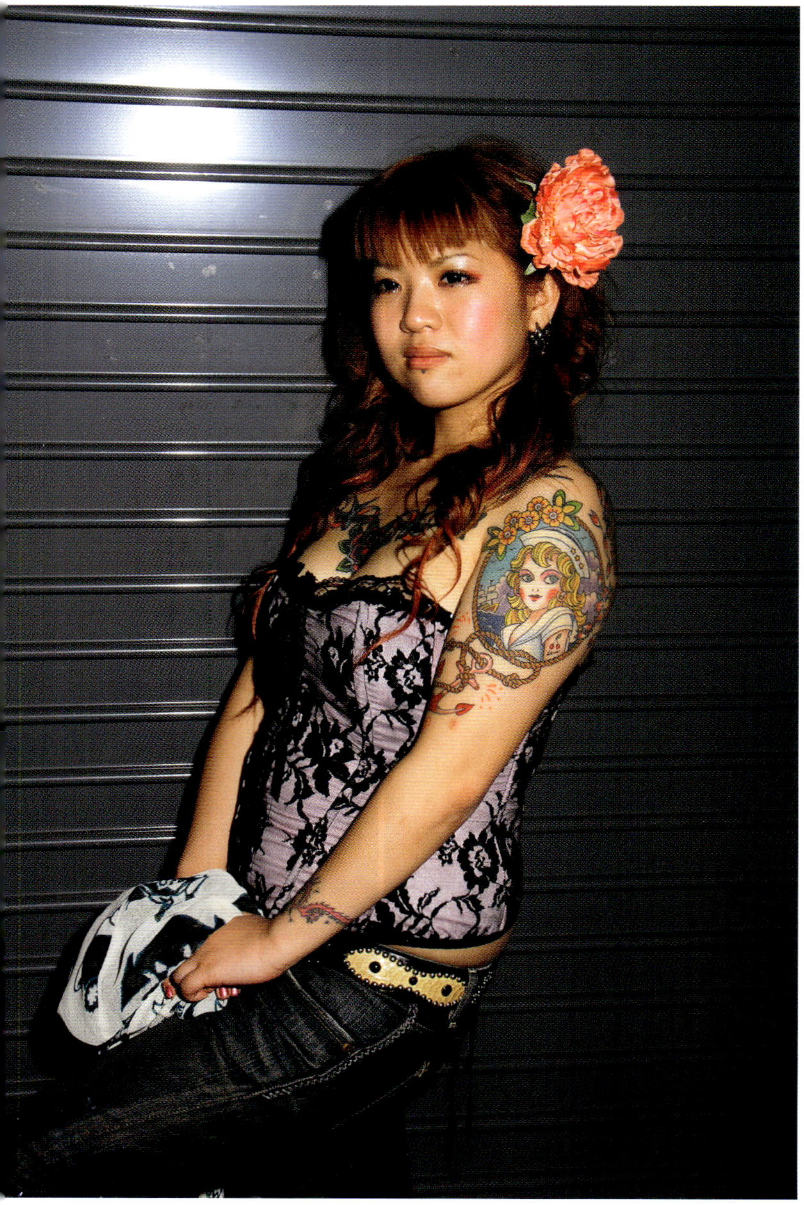

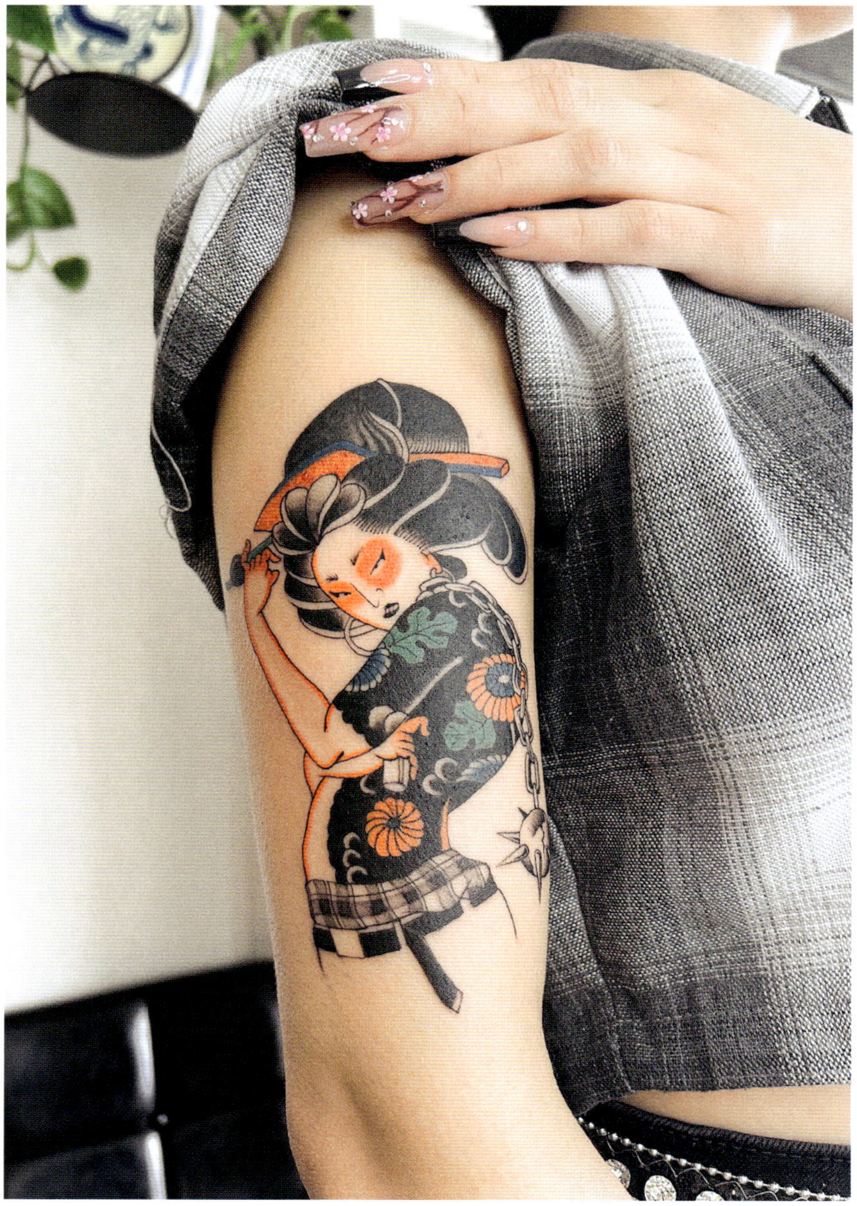

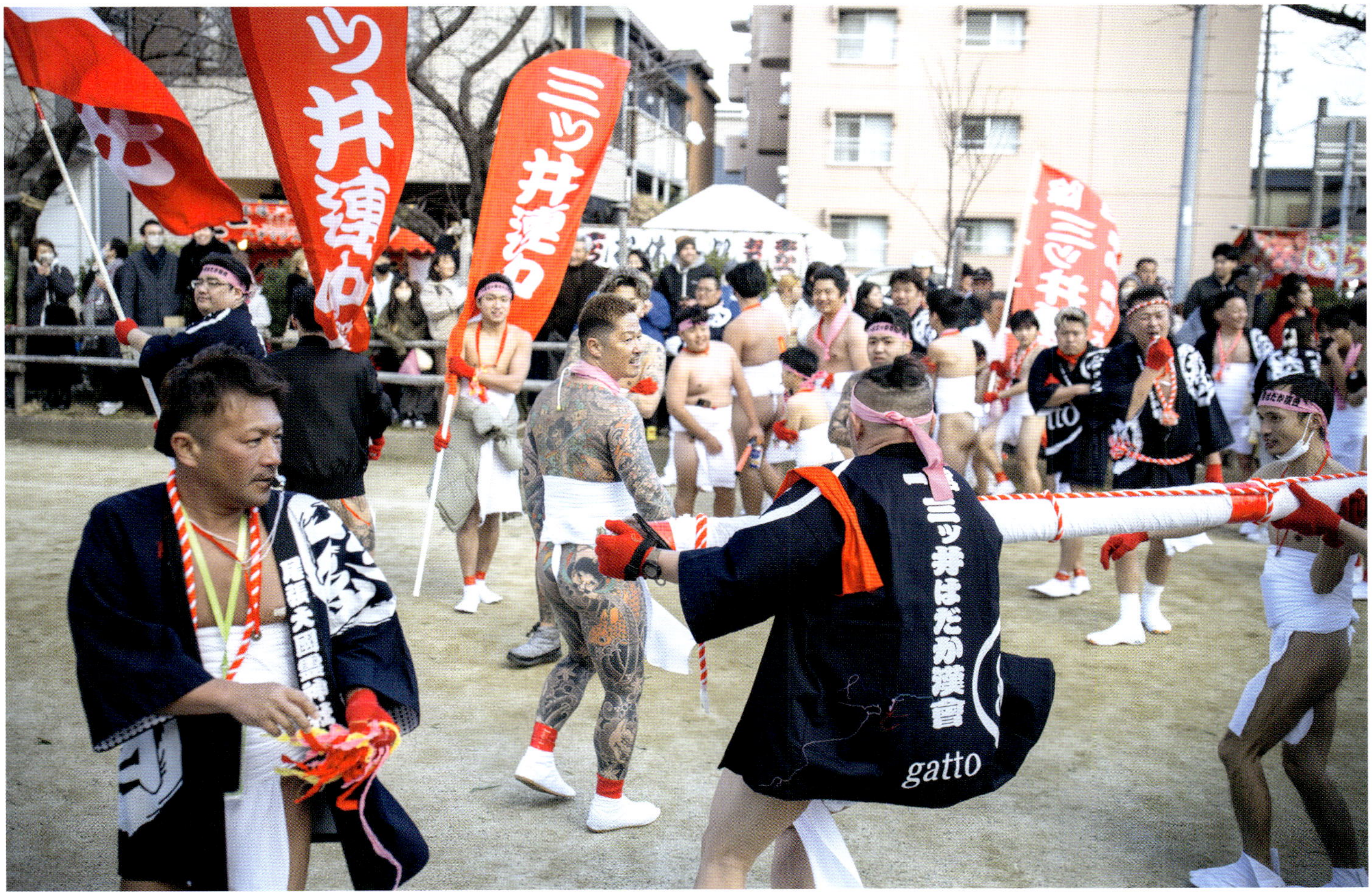

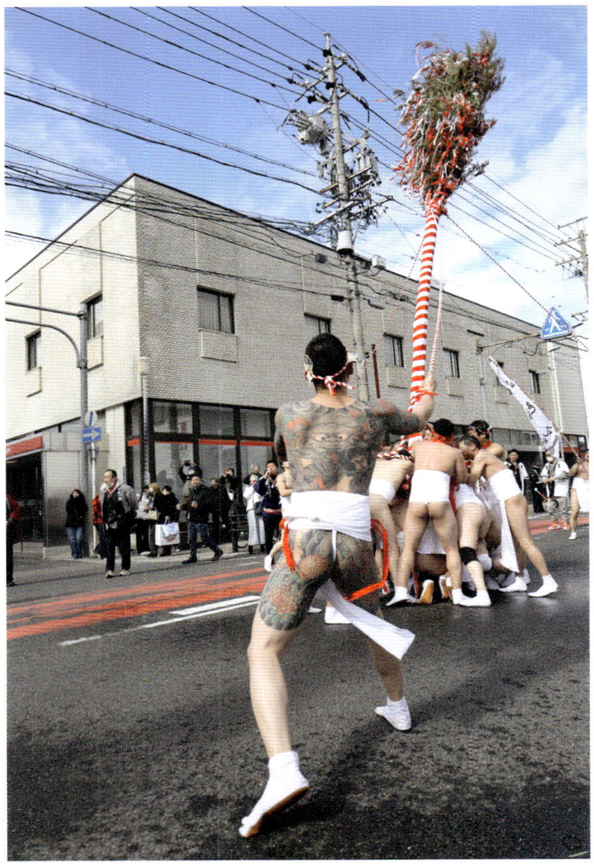

OPPOSITE LEFT
A staff member from the tattoo shop Hocus Pocus in Shizuoka prefecture is shown here attending a tattoo convention, where it's common to see many inked women who are part of various subcultures, from rockabilly to goth.

OPPOSITE RIGHT
Madoka is a female tattooer based in Kyoto who mixes Japanese motifs, like geishas and ghosts, with Western tattoo sensibilities.

ABOVE
In parallel to events such as conventions and shows, there are also many traditional festivals (*matsuri*) across Japan that are attended by tattooed people. These cultures exist side by side. For example, an incredible number of full bodysuits and *wabori* pieces are on display at the Konomiya Naked Festival.

RIGHT
The festival sees men of the ages of 25 and 42, which are considered unlucky years, wearing nothing but loincloths. They gather at Owari Okunitama shrine to try and dispel their bad fortune in the middle of winter, and are doused with cold water along the way.

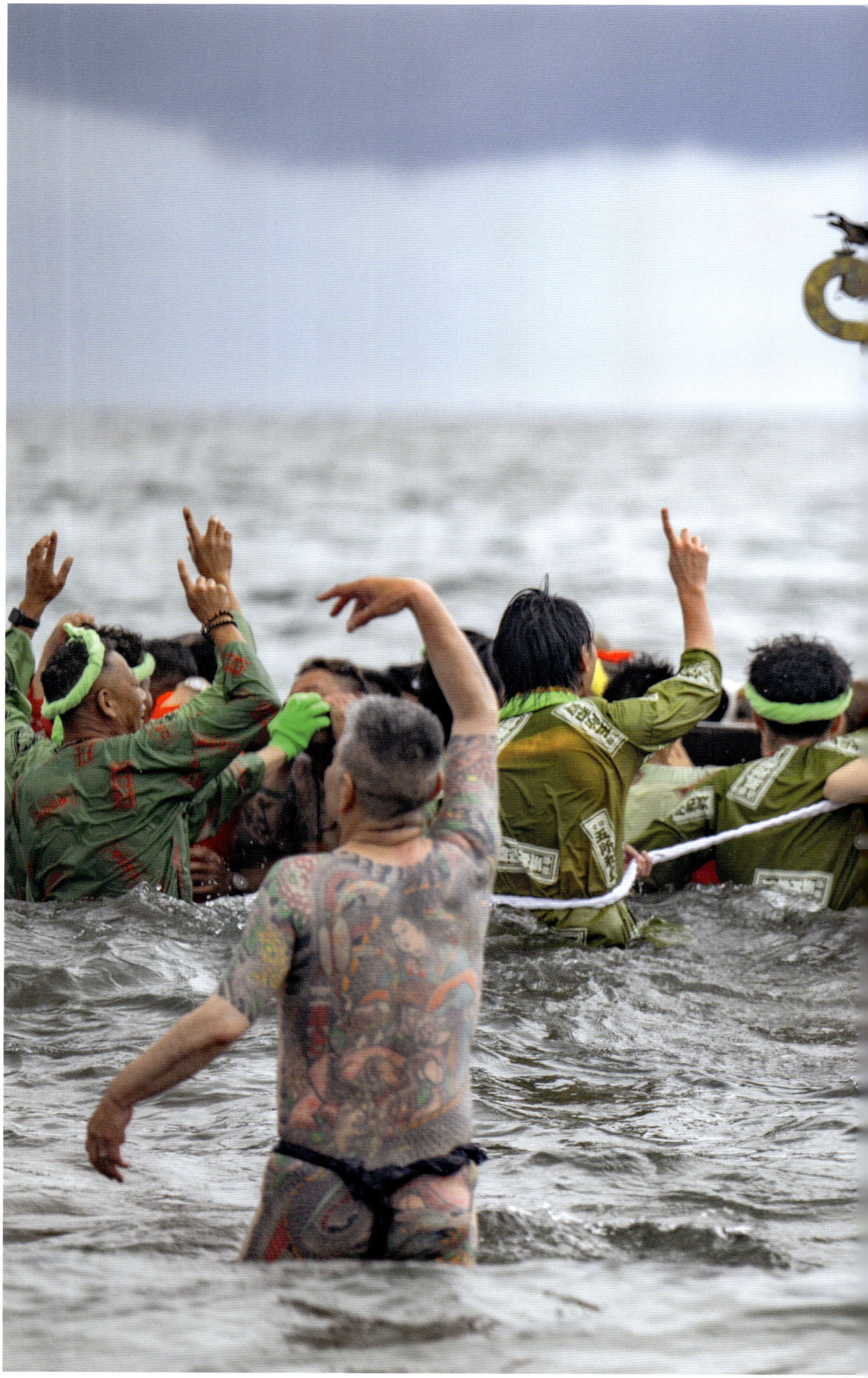

RIGHT
A *mikoshi* (portable shrine) is carried into the ocean at Kamakura, Kanagawa. Owing to the presence of *horishi* like Horiyoshi III in Yokohama, there are many top-tier tattoos on display at these coastal festivals.

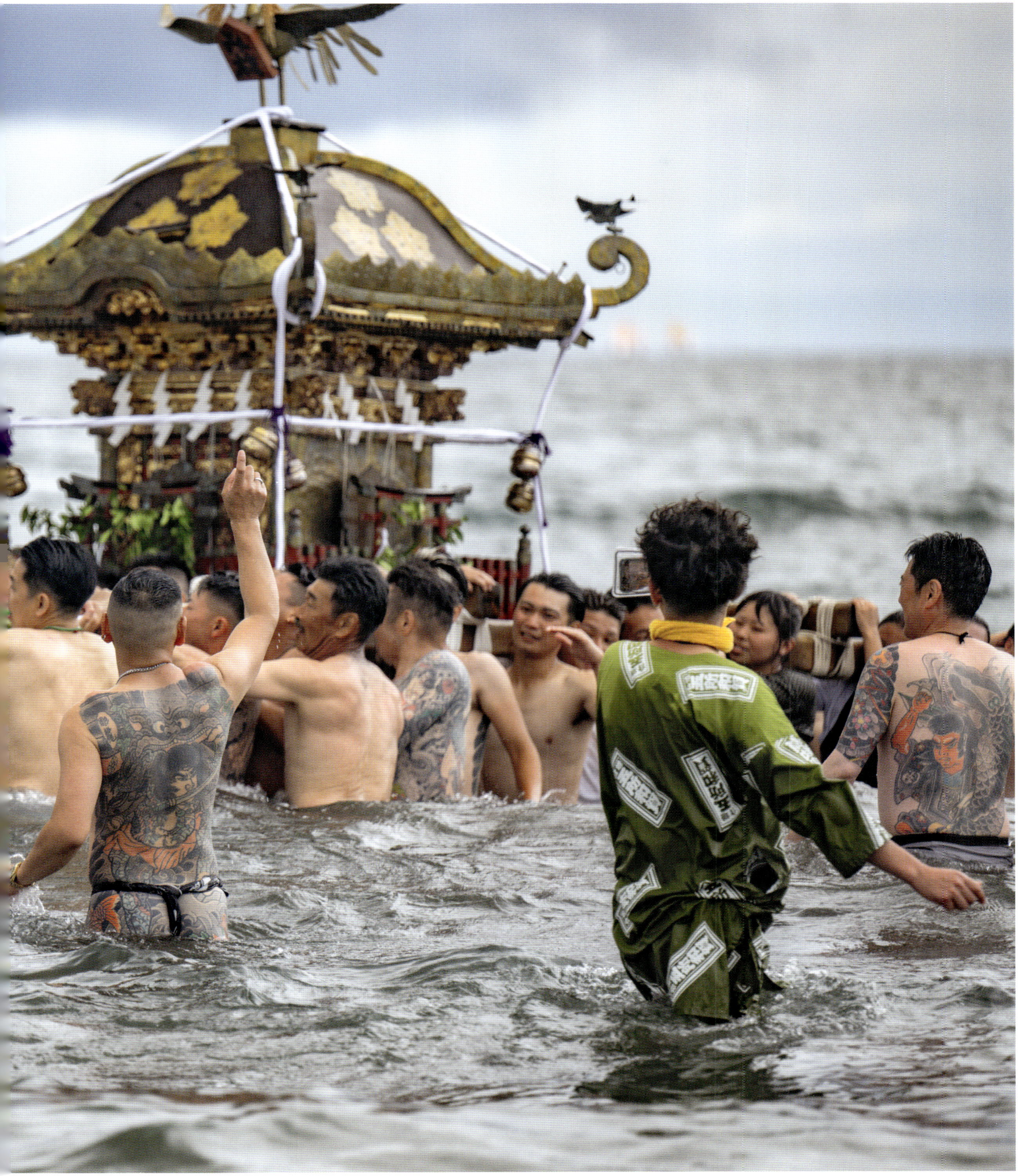

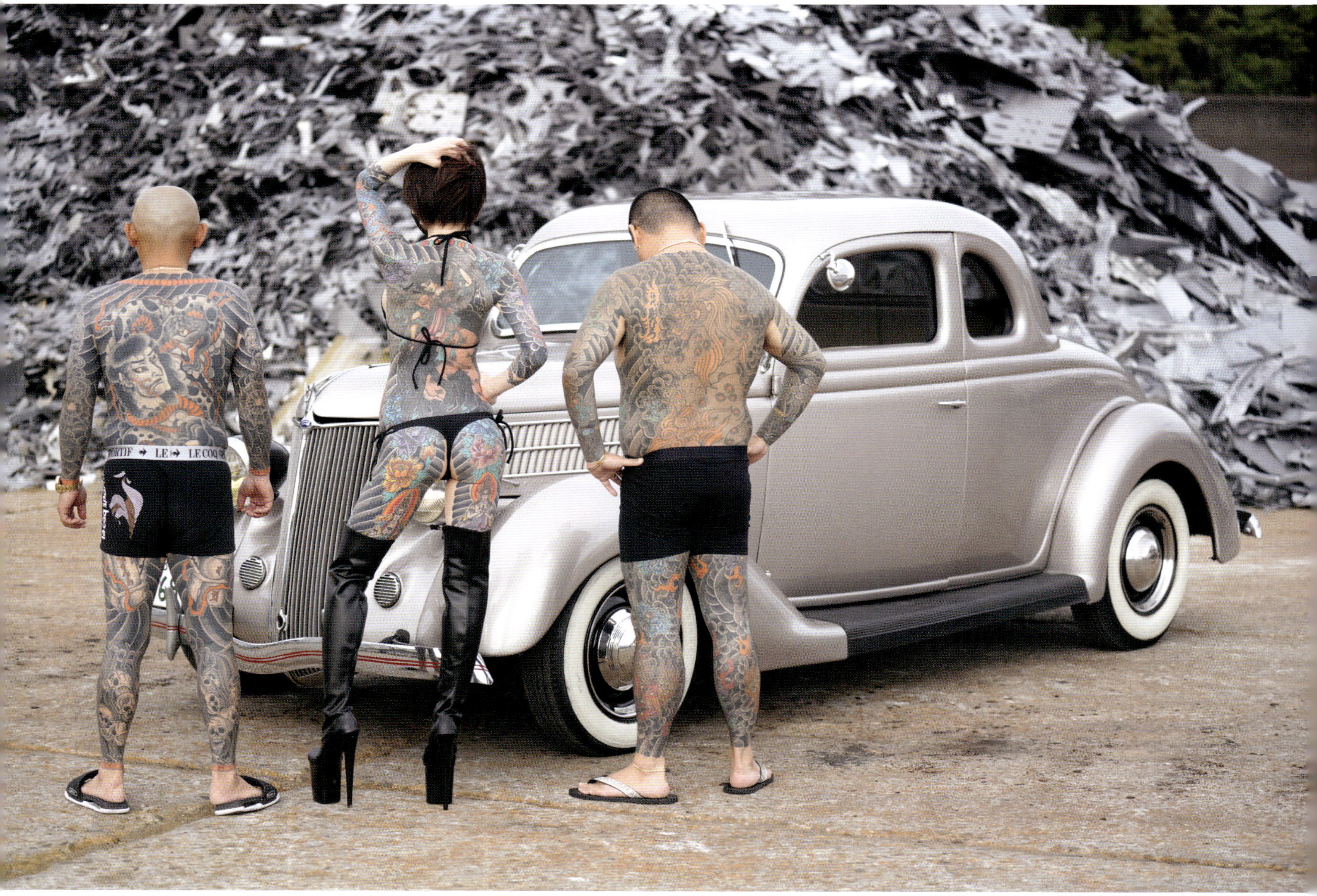

ABOVE

Clients of Horihiro in Shizuoka prefecture, where his studio is located. Horihiro specializes in *wabori*, but uses a machine for the entire process. Because of this, he is able to work with a speed and efficiency that make him popular with clients from across Japan. While many *horishi* in this book have more of an artisan-like mentality and see tattooing as part of their identity, Horihiro is quite straightforward about the fact he is just doing his job. He says that most of his clients are part of the underworld or military, as he is located close to an American base. 'My strategy is to tattoo fast and to finish them off efficiently, so I can take on the next person,' he explains. 'As a result, I am extremely busy and clients come from as far as Kobe.'

When he was a child his mother was a geisha, and at the *okiya* (geisha lodging) where they lived, there were a lot of *yakuza*. Of this time, he says, 'The people who looked after me were these kinds of people and I had opportunities to see them naturally. The only impression I had is that they were nice to me, and then I went on to do this kind of work. I have been tattooing since around primary school and am self-taught. When I was 11 years old, I was tattooing my leg. I started with *tebori* but it is so inefficient and hard to make money.'

OPPOSITE

A full bodysuit being completed at Horihiro's studio in 2008. Contemporary Japanese tattooing involves both criminal and pop-culture elements, and the two worlds exist in parallel.

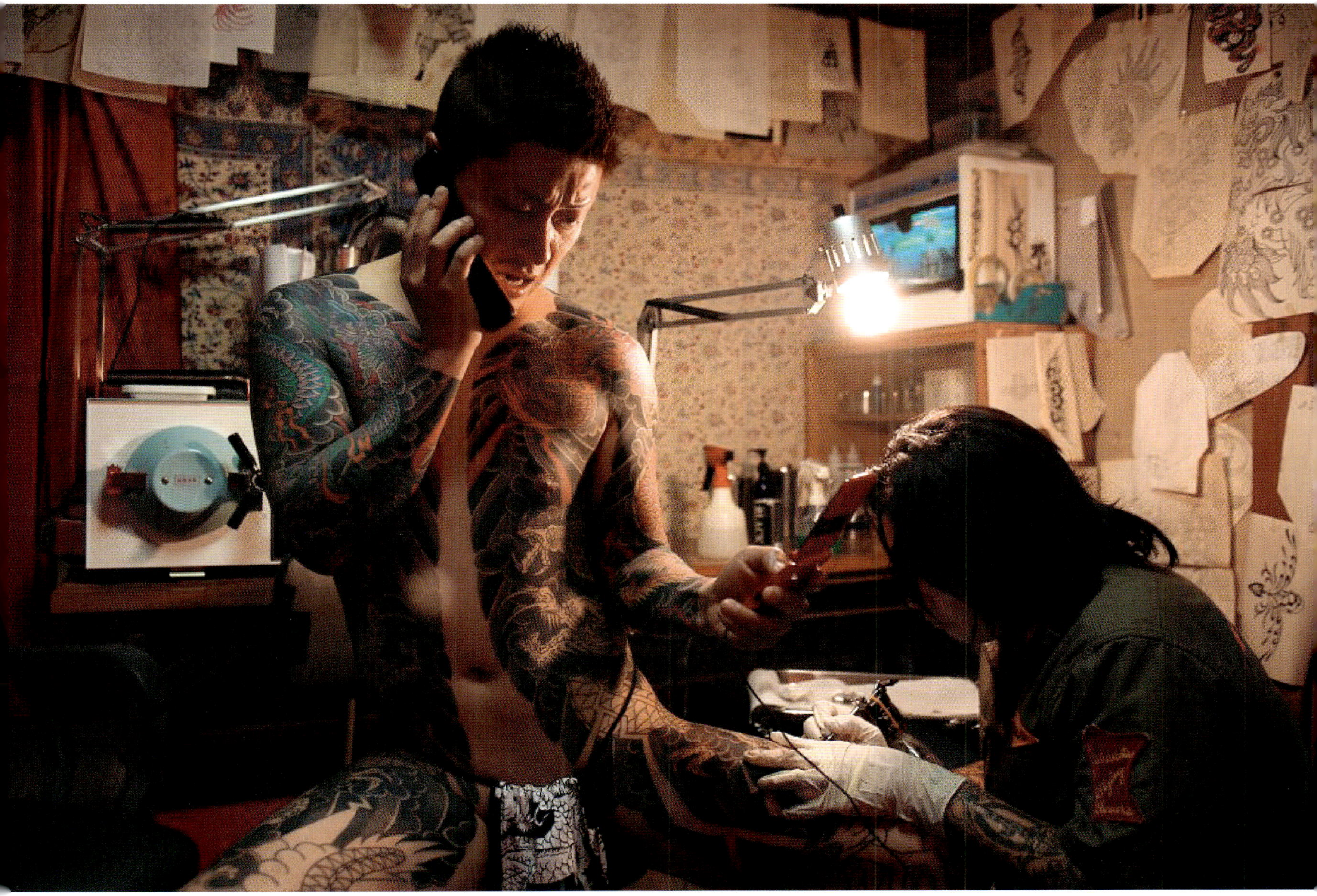

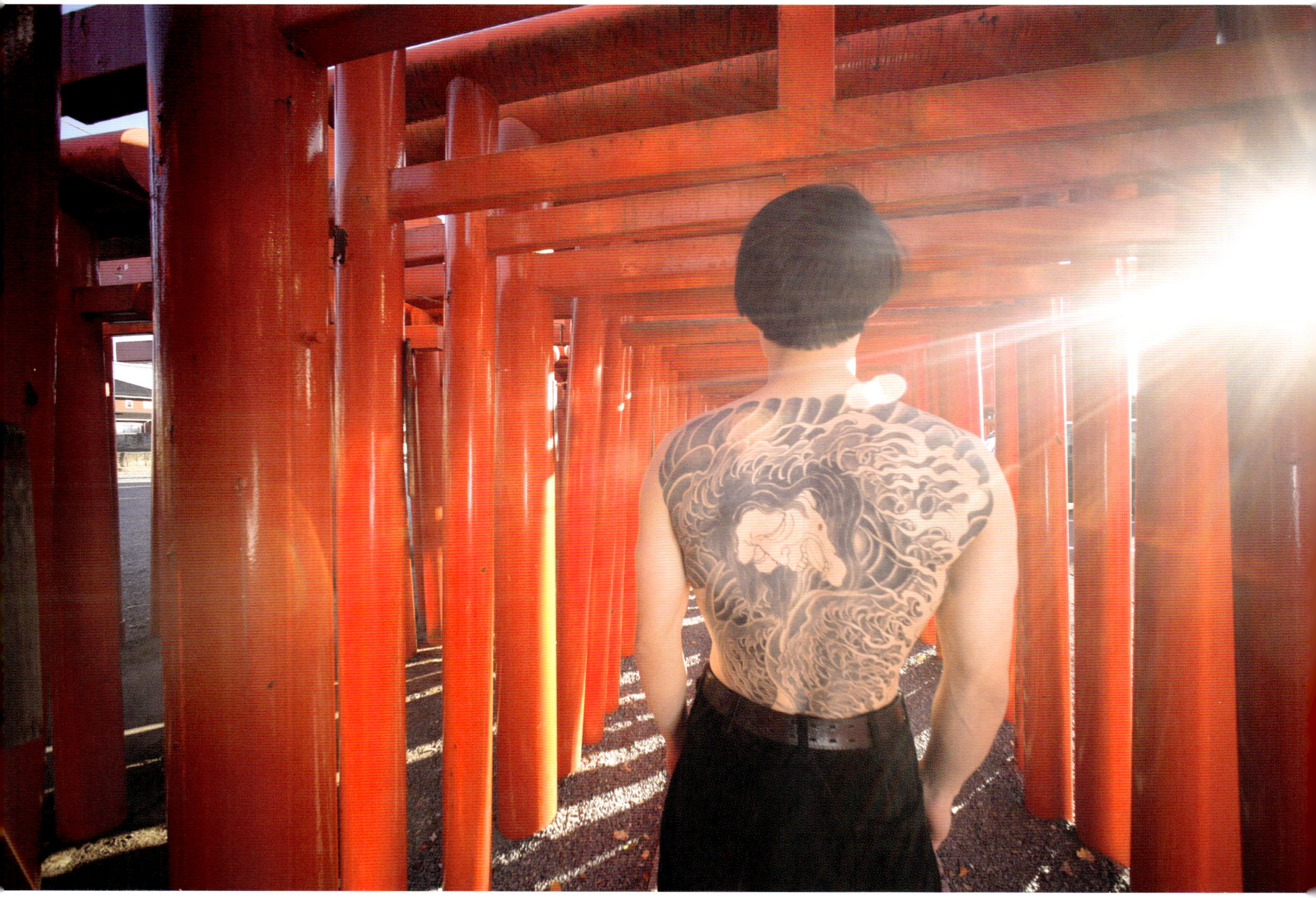

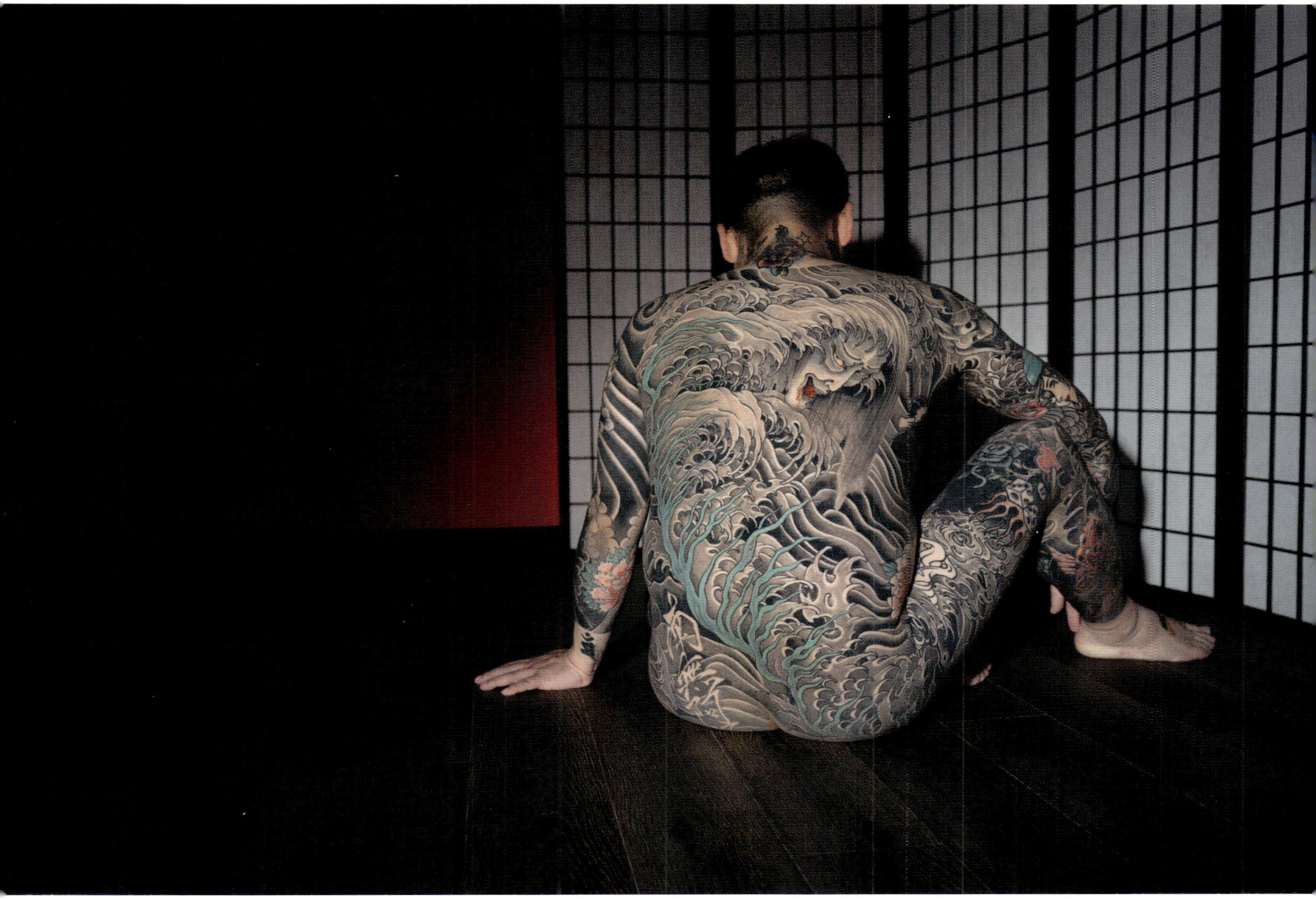

OPPOSITE
Backpiece by Horimasa, a *horishi* based in Gunma who has been working since 1993. During the Japanese tattoo boom of the early 2000s, he travelled overseas frequently and built up an international clientele. He is part of a trajectory of *horishi* who first got tattooed Western-style and are self-taught. Horimasa's clients are 'straight people' – he doesn't tattoo thugs or *yakuza*. Despite this, his portfolio includes dark, hardcore imagery, such as severed heads and ghosts, which have become quite trendy.

ABOVE
Horimasa excels at ghost imagery. A backpiece on another tattoo artist.

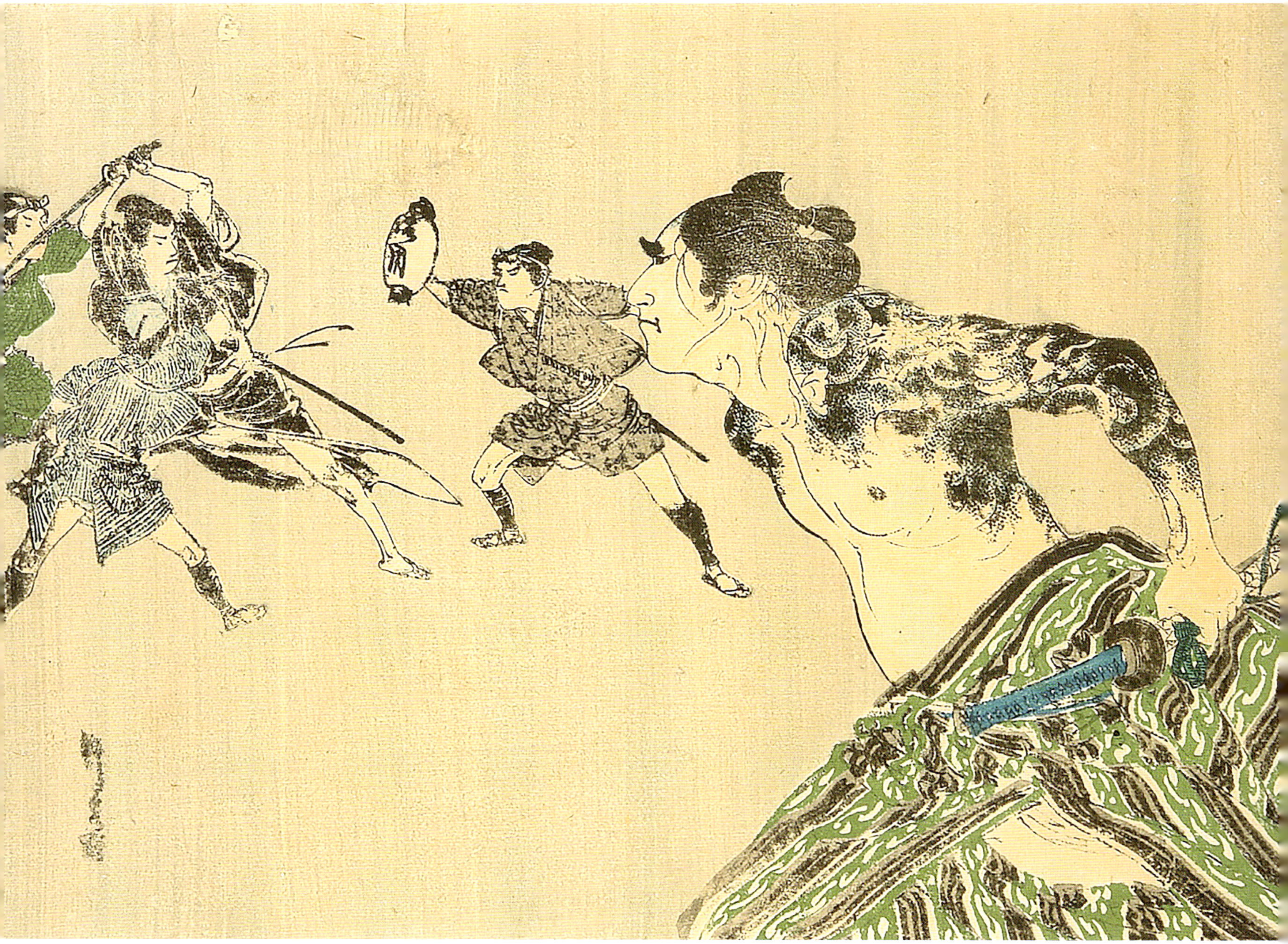

ABOVE
Suzuki Kinsen, *Tattooed Helper*, *c.* 1900–1910, woodblock print. A tattooed *yakuza* fights the police in order to help his friend.

OUTLAWS AND CRIMINAL TATTOOS

Tattooing in Japan has a long association with criminality, and this impacts how Japanese people view tattoos, even today. In fact, the words used, although they are interchangeable, indicate the existence of two types of tattooing: *horimono*, the elevated art form that aficionados acquire, and *irezumi*, which historically refers to criminal tattooing and has crude connotations. According to Asakusa-based *horishi* Horicho II, 'Usually people refer to traditional Japanese tattoos as *horimono*, or *sumi wo ireru* (to insert ink) if they want to make it sound more specialized and exclusive. *Irezumi* is used more by people that aren't from the tattoo world, like people who say, "Oh my god, that person has *irezumi*!" in a derogatory way.'

As early as 1720, tattoos were given to criminals as a form of punishment for petty crimes when the 8th shogun, Tokugawa Yoshimune, standardized the practice. The most common types of penal tattoos were bands around the arms, the symbol for 'dog' or the character for *aku* (bad, evil), tattooed on the forehead. According to the Meiji University Museum's Criminal Materials Department, other 'basic' punishments under the Tokugawa shogunate's laws included crucifixion, exile to an island or house arrest. More specific punishments like tattooing were reserved for crimes such as theft, and were sometimes done in public.

Marked people were seen as felons, and some used this reputation to commit acts such as intimidation. Many eventually got larger pieces to cover up their penal tattoos, giving rise to the concept of aesthetically pleasing tattoos. Because of the rapid spread of the practice, the shogunate restricted *irezumi* numerous times. However, due to anti-authoritarian attitudes among commoners, it became increasingly popular and visually resplendent.

Tattooing was banned in 1872 during the Meiji era, since the government was concerned about appearing uncivilized after the nation opened up to the rest of the world. This ban was only lifted after World War II under the US's occupation. During that time, US servicemen stationed in Japan got inked by local artists, and one of General Douglas MacArthur's officers even visited *horishi* master Horiyoshi II. Of this period, tattoo artist Horihide says, 'When I was an apprentice, the ban against tattooing was still in place, so anyone tattooing and getting tattooed was a criminal, basically.' According to *horishi* Horitoku, 'Old *yakuza* clients told me that, in the war, the military lined everyone up to do a health inspection, and tattooed folks were sent to the most dangerous places because it was illegal.'

Due to the criminal connotations of tattoos, *wabori* was eventually co-opted by organized crime groups

– the *yakuza* – who use them as part of their initiation rites and as a means of intimidating members of the public. Quite often, *yakuza* members are superstitious and concerned with tattoos' meanings. For example, the word *koi* (carp) sounds the same as 'come whenever,' so carp represent being prepared to die at any time, just as the gangsters are.

Up until around 2015, many master tattoo artists had a predominantly underworld clientele, sometimes close to 100 per cent. Most *yakuza* members were embellished with full bodysuits, and *yakuza* tabloid journals, which were openly sold at convenience stores, were filled with pages of tattoos (surprisingly, some of terrible quality). Shoko Tendo, author of the memoir *Yakuza Moon*, which describes her life as the daughter of a *yakuza* boss, says of the time: 'When I was a child, I was constantly surrounded by people with a lot of tattoos, so if a person didn't have any ink, it seemed strange to me. It was common sense that someone would be tattooed.'

Given the wider associations between tattoos and criminality, there was a notion that people who had *irezumi* took part in organized crime, or were linked with what are referred to as 'antisocial groups' by law enforcement. Horitoku says, 'My clients used to be introduced via word of mouth and they were almost all *yakuza*. The bosses would call me and send their young ones. They would enter and say they are from whatever syndicate, and the *shatei* (younger brother) of so-and-so, and give me their business cards. In prison, the inmates are all dressed the same. The only way to be stylish is with ink. Even if they are low-ranked on the outside, on the inside, if they have good ink, they are seen highly and get treated nicely by their superiors, and they can benefit in various ways. If people are halfway tattooed, when they come out, they come to me and get tattooed immediately because they realize how important it is to have good ink behind bars – in the past, prisoners were a form of advertisement. My chrysanthemums are real-looking, but other people were doing simple ones. The inspectors in prison would take one look at my chrysanthemums and would ask my clients, "That's a Horitoku chrysanthemum, right?" Those kinds of people were really common in the past, it is the ultimate status brand, and if you got a terrible piece you would probably get laughed at.'

From the 1970s to the '90s, old-school artists went around tattooing crime syndicates across Japan for weeks at a time. Tokai Horihiro, a traditional tattooer based in Gifu, notes that, in the past, these groups would pay for his travel, hotels and expenses (which also included massages) in places like Kansai, Suzuka and Wakayama. Horihiro explains of these types of work trips: 'In the past, if you became part of a crime organization, you would have to get inked; the boss would order you to do it. I'd already entered that world under those conditions, so it was the accepted thing to be doing. It was a time when the syndicates really had pride and there were never any issues with money – it was really fun, because they'd treat you really well. When you got to the hotel they took your bags, and when you woke up they were waiting in the corridor, and when you drove they would fill your tank to the top. When I left, my car boot (trunk) was filled with presents. With some groups that I have the longest affiliations with, I have seen the boss change three times. Over the course of twenty years, the guy that had initially carried my luggage became the top man.'

At the end of the day, outlaws have the perspective that they want to separate themselves from the rest. Horikazu says, 'I feel that, more than others, they are determined to make a name for themselves in this tough world. That is why I can put my all into it.'

Nowadays, even in the world of *wabori* there are fewer *yakuza* clients, as many top-tier *horishi* have made it their policy to not tattoo gangsters at all. There are a couple of reasons for this shift. For one, there is a growing demographic of young people who are getting tattoos for purely aesthetic reasons. And, at the same time, anti-organized crime laws mean that *yakuza* numbers are dropping. Lately, across the board, many artists report that the proportion of their clients who are gang-affiliated has gone from 100 per cent to 0–10 per cent.

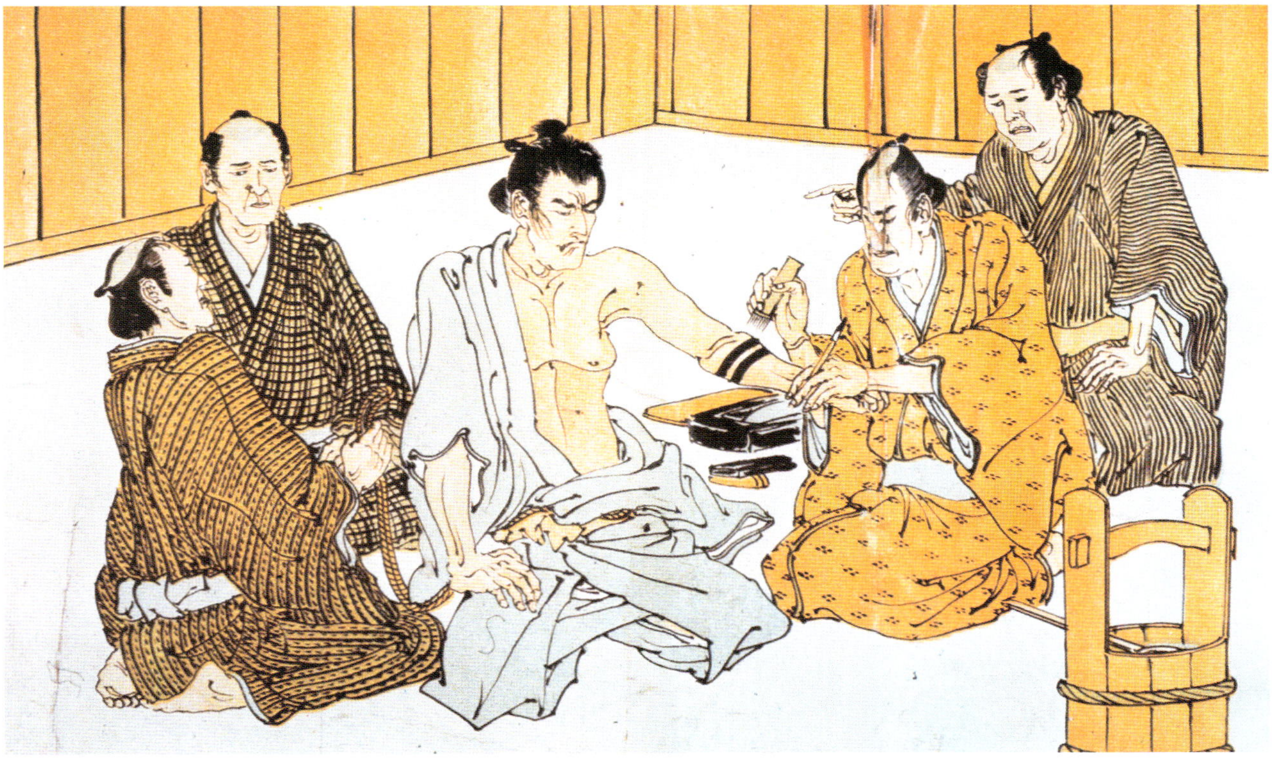

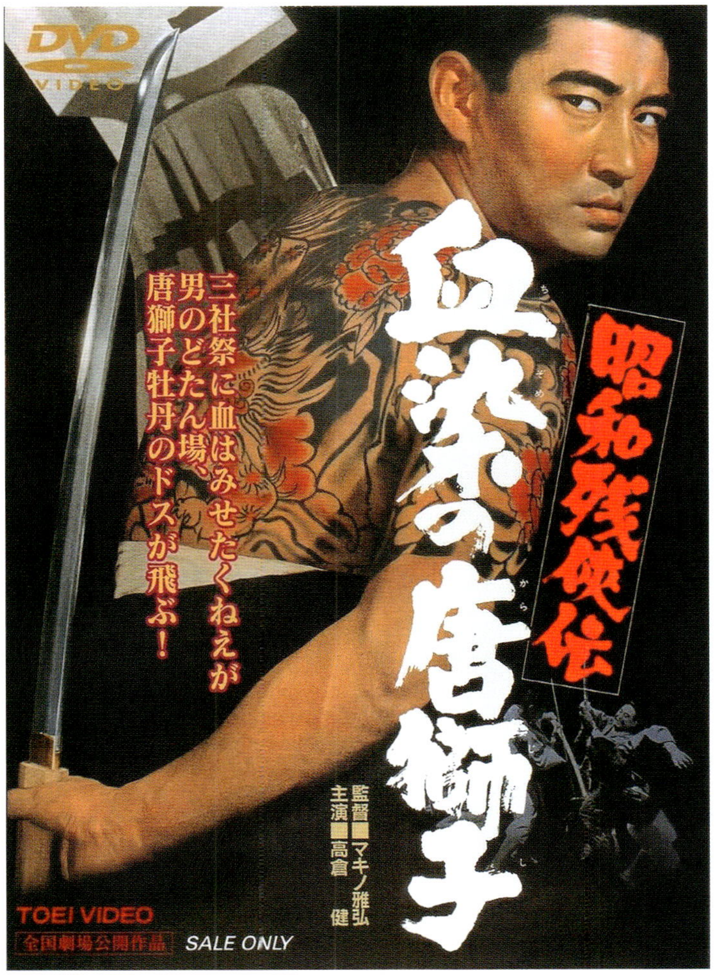

ABOVE
The Illustrated Guide to Punishments of the Tokugawa Shogunate by Shintaro Fujita (1893) shows the various punishments used by the Tokugawa Shogunate. Here a criminal is being given a punishment tattoo.

RIGHT
The popular tattooed samurai character Toyama no Kin-san appeared in 18 films, a series of books and a long-running TV show; depicted here is the poster for *Showa zankyo-den: Chizome no karajishi* (1967) starring the charismatic Ken Takakura. Many *yakuza* found these movies aspirational and wanted the same motifs.

Horiyoshi III, a famous Japanese tattoo artist, explains that when he started, maybe 60 per cent of his clients were *yakuza*, and the rest were craftsmen, construction workers or labourers. He adds, 'Now, it's nearly zero. It's a little sad. Matsuda Osamu, a historian at Hosei University, said that Japanese traditional tattoos are something that is outlawed or countercultural, that they shouldn't be socially acceptable, as that would be sacrilegious. I think that kind of theory holds true. There were a lot of rebels previously – well, even if they weren't outlaws, they had that kind of spirit. Now, it's not like that. It's mostly people into fashion, and the industries they are from are different too. The designs and the placement are also different. People get tattooed so that people can see it, so they show it really conspicuously, but in doing so, the charm of the tattoos disappears. It's not that it's popular now, it's just more visible. That sense of secrecy is lost, and it's become a bit cheap. For example, if you meet someone quite scary, they have something about them that is fascinating, a certain charm – and when that is gone, they are just a regular guy. That was one of the aspects of *irezumi* that is gradually being eradicated.'

Despite the majority of *horishi* saying that most of their clientele are regular folks these days, and the fact that people who get tattoos for fashion often flaunt them conspicuously, there is still a lot of discrimination and stigma against tattooed people in Japan. Most gyms, spas and pools do not allow tattooed people to enter, or if they have a small tattoo, they will ask guests to wear a plaster (Band-Aid) on top. For example, in 2013, New Zealand-based academic Erana Brewerton was asked to leave an *onsen* (hot spring bath) in Hokkaido because she had traditional Maori facial tattoos, making international news.

Nakamura, an artist in Kyushu, said in a 2008 interview that because no one would rent a house to a *horishi*, he ended up having to buy the house he lives in now. 'The mass media likes to introduce tattooing as something negative, it is not seen as an art form. I don't really announce that I am a *horishi*. I often hide it and say I am a driver, or a carpenter. Even though Japanese young people are getting them for fashion, the Japanese perspective on tattoos hasn't changed. A regular Japanese person doesn't know the difference between a Western tattoo and *wabori*, it is all same thing to them.'

Many people these days, however, get tattooed knowing the repercussions and don't seem to care how it is seen socially. Horicho II thinks change doesn't need to be imminent. While tattooers in the West are exalted as celebrities and even appear on tattoo-themed reality TV shows, Japanese masters align themselves with the humble world of artisans, describing themselves not as artists, but craftsmen. As a result, *wabori* culture is viewed as a kind of hidden beauty. 'I don't think it is appealing or cool to wear traditional *wabori* tattoos out in public,' he says. 'If it is a Western tattoo, it's fashionable and cool to show off.' He adds that, unlike the in-your-face designs of the West, Japanese tattooing is more like the patterning on the underside of a kimono. 'It is beautiful because you only get a glimpse of it.'

OPPOSITE TOP
Besides tattooing, the *yakuza* also engage in other rituals, such as removing portions of their own little fingers as a form of punishment or atonement.

OPPOSITE BOTTOM
In 2018, Yamaguchi syndicate member Shigehari Shirai, who had been on the lam in Thailand, was caught because his magnificent tattoo went viral on the internet.

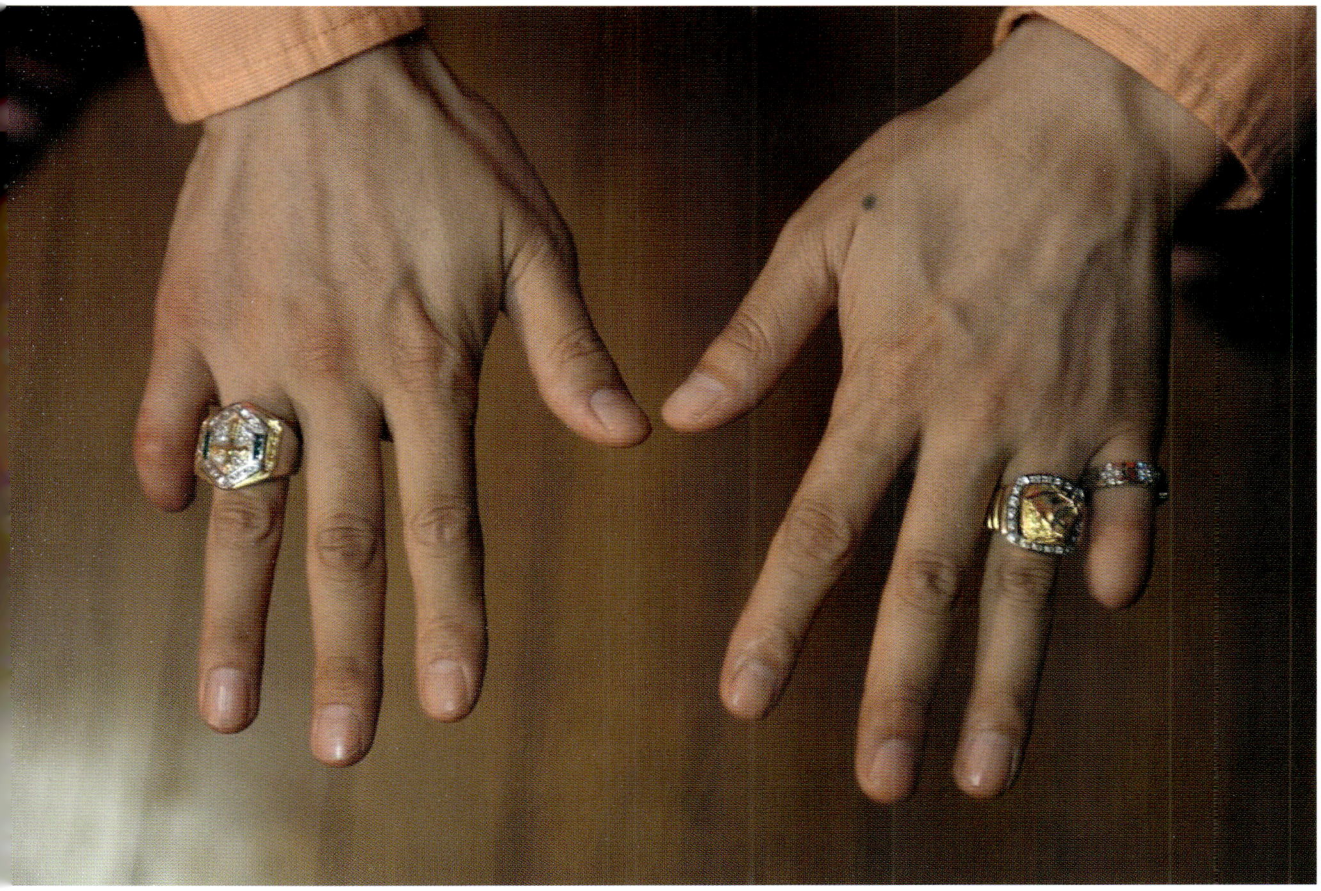

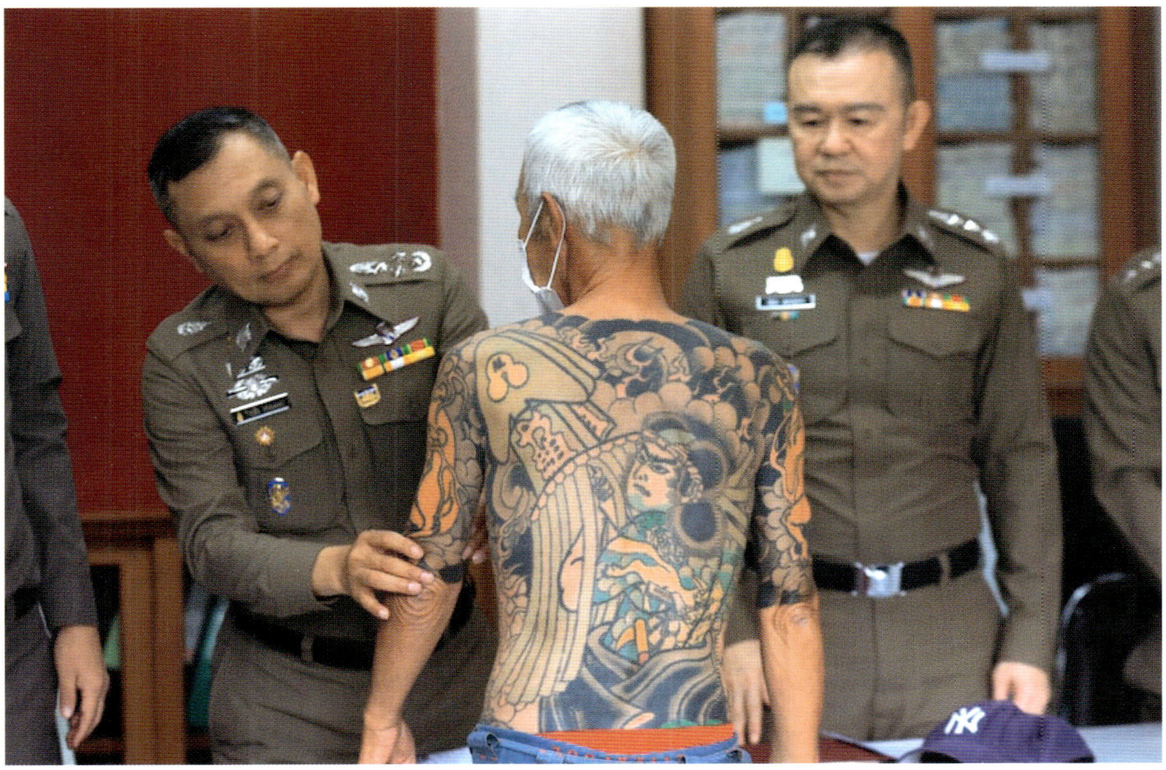

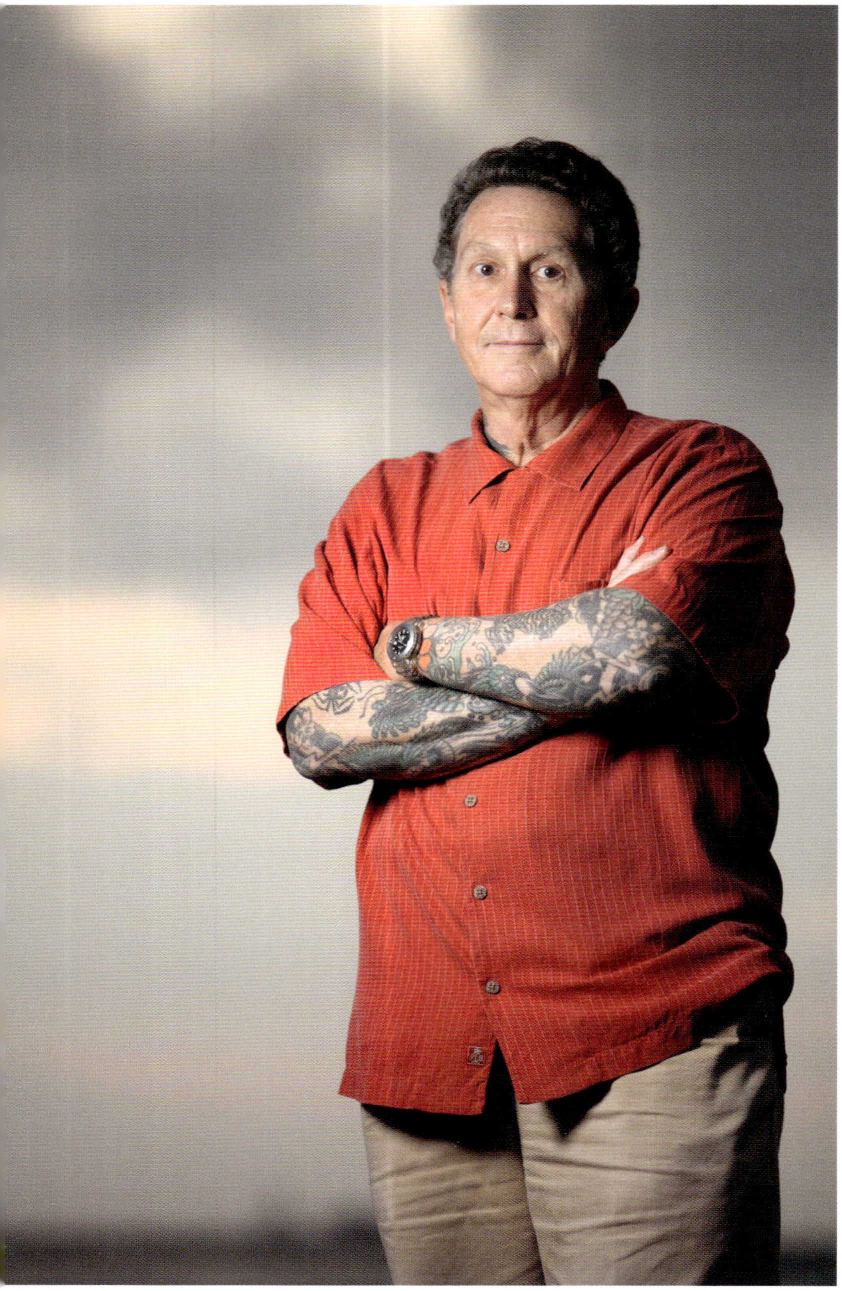

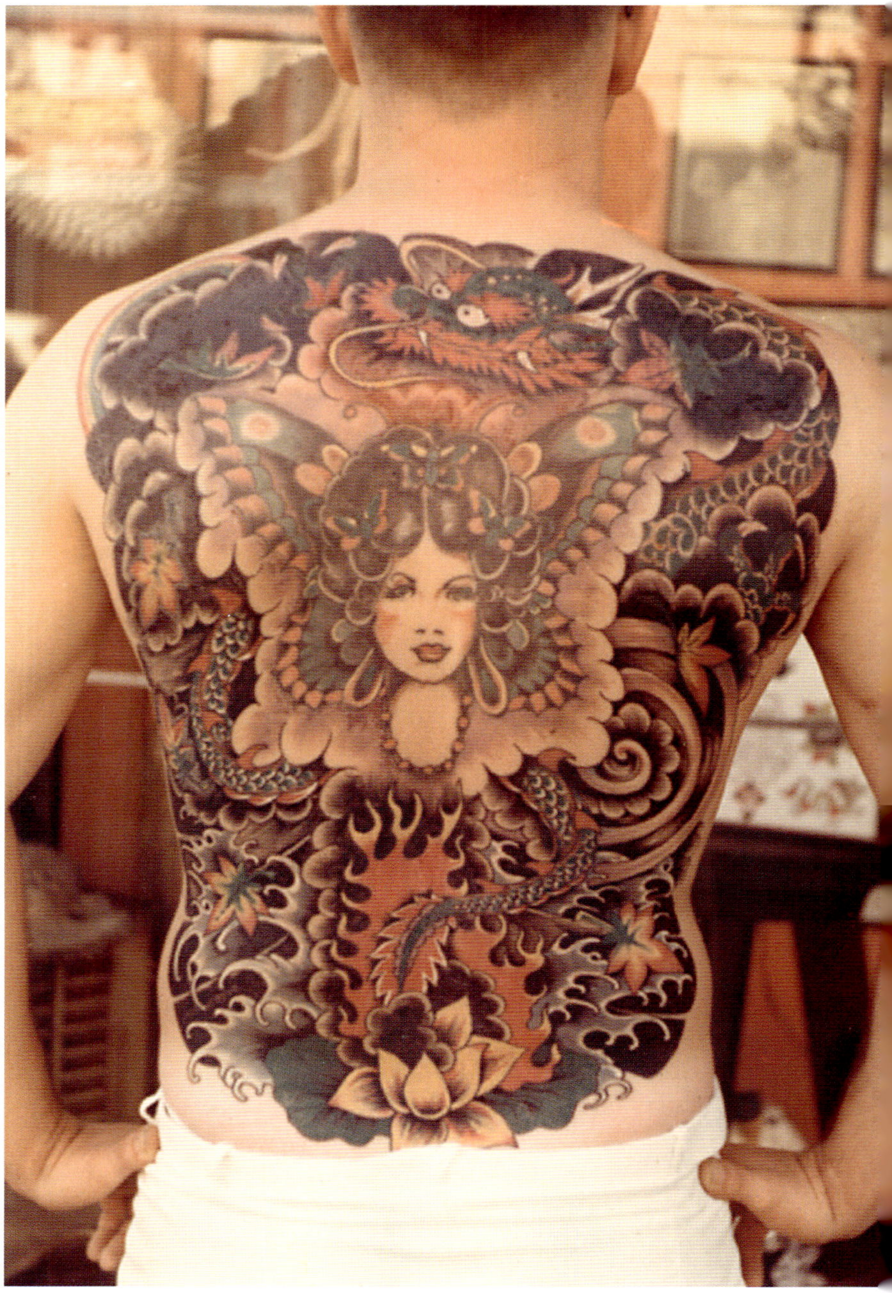

LEFT
Ed Hardy in Hawaii, 2007. He is often called the 'godfather of modern tattooing', and was integral to the exchange of Japanese and Western ideas about the art form.

RIGHT
The first backpiece tattooed by Ed Hardy, completed in 1969.

JAPANESE TATTOOS OVERSEAS

While Japanese tattoos are seen as clandestine and pushed underground in Japan, they have spread internationally. Although there was interaction between *horishi* and artists abroad earlier on, it was American tattooer Sailor Jerry's friendship with famed *horishi* Horihide in the 1970s that changed the tattooing landscape. Not only did Horihide visit Hawaii to learn about colours, but Sailor Jerry was able to learn about Japanese motifs from this exchange.

Ed Hardy, who is often called the 'godfather of modern tattooing', lived with Horihide in 1973 to study Japanese tattooing. Hardy only saw *wabori* in the flesh when he went to Japan, as it was such an 'insular' world. He explains that, the first time he saw Horiyoshi II's pieces, the 'psychic velocity that came off seeing the work on the skin was really amazing'. Around the 1990s, many tattoo artists overseas started to specialize in *wabori* and studios with Japanese-style artists flourished. This cemented *wabori* as a representative style that is pursued by tattoo artists globally, particularly in the Western world.

International artists like Filip Leu and Guy Aitchison started to forge new possibilities for Japanese tattoo art by creating original artworks that were inspired by *wabori*, but infused with their own creative spin.

Dirk-Boris Rödel, a tattoo researcher and former editor of Germany, Austria and Switzerland's largest tattoo publication, *TätowierMagazin*, explains, 'The popularity of Japanese tattooing in the West came along with a growing general interest in tattooing in the 1990s. Tattooing in the West slowly started to evolve from seafarers and subcultures like bikers, punks, skinheads and rockabillies into a more widespread form of culture. The "discovery" of these non-Western tattoo cultures gave people the possibility to get tattooed without the associations that came along with joining subculture communities. Japanese tattooing seemed relatable while still having an exotic aura.'

Rodel says that the greatest influence Japanese tattoos have had on the Western tattoo world is their composition and scale. '*Wabori* had connected and complementary designs on the body in a certain way, paying attention to how the design interacts with muscles, joints and the body in general – to not just put stickers on the body but create living, large-scale pictures on the skin.'

Hardy recalls, 'Back when we started [in the 1980s], there was only about four of us trying to do Japanese-inspired work. So people liked it; by and large, clients like things that are exotic to them. Even when I was tattooing the military in San Diego, I was trying to do bigger work on sailors and I would ask, "Can we integrate this into something?" I would try and get them to get something larger and more challenging.'

WOMEN IN THE JAPANESE TATTOO WORLD

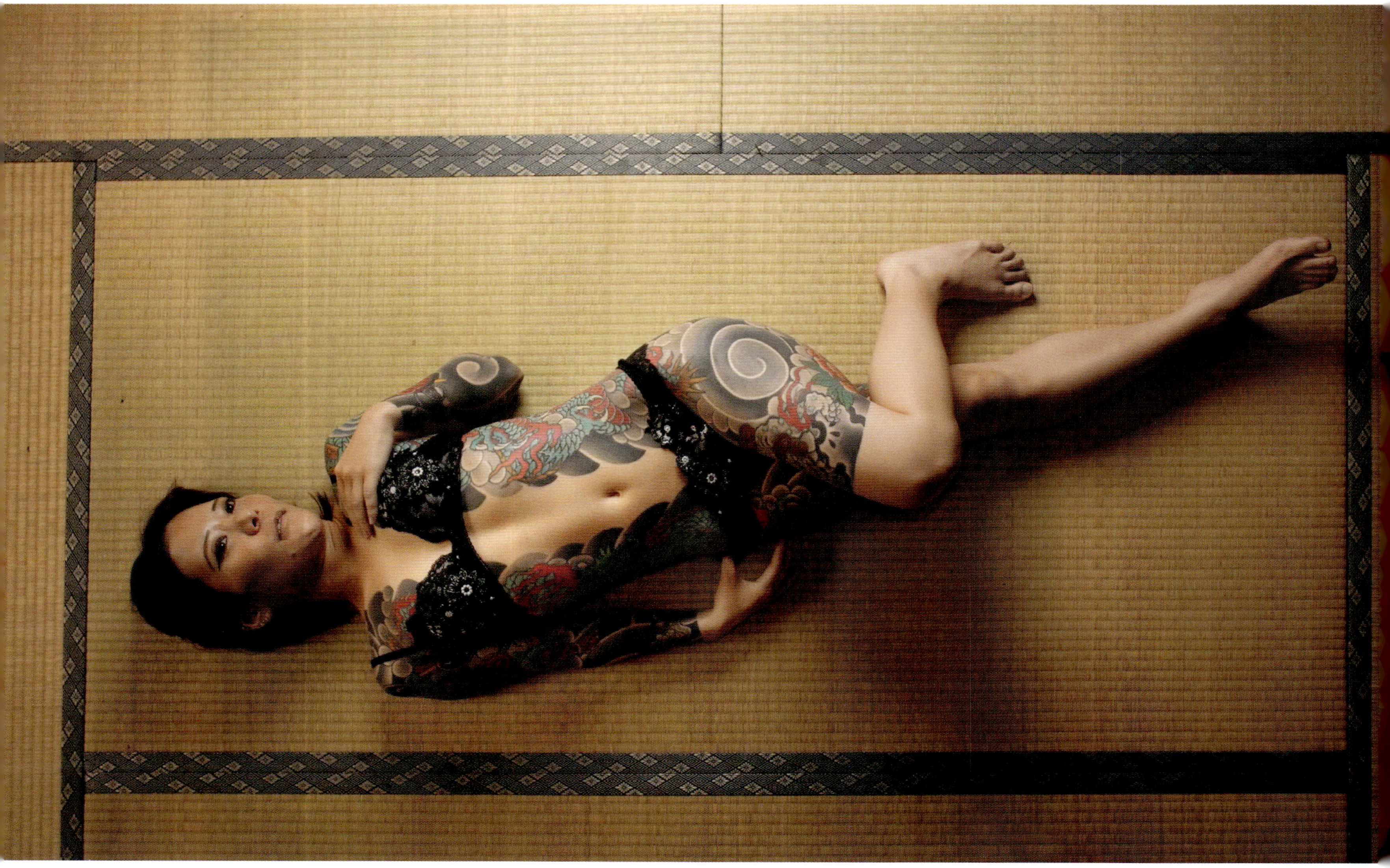

ABOVE
Although tattoos have always been much more popular among Japanese men, there is an ever-growing interest among women. Mei, pictured here, found her tattooer Akatsuki – who is also female – via social media.

In the world of traditional Japanese tattoos the clientele were, historically, overwhelmingly men. Although some *yakuza* wives and daughters are tattooed, there has usually been no requirement for the spouses of *yakuza* men to be tattooed – so there is less association between inked women and the underworld.

The reasons women get tattooed are more personal, and as the popularity of tattoos in general rose across Japan, so did the proportion of women with ink. Many top-tier Western-style tattooers are female, such as Kyoto-based Madoka, whose work is a cross between 1990s one-point delinquent tattoos and Japanese motifs, like geishas (see p. 44). *Tattoo Burst* former editor Miho Kawasaki points out, 'There are more tattoo genres in contemporary times, and if a female wants a *kawaii* (cute) tattoo, what a man thinks is cute is different. It has become easier to become a female tattoo artist because you can learn on your own without going into a traditional tattoo family and there is more demand. While I think, generally, people choose an artist because of the quality rather than gender, there are female clients who want to be tattooed by female artists too.'

Kawasaki notes that the increase in tattooing among Japanese women over time is connected to their economic standing and disposable income, as well as overall liberation, including via the 1985 Equal Employment Opportunity Act. The rise happened adjacent to the 1990s tattoo boom, when new subcultures that championed individuality and freedom came to Japan.

While most contemporary Japanese women who get tattooed are fans of Western and one-point tattoos (such as lettering, or small black-and-grey motifs), there are also women who get full body tattoos. Often, they are open about being tattooed on social media, garnering a lot of followers. Yet, despite this, the consequences of having tattoos are often higher for women and they can end up leading two lives: their tattooed life on social media, and their everyday life. Some even hide their faces online while baring their skin to flaunt their inked bodies. Kawasaki explains, 'I think the most difficult time for tattooed women is when they have kids. They have to network with other parents of various ages, some 20 years apart. There are differing values; there are a lot of people who don't want their kids to be exposed to tattoos and they will send complaints to the nurseries.'

Mei (see opposite) was driven to get tattoos through a desire for self-expression. She was specifically looking for a female artist and sought out Tokyo-based tattooer Akatsuki on Instagram. 'For tattooing you get naked, so I didn't want a man to tattoo me,' Mei says. 'For me, tattooing is an affirmation that there is only one of me. I gained confidence in myself from my tattoo, as I feel that tattoos are like armour.'

Ami (see overleaf) is a heavily tattooed woman with a sizeable Instagram presence who covers her ink at her day job. 'I first saw a tattoo when I was a teenager. Small Western tattoos were really in fashion then,' she recalls. 'I decided then I wanted to get my whole back done, but I got rejected when I went to Horihiro's studio because he said I was too young and told me to come back in my twenties. After I got my backpiece from Horihiro, a few years passed. I wanted my life to change, so I tattooed some peonies [which represent good fortune]. Over the years I've had a lot of problems and suffered, so I've really had the desire to transform. I use the goddess Benzaiten, the motif on my back [see p. 48], as a representation of myself, and the dragons around it are protecting me. There are seven in total for luck. I put eyes on the dragon on the front of my body – the dragon is looking on my behalf.' As for social pressure, she says, 'In Japan, the number of people with tattoos is increasing, and people are asking for a world without discrimination. But I am doing it to separate myself from everyone, so I think the discrimination is fine. I have no desire to be accepted.'

Miko (see p. 64) is a chocolatier at 6c3524, a confectioners' shop in Chiba prefecture, whose daughter is a tattoo artist. Miko is covered in nine dragons and started to get tattooed in 2020, after marrying and divorcing twice. She explains, 'Horitake in

Chiba was my artist; he is in the Horikyo family. I never regret getting my tattoos. Rather than having a desire to transform, I am trying to reclaim the person I originally wanted to be, not the repressed person I was when I was married and just at home. I had to stifle my curiosity about a lot of things, but now I can regain my sense of freedom.'

Otoha (see overleaf) has a full bodysuit by Horiyuki, whose work she finds appealing, as she thinks he 'accentuates female eroticism'. She says, 'Since getting tattoos, I've made a lot of friends with tattoos in their late twenties and early thirties. I don't think it is a trend, but there are a lot of people around me with heavy Japanese tattoo work. They are people who have strong convictions and are quite deep, so I find them interesting to talk to. My life has become richer as a result.'

In interviews, many tattoo artists mentioned that, from around the mid-1990s, they had a lot of female clients from the sex industry. Kawasaki says this is likely due to the fact that sex workers have a high disposable income and a job that is more open to being out of the tattoo closet. Veteran *horishi* Horihide recalls tattooing many women working at hostess clubs and bars, a lot of whom asked for permanent makeup. He explains that, while women historically wanted motifs like Japanese flowers, from around 1995, they started to ask for roses and designs like black cats on their breasts. 'In the beginning, it was mostly people in the sex industry,' he says, continuing, 'but now it really surprises me, the kind of people that get tattooed! I had a lot of geisha who were doing it to attract customers.'

According to *horishi* Horicho II, whose studio was previously located adjacent to Yoshiwara, Tokyo's red-light district, 'There are many women from the adult industry. The more they are tattooed, the more likely they are to be successful, and that is the reason they got inked. They have many clients who are tattoo fans and ask them to get more work. This is more just the preferences of Japanese perverts than Yoshiwara culture, per se! The clients probably don't have any tattoos, but they like to fantasize that the girl is a *yakuza* guy's girlfriend or something like that.'

Akira (see overleaf) is a dominatrix who works at Bar-Bara, a BDSM bar in Kyoto. She says that people interested in S&M and those who are tattooed are both minorities in Japan. While she isn't conscious of it at work, she explains that, once she steps outside of subcultural spaces, she feels that 'people are not socially progressive'. Her job provides a space, much like tattoo events, where she can 'say things that you can't say outside'. She continues, 'There is the notion that people who are tattooed are scary and associated with something antisocial. I definitely feel that there is a negative image. If I'm in the BDSM world I don't feel an issue, but in my regular life, if I go to a restaurant and my tattoos are showing, they might not be welcoming, and I can't go to large public spa facilities. I hide them usually, though; I don't want to be looked at. There was a time in my personal life when I invited someone to have sex, and he ran away when he saw my tattoos. Having said that, my soul is satisfied; it is proof that I can live freely and not be swayed. That is the reason I am tattooed. It is like makeup, it is decorative. I don't do it to be called beautiful, but rather to express my sense of beauty.'

Horimasa, a *horishi* in Gunma prefecture, says that while he used to tattoo many women during the 2000s tattoo boom – a lot of whom were cabaret club hostesses and sex workers – not many of his female clients have been getting large pieces in more recent years. His regulars are more interested in, as he says, 'looking the same, rather than standing out'. He explains: 'In the past, they were expressing themselves, but nowadays, they want to get paid as influencers rather than work a regular job. They want to look like the girls that aren't celebrities but are paid regardless to be on TikTok, girls that look like Korean idols with tiny black-and-grey tattoos. It is fundamentally a different era.'

Horiren (see pp. 66–67) is a female traditional Japanese tattoo artist who specializes in Buddhist deities. She first came across tattoos in Australia, where she collected a few souvenir tattoos from

OPPOSITE
Horihiro's client Ami outside his studio in Shizuoka. She prefers to cover her tattoos in public: 'I have a day job and no one at my work knows. I usually hide them and only show them on my social media,' she explains. 'I think the eroticism of a woman comes from the skin, so I leave a bit unfilled.'

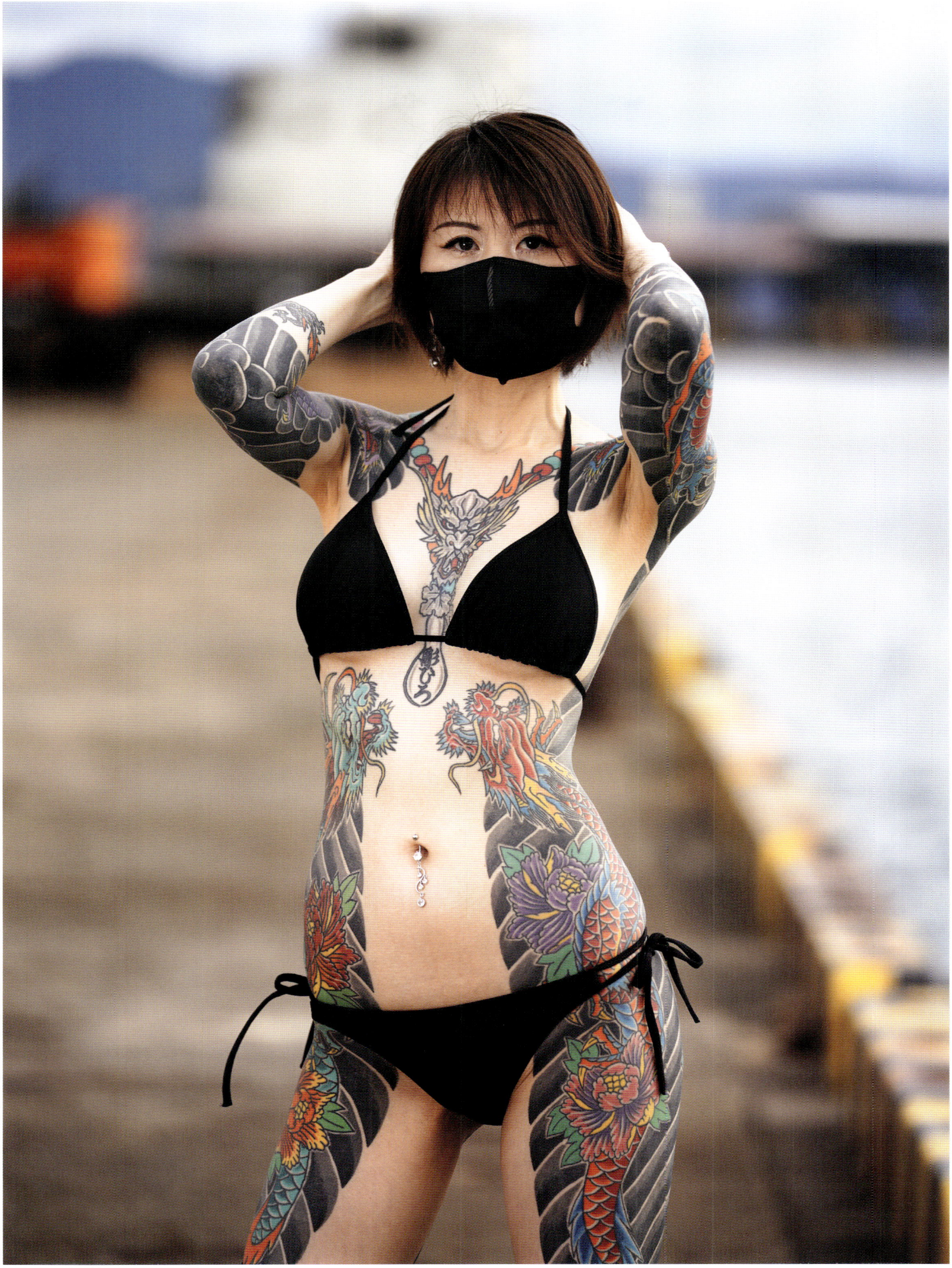

random shops across the country. Having worked in the graphic design industry, she started tattooing one-points for around eight years until she escalated to full body pieces. Since 2021 she has also been a priest in the Shingon sect, ordained with the Buddhist name Rensho, after she apprenticed under Ryozen Tateba, a priest in Mie prefecture. She was motivated to become a priest by the death of one of her first clients, who passed away in the 2011 Fukushima earthquake, as well as by the death of a woman who helped her get established in the tattoo profession in Osaka, where she works. Horiren explains, 'Firstly, my interest was in the visual aspect of the deities, they were just cool. For years I had wanted to become a priest, but I decided to actualize that wish during the 2011 Fukushima disaster. I wanted to be able to send people off [with Buddhist funeral rites] after they passed.'

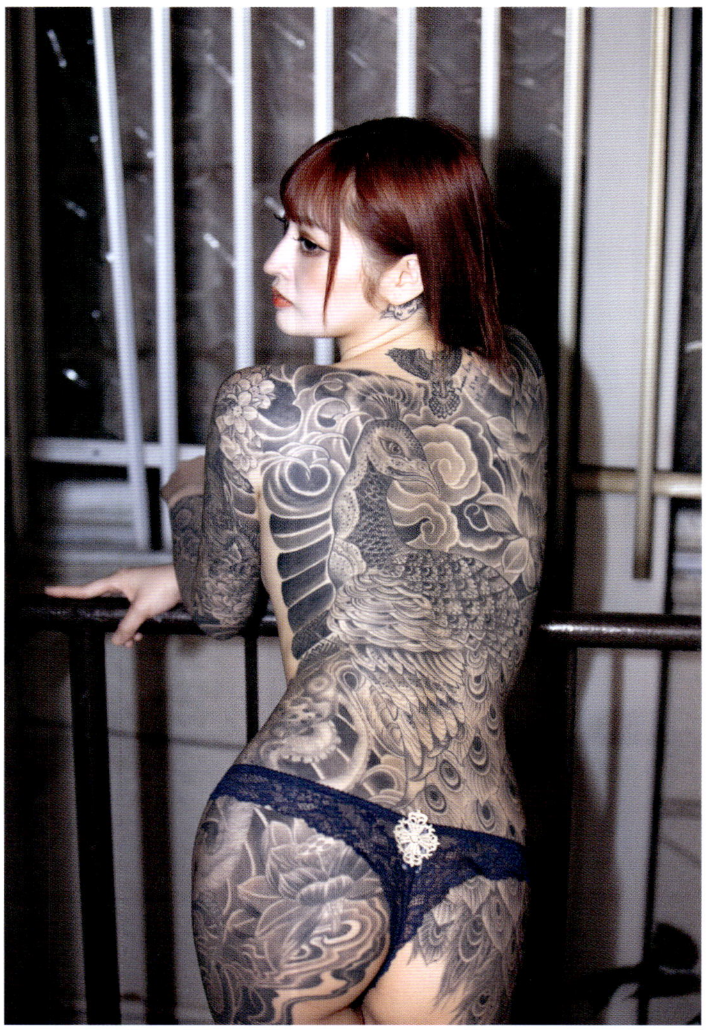

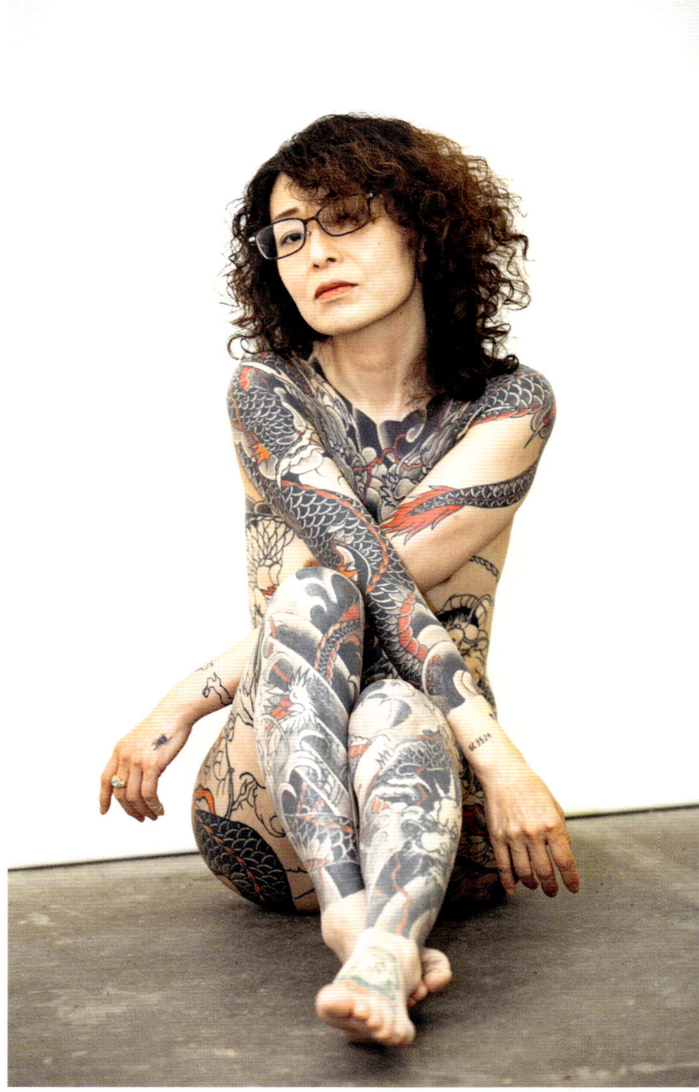

LEFT
Otoha's backpiece features a peacock, which is thought to provide protection from snakes and is associated with Buddhist deity Kujaku Myo-o, a female Myo-o with a kind face. This tattoo is neo-traditional in that it employs traditional Japanese motifs, but was made with a machine and has modern sensibilities.

ABOVE
Miko, who works as a chocolatier, has a large dragon backpiece by Horitake. Her daughter is also a tattooer who started out as part of a tattoo family (*ichimon*), but went independent because she found it hard to fit into the hierarchical, traditional Japanese system. She is now tattooing Miko.

OPPOSITE
Akira is a dominatrix working at Kyoto's oldest BDSM bar. She is drawn to the beauty of tattoos.

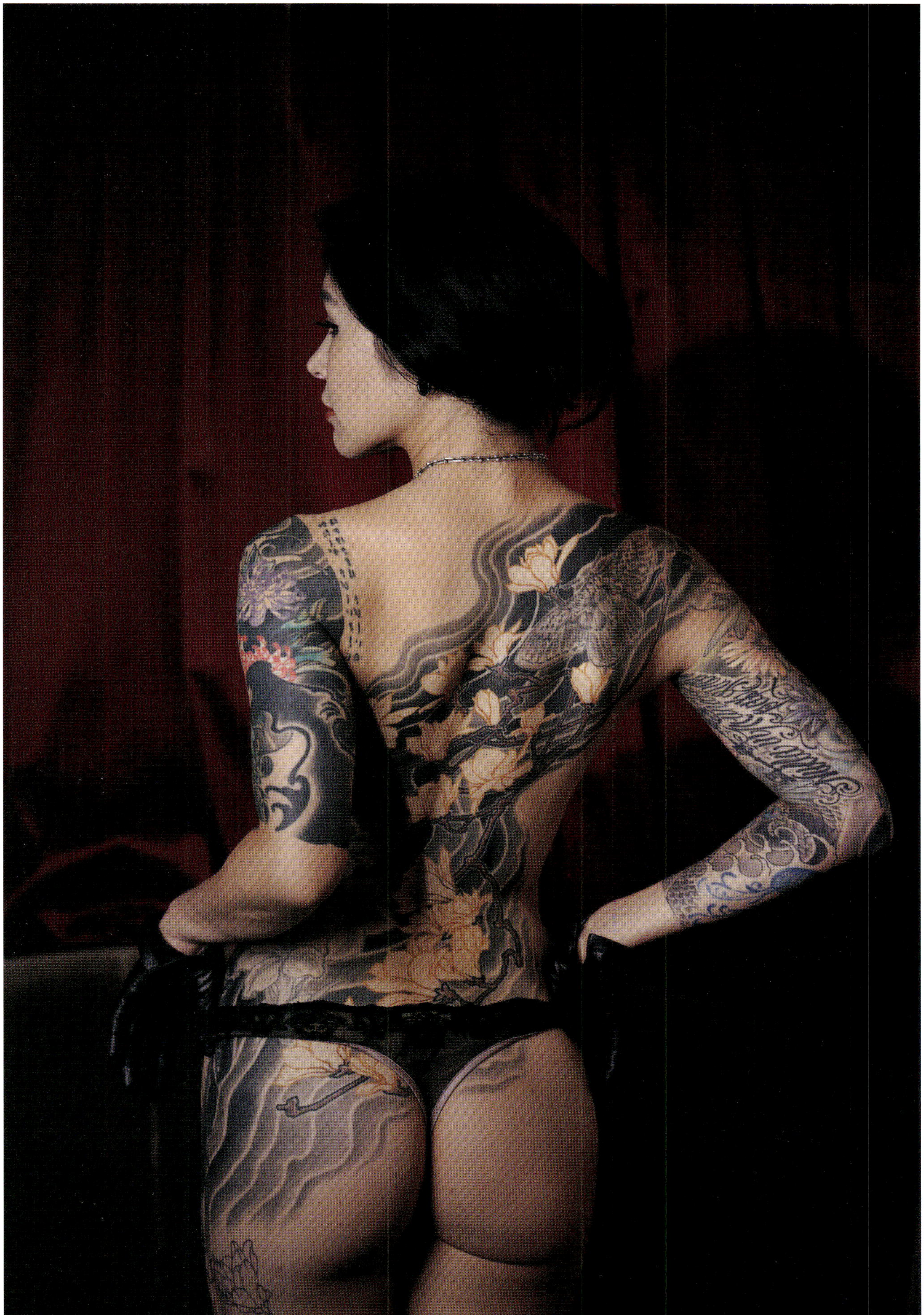

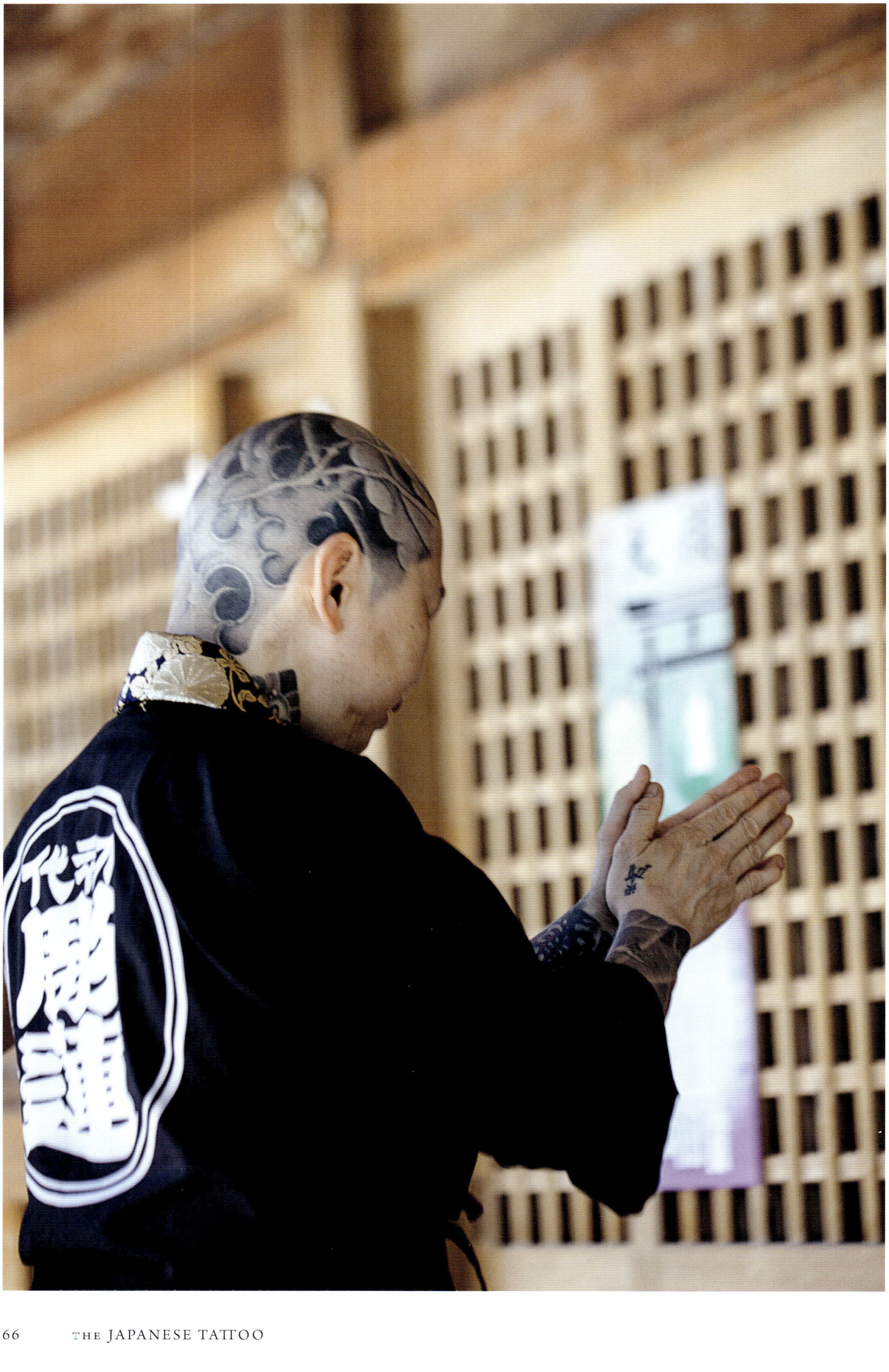

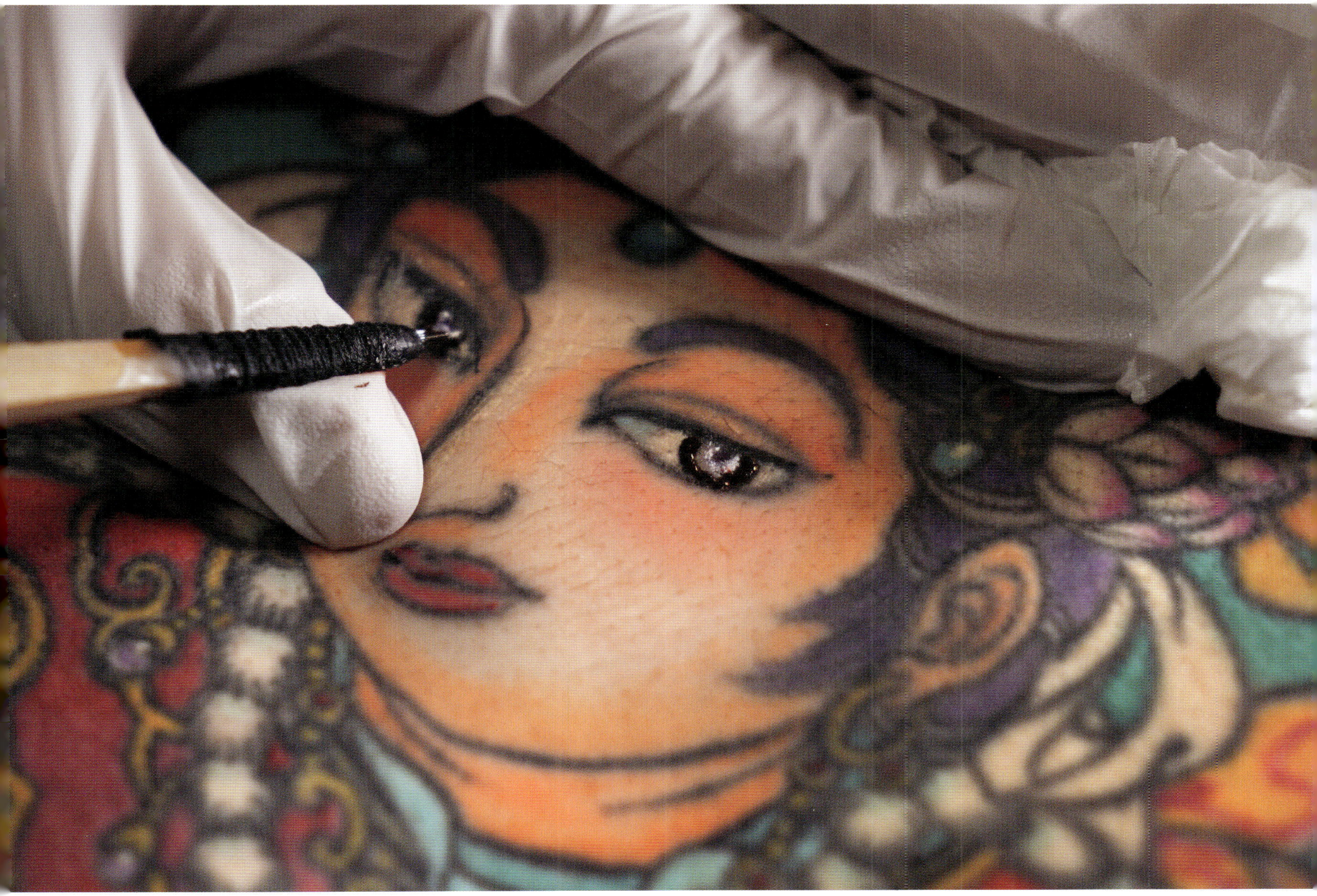

OPPOSITE
Horiren is a tattoo artist and Buddhist priest. Her head was tattooed by *horishi* Horimyo.

ABOVE
A client of Horiren's in her studio in Warabi, Saitama prefecture. This piece took eight years to complete. Filling in the eyes is the last step in the process.

ARTISANS AND AESTHETICS

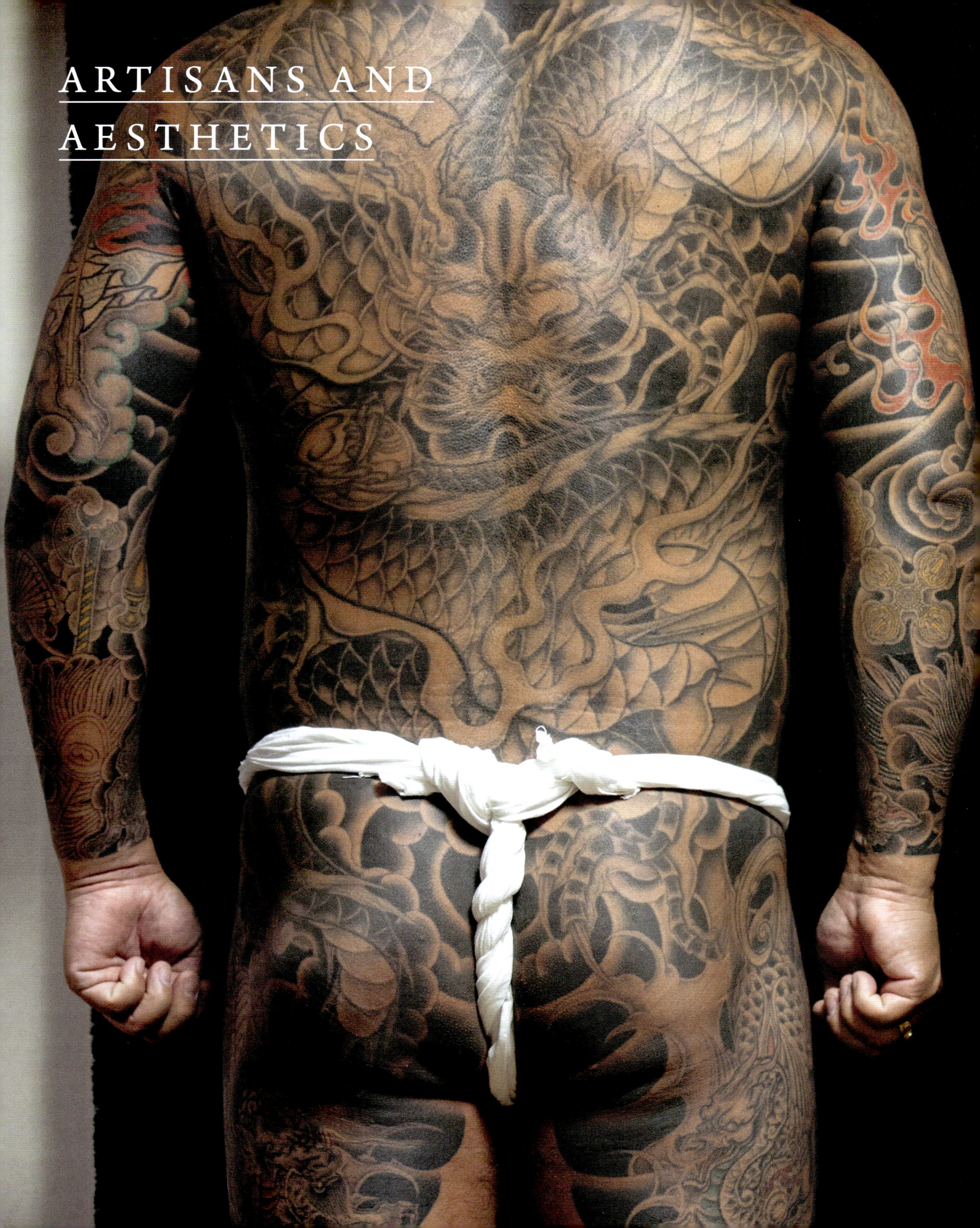

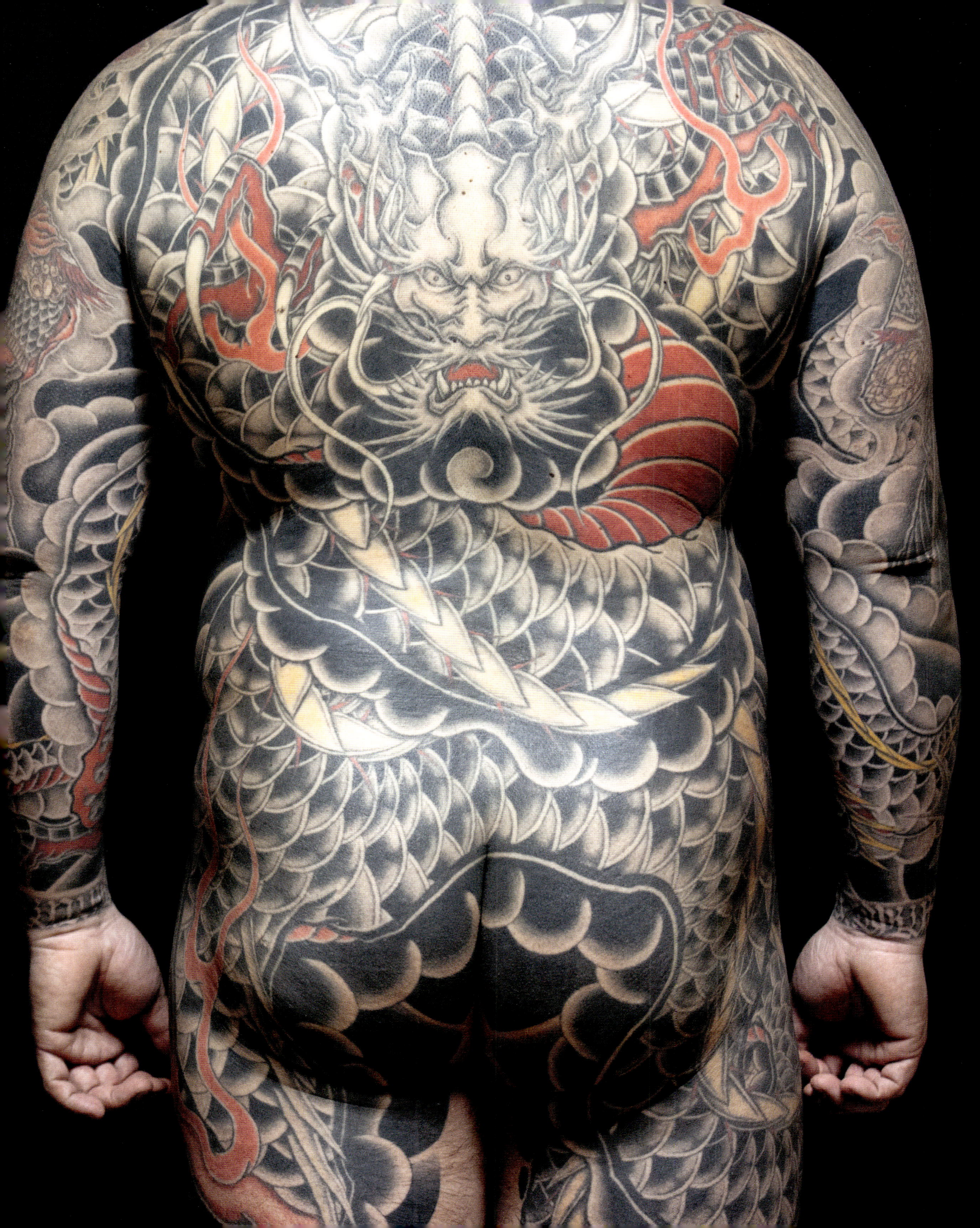

The art and craft of Japanese tattooing that is undertaken by *horishi* has many parallels with other Japanese artisanal cultures, such as woodworking, textile production and ceramics. These crafts are often connected to the local community and the identity of a district.

Japanese artisans are called *shokunin*, individuals who work on one specialized craft. While many artisans are self-taught, the skills and technical aspects of the trade are traditionally passed down generationally, through a master (*shisho*) and apprentice (*deshi*) system. Before the notion of trade schools spread, the system of apprenticeships that flourished in the Edo period enabled budding youths to garner skills from esteemed masters. This ensures that there is a level of competency before someone is able to work professionally, and there is also a degree of integrity that is imbued via the philosophy of artisanship, not just the ability to work with the relevant tools and make money.

The apprenticeships are gruelling and feudal, usually starting with cleaning and duties that are not directly related to the craft itself. Historically, an apprenticeship was an exchange of sorts, and would entail living at a master's house, cooking all the meals, cleaning and slowly 'stealing' the work through observation, as apprentices are not taught verbally how to tattoo. It is only after they are given menial tasks that they are allowed to progress to further steps, and if there are other apprentices, *deshi* are often taught by other *deshi*.

Rather than just passing down skills, however, the *deshi* system also entails bonds within the tattoo family (*ichimon*), and a commitment to a particular way of life. Individuals belonging to *ichimon* were in the past afforded a degree of protection from organized crime groups, too, who often came knocking on independent tattooers' doors, particularly if a tattooer was green and did a terrible job on one of their underlings. While it is not common now, *horishi* Horimasa recalls that, if someone of his generation opened up a shop, a gang member would often turn up to claim extortion and 'protection' money. 'It was sometimes every day. They wanted 20,000 yen a month, and for New Year's I was asked for *mochi* (sticky rice cakes)! Sometimes, they asked for pro wrestling and sumo tickets.'

The naming of *horishi* also follows an established system and is a quintessential part of passing on traditions. *Horishi* literally means 'person who engraves'. Most Japanese-style tattoo artists use the '*hori-*' prefix plus syllables from their real name. Sometimes a master will give them a name. The names of certain masters hold a kind of weight, and anyone who assumes those names receives the reputation, fame and charisma of the preceding artisans. Once an artisan achieves a certain level of mastery, they will seek to pass on their name to a member of the next generation. While it is rare, there are some tattoo dynasties, like Horikazu (see pp. 152–63), with bloodline relationships between father and son. However, the norm is for young people to enter the world of tattoos by approaching the master of their liking for an apprenticeship. Whether the master accepts them is determined on a case-by-case basis.

One of the central tenets of the artisanal mindset is the idea that a person is forever a student, no matter whether they are self-taught or studied in a family. Often, artisans will say that, after 10 to 20 years, they started to grasp an understanding of their craft. A common refrain among them is that they are perpetually in training and are never satisfied. There is a dedication to the process of learning, even if they have decades of experience and are considered masters. Seeking a path of improvement, the actual act of making things and a humble outlook are of paramount importance.

The tattoo production process itself is meditative to watch, and is executed with meticulous precision. The tattooers align themselves with artisans more than with artists, and focus with a stoic efficiency on their work. There is a methodical and smooth speed to their movements, requiring concentration and presence. There is an interplay between the medium and the *horishi*, which is akin to a type of communication. The quality of the work is reflective of the

PREVIOUS SPREAD
Two backpieces by Horimyo featuring dragons.

OPPOSITE
Nakamura is one of the few *horishi* who uses the *shamisenbori* technique.

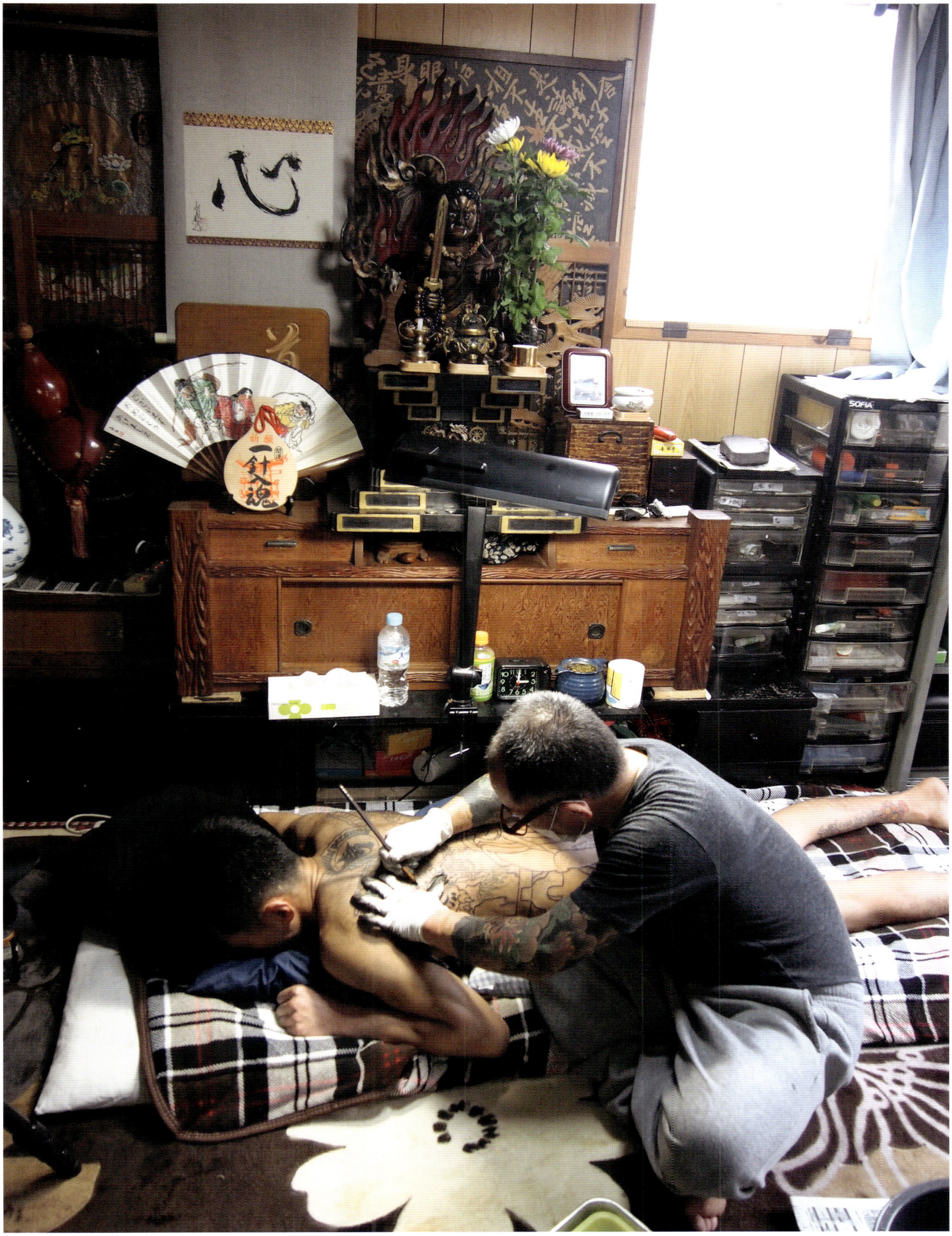
心
祈願
一針入魂
SOFIA

artisan's inner state – if they are not attentive, or they are in a bad mood, the work will also suffer, particularly when drawing facial expressions. The process describes their presence in the existential moment.

With the coming of the industrial revolution during Japan's Meiji period, slowly, the world of artisans became less common. Many young people living under the nation's current economic climate will find it hard to survive a traditional apprenticeship (and are usually simply too impatient for it), although tattoo masters do often have foreign apprentices driven by a passion for Japanese crafts. In the world of tattooing, progress in technology, such as pens, means that anyone can start working right after buying a kit online. Instead of having a master, many youths today say that the internet is their teacher.

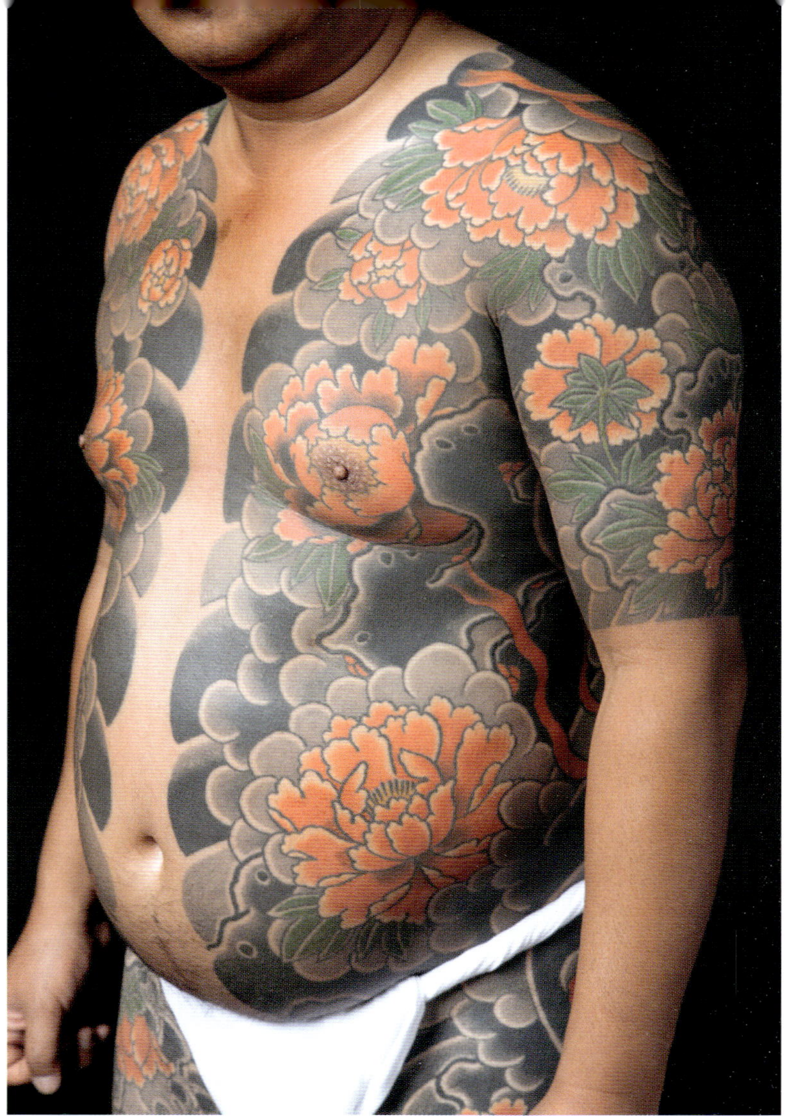

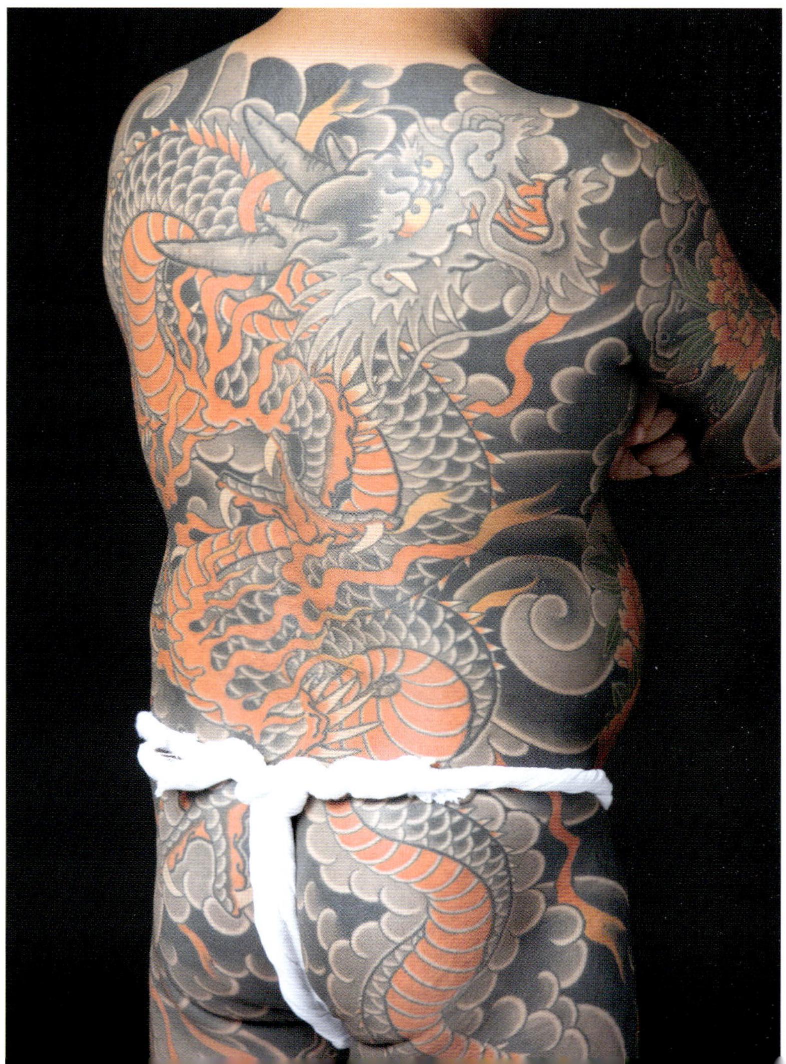

TOP
The front of a full bodysuit by Tokyo-based *tebori* artisan Bunshin Horitoshi, who first moved to the capital at age 18 and was inspired by what he saw at the famous Tokyo Tattoo convention. Nowadays, he is fluent in English and is active internationally, particularly in Europe.

BOTTOM
Bunshin Horitoshi says, 'I look at all kinds of things to compare them with my work, regardless of the genre, even tribal art. I look at it thinking, "Why does this look good?" I think that is the same across any art form, whether it is graphic design or interiors, fashion or street art.'

JAPANESE TATTOO TECHNIQUES

The world of Japanese tattoos is directly connected to *ukiyo-e* woodblock printing, which was historically comprised of forms that are expressed through flatness and lines, rather than the sense of 3D perspective and light seen in Western art. Historically, Japanese tattooing has been done by hand with *tebori* ('hand-carving') techniques, as opposed to the machines that are the norm for Western tattoo work. It is extremely rare, but in exceptional cases, there are *wabori* masters (such as Horiyasu in Asakusa) who use a machine for everything. Nowadays, most artisans use a machine at least for the *sujibori* (outlines) as a way to expedite the process. For inserting ink by hand, they use a tool called a *nomi* (or *sashibo*) that is either bamboo or metal, with *hari* needles attached. Elegant, curved lines are sometimes tattooed with *tebori* over the machine-made lines.

Given that human hands are inserting the ink, *tebori* work has an aesthetic that is proudly rustic and rugged; no two pieces are the same. While any discrepancies might seem like defects, with handcrafted work, tattoo clients feel an affinity with the 'imperfections'. These characteristics inherent in artisanal crafts are often referred to as 'warmth' (*nukumori*) in Japanese, and give the tattoos a rich flavour that aficionados are drawn to.

The primary goal of Japanese tattoos is to try and create a narrative within the limited space available. Their composition is formed from a *shudai* (central subject), which is the main motif. This usually involves folkloric characters, animals both mythical and real, or Buddhist deities. They all have symbolic meaning and are generally auspicious, offering luck or protection. *Keshobori* are the decorative elements that serve as visual accompaniments to the central subject – for example, flowers that are seasonally compatible with the main motif. *Gakubori* refers to the background, which frames the entire composition and consists of images like clouds, waves and wind. This serves to structure the motif and hold it together, while highlighting the central figure or subject. *Nukibori* are tattoos where the background is intentionally left blank; often, the negative space is an important element of the overall composition. There is a certain aesthetic of omission in Japanese art, and sometimes a tattoo is completed with no background, for example just a *koi* (carp) or dragons on the back.

The *mikiri* are the borders around a tattoo. These come in a variety of different shapes, such as *akebono mikiri*, which fades in intensity; *botan-giri*, which looks like waves and clouds; *matsuba mikiri*, which appears similar to pine needles; *bukkiri*, which is straight and looks like it was cut with a sword; and *jari mikiri*, which consists of small dots and looks like stones.

Finally, there are *kakushibori*, which are playful motifs that can make sexual innuendoes or are included as a kind of joke. They are usually placed in hidden areas like the armpit. Some people also have pop culture elements to their tattoos, like *Doraemon* characters. Sometimes, trends within *kakushibori* are started by a powerful *yakuza* boss, and then people who see them and find them aspirational will copy their motifs.

One of the most important elements within Japanese tattoos is the *bokashi*, or shading. *Usu bokashi* is shading with a soft black appearance and *tsubushi* is packed (dense, with a lot of ink inserted), while *akebono bokashi* features gradations from dark to light.

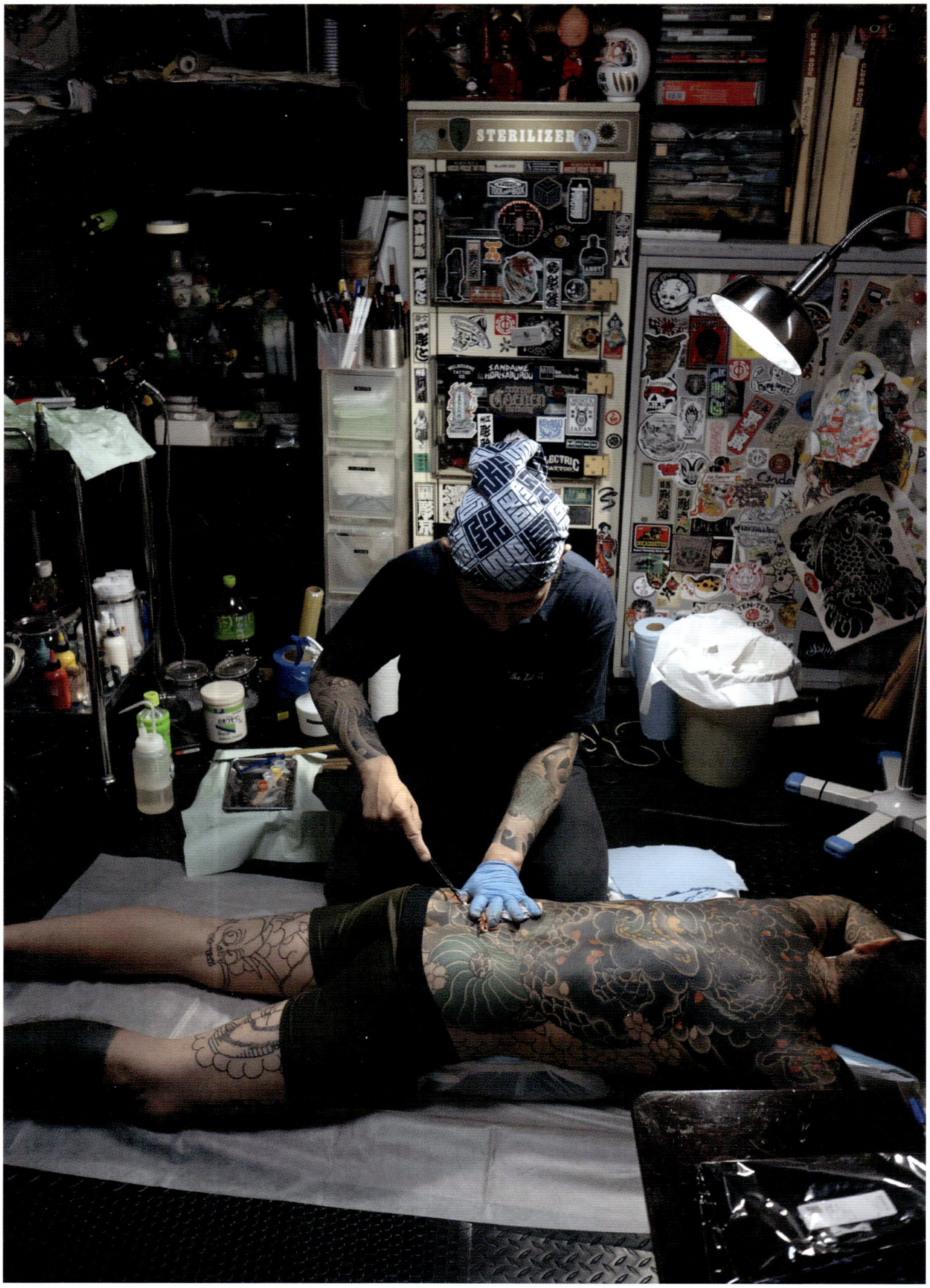

LEFT
Bunshin Horitoshi entered a traditional apprenticeship at a young age. Of that time, he says, 'The older apprentices were showing me, but basically, I was just cleaning. They would often say, "I can't teach you that," because there are steps that you have to do sequentially. It was a large family and some were real relatives, so some would teach me and some wouldn't. I was getting no pay for the first year and tattooing the other apprentices. Then I would find friends to tattoo and I would show my teacher the work. I was slow, so I didn't do big pieces. Once you get a name, like *hori*-something, you have become a member of the family and take responsibility.'

The ink is applied using several techniques. *Hanebori* is a technique where the ink is inserted by flicking the skin upwards with needles, allowing more ink to seep in. *Tsukibori* is when the ink is jabbed into the skin without flicking upwards and *imotsuki* is when the ink is inserted vertically, using an in-and-out motion. *Horishi* Nakamura from Kyushu prefecture and Horiren are also competent at *shamisenbori*, an unusual style of *tebori* wherein the main tool used resembles a *shamisen* pick (a Japanese musical instrument, like a lute) and moves upwards in a strumming motion.

OPPOSITE
Japanese tattoos usually have specific borders and backgrounds. However, a *nukibori* simply features a central subject with nothing to complement it. For certain themes, it can be quite striking. This piece by Horimyo is a collaboration with artist Ai Sawada.

SHAPES

Classic Japanese tattooing fits to the body's silhouette and flows across the corporeal form and muscles to create a holistic picture. There are several shapes that are typically used when creating a large-scale Japanese tattoo. *Soushinbori* is a full suit that covers most of the body. *Munewari* is typically a bodysuit that has an un-tattooed section down the chest to the bottom of the stomach. The shape is like a worker's coat, as opposed to a *donburi*, where the entire chest area is filled in. The *kame no kou* is a backpiece from the back to the thighs, and a *sewari* covers the entire back to the point where the buttocks start and then separates outwards towards the thighs.

All Japanese sleeves include a chest panel, or *hikae*. A fuller panel covers the whole pectoral area, and the shallow type covers the area just above the nipples (and looks particularly beautiful on women). A *nagasode* is a full sleeve, a *gobu* ends above the elbow and a *shichibu* reaches below the elbow.

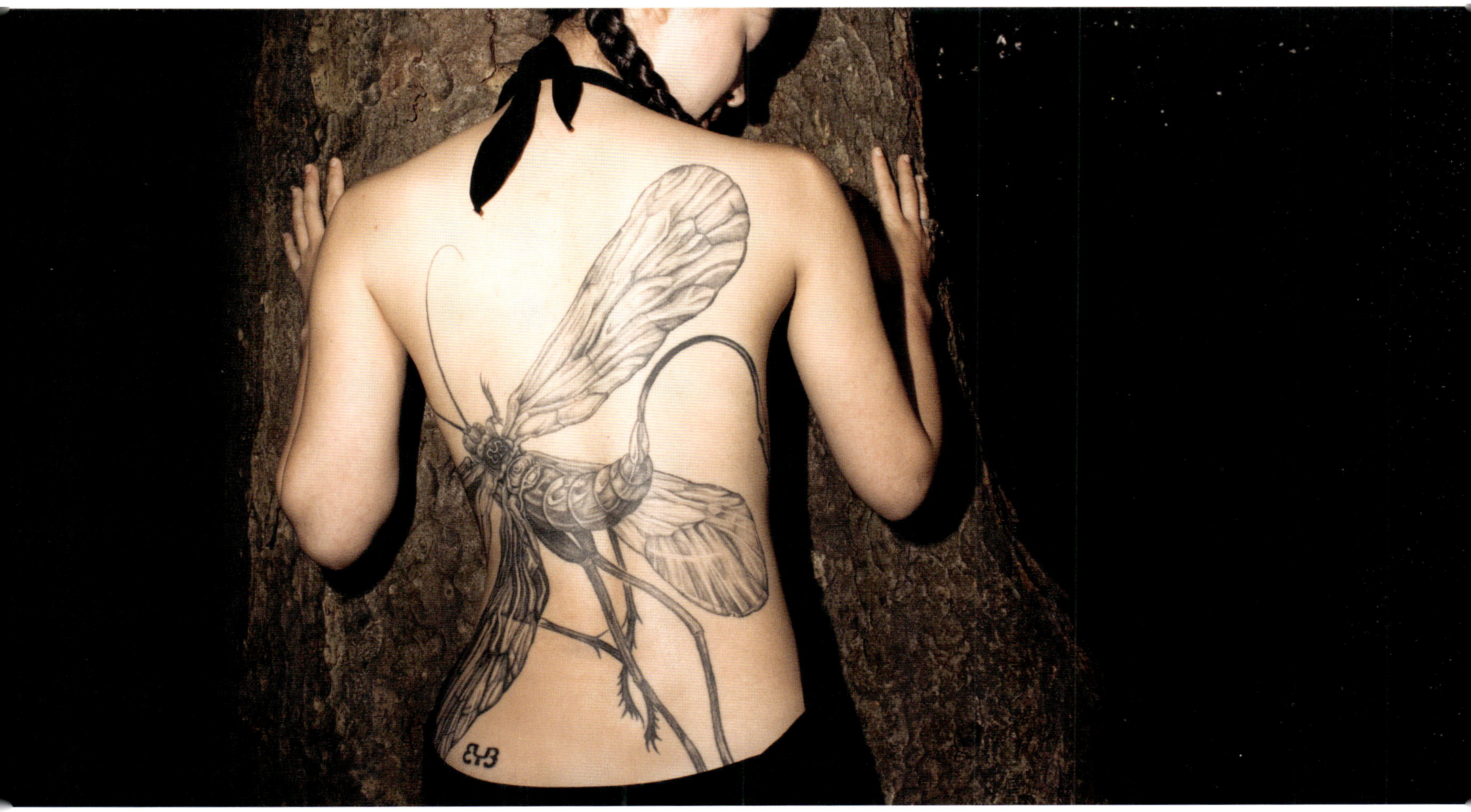

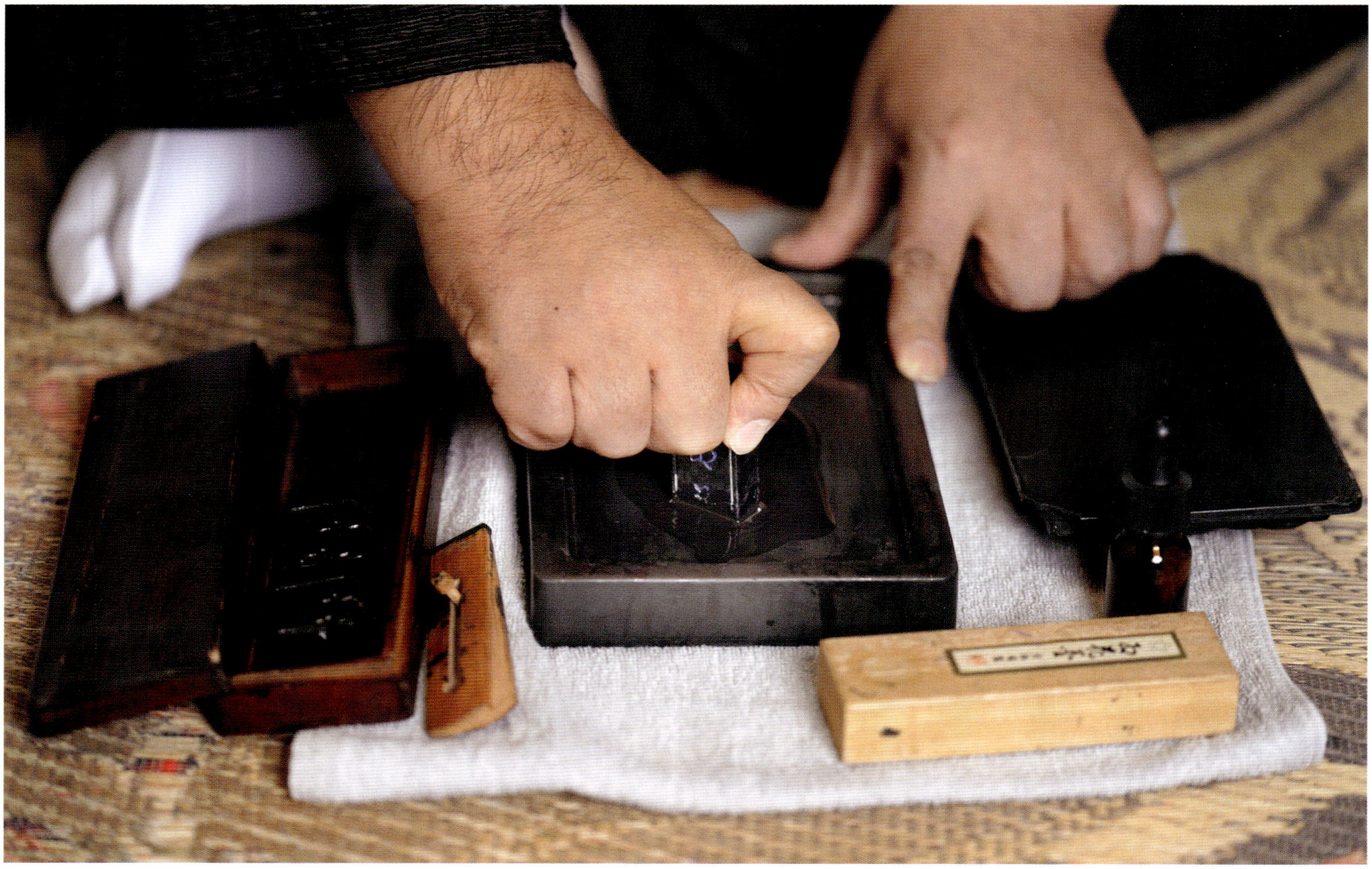

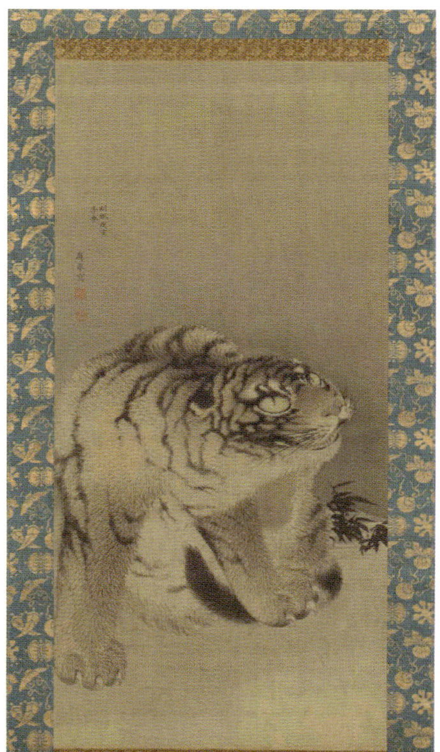

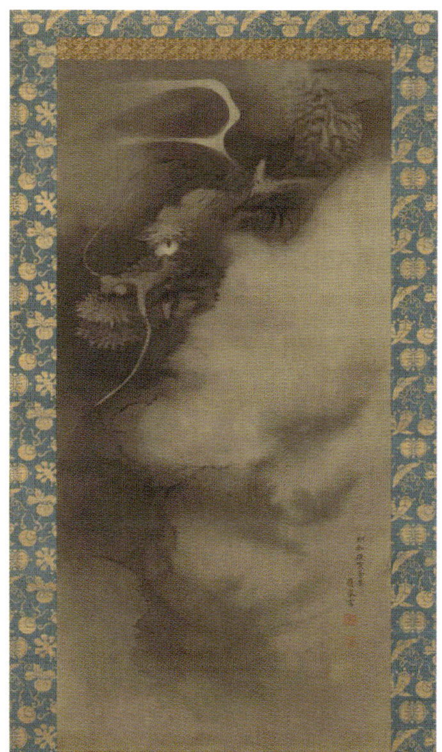

SUMI

OPPOSITE TOP
The *sumi* is bought in stick form and is ground on a specialized ink stone with water until the desired viscosity is produced. The result can be blue-black or brown-black.

OPPOSITE BOTTOM
Maruyama Okyo, *Dragon and Tiger*, 1770, pair of hanging scrolls, *sumi* ink on silk. *Sumi* is mostly used in calligraphy and painting.

While people are no doubt drawn in by the power of the motifs present in Japanese tattoos, the true allure of *wabori* is inextricably linked to the indelible beauty of *sumi*, the black ink used for the practice, which is made by collecting soot. Horimitsu (see pp. 122–29) describes the style of the elaborate shading as like making a woodblock print into a 'scene that depicts the night. The difference in Japanese and Western tattooing is that Western tattoos depict the day – they don't put things around the subject, and are vibrant and light. With Japanese traditional tattoos, the waves and the clouds are black and depict the night.'

Sumi was first brought to Japan by a Korean monk in AD 610. There are many temples in the Nara area and thus, during that era, there was demand there for writing script and sutras. This was aided by the availability of the raw materials needed, such as pine. Production historically flourished and Nara still remains the most important site for *sumi* production. There are two types of *sumi*: *shoenboku*, made from pine resin, and *yuenboku*, which is lampblack made from rapeseed, sesame or other oils. A glue is added to the soot, which allows it to be kneaded. *Sumi* ink sticks are sold at stores and are also used for other traditional arts, such as calligraphy and ink painting. Not all *sumi* is suitable for tattooing. There are some Japanese-style tattoo artists who also use Western bottled tattoo inks.

Before use, a *horishi* will grind a *sumi* ink stick in a vessel called a *suzuri*. The way in which it is ground, the water used and the weather outside will impact the ink. Like all artisanal crafts, *sumi* ages beautifully. Artists often talk about the organic ink's energetic properties. The *sumi* takes on a life of its own, metamorphosing, adopting an attractive patina. The tattoos either take on bluish-black or brownish-black hues as time passes, and there is an indescribable depth and atmosphere to them that can only be produced with *sumi*.

According to Horikazu, 'There is something about using *sumi* ink that I'm very particular about. I feel that the light bluish tint of Japanese ink makes the Japanese patterns look more attractive and deeper. I also like the way the ink gradually blends into the skin after the tattooing is finished, becoming more beautiful. I feel that the tattoo lives together with the bearer. Also, as those who use *sumi* ink will understand, I like the time I spend grinding. Sometimes I grind while thinking about various things, and sometimes I just concentrate on the act. I can smell the ink. Bottled tattoo ink is convenient to use right after opening the cap, but ink that you have to grind every time you use it is a hassle. Maybe I like things that are troublesome, but good things like tattooing and cooking take a lot of time and effort. I believe that putting one's soul into these things that ordinary people would skip over is what leads to good work.'

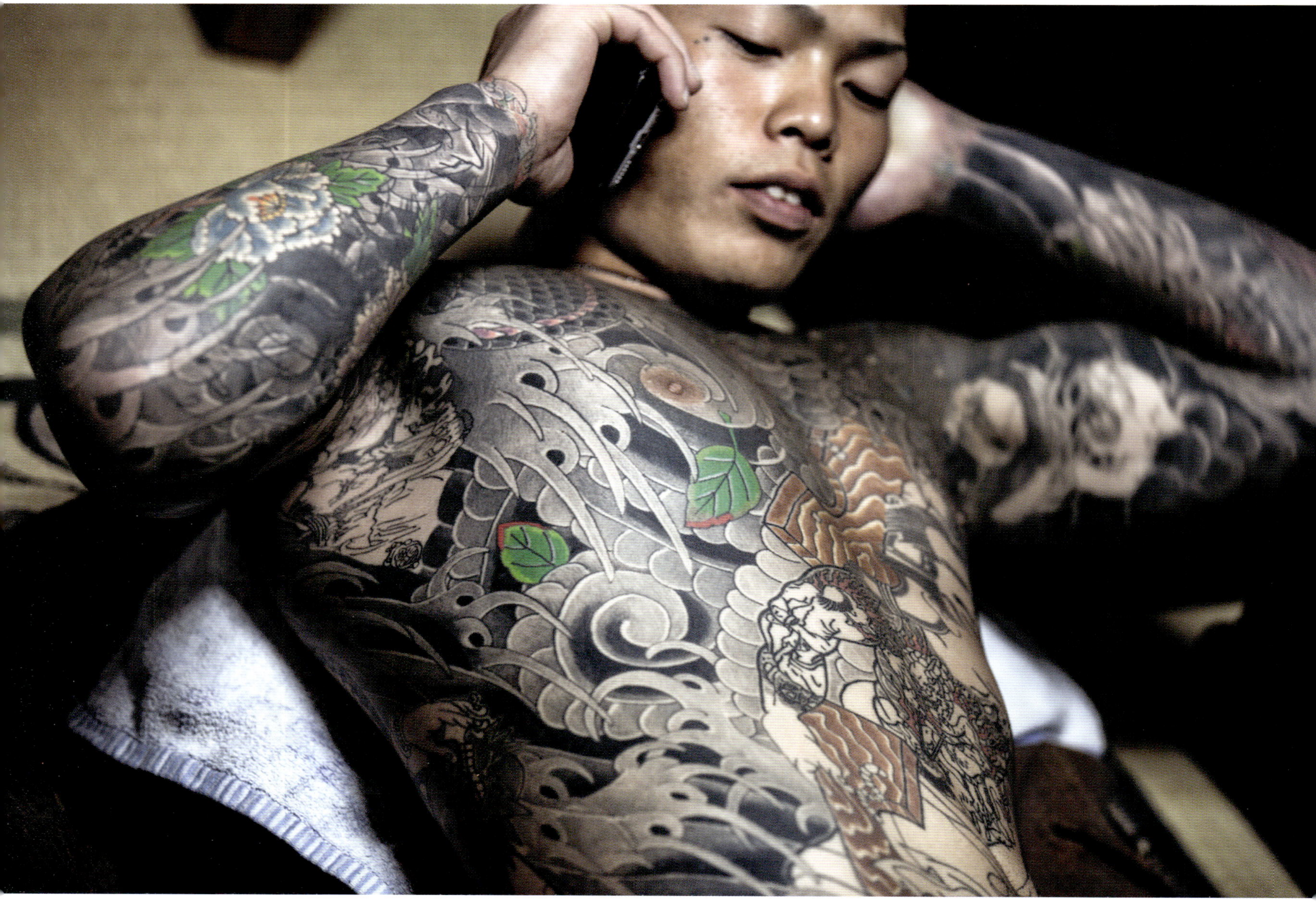

ABOVE
Chest piece by Horikazu. The heavy backgrounds add to the dark atmosphere of the work.

OPPOSITE
Suikoden heroes, with their anti-authoritarian attitude, were seen as the epitome of *iki*. Ichijosei Kosanjo, depicted here, is a female warrior who blocks a hail of arrows using a sword.

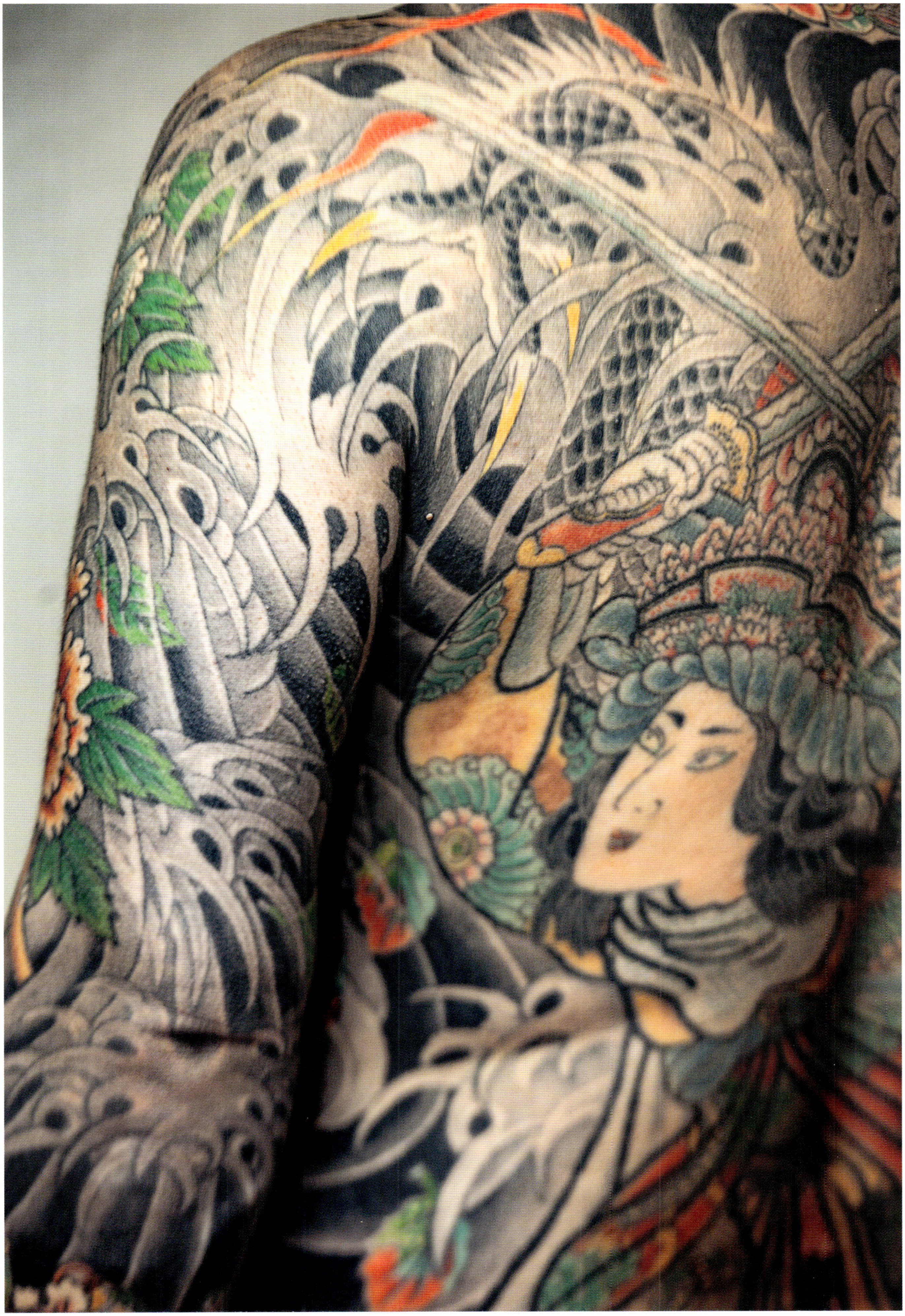

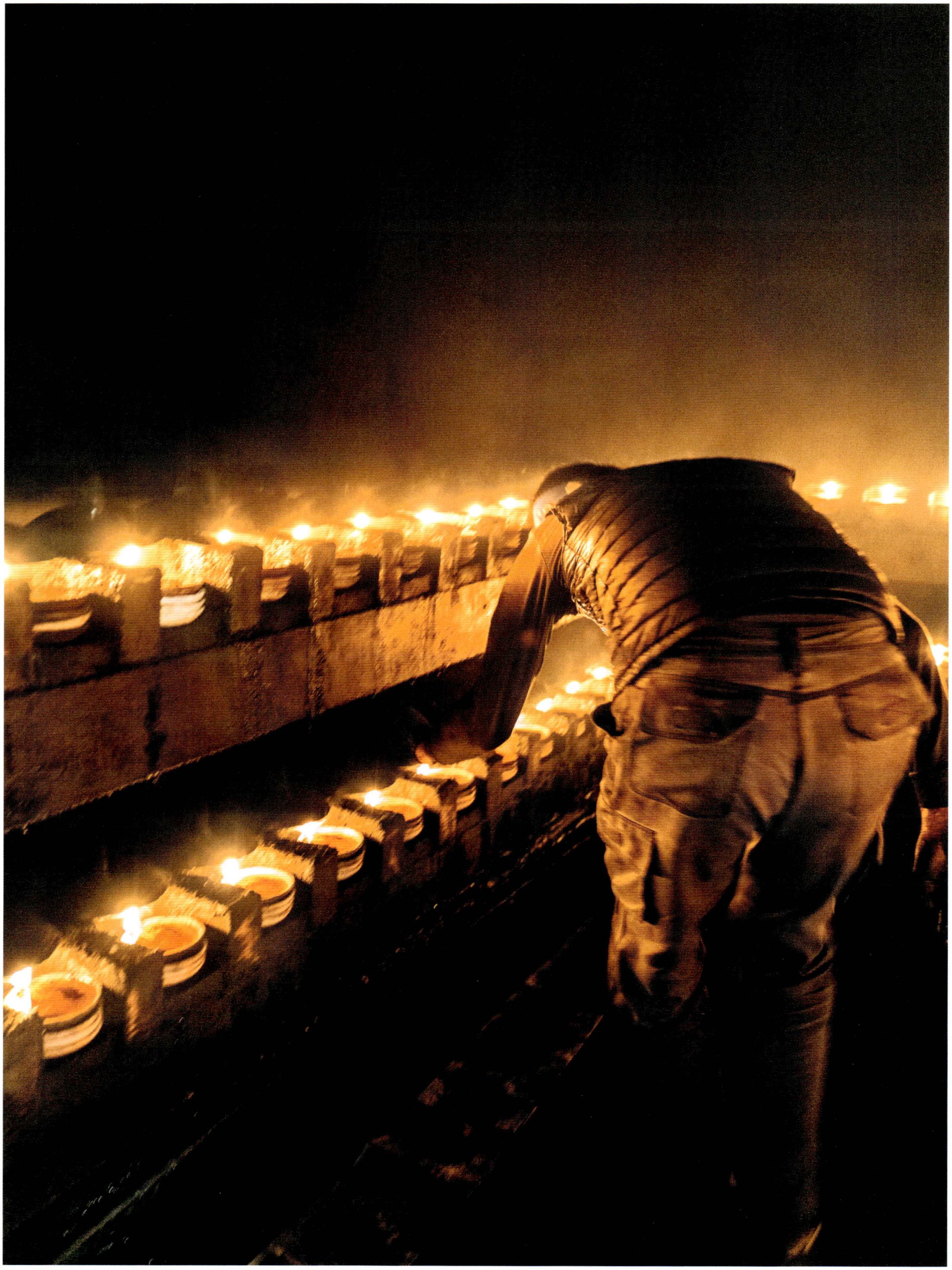

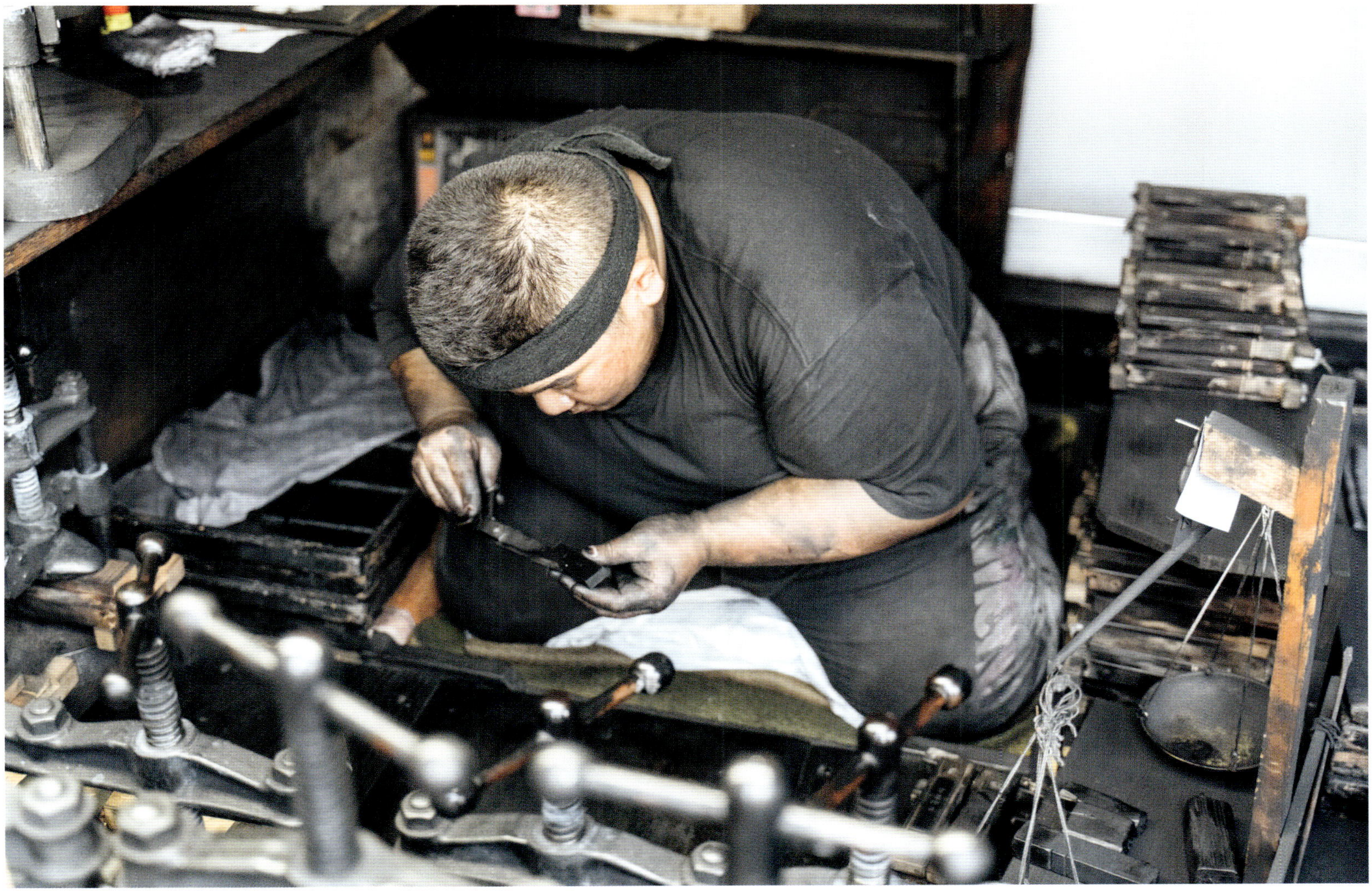

OPPOSITE
Artisans creating *sumi* ink at Kobaien in Nara prefecture.

ABOVE
Kobaien is a famous *sumi* store and Japan's oldest *sumi* manufacturer.

IKI, TOKYO'S 'COOL' AESTHETIC

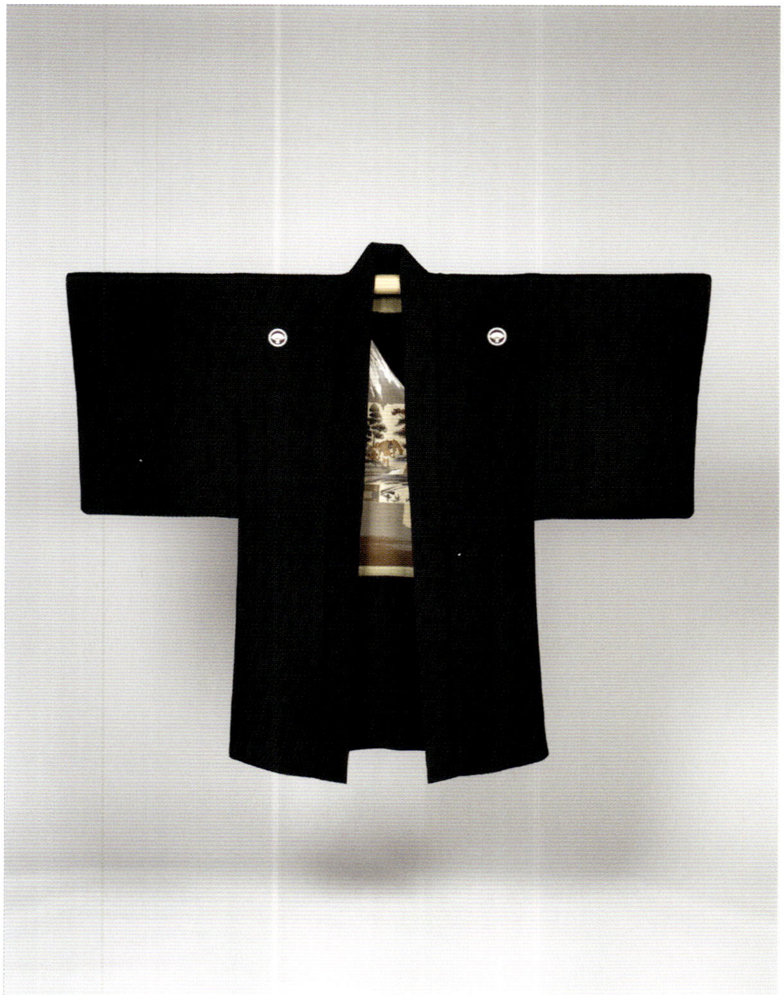

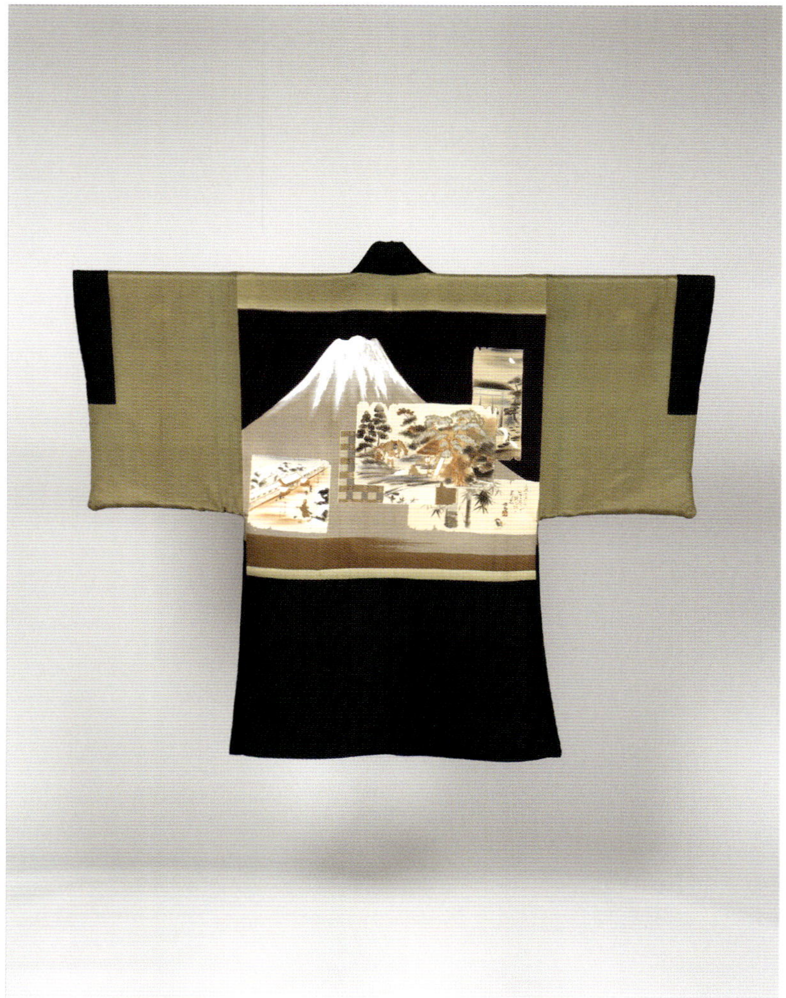

Poet and royal courtier Ki no Tsurayuki's description of the aesthetics of poetry in the introduction of the 10th-century anthology *Kokin Wakashu* includes a concise summary of Japanese sensibility and beauty: 'Effortlessly moving heaven and earth, arousing the sympathies of the demons and gods invisible to the eye, calming relations between men and women, and soothing the warrior's heart.' Indeed, Japanese culture is deeply concerned with aesthetics, and various types of visual qualities can be described as characteristic of Japanese sensibilities. Art academic Yukio Yashiro famously said in the 1920s that the hallmarks of Japanese aesthetics are to be impressionistic, decorative, symbolic and sentimental. French art critic Ernest Chesneau pointed out in the late 19th century that asymmetry, stylization and polychromatism are its common features.

There is no practical reason for people to get tattooed; unlike most crafts, tattoos have no utility. In terms of *irezumi*, the extreme sense of decadence, ornate splendour and commitment to beauty go beyond superficial fashion and entertainment. All Japanese tattoos are rich in meaning, too.

ABOVE
Iki is often used to describe a kind of coolness, or hidden beauty. It's exemplified here on the inside of a *haori* (jacket worn over a kimono) from the Meiji era.

OPPOSITE
Kikukawa Eizan, *Two Girls under an Umbrella*, from the series *Contemporary Flowers of the Southeast*, 1807, woodblock print. The term *iki* was first used to describe Tatsumi geisha, skilled female entertainers who flourished in the Edo era in the Fukagawa district of downtown Tokyo.

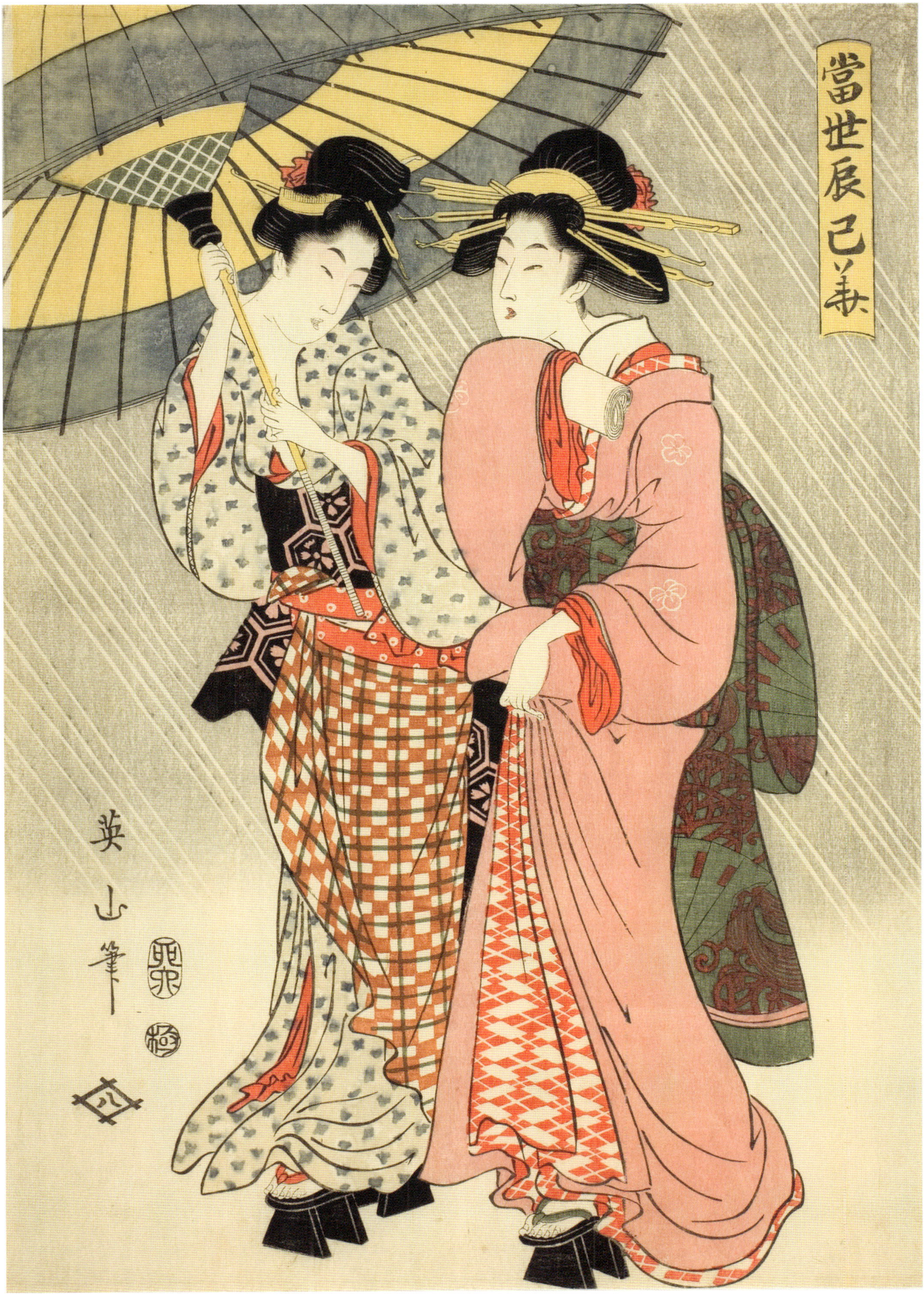
當世辰己美
英山筆

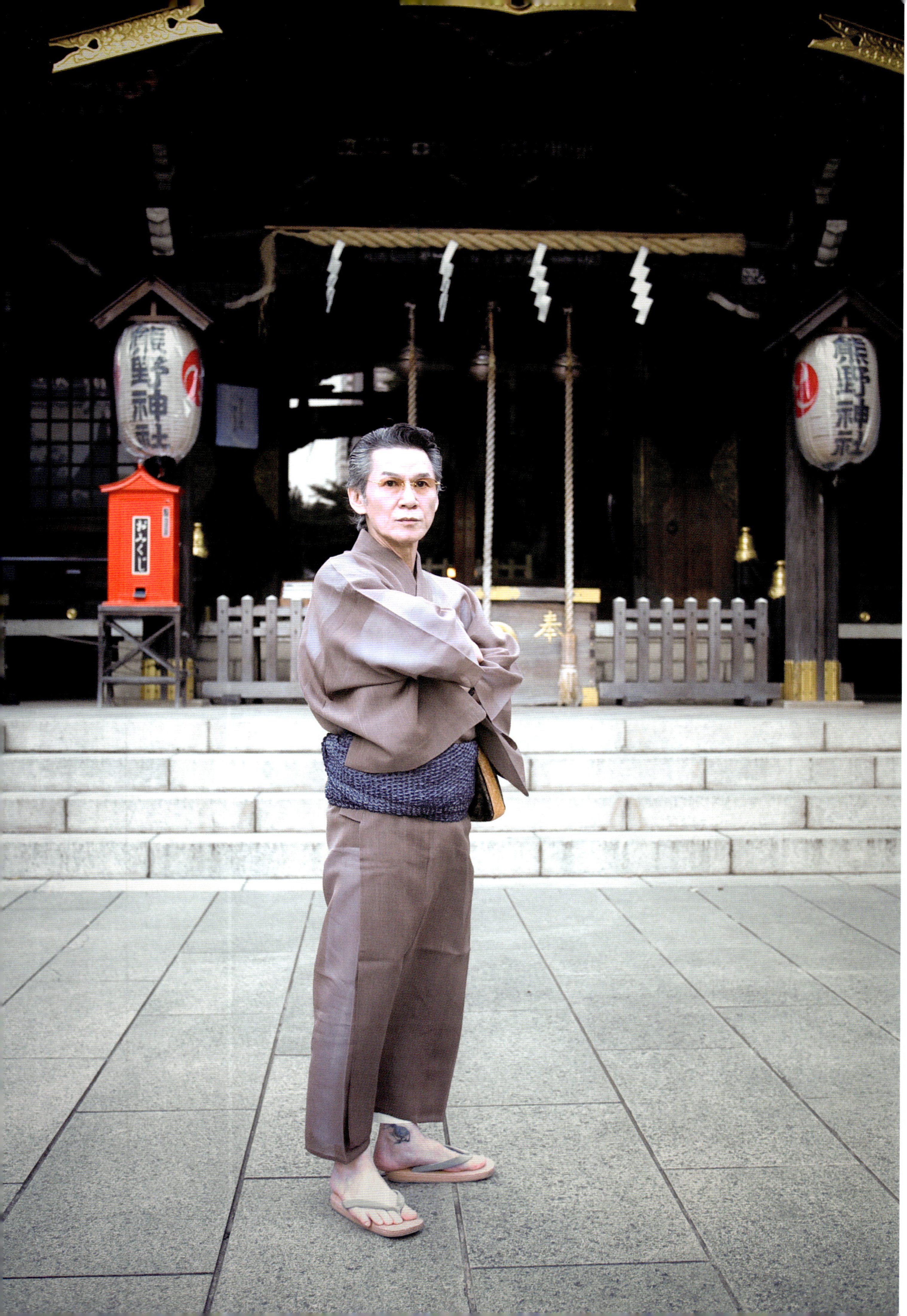
熊野神社
おみくじ
奉
熊野神社

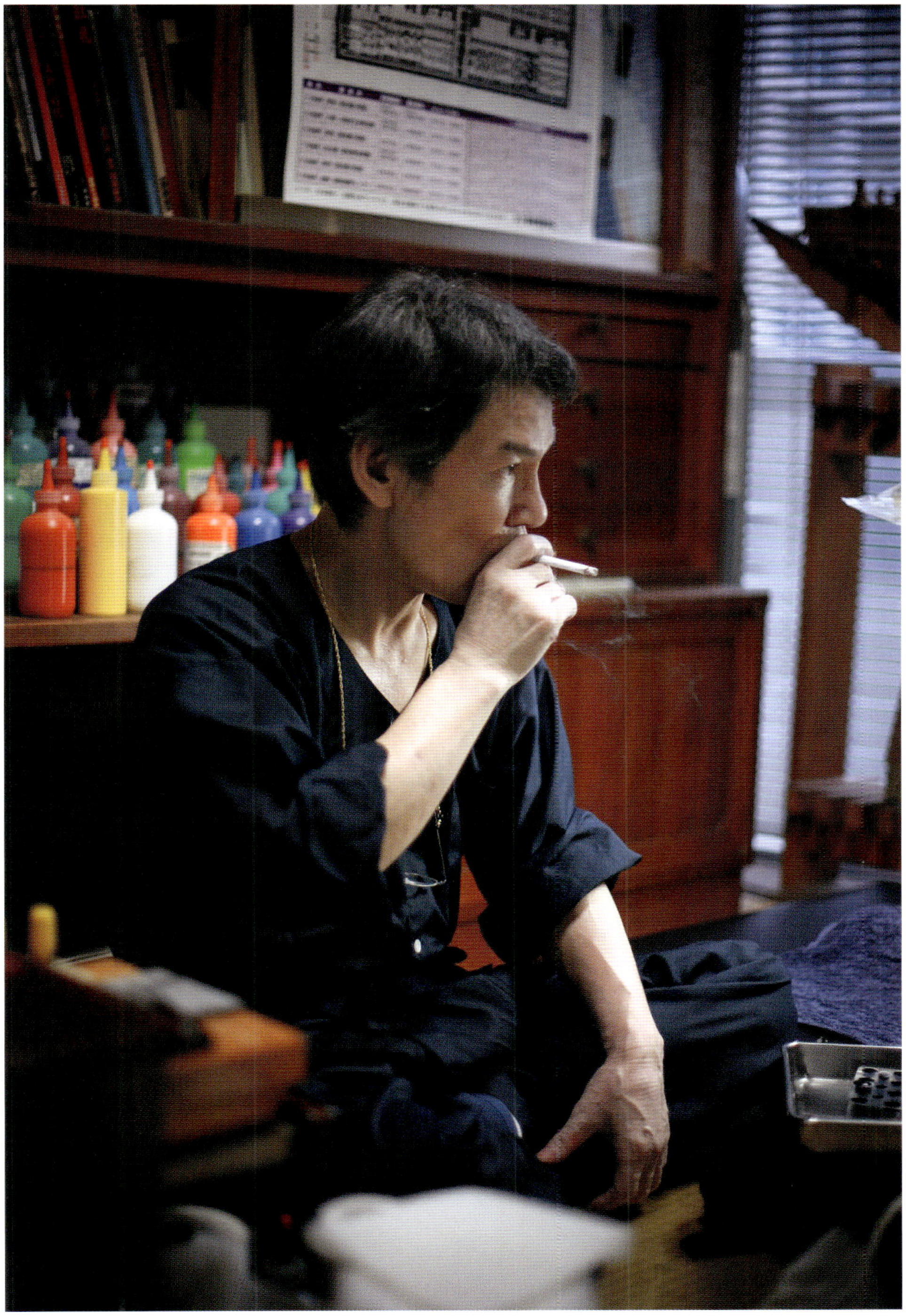

OPPOSITE
Horishi Horitoku's cool elegance is the epitome of *iki*.

ABOVE
Horitoku in his workwear at his Shinjuku studio.

Iki is the term most often used to describe *wabori* culture and the denizens of Tokyo who encapsulate the tattooed lifestyle. In the Edo era *iki* was utilized to characterize Fukagawa geisha, who were not prostitutes like the women of Yoshiwara, but performers who would entertain by playing the *shamisen* and dancing. They were seen as strong and sophisticated, wore men's clothing and were somewhat dapper and androgynous.

Japan's Edo era was a time of pleasure, hedonism and newfound wealth among the commoner class. However, sumptuary laws were often foisted on Edoites, forbidding them from practices and social pastimes deemed too decadent or conspicuous, such as wearing garments made from embroidered silk. In response, *iki* ('urban cool elegance') became the aesthetic norm. Invisible parts of a garment, such as the underside of a kimono, were opulently patterned, and fabrics were embellished with minute motifs that were difficult to see. This was partly to circumvent restrictions, but eventually evolved as a style statement of its own and was considered in vogue. Nowadays, tattoo artists will often describe the flash of a sleeve under a coat, rather than showing off a full suit, as *iki*.

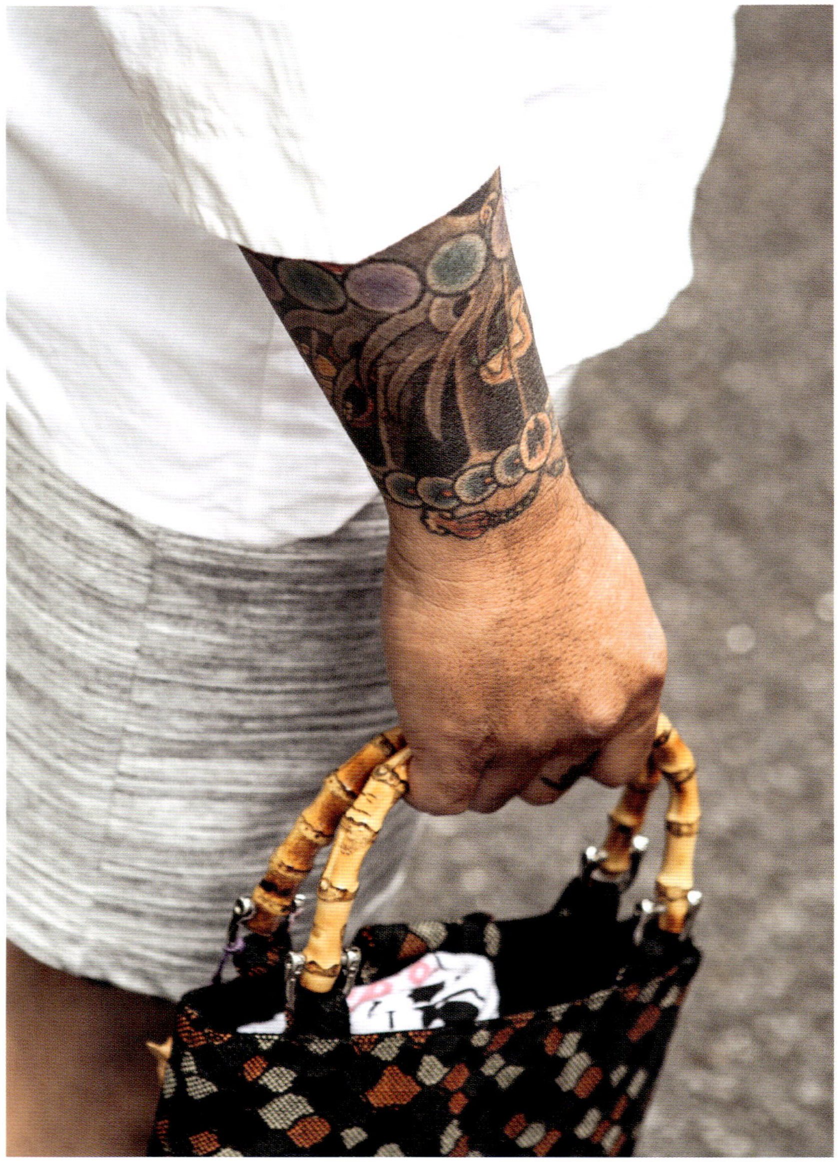

In his 2010 exhibition *Basara*, held in Tokyo, contemporary painter and curator Hisashi Tenmyouya showcased tattoos in his work as a form of *iki* style, which he deemed to have 'lavish and subversive' qualities. Tenmyouya explains that the beauty of tattoos is in stark contrast to the subdued, restrained beauty of Zen and its minimalistic sensibilities. He describes *iki* as a spirit encapsulated in people who rebel against authority but at the same time flaunt superior aesthetic sensibilities and flamboyant lifestyles (in this way, someone who is completely destitute would never be called *iki*).

Everything about Japanese tattoos is extraordinary. There is the basic fact that, in order to insert ink, a significant amount of pain is involved. The act itself necessitates discipline and a commitment that lasts over decades. Some of the recipients of extremely dense work, such as that of Horikazu, go to his studio three times a week for years to complete their suits. A degree of resolve is needed to finish a piece, and this sense of perseverance is one of the symbolic qualities imbued in tattoo art.

Notwithstanding, there is a profound impermanence inherent in the Japanese tattoo art form as well. As much as *irezumi* thrives on the skin, it only exists for as long as the carrier is alive, and when a tattooed person dies, so does the work. In his book, *Basara*, Tenmyouya states, 'Tattoos are something that is flesh and blood. In Japan, if you see it from the perspective of *bushido* philosophy, they see beauty in cherry blossoms and plums because they shed. There is the aesthetic notion that it is transient, and it's not forever, but that is seen as beautiful.'

The connotation of death, or rather, those that face it without fear, is heavily imbued in Japanese tattoos as well. During the Edo period, people like firefighters faced mortality every day. Groups of them, who were constantly competing with each other to fight fires, showed off their ink as a symbol of manliness. In the post-war era, ultra-violent films contained multitudes of romantic depictions of tattooed, chivalrous gangsters whose lifestyle was permanently on the edge. This sense of acceptance, and even the ritualization of transience, is one of the hallmarks of what can be described as *iki*.

ABOVE
The beauty of a tattoo that's only partially visible from the sleeve of the shirt is considered to be *iki* (a subdued sense of 'cool' born from commoner culture in Edo).

OPPOSITE
Goldfish swimming in *sumi* waves. Horikazu is known for his meticulous, hyper-detailed embellishments. This attention to parts no one can usually see is part of *iki* culture.

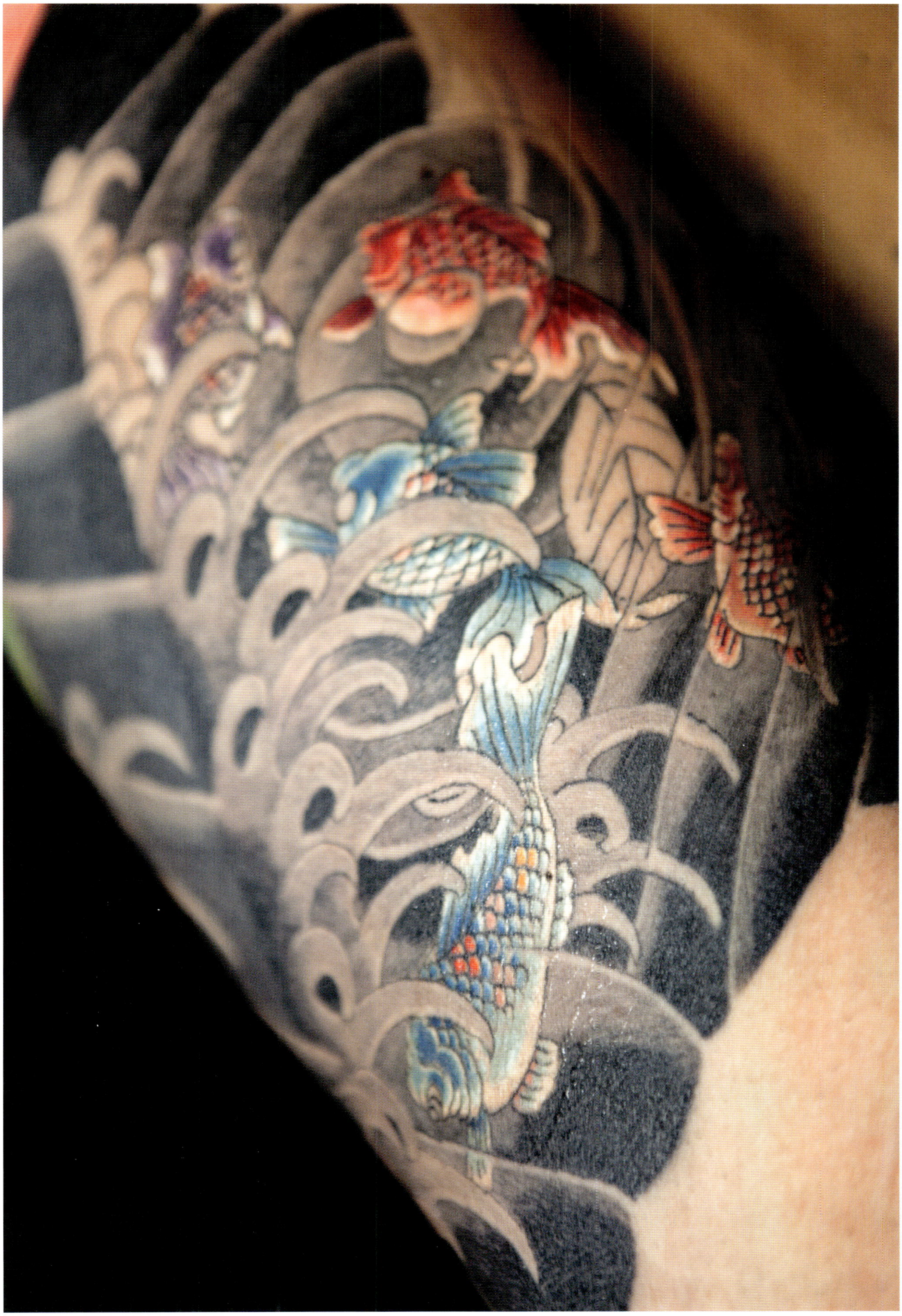

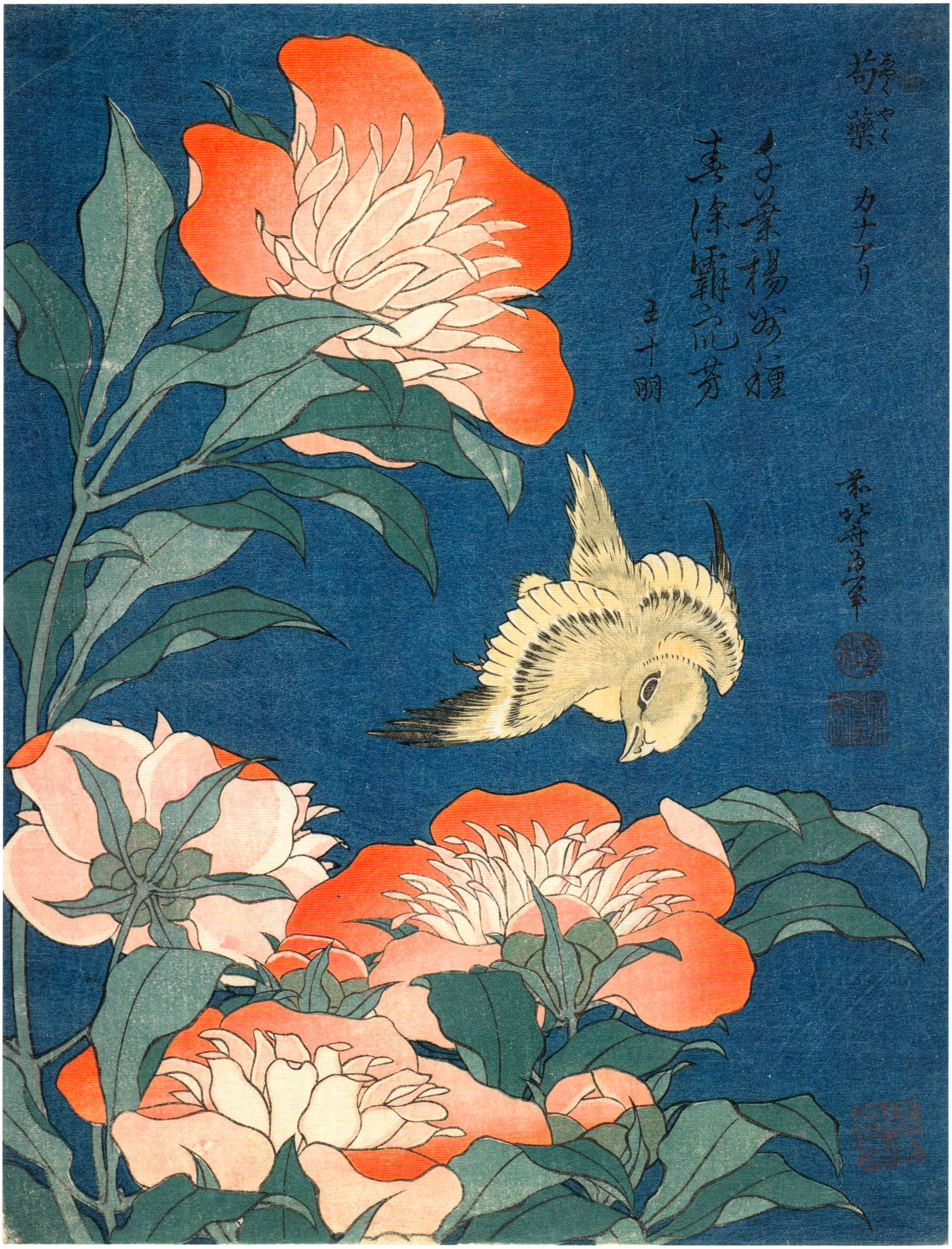
芍薬 カナアリ

SEASONALITY AND NATURE

Japanese cultural practices, aesthetic values and ideas about beauty are greatly influenced by nature. The Japanese lifestyle was historically almost entirely agricultural, and so led by the seasons. The nation's indigenous religion, Shinto, is animistic, and embraces the notion that everything in nature can be a god – thus, there is a sense in Japanese art that people wish to coexist with nature. Art forms like literature, poetry and painting often express seasons using a sensibility called *kachofugetsu* (literally 'flowers, birds, wind and the moon'). Each of these elements can change according to the season and are included in tattooing. The motifs usually represent spring or autumn and are symbolic, signifying certain traits. Here are some of those commonly used in tattoos:

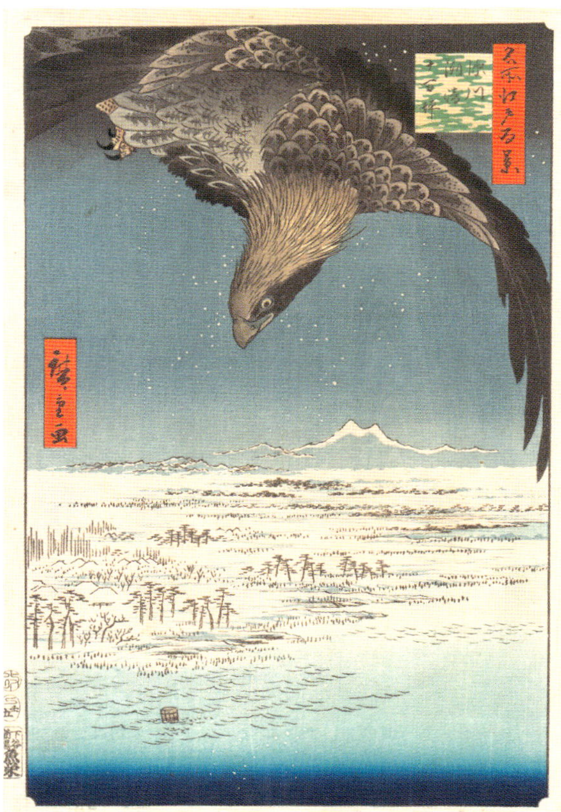

OPPOSITE
Katsushika Hokusai, *Peonies and Canary*, 1834, woodblock print. Traditional Japanese tattoos are heavily inspired by nature motifs.

RIGHT
A hawk features in Utagawa Hiroshige's *Jumantsubo Plain at Fukagawa Susaki*, from the series *One Hundred Famous Views of Edo*, 1856, woodblock print.

BIRDS OF PREY: Falcons and hawks are majestic birds commonly seen high in the air along the coast of Japan, gliding effortlessly or displaying impressive feats of hunting prowess. They were used as messengers and for falconry by the samurai, and so when used as a motif they are seen as a samurai bird, representing strength, the ability to soar and determination.

BUTTERFLIES: Represent rebirth, or metamorphosis. In Japan they have positive connotations of freedom, grace, femininity and the ephemeral nature of life. They can also mean pleasure and romance.

CARP: This fish embodies perseverance and strength as it swims upstream. It is considered an auspicious symbol. Phonetically, *koi* also sounds like 'love' in Japanese.

CHERRY BLOSSOMS: The most loved Japanese flower. They are considered a celebratory symbol and represent the yearly cycle of nature. Their rapid bloom and consequent shedding of petals is indicative of the idea of *mono no aware*, the transience of life, with its ephemeral beauty. There are various types of cherry blossom, such as the regular *somei yoshino* and weeping cherries.

CHRYSANTHEMUMS: A flower imported from China symbolizing long life. They bloom in autumn for much longer than many other flowers. They are depicted on the Japanese imperial family crest.

FOXES: Foxes can be either nefarious or benevolent characters in Japanese folklore and at shrines, as they are the messengers of Inari, the god of rice and harvests. They are also seen as shapeshifters – they can be deceptive, or helpful assistants.

GOLDFISH: Are thought to be incredibly auspicious and represent wealth. They were brought into Japan as pets for the aristocracy in 1502 and later became popular with people of all classes. It was a summer custom to buy goldfish sold by street vendors, and the game of scooping them caught on at festivals and fairs. Eventually, they came to be a common sight within *ukiyo-e* woodblock print scenes.

MAPLE LEAVES: The iconic image of autumn.

MONKEYS: Have a close resemblance to humans and are depicted in Japanese folk tales and art in a variety of guises. They can sometimes be more like actual animals, swinging from trees. In folklore, the most famous monkey story is that of the warrior magician Monkey King, or Songoku, a shapeshifter who can ride clouds. His feats of bravery and adventure were immortalized in a novel, as well as a manga and TV show.

PEONIES: With their large, gorgeous petals, peonies are considered to be the king of flowers. They bloom in spring, representing nobility and affluence. Often used in conjunction with butterflies and *shishi* (lions).

PLUMS: Bloom in winter, and are an indicator of the coming of spring. They are often paired with an *uguisu* (bush warbler) bird.

SNAKES: Represent longevity and resilience, as they can get into tight spaces. They are often tattooed alongside flowers such as cherry blossoms and peonies, and they herald the coming of spring after hibernation. They are auspicious, but also have connotations of virility and represent fertility.

TIGERS: A symbol of power, courage, strength, beauty and self-improvement. They are affectionate and protective towards their cubs. Tigers are most active at dusk, so can represent a dark soul as well. They are often depicted in bamboo groves. They are considered rivals to dragons, and can thus be used together in a tattoo, balancing out each other's characteristics.

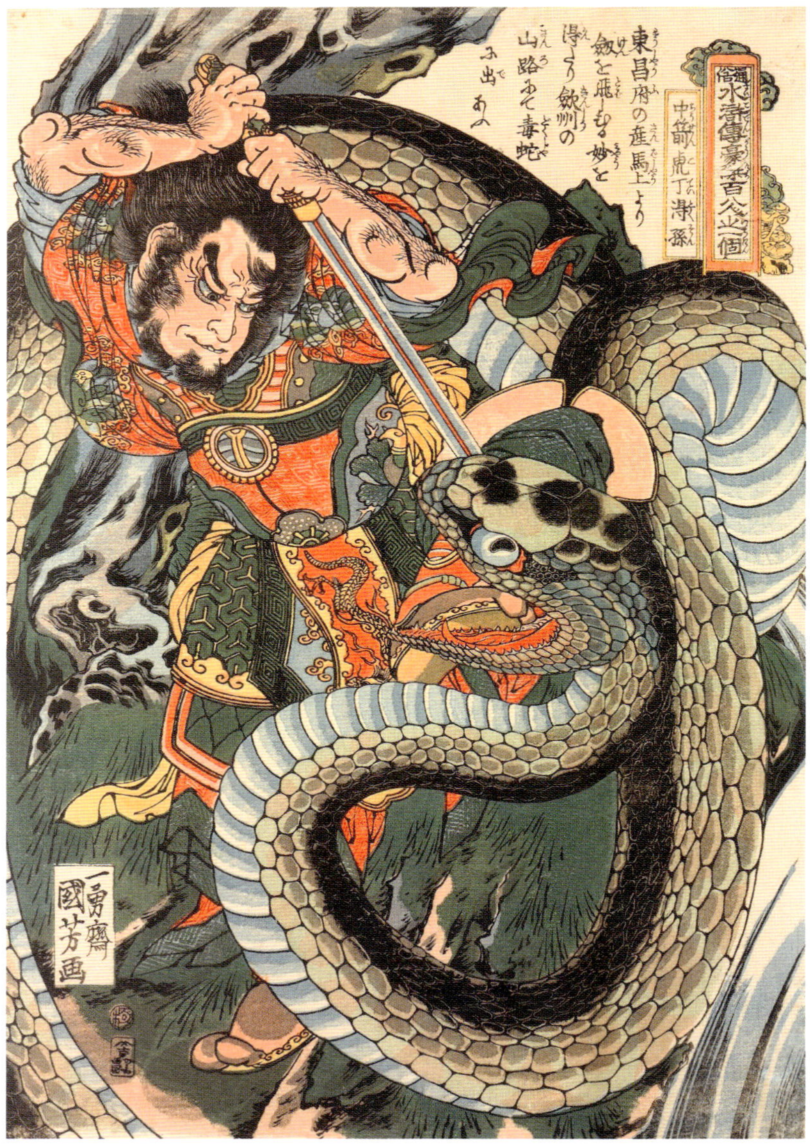

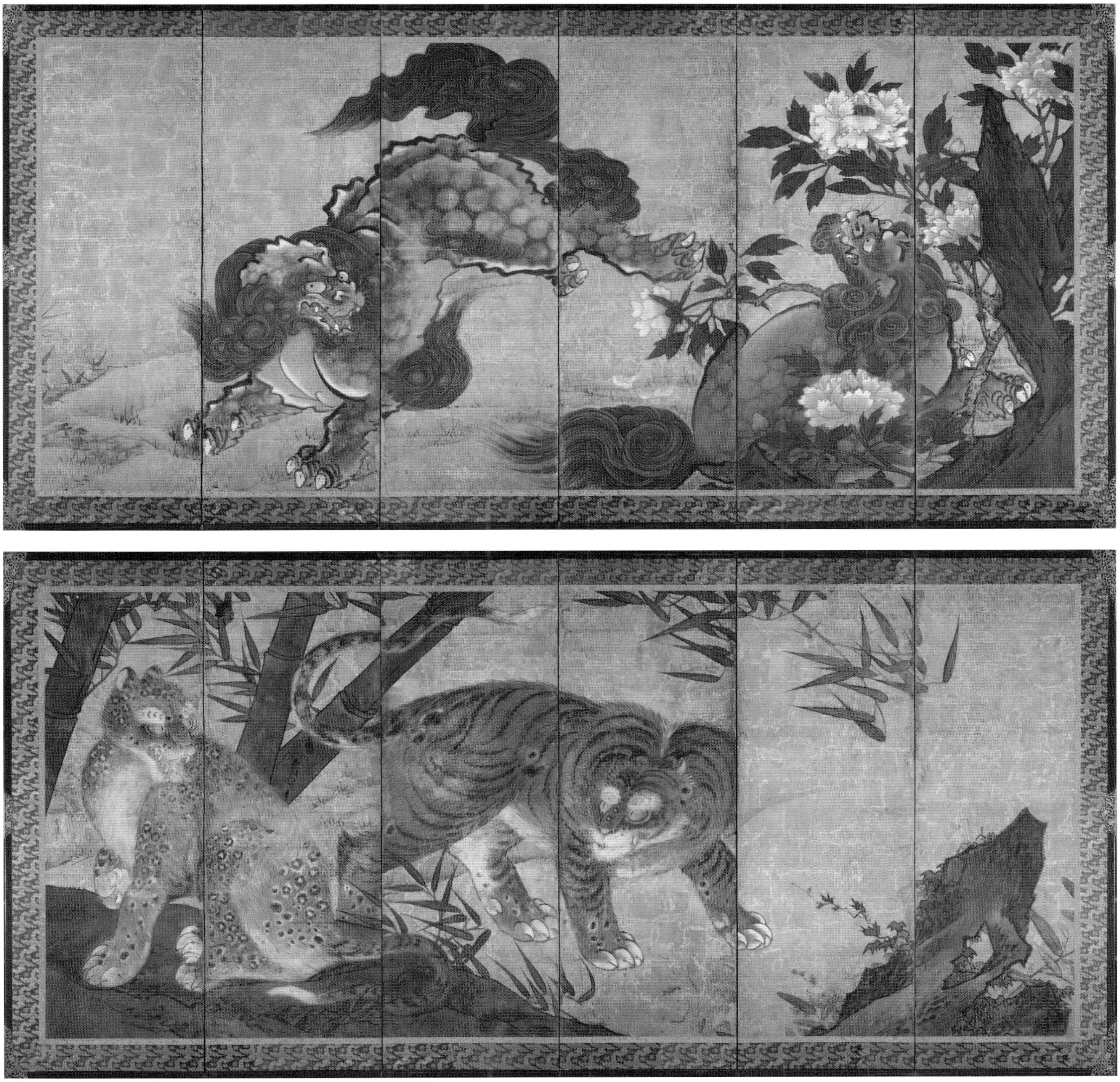

OPPOSITE
Snake in Utagawa Kuniyoshi, *Chusenko Tei Tokuson*, from the series *One Hundred and Eight Heroes of the Popular 'Water Margin'*, 1827–30, woodblock print.

ABOVE
Yamaguchi Sekkei, *Lions and Tigers in Peony and Bamboo*, 1668, woodblock print.

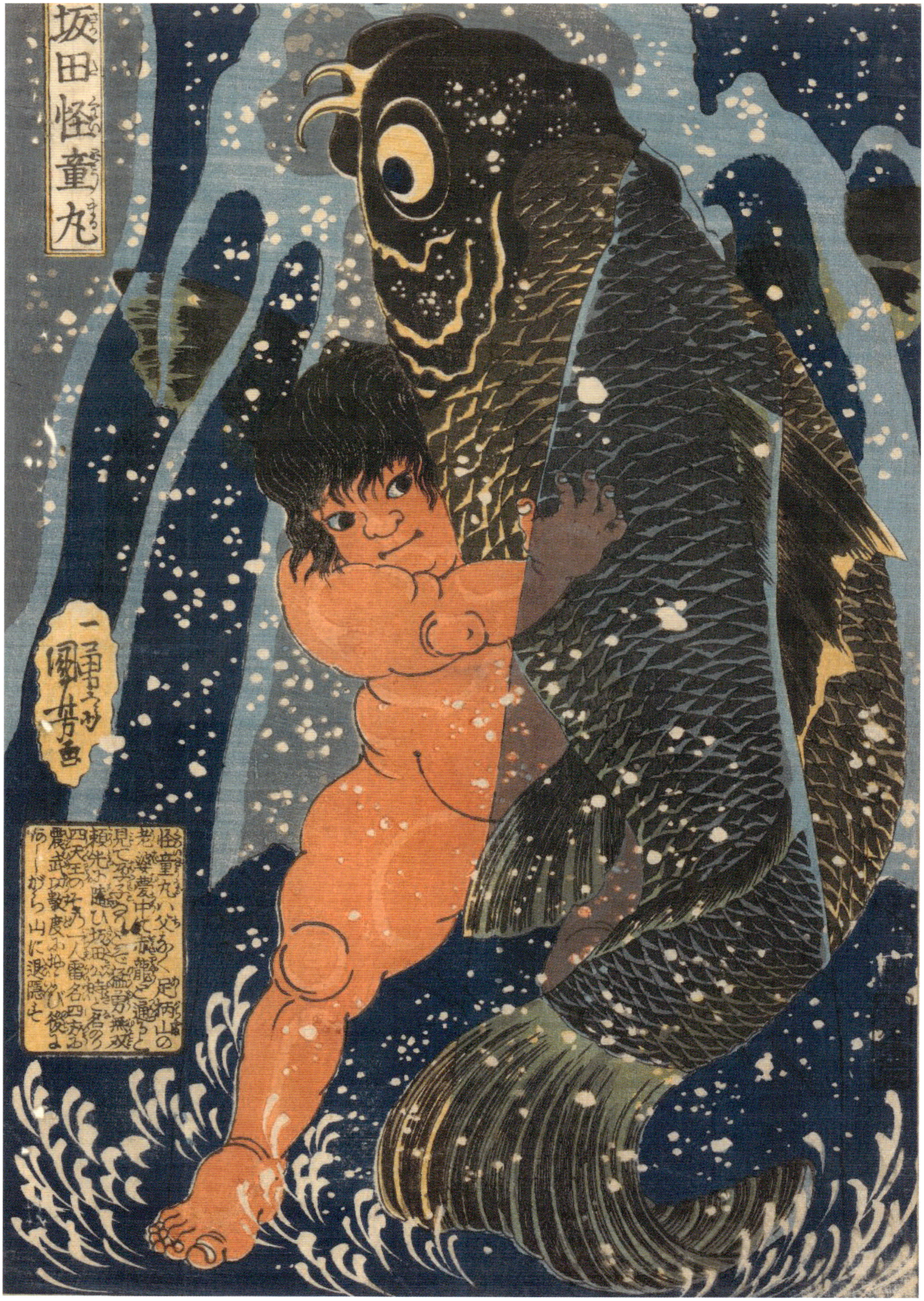
坂田怪童丸
一勇斎國芳画

FOLKLORE AND MYTHOLOGY

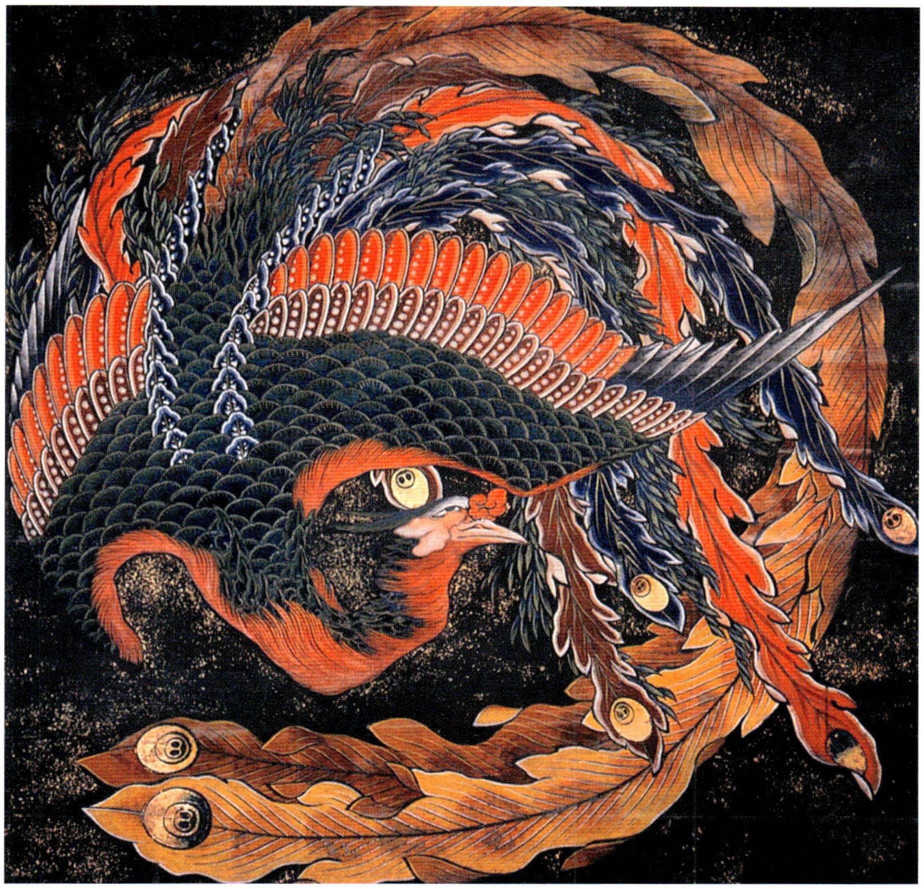

Folk tales and lore are a means through which the Japanese pass on cultural norms and customs, but are also valued for their aesthetics when shown in art. They encapsulate aspirational ideals, define whether behaviour is ethical or immoral, and cement in the popular consciousness how one should live. People feel emotionally connected to certain characters and their traits, and get tattooed with depictions of them, hoping to acquire their characteristics as well. Many folk tales evoke emotional archetypes, and animals are often expressed as anthropomorphic beings. According to *horishi* Horimyo (see pp. 146–51), even if a character is malevolent, like a nine-tailed fox, ironically, they are so wicked that they will scare other negative spirits off – so they are seen as protective. Here are some common folk tales that are often represented in tattoos:

DRAGONS: Japanese dragons have snake-like bodies with fish-like scales and bird-like talons (usually three), and are often associated with Buddhist temples. They are connected to water, as they are thought to bring rain, and are often depicted with storm clouds Dragons are considered to be heavenly creatures as well as symbols of imperial power. There are various types, such as ascending and descending dragons. Dragons fly upwards towards the heavens during the vernal equinox in spring. They fly downwards during the autumn equinox and are depicted in a body of water during winter.

Dragons in tattoos usually feature cool hues, like dark green or bluish-black, although according to the type they may have red, white and yellow colouring too. They are often paired with tigers or depicted

OPPOSITE
Utagawa Kuniyoshi, *Sakata Kaidomaru*, 1835, woodblock print. Another major type of inspiration for *wabori* comes from Japanese folktales and lore.

ABOVE
Katsushika Hokusai, *Phoenix Staring in Eight Directions*, 1848, ceiling painting at Gansho-in temple, Obuse.

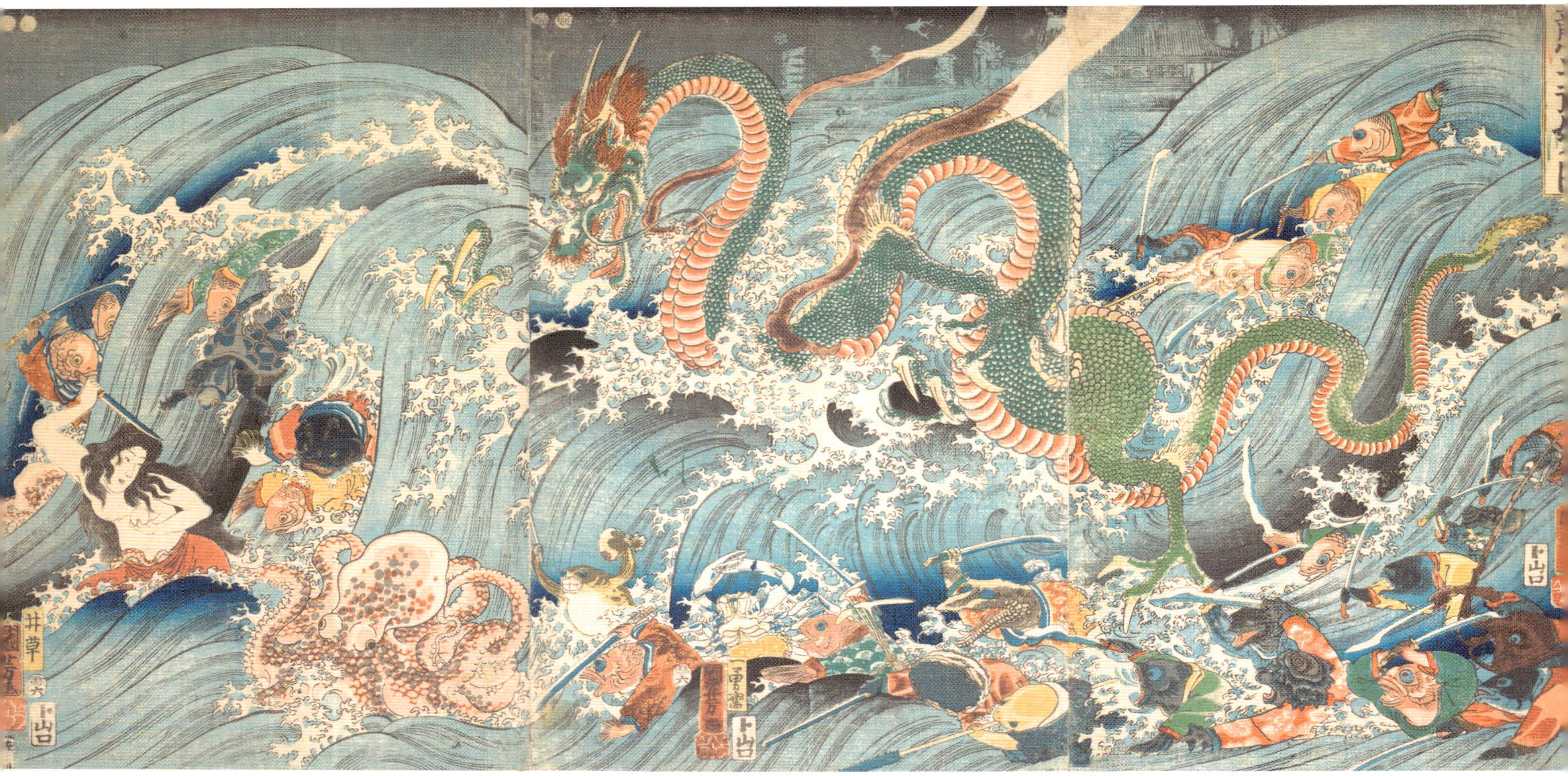

with swords. Another typical tattooed dragon motif derives from the *Suikoden* character Kyumonryu Shishin, who has a nine-dragon tattoo.

THE EIGHT DOG CHRONICLES: An epic 19th-century serial novel by Kyokutei Bakin, about a group of eight warriors whose father is a dog. It was immensely popular not only as a book, but in the form of *kabuki* theatre and in *ukiyo-e* prints by artists such as Utagawa Kuniyoshi.

GHOSTS: The Japanese attitude to ghosts is influenced by both Buddhism and Shintoism. Ghosts are connected to the animistic notion that all living beings also contain a god. When a person dies, their ghost can manifest if they are not given the right posthumous rituals. What ghosts exactly entail has changed over the course of Japanese history, but they still remain prominent in pop culture.

HANNYA: Once human, these female demons, who appear in traditional Noh theatre, are consumed with jealousy and spite. They seem sorrowful, but are also full of torment and rage. Hannya are adorned with two horns.

JIGOKU DAYU: The 'Hell Courtesan' was a legendary 15th-century woman living in Sakai, Osaka. She is usually depicted wearing a robe with images of Emma-O (the gatekeeper of hell), demons and divinities adorning the fabric. Legend has it that she was kidnapped and sold to a brothel. Folklore about Jigoku Dayu often involves Ikkyu, a famed monk who had a penchant for drink and women.

KINTARO: A character from a Japanese folk tale. As a young boy, he had superhuman strength. Kintaro grew up in the mountains befriending animals and eventually became a brave warrior. The image of him wrestling a giant carp is extremely popular in tattoo art. It is customary to decorate Kintaro dolls on Children's Day, a national holiday, in the hope that one's son will become as strong and brave as him.

PHOENIX: A bird of paradise that asks for love and has a feminine elegance. Coming from Chinese mythology, where it is an amalgamation of a duck, pheasant, peacock and swallow, the phoenix symbolizes peace, grace and benevolence.

***SHISHI* AND *KOMA-INU*:** Guardian lions and lion-like dogs are entirely imaginary, as Japan never had lions. Since the Heian period (794–1185), *shishi,* or guardian lions (without horns), and *koma-inu* lion-dogs (horned) have often been paired as protectors outside temples and shrines, one type with its mouth open, the other with its mouth closed. They are symbolic of royalty and power. *Shishi* are defensive yet playful, and are often pictured with peonies.

SKULLS: Skeletons and skulls are ubiquitous motifs in Japanese art, in which aesthetic value is placed on the ephemeral nature of beauty. Skulls represent mortal existence and are often seen in *ukiyo-e* woodblock prints. They were popular during the Meiji period, and were most often used as a form of embellishment on textiles in the Taisho (1912–26) and early Showa (1926–89) eras.

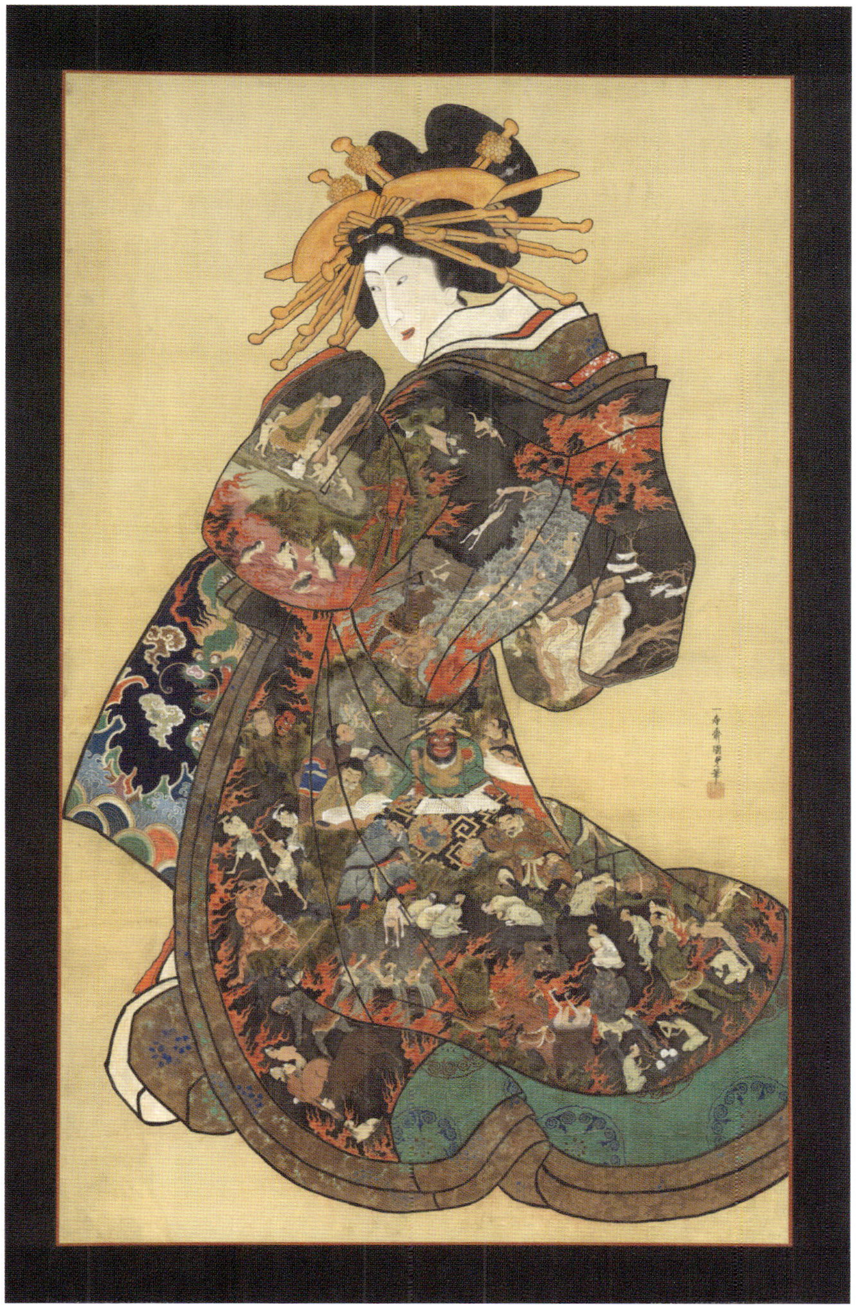

OPPOSITE
Utagawa Kuniyoshi, *Recovering the Stolen Jewel from the Palace of the Dragon King,* 1853, woodblock print.

RIGHT
Utagawa Kunisada II, *The Hell Courtesan,* late 1850s, woodblock print.

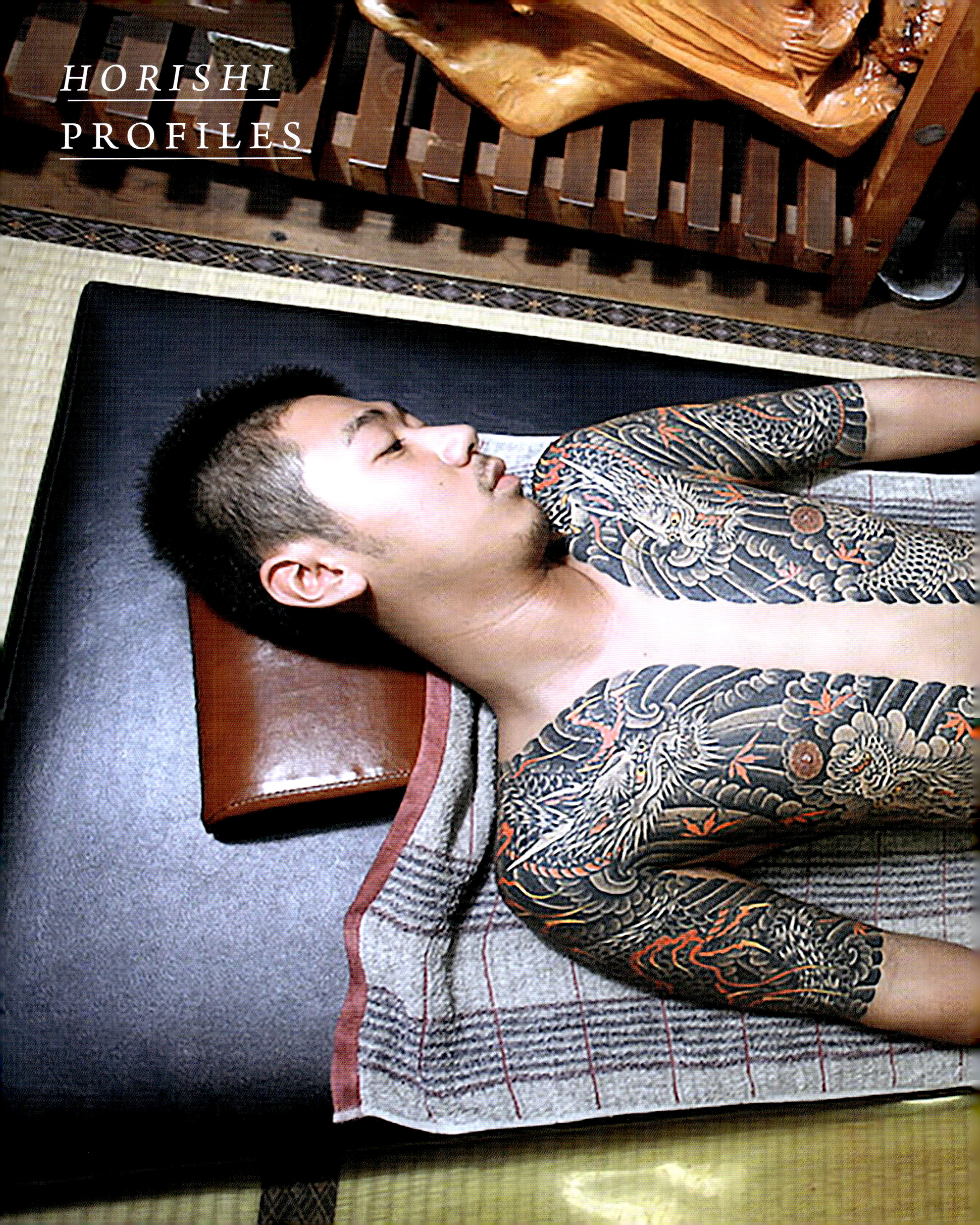

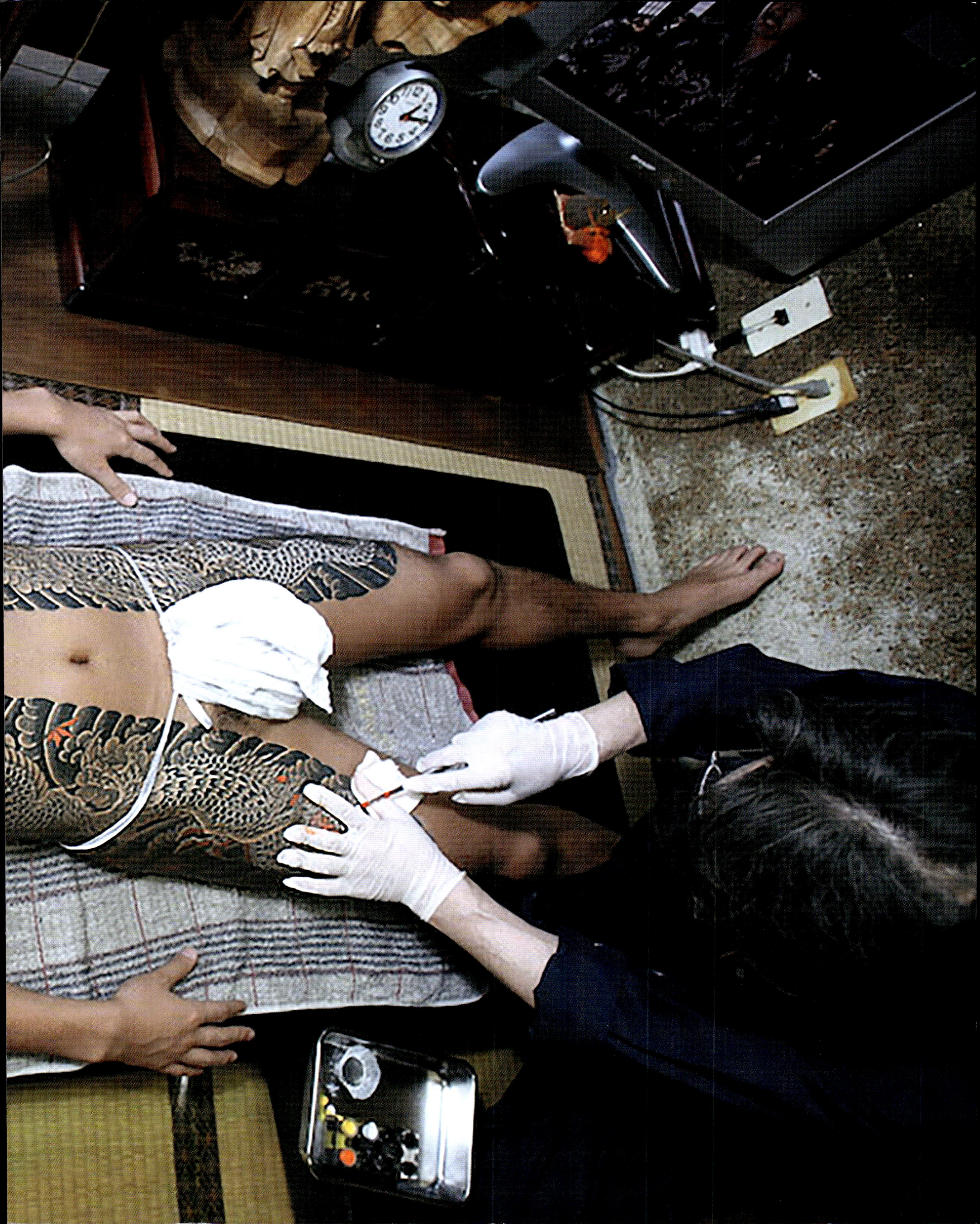

HORITOKU 彫徳

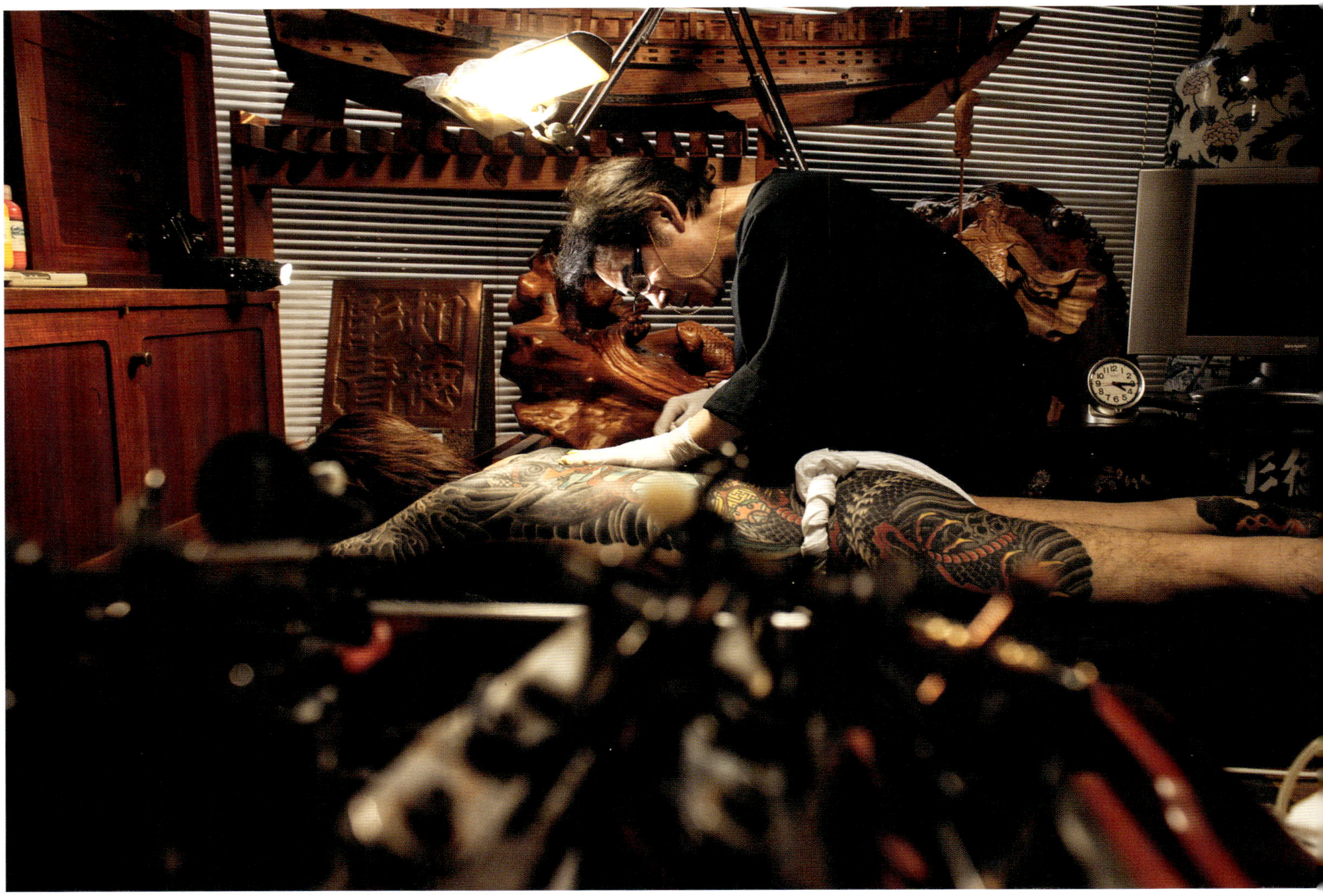

Horitoku is a veteran *horishi* based in Tokyo's Shinjuku neighbourhood who has a large *ichimon* of apprentices. He is known for his powerful work, such as white and gold dragons that seem almost alive, as well as for the subdued intensity of his colours and his deep bluish-black backgrounds. Through media appearances, he gained many apprentices early on, and as they opened their shops they went on to create the contemporary tattoo industry in Japan.

***How did you start as a* horishi?**

I taught myself. I wasn't anyone's student. I think it was rare for that time, but I wasn't really thinking I'd become a *horishi* – I was just playing around in junior high school and doing it on my friends. I saw a person with proper work and thought, 'At this rate, I will just be playing around forever' – I wasn't a real *horishi*. Eventually it escalated and I wanted to use colour, so I went to a *horishi* to get tattooed, and watched and stole the technique. I was also inspired by Horiyoshi I.

What are the characteristics of a good tattoo?

The appeal of Japanese traditional work is the *sumi* (ink). I like the combination of black, white and vermilion – it is really beautiful; it is a colour that was used a lot in the past and really suits black. There are meanings within the backgrounds around tattoos, too. To separate heaven and earth, water and rocks. The background is really important, whether it is in Japanese or Western painting.

Nowadays it is easy to get supplies from tattoo shops, but when you started, where did you get the needles?

PREVIOUS SPREAD
White dragons are characteristic of Horitoku's work.

ABOVE
Horitoku tattoos out of his studio in Tokyo's Shinjuku neighbourhood. When he first started, he used needles that were attached to chopsticks by being wrapped around with thread.

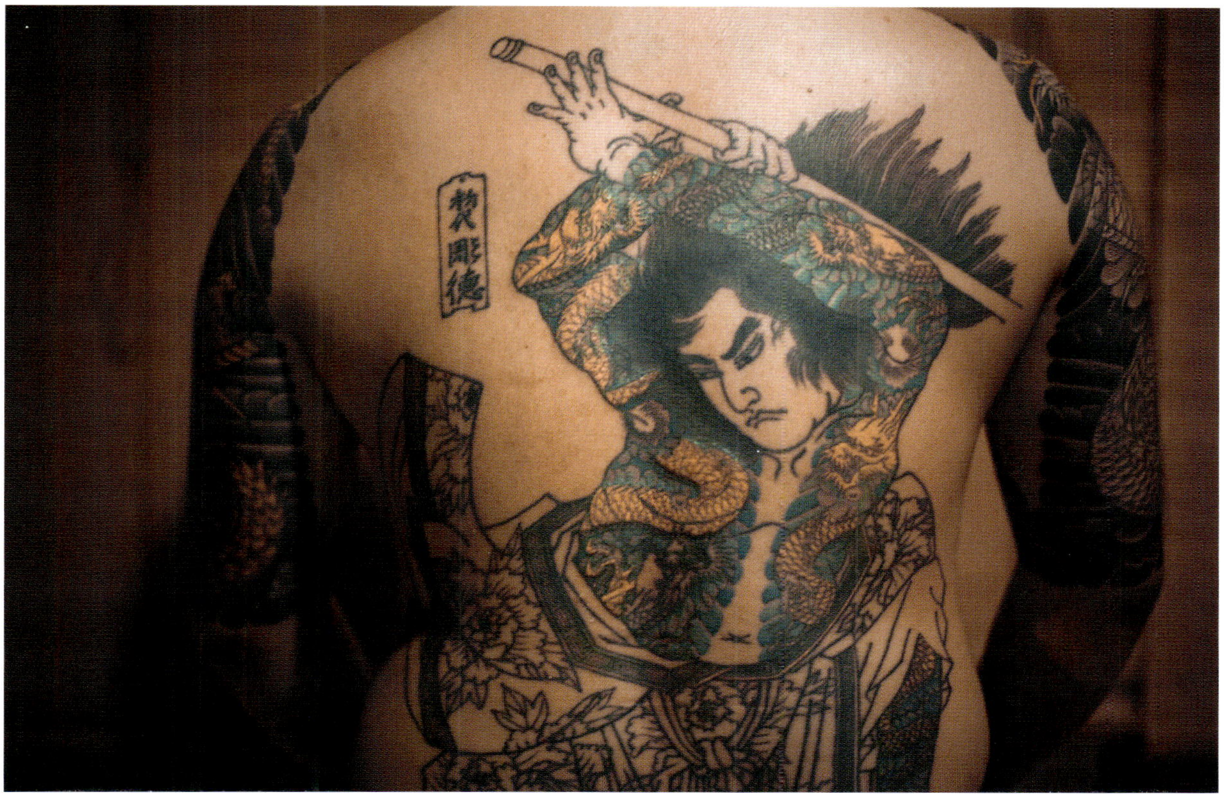

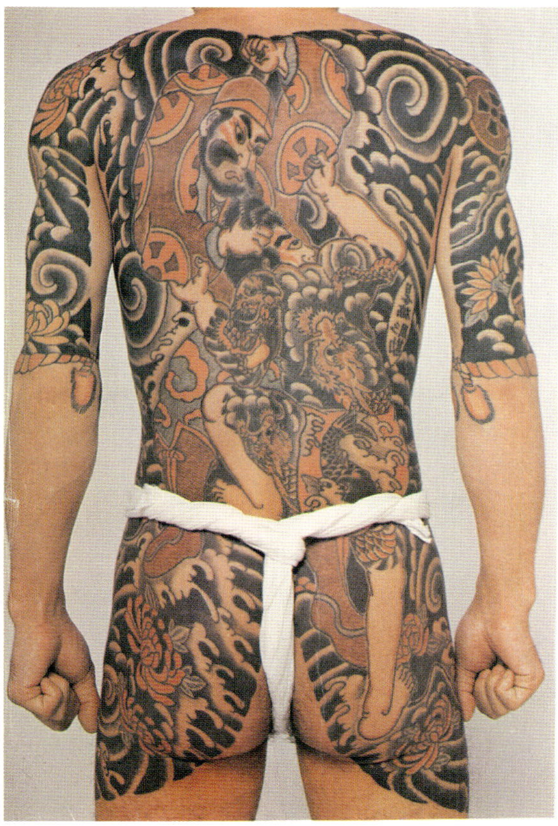

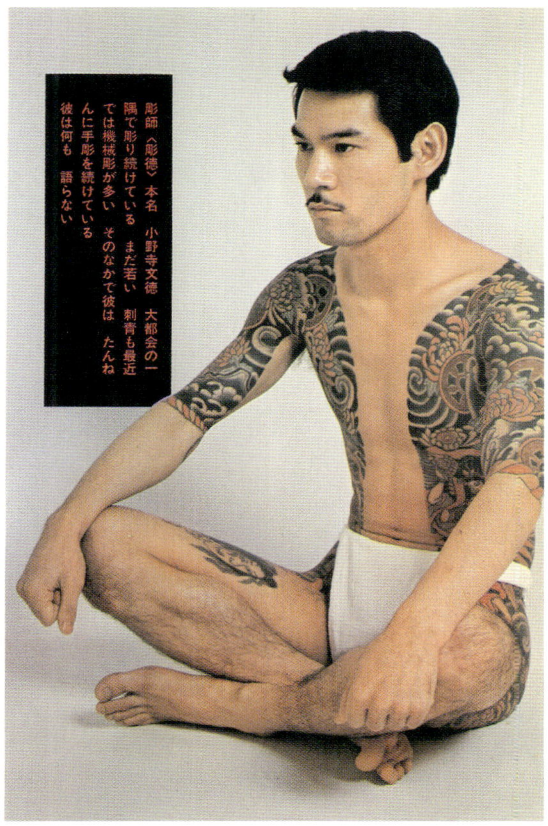

TOP
A *nijubori* motif is when the subject of a tattoo is also tattooed.

BOTTOM
In the late 1970s Horitoku had a moment as an *enka* (a form of Showa-era Japanese blues) singer after his friend said they would release an album of his work. This is despite Horitoku admitting that he can only sing one *enka* song. 'When I was told to record an album, I was gobsmacked – what? You can really record an album that easily!?' The cassette tape art is shown here.

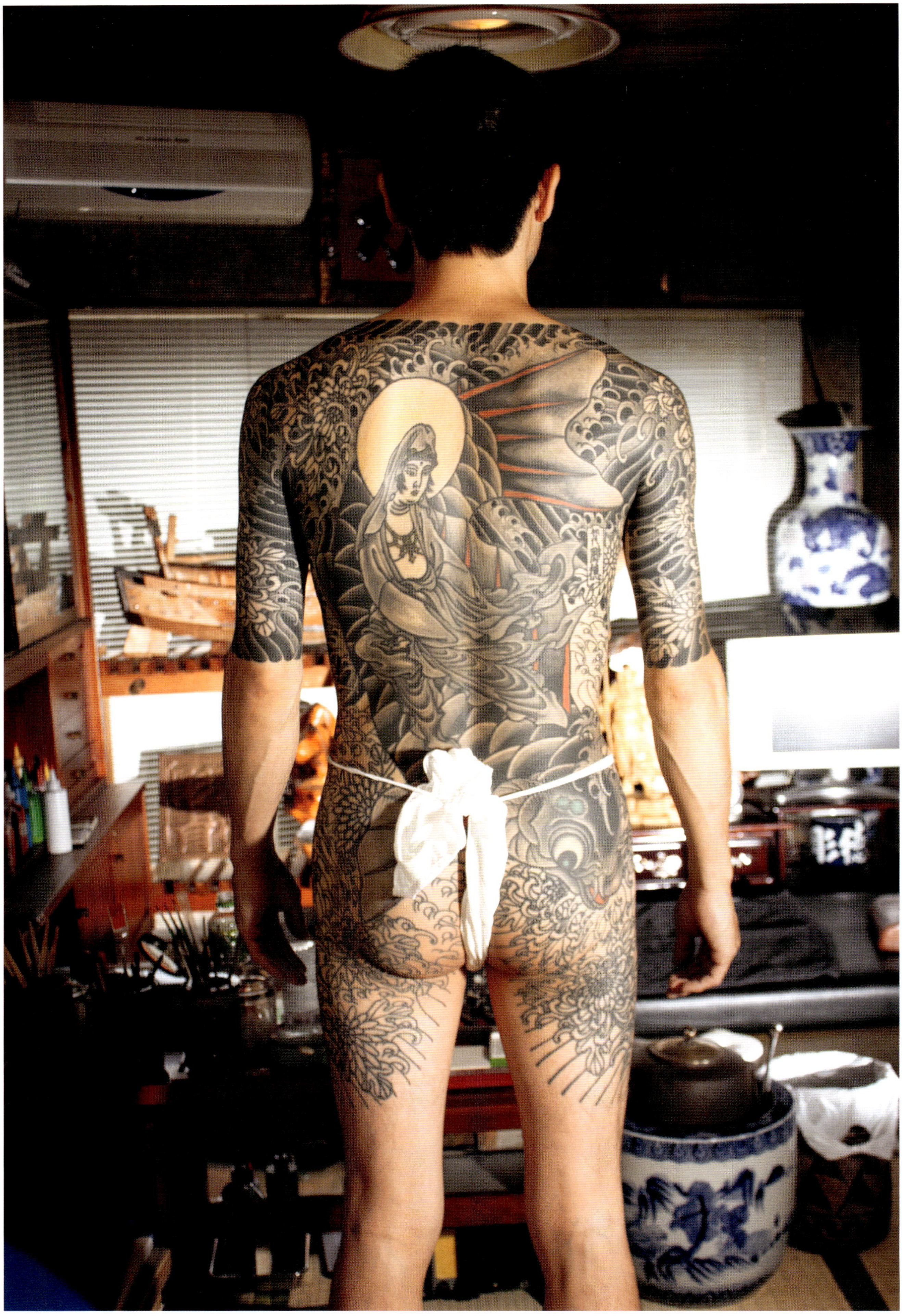

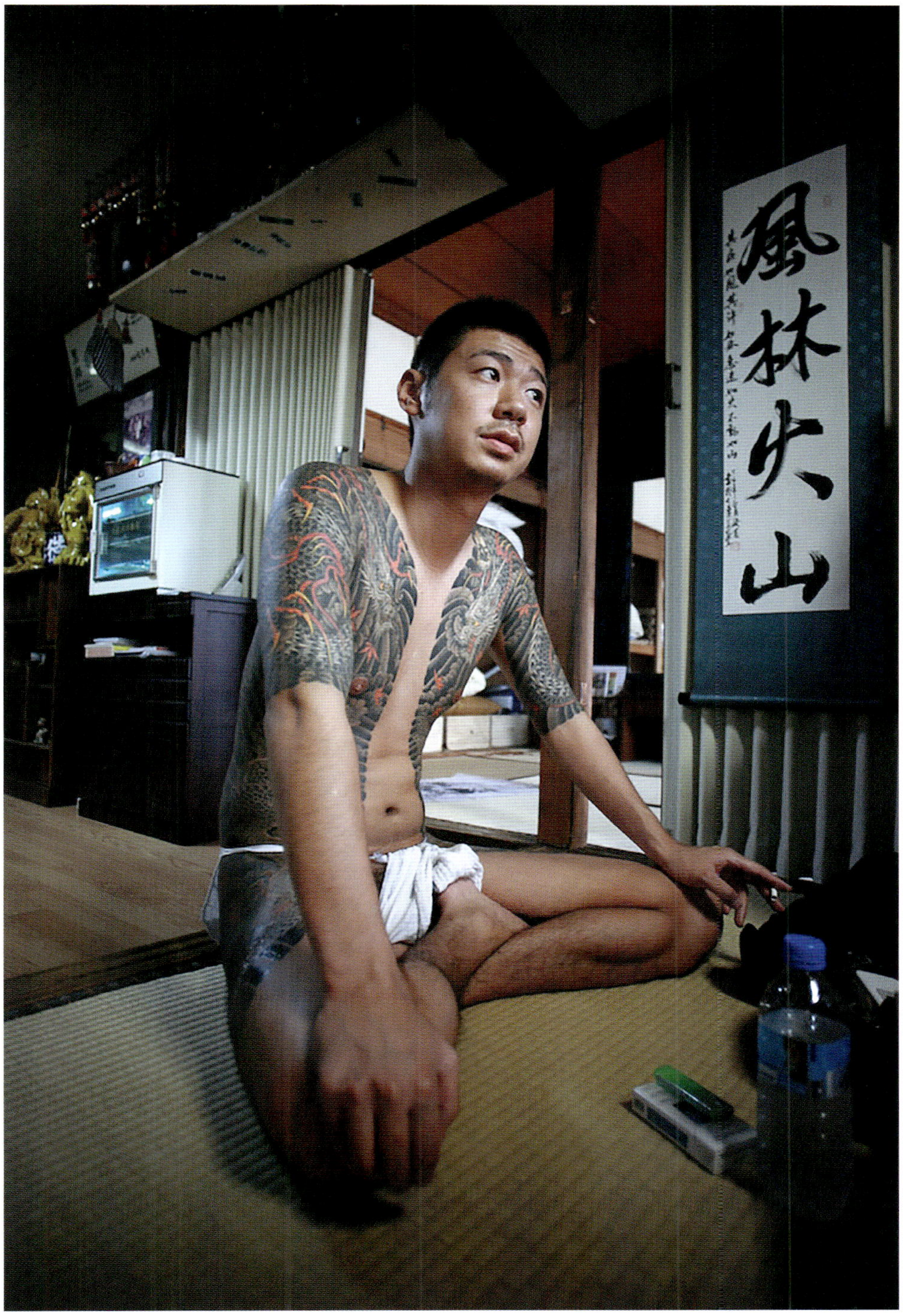

OPPOSITE
Horitoku has never taken part in a tattoo convention. He explains, 'For artisans, it is a battle with oneself, so by looking at other people's work, your own work will become diluted. You need to focus on your own work.'

ABOVE
A client has a cigarette break during a tattooing session.

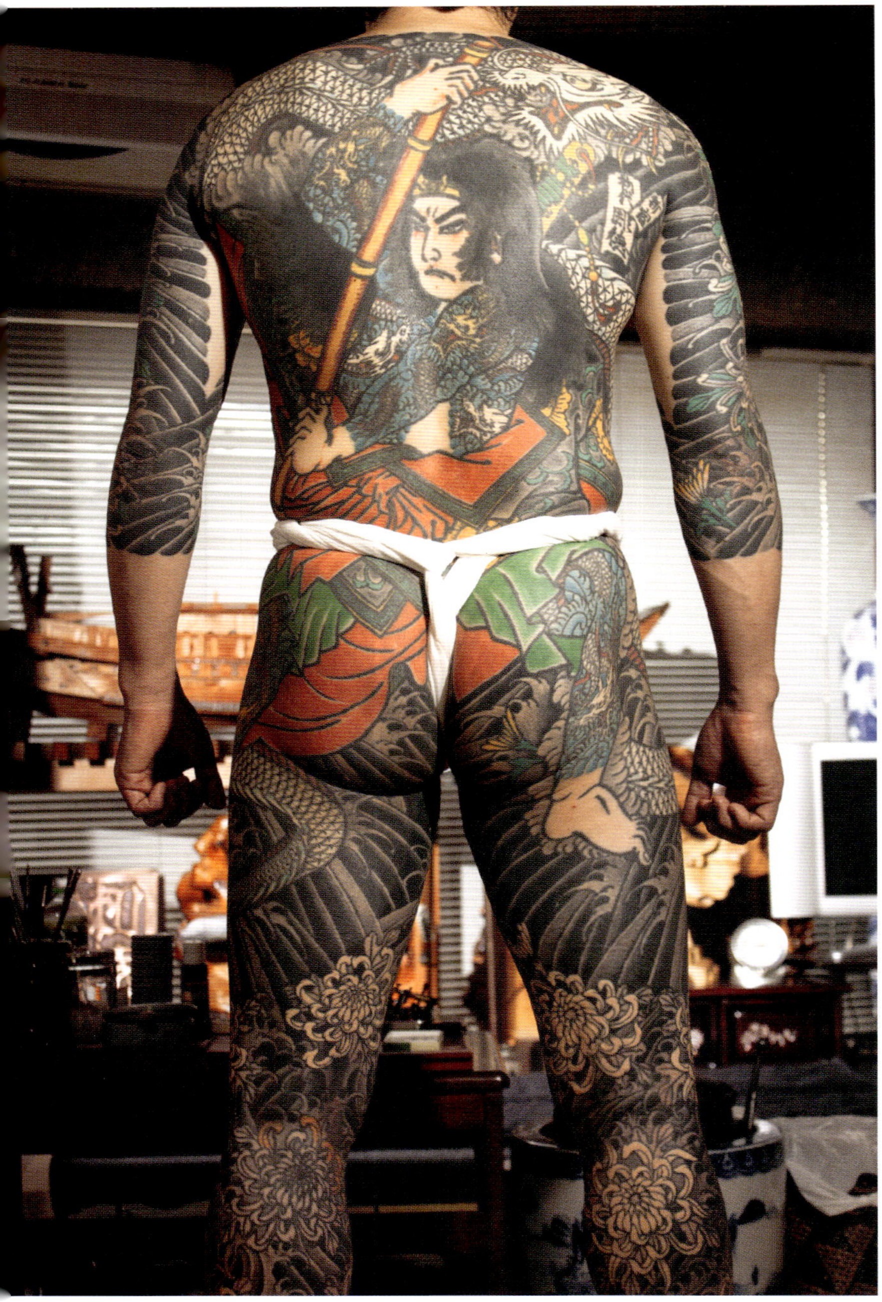

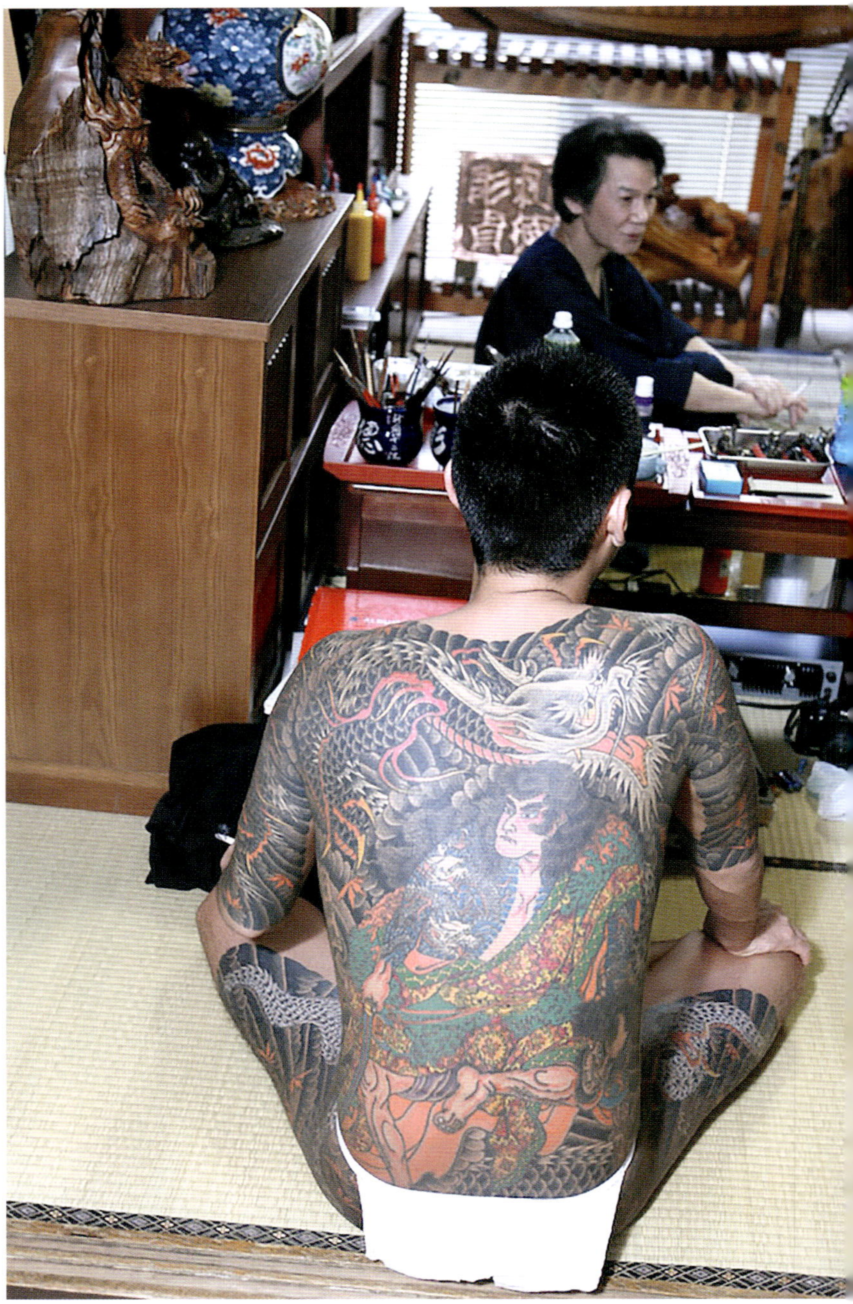

LEFT
Horitoku has one of the largest *ichimon* (tattoo families) in Japan, with around 20 apprentices. They are obligated to protect the nation's tattooing traditions. He says, 'If their eyes are wandering to Western tattoos, then the illustrations end up weird.'

RIGHT
Suikoden motif on a client's back.

I went to a needle factory. Needles called *beads bari* are the most narrow and I used them for a long time, but they are still too wide, so I didn't like to use them as-is. I would get a few and grind them to make the best tip and strength. In the past, the needles would snap quite easily, and it is no good if they are that brittle, because it will scar the skin when you flick the *tebori* tool up. So I would order them and get them customized just for me.

What about the ink?
I use ink from overseas now, but in the past it was pigment. There was an art supply business for Japanese paintings and the owner would research pigments and tell me, 'This colour will probably be broken down by the body, and won't be harmful.' In around 1985, I found out about ink in a bottle. The only problem is, when you use it with *tebori*, too much goes into the body, because it is the consistency of ink and not pigment. When you are flicking up the skin, the ink is absorbed by the skin – so tattoo ink really needs to be put in with a machine as the elements are too fine. Now I use National [brand] or whatever, but I get the inks with the most viscous texture, stuff that tattoo artists don't really want to use.

What would you tattoo for someone who wants to look stronger?
Something from *Suikoden*, and for someone who wants something beautiful, a courtesan or *tennyo* (Buddhist angel): they are the representative motifs. In the past, clients were very into the meanings and were really concerned if something was unlucky. For example, a morning glory flower will bloom in the morning but at night it will wilt, so they would ask me not to fill in the whole thing and leave open one leaf or a petal. Or they would ask me to leave one bead open in prayer beads on the wrist or on the neck, because otherwise it might be like being strangled. Nowadays, the clients like the visuals and don't really talk about whether they are lucky or not.

When you first started, where were you getting references?
Ukiyo-e books, and I also went to the Kanda book district [in Tokyo, the world's biggest bookshop district, with over 10 million books in their collective inventory]. I would go with my former apprentice Horitoshi and would tell him to scour one side of the road and I would search the other side. We would allocate a whole day for looking for Kintaro [see p. 94] references. And if Kanda didn't have anything, we would comb libraries and copy things from there. For Fudo Myo-o [a demonic-looking Buddhist deity] or Buddhist motifs, I can reference scrolls or a statue.

For our work, we are copying that era's illustrations and *ukiyo*-e designs. When you see *ukiyo-e* you really have to work things out, like how is this *obi* (kimono sash) tied? Where does it go and why? Why is a kimono tied a certain way and why are the sleeves like that? What is this wig? If you don't understand these things, you can't draw the designs. In order to understand them, you need to go to the *kabuki* and *sumo* and see the hairstyles in real life. I really encourage people to study the culture. When *horishi* who do that are around, Japanese culture will endure, and they can teach their apprentices. However, when these people disappear, the culture will die out.

How do you determine whether to take on an apprentice or not?
I ask them if they like illustrations, and observe what kind of personality they have and whether I think they will last. If they seem all right, I get them to come in. The speed at which they learn differs according to the individual, though. No matter how many years it takes, they can call me if they need to know something – but I have a lot of apprentices, so they teach each other and they learn quickly like that.

So, entering a family* (ichimon) *is quite beneficial?
Yes. No matter where they go, they can carry that name. It is a status symbol.

When members of the* yakuza *get tattooed, are the motifs they choose left up to the individual?
Yes. Occasionally they will get what the superior has. Or, conversely, there are superiors who will say, 'Don't get the same things as me!' In the past, the superiors paid for their underlings – it was a good era – but they were like, 'If you run away, you'll have to

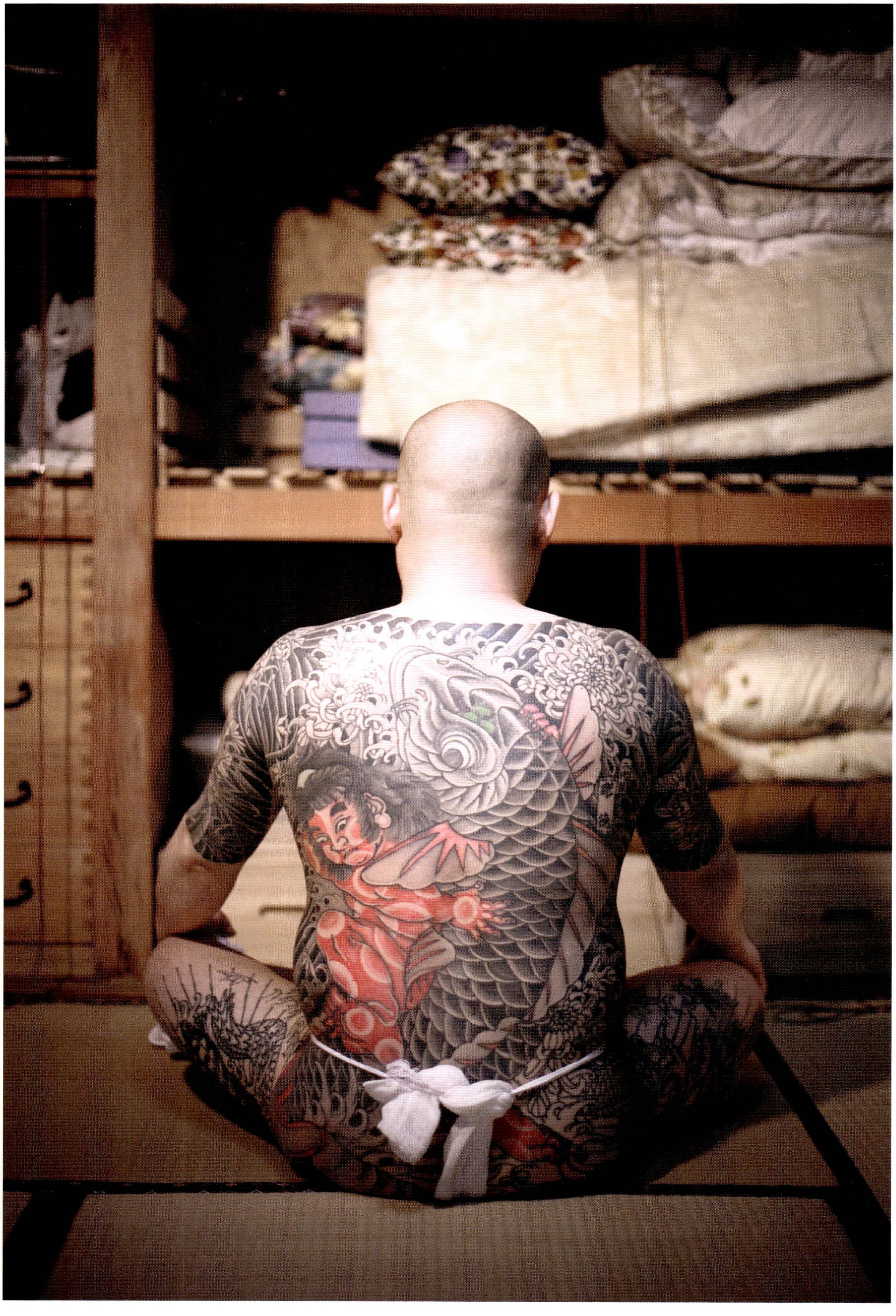

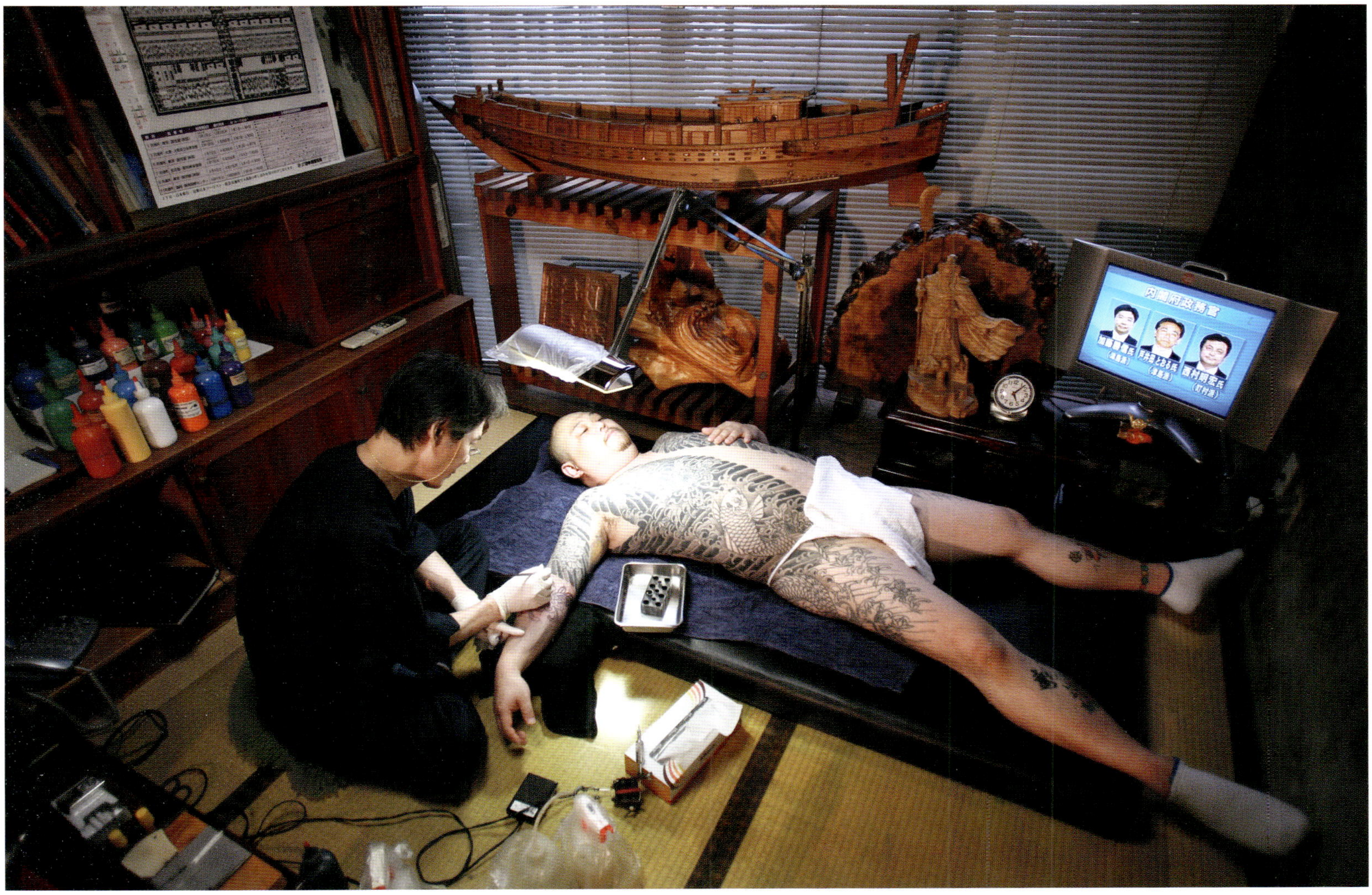

OPPOSITE
Horitoku is originally from Hokkaido. He first came to Tokyo in junior high school and found the tattoos he saw when he was young to be 'aspirational and masculine'. Here, Kintaro, a popular character from a Japanese folk tale, is wrestling a carp.

ABOVE
His studio is in Shinjuku, which is also home to Tokyo's largest entertainment and red-light district, Kabukicho, where a lot of underworld activity occurs. Horitoku, who was always incredibly busy owing to his location and skill, is now semi-retired and only takes on a few clients. He spends most of his time teaching his *deshi* and configuring old woodblock prints so that they are easy to use in tattoo designs.

peel your skin off and leave it behind. You can never run away!' It was all about hierarchical relationships.

When did you begin to see a mass decline in* yakuza *clients?
Nowadays, regular people walk around showing their tattoos off, so it isn't obvious who is who. If a *yakuza* member did that too, they'd look the same as a regular person, so there is no notion that doing something like that is scary anymore. In my case, I get regular people too, and that has been the case since the tattoo boom [in the late 1990s to 2000s]. It changed after the laws became strict. Flashing your *irezumi* and wearing a syndicate badge or showing your business card and intimidating someone would lead to arrest. After the laws changed, *yakuza* couldn't work, open bank accounts or rent rooms. And then, gradually, normal people started to increase as clientele.

Regular people are a bit out of it. They don't have a sense of tenseness, they come in like it's a shop. *Yakuza* have really good manners, and they bring two bottles of sake and talk in honorifics. However, the whole era has changed: *horishi* don't need to live off *yakuza* anymore. My students put on a tattoo convention recently as well.

Besides* yakuza*, who was primarily getting tattooed in the past?
Construction workers. You could tell from the way they dress. There was once a salaryman who was wearing a necktie and I said him, 'Why do you want to get tattooed?' I told him to go home and think about it. I told him, 'If you definitely want it, come back, but I think it's better if you don't, ha ha!'

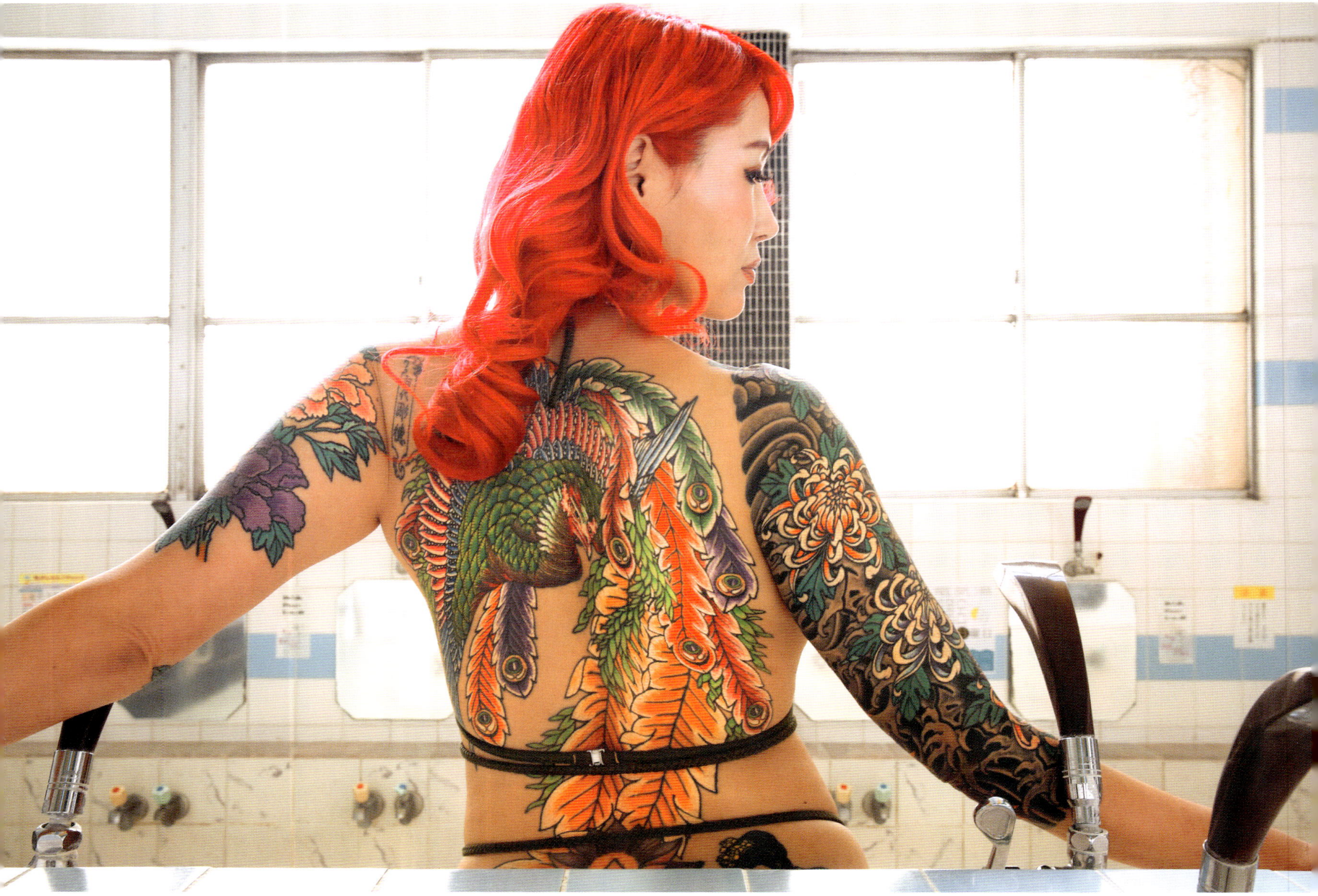

ABOVE
The culture of *sento* developed in the Edo era. *Sento* were initially intended to be places to wash, as individual Japanese homes didn't have their own bathrooms. Nowadays, they are used as places to relax and have a communal atmosphere, creating an unusual semi-public third type of space, neither home nor work. Tattooed people in downtown Tokyo use *sento* much in the same way that Edoites did, and they are still the best places to see tattoos on a daily basis. Many of the nation's top *horishi* say that the first place they ever saw a tattoo was at their local bathhouse and seeing these pieces left an indelible impression on them as children, providing the impetus for becoming *horishi*. This photo was taken at Denkiyu *sento* in Kyojima, which was also featured in Wim Wenders' film *Perfect Days*. The model, burlesque dancer Aya Mermaid, is suited for the photos but usually people bathe naked.

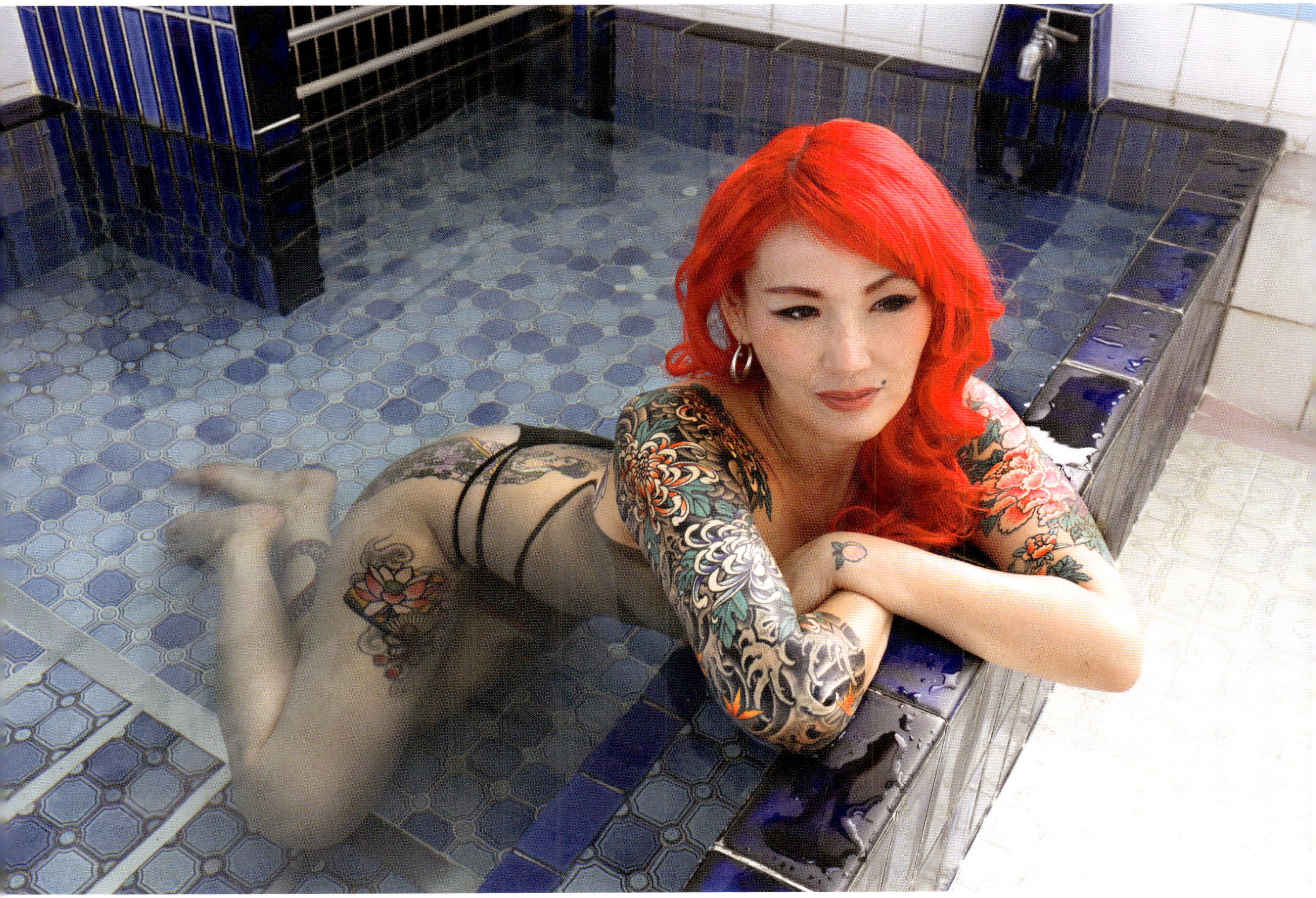

ABOVE
'I first saw Horitoku's work in 2018,' she says. 'I thought it was a miracle to be able to meet him through a mutual friend. He has a scary aura at first, but he is stoic and unwavering. Sometimes he has a gentle smile on his face. I used to be insecure about my body, but I began to like it after getting tattooed. I am proud to have the work of an important teacher. I want a lot of people to see his work, so I also persevere as a dancer so I can show it off on stage.'

HORIHIDE

彫秀

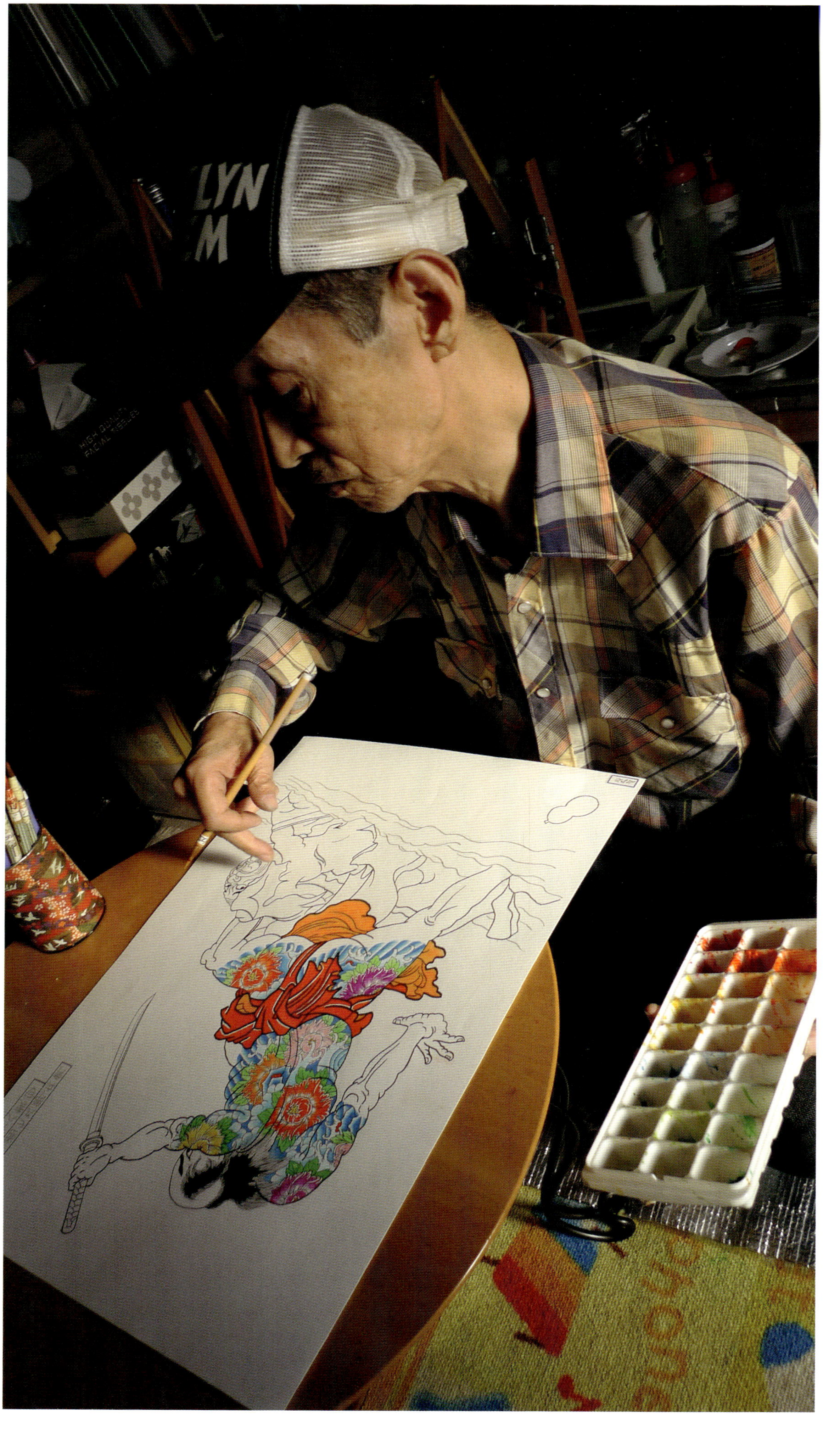

Horihide, a veteran *horishi* based in Gifu, is responsible for changing the course of tattoo history due to his interactions with Western tattoo artists. Through his meetings with Sailor Jerry in Hawaii in the 1970s, he brought colour to Japan (previously, Japanese tattoos were mostly black and vermilion). In turn, Japanese motifs were introduced to the lexicon of American tattoo designs.

How did you start as a horishi?

I stabbed someone and was on the run. I didn't have any money and there was a piece of paper on the wall saying, 'Looking for an apprentice.' I just thought, 'I need to eat,' and was there for six years. I was in hiding, I was worried I would get arrested, so I didn't go out at all, even though I was given pocket money and was told to go out. My teacher thought I was really just into working hard and diligent, so he said, 'I'll teach you properly.' After three years he said, 'You've become better than me at drawing.' I took that to heart and tried really hard.

When you were an apprentice, what was a typical day-to-day schedule?

I would wake up in the morning, finish my meal and then I would clean and get the tools ready. I'd see who had a booking. If I knew it was someone who wanted an outline, I would just grind the ink for that, prepare the needles and put them in a bag with their name on it. At the time, your master was

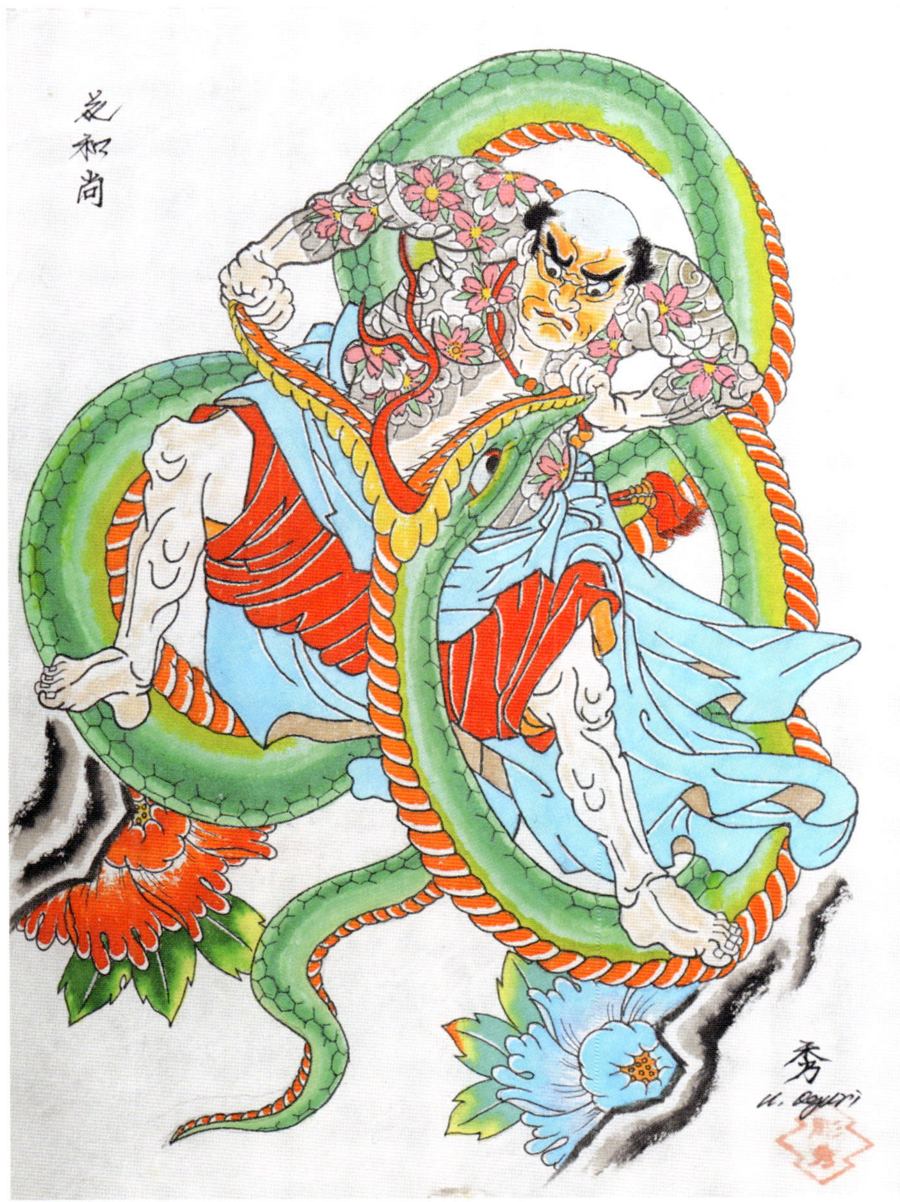

OPPOSITE
Horihide painting in his studio, 2012. He is now retired from tattooing and creates artwork that many tattooers around the world collect as memorabilia.

RIGHT
Lo-Chishin Fighting the Snake, from *Suikoden*. Horihide is concerned that many people tattoo without knowing the meanings behind the imagery, and for that reason has published books so that tattoo enthusiasts abroad can understand the iconography properly.

really like a king. Say he said something that was blatantly wrong, you wouldn't correct him. It was really strict when I was an apprentice. With any artisan trade, such as carpenters, you had to do a live-in apprenticeship for five years. It didn't matter if you could tattoo or not. For the first two years, you were doing the grunt work and you didn't learn anything. You would clean outside with a broom and wipe the inside of the house with a cloth, you would do it all. When the master started work, you sat still, kneeling next to him, and watched him – he wouldn't teach you verbally, it is more that you 'stole' the technique. After the second year, gradually he let you work the needles. There is no substitute for human skin, so he would let me practice on his leg. He would say, 'Hey, it hurts!' and hit me if I made him bleed.

That sounds nerve-wracking!

Yes, I was definitely nervous, and I would tense up. He would tell me to relax and do it. He was really strict, but that was the norm. This was in the post-war era, when these relationships were feudalistic and honorific, and it was almost a given that he would hit us. In my fourth year, I was allowed to tattoo my first client. The fifth year, I tried to earn money so I could pay back the amount that I had received in terms of eating and learning how to tattoo.

What tools were you using?

During that time, there were no needles specifically for tattooing. We were using sewing needles and the configurations were different according to the artist. There were some that used a rounded tip; there were many different methods. There is a needle shop in Nihonbashi [in Tokyo]. First I was taken by my teacher and he told me which ones to buy, as they are specified by symbols and numbers.

Coloured tattoos didn't exist in Japan at the time, so the pigment we used was meant for Japanese classical painting. It is actually poisonous when inserted into the body, as it is a mineral. In order to rectify this, you would have to boil it every day for a week and remove the mercury that floated up to the top until it didn't come out anymore. Then we would dry it and soak it in *shochu* [a type of Japanese alcoholic drink] and then use it on the clients.

Who are your most common types of clients since the tattoo boom?

Mostly firefighters, construction workers, carpenters and sushi chefs. Occasionally there are *yakuza* too. It is mostly people who work during the day. Construction workers and firefighters do the most dangerous work, like climbing up tall buildings, and they have seen their friends fall and die, so they get tattoos for protection to ward off bad luck. For example, they will get a hawk, thinking that they won't fall, but fly. They are really into the meanings and get things that ward off bad luck.

Who were your* yakuza *clients?

I was working in Asakusa but also around Tohoku, Kanazawa, Fukui and Gifu, for one month at a time. The Sumiyoshi [*yakuza* syndicate] boss was in Tokyo, and he seemed to like me, I have no idea why. He called me 'Hide Hide'.

One of the most memorable experiences was when I was tattooing a man upstairs at a *yakuza* office, and a guy from a rival gang came in yelling and brandishing a samurai sword. I was in the middle of tattooing when this guy came in and chopped off my client's arm. Blood sprayed all over my face like a shower and the bone was showing through. His arm was dangling by a thread! But when you are that injured, you are anaesthetized from the pain. He just got right up and ran after the guy. Later, in hospital, he begged them not to amputate his arm, because I had just tattooed it!

How did your relationship with Sailor Jerry come about in the 1970s?

For us artisans, the 2nd and the 15th of each month are days of rest, so I went to Asakusa to look at the magnificent art on the temple. When I went one time, there were three American GIs walking around with short sleeves. They had tattoos with colour in them and I was really astonished. Before they came to Japan, they'd had a week off and went to Hawaii and got tattooed by someone at the port. They said

OPPOSITE
Horihide tattooed as he went along, one part at a time, rather than creating the outline first as most *horishi* do.

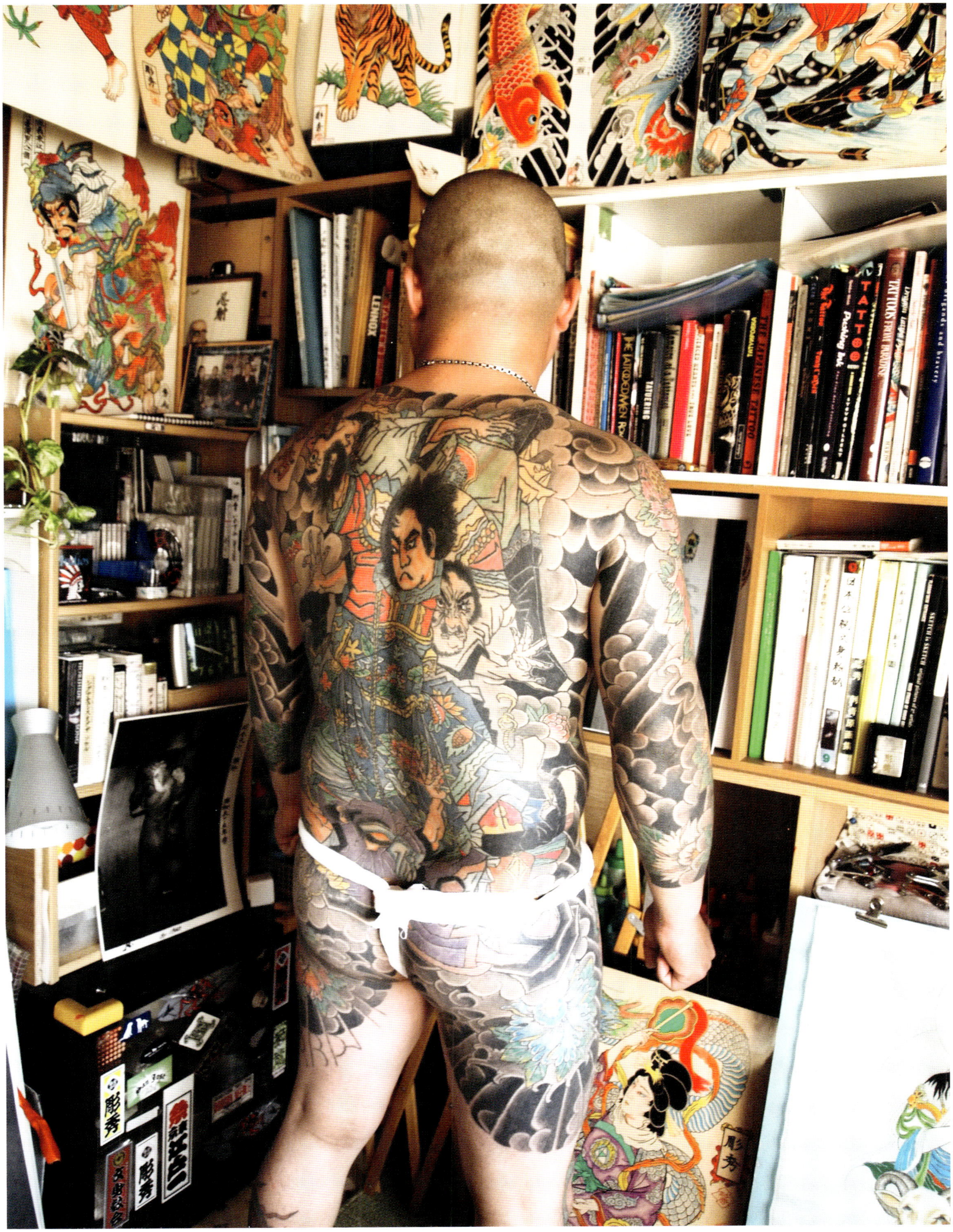
TATTOO
TATTOOS FROM BORNEO
LENNOX
彫秀

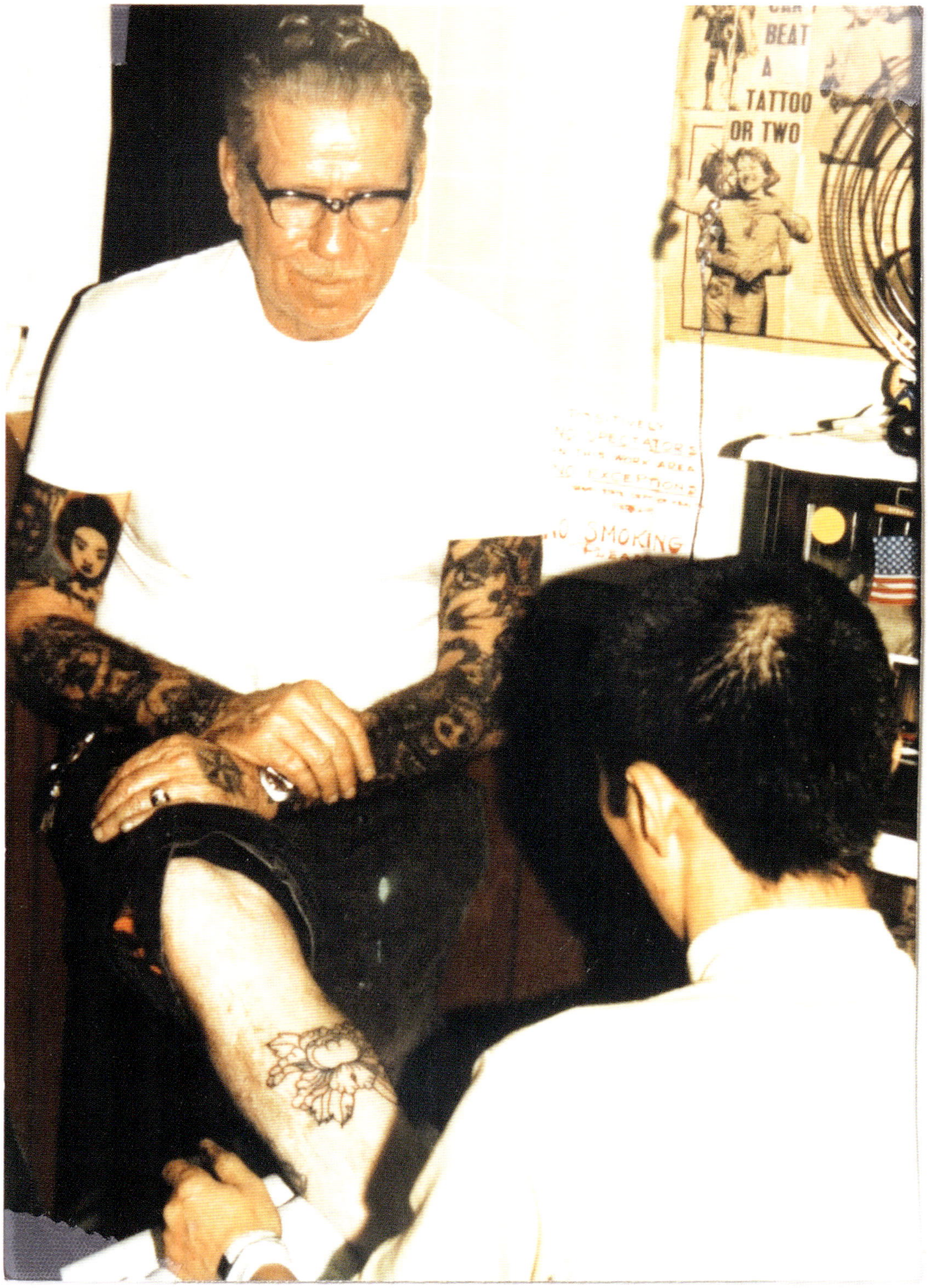

Tattooing to Sailor Jerry
at his studio by machine
in Hawaii 1970.

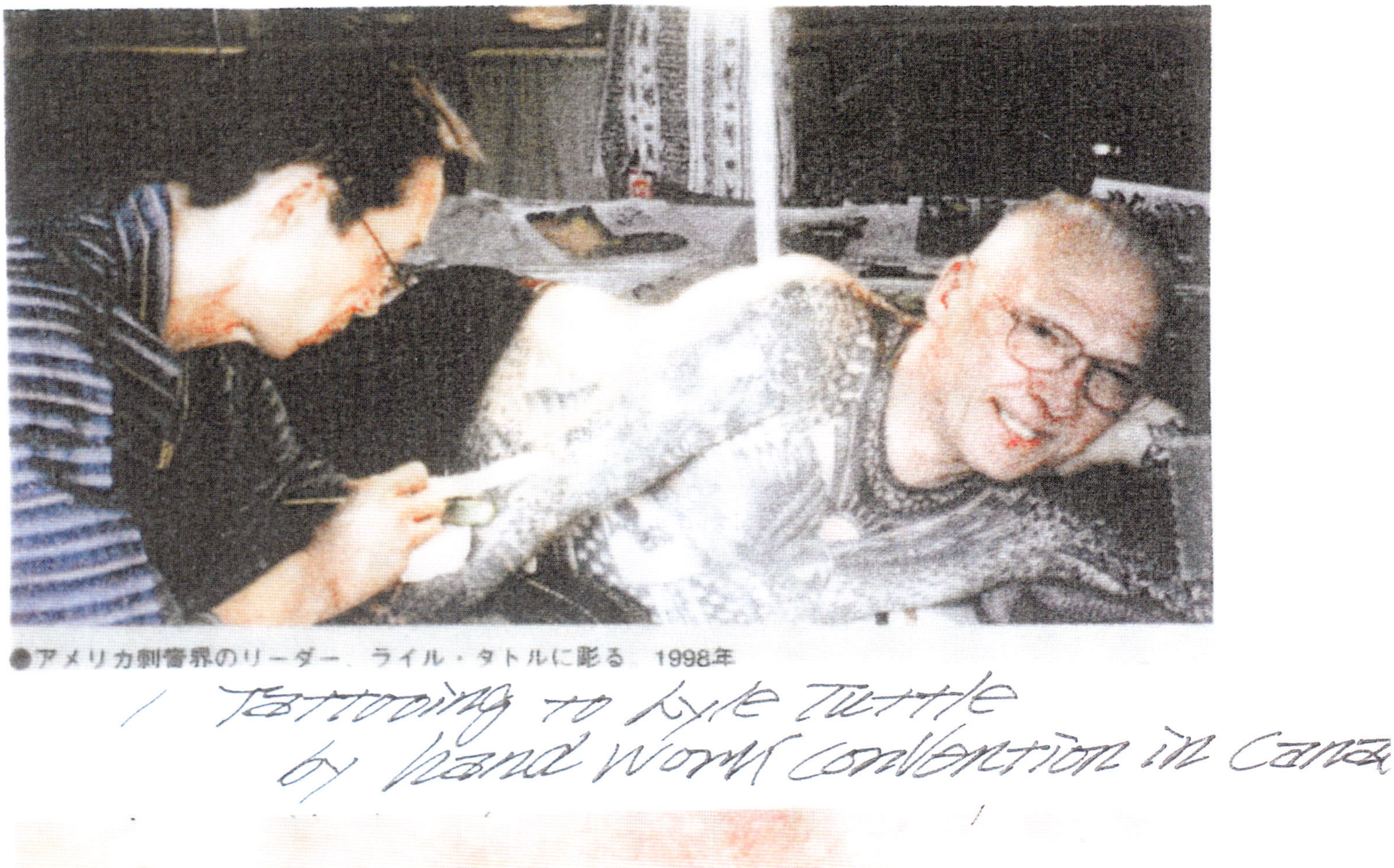

OPPOSITE
Horihide tattooing Sailor Jerry at his studio in Hawaii, 1970. He recalls that Sailor Jerry was surprised that his English was predominantly comprised of GI slang, as he'd worked as a driver for the Marine Corps when he was 17. After Horihide was able to acquire colours from the US, other Japanese tattoo artists asked him for colours as well.

ABOVE
Horihide inking American tattoo legend Lyle Tuttle in 1998.

they had the tattooer's business card and that was Sailor Jerry.

After that, I bought an English-language book and wrote letters to Jerry in English. I wrote saying there are no colours in Japan. He said he wanted Japanese motifs and told me to come to Hawaii – and in exchange for designs, he would give me the colours.

When you saw the tattoos on the GIs, you thought the colours were great, but how about the designs?
Oh, they were like sew-on patches. For example, Mickey Mouse, or the mark of the army group of the GI, or a grave with 'Mom' written on the gravestone, or a 'Fuck you'. Another guy showed me a dotted line, like dot, dot, dot, and then 'Cut here!' I found it so funny! I actually chuckled; it had no meaning!

Then you went to visit Sailor Jerry in Hawaii. How long were you there?
Ten days. Sailor Jerry smoked so much, his nickname was Hori Smoku. He was so busy, he would tell me to get burgers and tattoo while eating. I got to Hawaii and Jerry picked me up in his car. We went to his house to drop off my bags first and he showed me Pearl Harbor! I was like, 'I'm so sorry, I really do apologize,' and he said, 'Oh, it's not your fault!'

I was watching him tattoo his clients with a machine and the colours went in really easily and smoothly. I was so surprised and found it amazing. He taught me how to use a machine, and I practised on Jerry's leg – first the outline and then the colour – and I was like, 'This is great!' And that was the beginning of machines and colours in Japan, and I was the first to bring them in!

When did famed American tattooer Ed Hardy turn up at your place in Japan?

After that first trip, I became good friends with [modern tattoo pioneer] Zeke Owen. I went to San Diego because he has a studio out there. Close by was Ed Hardy's studio, who also learnt from Zeke, so it was after I went to Hawaii for the second time. He said he wanted to learn Japanese tattooing and to come to Japan and I was like, 'I will think about it.' He wanted to learn *tebori* and the illustrations.

After San Diego, I went to Oregon and Seattle. After a month, I went to San Francisco to meet up with Ed Hardy. Sailor Jerry told me, 'If you are coming back this way, could you please drop by Hawaii?' I told him I would, but Hardy was so excited, he wanted to go to Japan straight away, so we got a direct flight. Two weeks later, Sailor Jerry died on his Harley and his wife gave me the call. I really wanted to see him; it was a real pity we couldn't meet one last time.

Why did you still do* tebori *after learning about machine tattooing?

It's totally different. If you compare machine and *tebori* tattooing side-by-side, the machine work looks a bit weak. There are clients who don't want machine work: they don't want it unless it is by hand, and machines are more painful. Zeke and Ed Hardy tattooed me, but it was damn painful because they were fast and they covered so much area so quickly. When I went to America and saw Ed Hardy tattooing his clients' backs, I was surprised that they would sit through that pain! I even wondered if they were a bit masochistic. They would sit there with such an expressionless look on their faces like it was totally fine!

What would you say is the best thing about your work?

My best memories are of getting friendly with the ladies I have tattooed on my travels! With my female clients, they were embarrassed because they had to expose their skin to me when I was tattooing them, but that awkwardness went and we got friendly so quickly. They would ask me out after work. They would ask me if I had been to their area before, and if I said, 'No,' they would ask if I had a day off. Then they would kindly offer to guide me. And then it would be like, 'Instead of going to your hotel, why don't you come to mine and tell me some stories!' Tattoo artists do well with women. I guess it is because we are seen as being in a strange, mysterious world and it piques their curiosity.

OPPOSITE
Showa-era magazine featuring a geisha tattooed by Horihide.

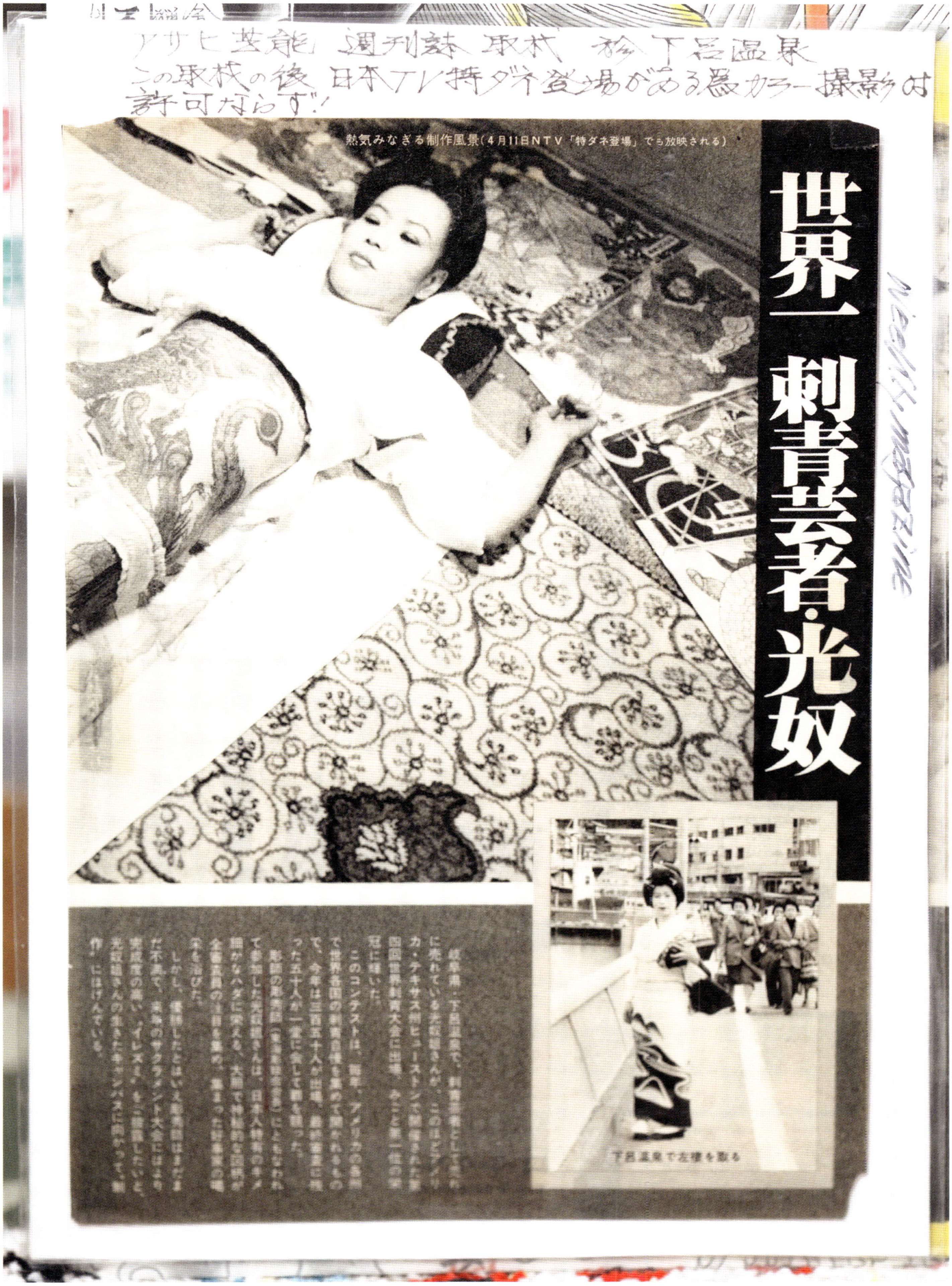

アサヒ芸能 週刊誌 取材 於 下呂温泉
この取材の後 日本TV特ダネ登場がある為カラー撮影は許可ならず!!

熱気みなぎる制作風景（4月11日NTV「特ダネ登場」でも放映される）

世界一 刺青芸者・光奴

岐阜県・下呂温泉で、刺青芸者として売れに売れている光奴姐さんが、このほどアメリカ・テキサス州ヒューストンで開催された第四回世界刺青大会に出場、みごと第一位の栄冠に輝いた。

このコンテストは、毎年、アメリカの各州で世界各国の刺青自慢を集めて開かれるもので、今年は三百五十人が出場、最終審査に残った五十人が一堂に会して覇を競った。

彫師の彫秀昭（東京都板橋区?）にともなわれて参加した光奴姐さんは、日本人特有のキメ細かなハダに映える、大胆で神秘的な図柄が全審査員の注目を集め、集まった好事家の喝采を浴びた。

しかし、優勝したとはいえ光奴姐はまだまだ不満で、来年のサクラメント大会にはより完成度の高い"イレズミ"を二度披露したいと、光奴姐さんの生きたキャンバスに向かって、"制作"にはげんでいる。

下呂温泉で左褄を取る

WEEKLY MAGAZINE

HORIYASU 彫やす

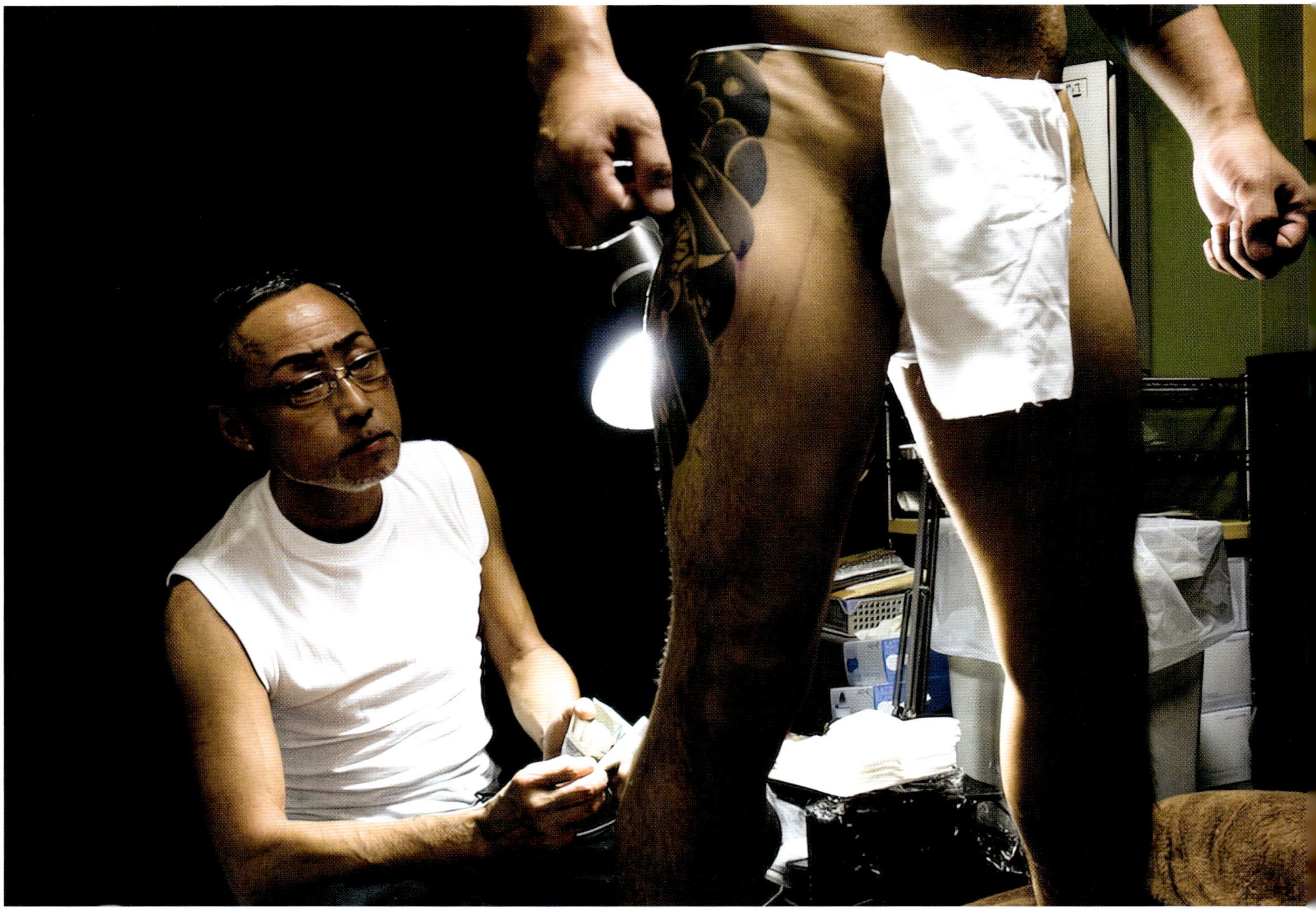

Horiyasu's work is typified by vibrant, graphically immaculate pieces that are executed with a machine. He started his career as a swordsmith, working the blades for 16 years, and switched to Japanese-style tattooing at the age of 37. Working out of Nishi (North) Asakusa, he has a large client base and doesn't tattoo *yakuza*.

When did you first get tattooed yourself?

When I was 21 years old. I was in Kofu prefecture and I was playing morning baseball. My colleague removed his shirt and I saw he was tattooed. The attraction I'd had to Japanese tattoos since I was a child was revived, and I asked where he'd had it done. The illustration and outline was probably Horiyoshi II, and Horiyoshi III did the colour gradations. It was done *donburi* style [a shape where the entire chest and stomach are filled in] and was really powerful. At the time *horishi* were limited in number – it was not like now, where there are lots of artists. It was a really specialized job and it was considered to be on a level much higher than regular artists – and even within these brilliant artists, Horiyoshi II's name really stood out. Horiyoshi II's illustrations were similar to Shodai (the first) Horiyoshi's, and they had a lot of emotional impact.

You also used to make samurai swords before becoming a tattoo artist.

Yes, I was a swordsmith for 16 years, starting when I was 21 years old, a year after I started getting tattooed. At the time, I liked swords too. I collected

ABOVE
Horiyasu is one of three prominent artists working in Nishi Asakusa, along with Horikazu and Horicho II. He is a former swordsmith, work that entailed polishing blades, removing rust and rendering the shape of the blade beautifully.

OPPOSITE
Horiyasu is known for his technical precision and his clean line work. He also does a lot of work without backgrounds, focusing on the central motif.

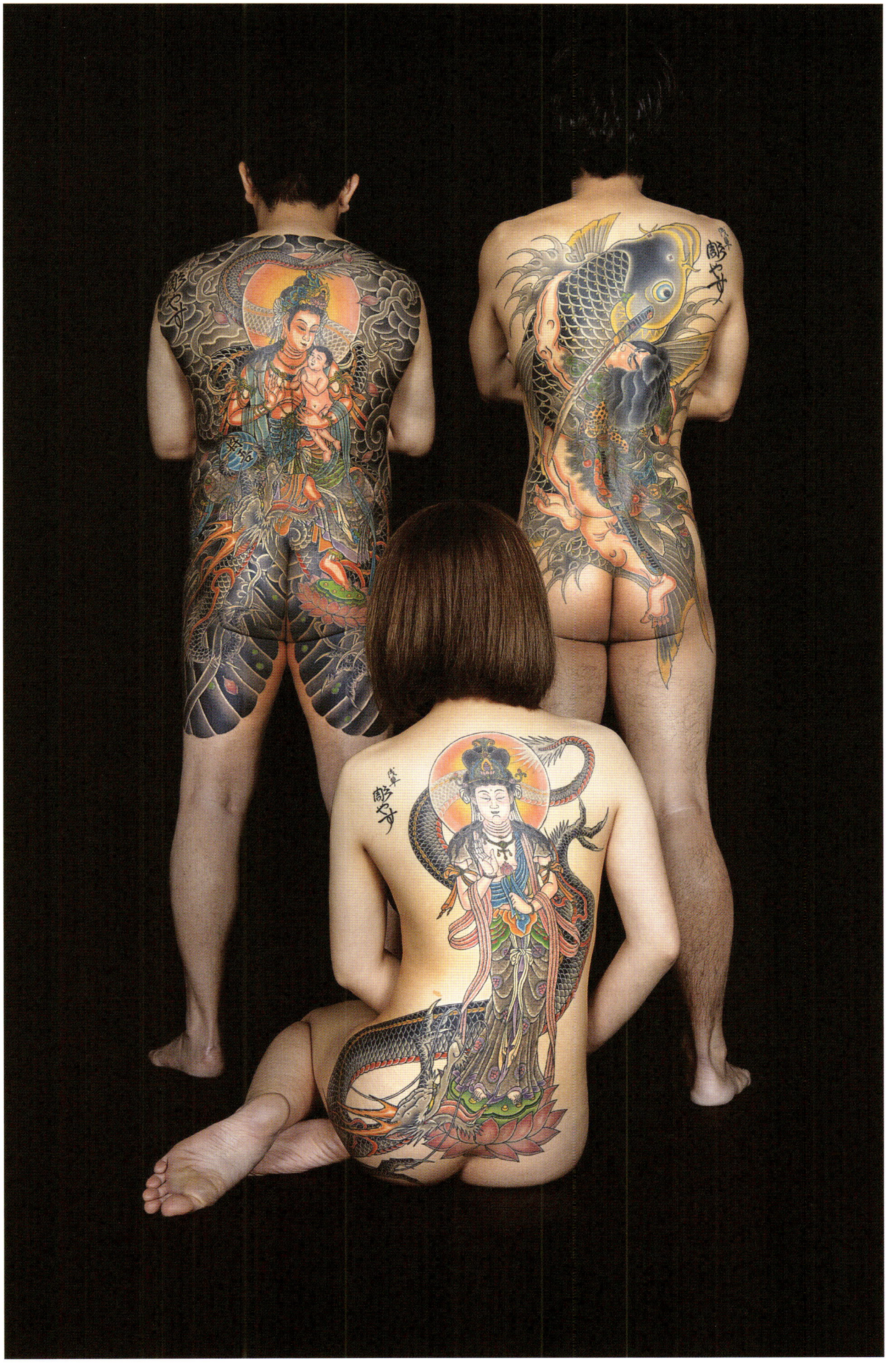
彫やす
彫やす

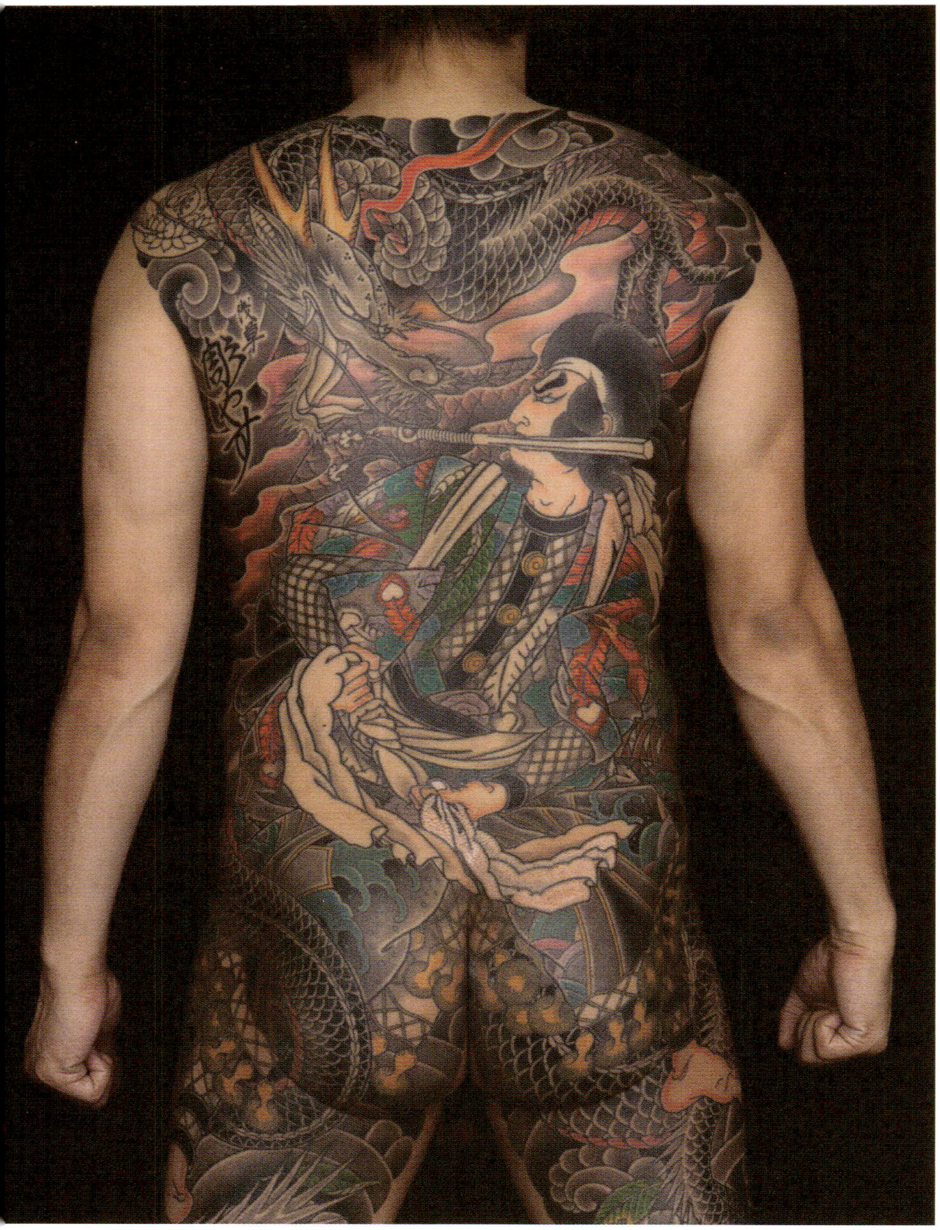

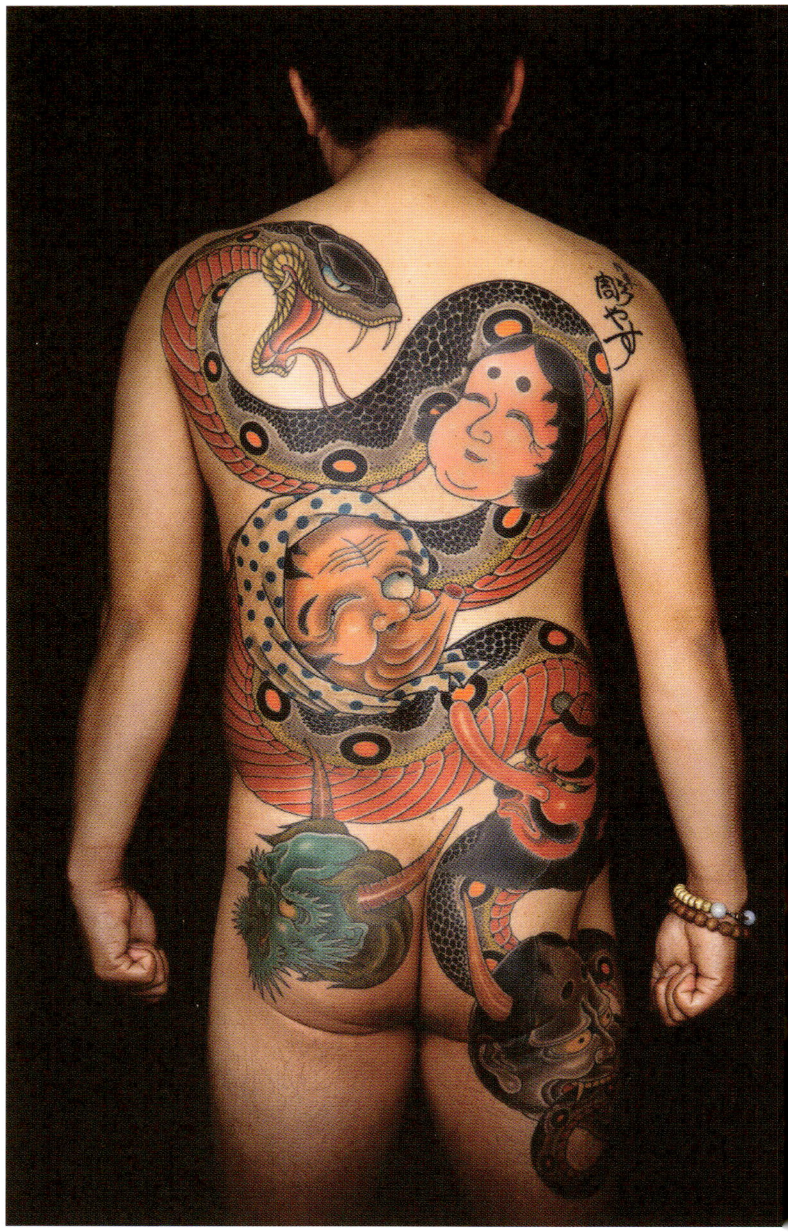

LEFT
Horiyasu is known for his impactful compositions. He used to travel internationally, winning many prizes for his work at conventions.

RIGHT
A snake and several types of theatrical mask.

them. Collectors were buying blades – the sky is the limit in terms of value, as some are artefacts from the Heian period.

In terms of traditional arts, swords are really on a high level. But they are expensive, so you can't make them as a hobby. In that way all the traditional crafts of Japan, not only swords but lanterns, tattoos, all these fantastic things, are disappearing. I always had an interest in tattoos and wanted to be a *horishi*. At the same time, I didn't want to give up my former profession prematurely, so I continued sharpening blades. The jump from swordsmith to crafting tattoos wasn't a huge problem though. I saw some progression in my swords and then I reached 36, which could be considered a landmark age. I thought hard about whether I wanted to do it and I may have had some hesitations, but I'd been wanting to do it for such a long time that I had a kind of confidence that I could.

How did you learn?

I was learning myself, but I didn't know anything. There was a *horishi* in Morioka who is a bit older, and I was going to him and watching and learning. After a year, I was able to obtain a machine, although at first I was doing it by hand.

I was introduced to Gifu Horihiro [an old-school and now-retired *horishi* based in Gifu and known for his clean machine work] and he told me how to set up the needles and how the machine moved. I went from Iwate prefecture to Gifu prefecture numerous times to learn. He did the outlines and the colour with a magnetic machine, the rest by hand. When I saw the speed at which he worked, I was astounded. Eventually, by watching these masters, I started to make my own machines.

What are the fundamental differences between Japanese and Western tattoos?

Wabori is traditional, so there are lots of meanings that go with it. As the body is a whole canvas, there is a tale behind each piece. *Ukiyo-e* woodblock illustrations are the basis, and the background, such as clouds and water, is of paramount importance. The artist I use the most for reference is Kuniyoshi; the work is intense and there is movement in it.

When I first saw Western tattoos, everything was basically different to Japanese ones. Also, the way the tattoos were inserted – the shading, the use of colour, the use of detail, the designs, that was all interesting. I liked seeing the differences, and how they could influence me.

Why do your clients get tattooed?

I am touched by some clients: for example, someone who lost their kid to a car crash, or is terminally ill and gets tattooed with their after-death name [some people receive these in Buddhist or Shinto tradition], then an image of Kannon. They can change their lives like this. Tattoos can be somewhat lighthearted, you can get them as souvenirs, but many Japanese get them at a turning point, when times are tough. At times like this, they often get inked to make them strong. I feel a lot of responsibility as a result. But because I feel responsibility, I make sure each line is given my fullest attention. When I am tattooing, I can forget everything and become immersed in the process. I can feel fulfilment and the client's joy.

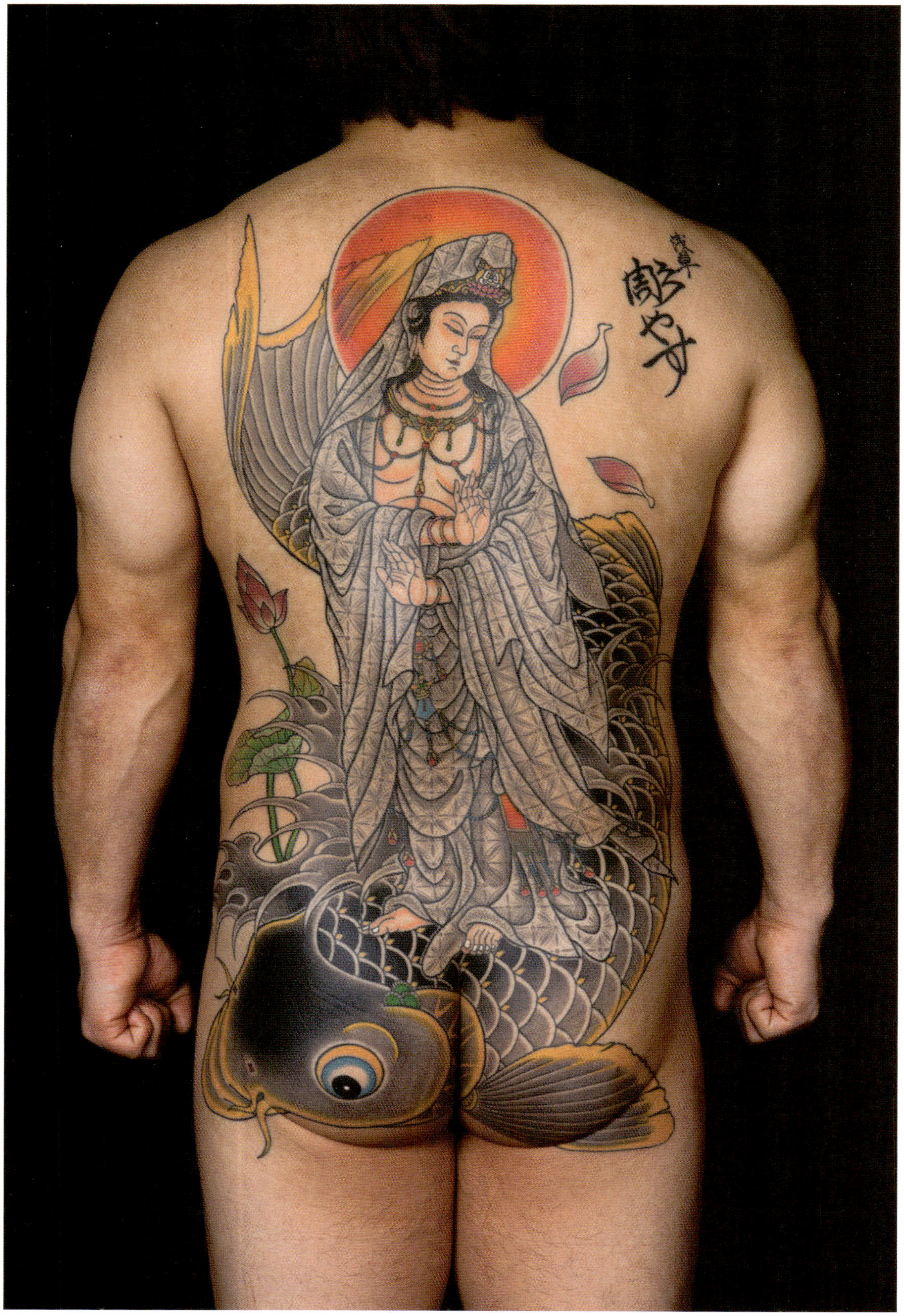

LEFT
The Buddhist goddess Kannon riding a carp.

OPPOSITE TOP
Horiyasu uses custom machines and is inspired by the work of Horihiro, a *horishi* from Gifu prefecture.

OPPOSITE BOTTOM
Horiyasu was nine years old when he first saw *wabori* at a sento. 'It had an emotional impact on me,' he says, 'and I got more and more interested in tattoos after I started getting them myself.'

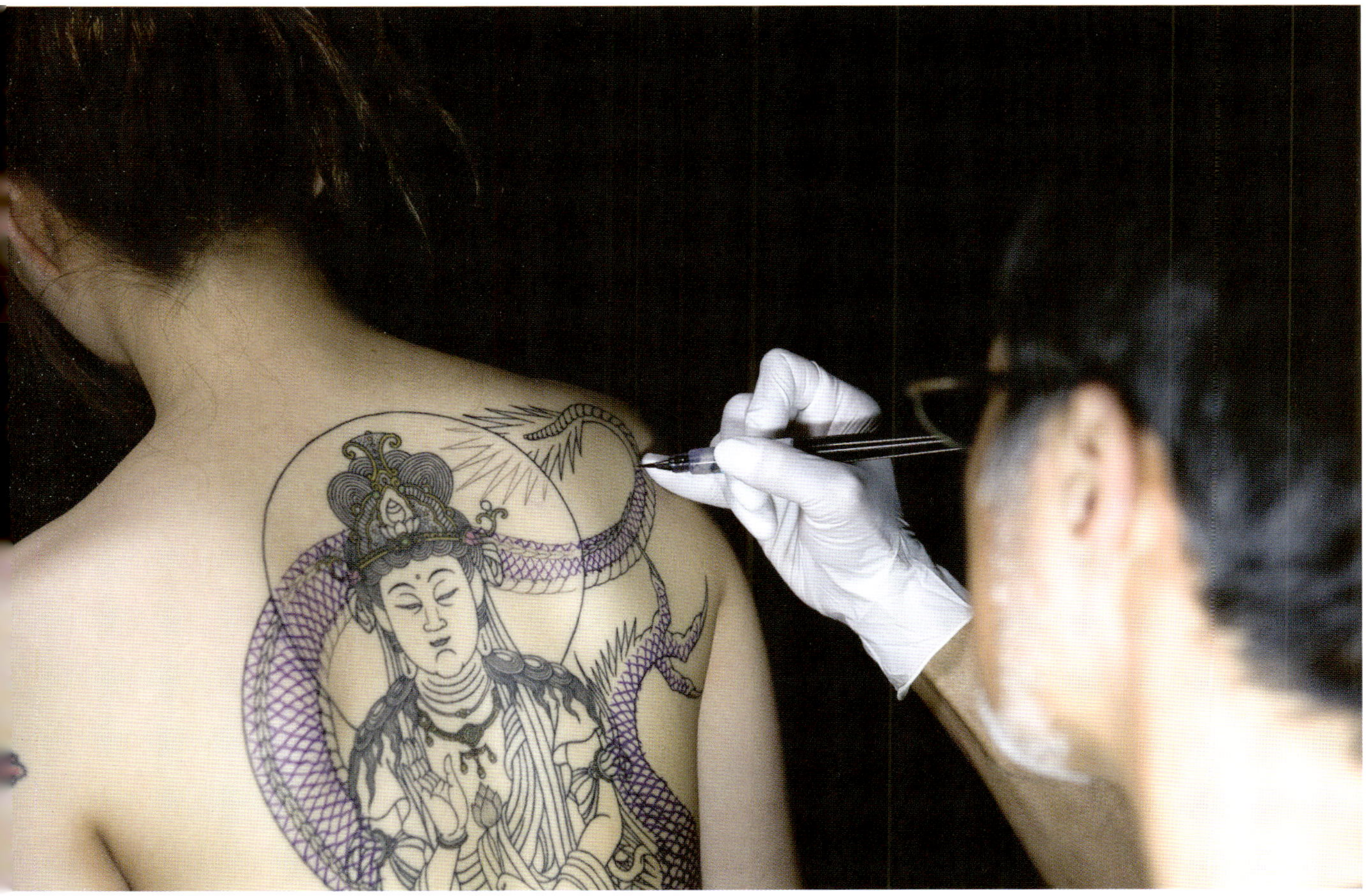

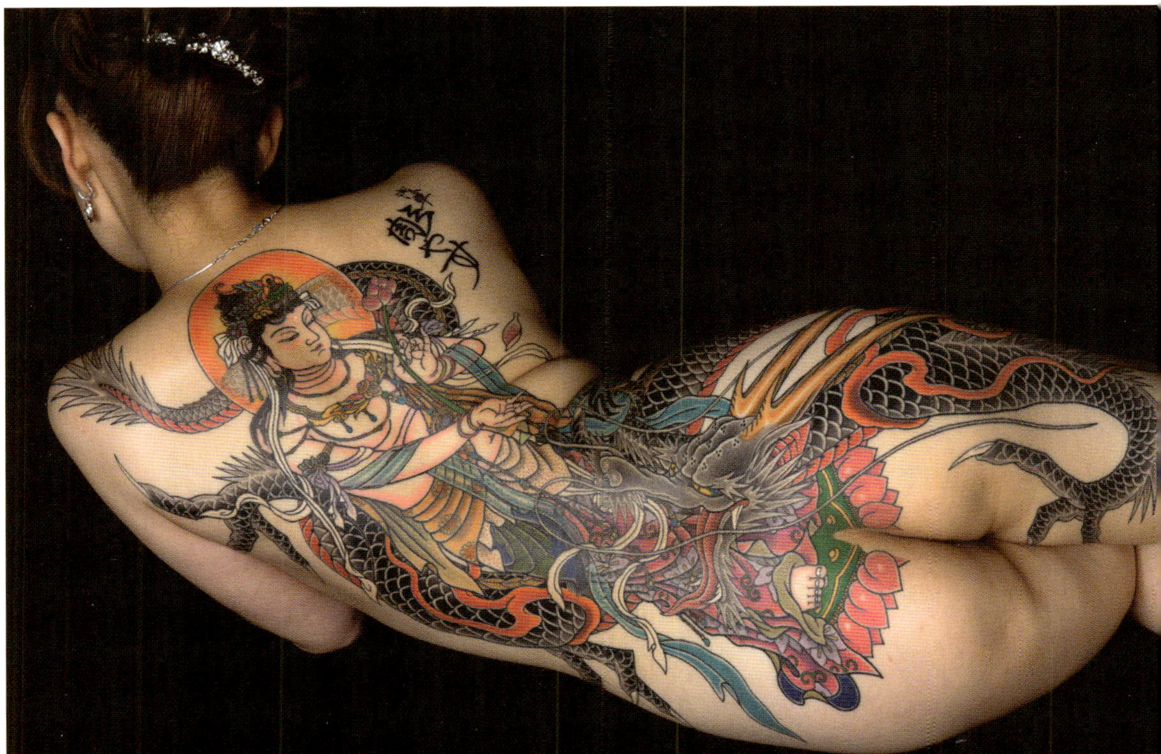

HORIMITSU 彫光

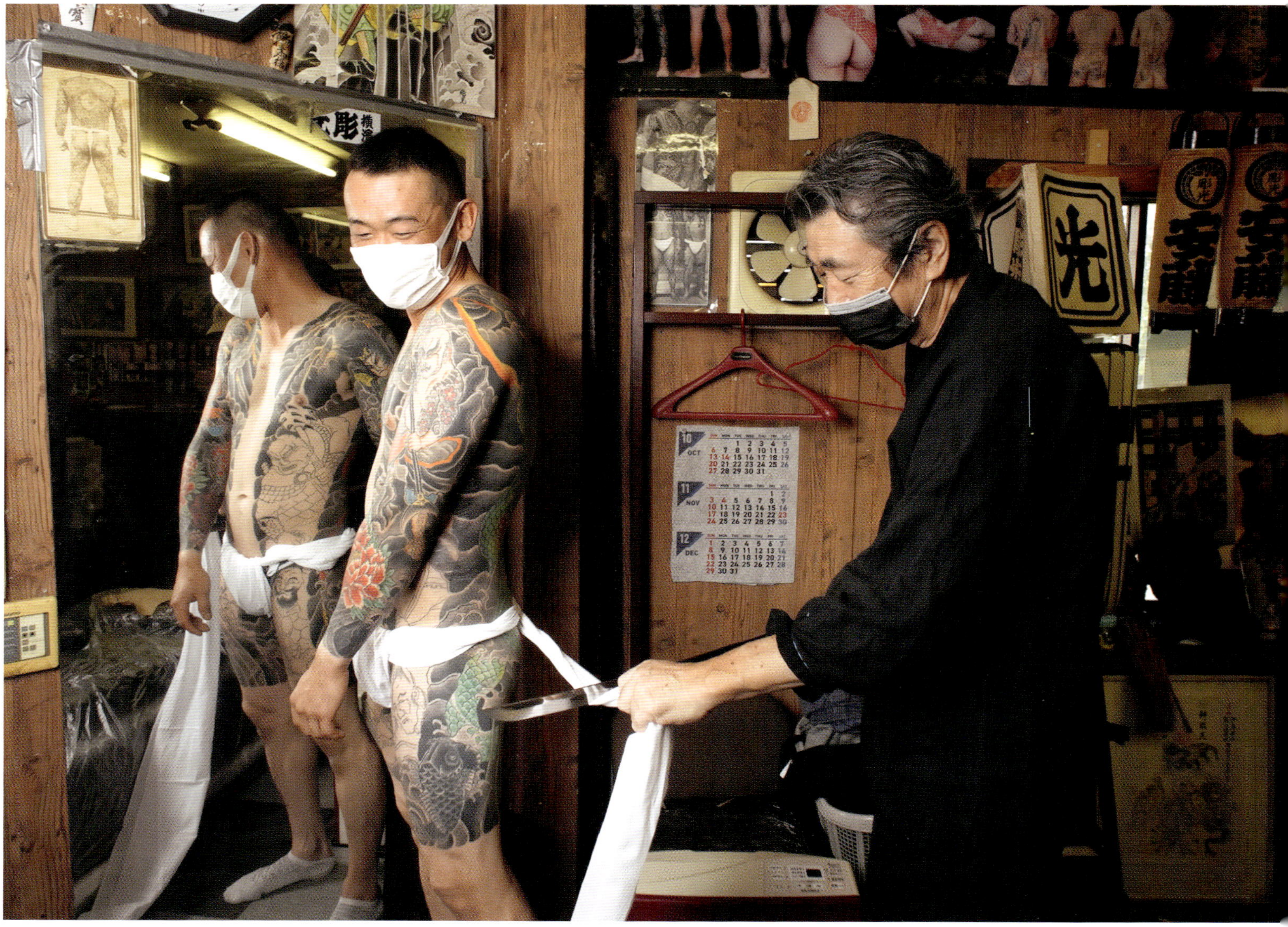

Horimitsu is a tattoo veteran with over 50 years' experience, since the mid-1970s. He is based in the port city of Yokohama, and has a largely underworld clientele. His work is dark and bold, and, in his words, 'depicts the night'.

What was your impression when you first saw a tattoo?

I was a delinquent and making fun of people with shit tattoos. But when I was 15, a person with a *nozarashi* [a skull, a type of memento mori] with snakes oozing out came into a bathhouse where I was, and that person was really scary. I thought, if that person has got tattooed with something frightening, they will be perceived in that way too. I was astounded that a design could be so grotesque and I thought the fact that art can do that is interesting – you can change a person. I was someone who couldn't really feel pain and never thought it was amazing to be able to withstand it. I could tattoo myself with no issue at all. I was more interested in the visuals and I think it connects with a desire to transform.

***How did you start working as a* horishi?**

I was 15 and tattooing at construction sites across Japan. The construction workers would stay in places temporarily and I would tattoo them. I would stay for three to four years and then move on. For example, when I went to a steel-production neighbourhood in Hiroshima, the workers were staying in a large room and I was tattooing in the main living room. They all wanted a tattoo. When I got to be 20 or so, I took

ABOVE
Horimitsu using a samurai sword to cut a *fundoshi* (traditional loincloth).

the name Horimitsu, and in my 30s, I got so busy I couldn't move. In my case it was over 90 per cent *yakuza*, a lot of whom were bosses. There are a lot of headquarters here [in Yokohama]. I am in between two headquarters; they are only 100 metres [330 ft] apart. There are offices everywhere. Having said that, with the changes in the law, there are fewer of the old-style *yakuza* doing things like getting protection money and gambling. Now it is more dangerous, because there are more thugs.

What makes a good traditional Japanese tattoo?

When you look at it from afar and you can see the motif properly. If you can't tell what it is unless you get up really close to it, that is no good. Lately, more and more hobbyists have been getting tattoos and looking at other people's, and because of that, there are beautiful detailed tattoos, but with *wabori* you get them to scare people, so strangers aren't looking at the work up close. You need to be able to see it from 3 metres [10 ft] away. If it is meant to scare someone, you need to tattoo in a way that is ominous, and if you put in a light background, the only reaction you will get is, 'Oh, it's pretty,' and that's it. That is no good!

I don't only tattoo old motifs, I also work on good contemporary things and make sure not to tattoo the same designs – if it is the same character, I try to make the next tattoo even better than the last. If you want heavy *wabori*, come to me, and if you want just pretty stuff that will make people say, 'Beautiful!', maybe go elsewhere.

What do* yakuza *usually want to have tattooed?

Usually the person himself will decide the motif. But, for example, if there is a syndicate that all have *Suikoden* heroes, then they will each have to get a *Suikoden* character, although there are 108 characters to choose from. Or, once I had a group that had to each choose a design with a tiger in it. There are specific syndicates in each region, but I've had clients from all over. A lot of *horishi* are specific to one group, but I don't like being tied down like that. I am really stubborn and I've never liked being told what to do!

How do they treat you?

They are really proper. The higher up they are, the more polite they are; the young delinquents don't seem to know how to behave.

Have you ever got into scary situations?

When I was young, I was really a fighter. I never had any problems with tattooing, but in my regular life I would often get into situations. My body is covered in knife scars. I've been stabbed in my stomach, cut all over the place to the bone! I really don't listen to people. As a student, I was doing Kendo and athletics, and up until the age of 30 I was doing martial arts, but I got busy with work so I stopped.

Explain your apprenticeship system.

Other *ichimon* receive money, but I don't take money from my apprentices. They get tattooed here, but I don't take money otherwise. I didn't learn from anyone myself. Lots of *horishi* are like a franchise, so the more students they have, the more profits they make. I just ask my students to clean the studio over New Year.

If you are doing Japanese tattoos, organized crime members will ask you who has your back. If you have someone with a famous name in your *ichimon*, they will tattoo the bosses of that syndicate so the apprentices will be protected. Otherwise, if you start on your own, they will come to you for sure. When you start and are no good and do a crappy tattoo, they will come over and ask, 'What the hell are you tattooing?'

What were the* yakuza *tabloids?

The tattoo pages in *Jitsuwa Document* [a *yakuza* gossip magazine] were really abysmal. But they didn't realize themselves how bad their tattoos were. My sketches got ripped off in that magazine and the editor was like, 'That is a sign that you are really good.' So nowadays I only do sketches that can't be applied as-is to the body as a transfer.

Explain your tattoos' backgrounds.

In the past, it wasn't common to have elements in the background that were transparent or blurry. Personally, I don't like to use those things that much

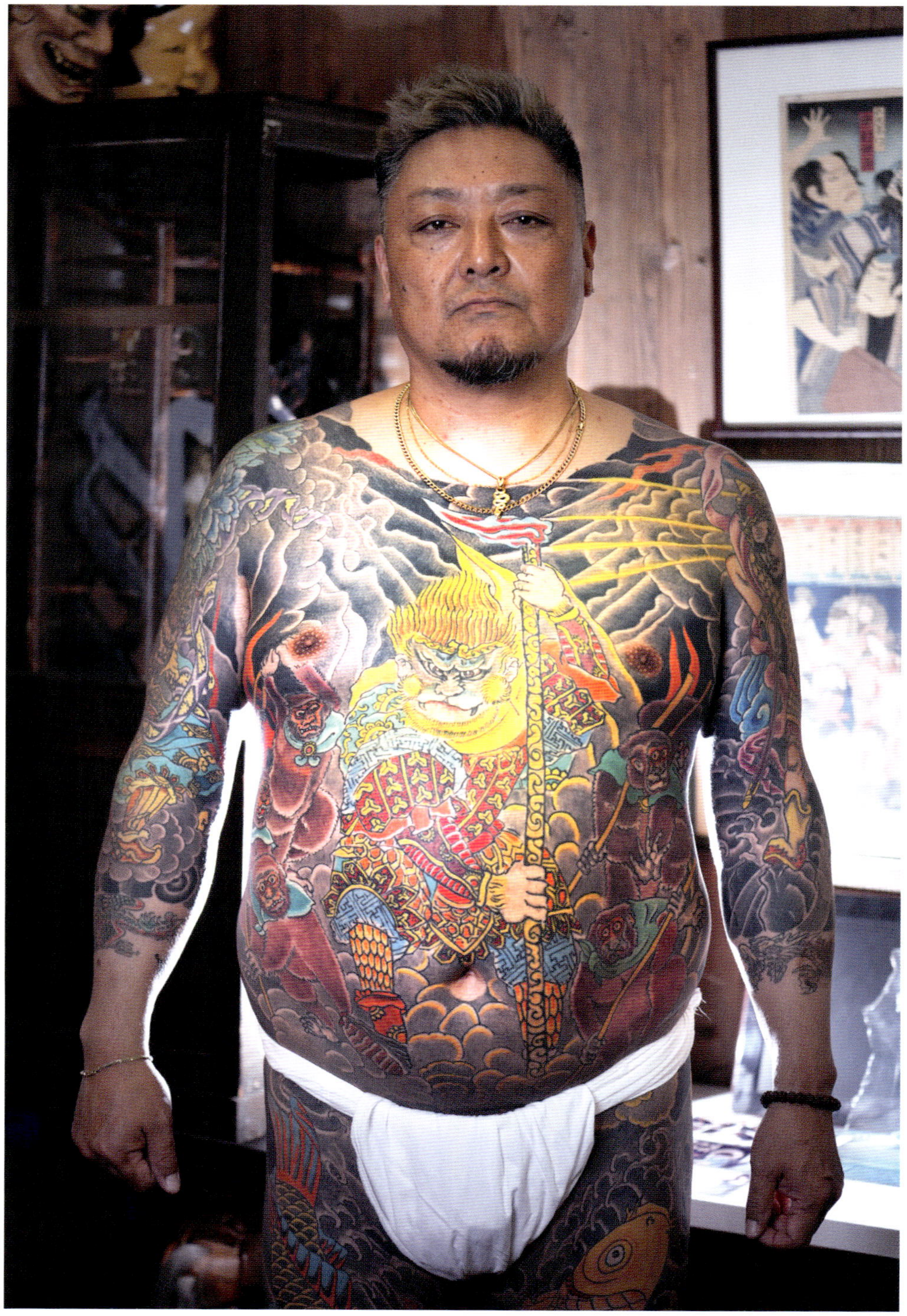

in my work, but nowadays, it's common to have water on the subject that you can see through. In the past, especially with the Japanese traditional style, it was basically hooligans doing the tattooing, and often people who knew nothing about illustrations – it was people who liked to tattoo. I think that is the reason they were so basic before. Nowadays, the tattoo artists really study!

What are the main characteristics of* tebori *tattoos?
The resulting work is deep. It is the same as in clothing, where you are really particular with the stitching. Also, the older the work is, the more depth you get, because I use a technique called *hane-tsuki*, where the ink goes in really thickly. If you use this technique, as time goes on, the ink blends into the body and gets deeper in colour.

ABOVE
A dense *soushinbori* (a suit that covers most of the body) with the Monkey King as the central motif, by Horimitsu.

OPPOSITE
He uses *itsutsuboshi* (literally 'five star') ink from Kobaien, a famous *sumi* store in Nara prefecture. They simmer rapeseed oil, not regular oil, to make it, and it is hard to grind.

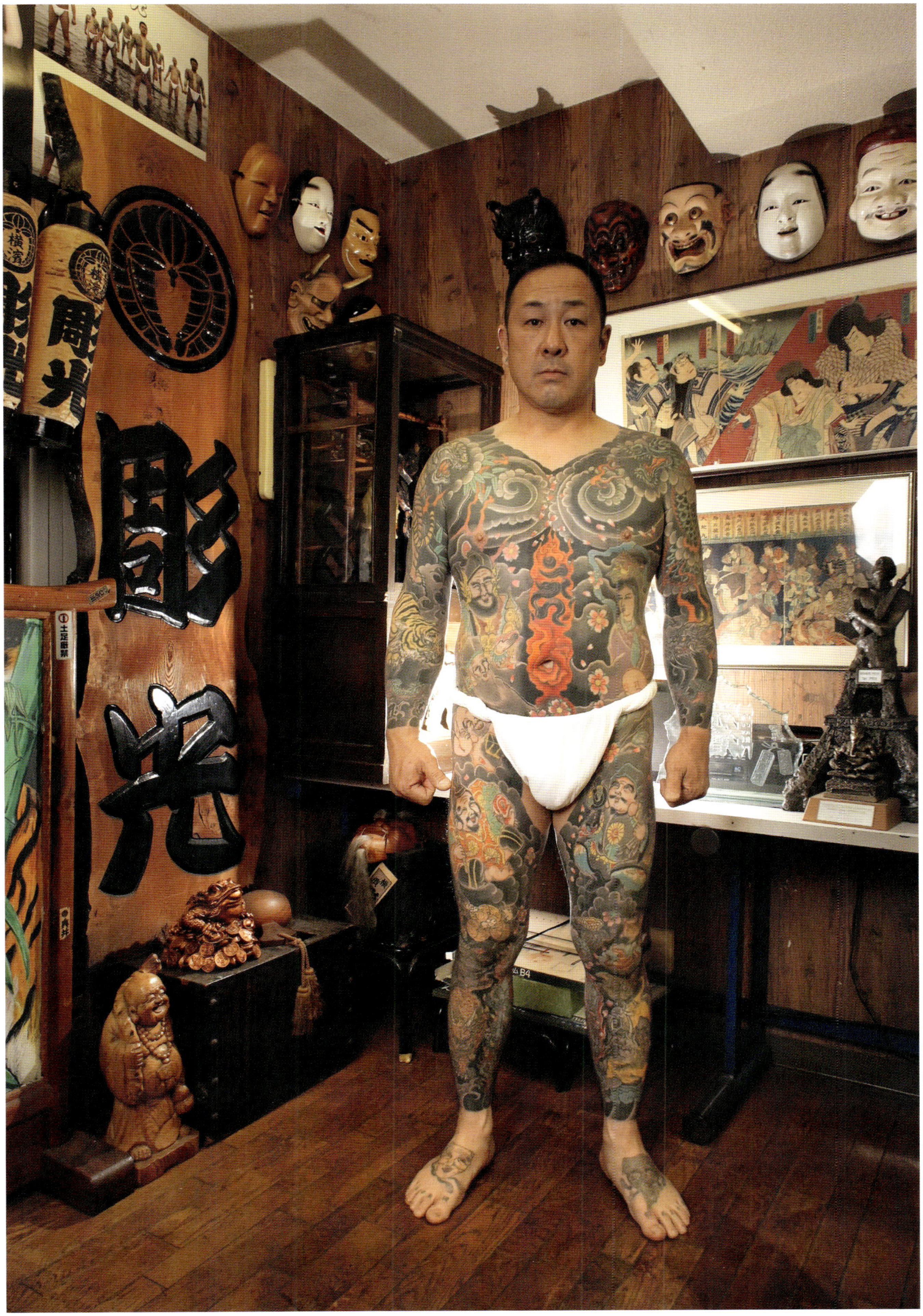
彫光

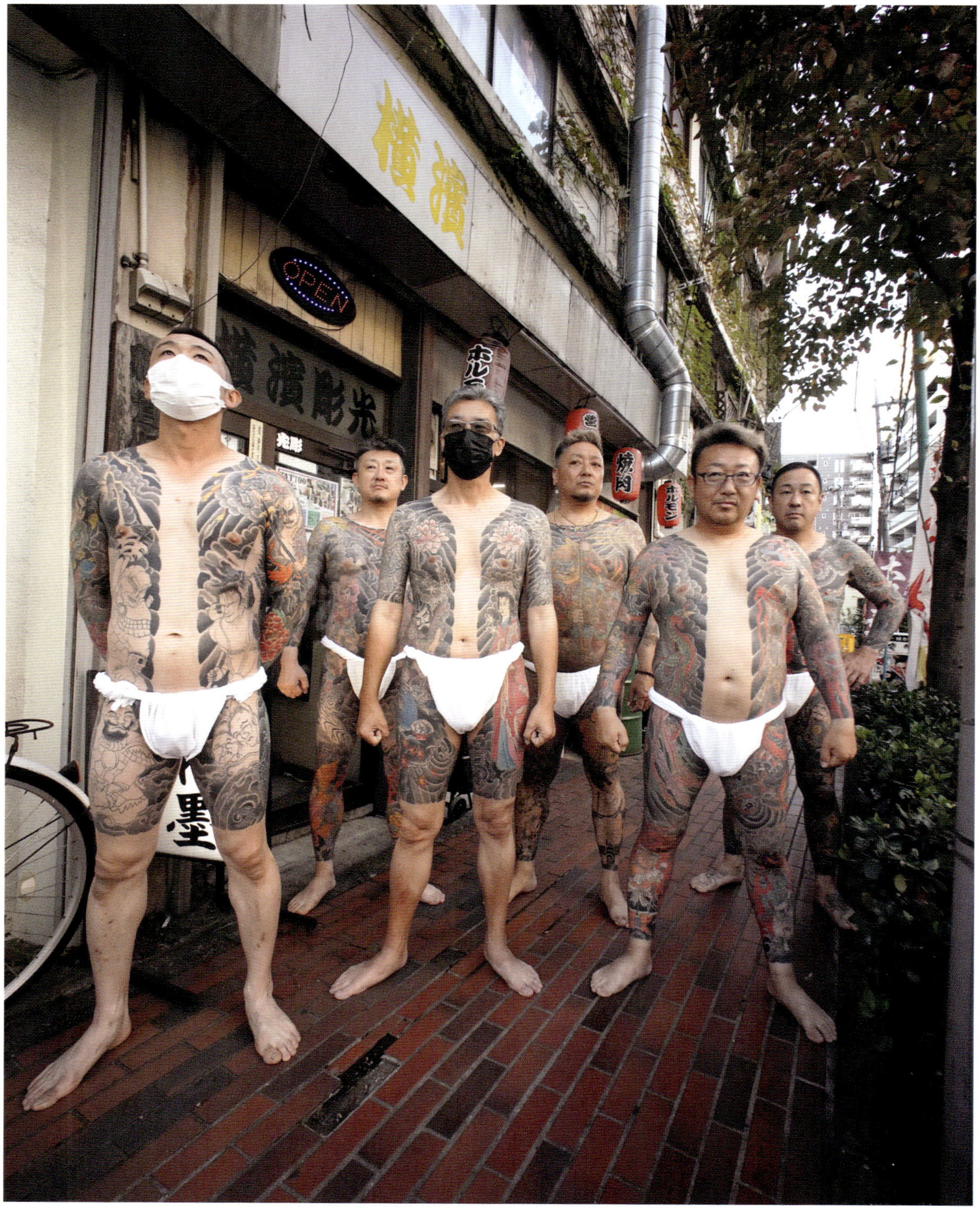

ABOVE
Outside Horimitsu's studio in Yokohama.

OPPOSITE
Horimitsu is known for hosting year-end gatherings called *bonenkai* at a Kanagawa prefecture hotpot eatery with his heavily tattooed clients.

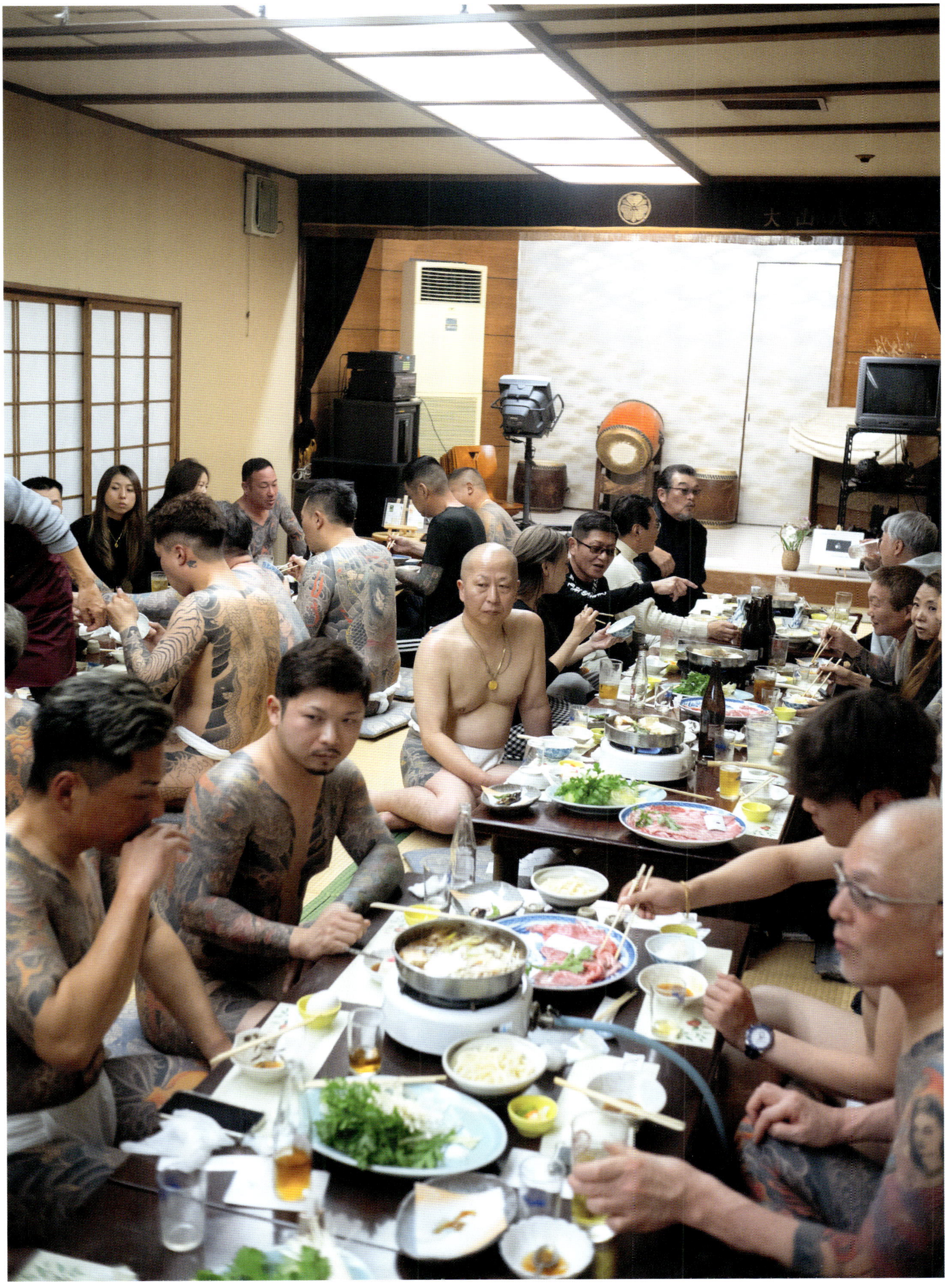

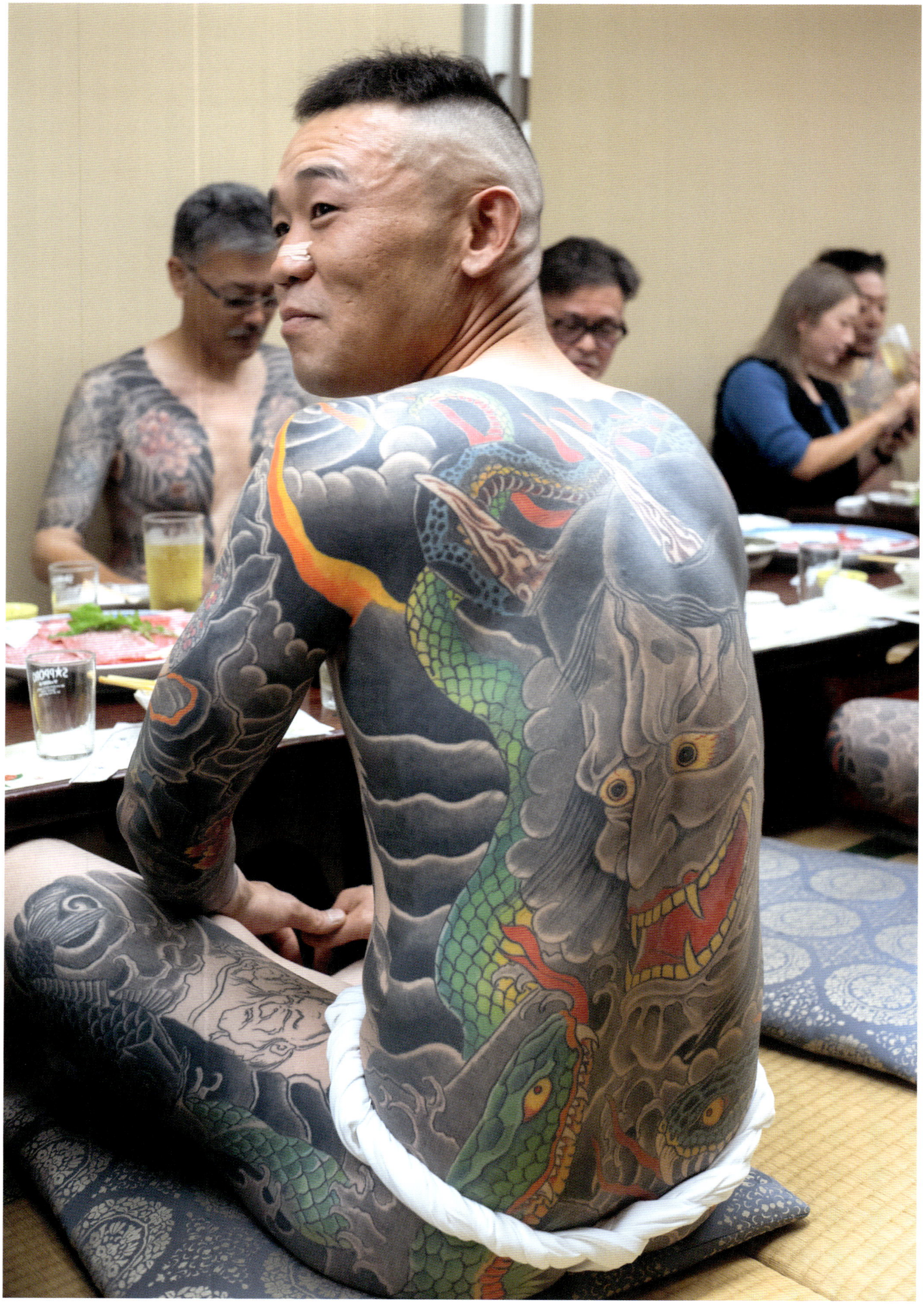

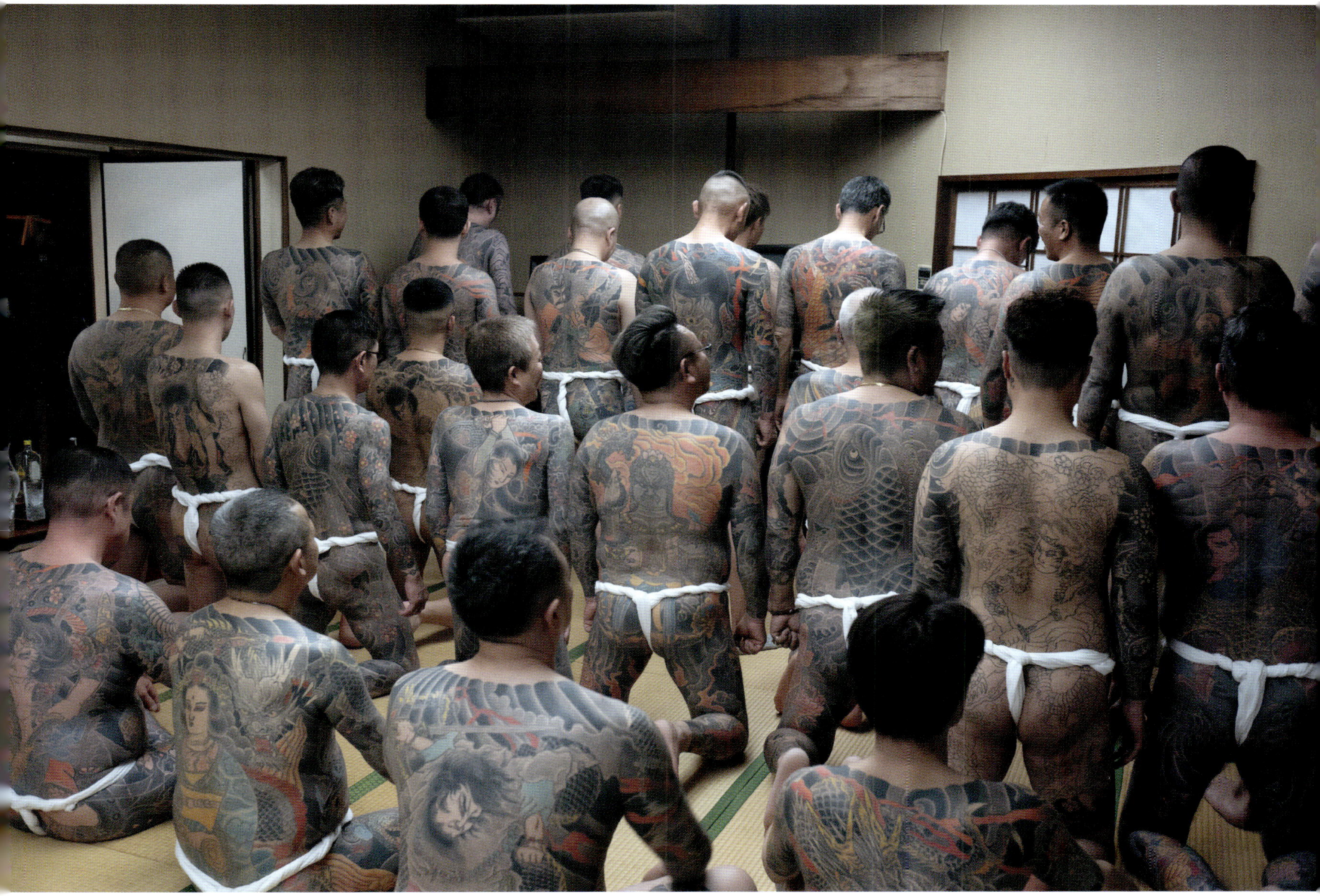

OPPOSITE
One of Horimitsu's clients at the *bonenkai*. With the *hanetsuki* technique, the work improves over time and the colours become more rich.

ABOVE
Horimitsu's clients at a *bonenkai* gathering.

HORICHO II 彫長

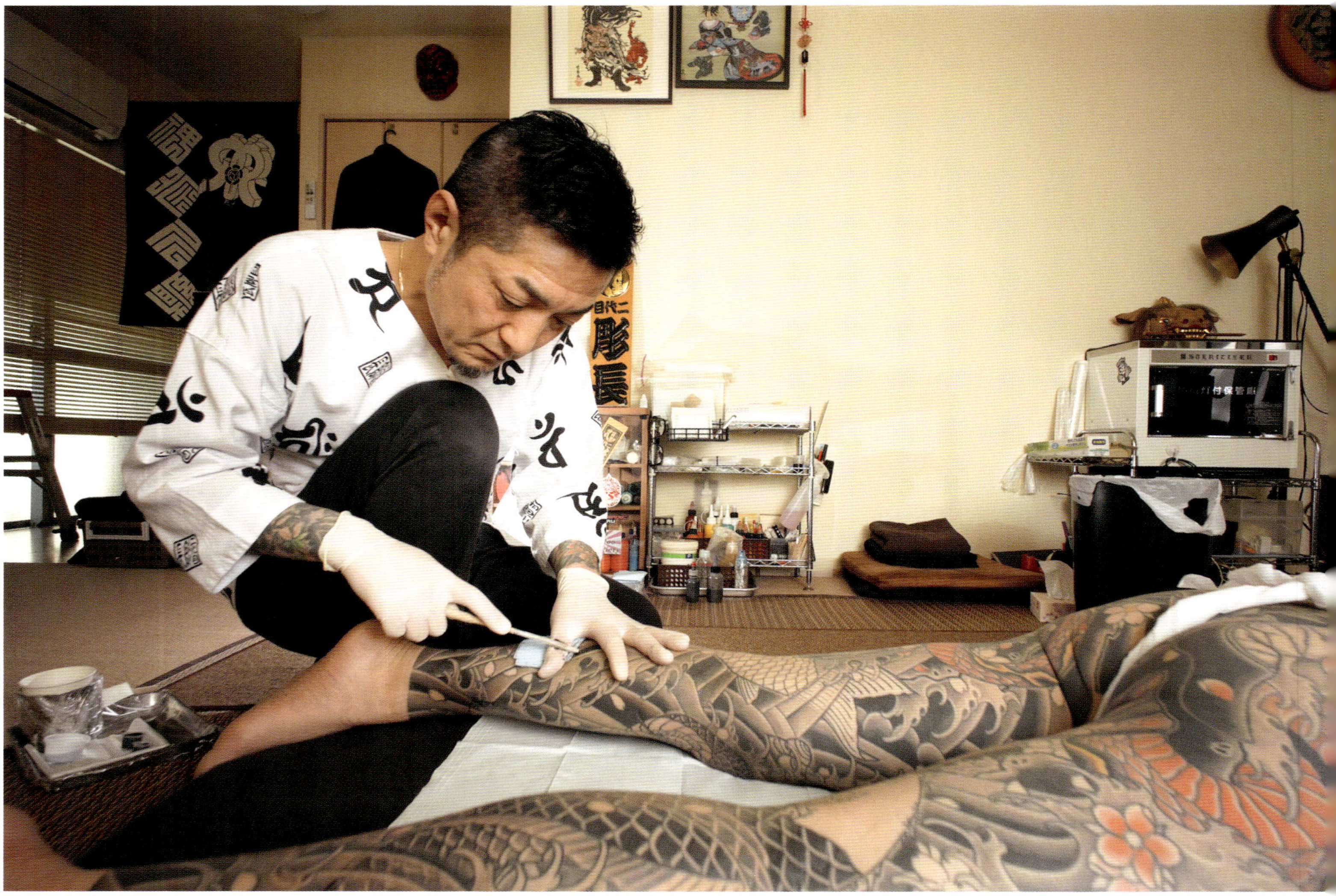

ABOVE
Horicho II at his apartment in Asakusa. Rather than tattoo shops, most *horishi* work out of discreet apartments.

OPPOSITE
He is best known for his *Suikoden* and warrior imagery.

Horicho II is based in the tattoo mecca of Japan, Tokyo's Asakusa area, and studied under the legendary *horishi* Horicho I, which is particularly evident in his dramatic backgrounds. He is known especially for his *Suikoden* and warrior imagery.

How did you meet Horicho I?

Horicho had a small museum in his studio's waiting room with artefacts, and I was getting a small tattoo from one of his apprentices. I thought the old-school *horishi* wouldn't meet, let alone tattoo, regular people, so I'd just be there looking at the items. When the apprentice went to Italy, I waited, but he didn't come back. I asked the shop manager, '*Sensei* (teacher) wouldn't tattoo a kid like me, right?' However, I was told he would with only a 3,000 yen [£16/$20] price difference. I'd seen his work in books, but in real life it just has a different atmosphere. I can't put it in words, but it is the colour of *sumi* (ink), it isn't pure black, and I felt that it was just right.

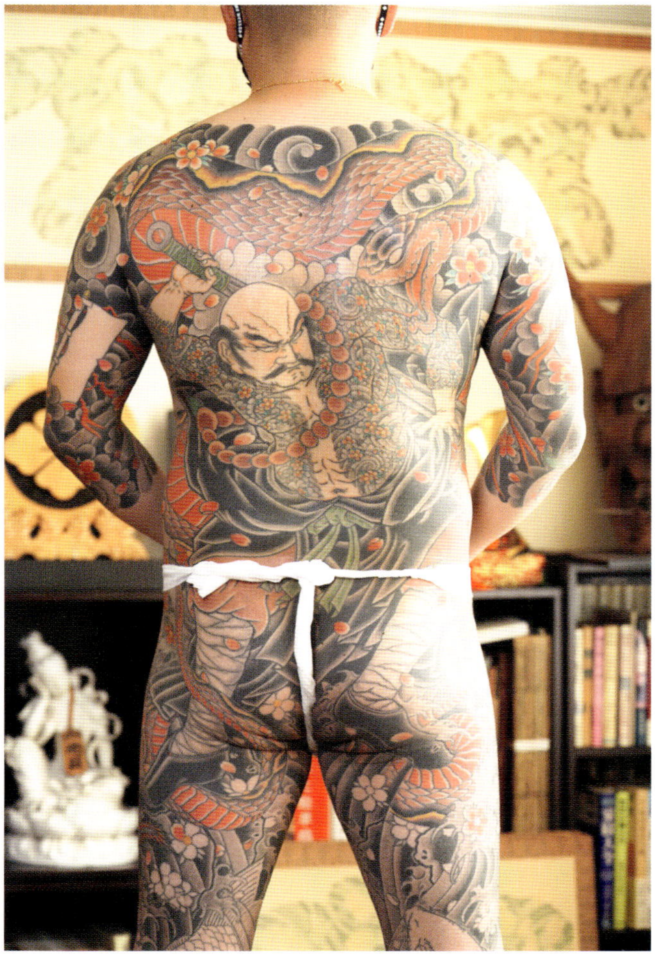

His backgrounds and the main characters are really distinctive. Overall, when you see his work from afar, rather than having that *yakuza*-like impact, his work is more subtle. I think that is what he is aiming for. Clients usually say that the background composition is good, and his gradations are outstanding.

I went three or four times and then asked to be an apprentice, and brought enough money so I could wait outside his door for three days. At first he said he wouldn't take on apprentices, but asked me to bring in some illustrations and he would have a look. He was like, 'Oh, you won't continue anyway, so why don't you come over?' He was strict and if you were five minutes late, he would say, 'Go home.' The *horishi* of the old days were like that.

What kinds of artefacts were in Horicho I's studio?

He would cut out pages from *yakuza* magazines like *Jitsuwa Document* and write comments on them, like, 'The scales are the wrong way up,' or there would be a tattoo of an emaciated Fudo Myo-o and he would write comments like, 'Is this Fudo on amphetamines?' It was an era where tattoo artists were really like kings.

What is the difference between your generation of tattooers and the next, who rely heavily on social media?

I would say there are the [tattoo magazine] *Tattoo Burst* types and the *Jitsuwa Document* types. The types that were around since the *Document* days, say people over 60, were basically apprentices in places that were exclusively tattooing the *yakuza*. These people were unlikely to have illustrative skill or knowledge, it was mostly delinquents. People in their 50s and younger remember the tattoo boom, but there was this notion that you had to enter a famous *ichimon*, like Horicho's or Horitoku's, to get protection. Tattoers now are the second generation of apprentices, in that the direct apprentices of the older generation now have their own *deshi* (apprentices).

If you are crazy about exposure then you will win with Instagram, but I don't think it is about numbers.

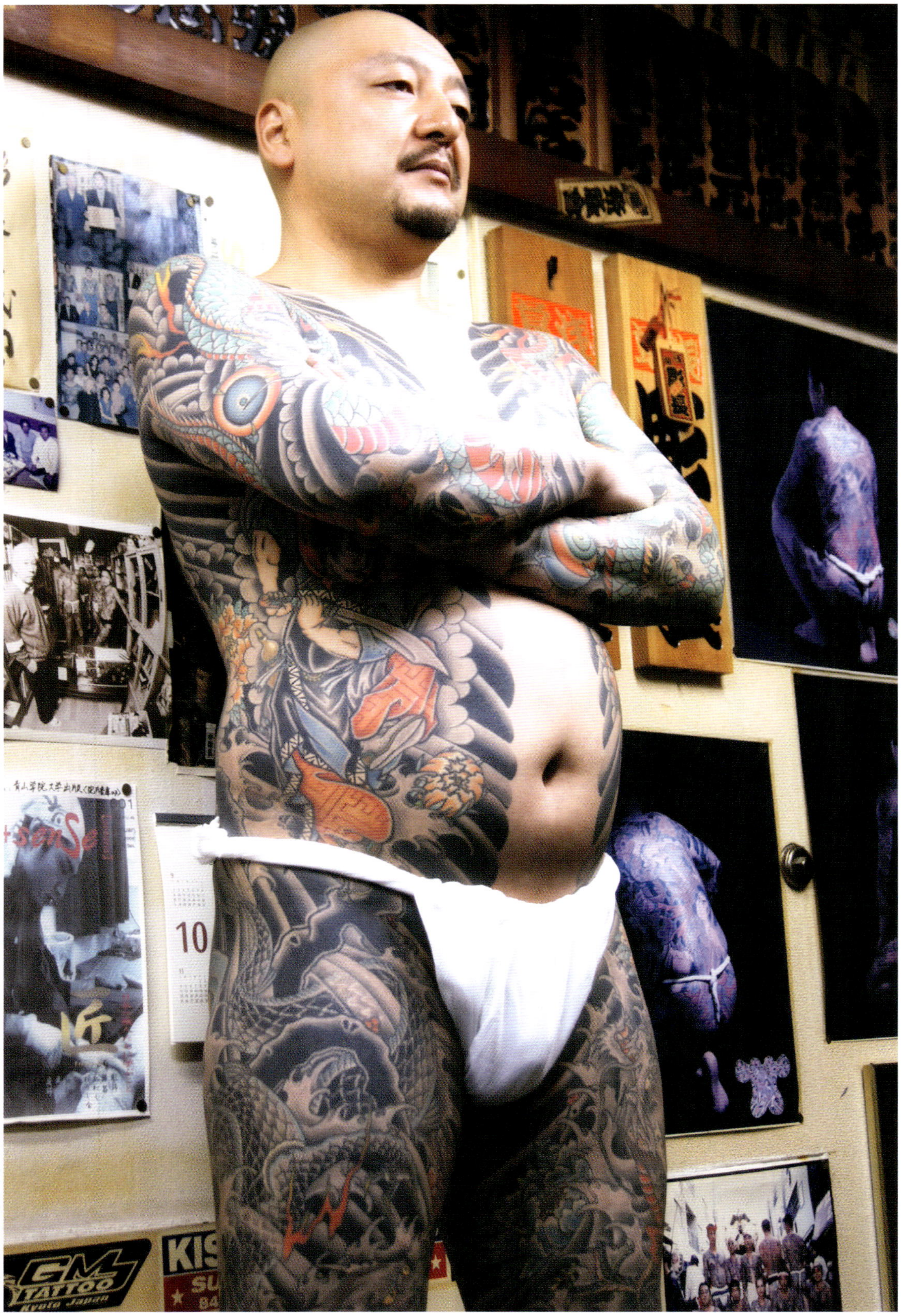

ABOVE
Horicho II deliberately degrades his colours to make them a bit old-looking, as he thinks the inks produced today are 'too pretty'.

OPPOSITE
The wall of Horicho II's former studio in Tokyo's Senzoku neighbourhood, next to Yoshiwara, the Edo-era red-light district.

It is more important to attract customers and to be able to complete pieces. Someone with 10,000 followers, I don't think they'll get 2,000 clients, unless it is only for one-points. Our world is about tattooing suits, and they don't make sense unless you complete them. I think the perspective is different. The younger generation are very much Western tattoo people. With YouTube *wabori* artists, I always think they say too much. Nowadays, it is people who blab that win, but I really wonder if there is no one above them to tell them to shut up.

Do you work with machines, or* tebori *(hand-poked) style?

I work *tebori*-style because I want to work in a characteristic style that is from Japan, and I will continue to tattoo in this way while I am physically able to! I occasionally have the feeling that I want to work with a machine and do more realistic tattoos, but there are so many people who do that already. However, I use a machine for the line work – that is the way it has been done since my teacher's time. To do everything in *tebori* makes the outline a bit staggered, and there are only a few people that want to take the time to do the whole thing only in *tebori*.

What is the basic difference in the outcome of the tattoo when you insert it by hand?

To be hyperbolic, the work with *tebori* might seem unrefined, as the machines are so good that the work looks like *nihonga* (Japanese classic painting), looks like paint, but when it gets exposed to the sun, it fades. With *tebori*, on the other hand, the colour gradually concentrates and blends with the skin. It is to do with the depth of the needles – we gently flick up the skin and the ink goes in underneath, as opposed to a machine that is on the surface. When you do it by machine, I mean no disrespect, but the machine moves on its own and assists you, whereas there is the sensation with *tebori* that you are inserting the ink each time, one movement by one, which is something I really appreciate.

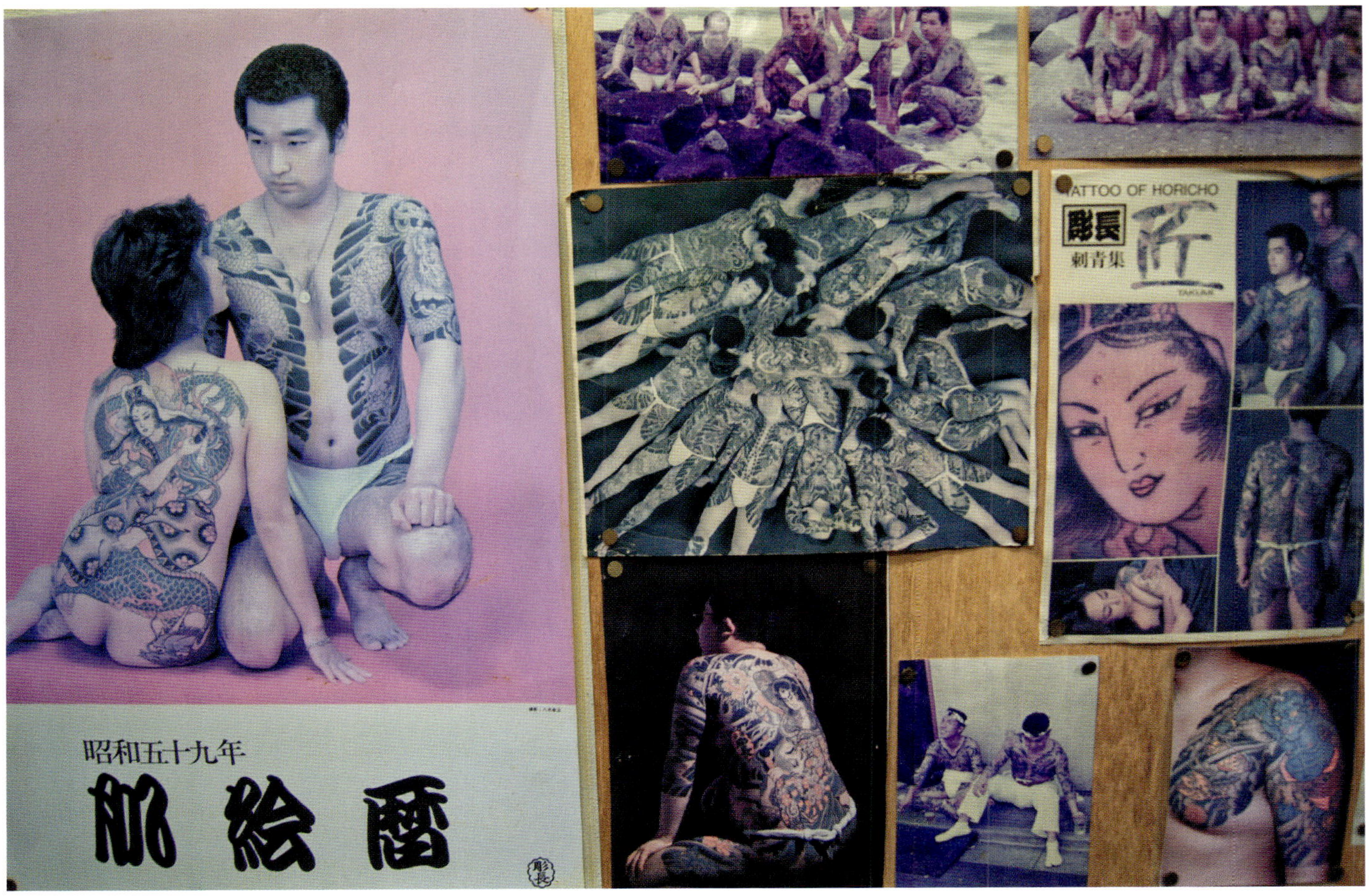

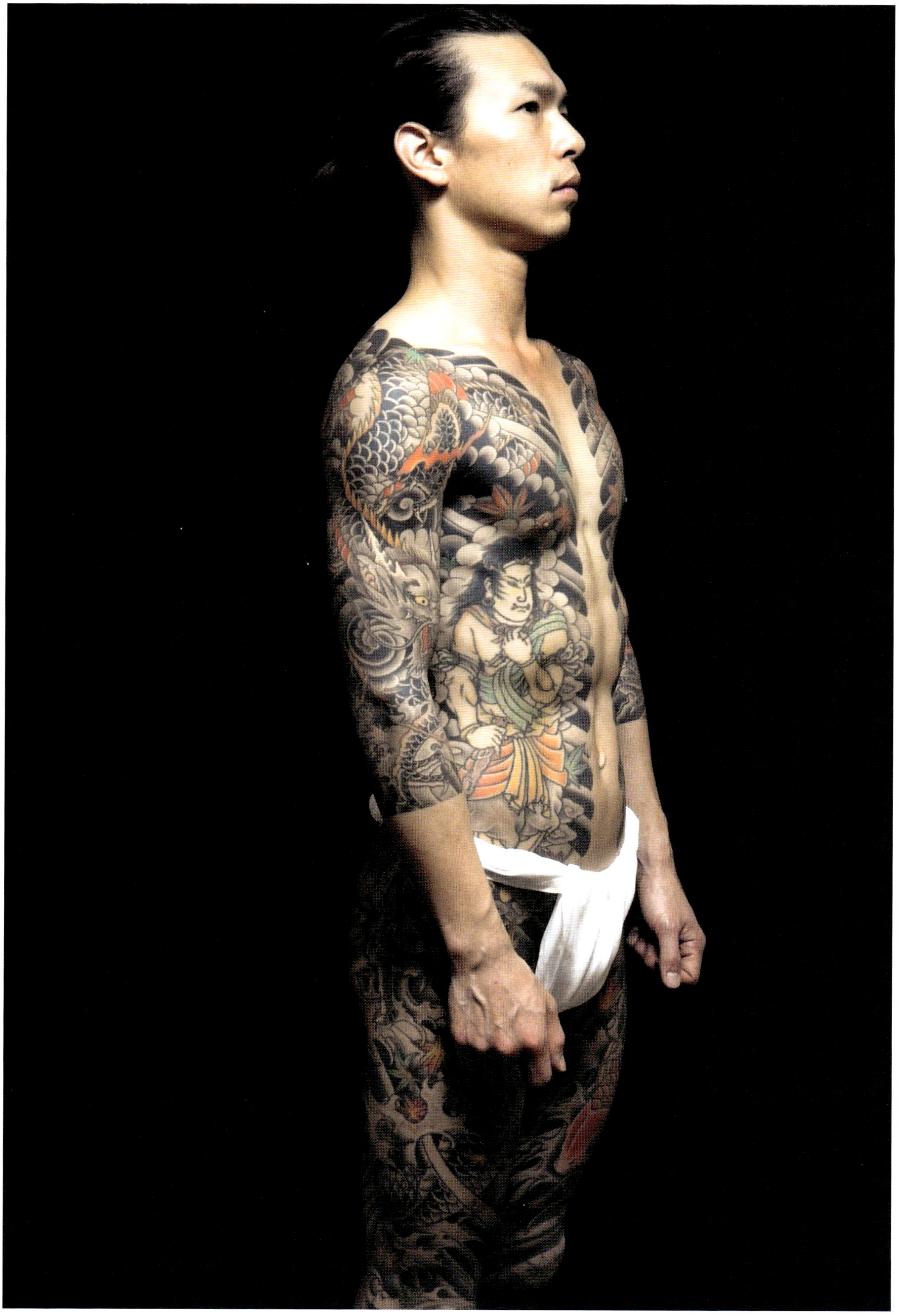

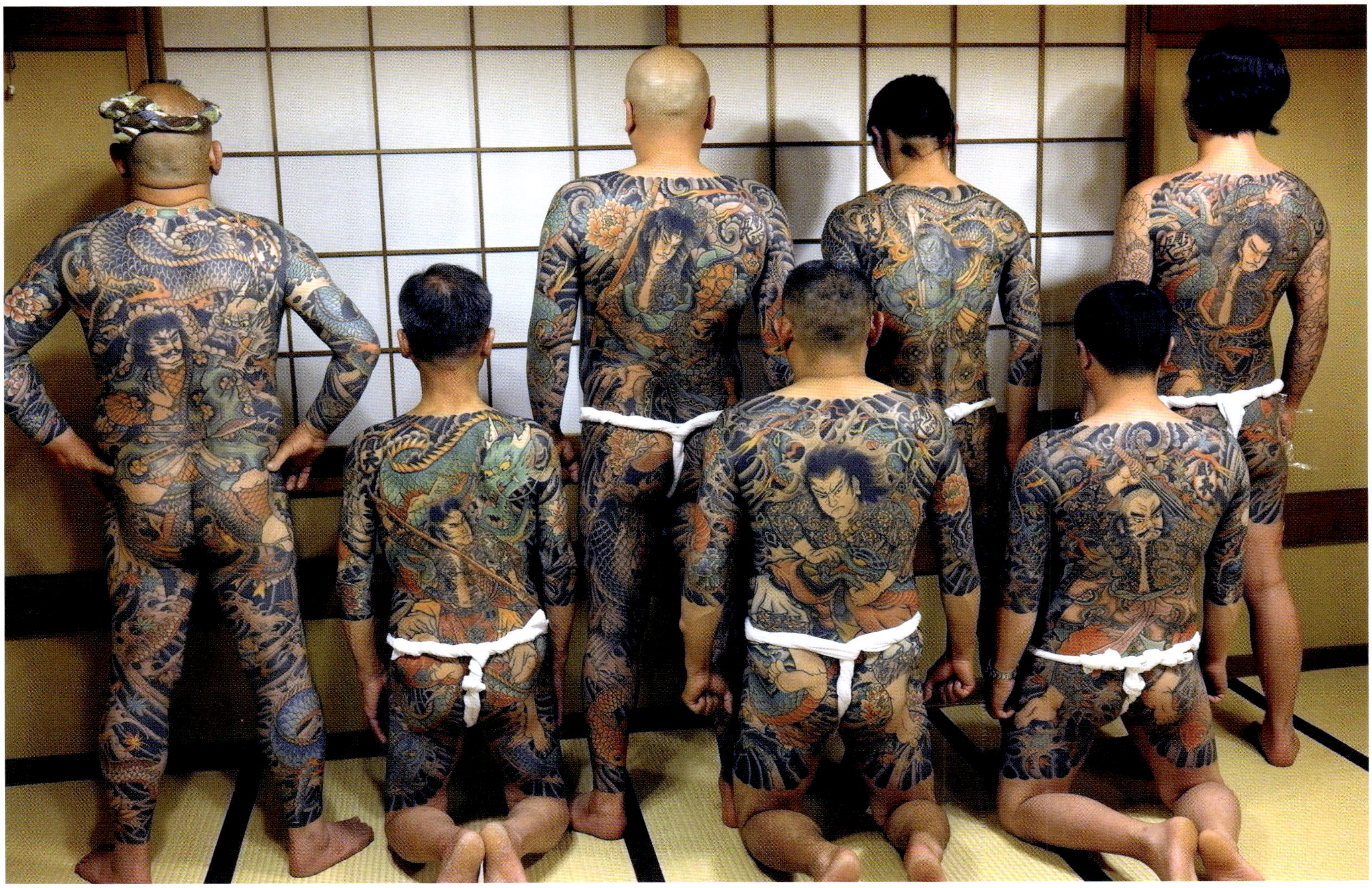

OPPOSITE
Horicho II's late master Horicho I was located in Asakusa, the mecca of Japanese tattoo culture. Many of his older clients are still heavily present at Japanese festivals. Horicho II takes on this lineage and his studio is located next door to Senso-ji temple.

ABOVE
Horicho II's clients at a restaurant in Asakusa. Almost all the motifs are *Suikoden* heroes. Kyokutei Bakin's version of the novel, published in 1805, had a lot of influence on the *irezumi* of the Edo period because of the *ukiyo-e* woodblock prints depicting its motifs by Katsushika Hokusai. Hokusai was the first to visualize the characters with simple tattoos. It was Utagawa Kuniyoshi who made them epic, full-body renditions in his series *One Hundred and Eight Heroes of the Popular 'Water Margin'*.

Who are your clients now?
A lot of my clients get tattooed when they become parents. I have older clients. I had one person who got tattooed for the first time at 70 years old. He retired from being a taxi driver and came to me for over a year. He didn't move at all, totally like an Edo-style guy, and would declare, 'It doesn't hurt at all!' He was so still, I wondered if he was dead. Some clients want a tattoo when their work is going well, for example, on their back, and after five years, if the business is going successfully, that person will then get the front. Or I had one client with two kids and he got two carps, things like that.

Nowadays, I get regular people – even a university teacher and a politician, although it is a real secret. Lately, there are very few scary people. At the moment I don't even have a small number of *yakuza* clients. In our case, however, *sensei* [Horicho I] wouldn't tattoo the local *yakuza*, only the ones from out of town, because if he went outside and bumped into them, it was a hassle, like, 'Let's go drinking!' and he couldn't even walk down the road picking his nose! If it was his day off, and he was eating soba noodles, they would be like, 'Look! He is eating that soba! He must be not busy these days!' He would only tattoo them if he liked the person, but if one person went to him, they would all want to go to him, so he tended to focus only on *yakuza* from Sendai and Ibaraki prefectures.

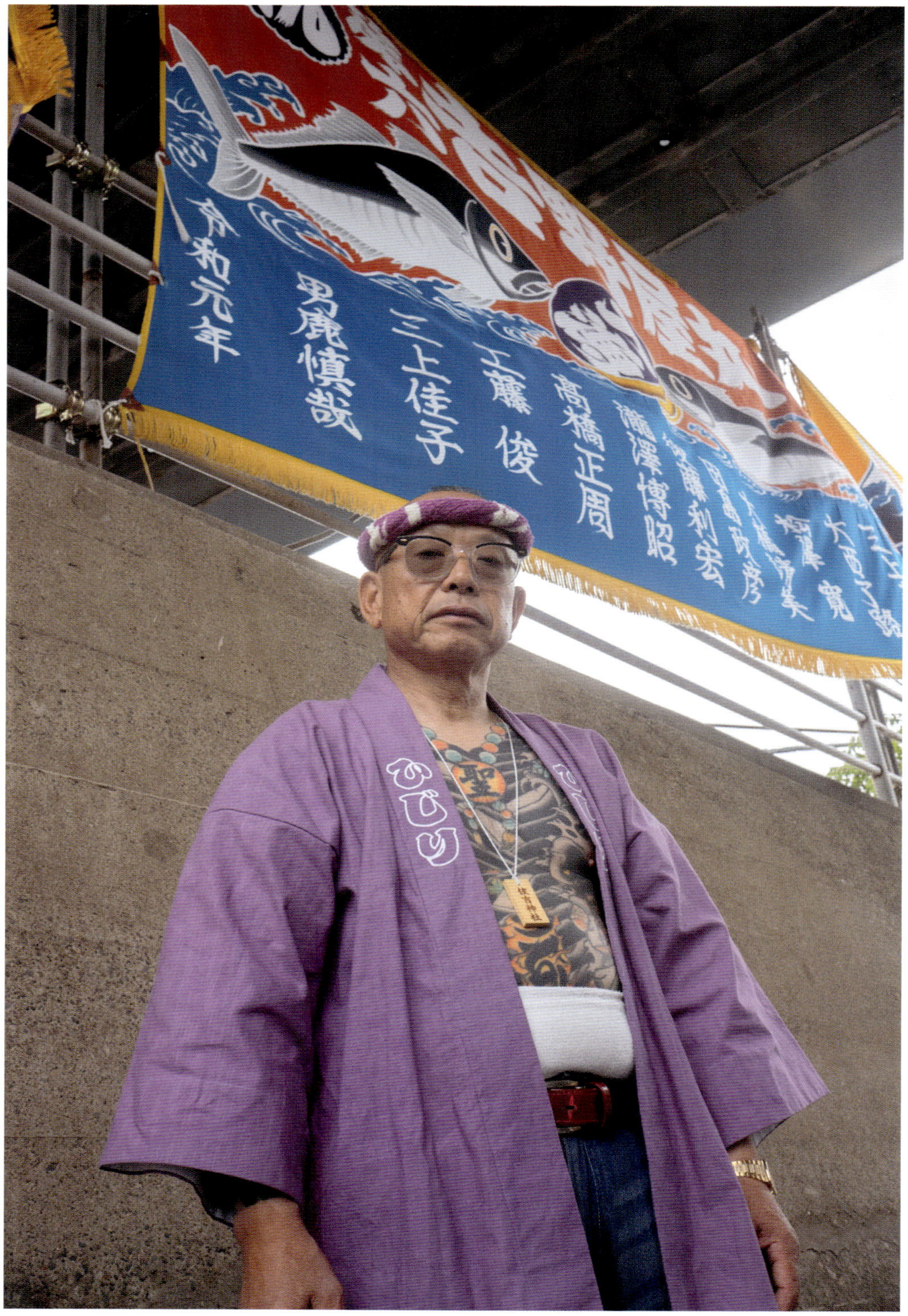

ABOVE
Fisherman in Chiba prefecture with a suit by Horicho II. A former Tsukiji fish market worker, many of his colleagues are tattooed as well. 'I wanted Horicho to tattoo me,' he explains. 'The tattoo has to have the artist's heart and soul. In Tsukiji fish market where I used to work, a lot of people had tattoos, but many of them have passed away. I wanted to be like those elders and to have a tattoo was aspirational. The *horishi* really needs to be able to draw well to do *Suikoden* motifs. My tattoo took five years, but I was really working hard to get my piece done. I was so motivated that overall, I ended up making more money than I spent on the tattoo. I think people with half-assed ink live half-assed lives.'

OPPOSITE
A fish market worker in Chiba prefecture with Horicho II's work.

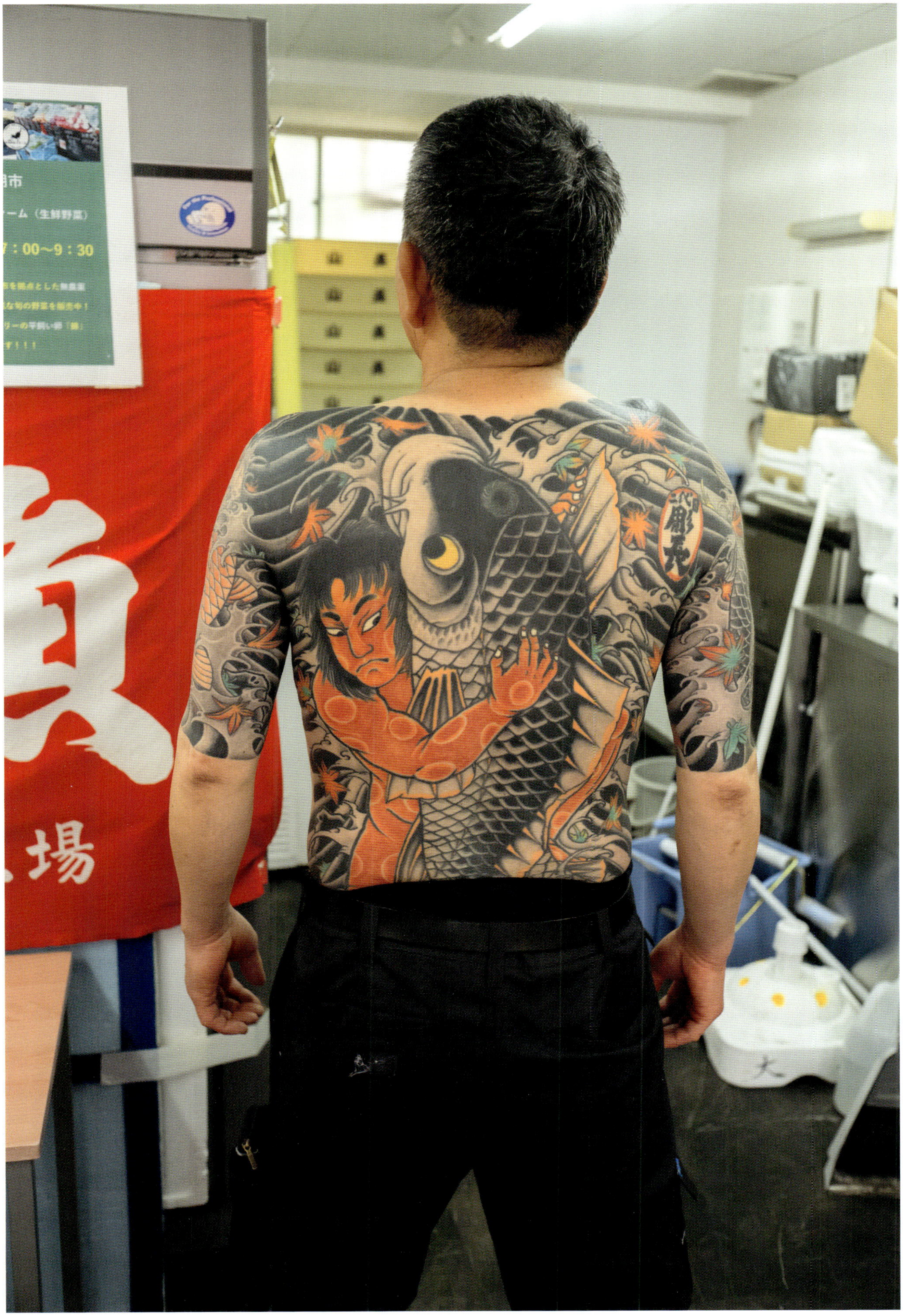
7：00～9：30
場

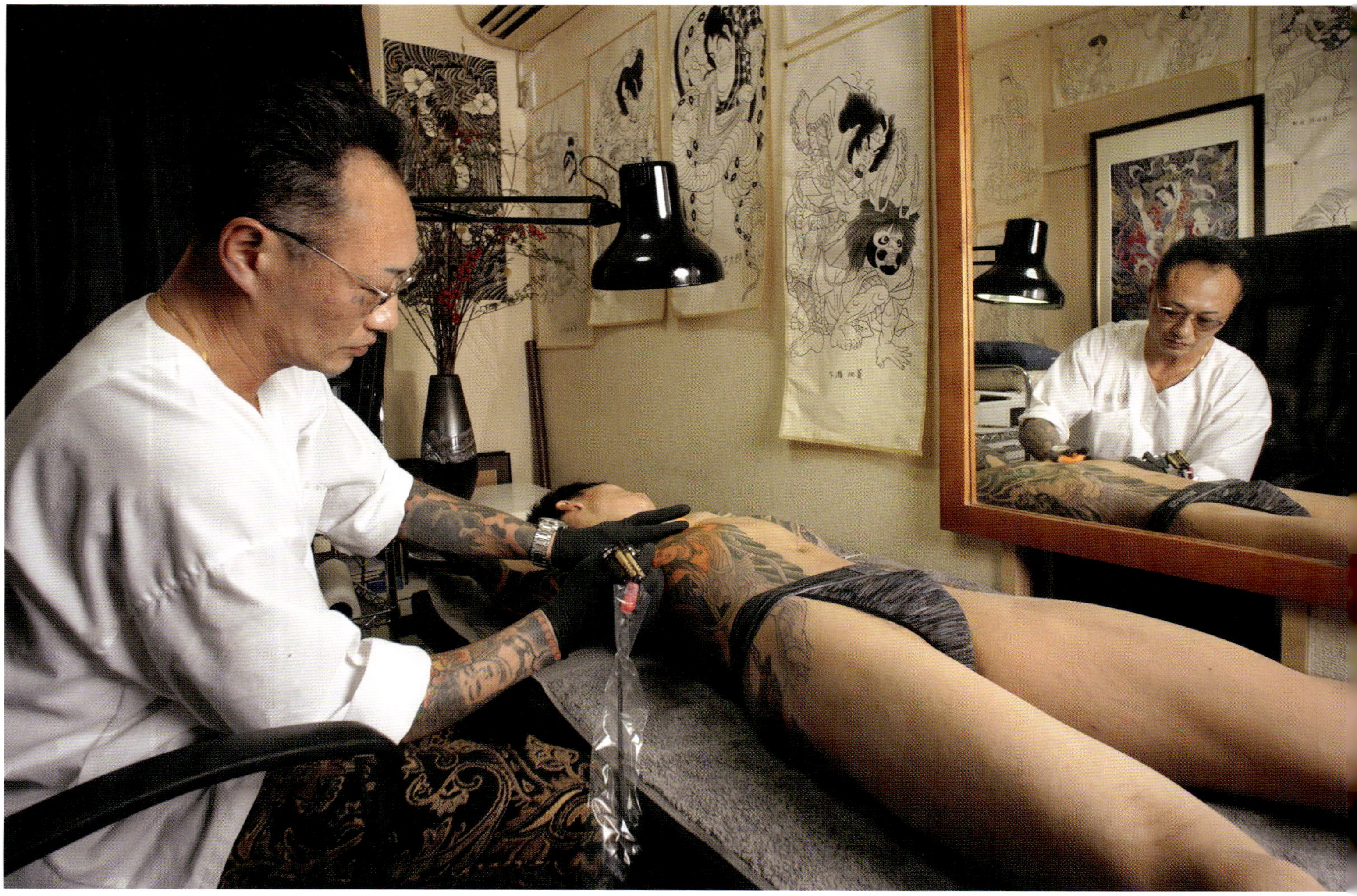

ABOVE
Horiken works with a machine, but uses *sumi* ink.

OPPOSITE
Sumi ink boxes at Horiken's studio's Shinto shrine in Machida.

Horiken is a *horishi* based in Machida, Kanagawa. He specializes in classic *irezumi* but uses a machine with *sumi* ink for the gradations. His work is intensely detailed and meticulous. His tattoos have the heavy atmosphere of underground work, but manage to appeal to young clients as well.

***How did you get started as a* horishi?**

I was a client of my teacher and then I asked to become his apprentice. It was an era when there weren't that many tattoos. I asked my teacher and he said, 'That's no problem, come in tomorrow.' I went independent after a year and a half, I was really fast. The other apprentices were living there but I was commuting. I've been doing this since 1993.

Bonten Taro began your tattoo family lineage. What are the characteristics of his work?

Shodai (the first) Bonten Taro was using a machine. He was making machines on his own; he was one of the pioneers of that in Japan. Machines are faster than *tebori*. He was a manga illustrator and drew *gekiga* (an adult-orientated dramatic manga style), so his work is more original than straight up *ukiyo-e*. I do pieces in his style as well, but I am the student of Bonten II and my work is based on *ukiyo-e*. I do a lot of *musha-e* (woodblocks that depict samurai and warriors).

***What are the benefits of being in an* ichimon?**

Horishi in the past had an outlaw kind of vibe and I was influenced by my master's personality. He was partial to manners and hierarchy. I think tattoos and *irezumi* are different in that *irezumi* has a hidden beauty. Particularly for women, it is better to do it in a place you can't see it. I don't tattoo past the

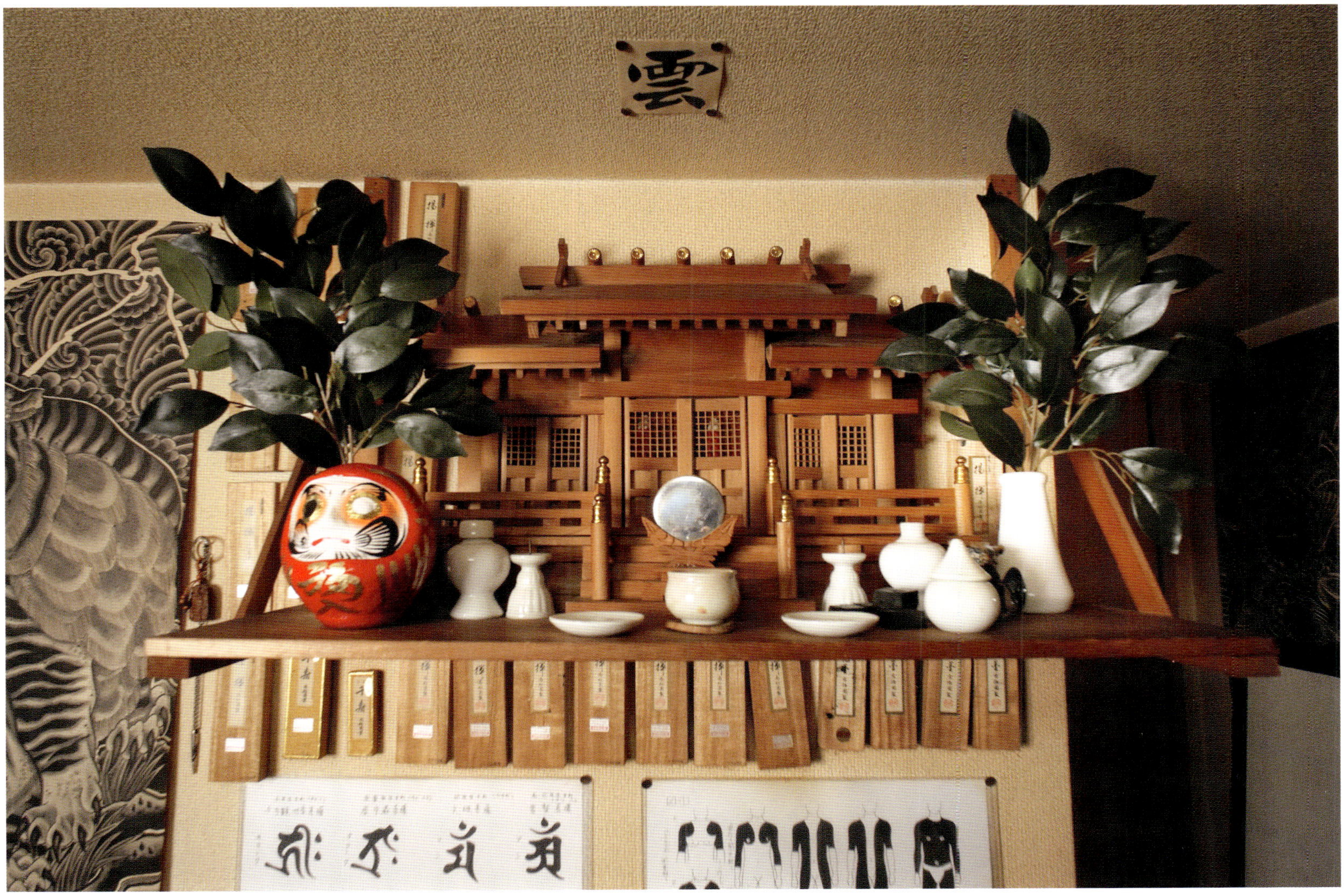

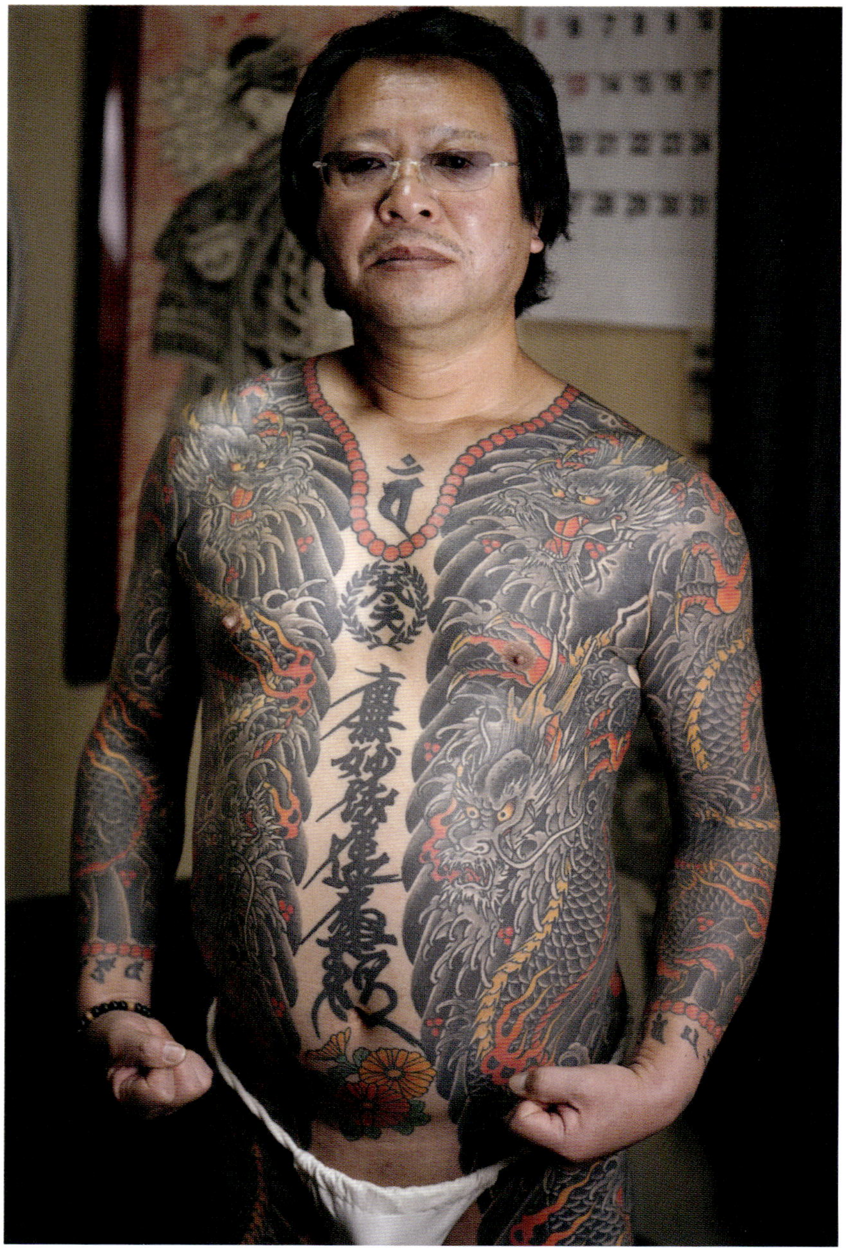

wrists on anyone, so there won't be any detriment to someone's daily life. I don't want them ever to regret getting inked.

Rather than being an artist, I am an artisan, and I do take these outlaw sensibilities into consideration, rather than just making something beautiful. With a *horishi* like Horitoku, for instance, his masculinity is present in his work.

What sorts of people are your clients?
Mostly artisans working in architecture or designers, people who have their own companies so have some flexibility in time. I get a lot of people in their late 20s and 30s, but I had a client in who was 65 and getting his first piece. One of my clients came in three to five times a week, three hours each session, and he finished his *munewari* (a full-body tattoo with a split down the middle) in 6 months. In the past, I was getting around 80 per cent organized crime members but now it is almost zero. It was a gradual shift. There are a lot of people who come from Instagram. I don't have any dips in work, I am just busy all the time.

ABOVE
Heavy and dense work on a client.

OPPOSITE
Meticulous details on a *nijubori* motif.

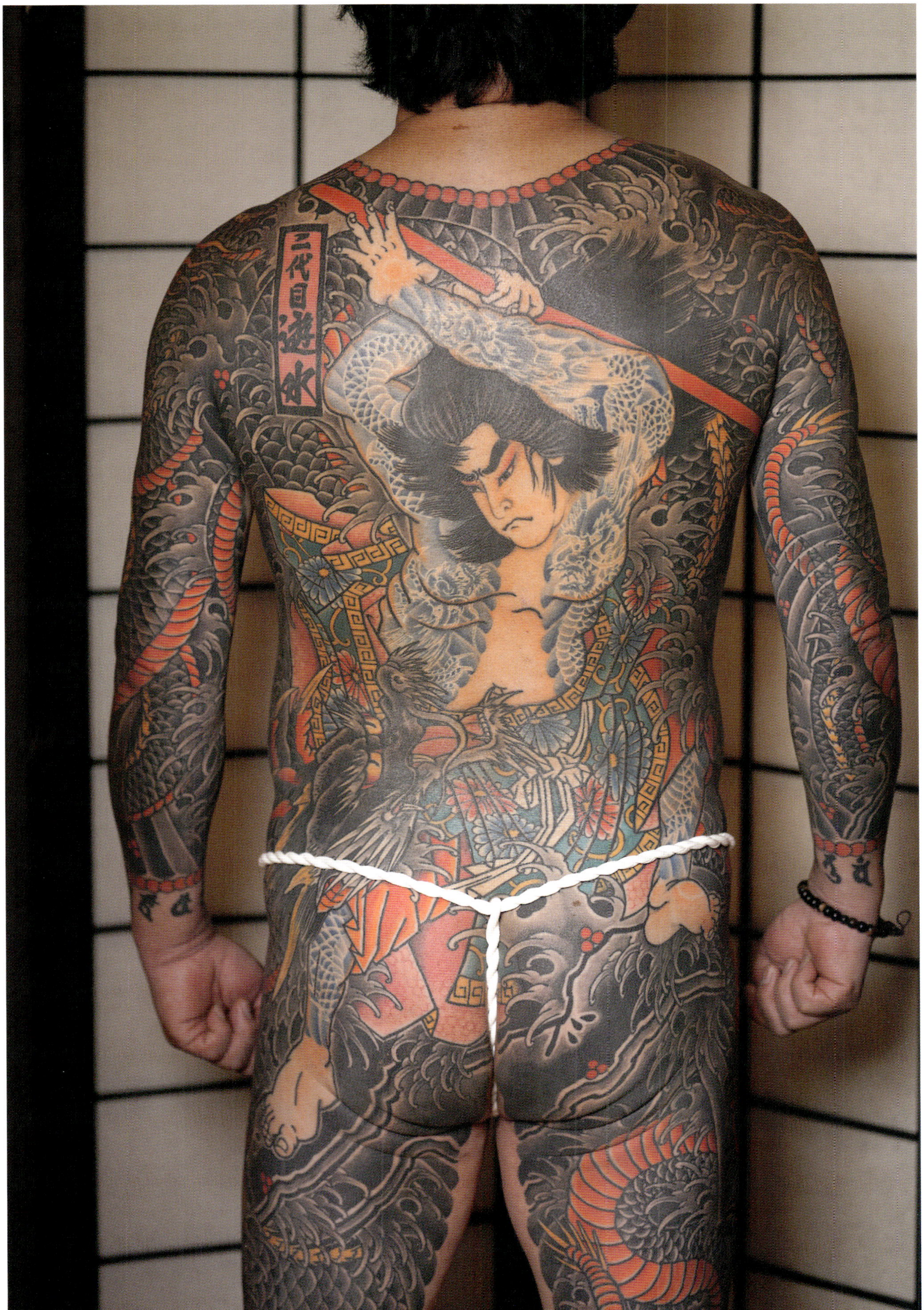
二代目遊水

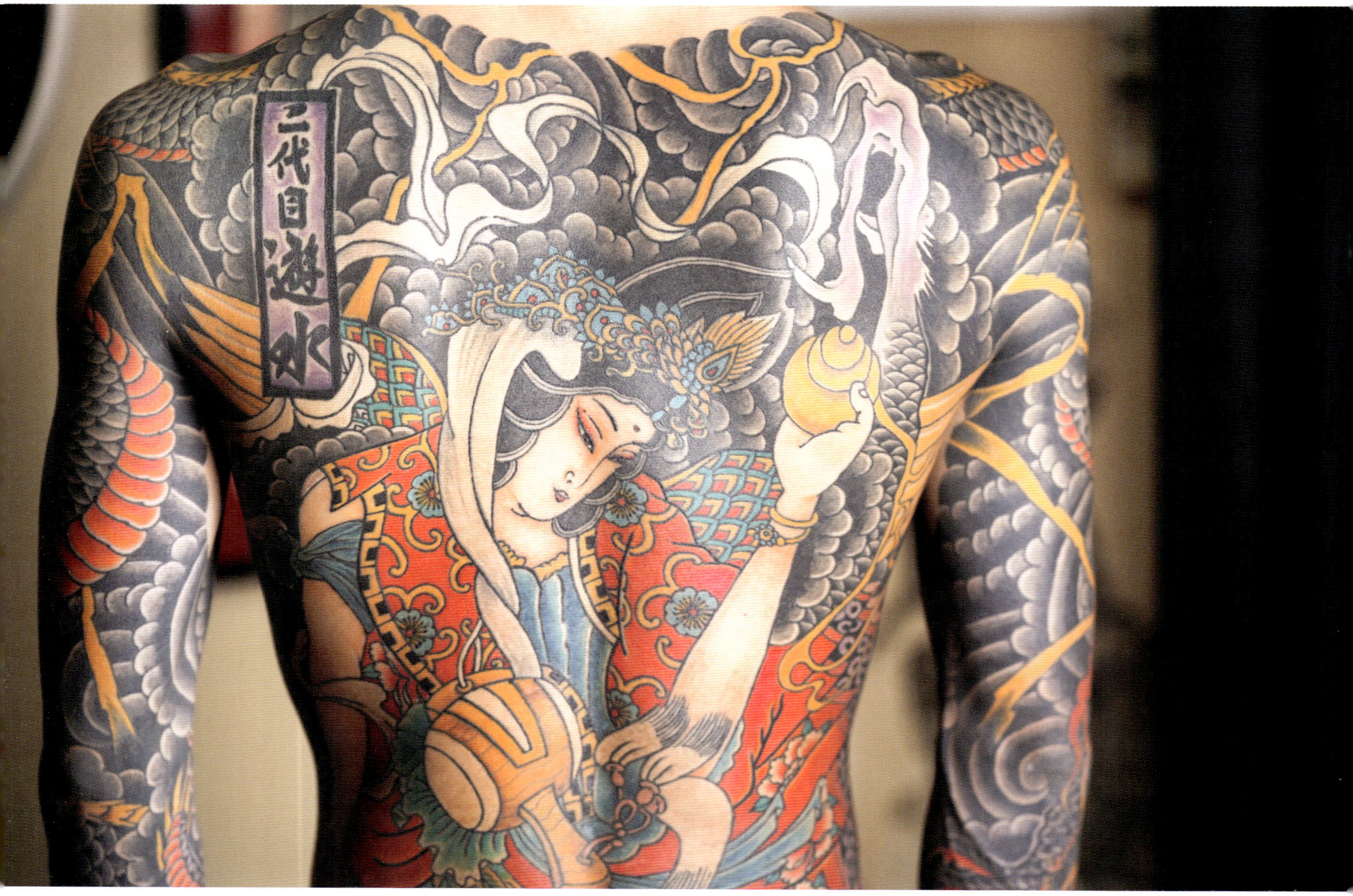

ABOVE
Backpiece featuring the goddess Benzaiten, one of the Buddhist Seven Lucky Gods. She is a popular tattoo motif.

OPPOSITE
Snake backpiece using only vermilion and *sumi*.

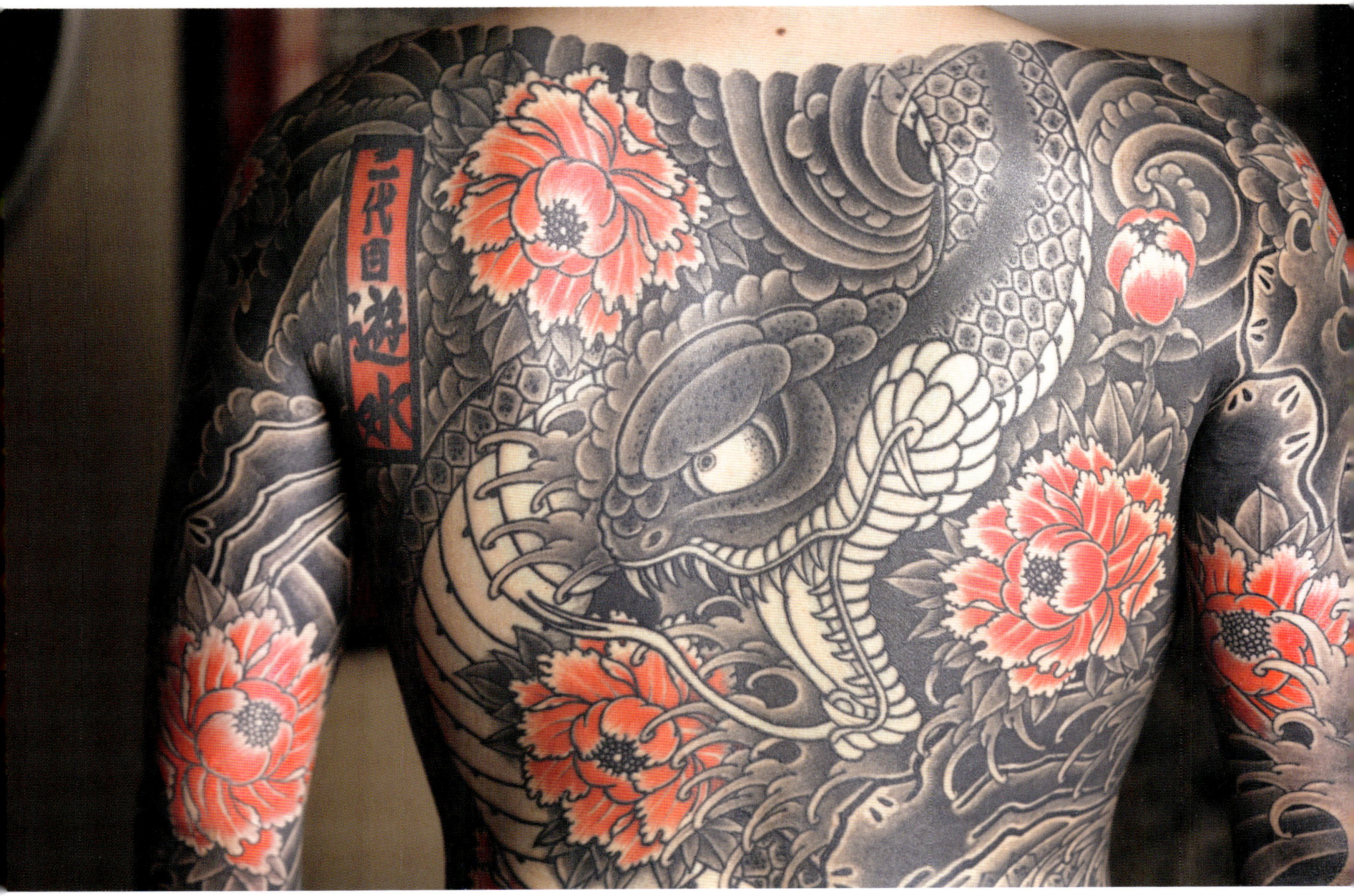

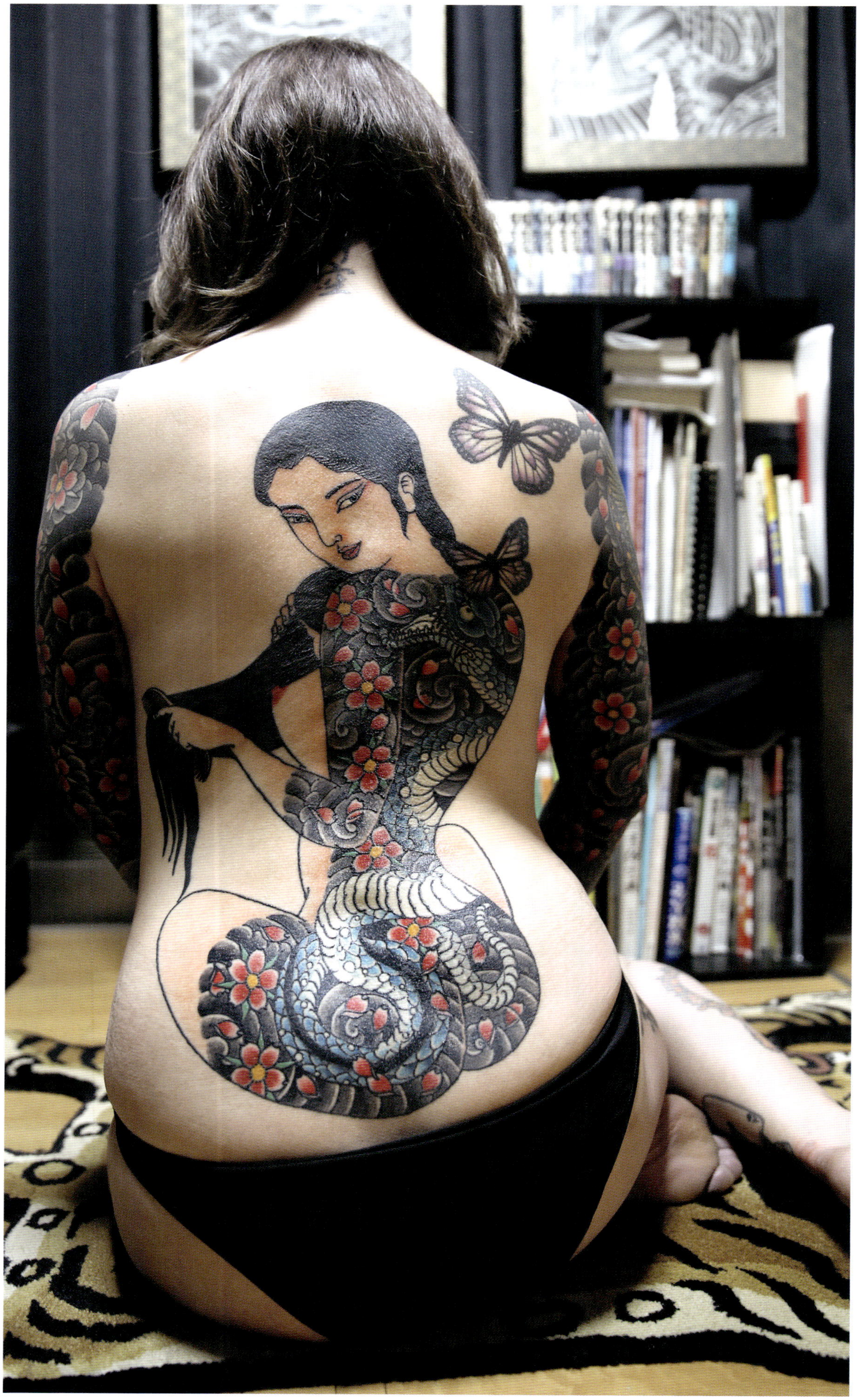

LEFT
Full body tattoo by Horiken.

OPPOSITE
Horiken with a client in his studio in Machida, Kanagawa prefecture. Many of his clients have full coverage but are quite young.

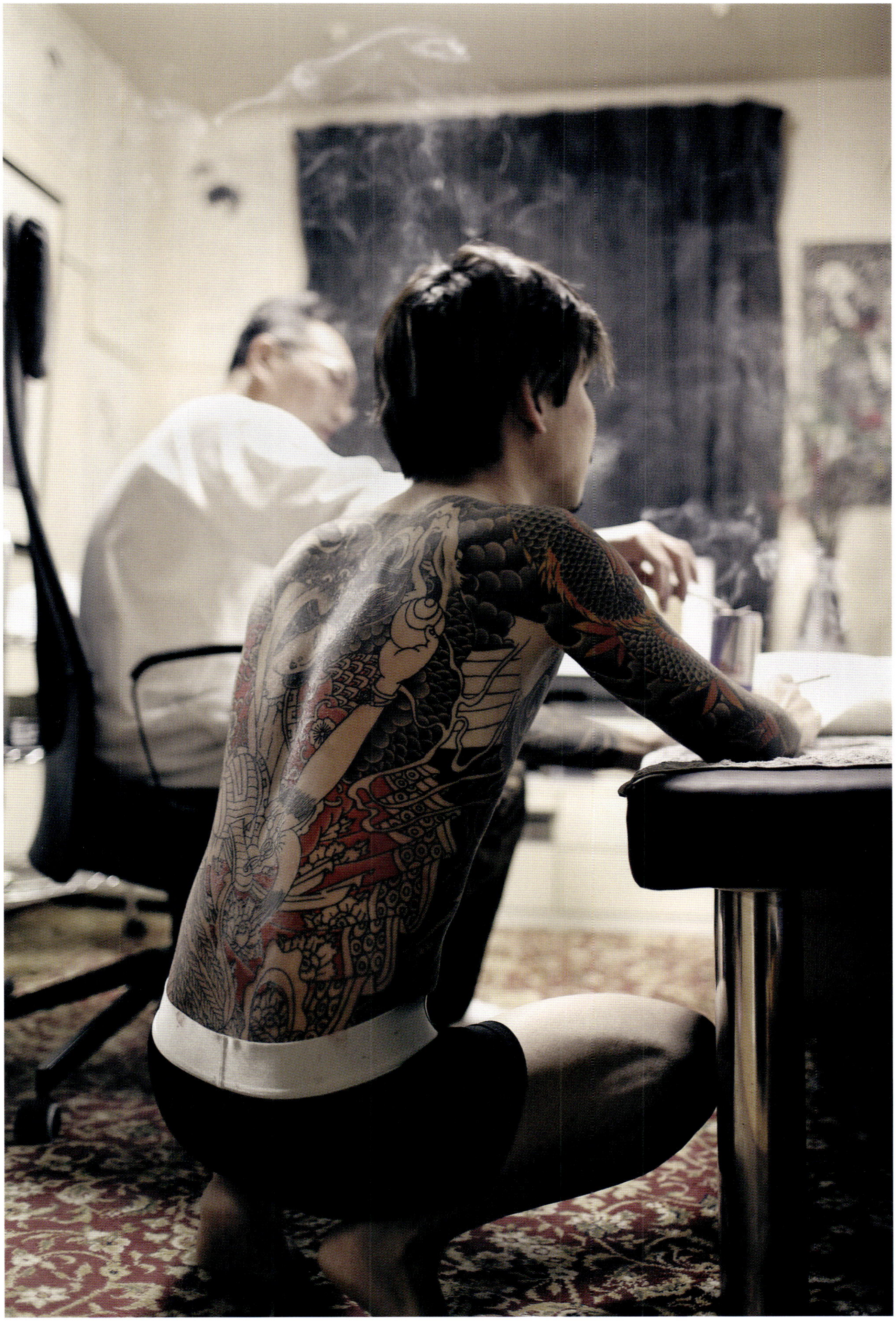

HORIMYO 彫妙

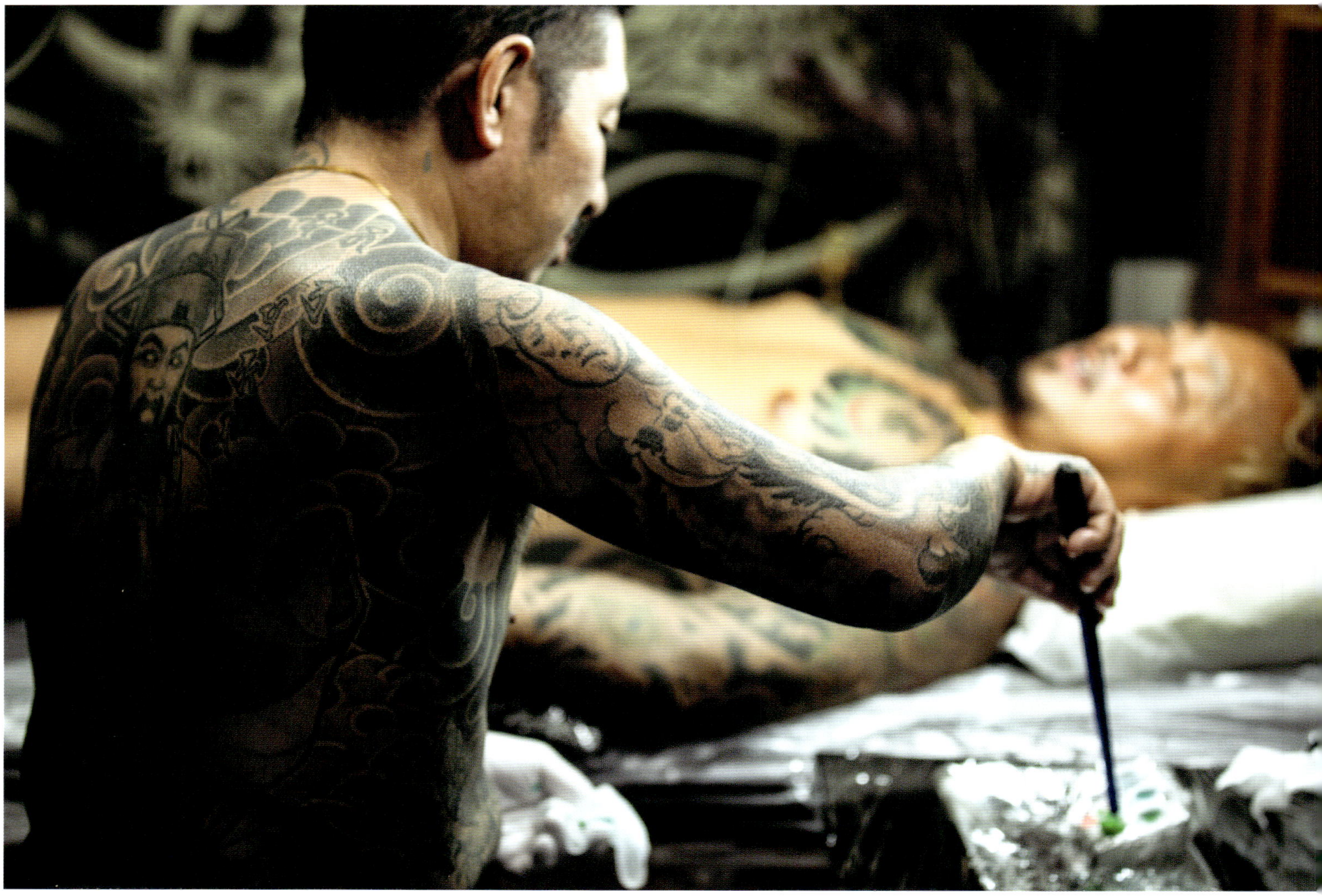

ABOVE
Horimyo is one of the few *wabori* artisans to use *tebori* techniques for all of his work, including the outlines. He is inspired by people like Kyushu-based *tebori* artisan Nakamura, known for his technical dexterity. Horimyo was also impressed by the speed of machine work he saw in Europe, so efficiency is something he focuses on.

Based in Saitama, Horimyo is one of the few *horishi* who does the entirety of his tattoos by hand (most do their outlines with a machine). He is extremely well-travelled, and has studied and worked with members of a number of tattoo cultures who use the hand-insertion method, thus enabling him to bring a variety of sensibilities to his designs. While visiting the USA and Mexico as a teen, Horimyo initially became interested in tattoos after being exposed to Chicano and hip-hop culture. This led him to question the value of Japanese culture and identity, and these are themes he constantly re-evaluates in his work.

How did you start tattooing?
I wanted to be a *horishi*, but during that time, it was the *yakuza* world – and I am not suited to those organizations, or even regular company structures. I always like to be free. I also wanted to contribute to society after the poverty I saw in Mexico. I learned English and went to the USA, and came across henna. On my way home, the person next to me on the plane had Japanese tattoos and he was a *horishi*. I went to the Yokohama Bay Hall Tattoo Convention and met my teacher then. I wanted to learn on my own, but we had an affinity for each other, and I also became increasingly interested when I realized how difficult *tebori* was. When I told my teacher I was thinking of doing the outlines with a machine he got really pissed off and told me *tebori* is not as easy as that. But a week later he told me he would take me on as an apprentice.

What are the difficulties in continuing as a* horishi *in this day and age?
A lot of the tattoo world is digital now, but I think it's important to meet people face-to-face and live in an analogue way. And I'm wondering how I can progress and how I can objectively master my craft. Of course my clients are going to praise me, but rather than letting that go to my head, I need to evaluate my strengths and weaknesses and remain humble.

I've had a few times when I was wondering how to proceed with my work and was worried about making a living. Once I consulted with a client and told him that I was thinking of advertising, and he said, 'Could you persevere a bit more? Because there is a lot of value in only working through word-of-mouth.'

Why are the tattoos' meanings important to you?
I talk to my clients and we decide on a motif together. I refuse people who just want to get tattoos for fashion; I steer them in the direction of understanding the meanings. Unlike clothing, you can't change them – tattoos are not disposable. People get meaningless things lightheartedly, and the tattooer agrees, so they end up trying to get rid of them eventually. There are a lot of people overseas who like the visuals, but I take meaning as the thing of paramount importance.

What do you think is the greatest difference between Western and Japanese work?
The history. I think the variety of the subject matter and using the entire body as a canvas, and that the subjects can be joined together. I think tribal work overseas is interesting too but there are no gradations in the work; the *bokashi* is an incredible aspect of Japanese tattooing.

Why is making an entire work with* tebori *important to you?
If you ask whether you want clothing made with a machine or a handmade item, everyone will choose the handmade item. I am thinking in terms of value. In order to make the most valuable work, I do the whole lot in *tebori*, plus I use Kobaien ink, the most valuable *sumi*. On top of that, I have word-of-mouth relationships.

What do you have in common with other artisans?
The hand-insertion methods are *tebori*, hand-poke, tapping and *sak yant*. They are all really slow, though.

What we have in common with other non-tattoo artisans is that everyone wants to do beautiful and time-efficient work [so they can earn a living]. If they are too focused on the beauty, the speed drops, but if they prioritize speed, the work gets rough. So it's the balance between these two elements.

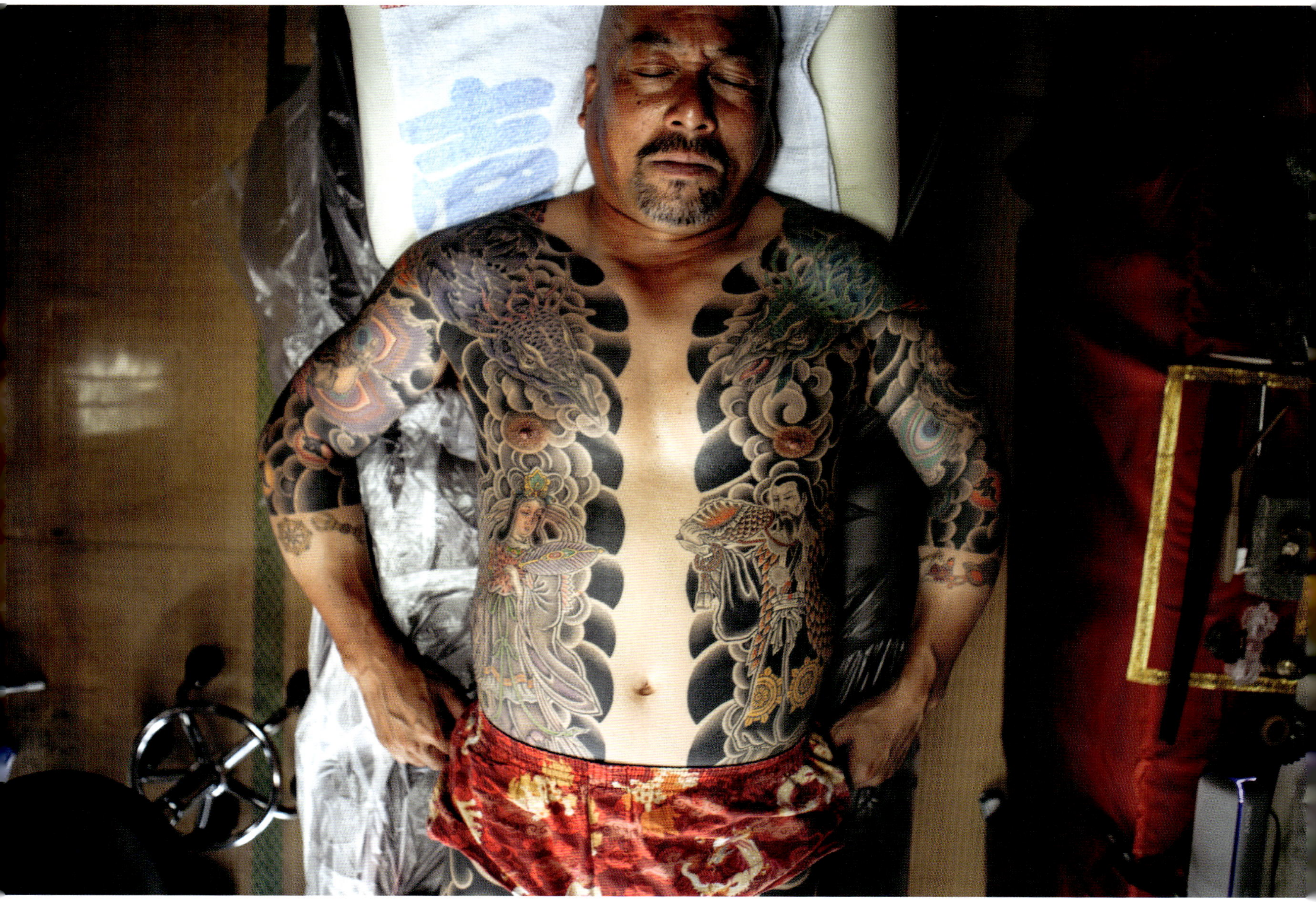

ABOVE
Beautiful, balanced work by Horimyo. The *munewari* shape of the tattoo has a split down the middle of the chest.

OPPOSITE
A majestic hawk motif decorated with *hanafuda* (playing cards). 'Hawk' is *taka* in Japanese, which is one of the characters in this client's name. He got this tattoo as a form of self-affirmation. In the *hanafuda* are the names of his wife and children.

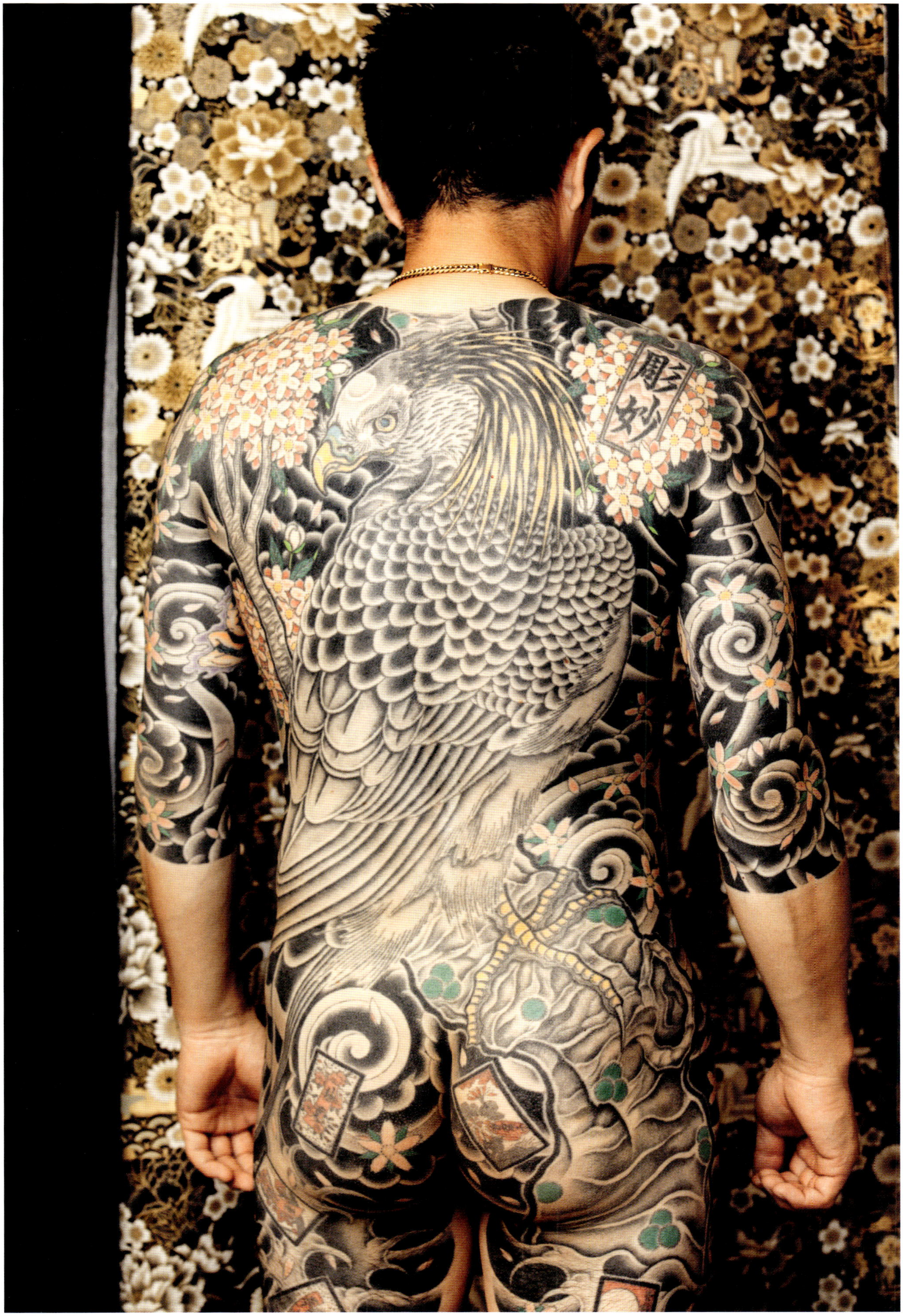
彫妙

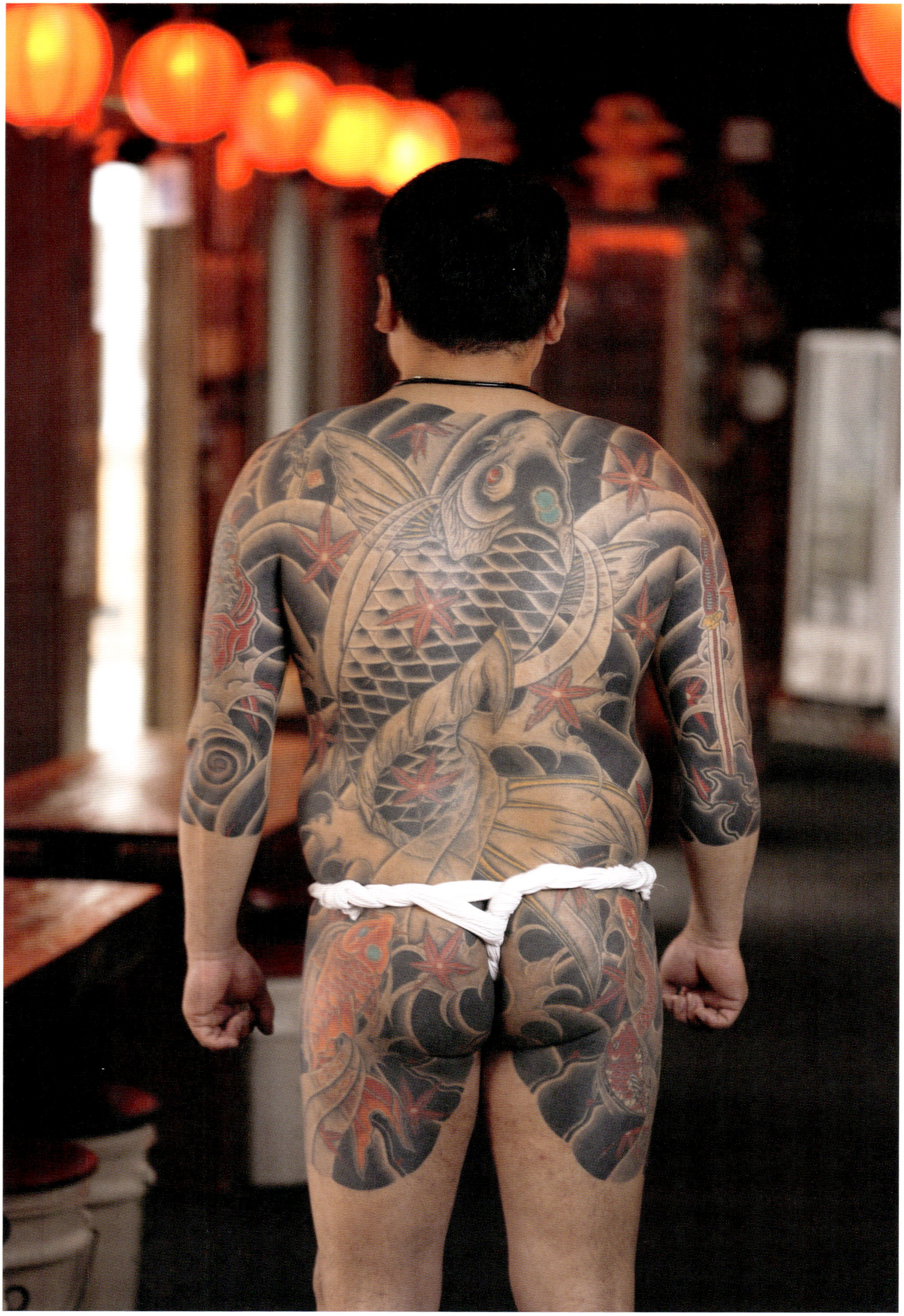

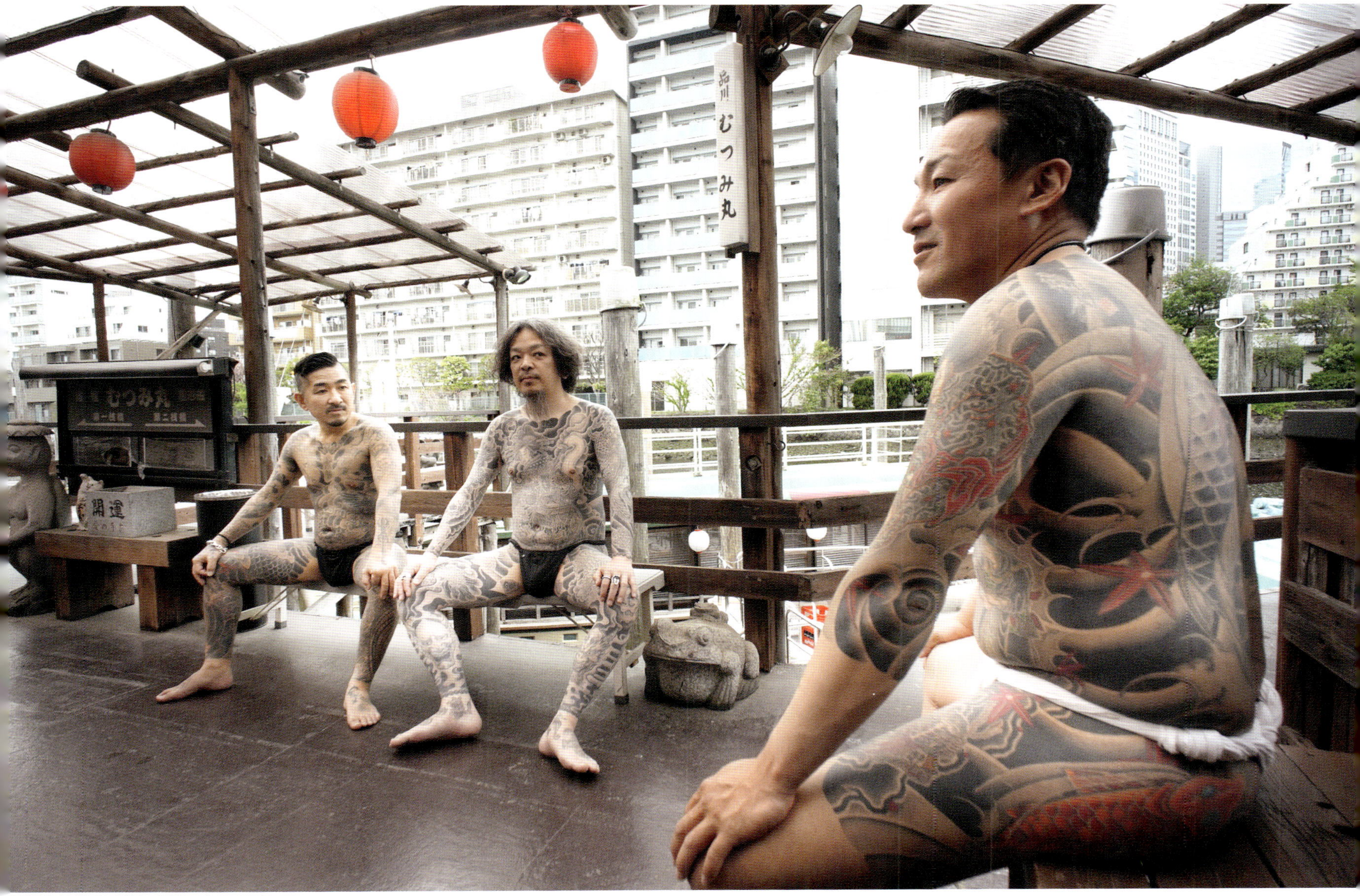

OPPOSITE
A carp, one of the most classic Japanese traditional motifs, using the timeless combination of vermilion and *sumi*.

ABOVE
Horimyo (left) with two clients.

PROFILE OF A DYNASTY: HORIKAZU

彫和

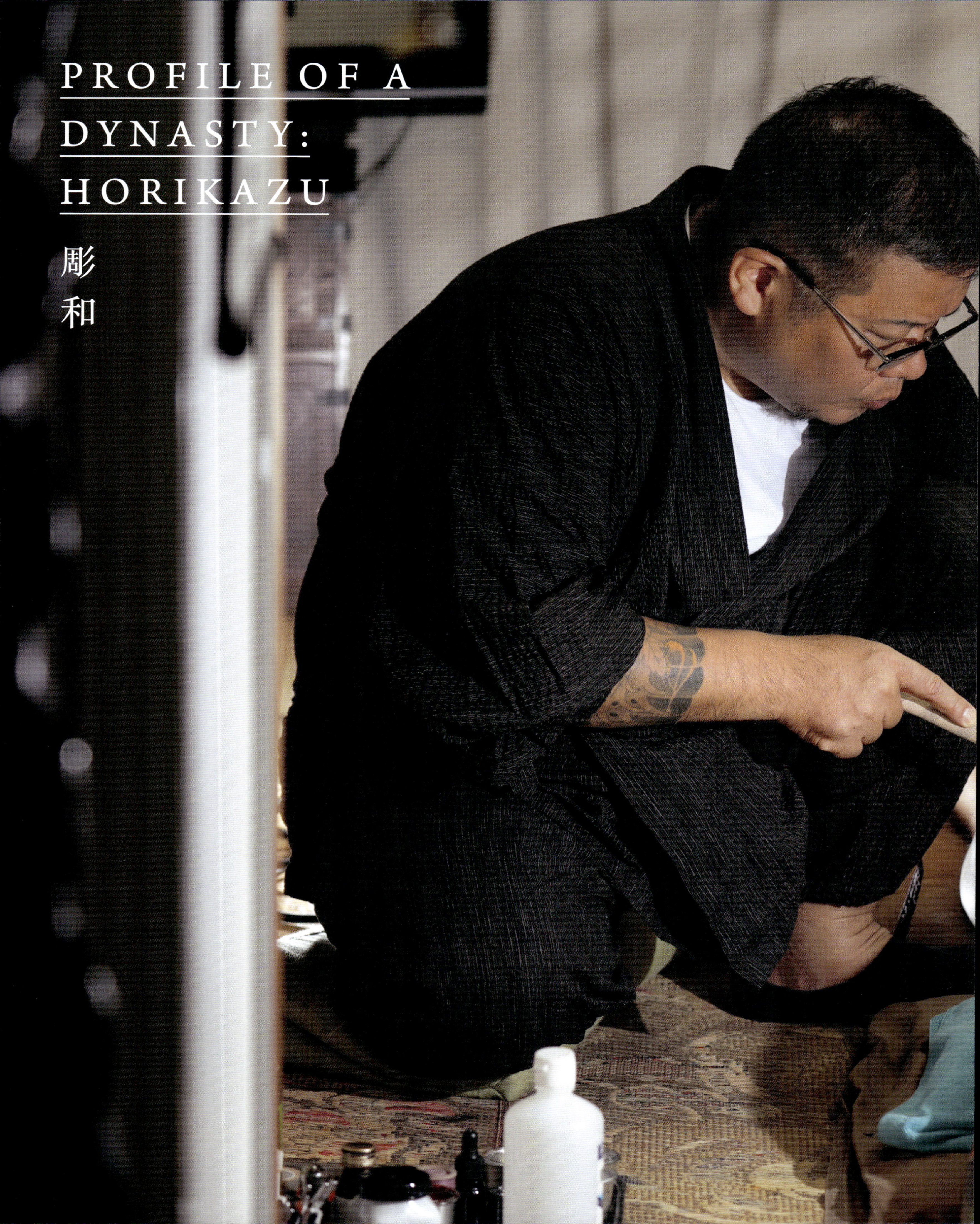

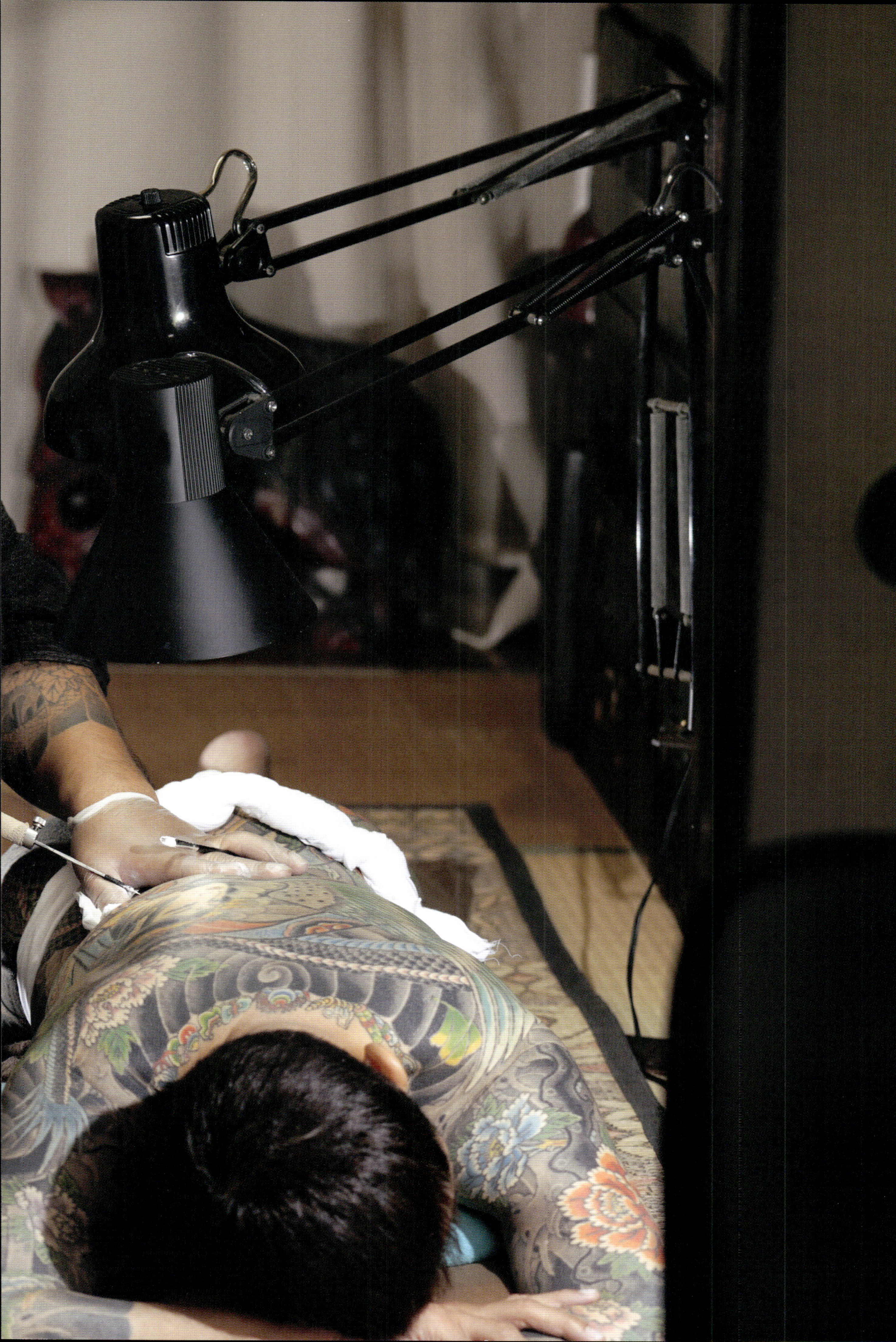

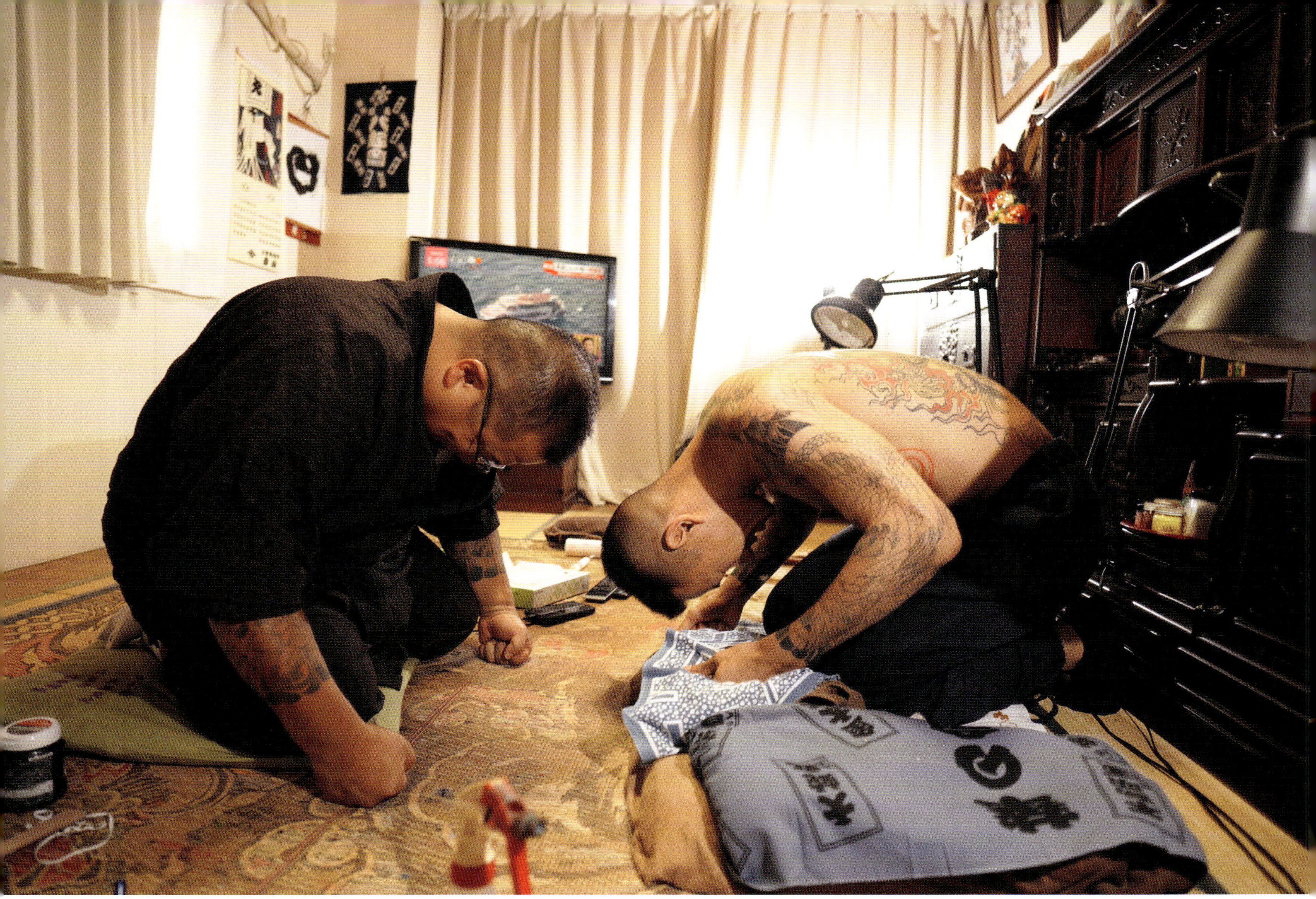

PREVIOUS SPREAD
Horikazu at work in his apartment in Asakusa, Tokyo's tattoo mecca.

ABOVE
Horikazu places a huge amount of importance on the relationships he has with his clients.

OPPOSITE
Horikazu aligns an illustration on a client's body to get a mental image of the overall composition.

Horikazu is a *horishi* based in Asakusa. The son of the late Shodai Horikazu, he follows in the footsteps of his father and takes on a lineage whose clientele and identity is firmly rooted in the east Tokyo downtown area. After Shodai Horikazu passed away from cancer in 2011, Horikazuwaka (literally 'Horikazu Junior'), as he was then known, became Horikazu, and took over his father's legacy. Much like his father, Horikazu is known for his intricate and detailed work, and for his eye for overall composition.

A *mikoshi* is a sacred portable Shinto shrine used at festivals, and Horikazu is also manager of a *mikoshi* group, a position he has held since 2000. The organization was formed by Shodai Horikazu and his clients in the late 1970s. Horikazu's community of clients are present at festivals across Japan, particularly during summer, continuing the historic connection between *matsuri* and *horimono*.

He is the only *horishi* who is currently actively involved in *mikoshi* organization and is largely known as the 'face' of Sanja *matsuri*, one of Tokyo's largest and most important *matsuri* festivals, which welcomes 2 million attendees annually. His larger-than-life presence and bevy of heavily tattooed customers dominate the streets during the three days of bedlam.

***When did you first see* horimono?**

Ever since I could remember, I would always see my father's work. I would serve tea when I was in primary school and help out around the studio. I always thought it was cool and liked it. Later on, I would get back home from work and just watch; I enjoyed that. The atmosphere was really tense, like a martial arts dojo. Most of his clients were architecture and construction company bosses or worked in the carpentry field. He was based in Asakusa, which was a *yakuza* mecca back then.

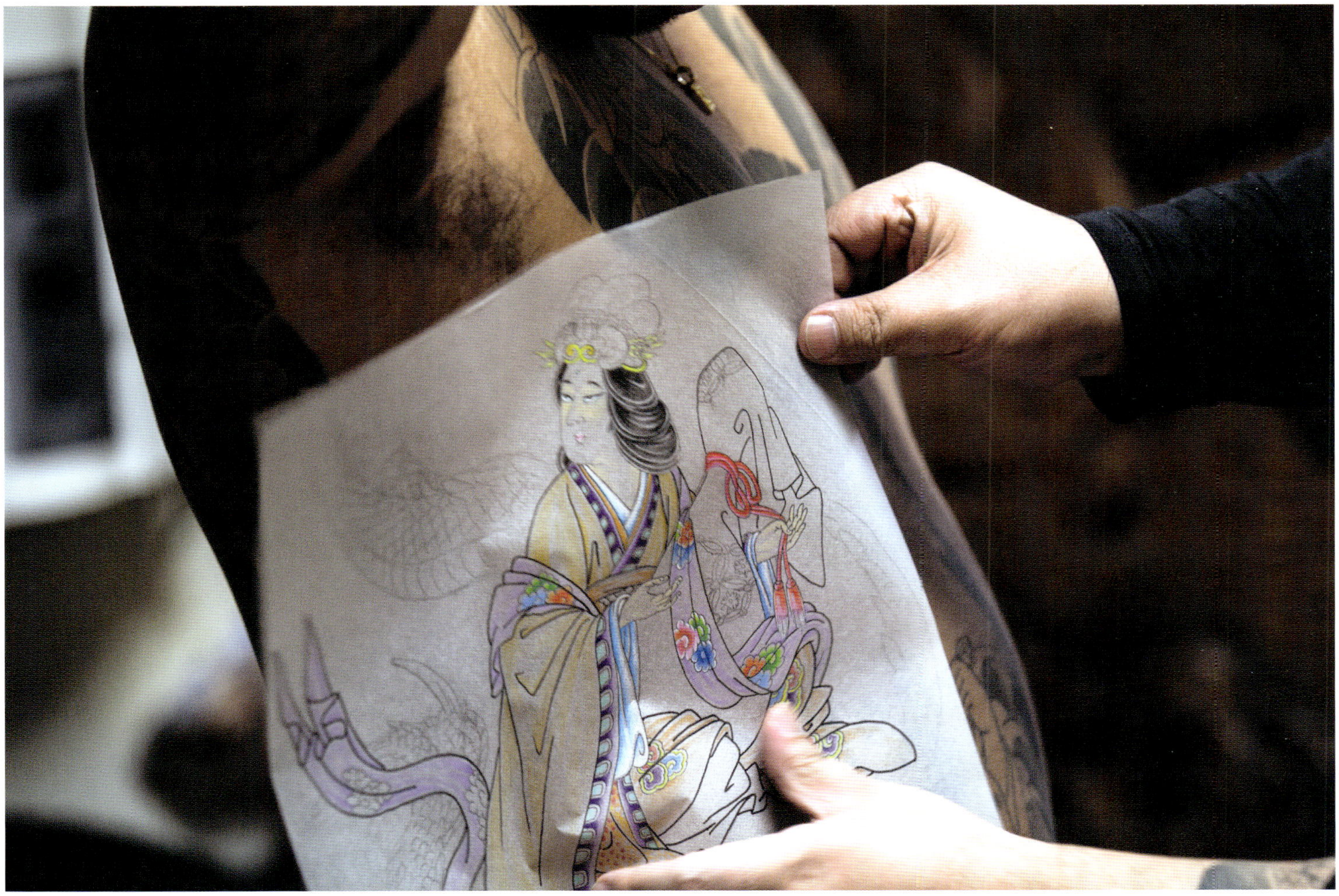

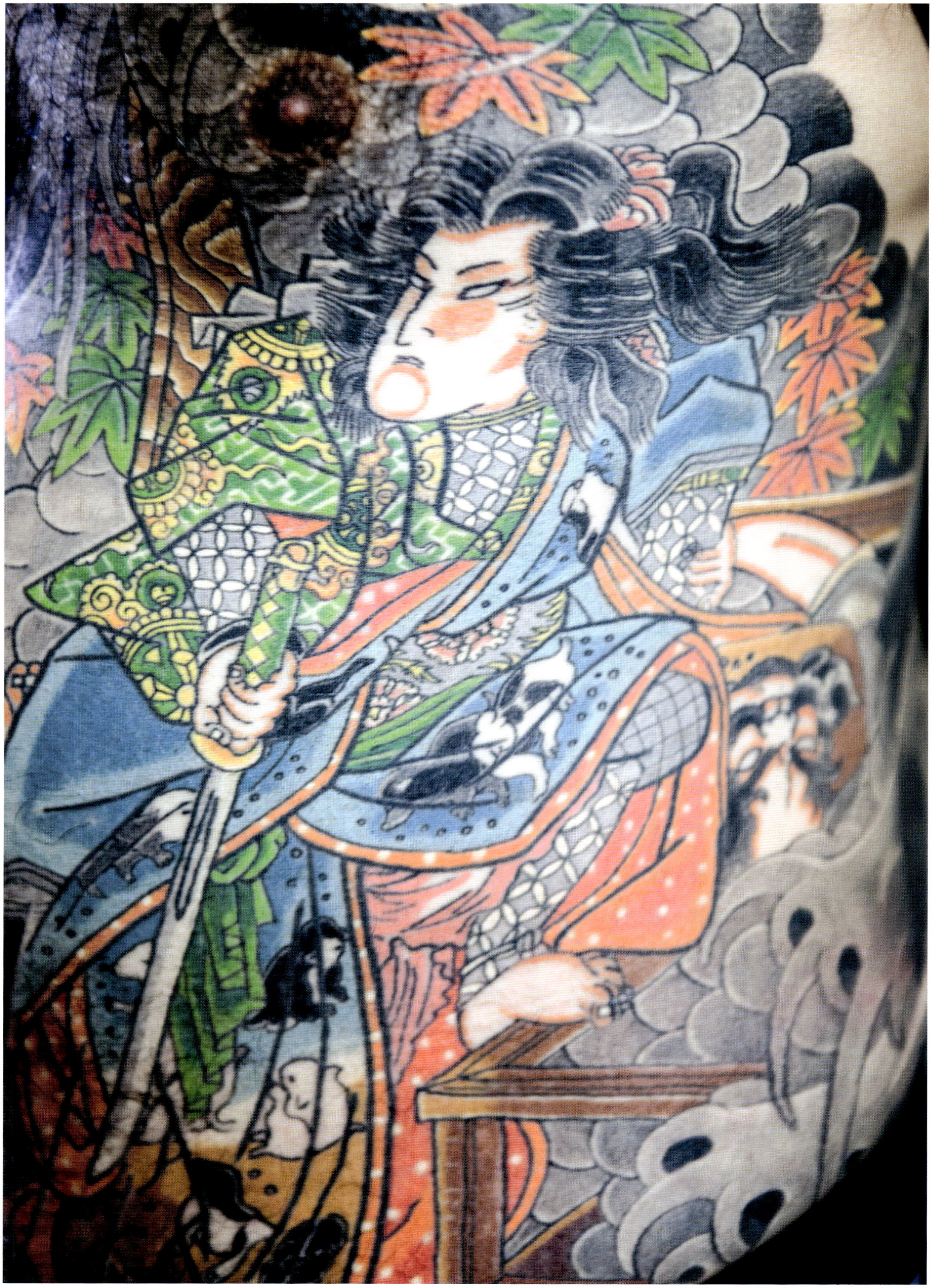

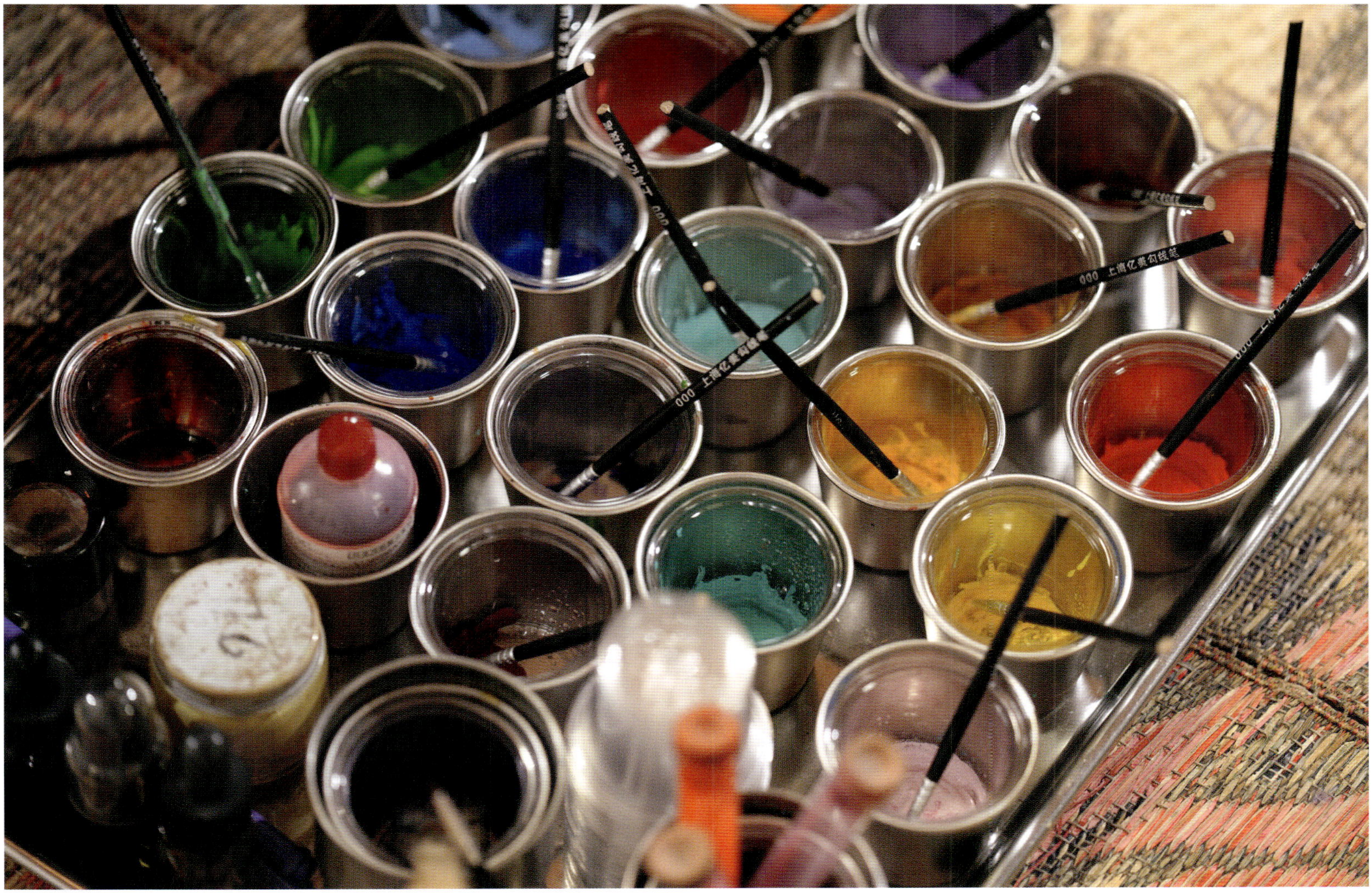

OPPOSITE
A protagonist from *The Eight Dog Chronicles* by Kyokutei Bakin, a 19th-century serial novel about a group of eight warriors whose father is a dog.

ABOVE
Horikazu is known for the vibrancy of his colours. Of his father Horikazu I's work, he says that 'the black ink gives the work a heavy presence. And yet, even in the smallest details, the tattooing is done with great care and attention to detail. His work is cool whether you look at it from afar or up close.'

When did you decide that you wanted to become a tattoo artist?

Since I was a child I wanted to be a *horishi* and that was my dream. My father taught me how to configure the needles. He had two other apprentices, they died. I was watching and learning and when I was a kid, I was practising on bananas and mandarin peels. I started tattooing when I was still at primary school. I was doing my own legs. I would tattoo my own body and he would say, 'Do it more like this, or that.'

An elderly client let me tattoo him when I was in my third year of primary school. I was told I should not tattoo for free, even back then, so he would give me 500 yen [£2.60/$3.50]. Shodai Horikazu would look with a magnifying lens to see if my tools were okay, and if not, he would let me use his. I did a lot of jobs like touch-ups.

Shodai Horikazu was omnipresent in downtown Tokyo. Was it difficult to take on his dynasty?

Shodai Horikazu wasn't just good at illustrating, it was the way he would interact with people, his clients. I don't think what we are doing is that different, in that our clients are the same and he ran the *mikoshi* association and would go to festivals.

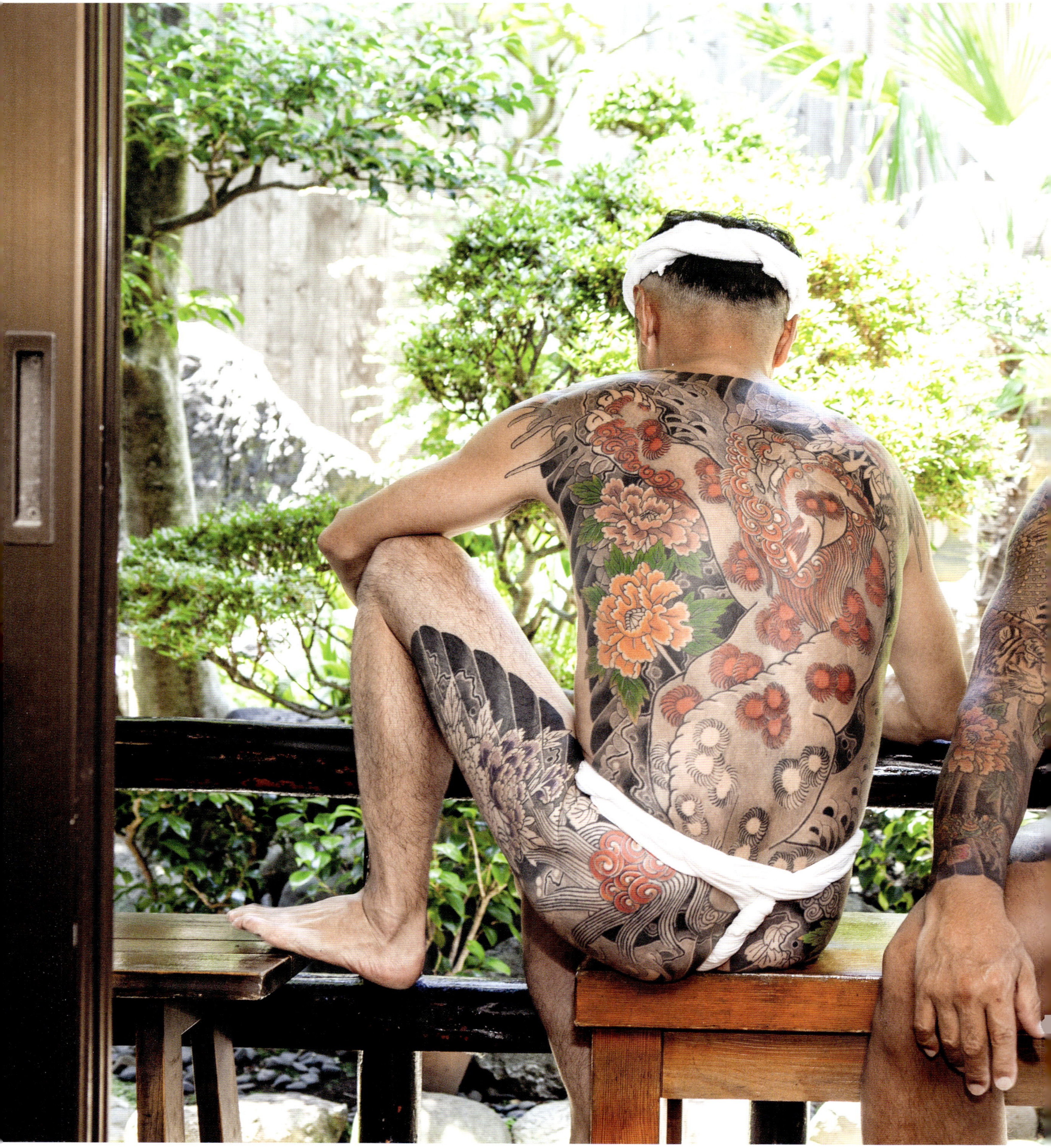

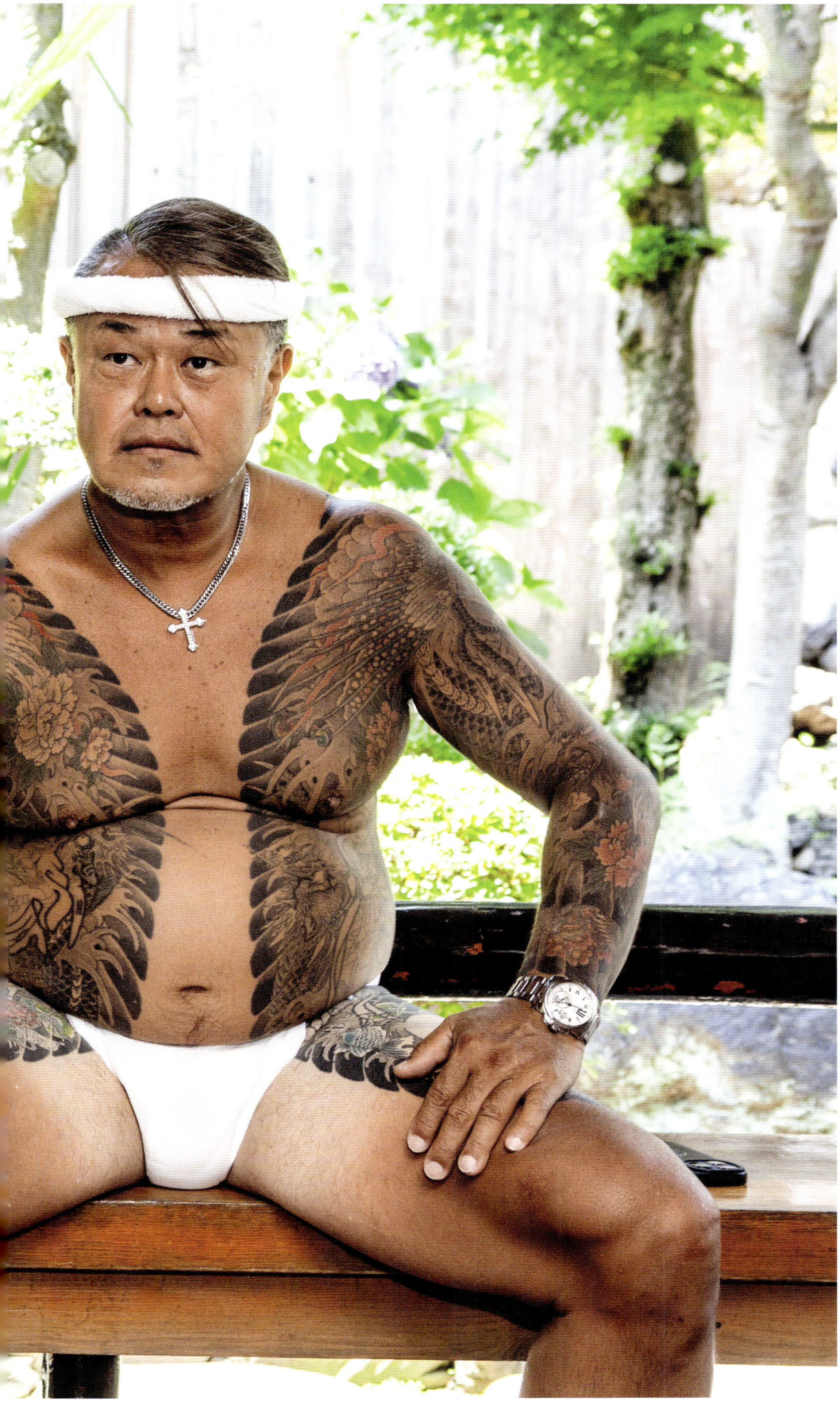

LEFT
Horikazu's clients relaxing at the *sento*. The man on the left has a *shishi* (guardian lion) piece.

When I was young I really liked tattoos, so I'd look at underground magazines with tattoos in the back pages and I would think, 'These tattoos are so bad' when I saw other people's work. I already knew Horikazu's work was amazing and was always copying the dragons and snakes. I also checked out his bookshelf to look at photo books. I really liked Azabu Horiyoshi's as well, in particular his drawings – even as an adult, I think these two are the greatest.

When did you start, officially?

I started tattooing as a job when I was 20 and had a shop in Shin Koiwa, but I didn't tell my father. He only found out when I was 22. He wouldn't have let me, for sure he would have said it was too early, and I didn't want to wait. I borrowed an apartment and was tattooing local hooligans. They were all *yakuza* youth and wanted tattoos because they found them aspirational. They would go to *matsuri* every year and would see tattoos peeking out from under the sleeves of coats. My father found out I was tattooing and then asked me to join him in Asakusa when I was 25. He was on the third floor and I was on the second. I would tattoo the underlings of his clients, such as their drivers and so on, as well as my friends. I only really tattoo people via introductions.

Why do many of your clients want Buddhist motifs?

They want protective motifs, or they want what a certain *yakuza* boss has. But generally in Asakusa it is aspirational, they want what they see on people at festivals or at the local *sento* (bathhouse). It is only these places where you can see my work. There are also many people in jail. I've had clients come to me because of the pieces they saw while locked up. While they are in jail, my work is the only thing they can take with them. I also get regular people who come in, such as *tobi* (construction workers) and *matsuri* folks, but they want the same things as the *yakuza*. Trends don't impact me because they all say, 'I want what so-and-so has.'

What is the appeal of Japanese tattoos?

I think it is *iki*. *Irezumi* is not something you parade around: it is a hidden aesthetic, you only show it at festivals and *sento*. Now people show them off and walk around, like a man would be walking his kid to the bus stop with his tattoos showing. But when you see these people, it is obvious they are not *yakuza*. For me, I would feel uneasy about it. It isn't that cool if an old man is showing his tattoos off and walking around, it would look like he was trying to scare someone, and it would be kind of crass. There are a lot of people who get tattoos as part of their lifestyle who are not *yakuza* but people like company bosses, *tonkatsu* chefs, sushi chefs, pot plant artisans and so on, who want to get work done after they finish bringing up their family. But at the end of the day, they are into the hidden beauty too.

How do you view the philosophy of the craftsman?

As a craftsman, I want to please the customers. For that reason, I give it my all. After listening to the customer's request, I do a better job than they imagined and make them happy. I'm always thinking about tattooing so I can do that kind of work. I think about motifs, needles, tools, the skin of the customer, books, going to museums when there is an interesting exhibition, looking at pictures of old work left by my father and going to a sauna after the last customer to relieve the fatigue of the day. I study, worry and struggle with the thought that everything I do is to do good work that will make customers happy. I live for good work. That is what the word 'craftsman' means to me. It is not only *horishi* but other people who do good work who live like that. I am able to have that way of thinking because of the influence of my teacher. He was really charismatic, both as a man and as a craftsman.

What are the basic characteristics of good Japanese tattooing?

I want to make backgrounds that not only enhance the subject, but create a natural flow in accordance with the body. I do not want to make backgrounds that merely fill in the gaps. I am conscious of how the backgrounds should look, so that even if you look at them from a distance, they will give a strong impression that they are the work of Asakusa Horikazu. I have been aiming to emulate Shodai Horikazu's work for a long time, but even when I look at pictures from the late 1980s or the '90s, I am still surprised

OPPOSITE
A client in the backstreets of Asakusa, near Horikazu's studio.

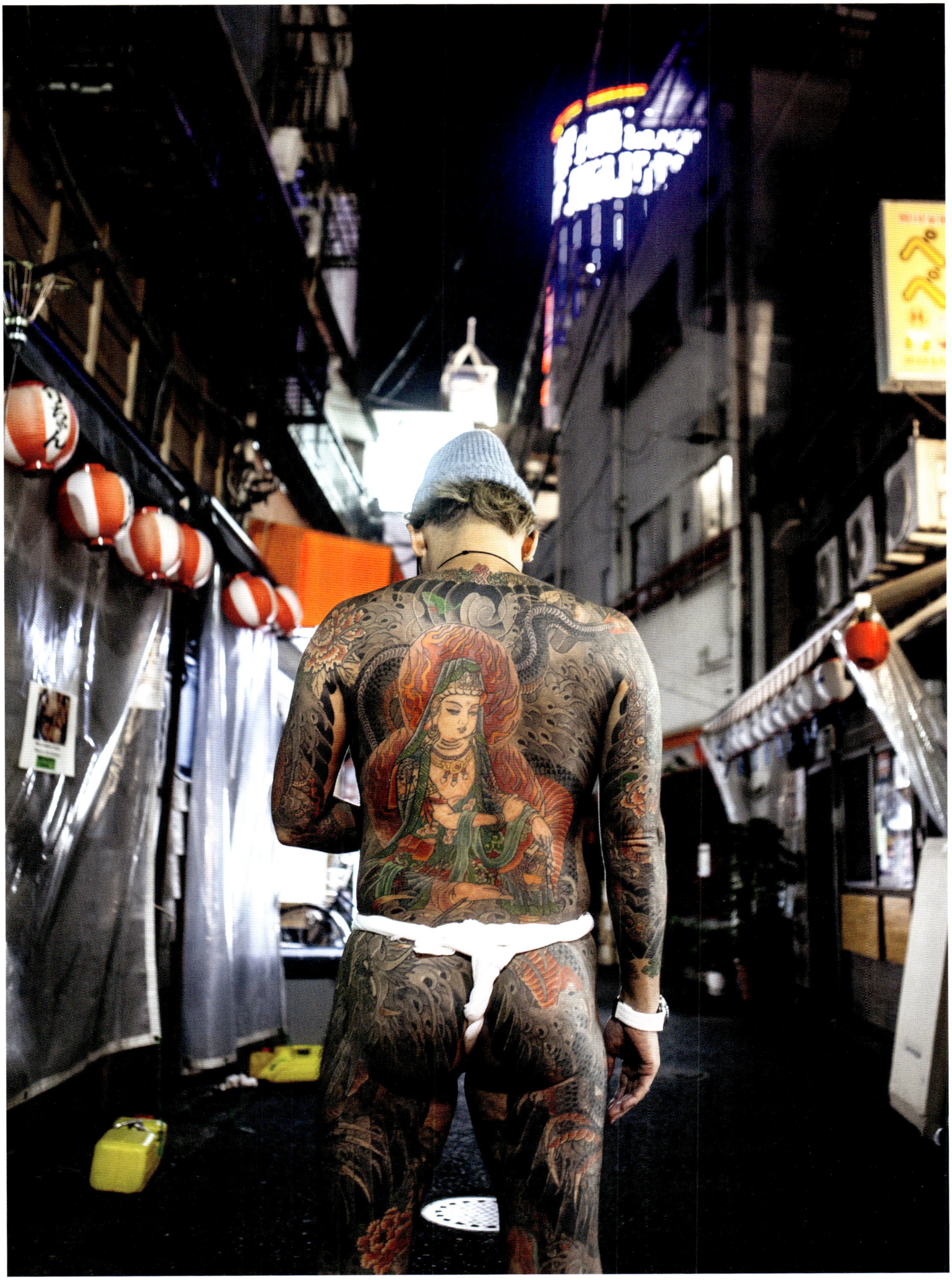

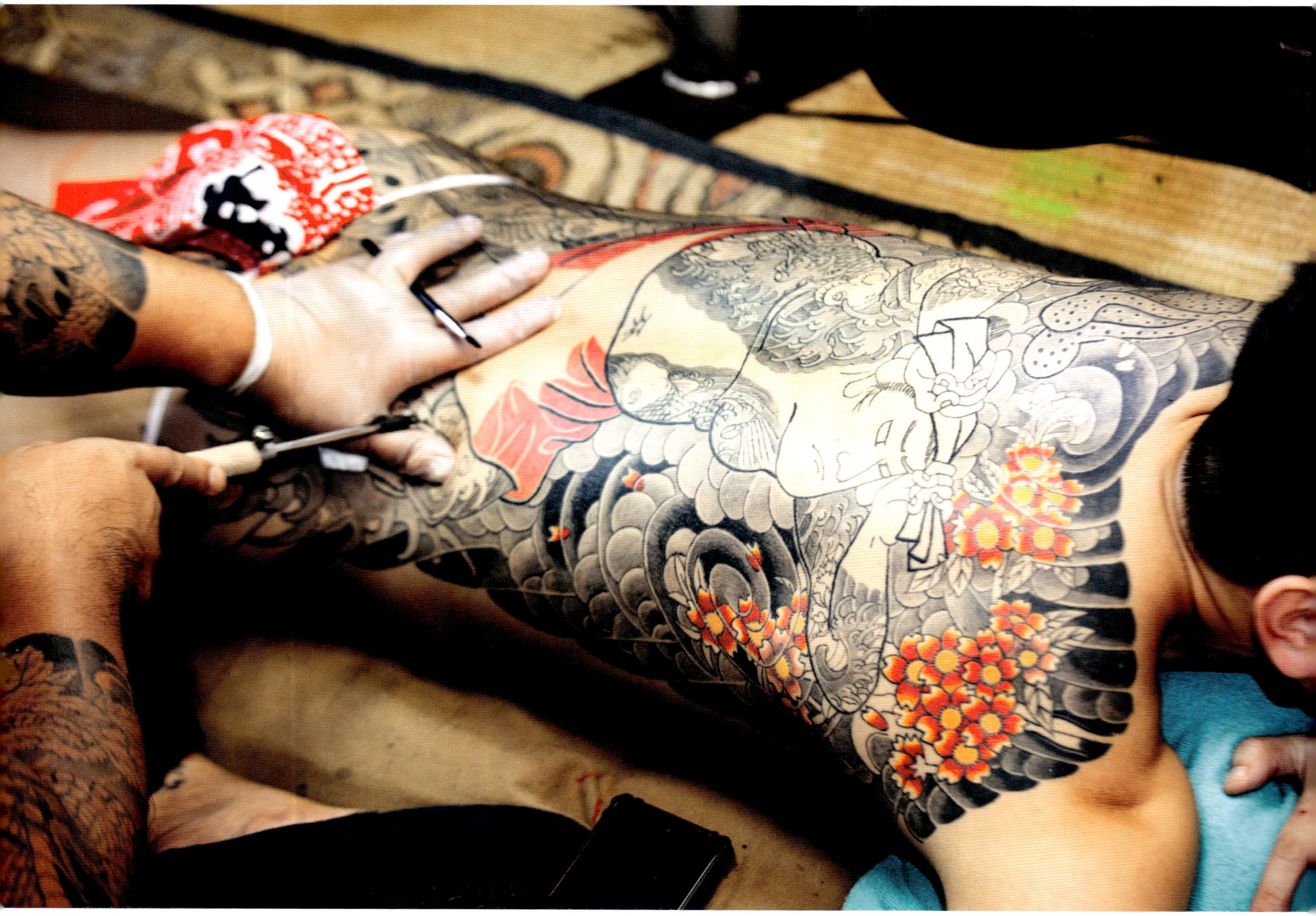

to discover that he was already expressing himself in that way at that time. I've been trying my best to surpass his work, but it's really difficult.

What is your relationship with your clients like?
For me, the relationship with the clients who come to me is as follows: they are my clients, friends, colleagues, seniors and juniors. We are different in age and background, and in that way, we each have something to learn from the other. We are both human beings, and I must not forget to thank them for entrusting their bodies to me. Because I want to make my life as a craftsman, tattooing people, don't I? To achieve this, it is essential to have customers who entrust their bodies to me. Moreover, the customers spend a lot of time, money and patience to endure pain, and they let me tattoo their bodies after offering me various kinds of compensation. How could I be more grateful? I think it is very natural for me to want to spend time with my customers, who are my benefactors, eating together, taking in saunas, carrying *mikoshi* at *matsuri*, going on trips and so on.

Of course, I will be angry if they misbehave. I apologize when I am not polite. Without a natural relationship as human beings, the relationship between *horishi* and customer will not exist, and good work for both parties will not be born. If more and more people think that just having a picture on the skin is enough when it comes to tattooing, and can't even socialize with others, then I think it would be a good idea to leave the profession of *horishi* and let AI take over. Perhaps people are drawn to things made by others because they sense an invisible current of shared emotions – an unspoken connection between creator and beholder – compelling them to lean in, bridge the gap, or even take a leap into the heart of that creation. People get tattooed for various reasons, but I feel pride that they choose me out of the many *horishi*, so I do my best for each and every one of them.

Why do your tattooed clients think* matsuri *are important?
Everyone has their own *matsuri* style: other districts are orthodox and wear their *obi*s (kimono sashes) tight and wear *waraji* (straw footwear), whereas our style is rougher and more rebellious. No matter the district, everyone is helping to keep *matsuri* culture alive and wants to pass it on to the next generation. However, if our crew disappeared, *matsuri* would become so quiet and boring. During the era of my father the festivals were so cool, and the relationships were really hierarchical and strict. Everything was so tense. It is only our generation that remembers that *iki* era. We feel like we have to maintain this intense atmosphere, and if we don't, it really won't be Sanja anymore and this part of Edo culture will disappear.

OPPOSITE
A *Suikoden* protagonist on a client who is blind.

WABORI AND FESTIVALS

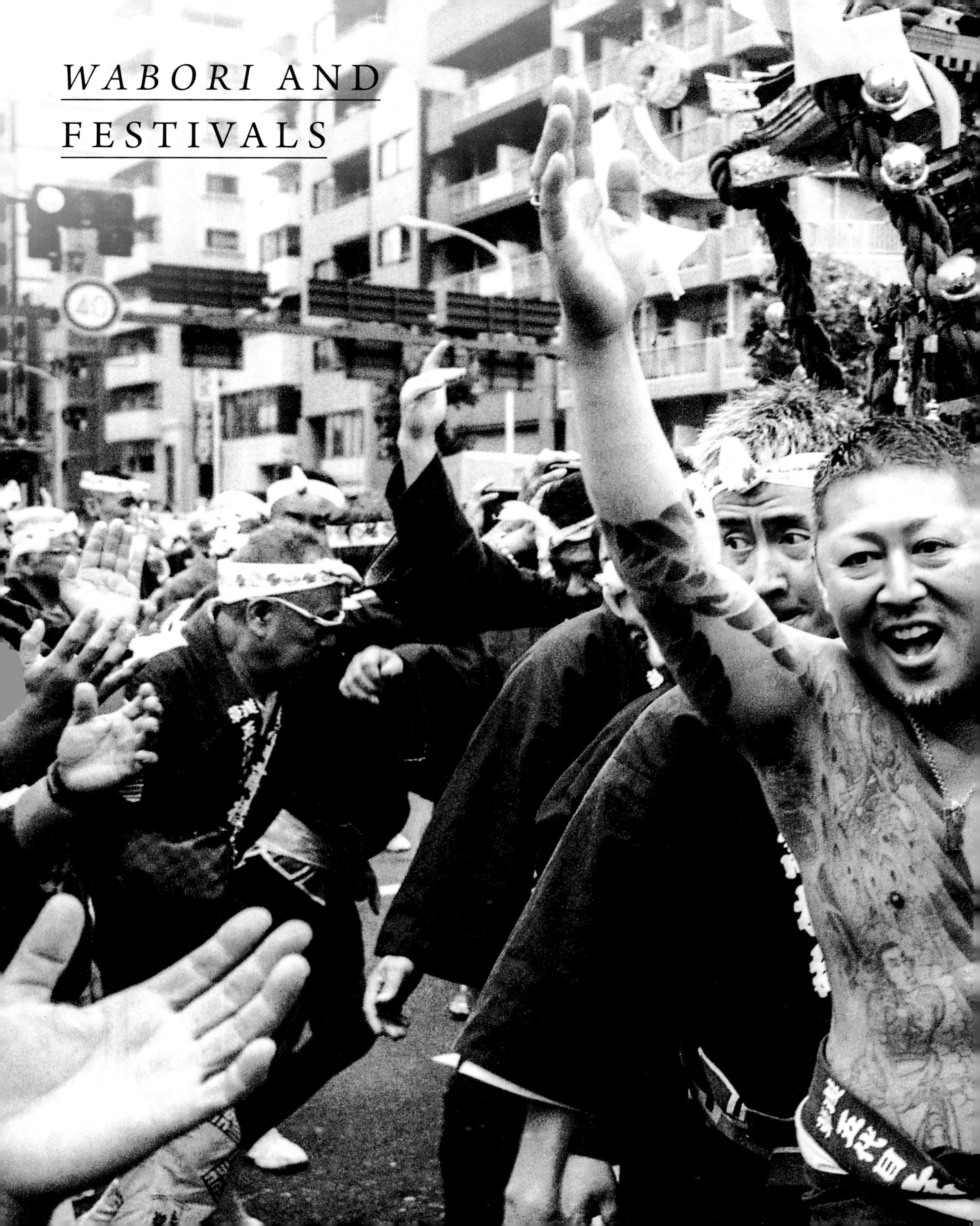

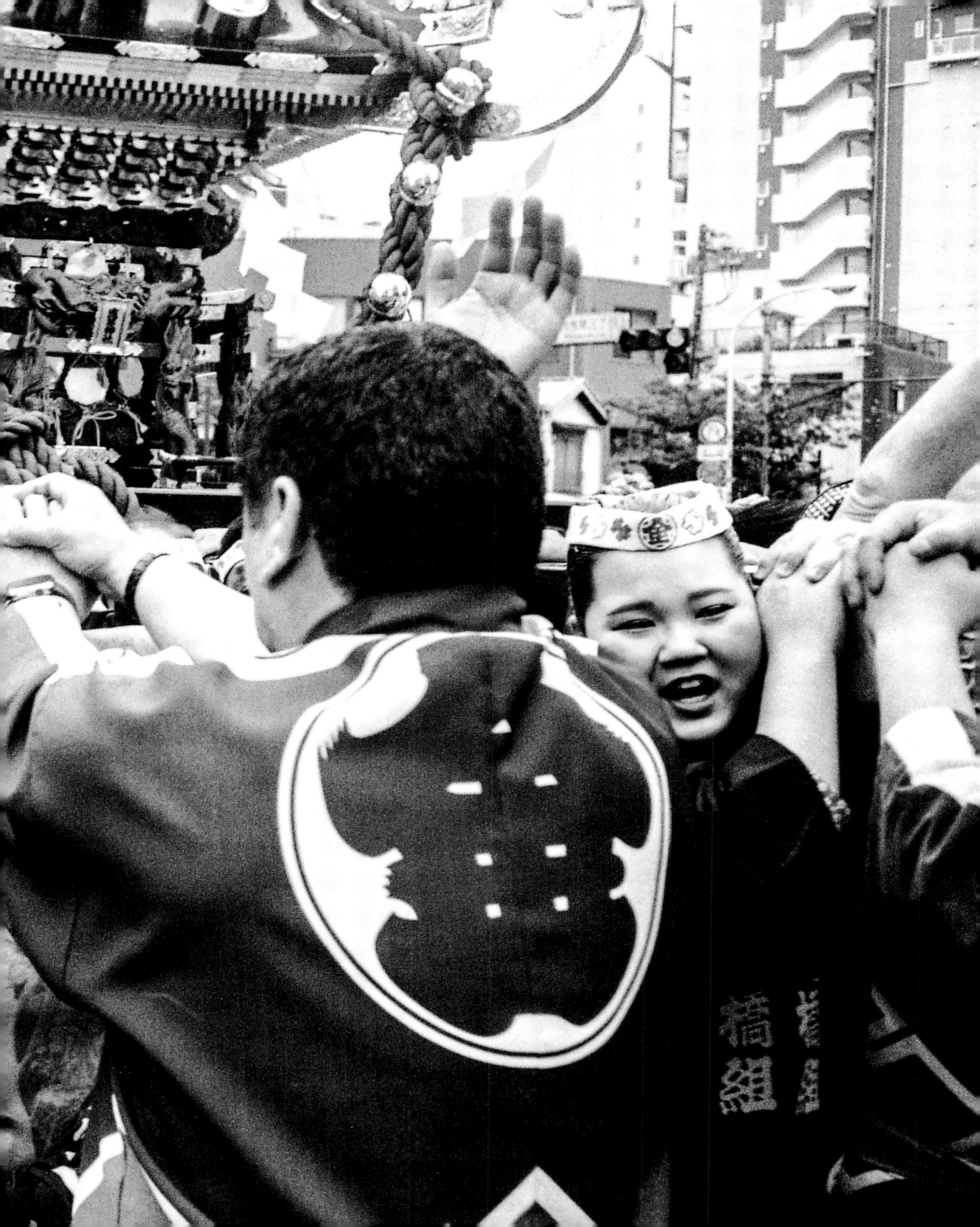

Rather than just serving as a form of fashion, *horimono* exists within a cultural context, and there is an inextricable link between it and Japanese spiritual life. Buddhist and Shinto iconography is the inspiration for some of the most common Japanese tattoo motifs, and many clients who get traditional work are passionate enthusiasts of *matsuri* festivals.

Matsuri are regional gatherings held on certain days of the month, usually relating to Buddhist or Shinto days of significance. They are the best places to see and experience modern Japanese culture intermingling seamlessly with traditional legacies. In essence, they are a way to express gratitude to the gods and engage in a performative rite to appreciate the seasons. They provide an ethereal aesthetic experience and are an important means through which to foster community between the participants. *Matsuri* involve a diverse range of characteristics, such as ornate floats, regional dances and music, and rituals determined by each particular district and its cultural customs (such as horseback archery, fire and water purification rites).

Despite the differences in format across the country, the central elements in most festivals are the *mikoshi* (shrines) that are said to house the gods and which are moved between shrines, *otabisho* (areas where shrines rest temporarily mid-journey) and places with spiritual significance. Because carrying the *mikoshi* has become more and more of a spectacle over time, with people jostling for a turn, they have grown increasingly elaborate.

According to Professor Takaaki Daito at Kokugakuin University Museum in Tokyo, '*Mikoshi* are vehicles that the gods ride, which makes them mobile. They make it possible for people to move deities at will. Festivals utilizing *mikoshi* were established in the middle of the Heian period and later spread to various regions. There are two ways that *mikoshi* are carried. One is in a long procession, and usually that is quiet. In Tokyo, at festivals like Sanja, there might be a manageable, serene procession, but others are in an excited state and jostle the shrine's *mikoshi*. Quite often, people are rowdy and it can be dangerous.'

Daito adds that while festivals 'connect gods and people', they also have the power to connect people with one another. 'When relationships between people or regions have been in crisis due to epidemics and natural disasters, the power of festivals has, at times, helped people to recover and rebuild. *Mikoshi* can also be seen as symbolic of this.'

When *matsuri* are being held, entire districts transform from the mundane to the otherworldly, and the usually reserved townsfolk drop their inhibitions to join celebrations that can last until the early hours of the morning. Streets are lined with Shinto protective paper talismans and hundreds of lanterns, and stalls are set up selling special *matsuri* food and drinks to add to the convivial atmosphere. At some festivals, massive sacred wooden effigies are built, only to be set on fire upon completion. *Matsuri* are of paramount importance to the locals, who anticipate the events months in advance and then reminisce about them feverishly afterwards.

Dr Ray Lucas, an anthropologist and architecture scholar who has researched Sanja *matsuri* for over a decade, says, 'Sanja has cultural significance, it is an expression of a long-held tradition. The continuity of culture manifests in the transformation of the space, from the hanging of paper lanterns or paper effigies through to the *mikoshi* and the hundreds and thousands of visitors. This transforms the space not just for those days, but for the next year. That cyclical nature of time is always talked about in Japanese architecture. [Famed Japanese architect] Arata Isozaki talks about Ise shrine, which is renewed every 20 years. What that means is that you need lumberjacks to cut that wood, you need the forest to be grown, you need the carpenters. The idea of cyclical renewal is really important and that is something that architectural literature is getting back to, instead of this European idea of, "We built this and it will be there forever." We exported modernism all over the world and it does a lot of damage wherever it goes. Actual life is not like that.'

Matsuri are so important to traditional craftspeople that they account for up to half of some artisans' work

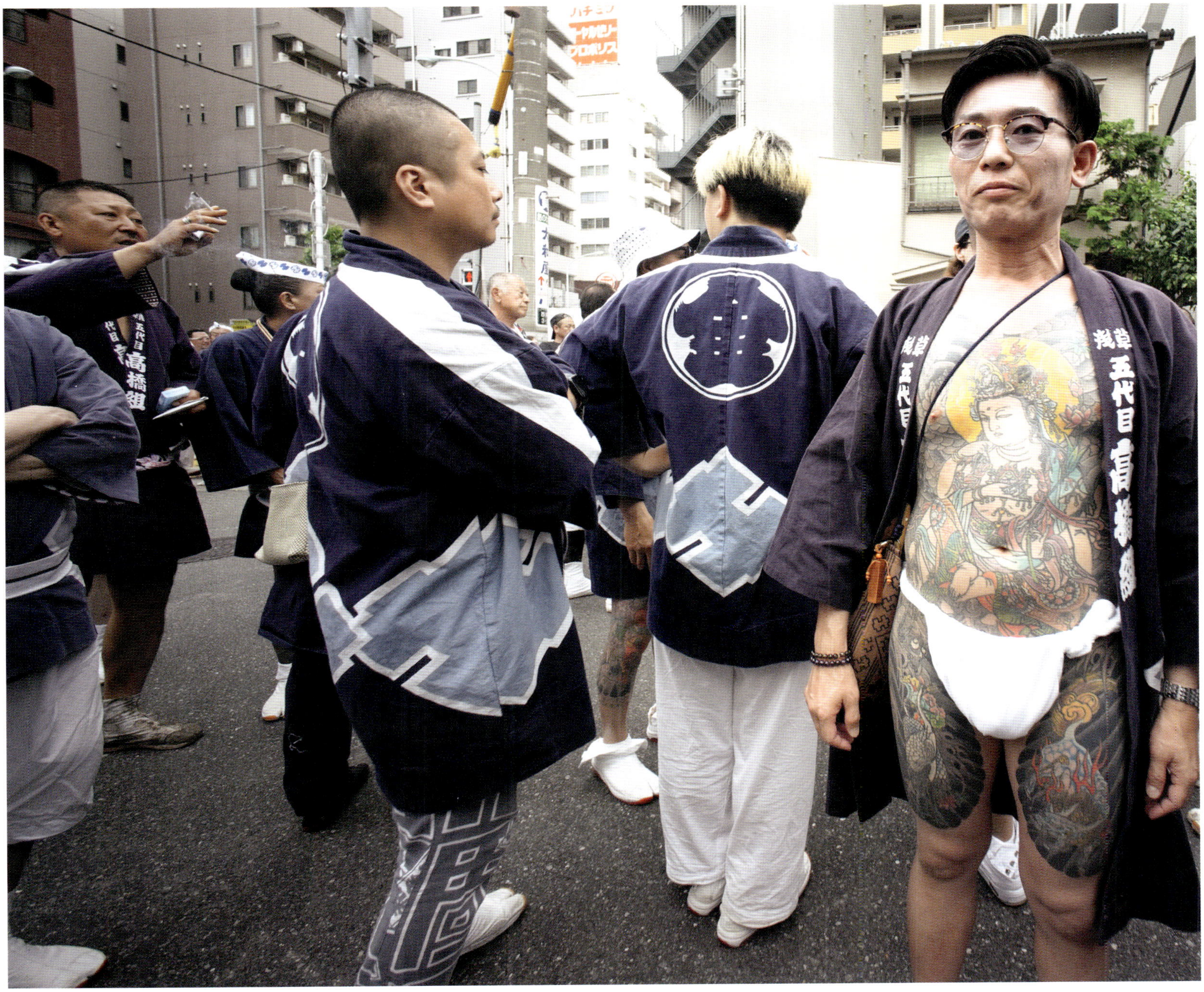

PREVIOUS SPREAD
Festival attendees jostle to carry a *mikoshi*, a portable wooden shrine that houses the gods. Japanese festivals, like the act of being tattooed, are experiential. Horikazu says, 'I think *matsuri* are significant and important. By experiencing the culture and customs of the localities where people are, one can get a deeper understanding of who one is as a person. There are many things you cannot understand just by observing from the outside.'

ABOVE
Nyoirin Kannon, one of the six Kannon Bosatsu manifestations, on the front of a Horikazu client, looking particularly powerful under his festival coat. The outfits worn at *matsuri* are called *happi* or *hanten* coats, and are short, loose-fitting garments that are open at the front. Wearing them enables people to carry a *mikoshi*. The lapels and back are usually decorated with symbols or text to designate affiliation. They were originally designed as workers' uniforms, for people like firefighters.

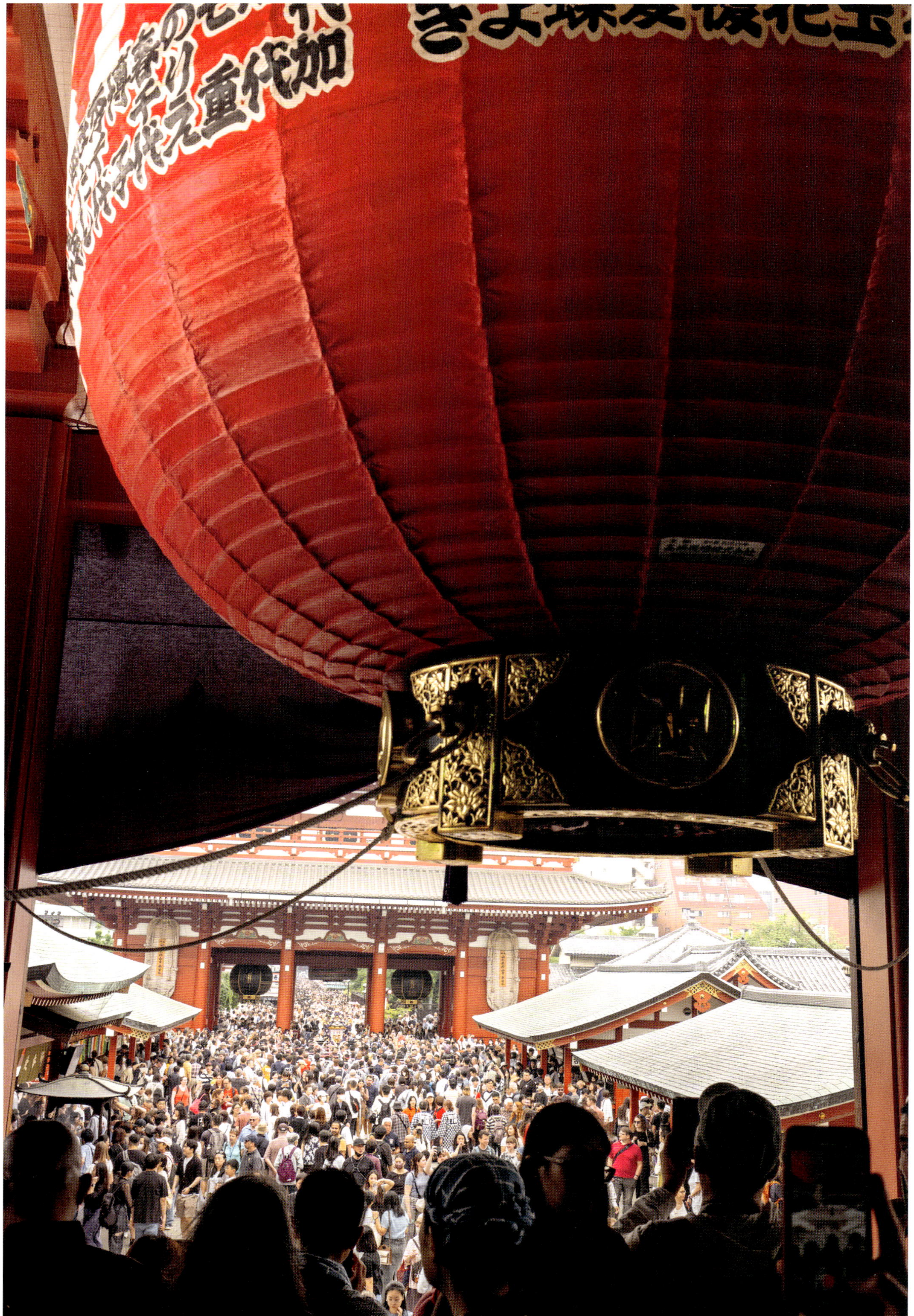

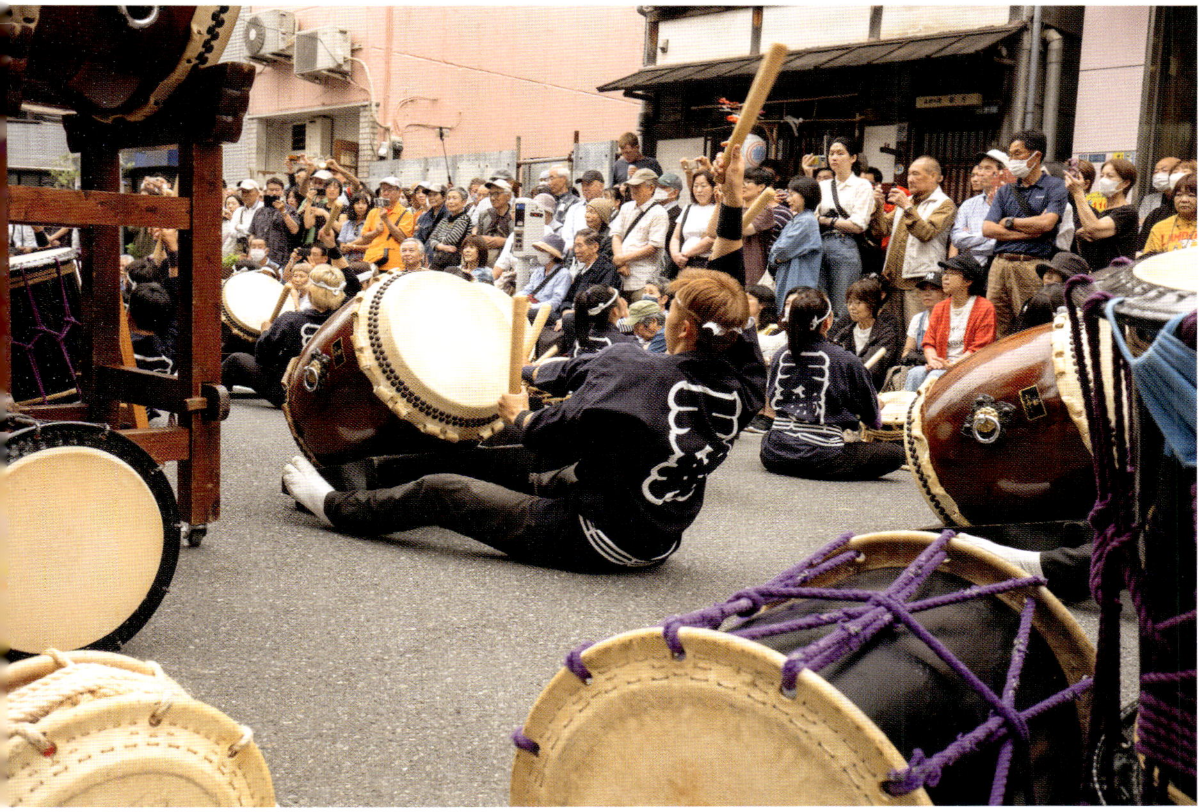

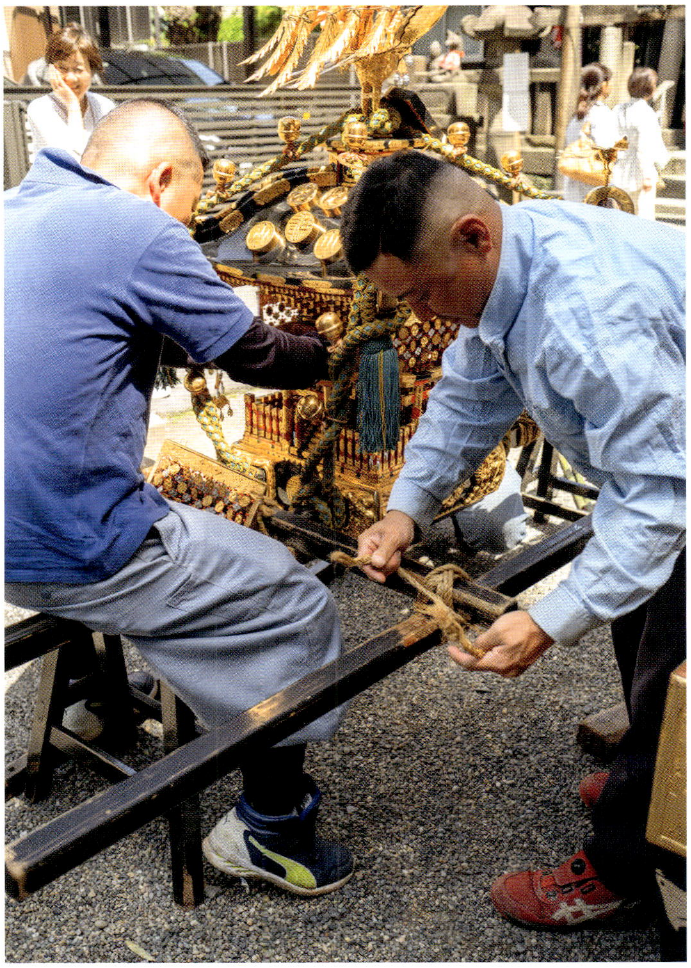

OPPOSITE
A giant lantern hangs from the centre of Senso-ji temple, with Sanja *matsuri* taking place below. Horikazu says that the people who attend the event were usually brought up in families that were enthusiasts, and are interested in a lifestyle that can be called *iki* (people with an Edo-era sense of style). He explains, 'There was this notion that it was cool to be able to carry the *mikoshi* in an aesthetic way.'

ABOVE
Many attendees are involved in festivals as participants and take turns carrying the *mikoshi*, playing musical instruments such as *taiko* drums, riding horses in full costume or helping tug floats down the street with ropes. Others are there just to soak in the atmosphere and drink copious amounts of sake.

RIGHT
Wooden *mikoshi* are a type of sacred palanquin. They often incorporate elements that resemble static shrines, such as a roof, and the ones used at Sanja are lavishly embellished with gold adornments. It takes around 20 steps to make a single *mikoshi*, requiring the skills of carpenters, lacquer artisans and people who apply gold leaf to the roof.

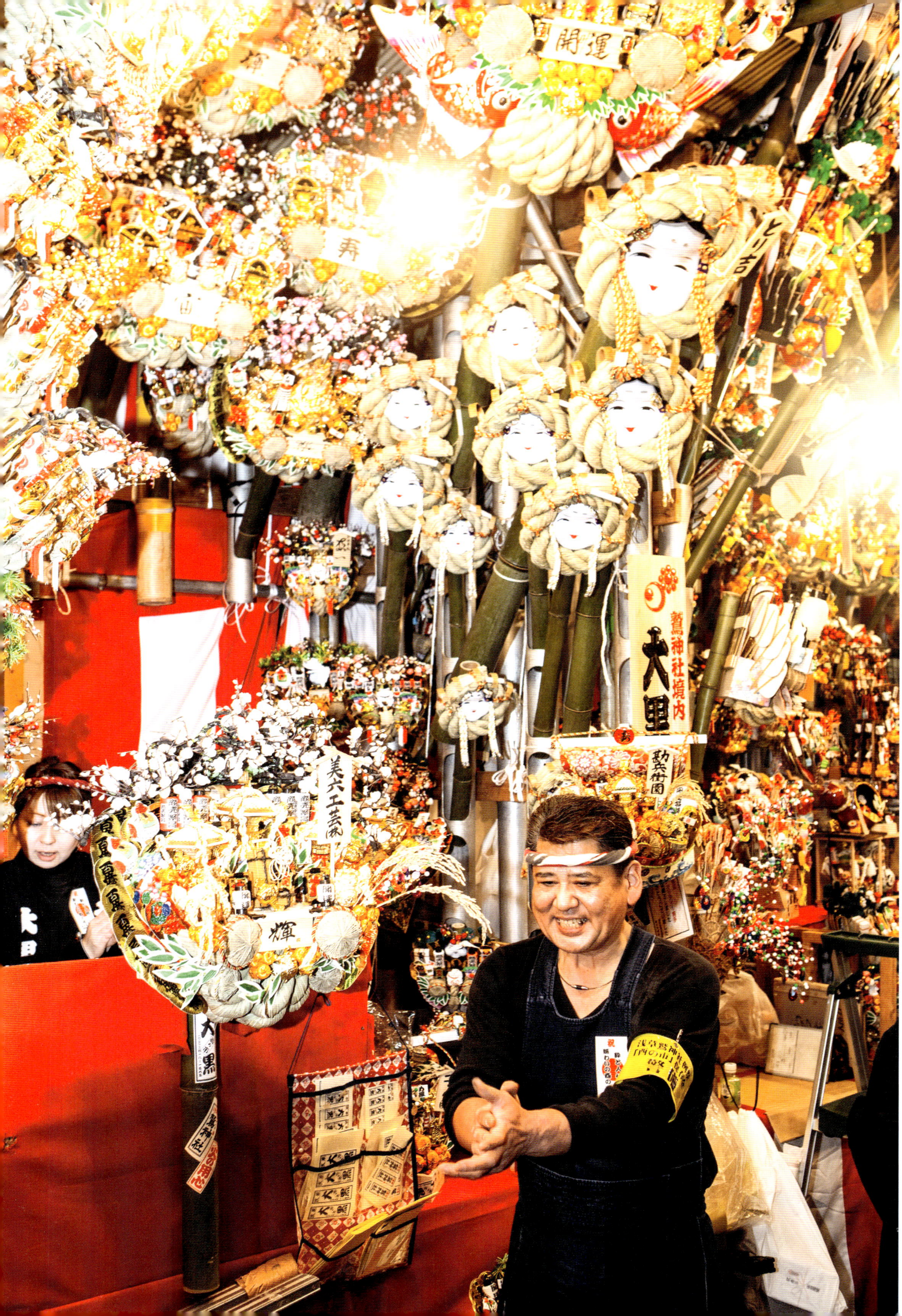
開運
寿
とり吉
鷲神社境内
大里
美六工芸
輝

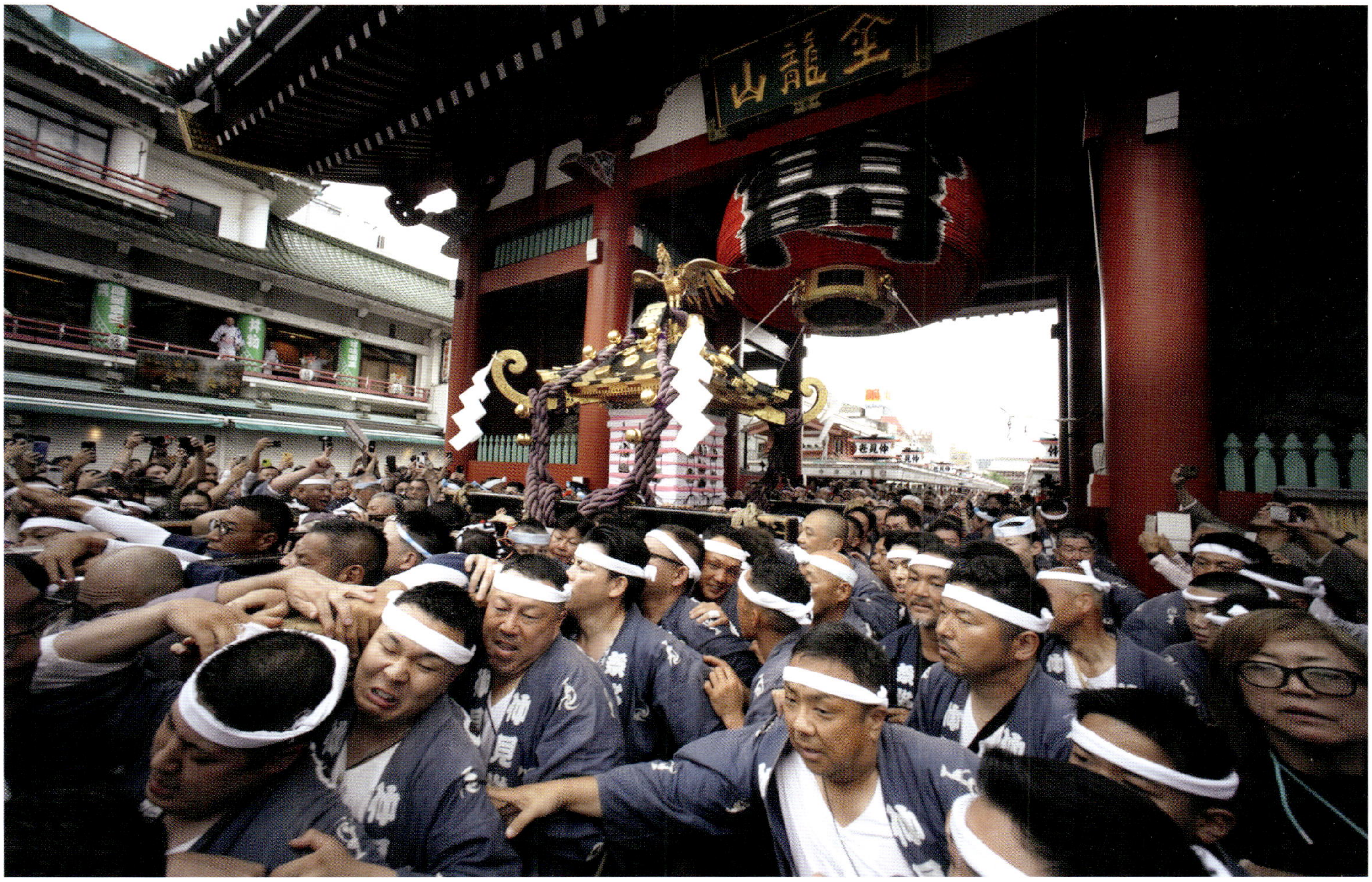

annually. For example, to prepare for just one event, lantern-makers will start crafting thousands of items at the previous year's end. Yukihiro Fujisawa, an indigo artisan in Tokyo's Kyojima neighbourhood, explains, 'We basically exist off *matsuri*. We make the outfits for festivals, such as the Sanja, Fukagawa and Torigoe festivals. There are 44 districts in Asakusa and I make about a third of their festival gear. As long as there are shrines, there will be festivals and the corresponding outfits.'

Likewise, many tattoo artists talk about the year in terms of 'before' and 'after' Sanja as their clients rush to finish their work in time for the festival; the entire calendar is determined by this single occasion as they hurry to complete all the backpieces that have been requested. Horikazu's regulars are some of the most avid *matsuri* enthusiasts, and these events provide a stage on which to see his work. Horikazu is also the only tattoo artist who runs a *mikoshi* association, so a large majority of the tattooed folk at *matsuri* are his patrons, who meet at almost weekly gatherings across Japan. His community of clients and tattoo enthusiasts helps keep the connection between Shinto and Buddhist festivals and Japanese tattoos alive.

OPPOSITE
Imbued in *iki* is the sense of the ephemeral or living for the moment. Festivals are a celebration of these sensibilities and are also visually opulent and decadent. Torinoichi is an annual festival in Tokyo where talismans in the shape of rakes are sold. Many people rely on the luck these rakes provide.

ABOVE
The huge lantern at the gate of Senso-ji temple is folded to make way for the *mikoshi*.

SANJA *MATSURI*

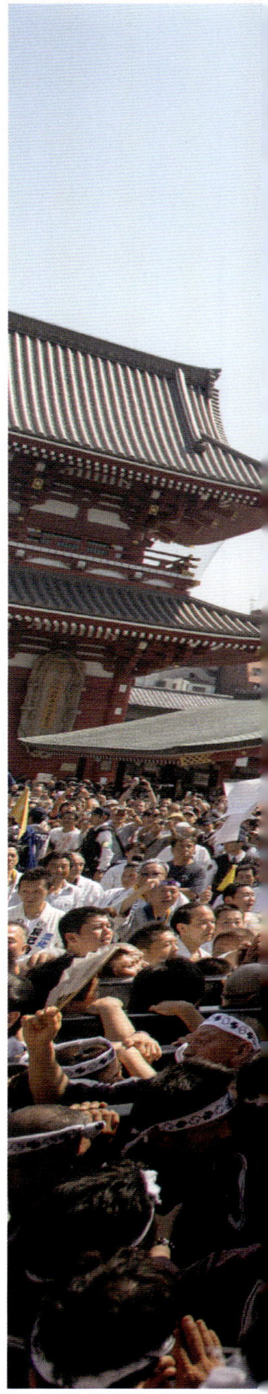

Senso-ji temple is one of the main tourist attractions in Tokyo and is usually overflowing with foreign travellers. However, on the third weekend in May each year, the usual crowds of visitors are overwhelmed by another type of pandemonium: that of Sanja *matsuri* participants, who take over the surrounding district for three days. The festival itself is the largest in Tokyo and attracts over 2 million attendees annually. It is an homage to the fishermen who established Senso-ji after they found a statue of goddess Kannon Bosatsu in their nets in 628.

During the Edo period, Asakusa was a downtown area of Tokyo that was home mostly to commoners. The region still houses many of those that make up the working class: artisans, merchants, craftsmen, carpenters, firemen, food vendors, geishas, gamblers and gangsters. While not every tattooed person at a *matsuri* is a *yakuza*, syndicate members are also heavily present – to the degree that, without them (at Sanja and Torigoe in particular), the festivals would have a completely different, rather tame atmosphere. Sanja *matsuri* ties all these people together and, as an event, encapsulates all walks of life.

Aside from enabling the continuation of traditional cultures, a salient feature of Sanja is that it resembles a massive street party, with the urban space fully reclaimed during the festival period. Entire blocks turn into epicentres of chaos, with the usually religiously ambivalent townsfolk celebrating with a fervour (and copious amounts of drinking) that can go on until the early hours of the morning. Spirits run so high that, quite often, brawls occur on full display. Although it is not legal, heavily inked mobsters often go all out and ride the *mikoshi*. The festival inspires a fierce parochial pride in the area with a gusto that represents the true character of downtown Tokyo.

'The conventional literature on festivals talks about a reversal of power,' Dr Lucas explains, 'but it could be more revealing, or showing the competing relationships. I like the idea of things being taut, in tension. There is something about the overall authority of police, government officials and firemen, and then the different versions of authority from the merchants to the *yakuza*. I don't think you can control something like Sanja – festivals are an implicit threat to the order. Any good festival has that reversal.'

Dr Lucas says there are elements to festivals that are common around the world, such as processions, costumes and 'people carrying things', but that there is a fierce territoriality about Sanja, a sensibility that is getting lost at festivals in other places. 'Whole streets get blocked off to protect *taiko* drummers, who are displaying astonishing levels of skill; there is a sense of ownership, simply being there and doing something, saying, "This is me and this is my neighbourhood." That identifying and grounding in a particular place suggests that all the traffic that is around the rest of the year is getting permission from the locals.'

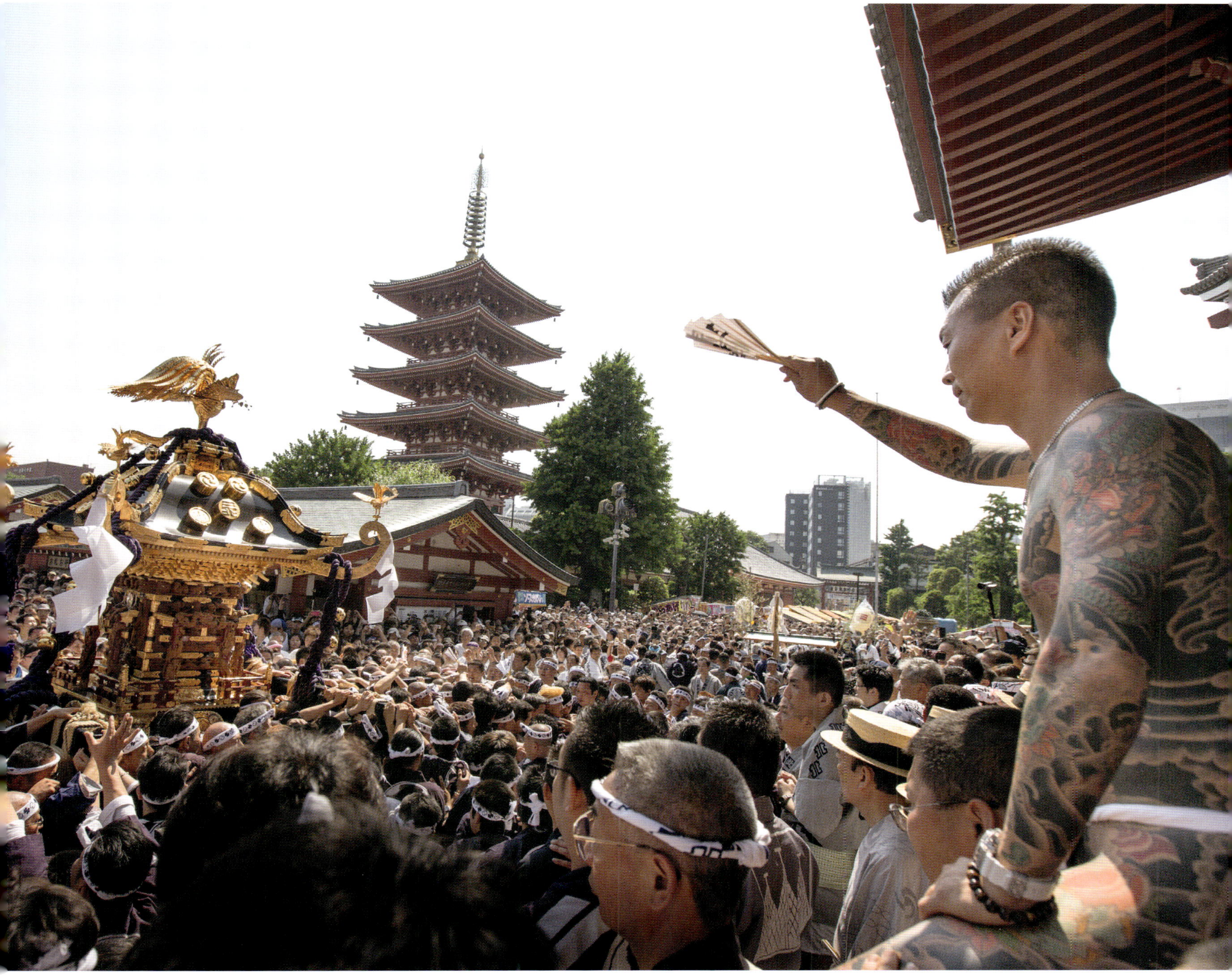

ABOVE
On the Saturday of Sanja *matsuri*, this *mikoshi* enters Senso-ji temple's grounds. It gets purified at Asakusa Shrine, then goes past Senso-ji and is finally returned to Nishi Asakusa, where it is normally parked.

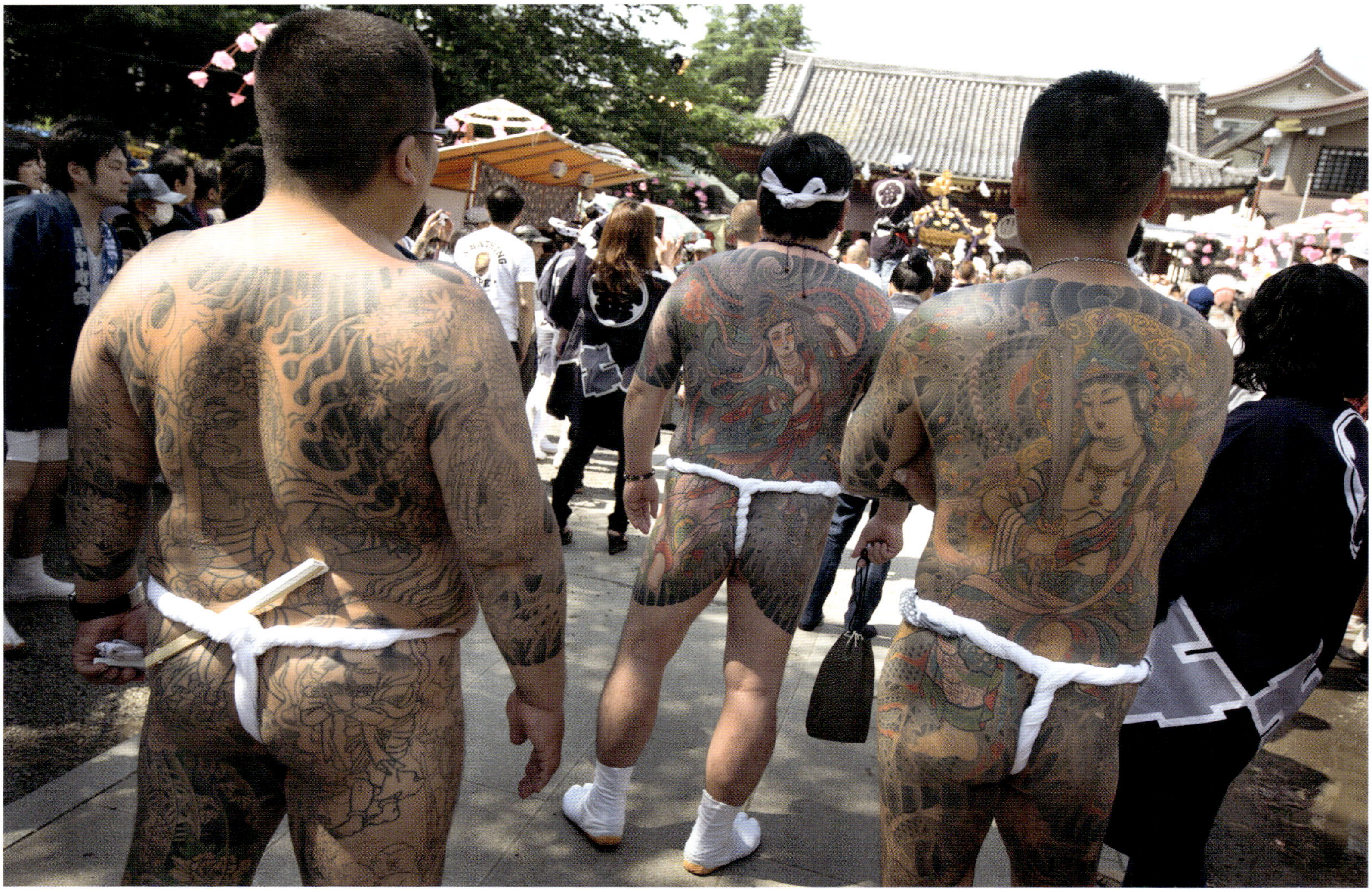

ABOVE
Horikazu (left) with two of his clients outside Asakusa shrine. His father, Shodai Horikazu, tattooed Fudo Myo-o on his back.

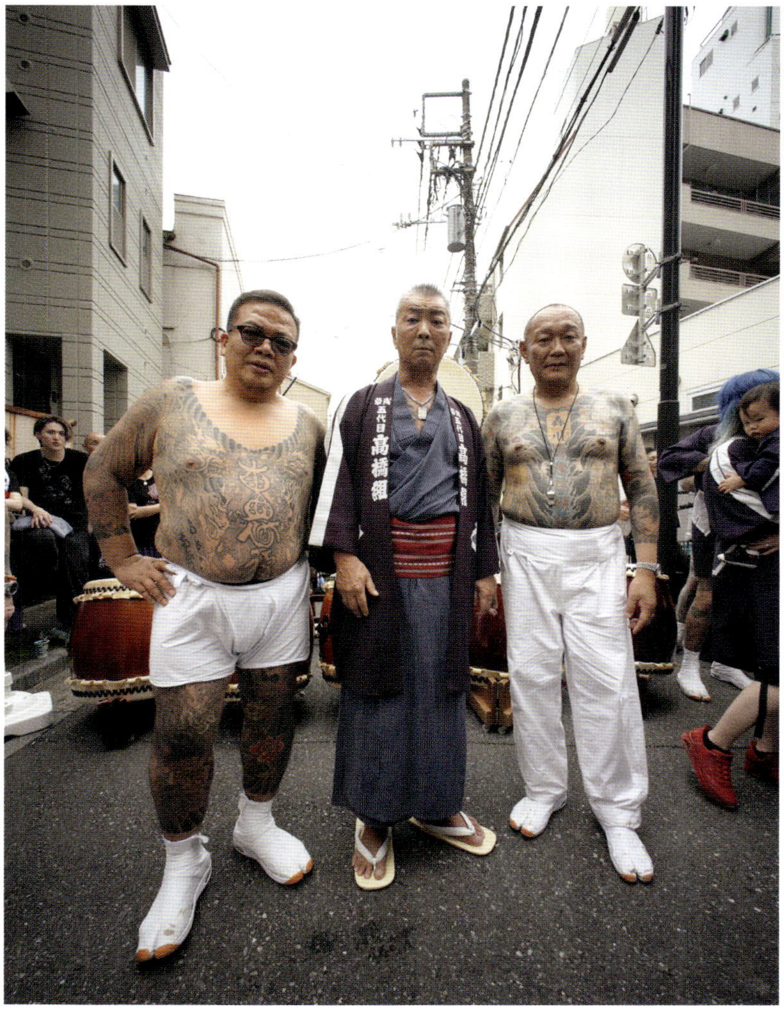

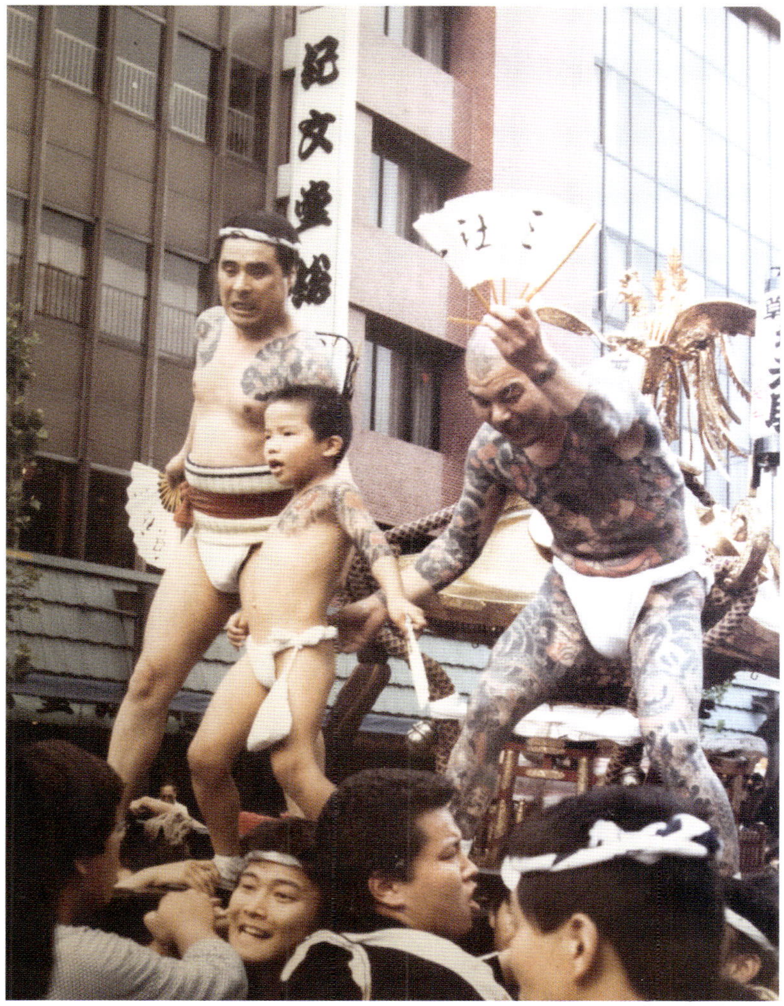

LEFT
A large majority of tattooed participants at Sanja are clients of the late Shodai Horikazu and his son, Horikazu, pictured here on the left. The Buddhist art on their backs adds to the mystery, power and intensity of the festival atmosphere. Besides Sanja and Torigoe, where they are considered to be some of the most visible participants, they also attend festivals elsewhere (and almost everyone depicted in all of the *matsuri* photos in this chapter is a client of Horikazu).

The months leading up to the festival are an excessively busy time for Horikazu, as everyone wants to finish their bodysuits for the occasion. He explains, 'Once I finish Sanja, I can head towards the New Year. I think most people in Asakusa have a cycle like this. It is a community event. Everyone has various roles like making food, standing guard. I am the *mikoshi* organizer and make sure that there are no issues throughout the festival and decide the yearly events. For us, *matsuri* are part of our lifestyles. Anyone can participate; it isn't just people from Asakusa, it is people who also like the fighting aspect as well. In our *mikoshi* group, it is mostly people who are tattooed by me; around 80 per cent of my clients are people interested in festivals too. They are people who were enamoured by what they have seen at festivals and found that aspirational – Sanja is good exposure for my tattoo work.

There are too many voices saying, "You can't cause trouble at *matsuri*," but in some ways the notion of *iki* overlaps with unrest. Yet, ever since the organized crime laws tightened in 1992, after which the Yamaguchi Gumi (*yakuza* syndicate) came to Tokyo, the police became really visible and started to arrest people over the tiniest fights. They are really going after people in *matsuri*. In the past, being unruly was seen as *iki* and it was seen as a show of bravado to go to the front and brawl, but now there are a lot of regulations. It is hard to do anything that is considered to be a nuisance because there are so many cameras everywhere and people film the event on their phones. Twice I have been arrested and locked up for nearly a month for riding a *mikoshi*. I have tattooed almost all of the *matsuri* associations' presidents. In our district, it is really good – they will get told to follow the rules from the shrine and the police, not to allow people to get naked or to show off their tattoos, and not to get into fights – but after the initial greetings, they will come up to us and tell us to take off our *hanten* (coats) and get on the *mikoshi*!'

RIGHT
Horikazu has attended Sanja since he was a young child, pictured here around 1988. He explains: 'I started pulling the *dashi* (floats) when I was in primary school. When I was a kid, my father painted me in Japanese tattoo motifs and made me wear a *fundoshi* (loincloth). I would start to hear the sounds of Sanja a week before it would start and I would be overcome with a sense of anxiety, until it started, which is when the fun began. The atmosphere of Sanja was really tense, the whole town was electric. I really felt that, even as a child.'

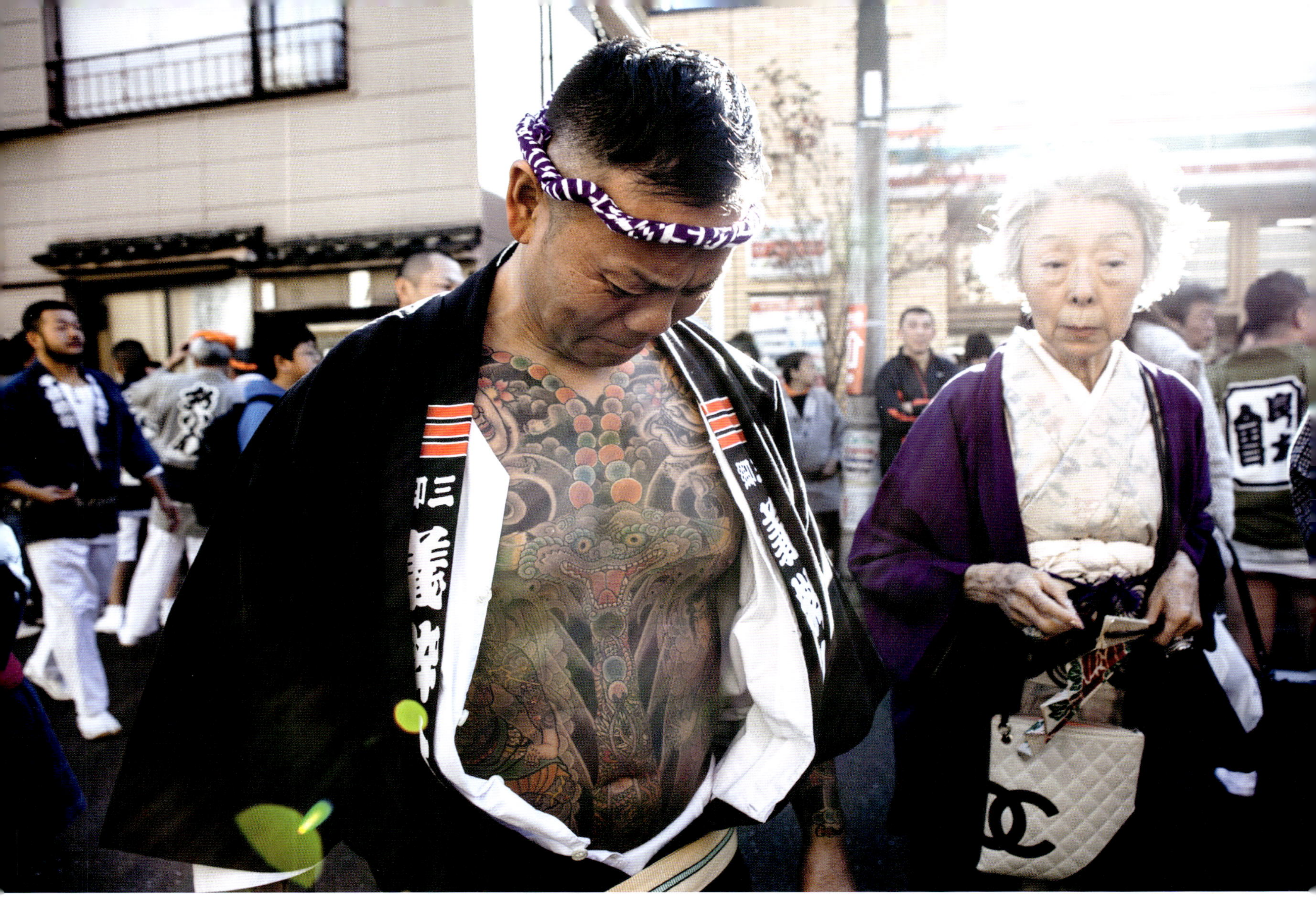

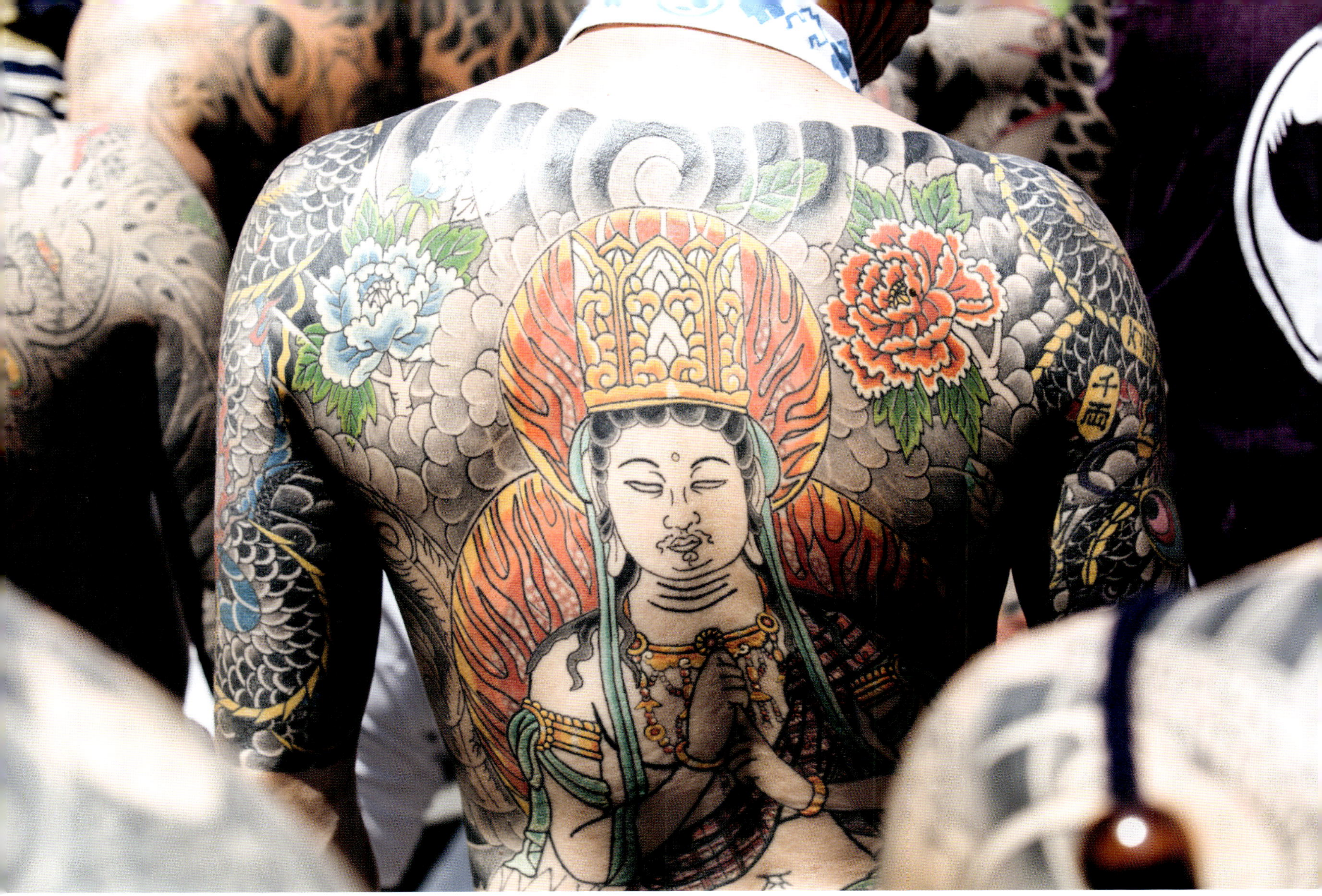
千両

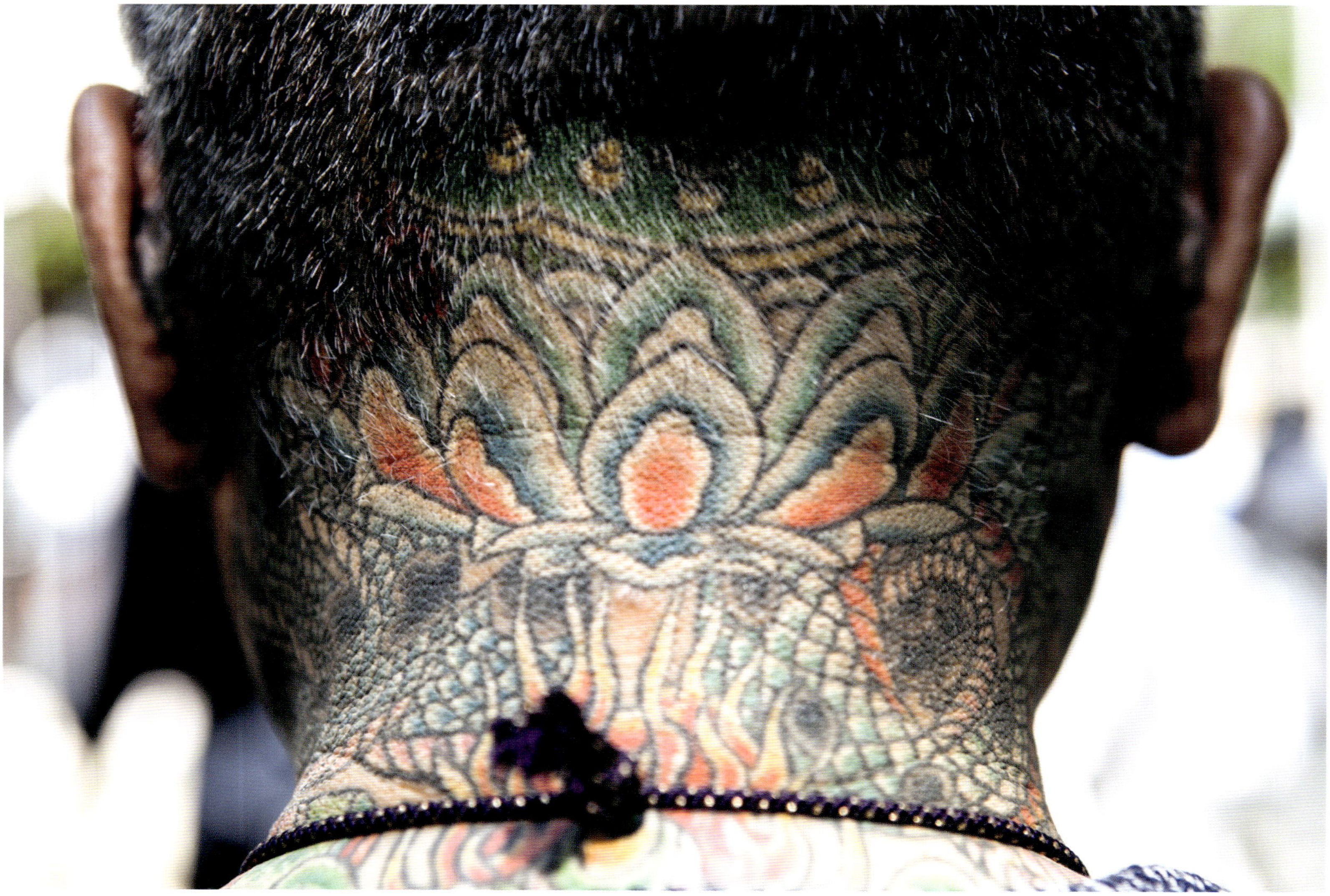

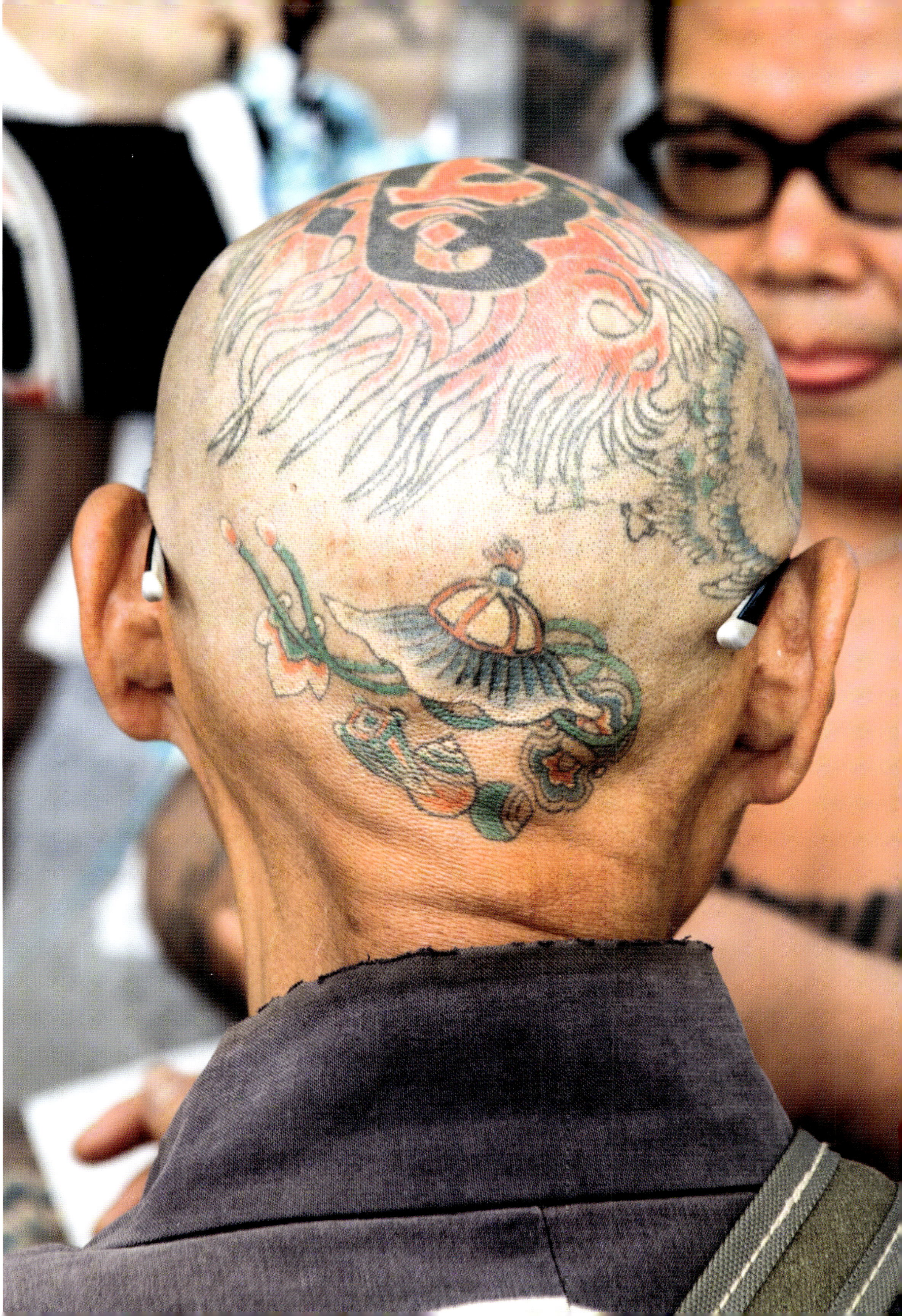

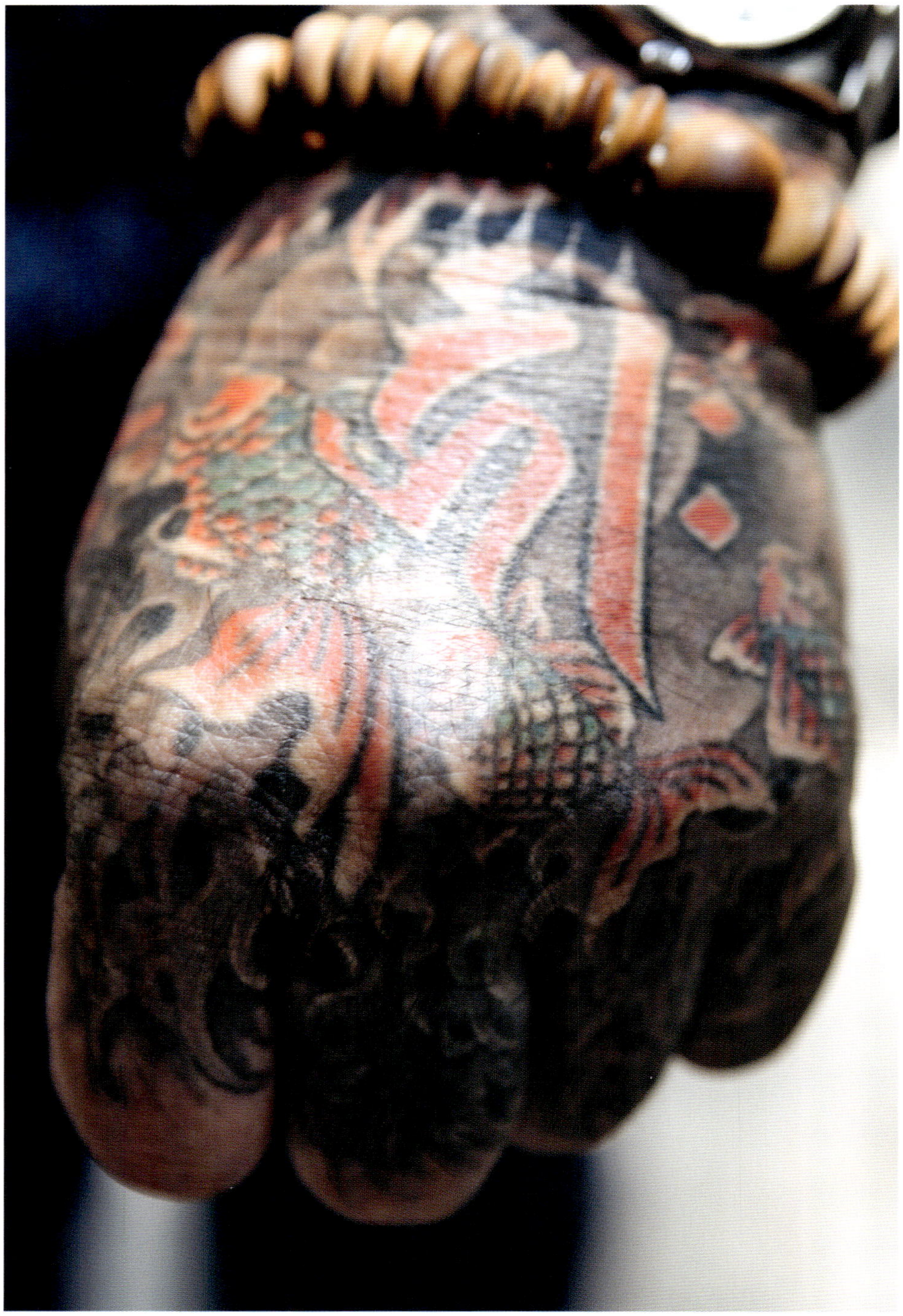

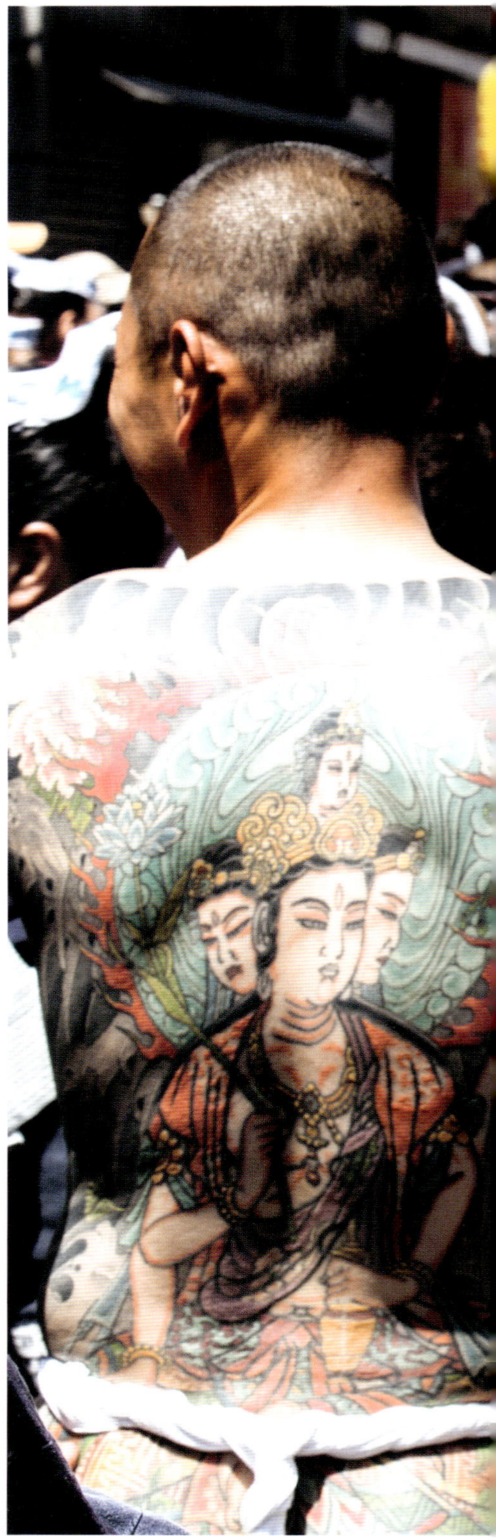

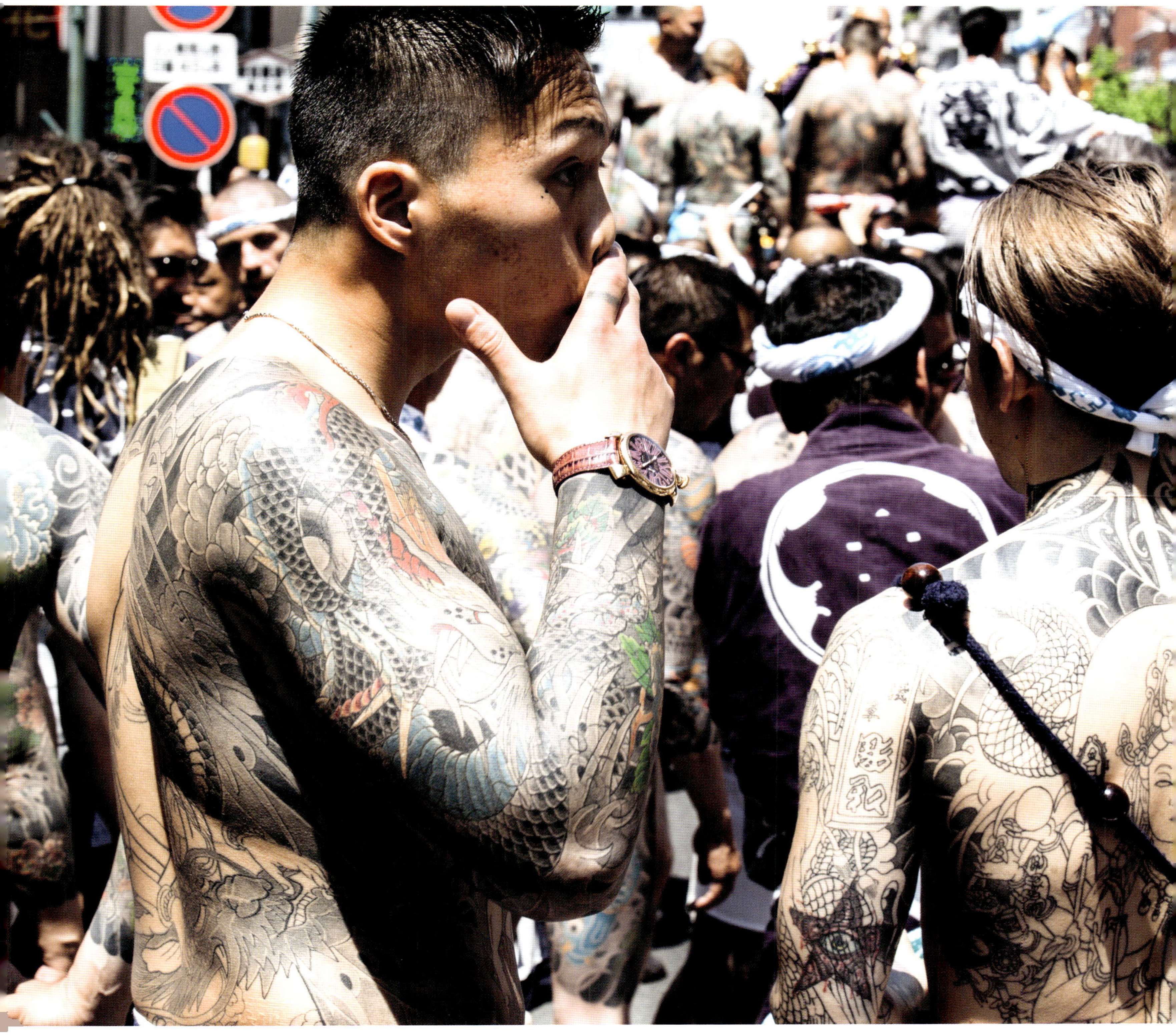

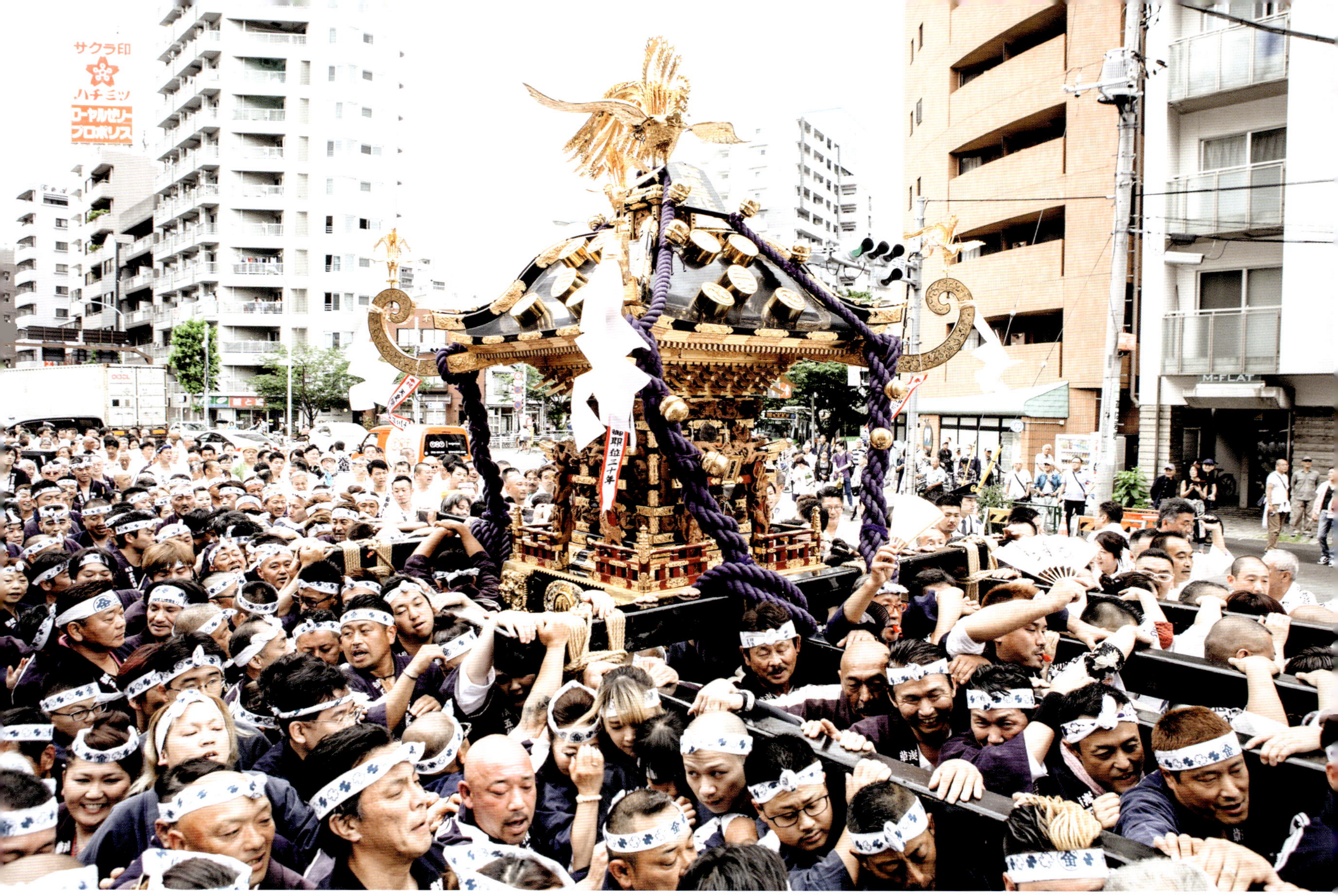
サクラ印
ハチミツ
ローヤルゼリー
プロポリス
M-FLAT

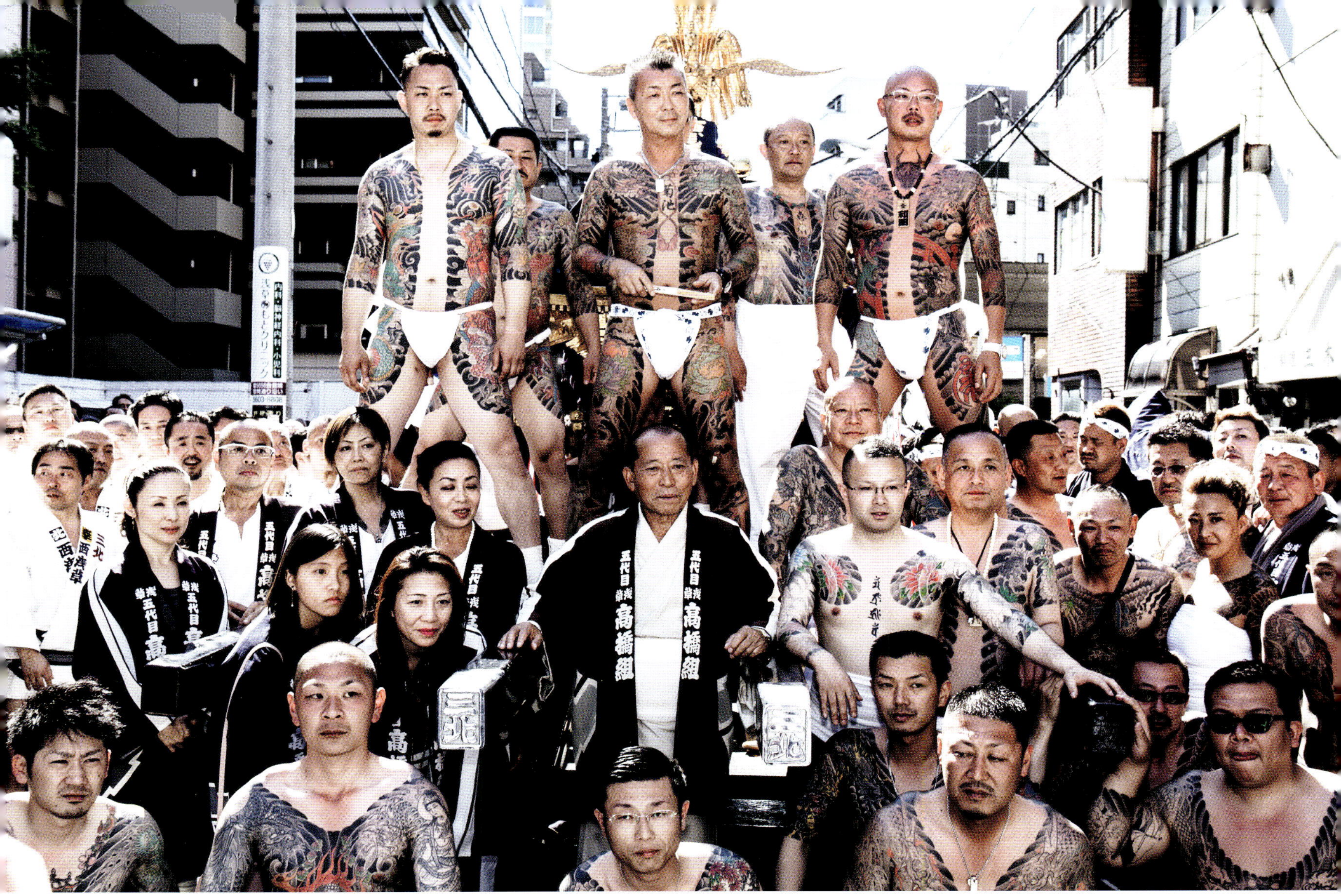

ABOVE
Many tattooed participants and traditional ink enthusiasts carry the *mikoshi* – and at times, even though it isn't allowed, also ride on top of it.

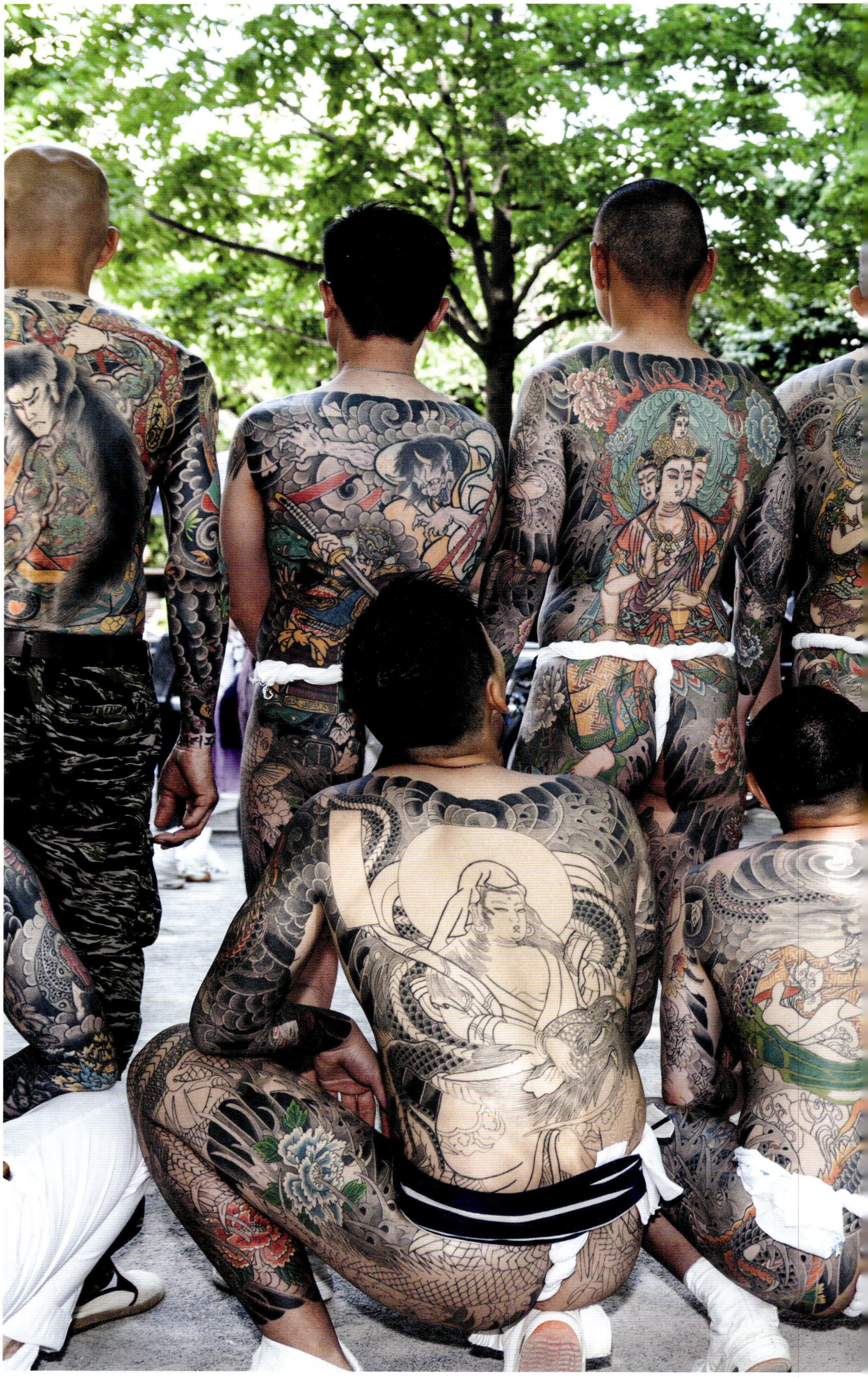

RIGHT
Horikazu explains that there is an aspirational aspect to his clients' requests, in that they see the heavily tattooed attendees at festivals and want to emulate their aesthetic.

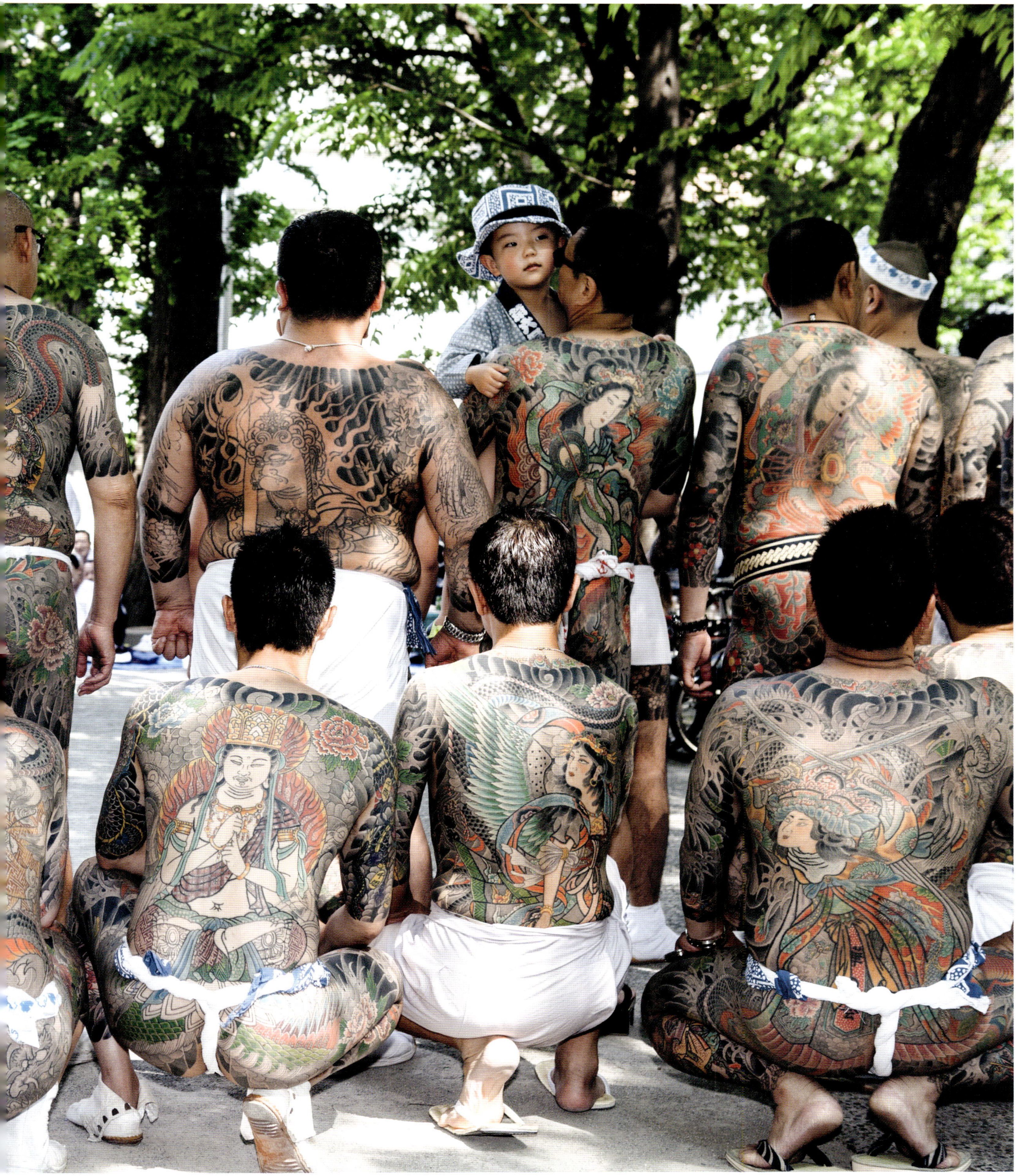

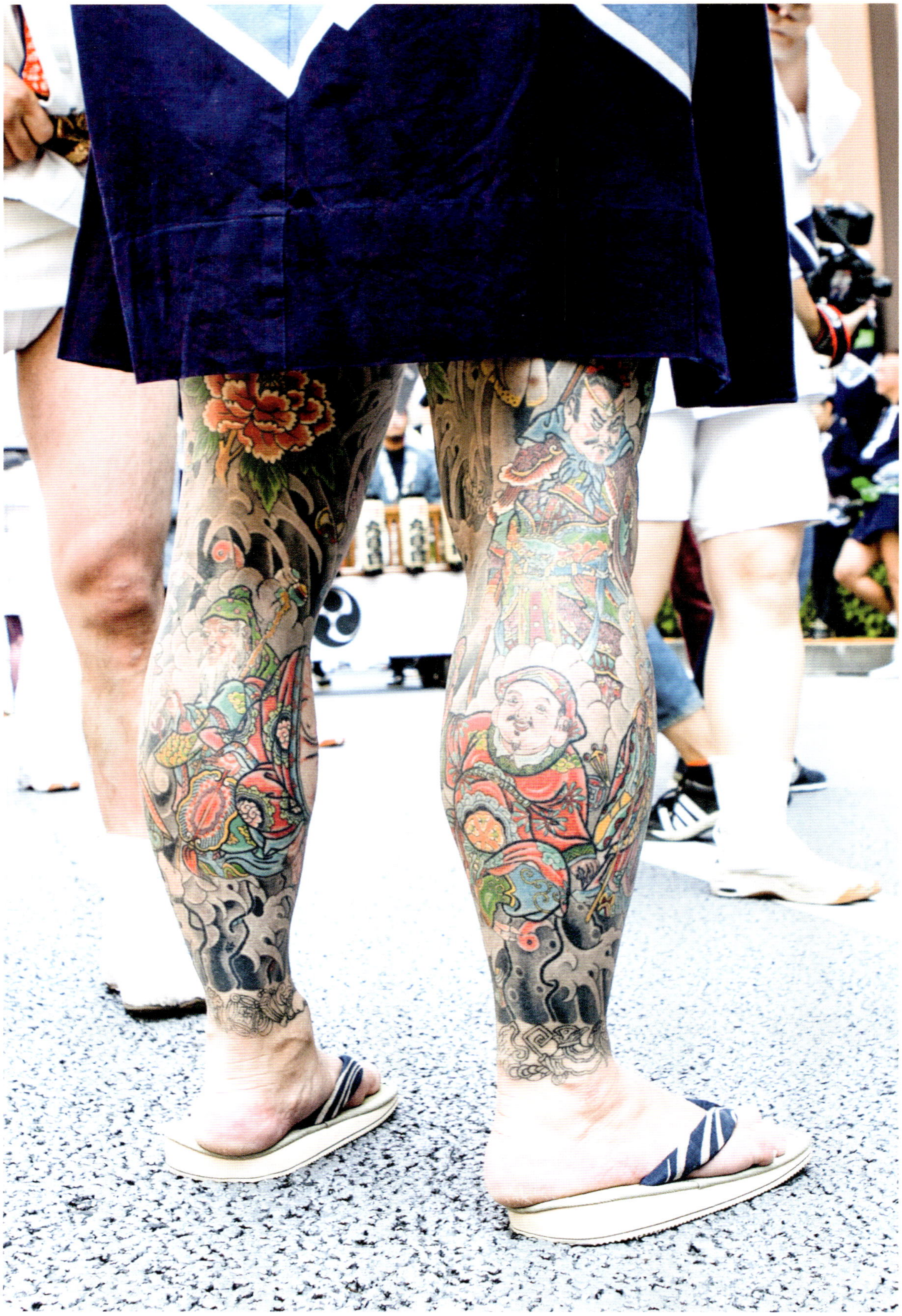

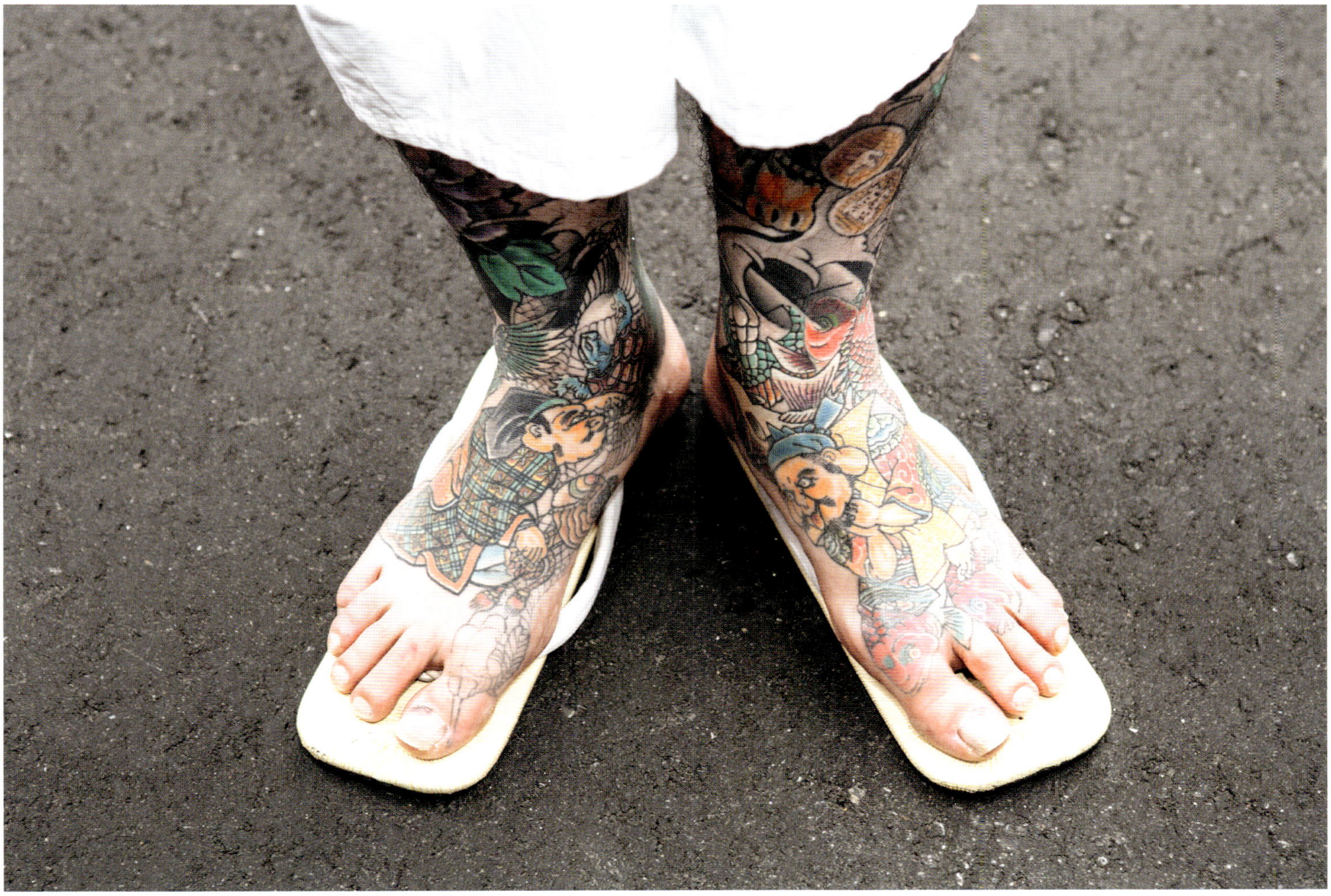

TORIGOE *MATSURI*

Torigoe shrine was founded in the year 651, and Torigoe *matsuri*, held in early June, is one of Tokyo's biggest festivals. Unlike Sanja – which has a large proportion of ogling tourists (many of whom are there to see tattoos) – it still retains a local atmosphere, as it is comprised mostly of participants rather than spectators. The festival was originally held to ward off plagues and protect against disasters.

Torigoe is famous for featuring some of the largest *mikoshi* used in Tokyo processions, the heaviest of which is known as Sengan *mikoshi*, which weighs around 3,600 kilograms (4 tons). *Mikoshi* from 23 town councils participate in the festival, all lit by gorgeous lanterns, but on the final day, the Sengan *mikoshi* leaves Torigoe shrine in the early morning and travels around the district. In the evening, the lanterns on the *mikoshi* are lit and it is returned to the shrine. The tone and overall aesthetic of the *matsuri* is quite intense. The solemn beat of the drums raises the tension and the darkness is illuminated with ethereal hand-held lanterns that are slowly carried up the street. Many of the core festival enthusiasts and associations who are present at Sanja also make an appearance at Torigoe, and the climax is rowdy and chaotic.

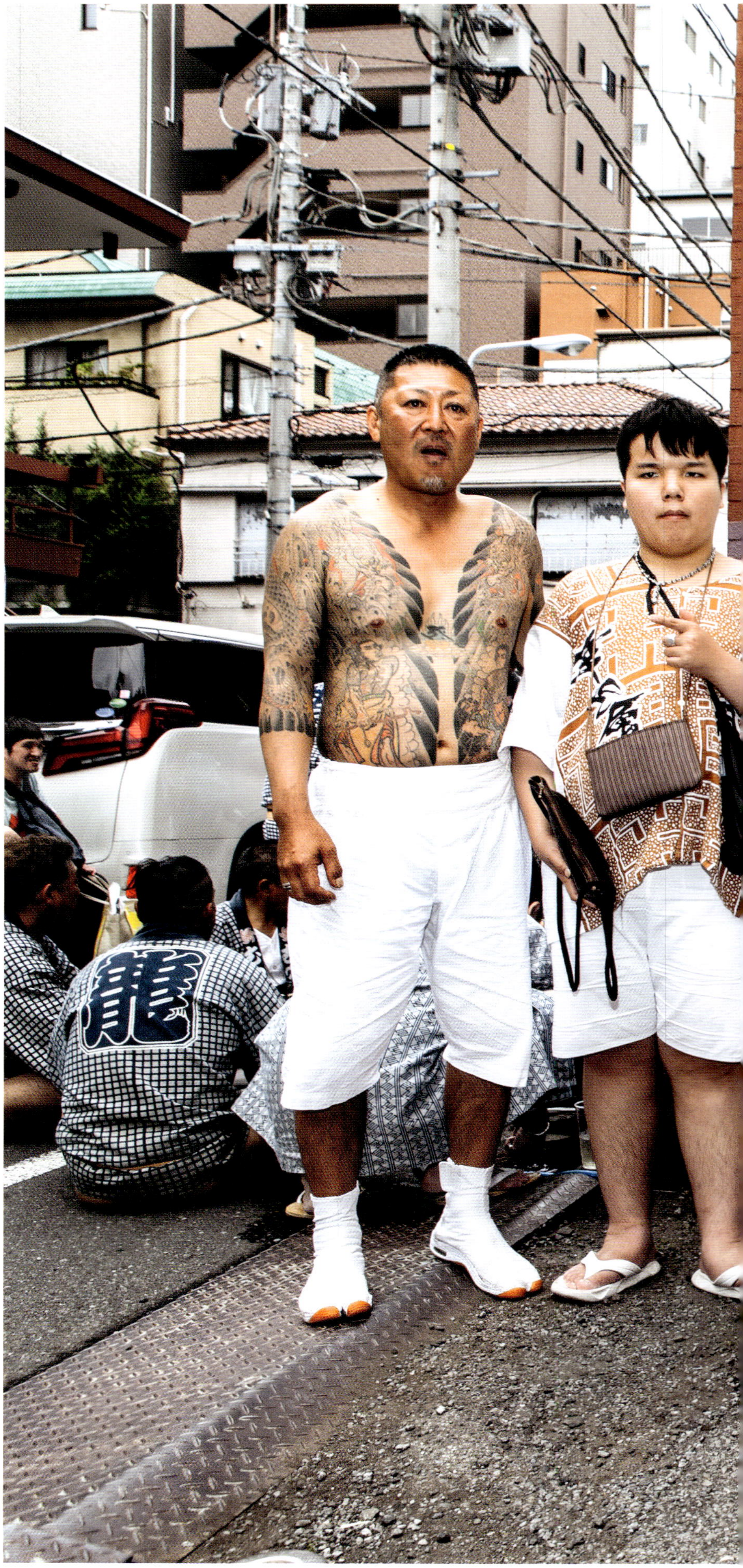

RIGHT
Before Torigoe *matsuri*, Horikazu (back row, second from the right) greets members of other *mikoshi* groups, which are managed by his comrades (who usually sport his tattoos as well).

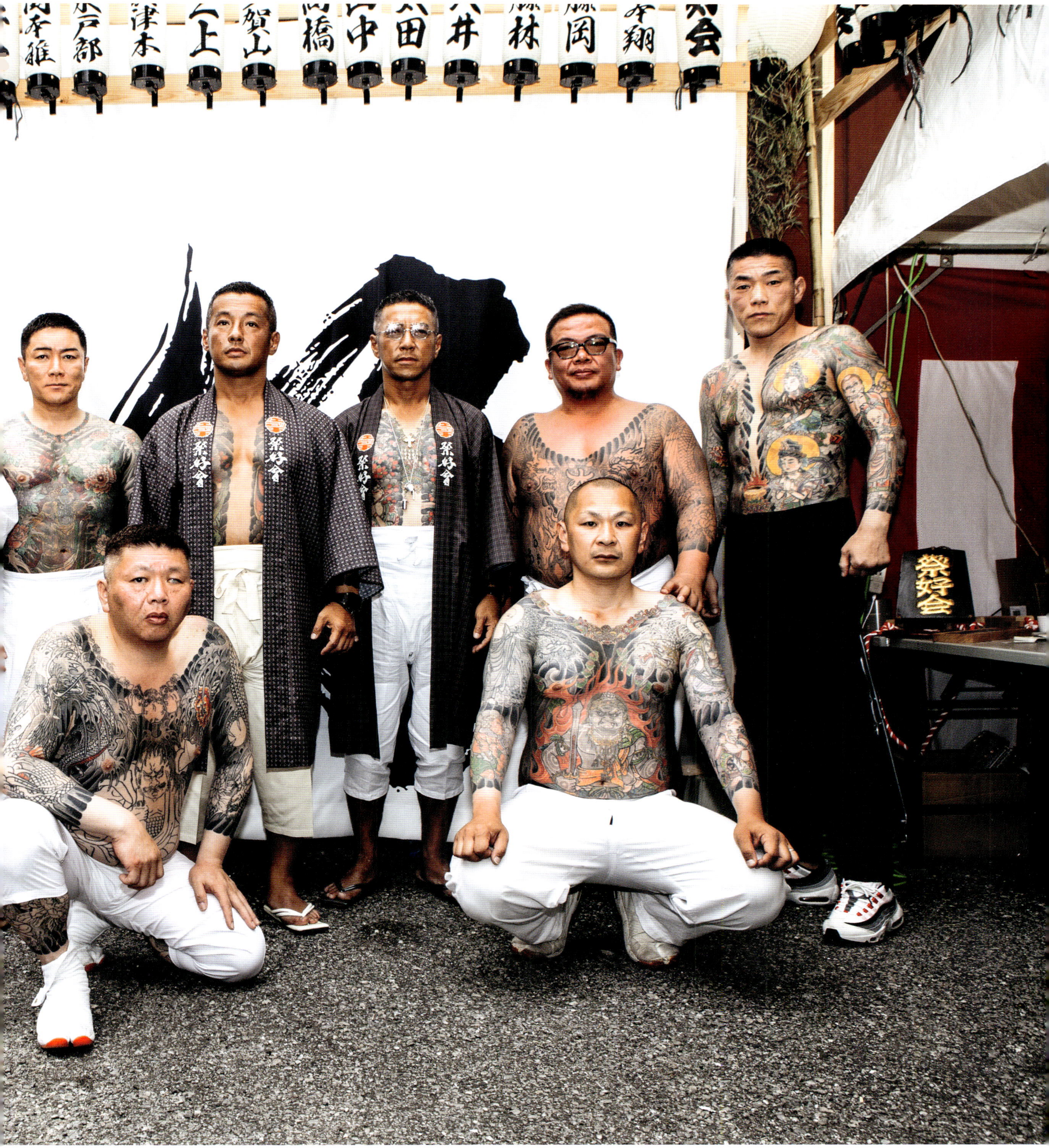
祭好會
祭好会

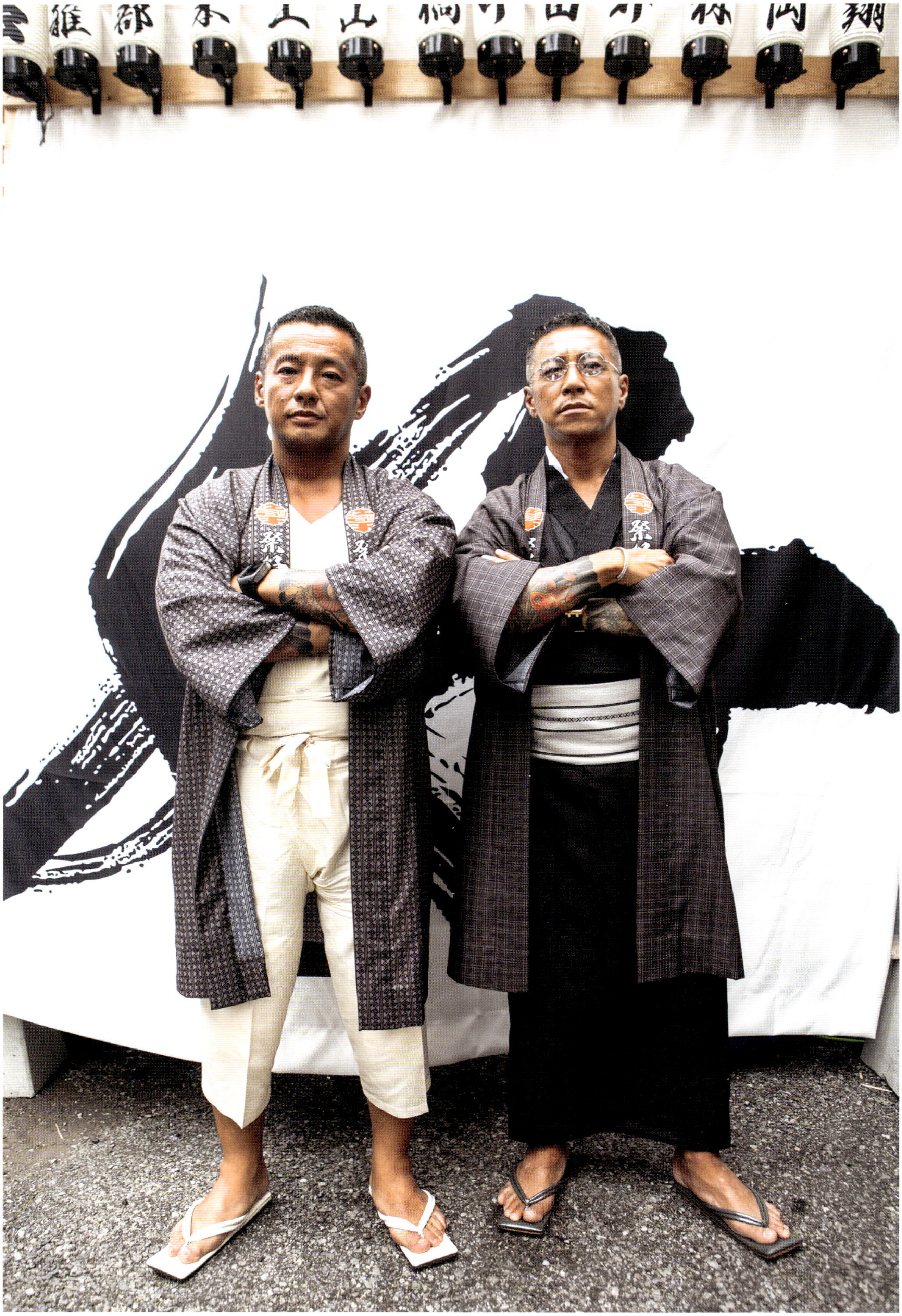

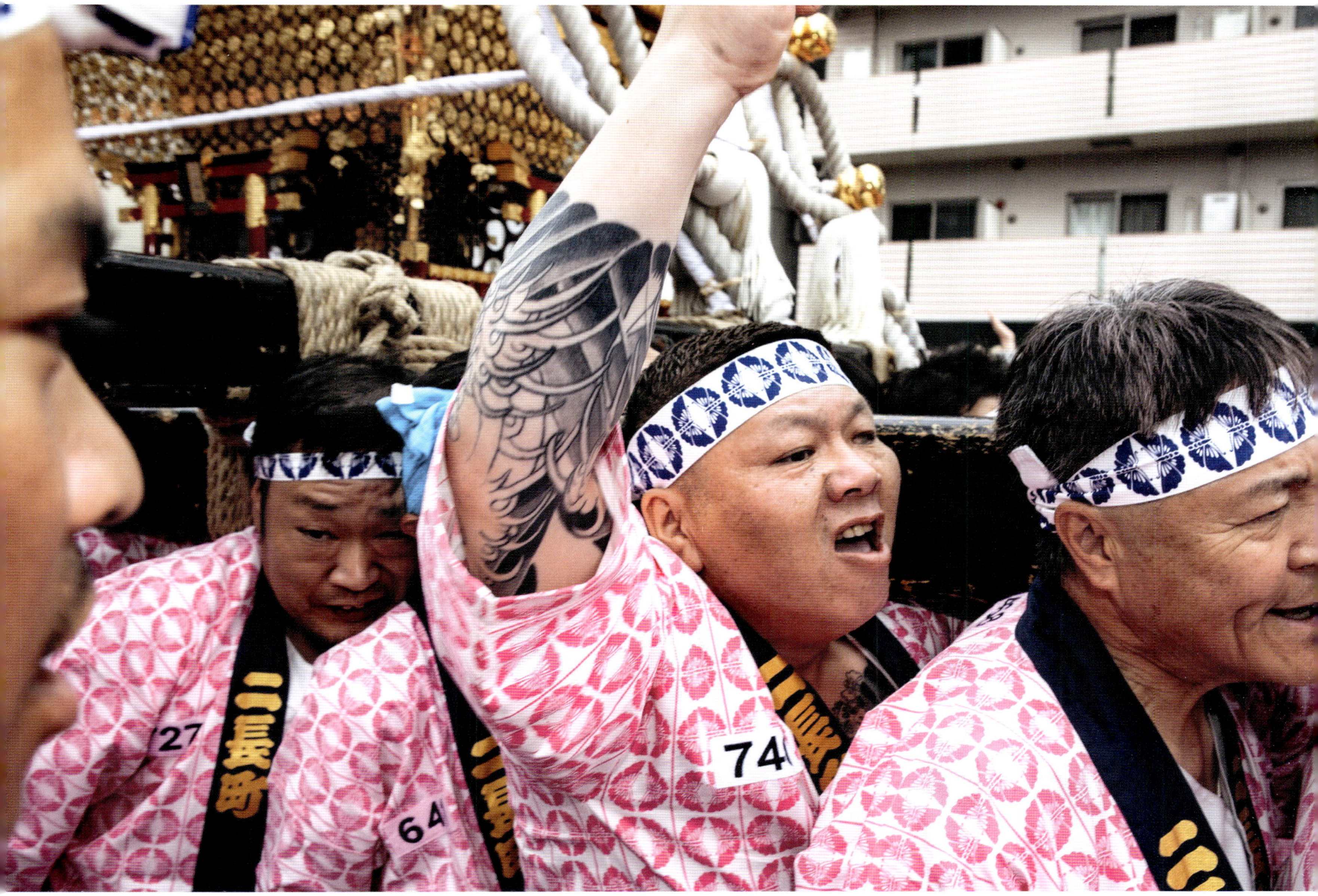
二長町
27
64
74

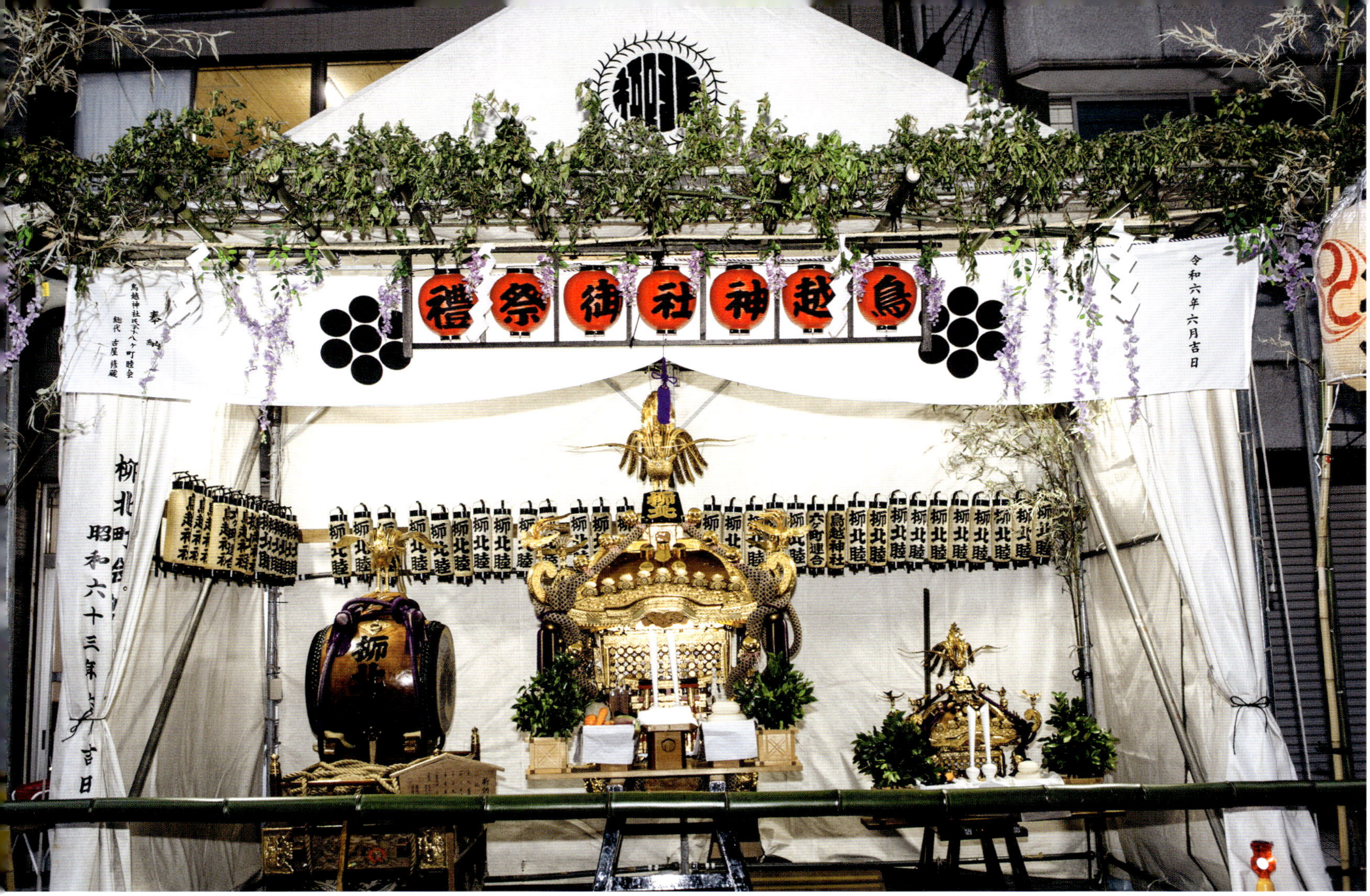
鳥越神社御祭禮
令和六年六月吉日

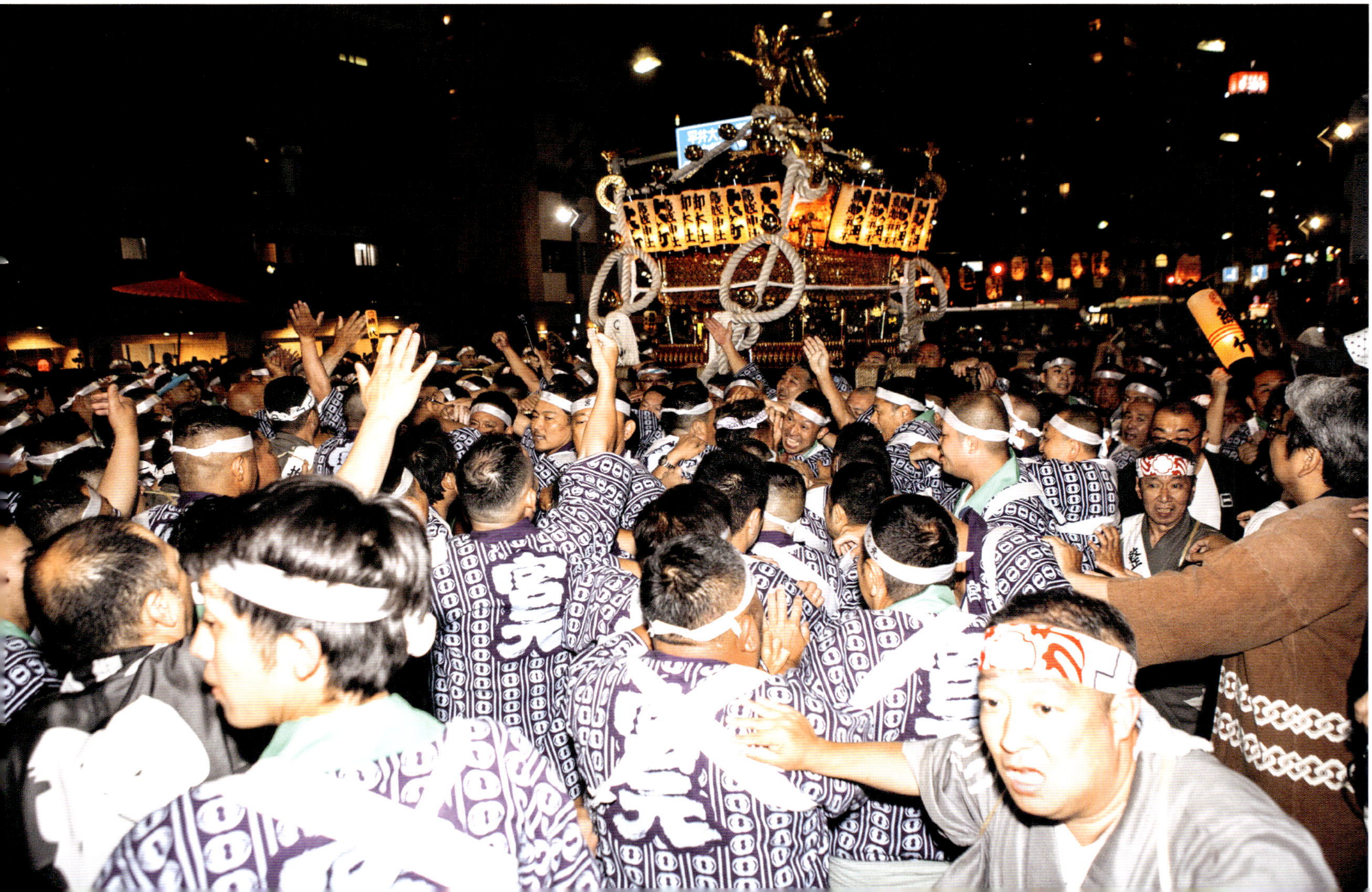

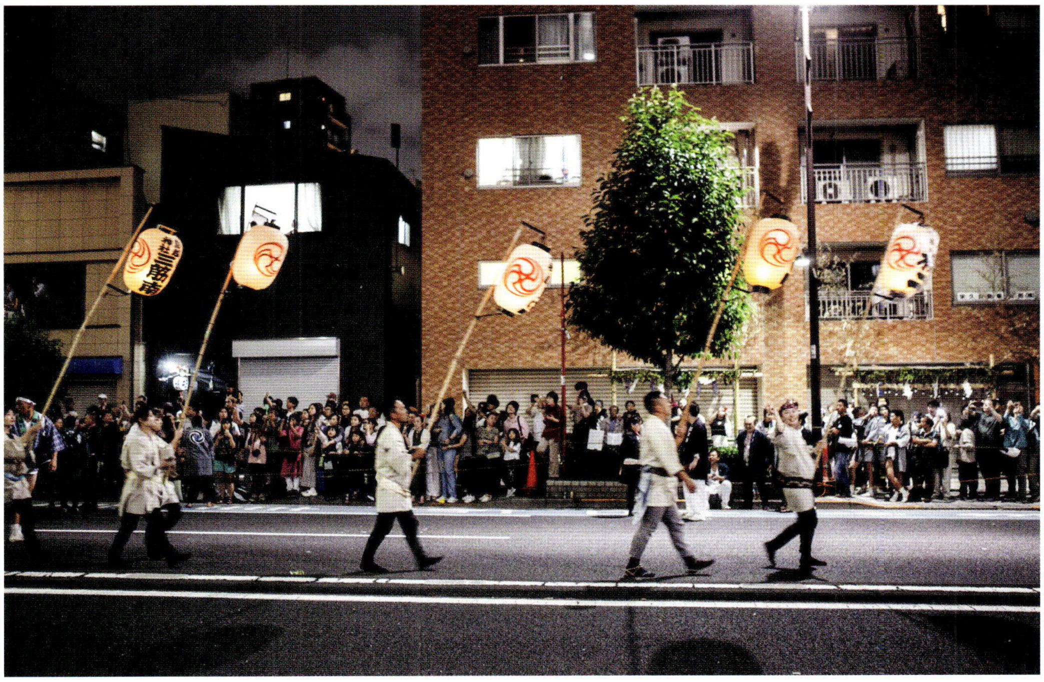

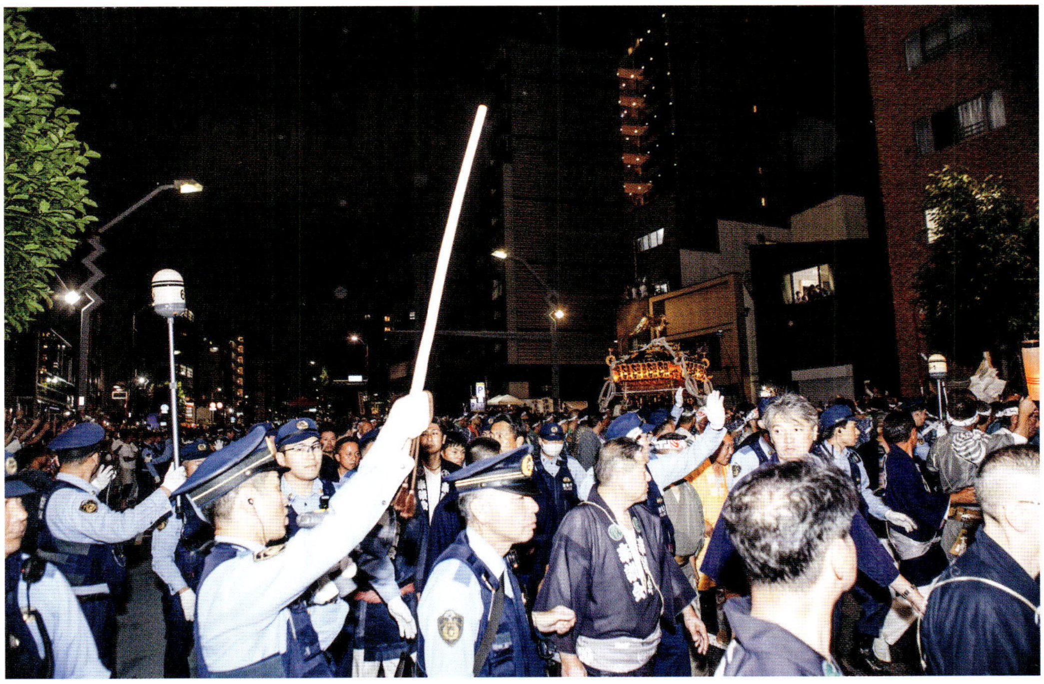

OPPOSITE TOP
Mikoshi are taken on a tour of sorts around the neighbourhood of Asakusa, with stops at *otabisho* (resting spots) along the way. The shrines go to get blessed and return to their homes.

OPPOSITE BOTTOM
Mikoshi are extremely heavy and are carried by many people at *matsuri*, who take turns. Several dozen members of the *mikoshi* association will also gather around it, shouting and chanting rhythmically, accompanied by drums and flutes. Torigoe is one of the most intense, chaotic *matsuri* in the Tokyo region.

TOP
Matsuri are ritualistic religious gatherings. Much emphasis is placed on aesthetic elements, such as lanterns, which provide an ethereal atmosphere.

BOTTOM
There is a heavy police presence at festivals, as high-spirited brawls often take place.

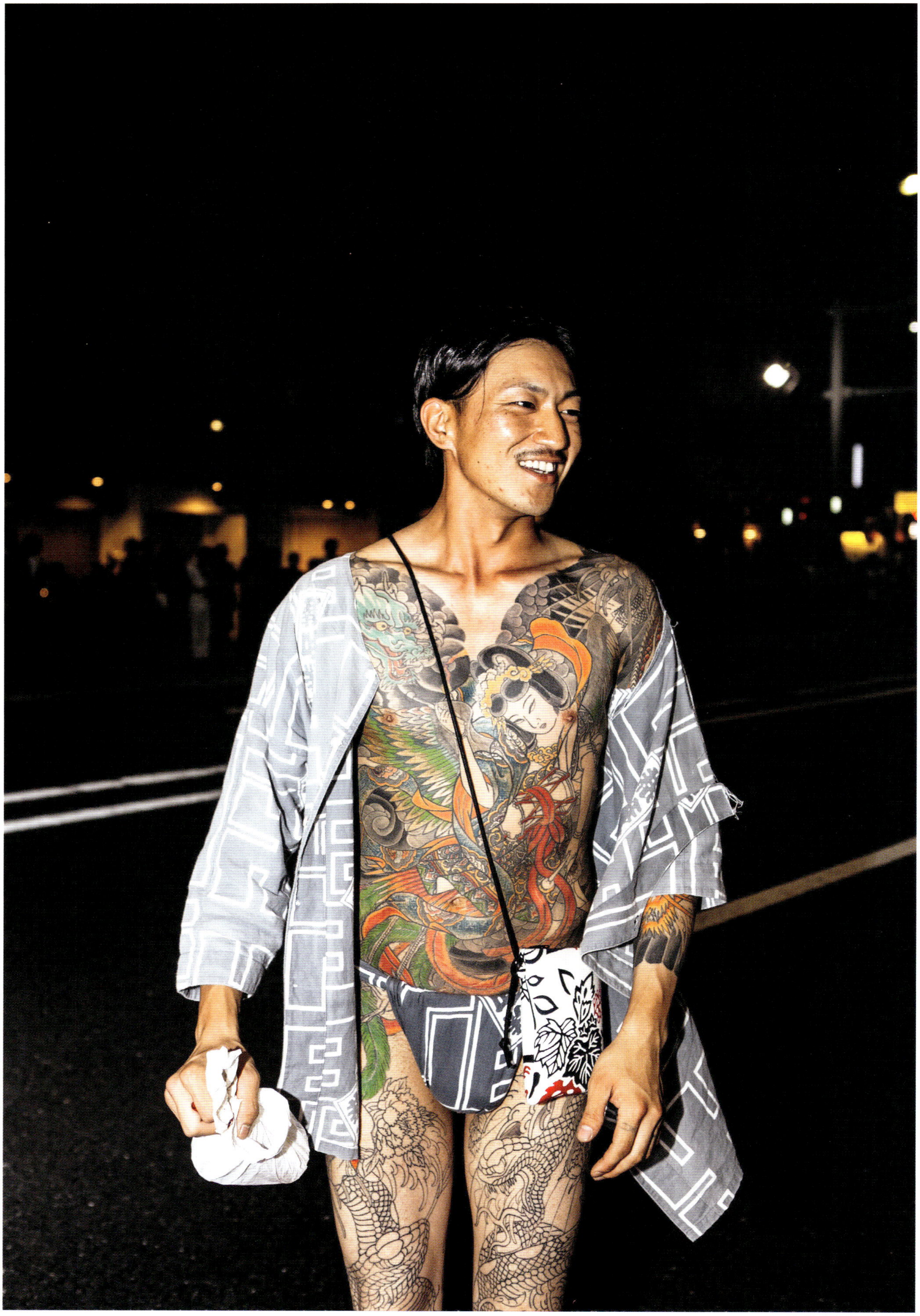

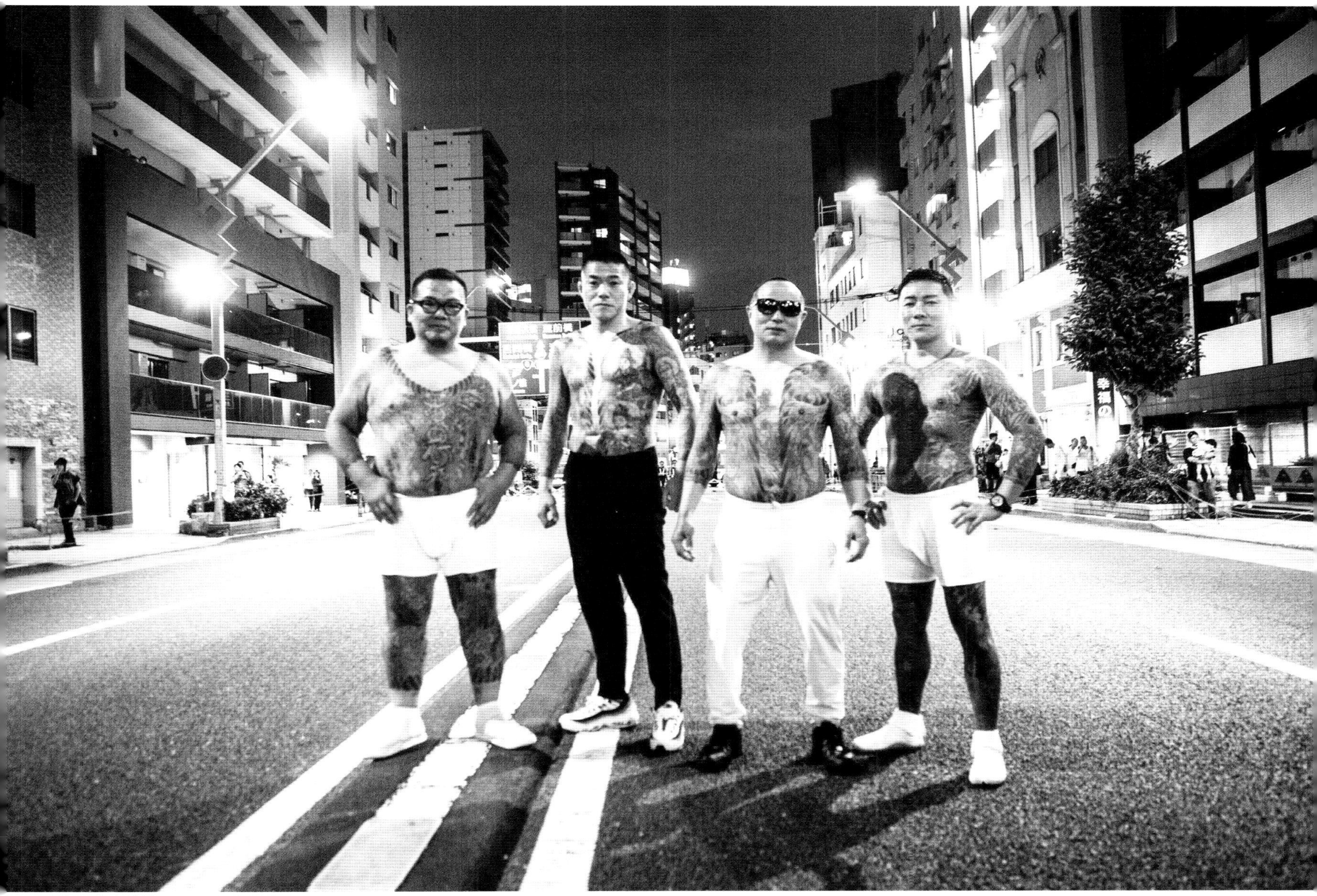

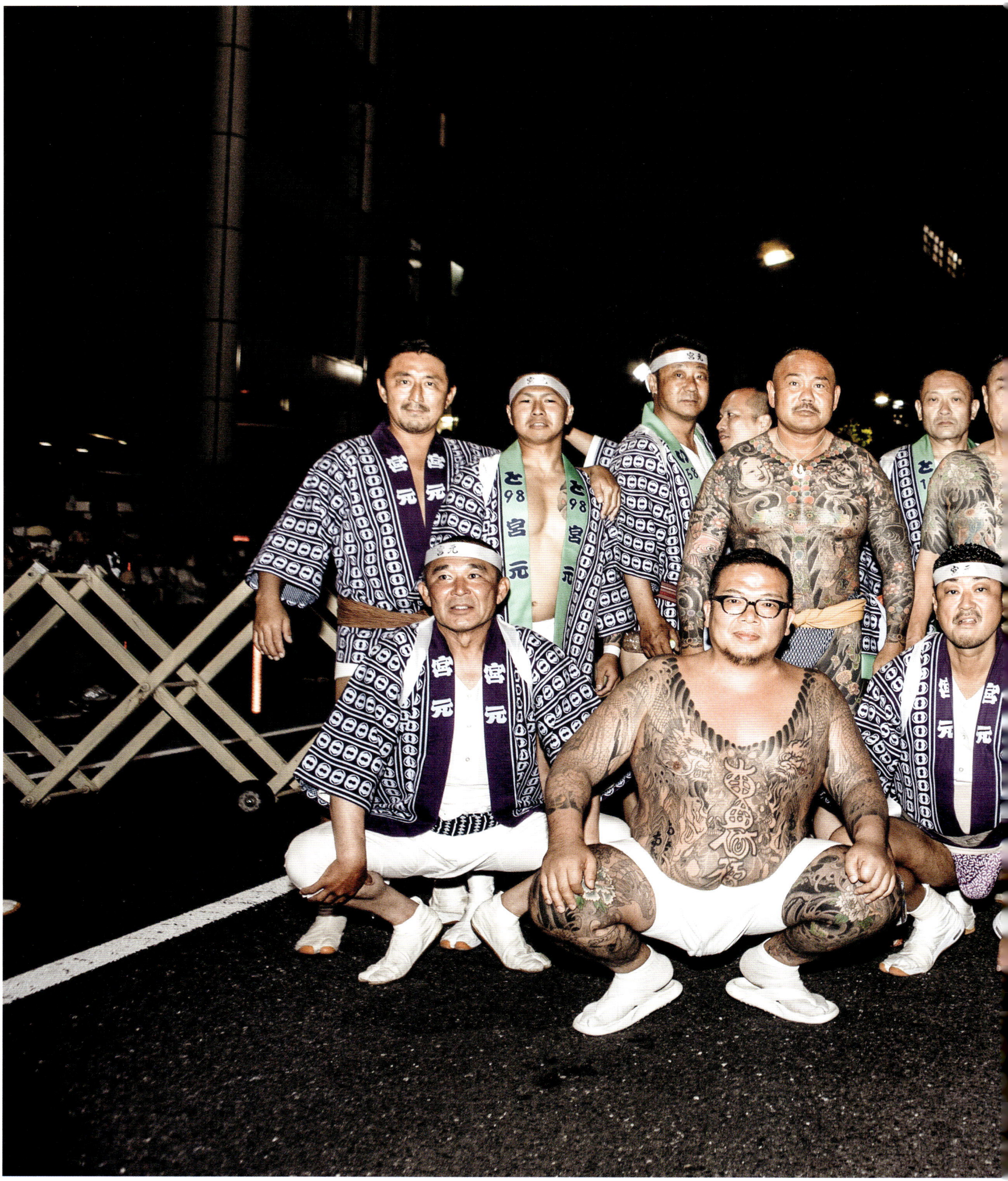
宮元
と 98 宮元

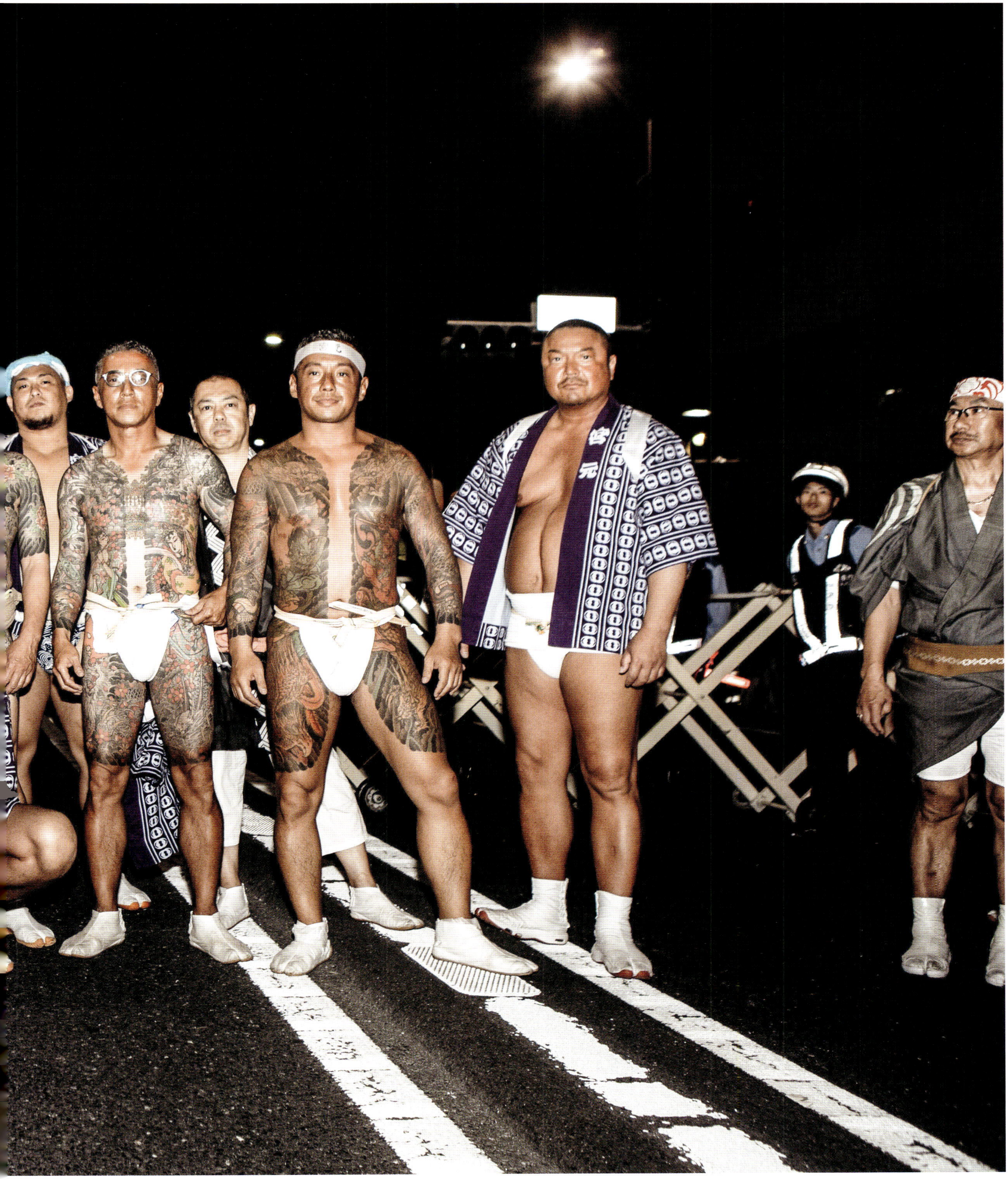

KAWAGOE *MATSURI*

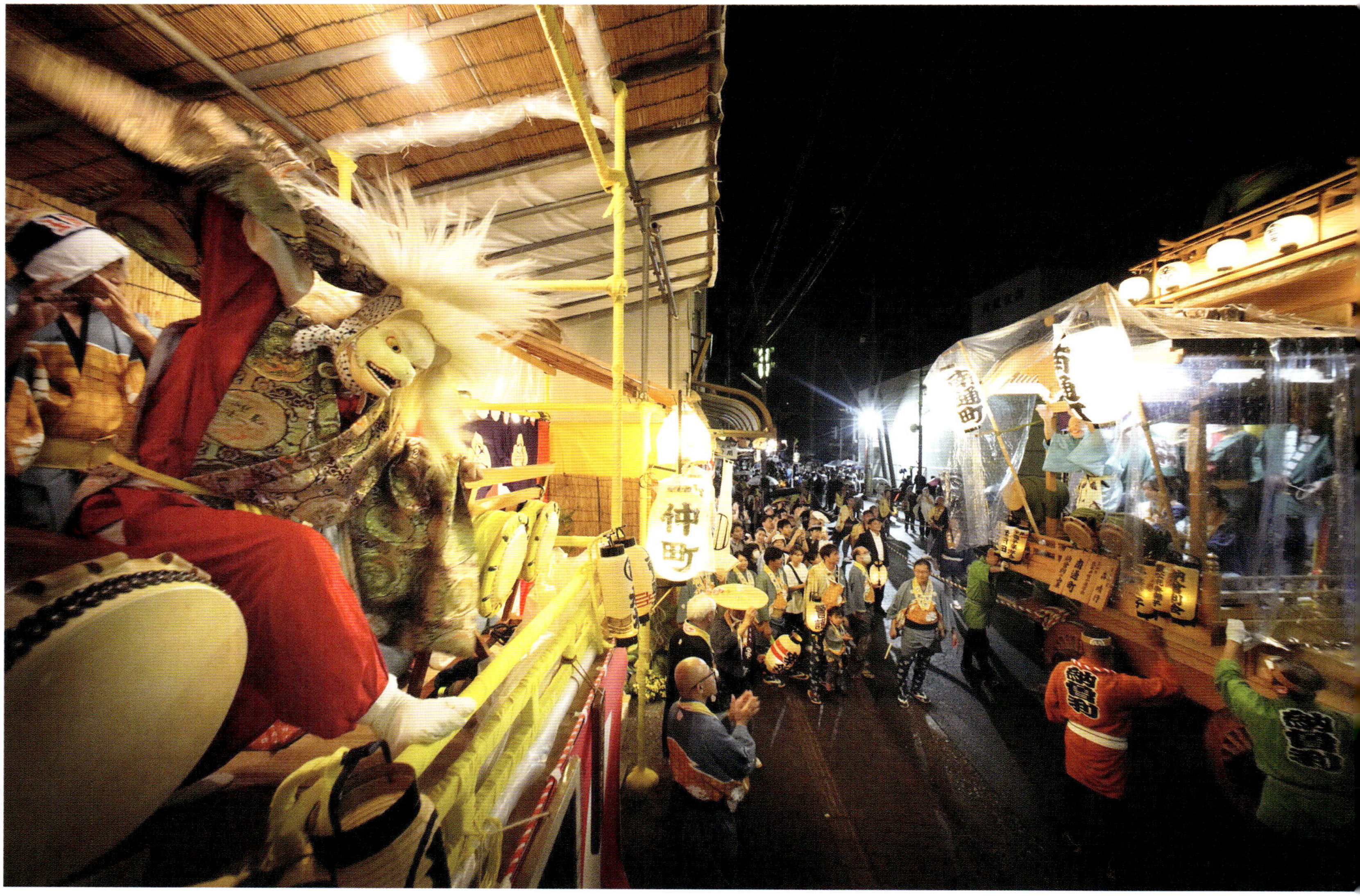

The Kawagoe district in Saitama, north of Tokyo, was established in the mid-17th century. It's known for its classic wooden architecture, as well as the atmospheric Kawagoe *matsuri* that takes place there every year during the third weekend of October. The *matsuri* features an event with 20 resplendent double-decker floats that are paraded around the old-town district. The tops of the floats have displays with dolls on them that are made in homage to famous theatre actors and folkloric figures. The festival is a dazzling spectacle and is recognized by UNESCO as an Intangible Cultural Heritage.

The lower levels of the floats have small decorated stages with roofs. These stages can revolve to face each other and partake in a musical competition of sorts, called *hikkawase*, wherein several floats battle each other in a performance with instruments and dancing. The dancers often wear fox masks, since foxes are the messengers of Inari, the Shinto rice god.

While most Japanese festivals are not tattoo events per se, they are attended by *mikoshi* groups, many of whom have full *horimono* coverage. As such, they end up being opportunities for enthusiasts to gather and show off their ink.

ABOVE
Rather than *mikoshi*, Kawagoe is known for its resplendent floats that often have performers riding on them.

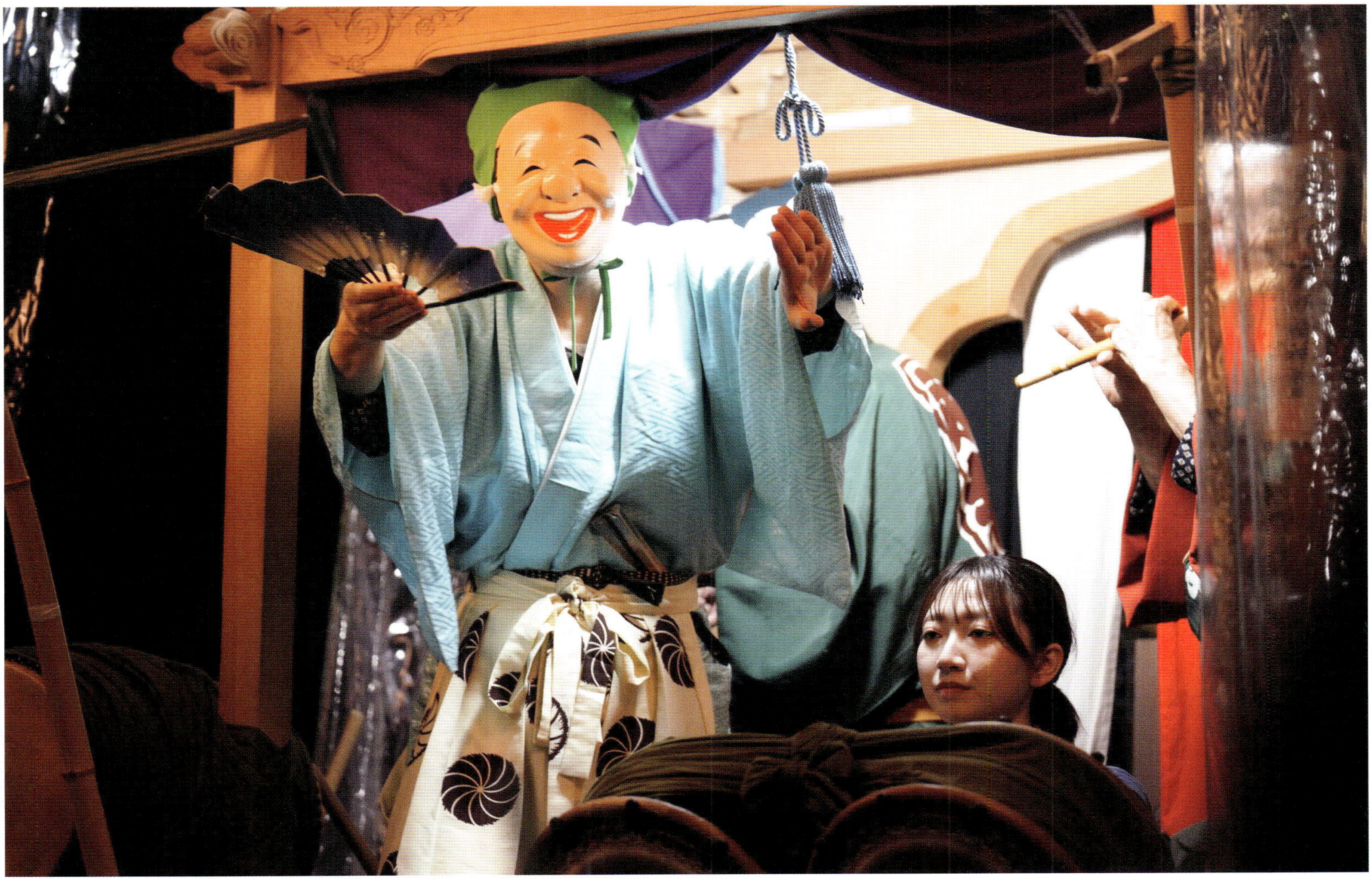

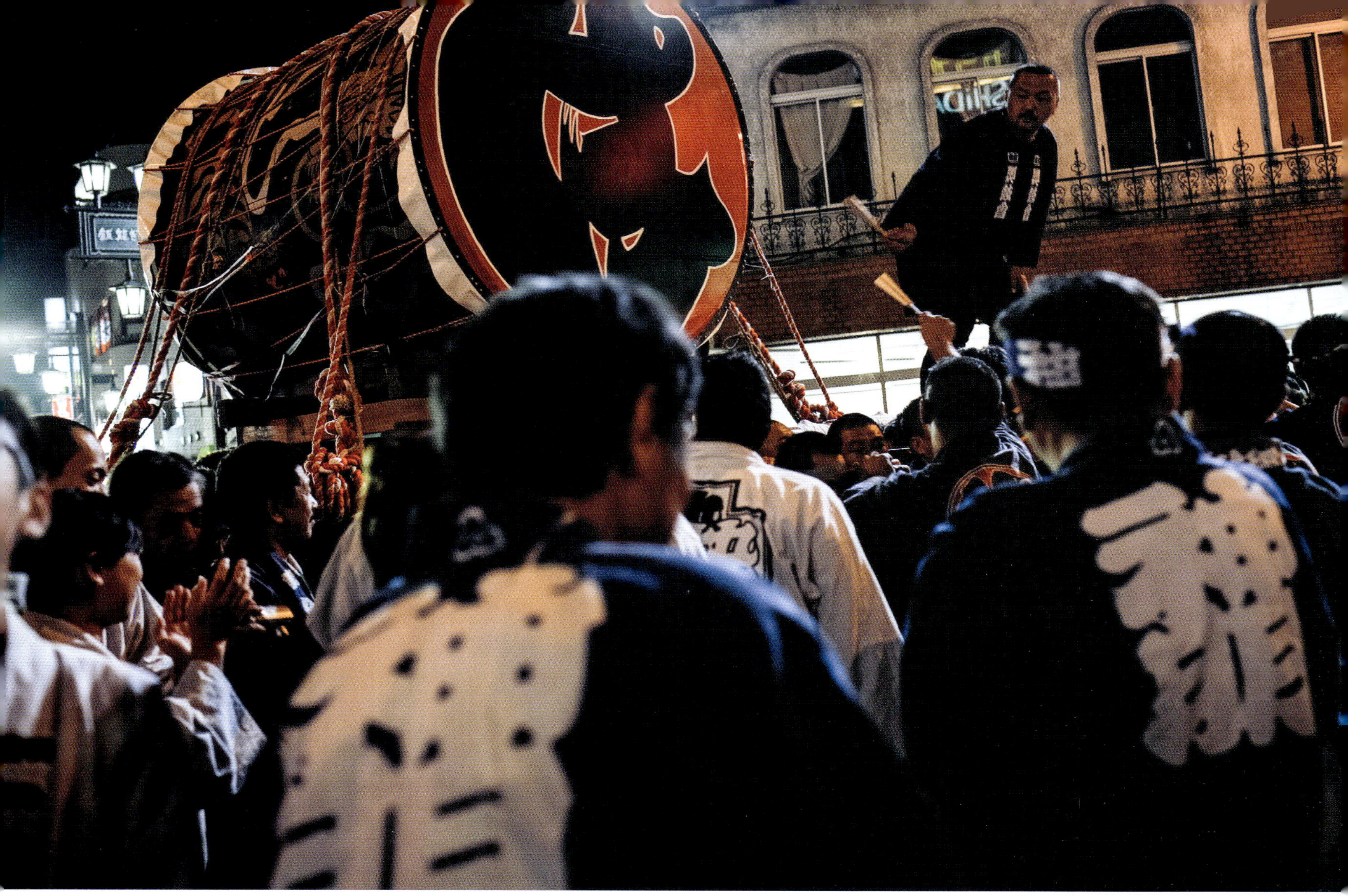

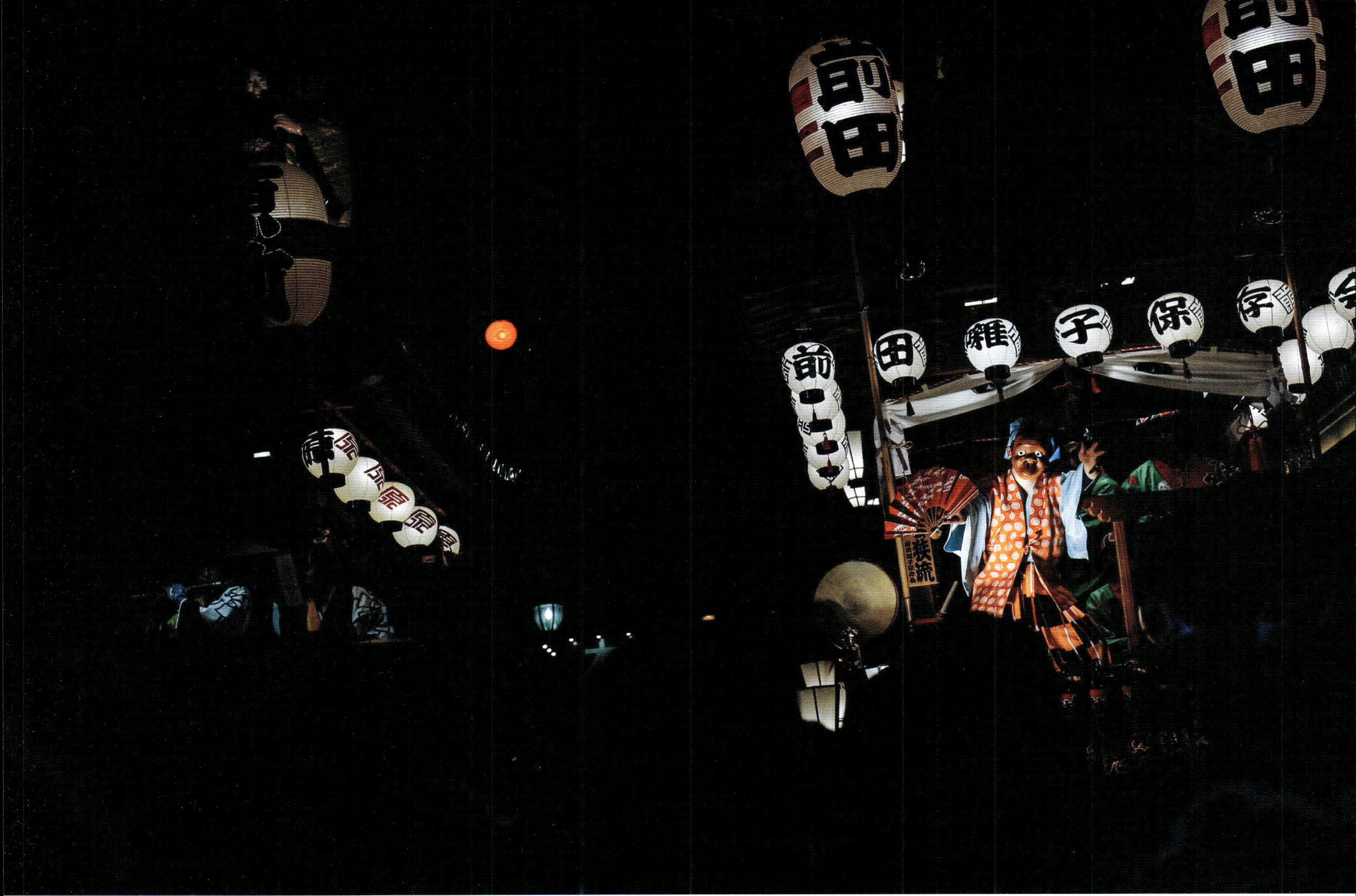
前田

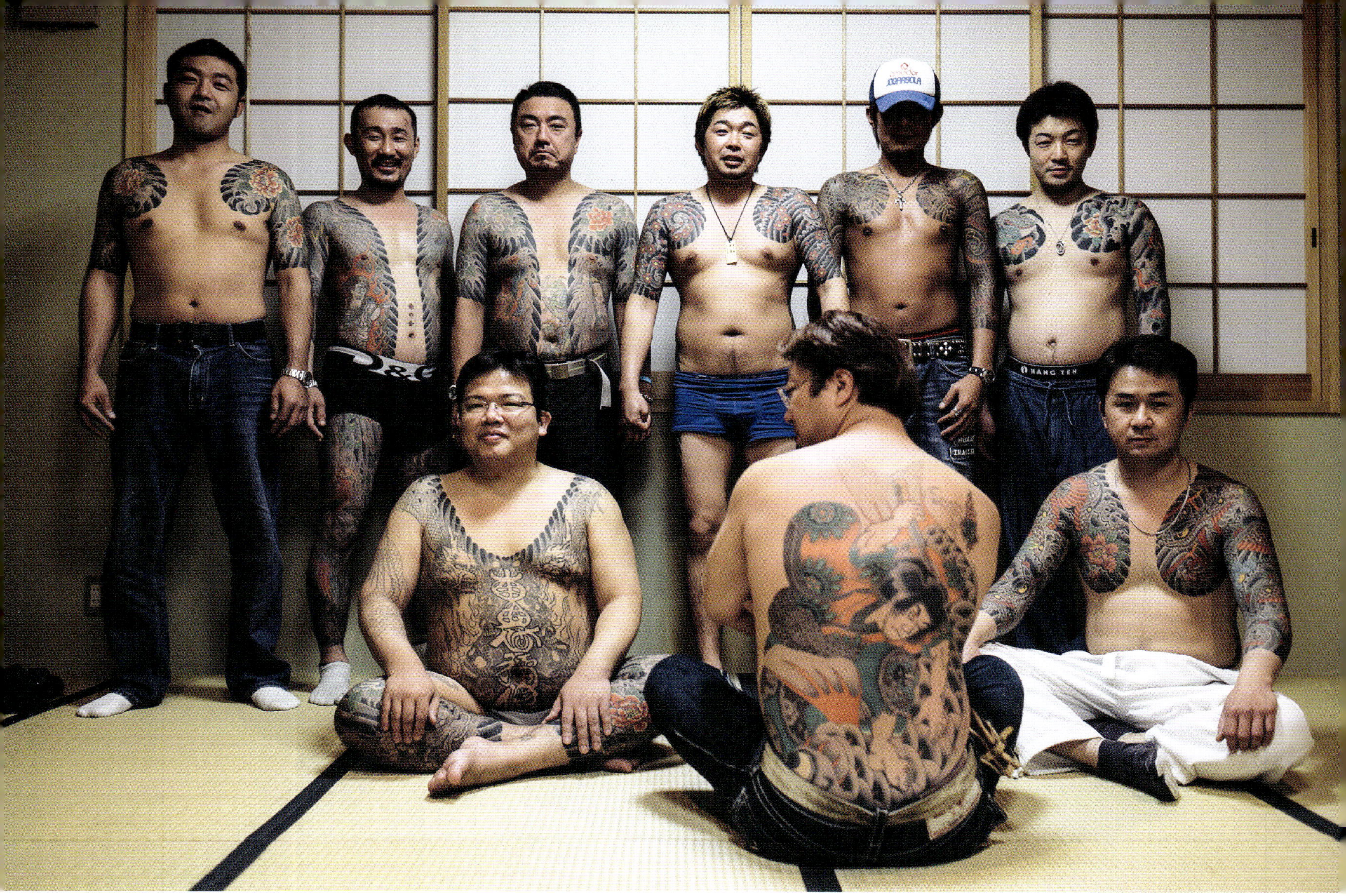

ABOVE
Large gatherings of participants over food and drinks are part of the *matsuri* experience. Horikazu's *matsuri* crew also attend festivals that are not their own local events, but those of their friends. As such, most of his summer weekends are spent at festivals somewhere in Japan.

OPPOSITE
Kakushibori are hidden motifs that are often comical. Here, Doraemon (a robot cat manga character) swims near the client's crotch.

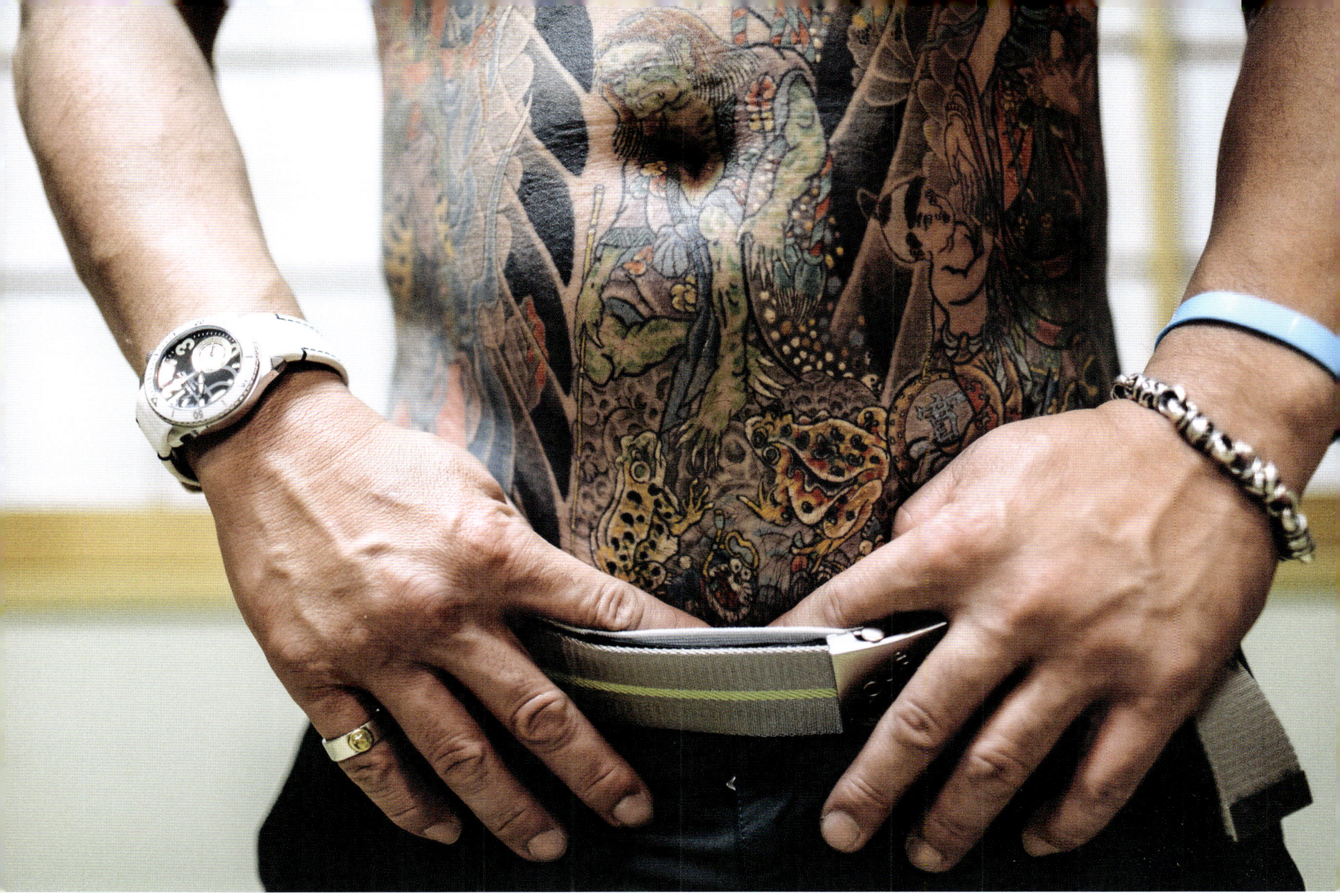

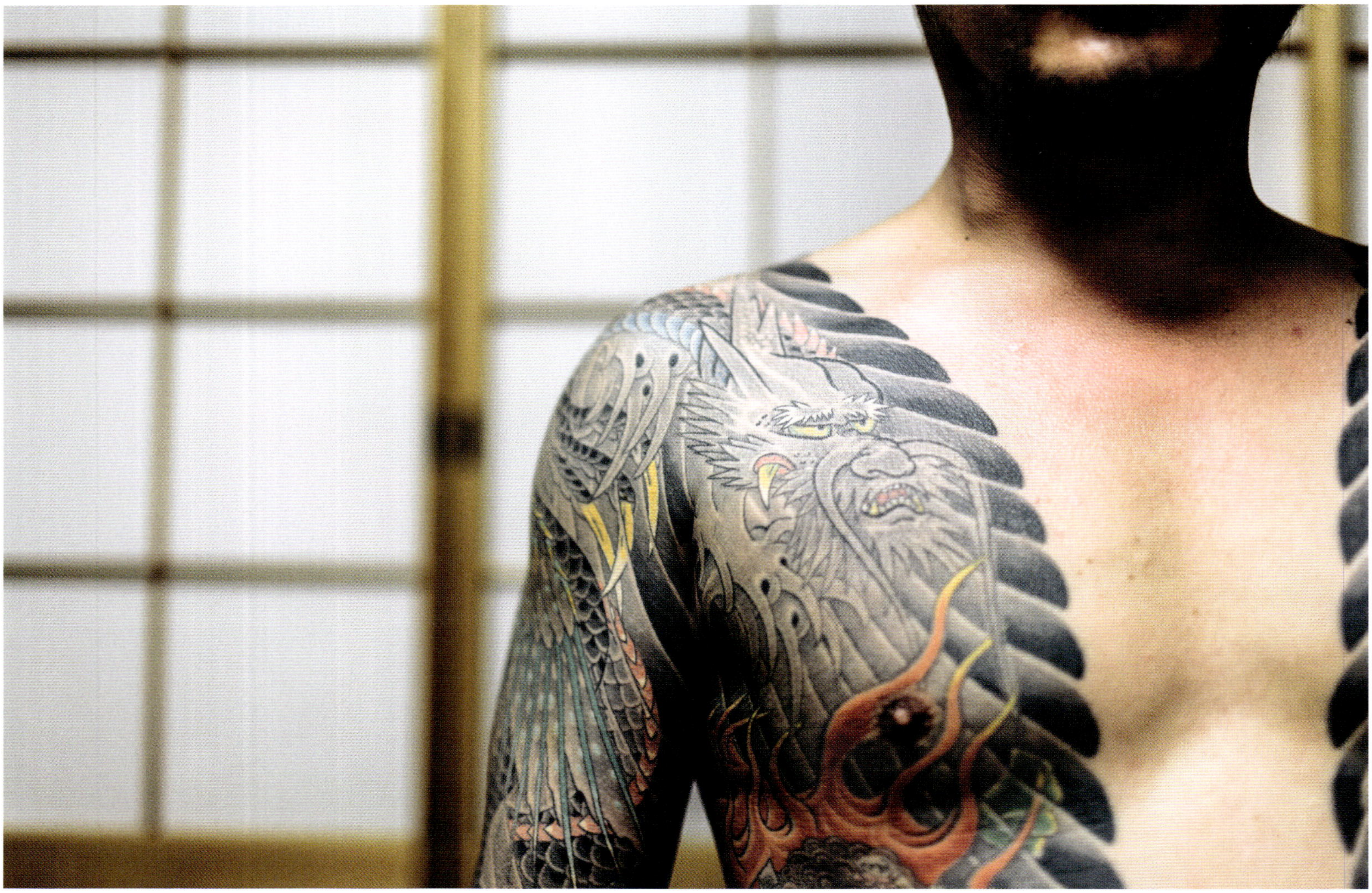

ABOVE
The *mikiri* is the edge of a tattoo. Here, the work of Shodai Horikazu shows the *bokashi* (gradations) of the *sumi* ink to highlight variations in lightness and darkness to full effect. The valley of untattooed skin running down the centre is called a *munewari*.

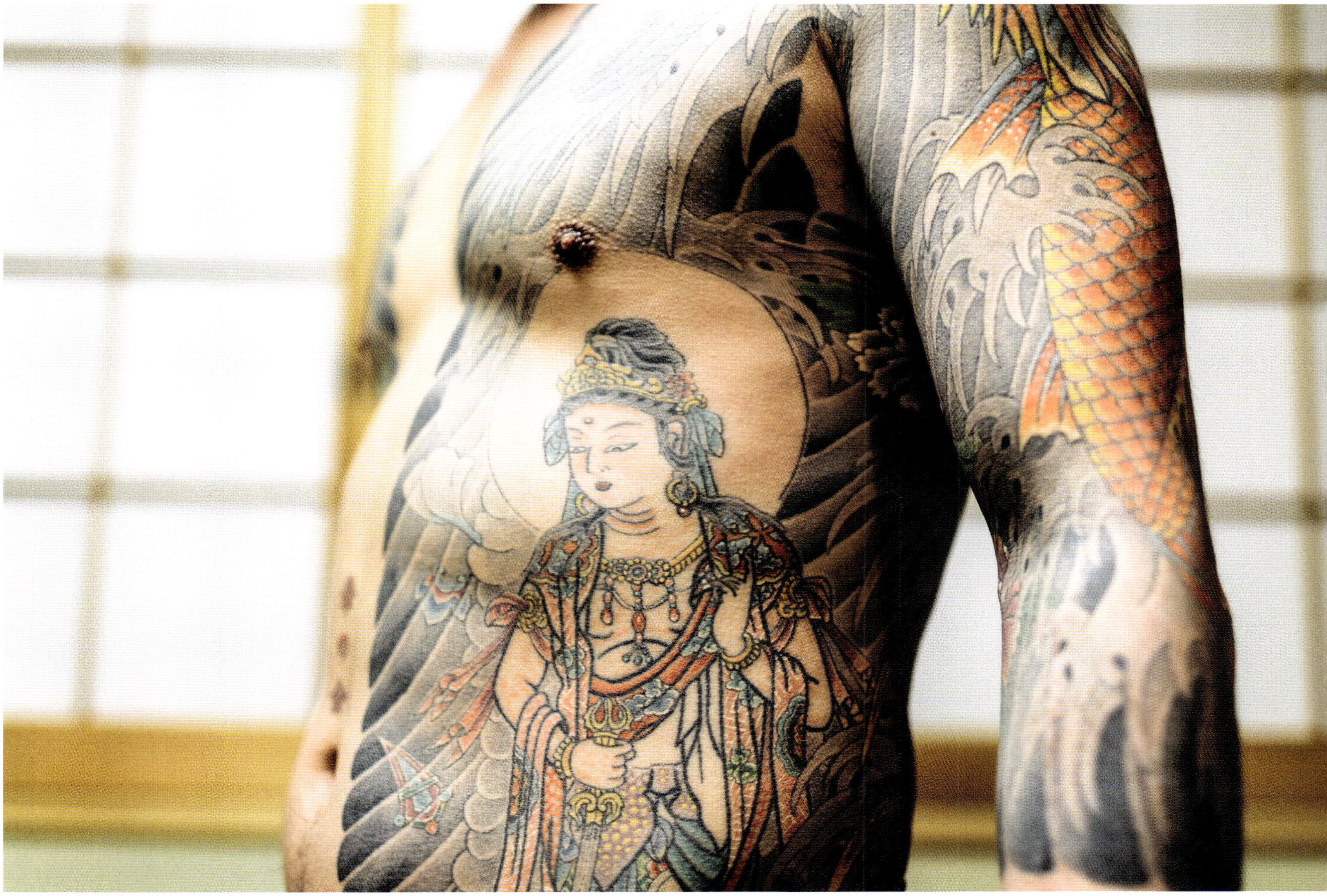

HAGOITA FAIR

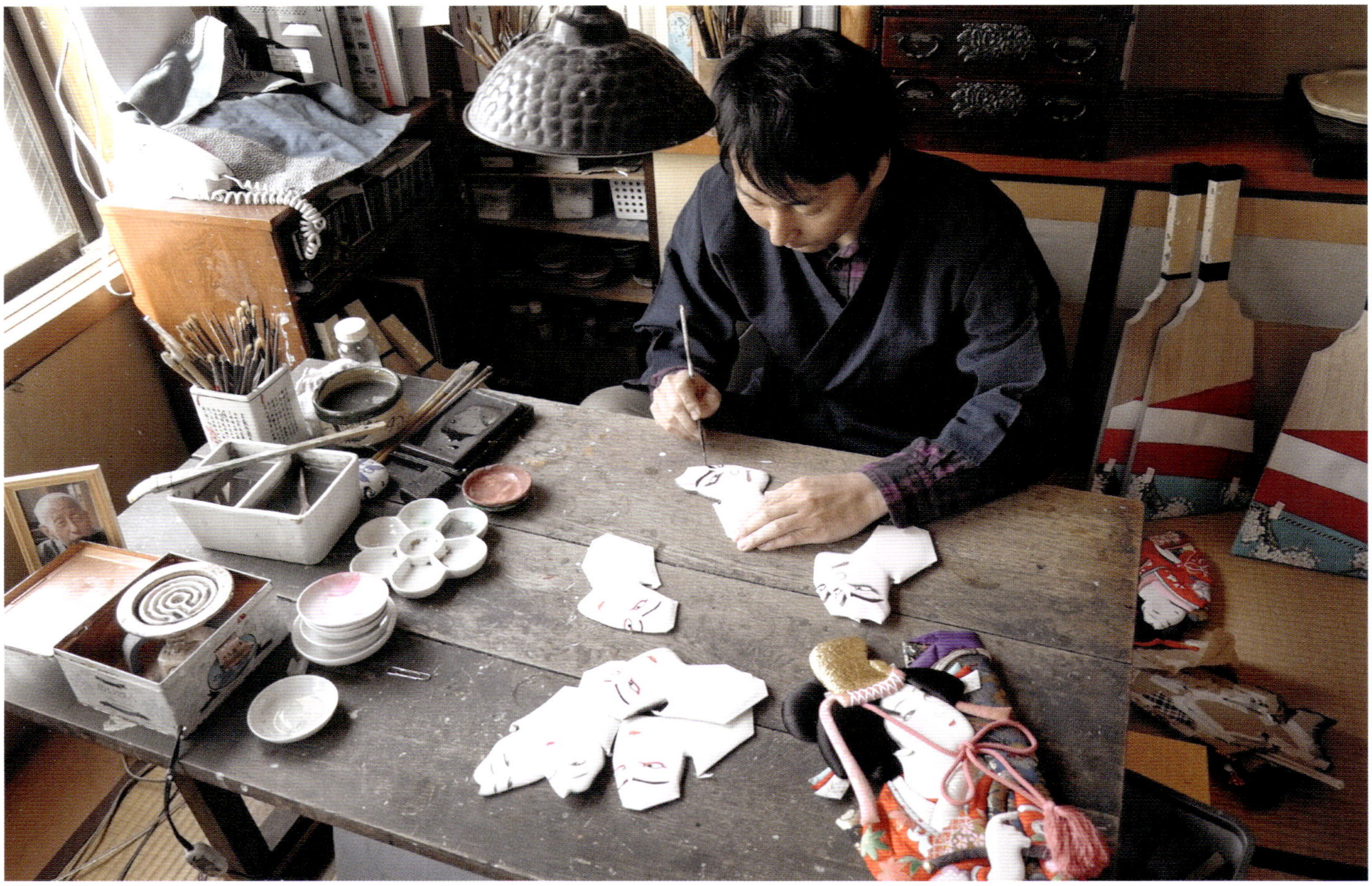

Hagoita are opulent wooden paddles that were historically used to play *hanetsuki*, a shuttlecock game. During the Muromachi era (1336–1573), this was a favourite pastime of the aristocracy who resided at the Imperial Palace. Plagues that were spread by mosquitoes were common during the time, and the shuttlecocks were a metaphor for dragonflies, which eat mosquitoes. Nowadays, the paddles are decorative and displayed as talismans. Artisan Kazuhiro Nishiyama, from the Hagoita Kougestu studio and shop in the Tokyo district of Mukojima, explains, 'There is a custom where grandparents or parents get a *hagoita* to celebrate girls that were born this year. The *hagoita* for this purpose feature cute motifs. Then there is another type of *hagoita* with *kabuki* motifs. In the Edo period, a *ukiyo-e* artisan put a *kabuki* actor's face on top of a shuttlecock – within the commoner class, *kabuki* was extremely popular, so the *ukiyo-e* artisan joined these two cultures together. They were simpler-looking than the ones now, though.'

The *hagoita* market in Asakusa's Senso-ji temple has stalls that attract people from across Japan at an annual festival held over the course of three days in mid-December. Since many of the featured characters are *kabuki* protagonists, there are a lot of tattooed figures depicted. After an artisan sells a *hagoita* at the fair, there is a *tejime* (clapping ritual). Nishiyama says, 'For a 10,000-yen [£52/$70] shuttlecock you make it cheaper, and so you say, "We will discount it to 8,000 yen," and the customer feels like they have lucked out, and our feelings of gratitude are transmitted. Then, they tip us more than we have discounted in an envelope. With this gesture, both parties feel good. It is an Edo-era way of buying things. We clap in a 3-3-4 rhythm, which adds up to ten, which is a nice round number, to signify that we rounded off a good deal.'

ABOVE
An artisan makes *hagoita* (decorative wooden paddles used as talismans). They often feature *kabuki* actor motifs and many of the figures are tattooed.

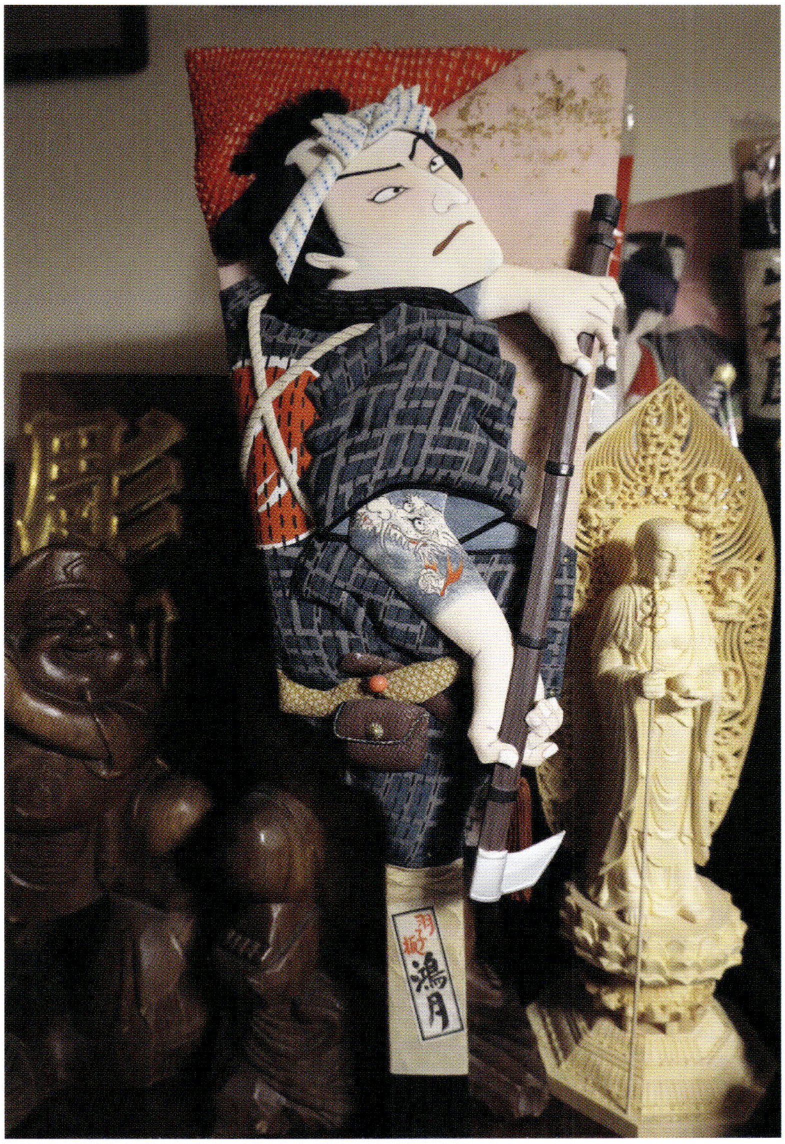
羽子板
鴻月

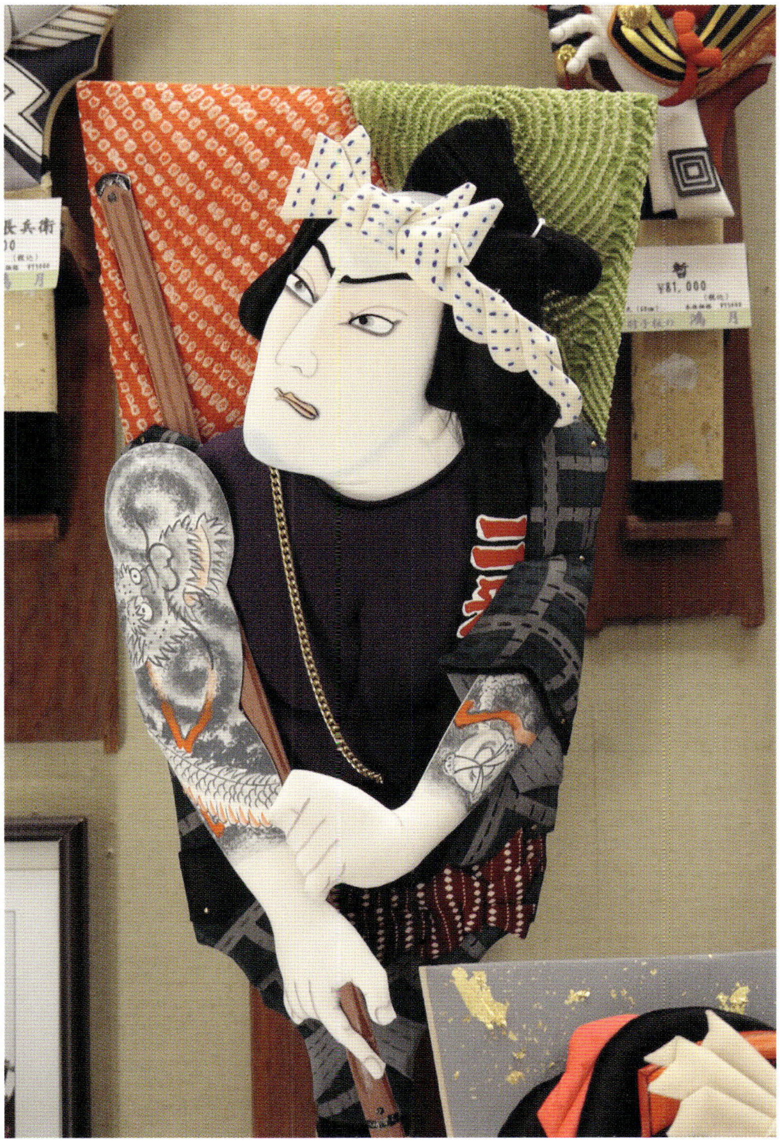
¥81,000

BUDDHIST AND SHINTO MOTIFS

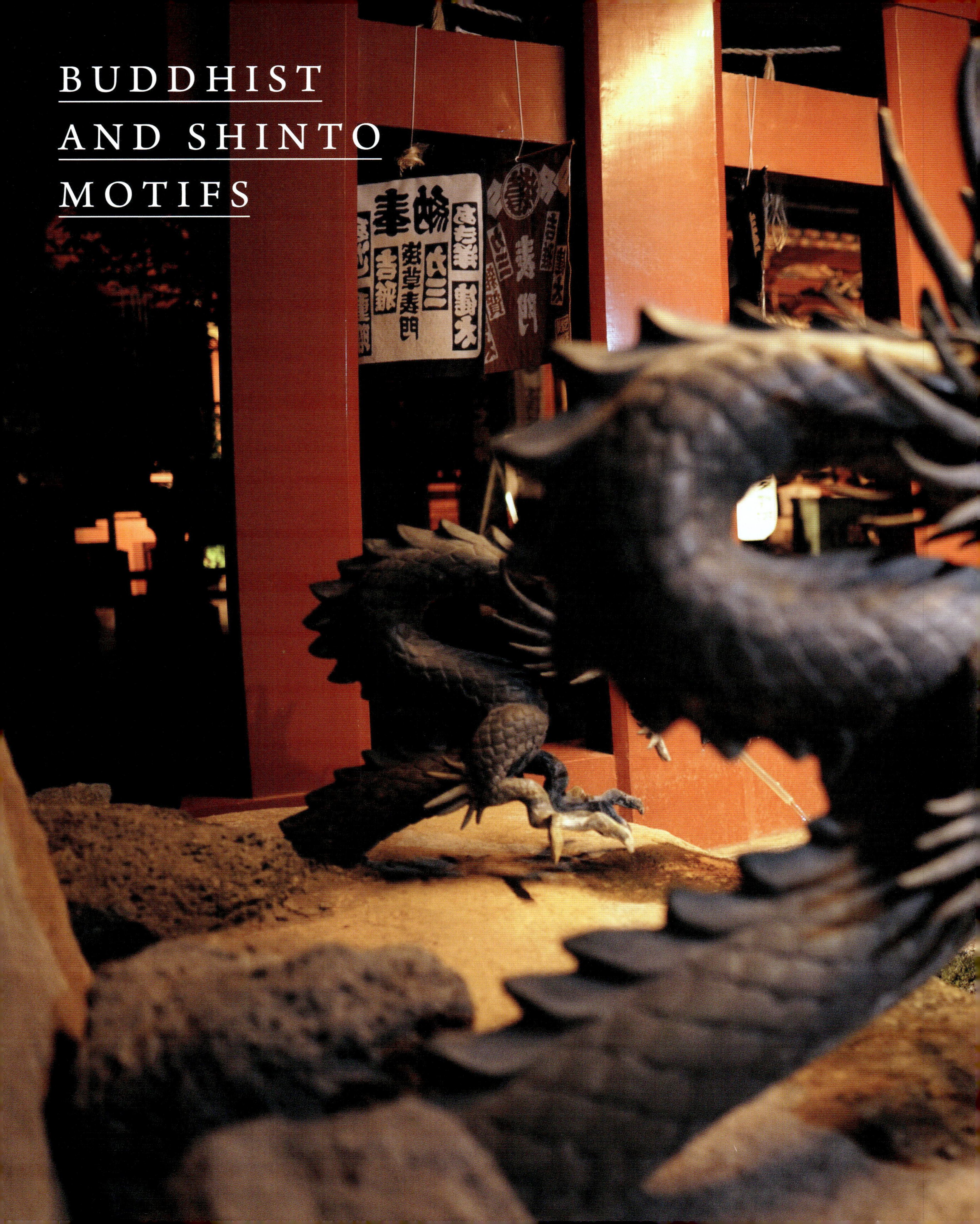

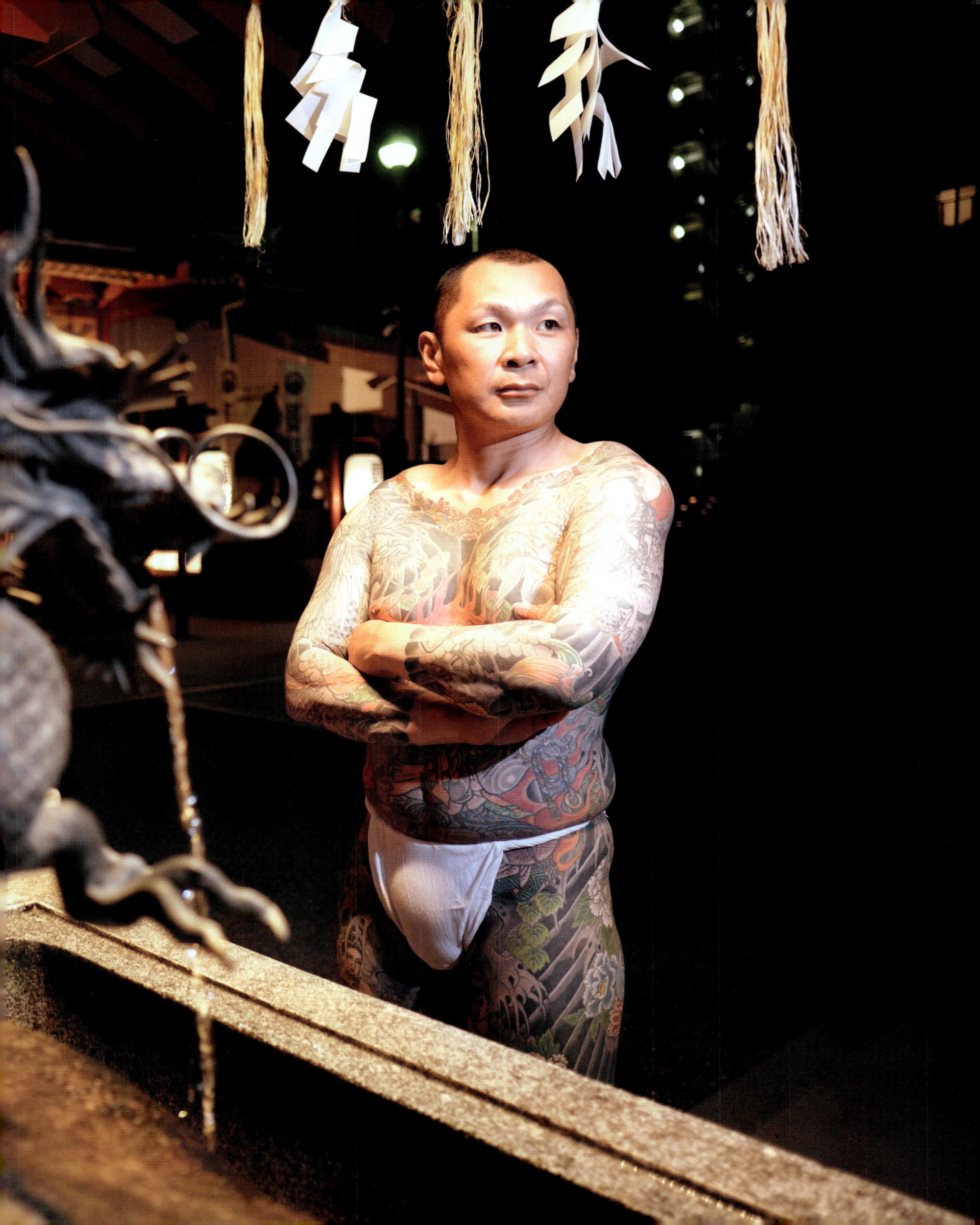

Religious imagery inspires some of the most common *wabori* motifs, particularly among those who attend festivals. A central deity is usually grouped with other religious elements to create a celestial tableau on subjects such as heaven, hell and famous meditation scenes. Paradoxically, the dark *sumi* backgrounds give even the most divine work a shadowy and ominous atmosphere.

Buddhism, which initially came to Japan via Korea in the 6th century, is a religious practice intended to help people attain an ideal state of being. It is said to exist when core fundamental elements are present: Buddha's teachings (the dharma), a community of believers, and symbols of faith and worship. The basic ideologies of Buddhism suggest that all things are impermanent and devoid of self, characterized by suffering, and that nirvana, or a state of enlightenment, is the goal. These laws are bound by the notion of causality – that everything is interdependent on everything else, and there is a cause-and-effect relationship among the world's various phenomena.

Shinto is Japan's indigenous belief system, which is predicated on animism and the notion that gods, or *kami*, are an omnipresent part of nature. In Japan, there is syncretism between the two religions and they have blended together, including their pantheons of gods. Buddhist deities are worshipped alongside Shinto divinities and they are often seen as incarnations of one another.

Buddhist gods and goddesses are often employed as narrative devices, or as reproductions of mystical visions. They are used to stimulate devotion, as practising Japanese Buddhism is a highly aesthetic experience. Making these images for Buddhist art is not traditionally a secular activity, but somewhat ritualistic, and meant primarily for religious contemplation. Buddhist imagery is rich with symbols, from hand gestures (*mudras*) to associated objects such as prayer tools and weapons meant to metaphorically cut down ignorance.

There are a mind-boggling number of Buddhist gods, and although the term 'Buddha' usually

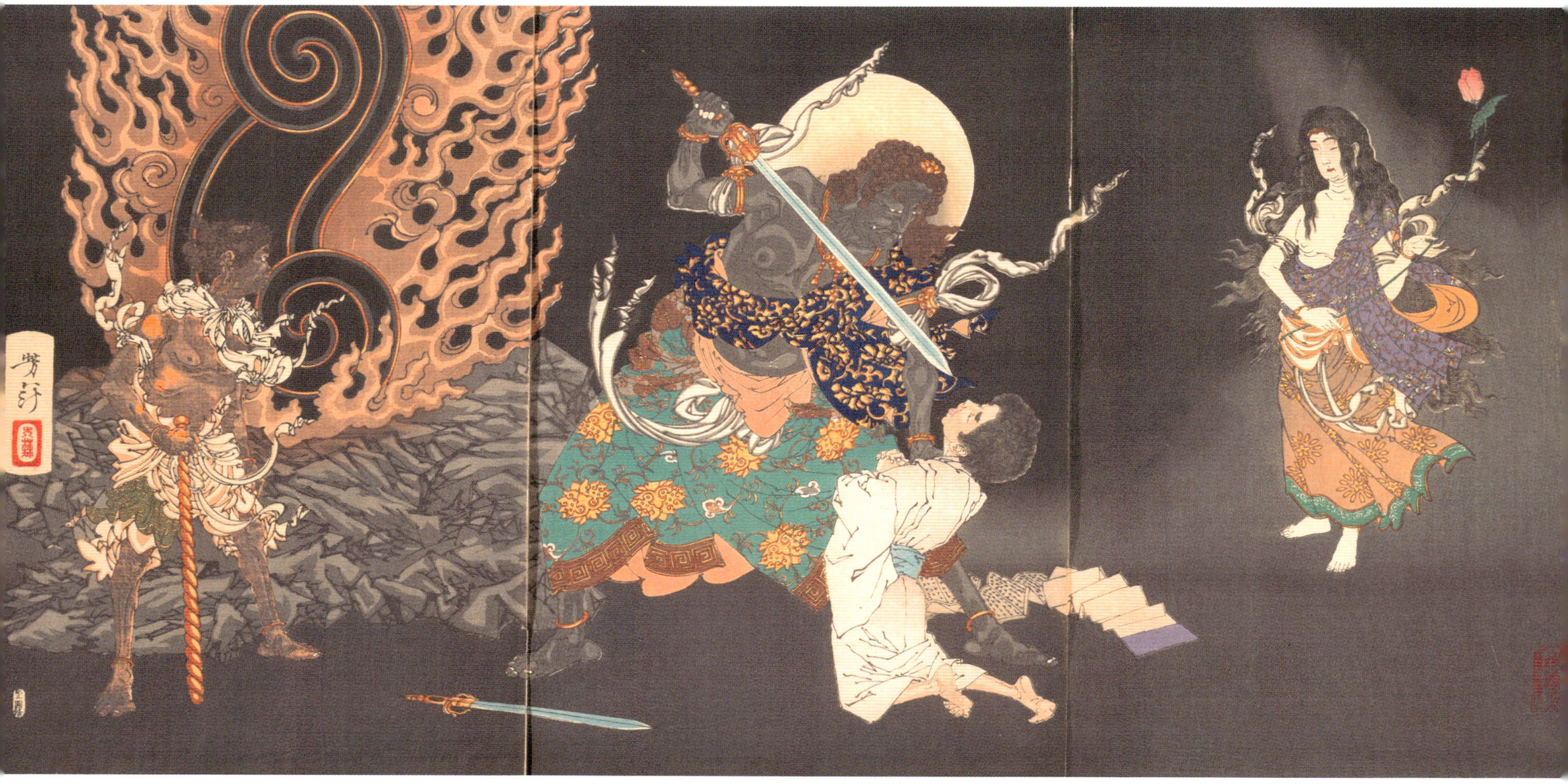

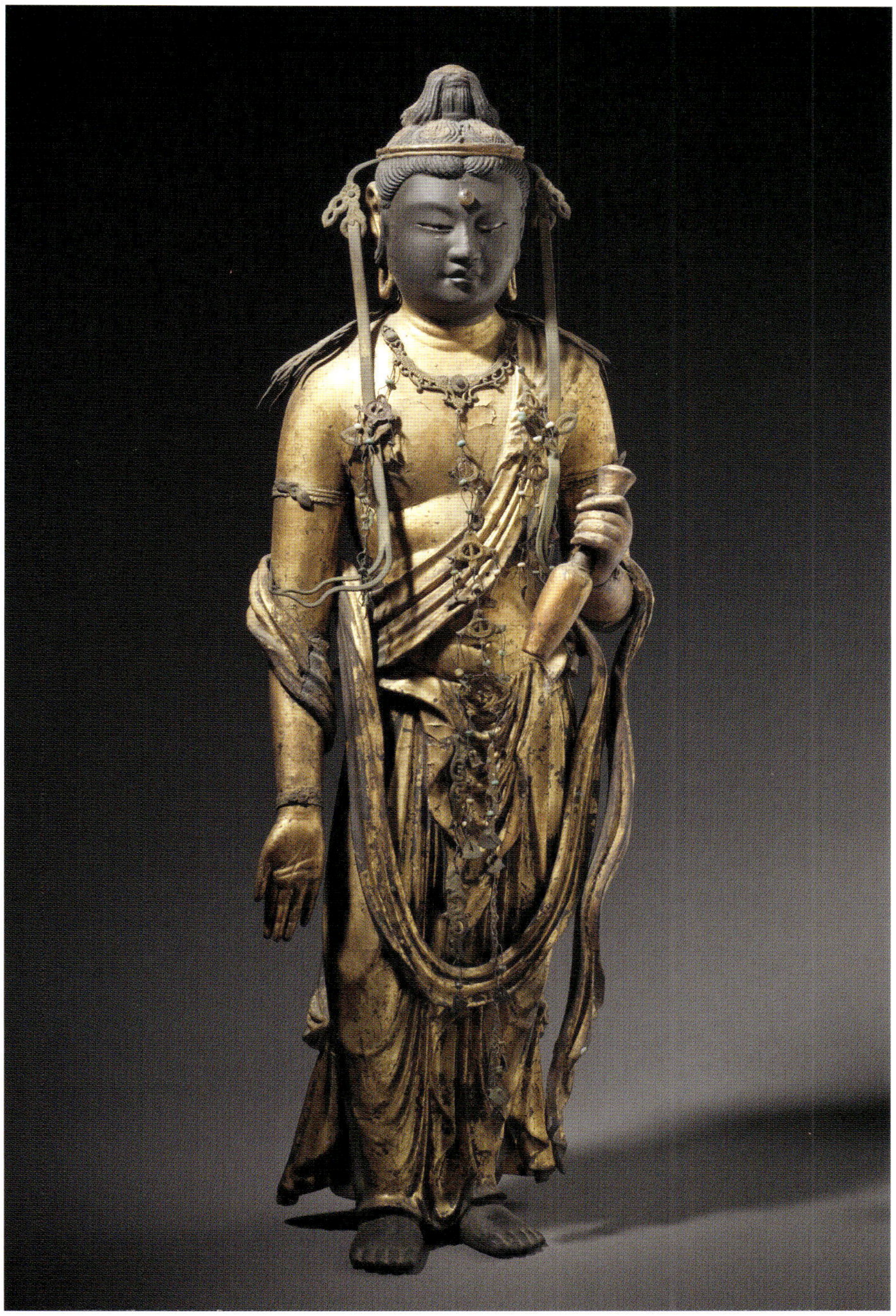

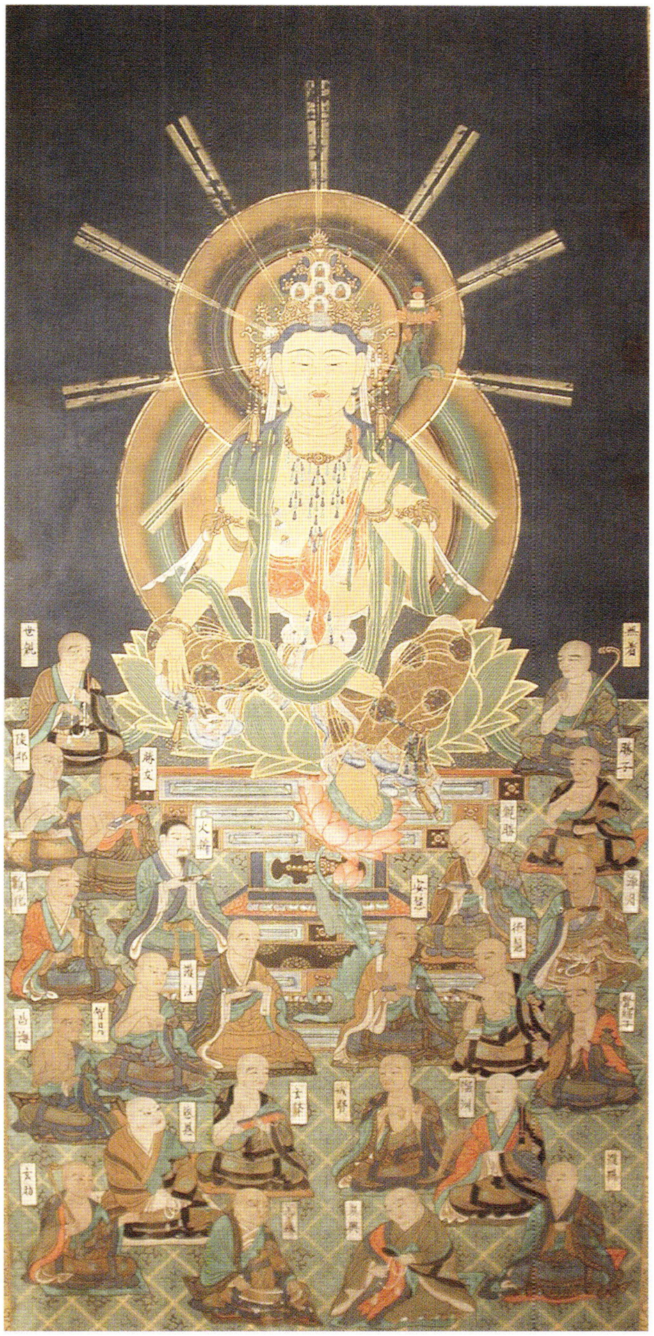

PREVIOUS SPREAD
One of Horikazu's clients at Asakusa Shrine.

OPPOSITE
Yoshitoshi Tsukioka, *Fudo Myo-o Threatens Yuten*, 1885, woodblock print. The Buddhist divinity Fudo Myo-o wields his sword that is used to slay non-believers. Yuten Shonin (1637–1718), a Jodo sect monk and eventual head of Zojoji temple, is depicted in his youth praying to Fudo Myo-o. By consuming the sword of wisdom, he is about to gain insight.

LEFT
Kei School, *Eleven-Headed Kannon*, early Kamakura period, 1200–1250, lacquered and gilt wood.

RIGHT
Hosso Mandala, 16th century, hanging scroll. The founder of the Hosso sect, Miroku Bosatsu, is the central deity.

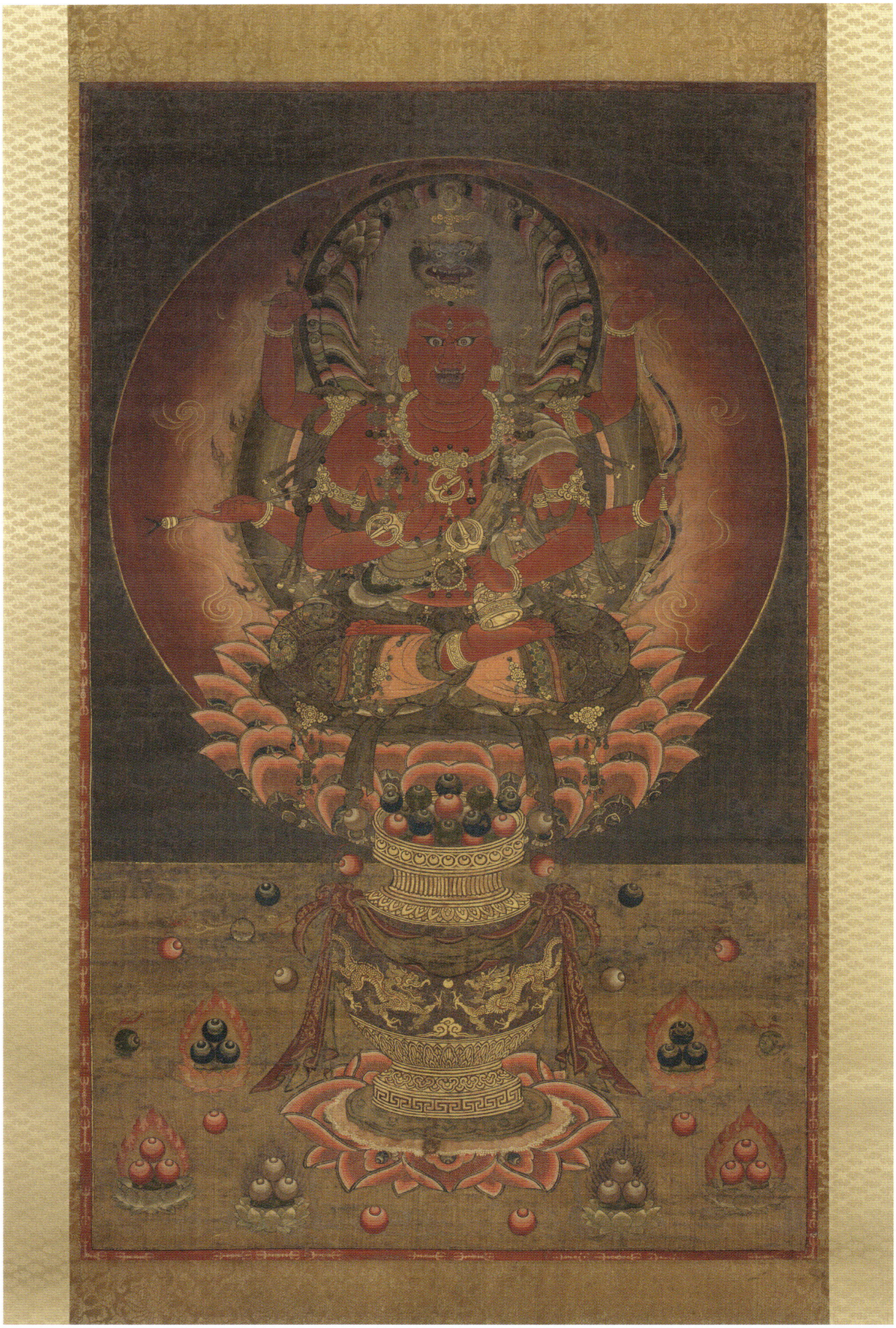

refers to the historic Buddha, Shaka Nyorai, a great number of Buddhas and Bosatsus (those who have postponed Buddhahood to help others) suit the specific needs of a wide range of people. In Japanese Buddhist art there are four categories of deities that may be present:

NYORAI: The Buddhas – the enlightened ones.

BOSATSU: Deities who seek wisdom and personify compassion. While Nyorai have attained enlightenment, Bosatsu are able to reach nirvana, but because of their compassionate nature, they have chosen to help sentient beings attain Buddhahood themselves.

MYO-O: Wrathful guardians who eliminate everything that stops one from reaching enlightenment. They possess mystical knowledge and are quite demonic in appearance, and unlike the soft and compassionate Bosatsu, they are more aggressive. They belligerently protect Buddhist principles and subdue evil, even if this requires force.

TEN: Celestial beings and protective divinities who help maintain Buddhist law. They can also act as guardians.

In Japanese tattoos, rather than Nyorai, the most common motifs are Bosatsu, such as Kannon and Monju Bosatsu, Fudo Myo-o, Aizen Myo-o, *tennyo* (Buddhist angels), the Seven Lucky Gods and the goddess Benzaiten.

This section depicts some of the most common Buddhist and Shinto motifs in Japanese tattoos. All of the people in these photographs are clients of Shodai Horikazu and Horikazu.

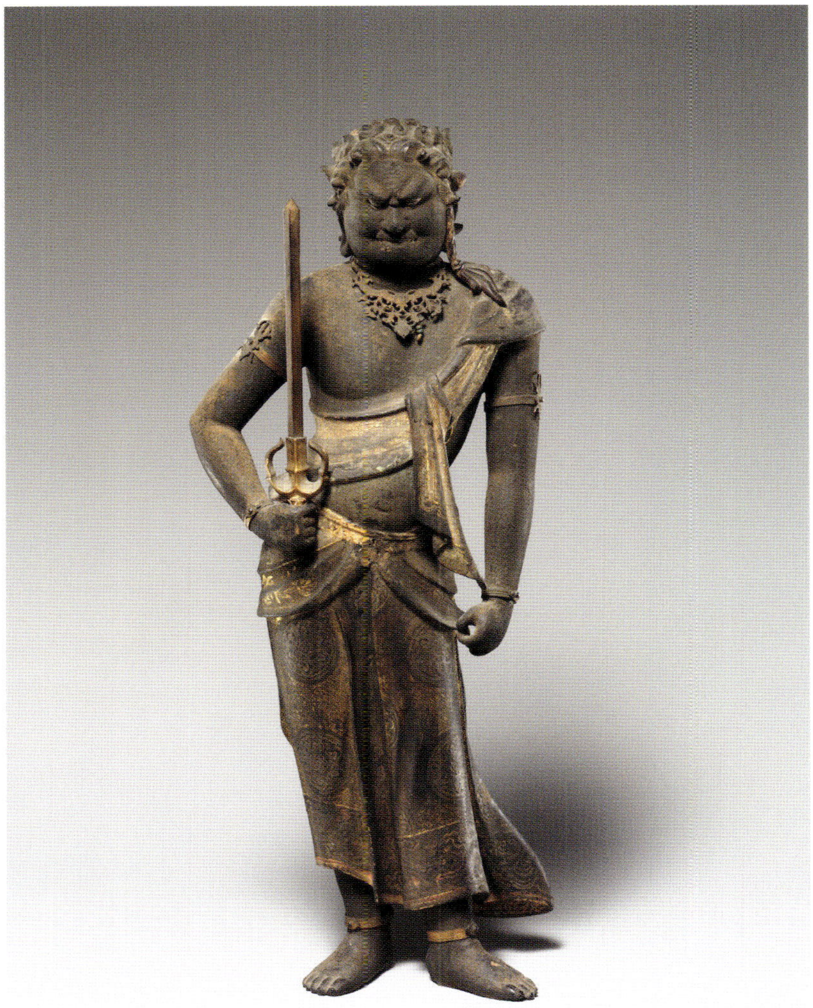

OPPOSITE
The Wisdom King, Aizen Myo-o, 14th century, hanging scroll.

RIGHT
Fudo Myo-o, 13th–14th century.

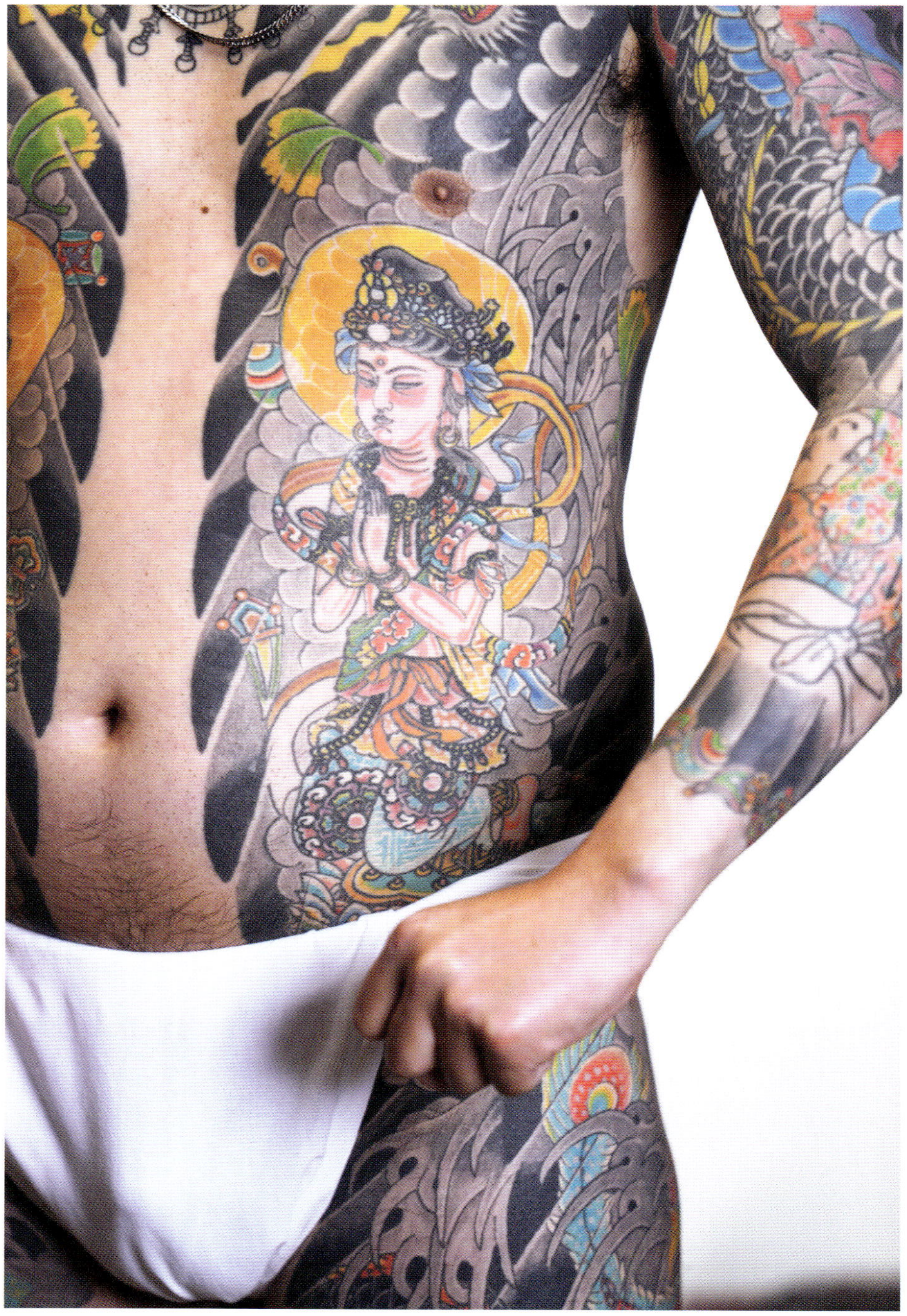

ABOVE
Horikazu is known for caring about a tattoo's overall composition. In his work, divinities often adorn the ribs on either side of the blank space in the centre.

OPPOSITE
In Japanese Buddhism, Nyorai are the Buddhas – the enlightened ones. This tattoo features a Dainichi Nyorai motif. Dainichi means 'Great Sun', suggestive of the light he emanates and the ability for Buddha's teachings to give warmth. Dainichi Nyorai is said to be able to convert ignorance to wisdom and is the personification of intelligence. In the Shingon sect of Buddhism, he represents everything in the cosmos and is essentially the centre of the universe. Dainichi Nyorai is also identifiable by the fact that he is always adorned with jewellery, a crown or ornaments, and looks somewhat like a Bosatsu (a different type of Buddhist deity). He wears silk robes. In art he is often depicted with Fudo Myo-o and Aizen Myo-o.

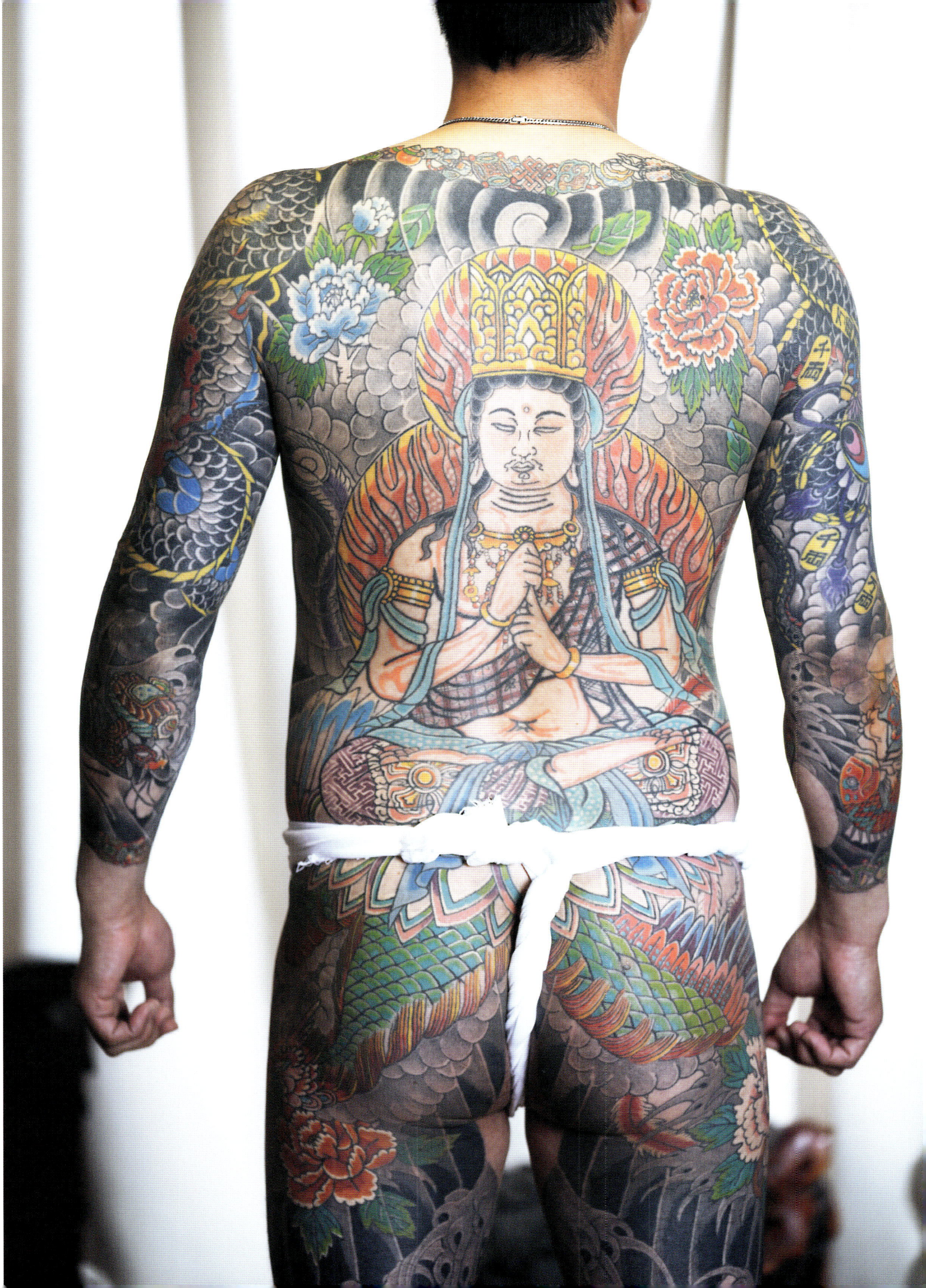

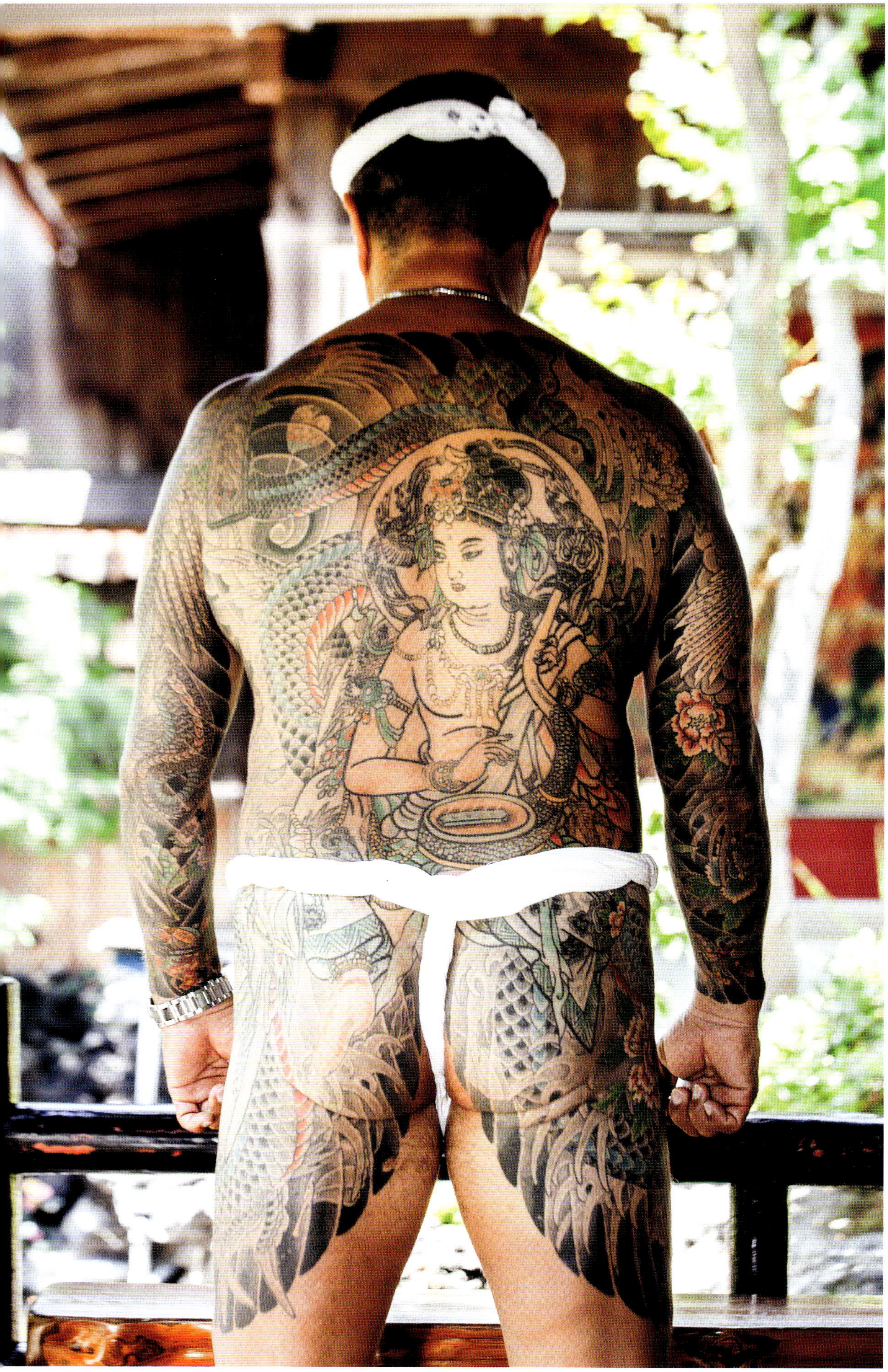

LEFT
Kannon Bosatsu is one of the most ubiquitous figures in Japanese Buddhist tattoo art. She is the goddess of mercy and compassion and is a mother figure, as well as a bestower of children. Kannon hears the concerns of the people, grants salvation to those who are suffering and helps them reach enlightenment. In Asakusa, clients frequently want Kannon Bosatsu tattoos because she is the goddess who is worshipped at Senso-ji temple.

In addition to the basic form of Kannon, Sho Kannon, she has 33 other forms, such as Juichimen Kannon (11-headed Kannon), Senju Kannon (1,000-armed Kannon, who protects from suffering and hungry ghosts), Bato Kannon (horse-headed Kannon) and Nyoirin (wish-fulfilling Kannon).

Kannon has a willowy figure, wears robes and is sometimes depicted holding a small child, lotus flower, jewel or vessel of water. Her face is usually soft and compassionate. She is also depicted in Buddhist art with Amida Nyorai, descending from the heavens to save people. If the person is deemed to be good, they will be taken to paradise.

OPPOSITE
Kokuzo Bosatsu represents wisdom and the ability to learn and memorize things, as well as giving luck and happiness. An important deity in esoteric Buddhist sects, Kokuzo Bosatsu enables people to access the wisdom of Buddha.

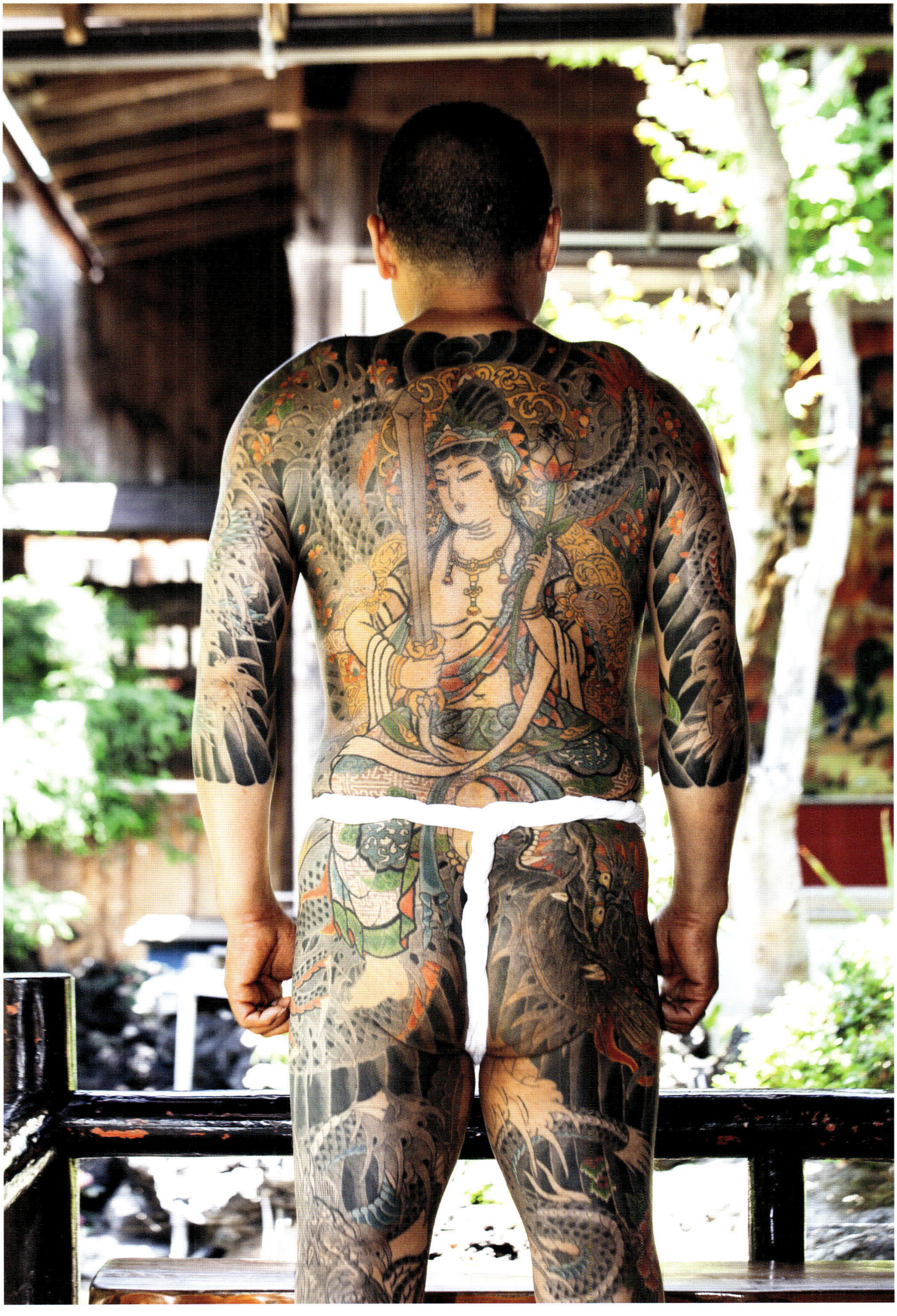

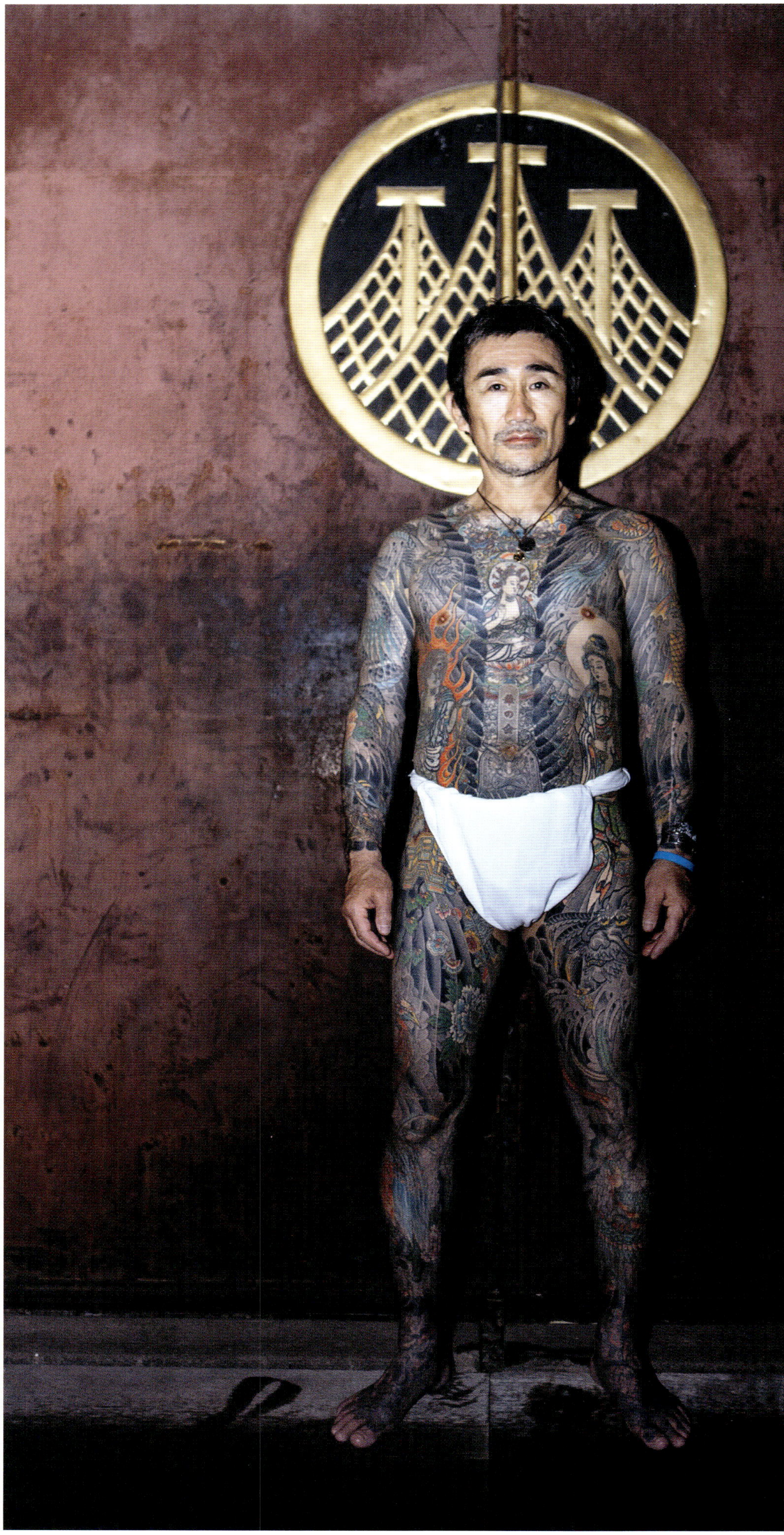

RIGHT
Left to right: Fudo Myo-o, Miroku Bosatsu, Kannon Bosatsu.

FAR RIGHT
Many clients of Horikazu – particularly those who are based in Asakusa – have Kannon Bosatsu tattoos, as she is the central deity of Senso-ji temple. Ichiyo Kannon, depicted here, is a rare manifestation of Kannon Bosatsu.

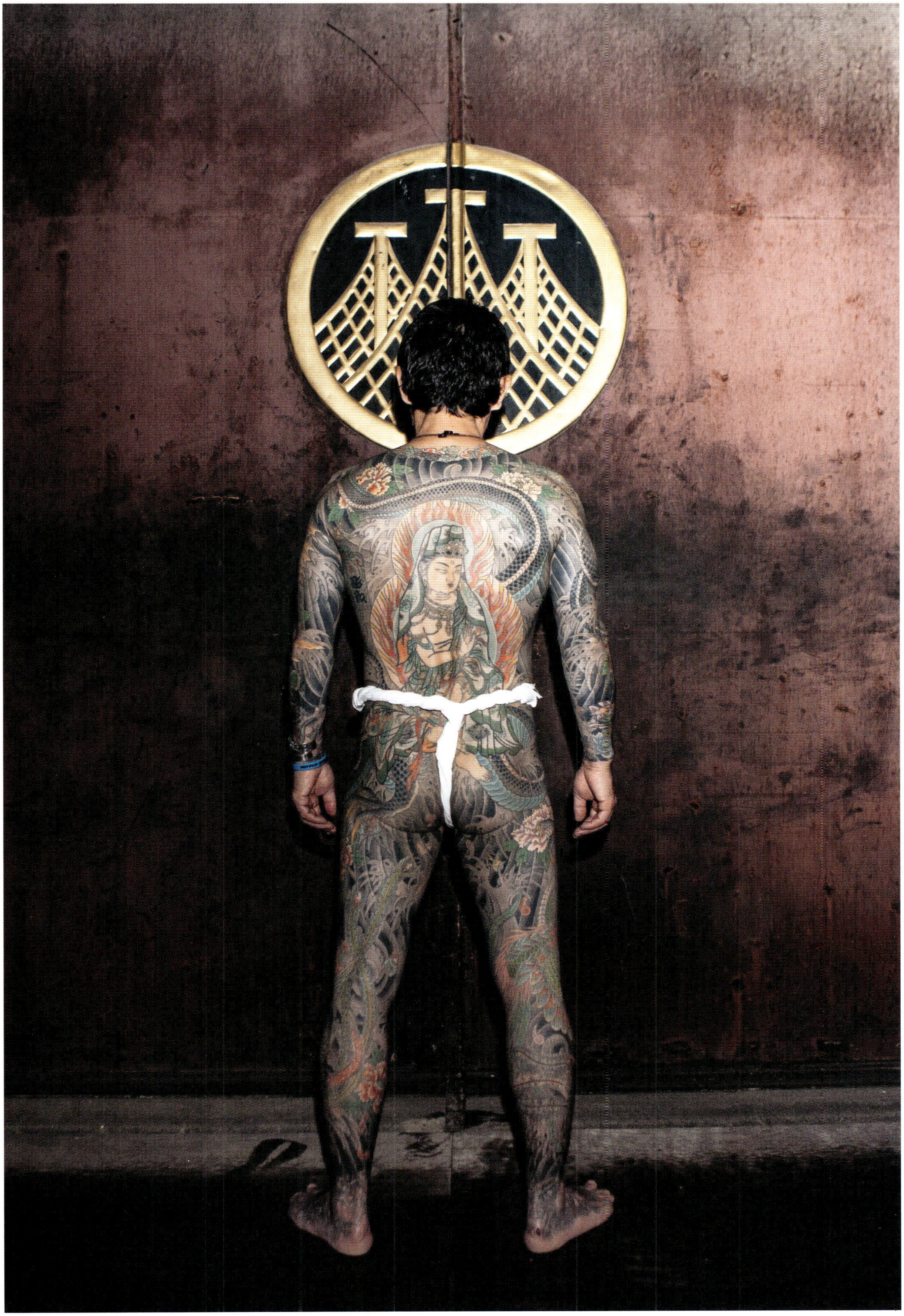

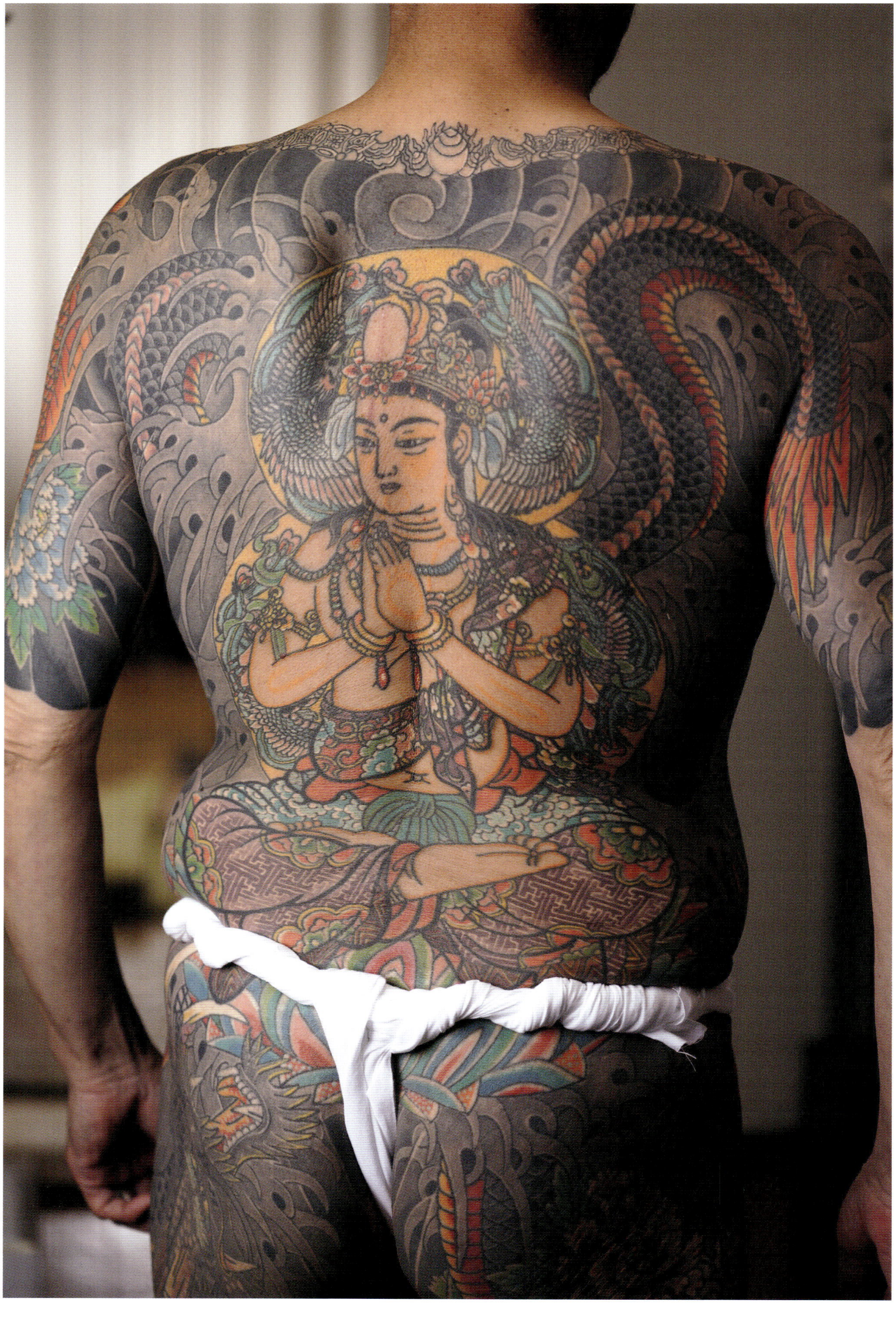

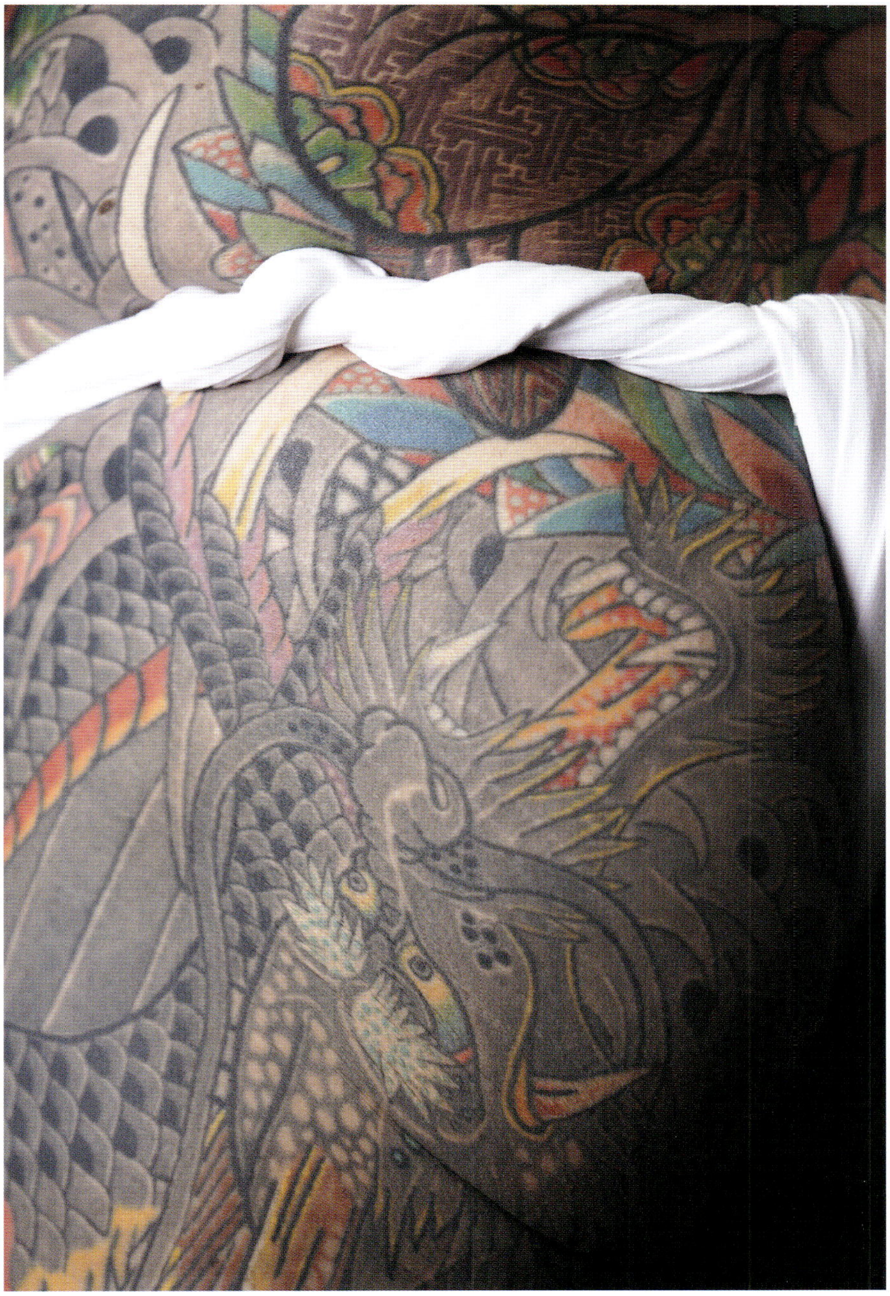

OPPOSITE
Fugen Bosatsu is a deity of meditation and action. A great teacher who encourages ethical conduct and service to others, he is also thought to bestow health and longevity. He often wears a crown, robes and jewellery, and sits with his hands clasped or in a *mudra* form. Most depictions of Fugen Bosatsu show him riding one or more elephants, which may have multiple heads. Alternatively, he is sometimes seated on a lotus, or standing on two lotuses.

ABOVE
The head of a dragon encircles the base of the lotus upon which Fugen Bosatsu is seated.

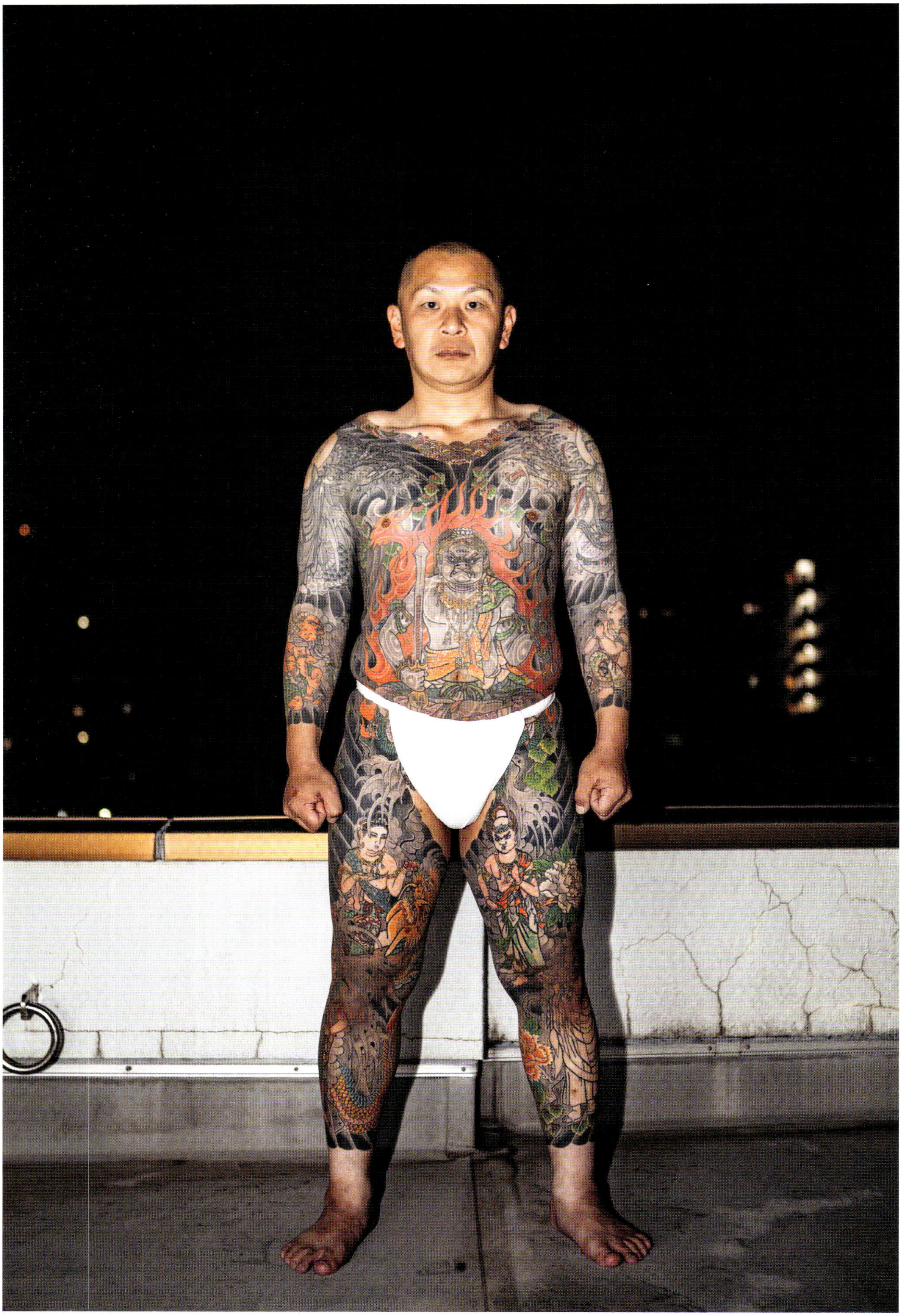

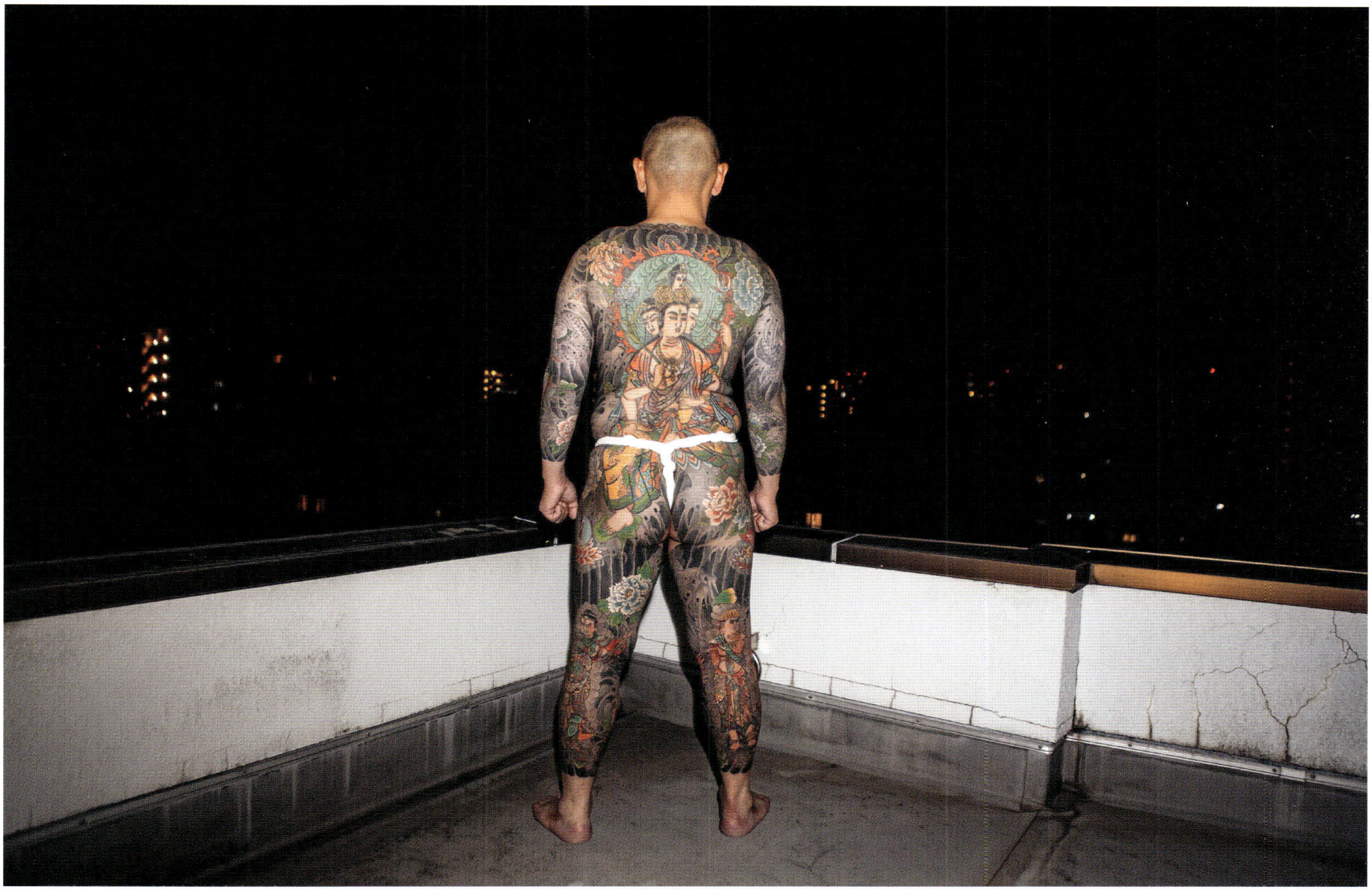

OPPOSITE
Fudo Myo-o converts anger into salvation, subdues evil and represents absolute determination. He has a menacing face and frightens non-believers into accepting the teachings of Buddhist law. He is also thought to bring money and prolong the lives of the devoted, in addition to assisting people to become Buddhas in the first seven days after death. Like most Myo-o, he is often shown surrounded by flames, which burn away all material desires and destroy karmic hindrances; sometimes, there are also waterfalls present. He is frequently accompanied by two attendants, Kongara Doji and Seitaka Doji. He carries a sword to slay devils, representing wisdom cutting through ignorance. Sometimes his sword is surrounded by flames, with a dragon winding upwards depicted on it. He also holds a rope to catch and bind demons, as well as to pull in reluctant believers.

ABOVE
Bonten is a deity of wisdom and a lord of the realm of rebirth. Historically, he is a protector of the Buddha, ever since Buddha's earliest stages. He also encouraged Buddha to teach after he reached enlightenment. As time went on, Bonten came to be regarded as a protective deity.

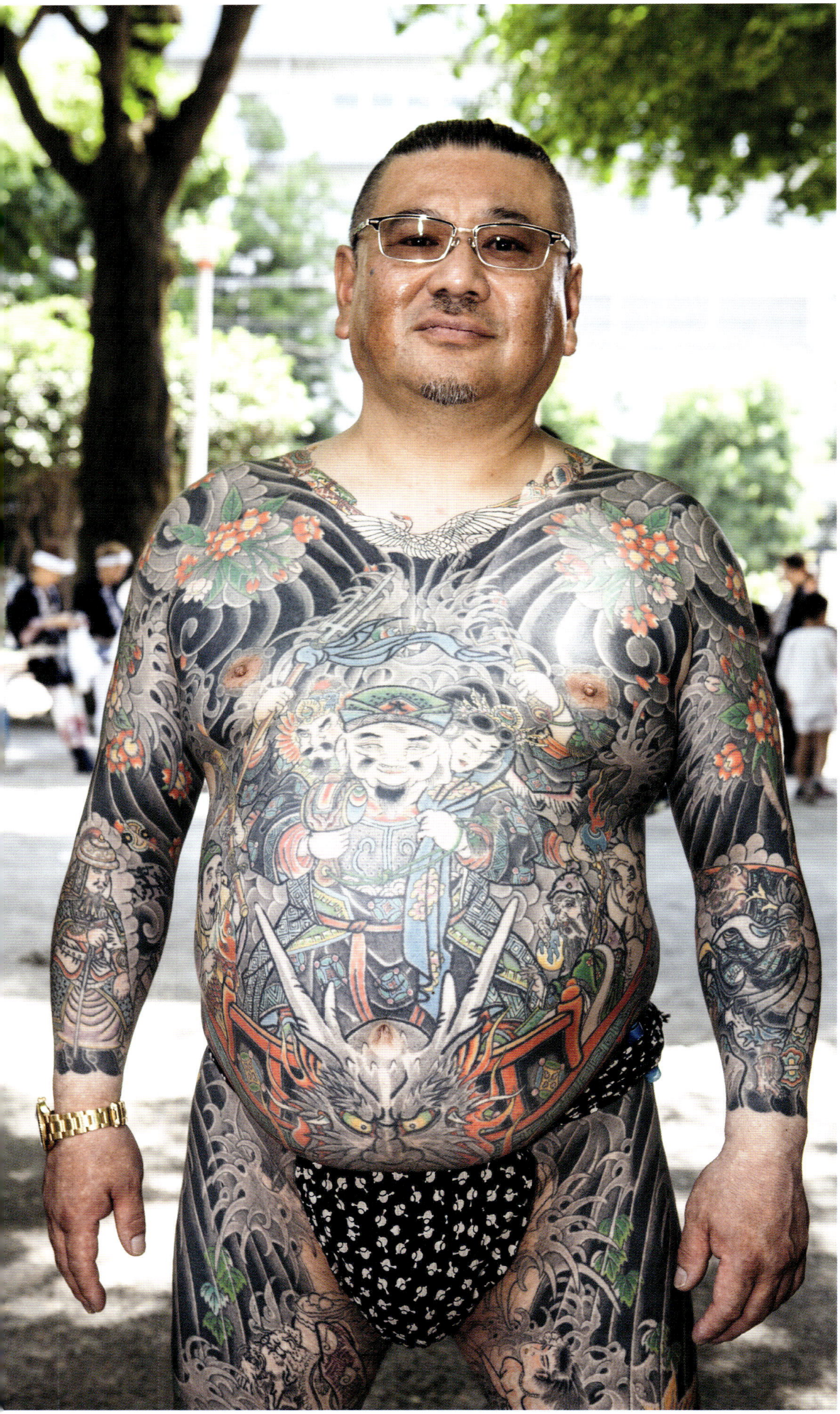

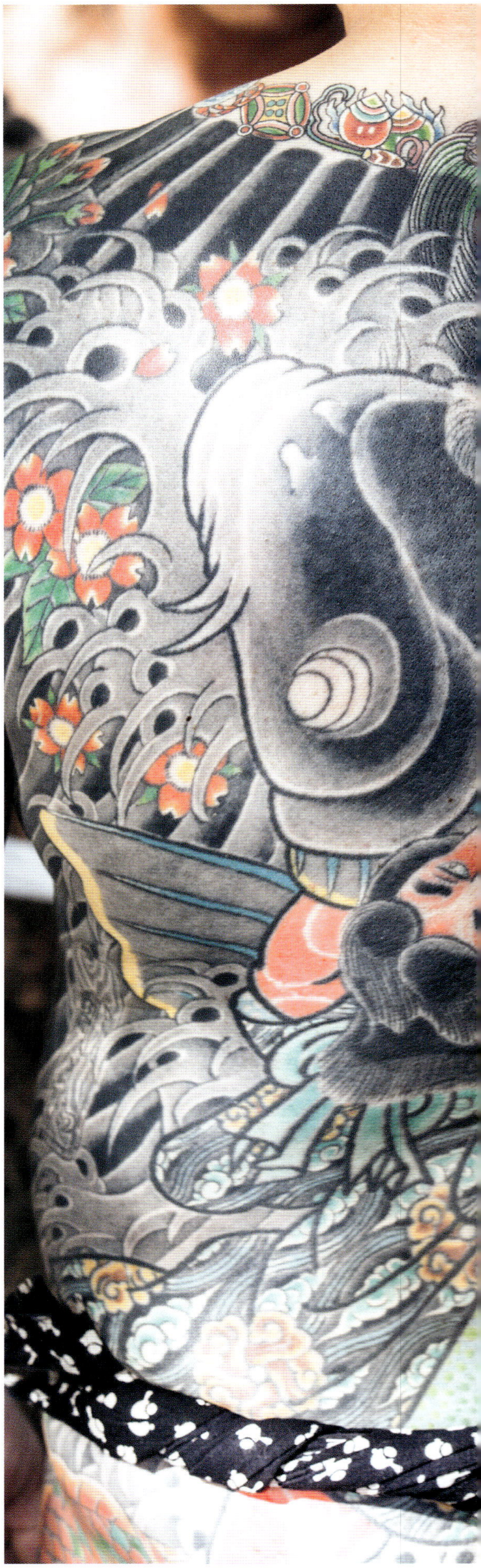

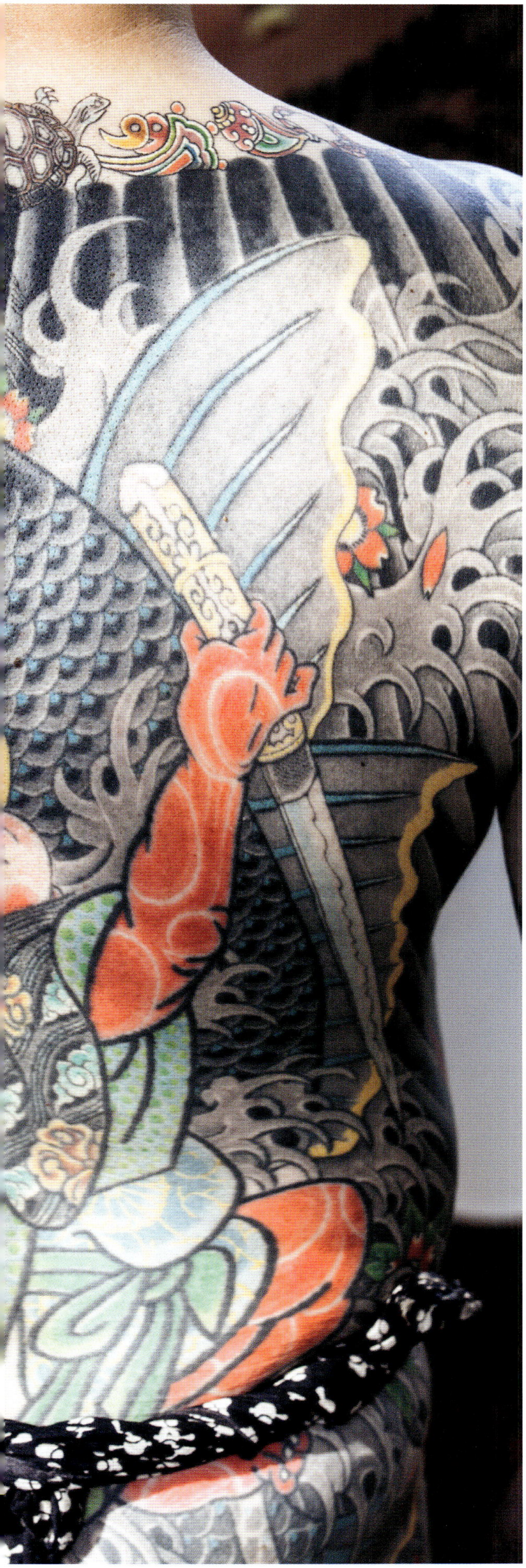

FAR LEFT
The Seven Lucky Gods are a jovial bunch of Ten deities that originate from various countries, and existed independently for thousands of years before being joined together in a boat by a monk named Tenkai during the 17th century. Ebisu, Bishamonten, Daikokuten, Hotei, Jurojin, Fukurokuju and Benzaiten sail around on their treasure ship and bring luck, fortune and longevity. As in many countries, seven is considered a significant number in bringing good fortune to Japanese people. The Seven Lucky Gods represent the seven essential human virtues of prosperity, popularity, integrity, goodwill, dignity, generosity and longevity.

Ebisu, who is the only indigenous Japanese god of the group, is a smiling, fat man with a beard who wears court clothing; he often has a fishing rod and a red snapper. He represents frankness, luck and fortune and is the god of fishermen, rice and sailors. Bishamonten protects from disaster and evil and is a divinity of warfare; Daikokuten is a god of food, agriculture and wealth and is depicted with a mallet; Hotei is the god of happiness and wealth and resembles a content, large man; Jurojin brings longevity and is often accompanied by a deer; Fukurokuju is the god of wisdom and longevity; and Benzaiten is the only female in the group and is a goddess of the arts, literature, wealth, femininity and music. She is often accompanied by a dragon and carries a *biwa* (lute). She is also a popular tattoo motif on her own.

LEFT
Besides divinities, another genre of Buddhist art that appears in tattoos features famous monks, such as Oniwakamaru (the childhood name of the 12th-century folkloric monk Saito Musashibo Benkei). He is often depicted as a child dramatically subduing a giant carp who swallowed his mother.

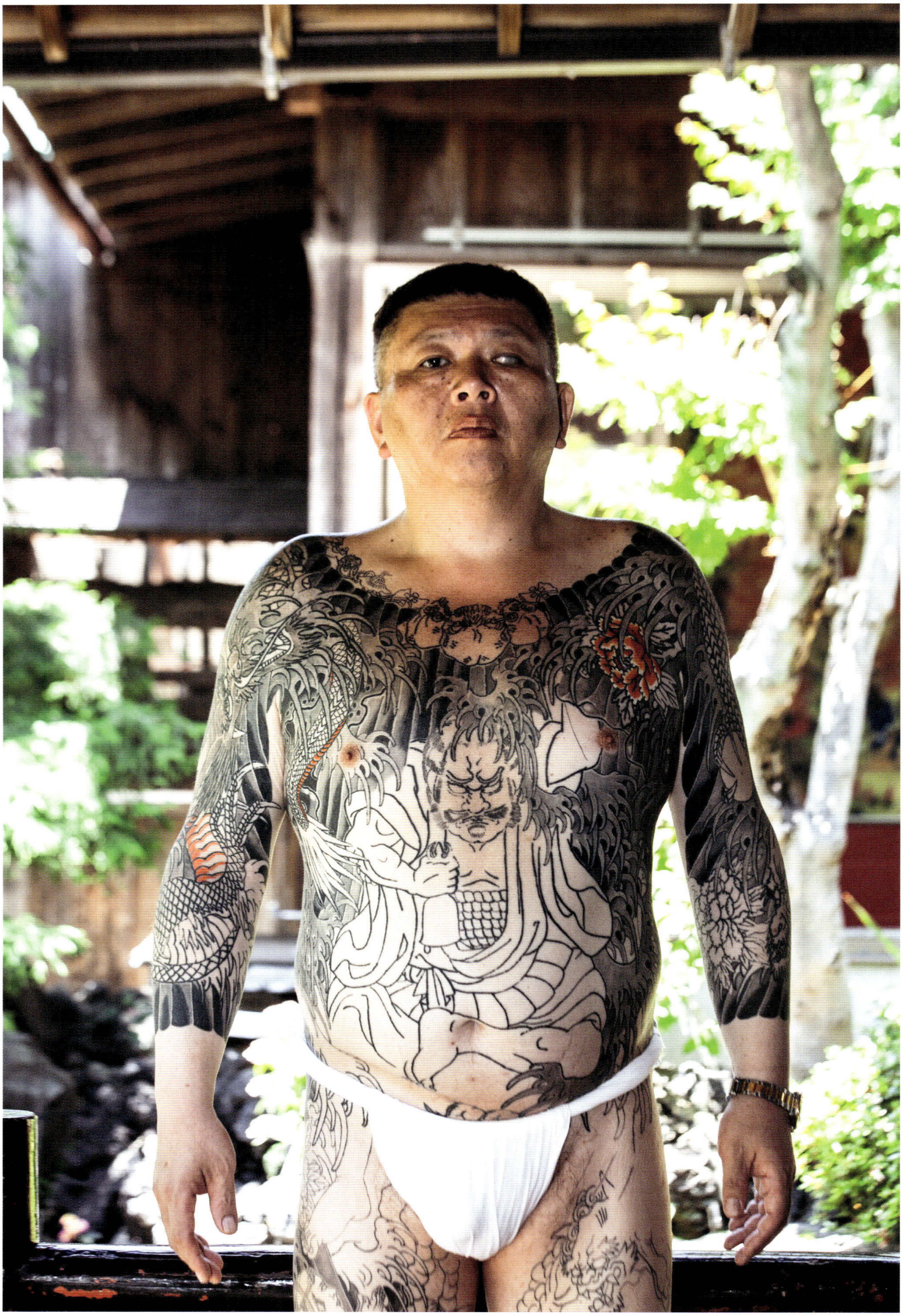

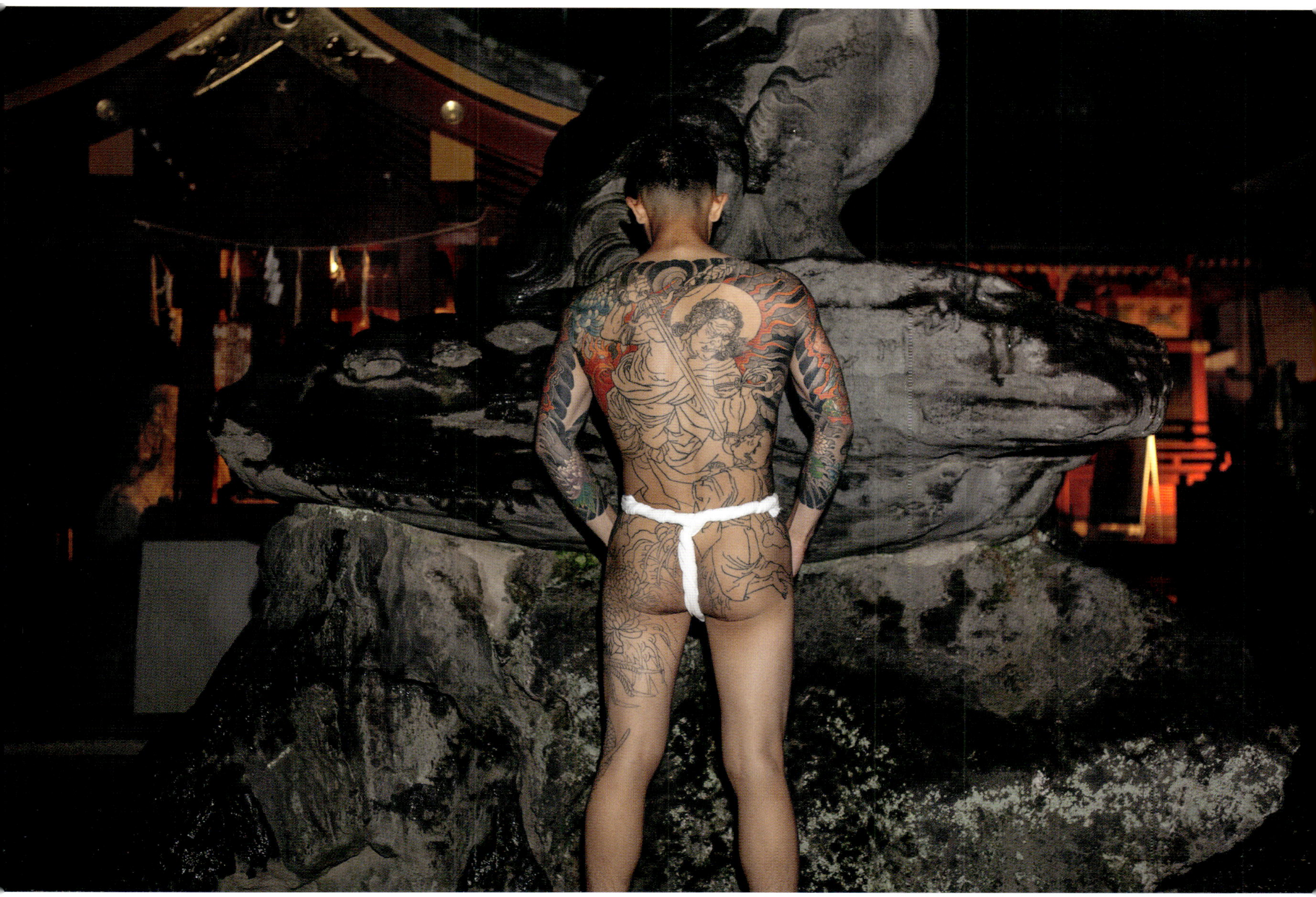

OPPOSITE
Another well-known monk represented in tattoo art is Mongaku, who was also a Japanese samurai in the late Heian and early Kamakura eras. One powerful and popular motif is based on a commonly depicted scene in which he did penance under Nachi waterfall for 21 days after mistakenly beheading his beloved, Kesa Gozen. Afterwards, he renounced his evil ways and became a monk.

ABOVE
Outlines of a piece based on Yoshitoshi Tsukioka's *Fudo Myo-o Threatens Yuten*, depicted at the start of this section.

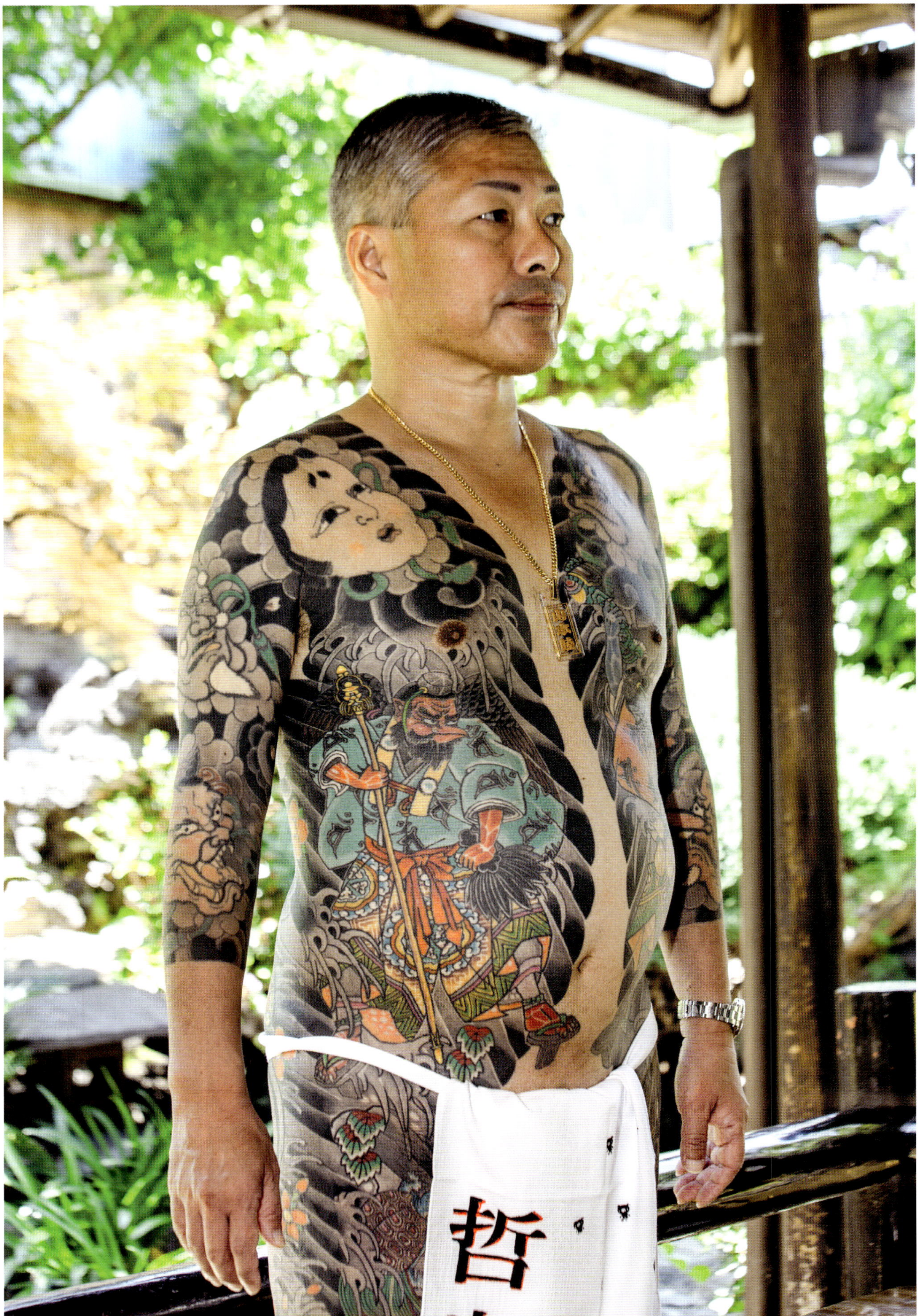
哲

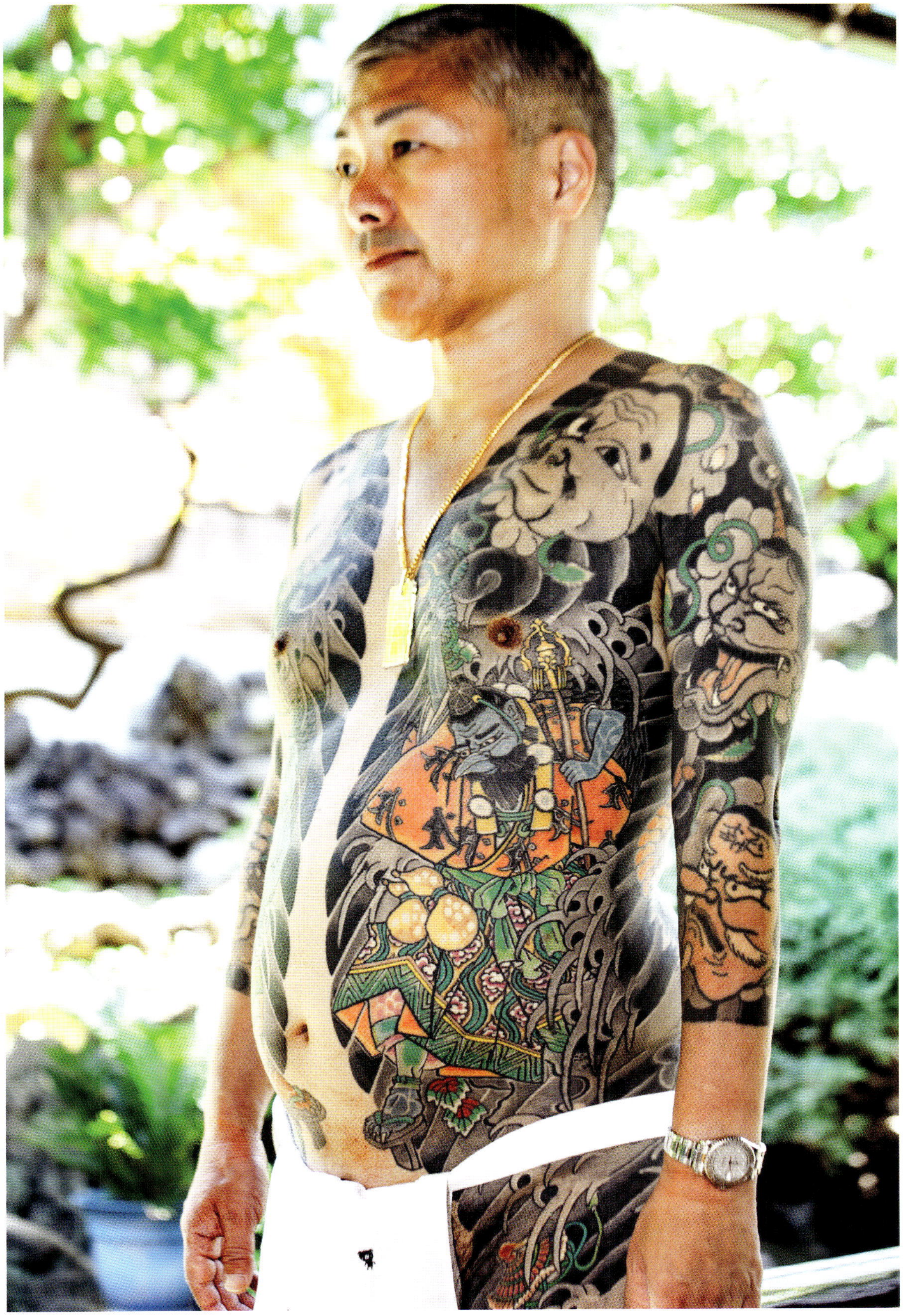

OPPOSITE
Tengu are mythical creatures with long noses, wings and red faces. They dress like mountain priests, wearing a single-toothed *geta* clog, and hold a fan. Some of these types of priests were seen as arrogant (hence the long noses), seeking fame and profit. The historic Japanese chronicles the *Nihon Shoki* describe a meteor-like event in the sky in 637, which was thought to have been a *tengu*.

RIGHT
From the Heian period onwards, *tengu* were depicted as more birdlike, but by the Edo era, they took on a human appearance and were seen more as divinities than ghouls. There are two main types of *tengu*: the territorial *karasu* (crow) *tengu* shown here is often depicted with a beak and wings and carries a sword, while the *hanadaka tengu* has a human face, large wings, a long nose and carries a fan.

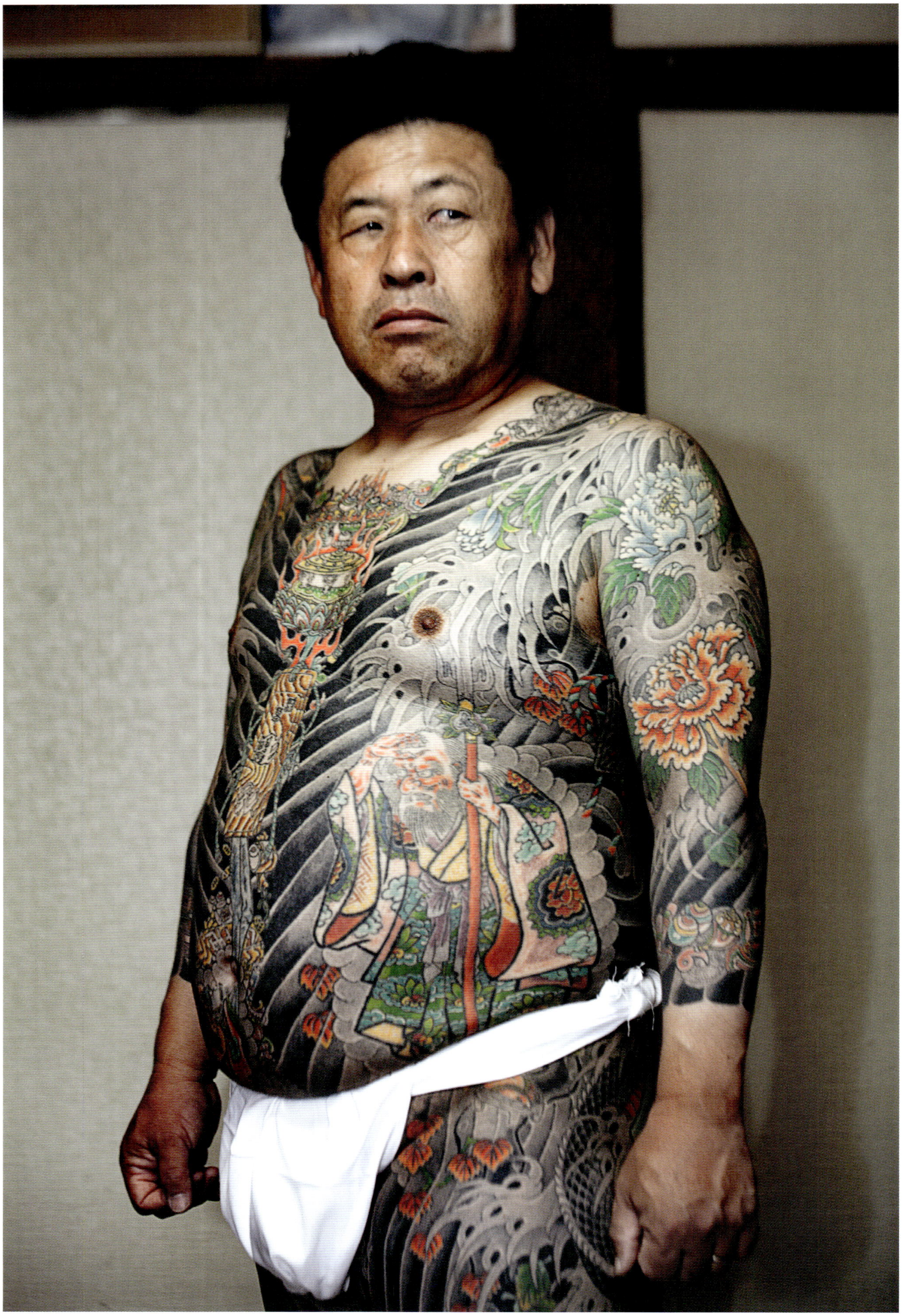

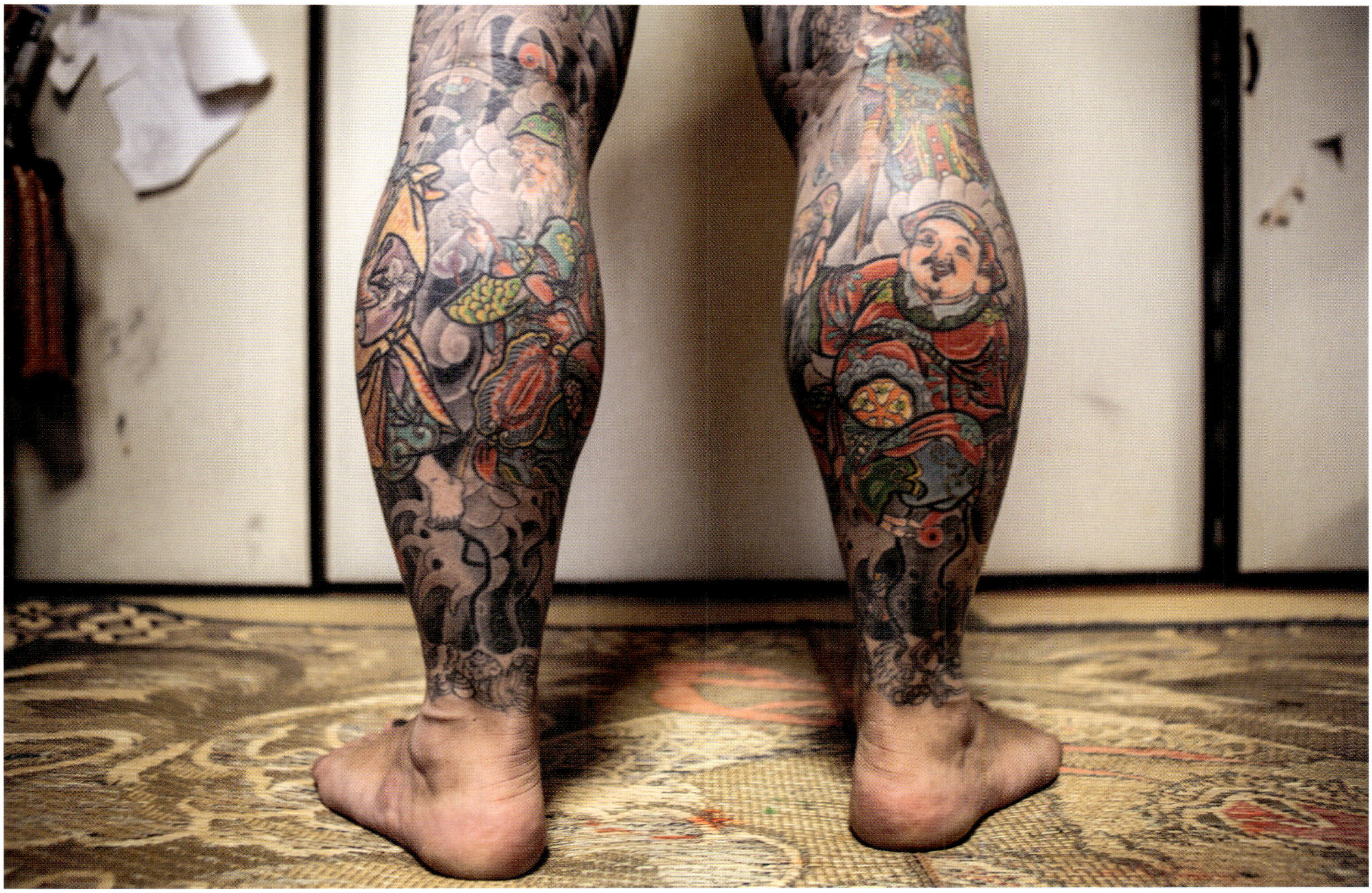

OPPOSITE
Sarutahiko Okami is a Shinto purification deity, and also a guide that enables Shinto gods to descend to earth. He acts as a guardian in between these boundary lands and is often venerated by travellers. Sarutahiko is considered to be the origin of the *tengu*'s appearance: in the *Nihon Shoki*, he is said to be tall, with a red mouth, long nose and bright, shining eyes.

ABOVE
Members of the Seven Lucky Gods adorn the legs.

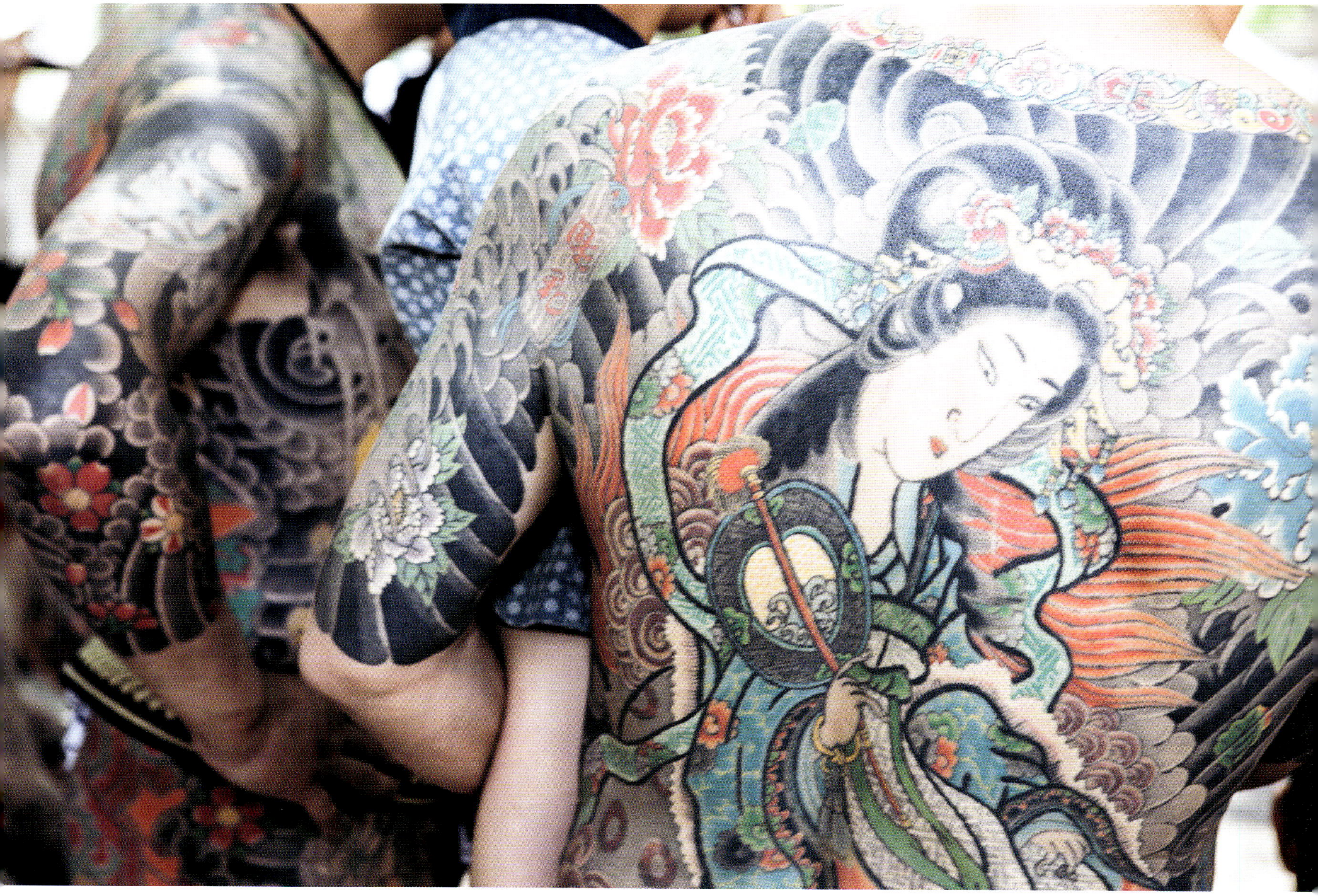

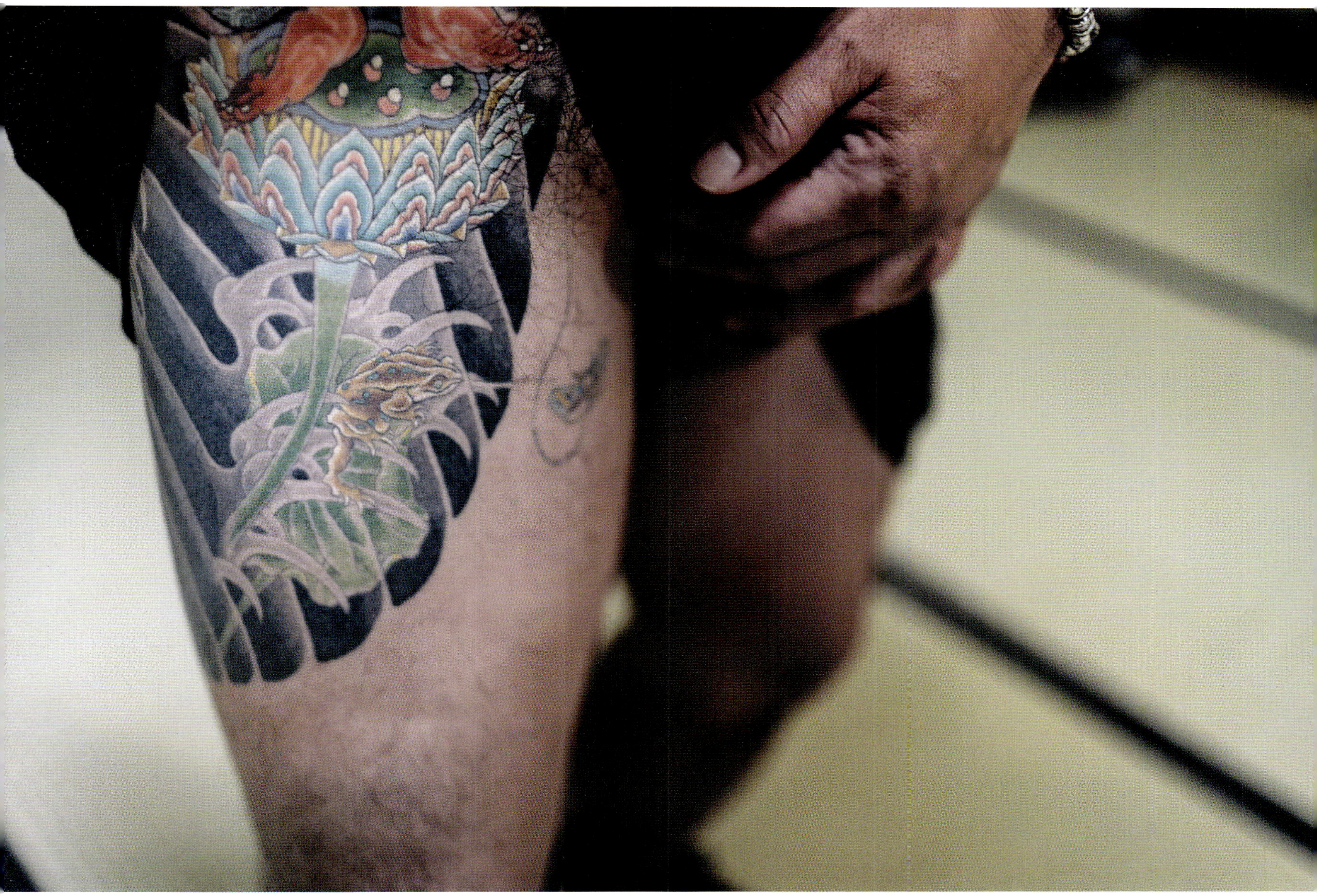

OPPOSITE
Kisshoten (Kichijoten) is a female deity who is the goddess of abundant harvest, fertility, beauty and happiness. She is elegant, with a tender face, and often wears layered, embroidered robes. Her appearance is similar to Benzaiten, but she holds a wish-granting jewel that can bestow good luck. Some also believe that she is the wife of Bishamonten.

ABOVE
The most important Buddhist flower is the lotus, as it blooms in muddy marshes and ponds – and is analogous to the idea that beauty can arise from darkness. It is said that after birth, the Buddha took seven steps and a lotus appeared beneath his foot at each step.

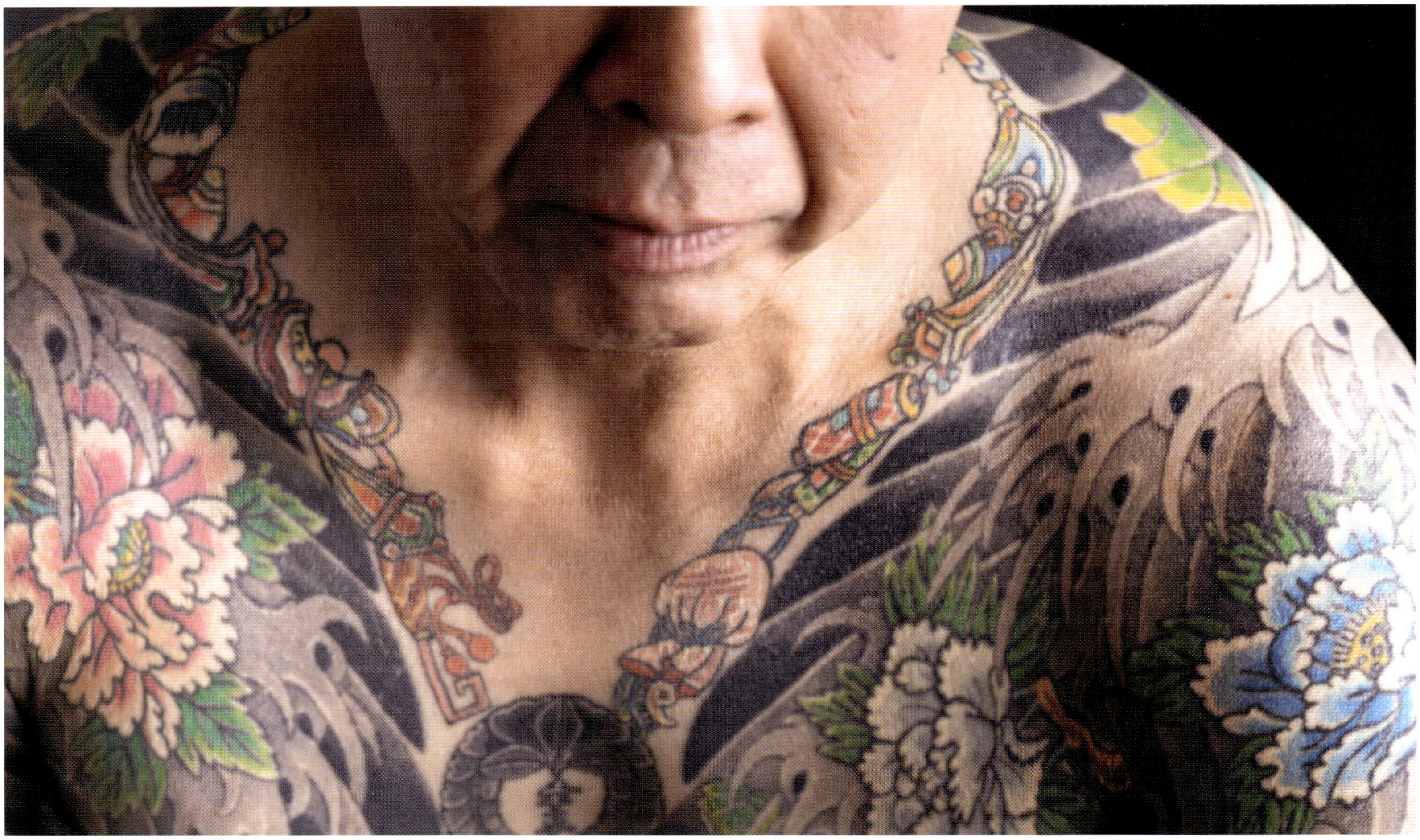

ABOVE
Various objects, ritual spectres, scrolls and symbols from Buddhist art adorn the neck.

RIGHT
Tattoo featuring Fudo Myo-o.

OPPOSITE
Tennyo are beautiful celestial beings who attend to Nyorai and Bosatsu. They take on various forms, usually appearing as musicians and dancers in female guises, and look like angels. They play music in the heavens and might carry or play a *biwa*, drum or flute, dance and fly through the air, and glide gracefully through the clouds. They might hold a lotus, scatter flowers or pray. They are usually adorned with flowing garments and decked out with jewellery, and sometimes have wings.

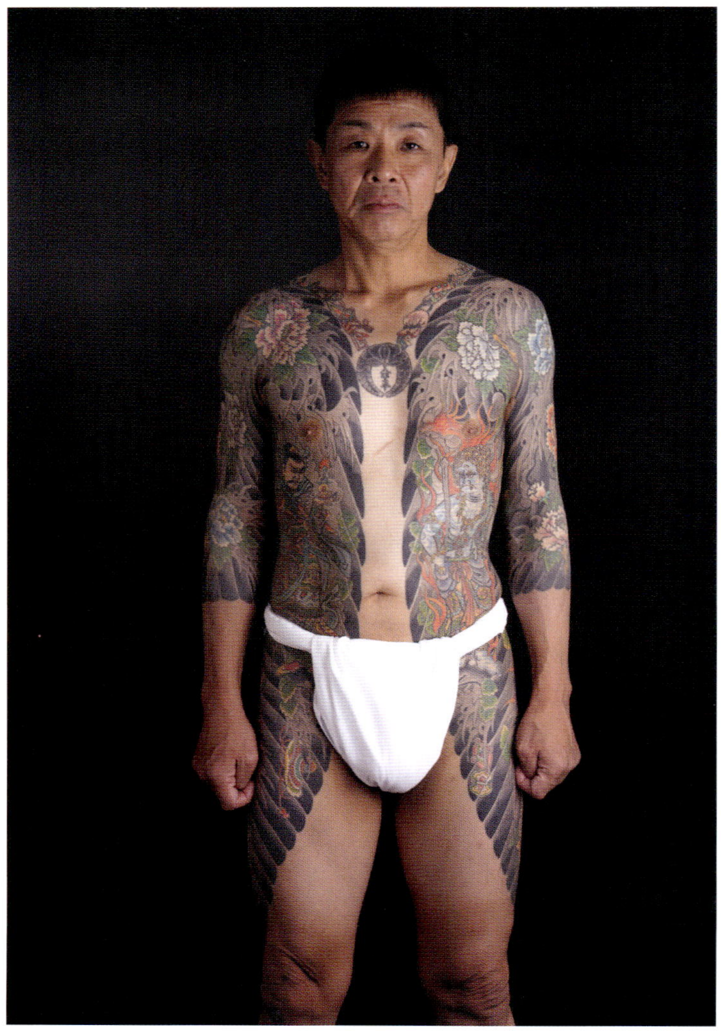

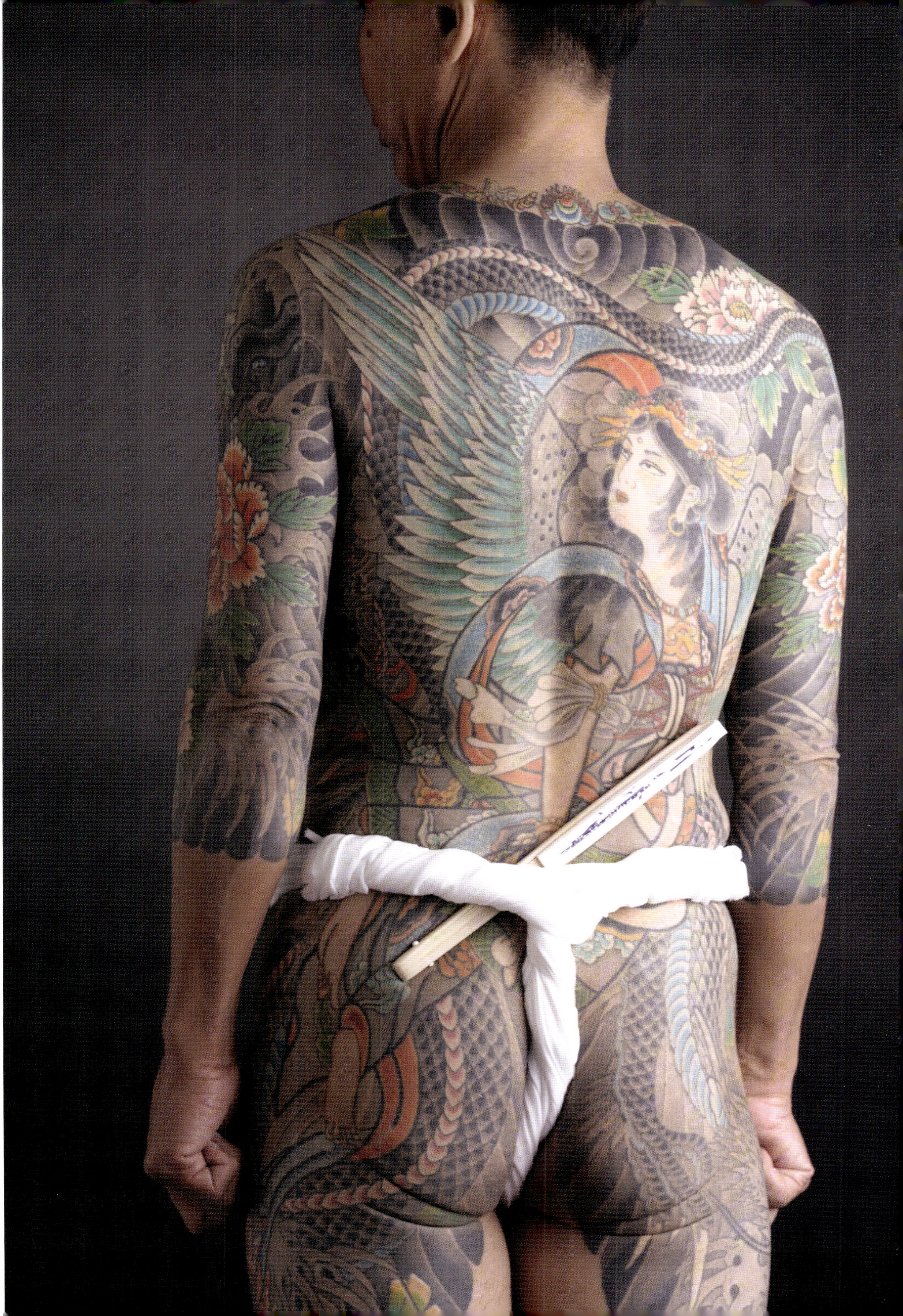

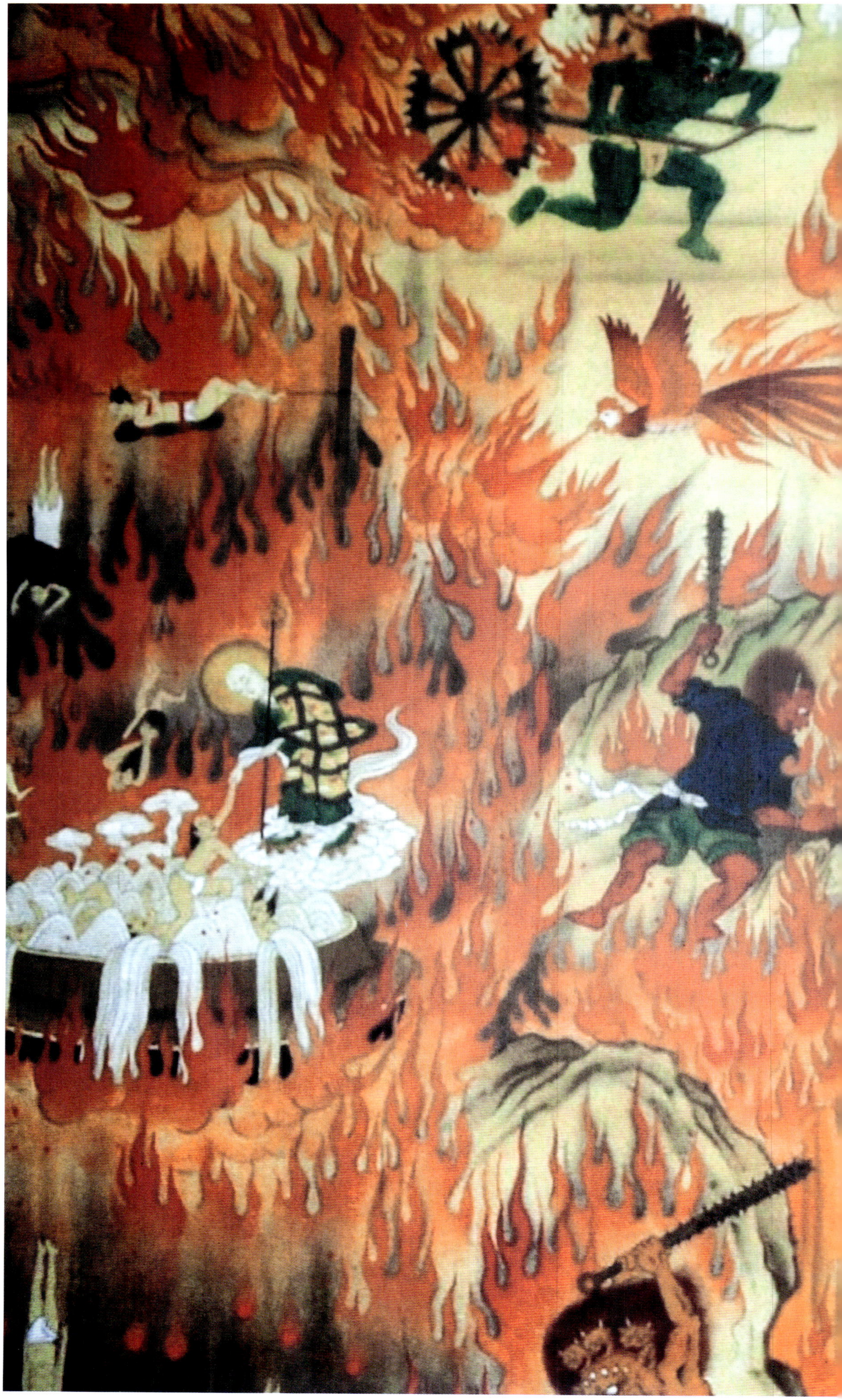

RIGHT
While it seems contradictory to Buddhist beliefs, which are predicated on the idea of karma and reincarnation, a posthumous heaven and hell do indeed exist in Buddhism. They are frequently portrayed in art, but damnation is not considered to be permanent. Buddhist hell is where people end up as a karmic consequence of their evildoings. Hell scenes like the ones in this tattoo are graphic and horrific, rife with monsters and demons torturing humans in various gruesome ways. They are meant to deter people from committing immoral acts.

Emma-O, here on the upper left thigh, is the Japanese Buddhist judge of the dead, who is assisted by two disembodied heads; he condemns people to hell. It is thought that a small, monk-like deity called Jizo has the power to guide people away from hell, as do the prayers of a hell-bound person's relatives. Jizo is a Bosatsu and can help those trapped in hell, including those that were condemned to go there by Emma-O.

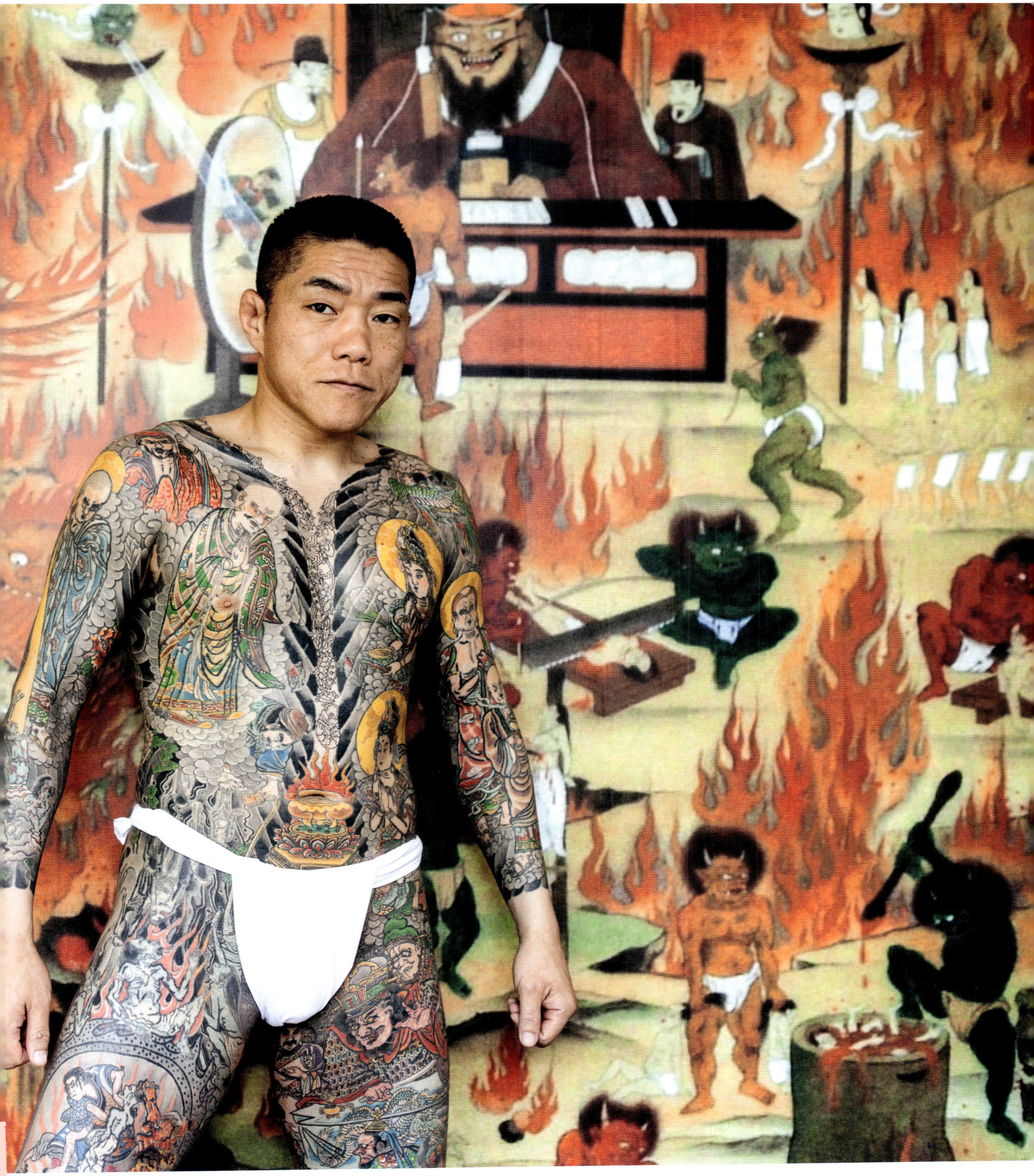

PICTURE CREDITS

Cover: © Ronin de Goede.

Introduction: pp. 6–9, 12–13 © Ronin de Goede; pp. 10 left and right, 16–17 © Cory Lum; pp. 14–15 © REUTERS/Kim Kyung-Hoon.

History: pp. 18–20 © Minneapolis Institute of Art; pp. 21, 30 right, 34 © The Metropolitan Museum of Art; p. 22 © Alamy; p. 23 top and bottom © Risa Hoshino; pp. 24, 26, 35 © Smithsonian National Museum of Asian Art; p. 27 top © Emil Pacha Valencia; pp. 27 bottom, 36–37 left and right © Cory Lum; pp. 28, 32–33 © The British Museum; p. 30 left © The Art Institute of Chicago; p. 31 © Brooklyn Museum.

Contemporary Tattoo Culture: pp. 38–39, 64 left and right, 66 © Ronin de Goede; pp. 40 left, 41, 57 bottom © Alamy; p. 40 right © The British Museum; p. 42 © Archive Photos, Getty Images; p. 43 © Three Lions, Hulton Archive, Getty Images; p. 44 left © John Harte; p. 44 right © Madoka; p. 45 top © Julian Krakowiak; p. 45 bottom © Manami Okazaki; pp. 46–47 © Mariella Kai; pp. 48, 50, 58 left, 60, 63, 65, 67 © Cory Lum; pp. 49, 57 top © Geoff Johnson; p. 51 © Giorgio Fragiacomo; p. 52 © Chronicle of World History; p. 55 top © Wikimedia Commons; p. 55 bottom © Toei; p. 58 right © Ed Hardy.

Artisans and Aesthetics: pp. 68–69, 78–79, 86–87 © Ronin de Goede; p. 71 © Manami Okazaki; p. 72 top and bottom © Bunshin Horitoshi; p. 74 © Emil Pacha Valencia; p. 75 © Ivan Toscanelli; p. 76 top © Cory Lum; pp. 76 bottom, 82, 92, 94–95 © The Metropolitan Museum of Art; pp. 80–81 © Minechika Endo; p. 83 © The Art Institute of Chicago; pp. 84–85 © Geoff Johnson; pp. 88–89 © Minneapolis Institute of Art; p. 90 © The British Museum; p. 91 © Cleveland Museum of Art; p. 93 © Wikimedia Commons.

Horishi Profiles: pp. 96–97, 99 top, 101, 102 right, 104–105 © Geoff Johnson; pp. 98, 100, 102 left © Ivan Toscanelli; p. 99 bottom © Horitoku; pp. 106–107, 144–45 © Zoetica Ebb; pp. 108, 111, 132–35 © Manami Okazaki; pp. 109, 112–13, 115, 122, 124–25, 130–31, 138–43, 150–151 © Cory Lum; pp. 116–21 © Horiyasu; pp. 127–29, 136–137 © Emil Pacha Valencia; pp. 146, 148–49 © Ronin de Goede.

Profile of a Dynasty: Horikazu: pp. 152–54, 157 © Cory Lum; pp. 155–56, 158–62 © Ronin de Goede.

Wabori and Festivals: pp. 164–65, 170, 175 right, 176–97 © Ronin de Goede; pp. 167, 171, 175 left, 198–99 © Cory Lum; pp. 168–69 top and bottom © Emil Pacha Valencia; pp. 173–74 © Jeremy Sutton Hibbert; pp. 200–205 © Michael Rubenstein; pp. 206–207 left and right © Manami Okazaki.

Buddhist and Shinto Motifs: pp. 208–209, 214–15, 220–21, 234 top and bottom, 235 © Cory Lum; p. 210 © Smithsonian National Museum of Asian Art; p. 211 left © Los Angeles County Museum of Art; pp. 211 right, 212–13 © The Metropolitan Museum of Art; pp. 216–19, 222–32, 236–37 © Ronin de Goede; p. 233 © Michael Rubenstein.

AUTHOR BIOGRAPHY

Manami Okazaki is a journalist who has published several books on Japanese culture, including *Tattoo in Japan: Traditional and Modern Styles, Japanese Buddhism x Horiyoshi III, Land of the Rising Cat: Japan's Feline Fascination* and *Oishii: Japanese Food Style,* and has researched tattoos in Japan since the early 2000s. Her tattoo-related writing has appeared in the *Japan Times,* the *Wall Street Journal,* the *South China Morning Post, MSN News,* academic journals and documentary projects for national TV networks, as well as fashion and street-culture magazines. She has contributed to many international tattoo magazines, has given talks at Aoyama Gakuin University and has hosted tattoo-related events at the Foreign Correspondents' Club of Japan in Tokyo and the Japan Society in London. She lives in Tokyo.

ACKNOWLEDGEMENTS

Putting this book together was not easy. Besides looking into *wabori* culture, it also provided a glimpse into Japan's underworld. Some subjects were interviewed multiple times over many years. The process entailed wading through the heavy police presence at tattoo studio visits and playing a constant cat-and-mouse game, chasing clients with exquisite work in order to photograph them, as they perpetually went in and out of prison. Many of the masterpieces of top *horishi* are currently incarcerated, so the making of this book also required visits to penitentiaries. The tattoo studios themselves felt like sanctuaries of sorts, a moment of calm from the chaos outside.

It was also a time of extreme beauty and moments that were nothing short of ethereal: seeing tattooed folks within a crowd of millions at a festival, witnessing the magic of the *sumi* entering the skin and late nights with hospitable people. Every single evening entailed a bathhouse sojourn.

Thank you to Shodai Horikazu (RIP) and Horikazu for upholding this culture, providing so many models for the shoots and being so incredibly real. Thank you to Horitoku for introducing me to the world of *wabori* and for the countless interviews. Thank you to Horimyo, who is one of my greatest collaborators and with whom I have done countless pieces of press and many overseas trips for events.

Thank you to the photographers, in particular Cory Lum, Ronin de Goede, Emil Pacha Valencia and Zoetica Ebb. To my editor Ali Gitlow, copyeditor Martha Jay, designer Sebit Min and the Prestel crew, for supporting this project. To all the *horishi* involved. To the editors from my stints working at tattoo magazines: Miho Kawasaki at *BURST,* Neil Dalleywater and Sion Smith at *Skin Deep,* Dirk Boris at *TätowierMagazin* and *TätowierErotica,* Miki at *Tattoo Life,* Rocky Rakovic, Toby Thompson and Amy Higgins at *Inked* magazine, Missy at suicidegirls.com and Bob at Skin and Ink. To all the other publications and media outlets who commissioned tattoo-related articles and media productions: the *Wall Street Journal,* the *South China Morning Post, MSN News,* the *Japan Times,* Waseda University, *Bizarre* magazine, *Acclaim* magazine, *FHM, MAXIM* Media Corp and artist Dr Lakra. To all the other organizations that have commissioned tattoo-related work over the years: the Japan Society in London, the Foreign Correspondents' Club of Japan, and Japan Expo in Paris for hosting my Japanese tattoo events and talks. To Marc Menish at Aoyama Gakuin University and Dominic Steavu.

produktsicherheit@penguinrandomhouse.de
The above information is mandatory information according to GPSR and should be used for all queries relating to the safety of our books

A Library of Congress Control Number is available.

A CIP catalogue record for this book is available from the British Library.

Editorial direction:
ALI GITLOW

Copyediting and proofreading:
MARTHA JAY

Design and typesetting:
SEBIT MIN

Production:
LUISA KLOSE

Origination:
Schnieber Graphik, Munich

Printing and binding:
Livonia Print SIA, Riga

MIX
Paper | Supporting responsible forestry
FSC® C002795

Penguin Random House Verlagsgruppe
FSC® N001967

Printed in Latvia

ISBN 978-3-7913-9378-0
www.prestel.com